BARRON'S

VERBAL WORKBOOK FOR THE

NEW SAT®

11TH EDITION

Mitchel Weiner
Former Member, Department of English
James Madison High School, Brooklyn, New York

Sharon Weiner Green
Former Instructor in English
Merritt College, Oakland, California

BARRON'S

ACKNOWLEDGMENTS

The authors gratefully acknowledge the following copyright holders for permission to reprint material used in reading passages:

Page 4: From *A Handbook to Literature, 6/E* by Holman. © 1992. Reprinted by permission of Prentice-Hall, Inc.

Pages 25–26: From "Symbolic Language of Dreams" by Erich Fromm in *Language: An Enquiry into Its Meaning and Function* by Ruth Nanda Anshen, ed. Copyright 1957. HarperCollins Publishers, Inc.

Pages 39–40: From "The Spider and the Wasp" by Alexander Petrunkevitch. Copyright © 1952 by *Scientific American, Inc.* All rights reserved.

Page 43: From *Small Town America* by Richard Lingerman. Copyright © 1980 with permission of Putnam Publishing Group.

Page 44: From *A Pocket History of the United States* by Alan Nevins and Henry Steele Commager. Copyright 1991. Alfred A. Knopf, New York.

Pages 111–112: From *The Most Beautiful House in the World* by Witold Rybczynski. Copyright 1989. With permission of Viking Penguin.

Page 114: From *La Vida* by Oscar Lewis. Copyright 1965. Random House, New York.

Pages 114–115: From "What is Poverty?" by Jo Goodwin Parker. Originally published in *America's Other Children: Public Schools Outside Suburbia* by George Henderson, ed. Copyright 1971. University of Oklahoma Press.

Page 117: From "Living in Two Cultures" by Jeanne Wakatsuki Houston in *Outlooks and Insights*. Copyright 1983. St. Martin's Press.

Pages 118–119: From "Introduction" by Antonio Castro Leal to *Twenty Centuries of Mexican Art*. Copyright 1940 by the Museum of Modern Art.

Pages 120–121: From *The Press and the Presidency* by John Tebbel and Sarah Miles Watts. Copyright 1985. Oxford University Press, New York.

Page 123: From "The Desert Smells Like Rain: A Naturalist in Papago Indian Country" by Gary Nabhan. With permission of North Point Press; div. of Farrar, Straus & Giroux, Inc.

Pages 125–126: "Native Earth," from *Indian Country* by Peter Matthiessen, copyright © 1979, 1980, 1981, 1984 by Peter Matthiessen. Used by permission of Viking Penguin, a division of Penguin Group (USA) Inc.

Pages 126–127: From "Social Characteristics and Socialization of Wild Chimpanzees" by Yukimaru Sugiyama in *Primate Socialization* by Frank E. Poirer, ed. Copyright 1972. Random House, New York.

Pages 128–129: From *War, Peace and International Politics* by David W. Zeigler, Copyright 1977. Reprinted by permission of Addison-Wesley Educational Publishers, Inc.

Page 131: From *Picasso on Art: A Selection of Views* by Dore Ashton. Copyright 1972. The Viking Press, New York.

Pages 131–132: From *Picasso: The Early Years* by Jiri Padrta. Undated. Tudor Publishing Co., New York.

Pages 135–136: From "The Dynamic Abyss" by Charles D. Hollister, Arthur R. M. Nowell, and Peter A. Jumars. Copyright © 1984 by *Scientific American, Inc.* All rights reserved.

Pages 136–138: From *Organizing the World's Money* by Benjamin J. Cohen. Copyright 1977. Basic Books, a div. of HarperCollins Publishers, Inc.

Pages 139–140: From *F. Scott Fitzgerald* by Kenneth Eble. Copyright 1963. Twayne Publishers, an imprint of Simon & Schuster Macmillan.

Page 155: From "F. Scott Fitzgerald" by Edmund Wilson in *Shores of Light*. © 1985 with permission from Farrar, Straus & Giroux, Inc.

Pages 281–282: From *Picasso: Fifty Years of His Art* by Alfred H. Barr. Copyright 1946 by the Museum of Modern Art.

Page 287: From *The Magic Years* by Selma H. Fraiberg. Copyright 1959. By permission of Scribner, a division of Simon & Schuster.

Pages 287–288: From *Essentials of Psychology and Life* by Philip G. Zimbardo. Reprinted with permission of Addison-Wesley Educational Publishers, Inc. Copyright 1980. Scott, Foresman and Co., Glenview, Illinois.

Pages 313–314: From *The Joy of Music* by Leonard Bernstein. Copyright 1959. Used by permission of Doubleday, a div. of BDD Publishing Group.

Page 325: From "The Canopy of the Tropical Rain Forest" by Donald R. Perry. Copyright © 1984 by *Scientific American, Inc.* All rights reserved.

Page 330: From *The Politics of Prejudice* by Roger Daniels. Copyright 1962. University of California Press, Berkeley.

Pages 330–331: From "American Antisemitism Historically Reconsidered" by John Higham, in *Jews in the Mind of America* by Herbert Stember, et al, eds. Copyright 1966. American Jewish Committee, Basic Books, New York. Reprinted in *Antisemitism in the United States* by Leonard Dinnerstein, ed. Copyright 1971. Holt, Rinehart, and Winston, Inc., New York.

Pages 355–356: From "The Man Who Hitched the Reindeer To Santa Claus's Sleigh" by X. J. Kennedy in *The New York Times Book Review*, December 5, 1993. © 1993 The New York Times Co.

Page 367: From *The Way to Rainy Mountain* by N. Scott Momaday. Copyright 1969. University of New Mexico Press.

Pages 368–369: From *Mortal Lessons: Notes on the Art of Surgery* by Richard Selzer. Copyright © 1974, 1975, 1976 by Richard Selzer. Reprinted by permission of Georges Borchardt, Inc. for the author.

Page 372: From *Montana 1948* by Larry Watson. Copyright © 1993 by Larry Watson. (Milkweed Editions, 1993)

All inquiries should be addressed to:
Barron's Educational Series, Inc.
250 Wireless Boulevard
Hauppauge, New York 11788
http//www.barronseduc.com

Library of Congress Catalog Card No. 2004057384

International Standard Book No. 0-7641-2411-0

Library of Congress Cataloging-in-Publication Data

Weiner, Mitchel, 1907–
    Barron's verbal workbook for the new SAT / Mitchel Weiner, Sharon Weiner Green. — 11th ed.
        p.   cm.
    Rev. ed. of: Barron's verbal workbook for the SAT I. 10th ed. c2001.
    ISBN 0-7641-2411-0
    1. English language—Examinations—Study guides.
2. Universities and colleges—United States—Entrance examinations—Study guides.   3. Scholastic Assessment Test—Study guides.
I. Title: Verbal workbook for the new SAT.   II. Green, Sharon, 1939–
III. Weiner, Mitchel, 1907– Barron's verbal workbook for the SAT I.
IV. Title.

LB1631.5 .W45 2005
378.1'662—dc22   2004057384

Printed in the United States of America
9 8 7 6 5 4 3 2

CONTENTS

PART VII   WRITING A 25-MINUTE ESSAY

PART VIII TESTS FOR PRACTICE

PREFACE

Welcome to the world of the SAT, where *air* and *lumber* can be verbs, and *apathy* and *phenomena* are common everyday words. Welcome to the eleventh edition of Barron's *Verbal Workbook*. If you are preparing for the critical reading and writing skills sections of the new SAT, this is the book you need.

- It features four complete reading and writing skills tests, each six sections long. Here are four crucial "dress rehearsals" for the day you walk into the examination room.
- It briefs you on the vocabulary-in-context and reading comprehension questions, giving you key tips on how to tackle these important types of questions.
- It takes you through the double reading passages, showing you how to work your way through a pair of passages without wasting effort or time.
- It introduces you to the new writing skills section of the test and familiarizes you with its three types of questions, teaching you how to identify errors, improve sentences, and polish paragraphs. Finally, it leads you step by step through the process of writing an essay in just 25 minutes, providing you with a wide variety of SAT-modeled practice topics.
- It offers you enough material for a year-long study program so that you don't have to settle for last-minute cram sessions. Pace yourself as you work your way through the wealth of practice exercises designed for you.
- It gives you the SAT High-Frequency Word List, incorporating vocabulary from actual SAT tests through 2003. These words are *vital*—computer analysis shows that they occur test after test on actual SATs. Master them, and you'll be well on your way to building a college-level vocabulary.

With dozens of clear, helpful pointers and hundreds of brand-new questions modeled closely on questions appearing on today's SAT, Barron's *Verbal Workbook* gives you a down-to-earth introduction to the sometimes intimidating world of the SAT. Don't let the new SAT get you down. With the Barron's team behind you, go for your personal best: take time today to build your skills for the new SAT.

This eleventh edition of Barron's *Verbal Workbook* is a sign of Barron's ongoing commitment to make this publication America's outstanding guide to the reading and writing skills sections of the SAT. It has benefited from the dedicated labors of the editorial staff of Barron's, in particular Linda Turner and Ruth Flohn, and from the research and writing skills of Lexy Green. We are greatly indebted to them.

PART I

INTRODUCING THE NEW SAT: CRITICAL READING AND WRITING SKILLS

NATURE OF THE TEST

The SAT is a standardized test designed to help predict how well you are likely to do in your academic work as a college freshman. By looking at your school grades and your SAT scores, college admissions officers get a sense of you as a potential student—a person they'd like to have in their school.

The SAT tries to measure your ability to reason using facts that are part of your general knowledge or facts that are included in your test booklet. You're not required to recall great chunks of history or literature or science. You're not even required to recall most math formulas—they're printed right in the test booklet.

Assessment tests are essentially multiple-choice tests. Your score depends upon how many correct answers you get within a definite period of time. Speed is important, but so is accuracy. You have to pace yourself so that you don't sacrifice speed to gain accuracy (or sacrifice accuracy to gain speed).

OVERVIEW AND CONTENT

This is the actual format of the new SAT. The total testing time allowed is 3¾ hours. There are ten sections on the test. You are given 25 minutes apiece to complete seven of them. They are:

- 1 essay-writing section
- 2 critical reading sections
- 2 mathematics section
- 1 writing skills section
- 1 "experimental" section (critical reading, writing skills, or mathematics)

The eighth and ninth sections take 20 minutes apiece. They are:

- 1 critical reading section
- 1 mathematics section

Finally, there is an additional 10-minute section. It is:

- 1 writing skills section

These sections should all appear on the new SAT, as they do on the recently released SAT practice test. However, the order in which they appear is likely to vary from test to test.

Not counting the experimental section, the three critical reading sections should contain a total of 19 sentence completion questions and 48 reading comprehension questions. *More than half* of the critical reading questions on the new SAT directly test your reading comprehension.

Pay particular attention to how these critical reading sections are organized. All three sections contain groups of sentence completion questions followed by groups of reading comprehension questions. The sentence completion questions are arranged in order of difficulty: they start out with easy "warm-up" questions and get more and more difficult as they go along. (The reading comprehension questions, however, do not necessarily get more difficult as they go along. They are generally arranged to follow the passage's organization; questions about material found early in the passage come before questions about material occurring later. Nonetheless, in two of the three sections, questions based on short reading passages—100 words or so—precede questions based on longer passages of 500 to 800 words, and students may find answering questions about material in a short passage easier than answering questions about material in a long passage.)

THE CRITICAL READING SECTIONS

Here are examples of the two types of critical reading questions you can expect:

SENTENCE COMPLETION QUESTIONS

Sentence completion questions ask you to fill in the blanks. Your job is to find the word or phrase that best completes the sentence's meaning.

> Directions: Choose the word or set of words that, when inserted in the sentence, *best* fits the meaning of the sentence as a whole.

Brown, this biography suggests, was an ____ employer, giving generous bonuses one day, ordering pay cuts the next.

(A) indifferent
(B) objective
(C) unpredictable
(D) ineffectual
(E) unobtrusive

If you insert the different answer choices in the sentence, (C) *by definition* makes the most sense. Someone who gives bonuses one day and orders pay cuts the next clearly is *unpredictable*—no one can tell what he's going to do next.

To learn how to handle sentence completion questions, turn to Part III.

READING COMPREHENSION QUESTIONS

Reading comprehension questions ask about a passage's main idea or specific details, the author's attitude to the subject, the author's logic and techniques, the implications of the discussion, or the meaning of specific words.

> Directions: The passage below is followed by questions based on its content. Answer the questions on the basis of what is *stated* or *implied* in that passage.

Certain qualities common to the sonnet should be noted. Its definite restrictions make it a challenge to the artistry of the poet and
Line call for all the technical skill at the poet's
(5) command. The more or less set rhyme patterns occurring regularly within the short space of fourteen lines afford a pleasant effect on the ear of the reader, and can create truly musical effects. The rigidity of the form precludes a
(10) too great economy or too great prodigality of words. Emphasis is placed on exactness and perfection of expression. The brevity of the form favors concentrated expression of ideas or passion.

1. The author's primary purpose is to
   (A) contrast different types of sonnets
   (B) criticize the limitations of the sonnet
   (C) describe the characteristics of the sonnet
   (D) explain why the sonnet has lost popularity as a literary form
   (E) encourage readers to compose formal sonnets

2. The word "afford" in line 7 means
   (A) initiate
   (B) exaggerate
   (C) are able to pay for
   (D) change into
   (E) provide

3. The author's attitude toward the sonnet form can best be described as
   (A) amused toleration
   (B) grudging admiration
   (C) strong disapprobation
   (D) effusive enthusiasm
   (E) scholarly appreciation

The first question asks you to find the author's main idea. In the opening sentence, the author says certain qualities of the sonnet should be noted or observed. He then goes on to tell you which of these qualities deserve your attention, characterizing them in some detail. Thus, he *describes certain of the sonnet's* qualities or *characteristics*. The correct answer is (C). You can eliminate the other answers with ease. The author is upbeat about the sonnet: he doesn't say that the sonnet has limitations or that it has become less popular. Similarly, he doesn't discuss different types of sonnets. And while he talks about the challenge of composing formal sonnets, he never invites his readers to try writing them.

The second question asks you to figure out a word's meaning from its context. The rhyme patterns have a pleasant effect on the ear of the listener; indeed they *provide* or afford this effect. The correct answer is (E).

The third question asks you to determine how the author feels about his subject. All the author's comments about the sonnet form are positive, but he doesn't go so far as to gush (he's not *effusive*). The only answer that reflects this attitude is (E), *scholarly appreciation*.

See Part IV for tactics that will help you handle the entire range of reading comprehension questions.

THE WRITING SKILLS SECTIONS

There are three types of questions on the multiple-choice writing skills sections of the SAT: (i) sentence improvement questions, (ii) error identification questions, and (iii) paragraph improvement questions.

Examples of each type appear in this chapter. Later, in Part VI, you will find some tips on how to handle each one.

The writing skills sections on your test should include approximately 49 questions. The two sections will most likely break down as follows:

<u>35-Question Writing Skills Section</u>

Questions 1–11	sentence improvement questions
Questions 12–29	error identification questions
Questions 30–35	paragraph improvement questions

<u>14-Question Writing Skills Section</u>

| Questions 1–14 | sentence improvement questions |

Here are examples of each type of writing skills questions you can expect.

SENTENCE IMPROVEMENT QUESTIONS

Sentence improvement questions ask you to spot the form of a sentence that works best. Your job is to select the most effective version of a sentence.

> Directions: Some or all parts of the following sentences are underlined. The first answer choice, (A), simply repeats the underlined part of the sentence. The other four choices present four alternative ways to phrase the underlined part. Select the answer choice that produces the most effective sentence, one that is clear and exact.

Walking out the hotel door, the Danish village with its charming stores and bakeries beckons you to enjoy a memorable day.

(A) Walking out the hotel door, the Danish village with its charming stores and bakeries beckons you to enjoy a memorable day.
(B) Walking out the hotel door, the Danish village with its charming stores and bakeries is beckoning you to enjoy a memorable day.
(C) While you were walking out the hotel door, the Danish village with its charming stores and bakeries beckons you to enjoy a memorable day.
(D) As you walk out the hotel door, the Danish village with its charming stores and bakeries beckons you to enjoy a memorable day.
(E) Walking out the hotel door, the Danish village with its charming stores and bakeries beckon you to enjoy a memorable day.

Look at the answer choices to see what changes have been made to the original sentence. Choices B and E change the verb. Choices C and D change the opening participial phrase, turning it into a subordinate clause. First, identify the simple subject of the sentence. It is *village*, a singular noun. Don't let the phrase *with its charming stores and bakeries* confuse you. The singular subject requires a singular verb. Choice E is incorrect because it uses the verb's plural form, *beckon*; therefore, you can eliminate Choice E. Choices A and B both correctly use singular forms of the verb; since there cannot be two correct answer choices, the error you're looking for must involve the opening participial

phrase, not the verb. Who or what is walking out the hotel door? Certainly not the village! To improve the sentence, you must eliminate the dangling participle, replacing the participial phrase *Walking out the hotel door* with a clause. Both Choices C and D do so. However, Choice C introduces an error involving the sequence of tenses: the verb *were walking* is the past tense, not the present. Only Choice D corrects the dangling participle without introducing any fresh errors. It is the correct answer.

ERROR IDENTIFICATION QUESTIONS

Error identification questions ask you to spot something wrong. Your job is to find the error in a sentence, not to fix it.

> Directions: These sentences may contain errors in grammar, usage, choice of words, or idioms. Either there is just one error in a sentence, or the sentence is correct. Some words or phrases are underlined and lettered; everything else in the sentence is correct.
>   If an underlined word or phrase is incorrect, choose that letter; if the sentence is correct, select No error.

After the incident was over, neither the passengers
 A   B
nor the bus driver were able to identify the
                     C
youngster who had created the disturbance.
                    D
No error
 E

The error here is the lack of agreement between the subject and the verb. In a *neither-nor* construction, the verb agrees in number with the noun or pronoun that comes immediately before it. Here, the noun that immediately precedes the verb is the singular noun *driver*. Therefore, the correct verb form is the singular verb *was*. The error is in C.

PARAGRAPH IMPROVEMENT QUESTIONS

Paragraph improvement questions require you to correct the flaws in a student essay. Some questions involve rewriting or combining separate sentences to come up with a more effective wording. Other questions involve reordering sentences to produce a better organized argument.

> Directions: The passage below is the unedited draft of a student's essay. Parts of the essay need to be rewritten to make the meaning clearer and more precise. Read the essay carefully.
>
> The essay is followed by six questions about changes that might improve all or part of the organization, development, sentence structure, use of language, appropriateness to the audience, or use of standard written English. Choose the answer that most clearly and effectively expresses the student's intended meaning.

(1) This fall I am supposed to vote for the first time. (2) However, I do not know whether my vote will count. (3) Ever since the 2000 presidential election, I have been reading in the newspapers about problems in our voting system. (4) Some days I ask myself whether there is any point in me voting at all. (5) From the papers, I know our methods of counting votes are seriously flawed. (6) We use many different kinds of technology in voting, and none of them work perfectly. (7) And the newest method, electronic voting technology, is the worst of all.

Sentence 3 would make the most sense if placed after

(A) Sentence 1
(B) Sentence 4
(C) Sentence 5
(D) Sentence 6
(E) Sentence 7

The best way to improve this opening paragraph is to place sentence 3 immediately after sentence 4. The opening section would then read: *This fall I am supposed to vote for the first time. However, I do not know whether my vote will count. Some days I*

ask myself whether there is any point in me voting at all. Ever since the 2000 presidential election, I have been reading in the newspapers about problems in our voting system. From the papers, I know our methods of counting votes are seriously flawed. Rewritten in this fashion, the paragraph moves from the general ("voting") to the specific ("problems in our voting system"). The student author is gradually introducing her topic, the problems inherent in today's electronic voting technology.

THE 25-MINUTE ESSAY

The writing skills sections of the SAT test not only your quickness at spotting grammatical errors and awkwardly written prose but also your ability to write an essay under severe time pressure. You have 25 minutes. In these 25 minutes you must take a position on a particular topic or issue and write a first-draft essay that coherently develops your point of view.

In the essay-writing section, you are not being tested on how neatly you write (although legibility helps!), nor on how much you get down on paper (although longer papers often treat the topic more thoroughly than shorter ones do, and may receive higher scores). You are being tested on how effectively you express your ideas.

The essay questions on the new SAT are similar to the essay questions on the SAT II Writing Test. Most of them simply ask you to respond to a statement. Here is a typical essay prompt, followed by the assignment based upon it.

The harder the conflict, the more glorious the triumph. What we obtain too cheap, we esteem too lightly. —Thomas Paine

Assignment: The excerpt above argues that we most value that which is difficult to attain. Write an essay supporting, disputing, or qualifying this view. You may use examples from history, literature, popular culture, current events, or personal experience to support your position.

To learn how to handle writing an essay in 25 minutes, turn to Part VII.

BEFORE THE TEST

What you do on your actual test day clearly matters greatly. However, what you do *before the test*, as you organize yourself and learn how to handle tests such as the SAT, may in the long run matter even more.

SIX MONTHS BEFORE

Expand Your Verbal Horizons

If you haven't started studying for the test by this time, you'd better get started now. There's no point killing yourself with last-minute cramming sessions and overnight flash-card marathons. Now's the time to pick up some good habits that will expand your verbal horizons and increase your verbal skills.

Make a habit of reading a high-quality newspaper every day. Try *The Christian Science Monitor*, *The New York Times*, or *The Washington Post*, not something written in short sound bites like *U.S.A. Today*. Good newspapers, written for **discriminating** readers, **exemplify** what is best in journalism today. Note how their editorials address the day's issues **dispassionately**, **delineating** schemes to **rectify** society's ills.

Note also the number of boldface words in the preceding two sentences. We have highlighted them because they are key SAT words: you can find them all on our SAT High-Frequency Word List (Part V). Were any of them unfamiliar to you? Then turn to the high-frequency list. You can jump-start your SAT preparations if you follow the directions given there for building your vocabulary. You have the time—get to it!

TWO MONTHS BEFORE

Register

First, get the paperwork out of the way. Unless you like paying late registration fees, be sure to pick up a test registration form at your high school guidance office and send it in to the College Board at least 6 or 7 weeks before the date on which you want to take the test. Plan ahead: if you want to take the test in October, you have to mail your form in early September, when you are bound to be busy getting off to a good start with your new classes at school.

To get a registration form, or to order a copy of *The Sat Preparation Booklet,* a guide to the test including a sample SAT, call, e-mail, or write the College Board:

(609) 771–7588
(8:30 A.M.–9:30 P.M. weekdays)
www.collegeboard.com

College Board SAT
P.O. Box 6200
Princeton, NJ 08541-6200

Rehearse

The best way to practice for a race is to run the course in advance. Likewise, the best way to practice for a test is to take a simulated test, going over all the different question types in advance.

First, memorize the directions in this book for each type of question. These are only slightly different from the exact words you'll find on the SAT. The test time you would normally spend reading directions can be better spent answering questions.

Then take your practice test. In this workbook, you have four model tests—one self-assessment test in the next chapter, plus three more at the end of the book. To get the most out of these tests, try taking them under test conditions—no breaks in midsection, no talking, no help from friends.

You'll find this kind of run-through will help build your test-taking stamina and strengthen you for those four vital hours after you walk through the test-center door.

Learn to Pace Yourself

In taking the SAT, your job is to answer as many questions as you can, rapidly, economically, *correctly*, without getting hung up on any one question and wasting time you could have used to answer two or three additional ones.

As you go through this book, if you find you do get bogged down on an individual question, think things through. First, ask yourself whether it's a question you might be able to answer if you had a bit more time or whether it's one you have *no* idea how to tackle. If you think it's one you can answer if you give it a second try, mark it with a check or an arrow, and plan to come back to it after you've worked through the easy questions in the section. If, however, you think it's a lost cause, mark it with an X and come back to it only after you've answered all the other questions in the section and double-checked your answers. With practice, you should be able to distinguish a "second chancer" from a lost cause. In any case, if you're taking too long, your best bet is to move on.

Learn When (and When Not) to Guess

Students always worry about whether they should or shouldn't guess on standardized tests. Because wrong answers do count fractionally against you on the SAT, you may think that you should never guess if you aren't sure of the right answer to a question. But even if you guessed wrong four times for every time you guessed right, you would still come out even. A wrong answer costs you only $1/4$ of a point. *On the multiple-choice questions,* the best advice for top students is to guess if you can eliminate one or two of the answer choices. You have a better chance of hitting the right answer when you make this sort of "educated" guess.

As you go through this book, try this experiment to find out what kind of guesser you are. Take part of any test that you have not taken before. You don't have to take an entire test section, but you should tackle at least 25 questions. First, answer only the questions you are sure about. Then, with a different color pen, answer the remaining questions for which you can make educated guesses. Finally, with yet another color pen, guess blindly on all the other questions.

Score each of the three tests separately. Compare your scores from the three different approaches to the test. For many people, the second score (the one with the educated guesses) will be the best one. But you may be different. Maybe you are such a poor guesser that you should never guess at all. That's okay. Or maybe you are such a good guesser that you should try every question. That's okay, too. The important thing is to know yourself.

Learn to Concentrate

Another important technique for you to work on is building your powers of concentration. As you go through the practice exercises and model tests, notice when you start to lose your focus. Does your mind drift off in the middle of long reading passages? Do you catch yourself staring off into space, or watching the seconds ticking away on the clock? The sooner you spot these momentary lapses of concentration, the sooner you'll be back working toward your goal.

By the way, there's nothing wrong with losing focus for a moment. Everybody does it. When you notice you're drifting, smile. You're normal. Breathe in slowly and let the air ease out. Then take a fresh look at that paragraph or question you were working on. You've had your minibreak. Now you're ready to pick up a few points.

Learn There's No Need to Panic

Despite all rumors to the contrary, *your whole college career is not riding on the results of this one test.* The SAT is only one of the factors that colleges take into account when they are deciding about admissions. Admissions officers like the test because the scores give them a quick way to compare applicants from different high schools without worrying whether a B+ from the district high school is the equivalent of a B+ from the elite preparatory school. But colleges never rely on SAT scores alone. Admissions officers are perfectly well aware that there are brilliant students who fall apart on major tests, that students who are not feeling well can do much worse than normal on a test, and that all sorts of things can affect SAT scores on any given day. What's more, every college accepts students with a *wide* range of SAT scores.

You do not need to answer every question on the SAT correctly to be accepted by the college of your choice. In fact, if you answer only 50–60 percent of the questions correctly, you'll get a better than average score, and that, plus a decent GPA, will get you into most colleges.

As you can see, *there's no need to panic about taking the SAT.* However, not everybody taking the SAT realizes this simple truth.

It's hard to stay calm when those around you are tense, and you're bound to run into some pretty tense people when you take the SAT. (Not everyone works through this book, unfortunately.) If you do experience a slight case of "exam nerves" just before the big day, don't worry about it.

- Being keyed up for an examination isn't always bad; you may outdo yourself because you are so worked up.
- Total panic is unlikely to set in; by the time you face the exam, you'll know too much.

Keep these facts in mind, and those tensions should just fade away.

THE NIGHT BEFORE

Rest

The best thing you can do for yourself before any test is to get a good night's sleep. If you find you're so keyed up that you don't think you'll be able to sleep, try listening to relaxing music, or exercising and then taking a warm bath. If you're lying in bed wakefully, try concentrating on your breathing: breathe in for 4 to 6 counts, hold your breath for another 4 to 6 counts, exhale for 4 to 6 counts. Concentrating on breathing or on visualizing an image of a person or place often helps people to block out distractions and enables them to relax.

Organize Your Gear

The night before the test, set out everything you're going to need the next day. You will need your admission ticket, a photo ID (a driver's license or a nondriver picture ID, a passport, or a school ID), four or five sharp No. 2 pencils (with erasers), plus a map or directions showing how to get to the test center. Set out an accurate watch as well, plus a calculator with charged batteries to use on the math sections.

Lay out comfortable clothes for the next day, including a sweater in case the room is cold. Consider bringing along a snack, a treat you can munch on during the break.

Plan Your Route

Allow plenty of time for getting to the test site. If you haven't been there before, locate the test center on a map and figure out the best route. If you're using public transportation, check your bus or subway schedule, and be sure you've got a token or ticket or the correct change. If you're driving, check that there's gas in the car. Your job is taking the test. You don't need the extra tension that comes from worrying about whether you will get to the test on time, or the extra distraction that comes from kicking yourself for losing test time by being late.

DURING THE TEST

USE TIME WISELY

In the course of working through the model tests and practice exercises in this book, you should develop your own personal testing rhythm. You know approximately how many questions you need to get right to meet your academic goals.

Don't get bogged down on any one question. By the time you get to the SAT, you should have a fair idea of how much time to spend on each question (about 30–40 seconds for a sentence completion or sentence error identification question, 75 seconds for a reading comprehension or paragraph improvement question if you average in your passage reading time). If a question is taking too long, leave it and move on to the next ones. Keep moving on to maximize your score.

Note Down Questions You Skip

Before you move on, put a mark in your test booklet next to the question you're skipping. You're probably going to want to find that question easily later on.

What sort of mark? First, ask yourself whether it's a question you might be able to answer if you had a bit more time or whether it's one you have *no* idea how to tackle. If you think it's one you can answer if you give it a second try, mark it with a check or an arrow and plan to come straight back to it after you've worked through the easy questions in the section. If you think it's a lost cause, mark it with an X and come back to it only after you've answered all the other questions in the section and double-checked your answers. Either way, mark the test booklet and move on.

Whenever you skip a question, check frequently to make sure you are answering later questions in the right spots. No machine is going to notice that you made a mistake early in the test, by answering question 9 in the space for question 8, so that all your following answers are in the wrong places. Line up your answer sheet with your test booklet. That way you'll have an easier time checking that you're getting your answers in the right spots.

Never just skip for skipping's sake. Always try to answer each question before you decide to move on. Keep up that "can do" spirit—the more confident you are that you can answer the SAT questions, the more likely you are to give each question your best shot.

Answer Easy Questions First

First answer all the easy questions; *then* tackle the hard ones if you have time. You know that the questions in each segment of the test get harder as you go along (except for the reading comprehension questions). But there's no rule that says you have to answer the questions in order. You're allowed to skip; so, if the last three sentence completion questions are driving you crazy, move on to the reading passages right away. Take advantage of the easy questions to boost your score.

Tackle Shorter Questions Before Longer Ones

If you're running out of time on a critical reading section and you're smack in the middle of a reading passage, look for the shortest questions on that passage and try answering them. Aim for questions with answer choices that are only two or three words long. You don't need much time to answer a vocabulary-in-context question or a straightforward question about the author's attitude or tone, and one or two extra correct answers can boost your score an additional 10 to 20 points.

Eliminate Wrong Answers as You Go

Eliminate as many wrong answers as you can. Sometimes you'll be able to eliminate all the choices until you have just one answer left. Even if you wind up with two choices that look good, deciding between two choices is easier than deciding among five. What's more, the reasoning that helped you decide which answer choices to eliminate may also give you new insights into the question and help you figure out which of the remaining answer choices is correct.

Draw a line through any answer you decide to eliminate. Then, if you decide to move on to another question and come back to this one later, you won't forget which answer choices you thought were wrong. (However, when you cross out an answer choice, do so *lightly*. Don't obliterate it totally. You may want to look it over again later if you decide your first impulse to eliminate it was wrong.)

Even if you can't settle on a correct answer and decide to guess, every answer you eliminate as definitely wrong improves your chances of guessing right.

CENTER ON THE TEST

Focus on the question in front of you. At this moment, it's all that matters. Answer it and fill in your answer choice, *being careful you're filling in the right space*. Then move on to the next question, and the next. Find your steady, even testing rhythm and keep it going.

Block Out Distractions

When Tiger Woods plays golf, he has his mind on one thing: the game, not the movements of the enthusiastic crowd, not the occasional plane flying overhead, not the applause of the spectators, not even the photographers in the gallery. He blocks them out.

The SAT is your game. To play it well, block out the distractions. Don't start looking around at the other students taking the test. You don't get any points for watching other people answer questions. You get points only for answering questions yourself. Keep your eye on the test booklet and your mind on the game.

When Things Get Tight, Stay Loose

Sooner or later, as you go through the test, you're going to hit a tough spot. You may run into a paragraph that seems totally unintelligible, or a couple of hard questions that throw you, so that you stop thinking about the question you're working on and sit there panicking instead.

If you come to a group of questions that stump you, relax. There are bound to be a few brain-benders on a test of this nature. *Remember: you don't have to answer every question correctly to do just fine on the test.*

There will be a break about halfway through the test. Use this period to clear your thoughts. Take a few deep breaths. Stretch. Close your eyes and imagine yourself floating. In addition to being under mental pressure, you're under physical pressure from sitting so long in a hard seat with a No. 2 pencil clutched in your hand. Anything you can do to loosen up and get the kinks out will ease your body and help the oxygen get to your brain.

Keep a Positive Outlook

The best thing you can do for yourself during the test is to keep a positive frame of mind. Too many people walk into tests and interviews defeated before they start. Instead of feeling good about what they have going for them, they worry about what can go wrong instead. They let negative thoughts distract them and drag them down.

You are a motivated, hard-working student. That's why you've chosen to work through this book. You're exactly the sort of person for whom colleges are looking. For you, the SAT isn't an unknown terror. It's something you can handle, something for which you are prepared. It's okay for you not to answer every question. It's okay to get some questions wrong. You'll do better figuring out the answers to the questions you tackle if you know you're doing okay. Have confidence in yourself.

Note What's Going Right

Whenever you cross out an answer you *know* is incorrect, whenever you skip a question so that you can come back to it later, notice that you're doing the right thing. Whenever you catch yourself drifting off and quickly get back to work, whenever you stretch to get out the kinks, recognize how much you're in control. In applying these tactics you've mastered, you're showing you know how to do the job and do it right.

Pat Yourself on the Back

As you go through the test, each time you get a correct answer, pat yourself on the back. "Yes! Ten more points!" Enjoy your successes, and keep an eye out for more successes, more correct answer choices ahead. Feel good about the progress you're making and the rewarding college years to come.

PART II

SELF-ASSESSMENT

INTRODUCTION

How do you get a high score on the new SAT? Practice, practice, practice.

Call this chapter "130 Minutes to a Better Score on the SAT." Just a little over 2 hours from now you will have a much better idea of how well prepared you are to face the critical reading and writing skills portions of the new SAT.

This chapter contains a full test's worth of critical reading and writing skills test sections, just like the ones on the official practice test for the new SAT. There are three critical reading sections, and three writing skills sections. You are allowed 25 minutes each for Sections 1 through 4, 20 minutes for Section 5, and just 10 minutes for Section 6. Make every minute count. Take each test section under exam conditions, or as close to exam conditions as possible—no talking, no consulting dictionaries, no taking soda breaks. Limit yourself to the time allowed; that way you'll develop a sense of how to pace yourself on the SAT.

As soon as you've completed all six sections, see how many questions you've answered correctly. (The correct answers are given on page 51.) Then read the answer explanations and go back over any questions you got wrong. Note unfamiliar words you came across so that you can look them up in your dictionary. Check to see whether any particular question types are giving you special trouble. Do this follow-up thoroughly to get the most out of the time you've spent.

ANSWER SHEET FOR SELF-ASSESSMENT TEST

Section 1   **ESSAY**   Time allowed: 25 minutes

Essay (continued)

Section 2

1. Ⓐ Ⓑ Ⓒ Ⓓ Ⓔ   9. Ⓐ Ⓑ Ⓒ Ⓓ Ⓔ   17. Ⓐ Ⓑ Ⓒ Ⓓ Ⓔ   25. Ⓐ Ⓑ Ⓒ Ⓓ Ⓔ
2. Ⓐ Ⓑ Ⓒ Ⓓ Ⓔ   10. Ⓐ Ⓑ Ⓒ Ⓓ Ⓔ   18. Ⓐ Ⓑ Ⓒ Ⓓ Ⓔ   26. Ⓐ Ⓑ Ⓒ Ⓓ Ⓔ
3. Ⓐ Ⓑ Ⓒ Ⓓ Ⓔ   11. Ⓐ Ⓑ Ⓒ Ⓓ Ⓔ   19. Ⓐ Ⓑ Ⓒ Ⓓ Ⓔ   27. Ⓐ Ⓑ Ⓒ Ⓓ Ⓔ
4. Ⓐ Ⓑ Ⓒ Ⓓ Ⓔ   12. Ⓐ Ⓑ Ⓒ Ⓓ Ⓔ   20. Ⓐ Ⓑ Ⓒ Ⓓ Ⓔ   28. Ⓐ Ⓑ Ⓒ Ⓓ Ⓔ
5. Ⓐ Ⓑ Ⓒ Ⓓ Ⓔ   13. Ⓐ Ⓑ Ⓒ Ⓓ Ⓔ   21. Ⓐ Ⓑ Ⓒ Ⓓ Ⓔ   29. Ⓐ Ⓑ Ⓒ Ⓓ Ⓔ
6 Ⓐ Ⓑ Ⓒ Ⓓ Ⓔ   14. Ⓐ Ⓑ Ⓒ Ⓓ Ⓔ   22. Ⓐ Ⓑ Ⓒ Ⓓ Ⓔ   30. Ⓐ Ⓑ Ⓒ Ⓓ Ⓔ
7. Ⓐ Ⓑ Ⓒ Ⓓ Ⓔ   15. Ⓐ Ⓑ Ⓒ Ⓓ Ⓔ   23. Ⓐ Ⓑ Ⓒ Ⓓ Ⓔ
8. Ⓐ Ⓑ Ⓒ Ⓓ Ⓔ   16. Ⓐ Ⓑ Ⓒ Ⓓ Ⓔ   24. Ⓐ Ⓑ Ⓒ Ⓓ Ⓔ

Section 3

1. Ⓐ Ⓑ Ⓒ Ⓓ Ⓔ   10. Ⓐ Ⓑ Ⓒ Ⓓ Ⓔ   19. Ⓐ Ⓑ Ⓒ Ⓓ Ⓔ   28. Ⓐ Ⓑ Ⓒ Ⓓ Ⓔ
2. Ⓐ Ⓑ Ⓒ Ⓓ Ⓔ   11. Ⓐ Ⓑ Ⓒ Ⓓ Ⓔ   20. Ⓐ Ⓑ Ⓒ Ⓓ Ⓔ   29. Ⓐ Ⓑ Ⓒ Ⓓ Ⓔ
3. Ⓐ Ⓑ Ⓒ Ⓓ Ⓔ   12. Ⓐ Ⓑ Ⓒ Ⓓ Ⓔ   21. Ⓐ Ⓑ Ⓒ Ⓓ Ⓔ   30. Ⓐ Ⓑ Ⓒ Ⓓ Ⓔ
4. Ⓐ Ⓑ Ⓒ Ⓓ Ⓔ   13. Ⓐ Ⓑ Ⓒ Ⓓ Ⓔ   22. Ⓐ Ⓑ Ⓒ Ⓓ Ⓔ   31. Ⓐ Ⓑ Ⓒ Ⓓ Ⓔ
5. Ⓐ Ⓑ Ⓒ Ⓓ Ⓔ   14. Ⓐ Ⓑ Ⓒ Ⓓ Ⓔ   23. Ⓐ Ⓑ Ⓒ Ⓓ Ⓔ   32. Ⓐ Ⓑ Ⓒ Ⓓ Ⓔ
6 Ⓐ Ⓑ Ⓒ Ⓓ Ⓔ   15. Ⓐ Ⓑ Ⓒ Ⓓ Ⓔ   24. Ⓐ Ⓑ Ⓒ Ⓓ Ⓔ   33. Ⓐ Ⓑ Ⓒ Ⓓ Ⓔ
7. Ⓐ Ⓑ Ⓒ Ⓓ Ⓔ   16. Ⓐ Ⓑ Ⓒ Ⓓ Ⓔ   25. Ⓐ Ⓑ Ⓒ Ⓓ Ⓔ   34. Ⓐ Ⓑ Ⓒ Ⓓ Ⓔ
8. Ⓐ Ⓑ Ⓒ Ⓓ Ⓔ   17. Ⓐ Ⓑ Ⓒ Ⓓ Ⓔ   26. Ⓐ Ⓑ Ⓒ Ⓓ Ⓔ   35. Ⓐ Ⓑ Ⓒ Ⓓ Ⓔ
9. Ⓐ Ⓑ Ⓒ Ⓓ Ⓔ   18. Ⓐ Ⓑ Ⓒ Ⓓ Ⓔ   27. Ⓐ Ⓑ Ⓒ Ⓓ Ⓔ

Section 4

1. Ⓐ Ⓑ Ⓒ Ⓓ Ⓔ   9. Ⓐ Ⓑ Ⓒ Ⓓ Ⓔ   17. Ⓐ Ⓑ Ⓒ Ⓓ Ⓔ   25. Ⓐ Ⓑ Ⓒ Ⓓ Ⓔ
2. Ⓐ Ⓑ Ⓒ Ⓓ Ⓔ   10. Ⓐ Ⓑ Ⓒ Ⓓ Ⓔ   18. Ⓐ Ⓑ Ⓒ Ⓓ Ⓔ   26. Ⓐ Ⓑ Ⓒ Ⓓ Ⓔ
3. Ⓐ Ⓑ Ⓒ Ⓓ Ⓔ   11. Ⓐ Ⓑ Ⓒ Ⓓ Ⓔ   19. Ⓐ Ⓑ Ⓒ Ⓓ Ⓔ   27. Ⓐ Ⓑ Ⓒ Ⓓ Ⓔ
4. Ⓐ Ⓑ Ⓒ Ⓓ Ⓔ   12. Ⓐ Ⓑ Ⓒ Ⓓ Ⓔ   20. Ⓐ Ⓑ Ⓒ Ⓓ Ⓔ   28. Ⓐ Ⓑ Ⓒ Ⓓ Ⓔ
5. Ⓐ Ⓑ Ⓒ Ⓓ Ⓔ   13. Ⓐ Ⓑ Ⓒ Ⓓ Ⓔ   21. Ⓐ Ⓑ Ⓒ Ⓓ Ⓔ   29. Ⓐ Ⓑ Ⓒ Ⓓ Ⓔ
6 Ⓐ Ⓑ Ⓒ Ⓓ Ⓔ   14. Ⓐ Ⓑ Ⓒ Ⓓ Ⓔ   22. Ⓐ Ⓑ Ⓒ Ⓓ Ⓔ   30. Ⓐ Ⓑ Ⓒ Ⓓ Ⓔ
7. Ⓐ Ⓑ Ⓒ Ⓓ Ⓔ   15. Ⓐ Ⓑ Ⓒ Ⓓ Ⓔ   23. Ⓐ Ⓑ Ⓒ Ⓓ Ⓔ
8. Ⓐ Ⓑ Ⓒ Ⓓ Ⓔ   16. Ⓐ Ⓑ Ⓒ Ⓓ Ⓔ   24. Ⓐ Ⓑ Ⓒ Ⓓ Ⓔ

Section 5

1. Ⓐ Ⓑ Ⓒ Ⓓ Ⓔ
2. Ⓐ Ⓑ Ⓒ Ⓓ Ⓔ
3. Ⓐ Ⓑ Ⓒ Ⓓ Ⓔ
4. Ⓐ Ⓑ Ⓒ Ⓓ Ⓔ
5. Ⓐ Ⓑ Ⓒ Ⓓ Ⓔ
6. Ⓐ Ⓑ Ⓒ Ⓓ Ⓔ
7. Ⓐ Ⓑ Ⓒ Ⓓ Ⓔ
8. Ⓐ Ⓑ Ⓒ Ⓓ Ⓔ

9. Ⓐ Ⓑ Ⓒ Ⓓ Ⓔ
10. Ⓐ Ⓑ Ⓒ Ⓓ Ⓔ
11. Ⓐ Ⓑ Ⓒ Ⓓ Ⓔ
12. Ⓐ Ⓑ Ⓒ Ⓓ Ⓔ
13. Ⓐ Ⓑ Ⓒ Ⓓ Ⓔ
14. Ⓐ Ⓑ Ⓒ Ⓓ Ⓔ
15. Ⓐ Ⓑ Ⓒ Ⓓ Ⓔ
16. Ⓐ Ⓑ Ⓒ Ⓓ Ⓔ

17. Ⓐ Ⓑ Ⓒ Ⓓ Ⓔ
18. Ⓐ Ⓑ Ⓒ Ⓓ Ⓔ
19. Ⓐ Ⓑ Ⓒ Ⓓ Ⓔ
20. Ⓐ Ⓑ Ⓒ Ⓓ Ⓔ
21. Ⓐ Ⓑ Ⓒ Ⓓ Ⓔ
22. Ⓐ Ⓑ Ⓒ Ⓓ Ⓔ
23. Ⓐ Ⓑ Ⓒ Ⓓ Ⓔ
24. Ⓐ Ⓑ Ⓒ Ⓓ Ⓔ

25. Ⓐ Ⓑ Ⓒ Ⓓ Ⓔ
26. Ⓐ Ⓑ Ⓒ Ⓓ Ⓔ
27. Ⓐ Ⓑ Ⓒ Ⓓ Ⓔ
28. Ⓐ Ⓑ Ⓒ Ⓓ Ⓔ
29. Ⓐ Ⓑ Ⓒ Ⓓ Ⓔ
30. Ⓐ Ⓑ Ⓒ Ⓓ Ⓔ

Section 6

1. Ⓐ Ⓑ Ⓒ Ⓓ Ⓔ
2. Ⓐ Ⓑ Ⓒ Ⓓ Ⓔ
3. Ⓐ Ⓑ Ⓒ Ⓓ Ⓔ
4. Ⓐ Ⓑ Ⓒ Ⓓ Ⓔ
5. Ⓐ Ⓑ Ⓒ Ⓓ Ⓔ
6. Ⓐ Ⓑ Ⓒ Ⓓ Ⓔ
7. Ⓐ Ⓑ Ⓒ Ⓓ Ⓔ
8. Ⓐ Ⓑ Ⓒ Ⓓ Ⓔ

9. Ⓐ Ⓑ Ⓒ Ⓓ Ⓔ
10. Ⓐ Ⓑ Ⓒ Ⓓ Ⓔ
11. Ⓐ Ⓑ Ⓒ Ⓓ Ⓔ
12. Ⓐ Ⓑ Ⓒ Ⓓ Ⓔ
13. Ⓐ Ⓑ Ⓒ Ⓓ Ⓔ
14. Ⓐ Ⓑ Ⓒ Ⓓ Ⓔ
15. Ⓐ Ⓑ Ⓒ Ⓓ Ⓔ
16. Ⓐ Ⓑ Ⓒ Ⓓ Ⓔ

17. Ⓐ Ⓑ Ⓒ Ⓓ Ⓔ
18. Ⓐ Ⓑ Ⓒ Ⓓ Ⓔ
19. Ⓐ Ⓑ Ⓒ Ⓓ Ⓔ
20. Ⓐ Ⓑ Ⓒ Ⓓ Ⓔ
21. Ⓐ Ⓑ Ⓒ Ⓓ Ⓔ
22. Ⓐ Ⓑ Ⓒ Ⓓ Ⓔ
23. Ⓐ Ⓑ Ⓒ Ⓓ Ⓔ
24. Ⓐ Ⓑ Ⓒ Ⓓ Ⓔ

25. Ⓐ Ⓑ Ⓒ Ⓓ Ⓔ
26. Ⓐ Ⓑ Ⓒ Ⓓ Ⓔ
27. Ⓐ Ⓑ Ⓒ Ⓓ Ⓔ
28. Ⓐ Ⓑ Ⓒ Ⓓ Ⓔ
29. Ⓐ Ⓑ Ⓒ Ⓓ Ⓔ
30. Ⓐ Ⓑ Ⓒ Ⓓ Ⓔ

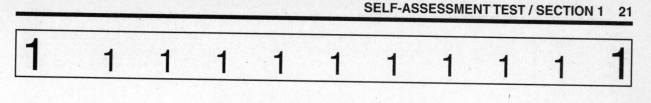

SELF-ASSESSMENT TEST
Section 1
Essay

Turn to your answer sheet and write your essay on the lined portion of the page. To receive credit, you must write your essay in the area provided.

Write on the assigned topic below. If you write on any other topic, your essay will be given a score of zero.

Write or print legibly: your readers will be unfamiliar with your handwriting, and you want them to be able to read what you write.

> The excerpt appearing below makes a point about a particular issue. Read the passage carefully, and think about the assignment that follows.

How can one learn to know oneself? Never by introspection, rather by action. Try to do your duty, and you will know right away what you are like. —Johann Wolfgang Von Goethe

Assignment: The excerpt above implies that we cannot know who we are and what we are capable of without testing ourselves. Write an essay supporting, disputing, or qualifying this view. You may use examples from history, literature, popular culture, current events, or personal experience to support your position.

BEGIN WRITING YOUR ESSAY ON THE ANSWER SHEET

2 2 2 2 2 2 2 2 2 2 2

Section 2

TIME—25 MINUTES
24 QUESTIONS

For each of the following questions, select the best answer from the choices provided and fill in the appropriate circle on the answer sheet.

Each of the following sentences contains one or two blanks; each blank indicates that a word or set of words has been left out. Below the sentence are five words or phrases, lettered A through E. Select the word or set of words that best completes the sentence.

Example:

Fame is ----; today's rising star is all too soon tomorrow's washed-up has-been.

(A) rewarding   (B) gradual
 (C) essential   (D) spontaneous
  (E) transitory

Ⓐ Ⓑ Ⓒ Ⓓ ●

---

1. While there were some tasks the candidate could _____, others she had to attend to herself.
   (A) perform
   (B) endorse
   (C) delegate
   (D) misconstrue
   (E) rehearse

2. Although caterpillars and spiders belong to distinctly different classes of arthropods and come to produce silk quite independently, the silks they produce have remarkably _____ compositions.
   (A) delicate
   (B) diaphanous
   (C) mutable
   (D) similar
   (E) durable

3. Concrete actually is _____, like a sponge—it can absorb up to 10 percent of its weight in water.
   (A) delicate
   (B) elastic
   (C) porous
   (D) ubiquitous
   (E) washable

4. His dislike of _____ made him regard people who flaunted their wealth or accomplishments as _____.
   (A) flattery...charlatans
   (B) poverty...misers
   (C) boasting...braggarts
   (D) failure...opportunists
   (E) procrastination...spendthrifts

5. Some of Kandinsky's artistic innovations are now so much a part of our visual world that they appear on everything from wallpaper to women's scarves without causing the slightest _____.
   (A) profit
   (B) remorse
   (C) boredom
   (D) effort
   (E) stir

6. Short stories, in Hemingway's phrase, have plots that show only "the tip of the iceberg"; such stories _____ a _____ shape below but do not describe that shape in detail.
   (A) cover up...distinctive
   (B) hint at...bulkier
   (C) depart from...nebulous
   (D) thaw out...colder
   (E) revolve around...grimmer

GO ON TO THE NEXT PAGE ⟶

2   2   2   2   2   2   2   2   2   2   2

7. The title *Rage of a Privileged Class* seems
   _____, for such a privileged group would
   seem on the surface to have no _____
   sustained anger with anyone.

   (A) incongruous...time for
   (B) paradoxical...reason for
   (C) ambiguous...familiarity with
   (D) ironic...indifference to
   (E) witty...capacity for

8. Darwin's ideas, which viewed nature as the
   result of cumulative, _____ change, tri-
   umphed over the older, catastrophist theories,
   which _____ that mountains and species
   were created by a few sudden and dramatic
   events.

   (A) gradual...maintained
   (B) drastic...anticipated
   (C) regular...denied
   (D) frequent...disproved
   (E) abrupt...insinuated

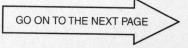

GO ON TO THE NEXT PAGE

2 2 2 2 2 2 2 2 2 2 2

Read each of the passages below, and then answer the questions that follow the passage. The correct response may be stated outright or merely suggested in the passage.

Questions 9 and 10 are based on the following passage.

How did the term "spam" come to mean unsolicited commercial e-mail? Flash back to 1937, when Hormel Foods creates a new
Line canned spiced ham, SPAM. Then, in World
(5) War II, SPAM luncheon meat becomes a staple of soldiers' diets (often GIs ate SPAM two or three times a day). Next, SPAM's wartime omnipresence perhaps inspired the 1987 Monty Python skit in which a breakfast-
(10) seeking couple unsuccessfully tries to order a SPAM-free meal while a chorus of Vikings drowns them out, singing "Spam, spam, spam, spam . . . ." To computer users drowning in junk e-mail, the analogy was obvious.
(15) "Spam," they said, "it's spam."

9. The tone of the passage can best be character-ized as

(A) nostalgic
(B) sardonic
(C) detached
(D) chatty
(E) didactic

10. The parenthetic remark in lines 6 and 7 ("often . . . day") serves primarily to

(A) establish the soldiers' fondness for SPAM
(B) provide evidence of SPAM's abundance
(C) refute criticisms of wartime food shortages
(D) illustrate the need for dietary supplements
(E) point out the difference between military and civilian diets

Questions 11 and 12 are based on the following passage.

Exquisitely adapted for life in one of Earth's harshest environments, polar bears can survive for 20 years or more on the Arctic
Line Circle's glacial ice. At home in a waste
(5) where temperatures reach minus 50 degrees Fahrenheit, these largest members of the bear family are a striking example of natural selec-tion at work. Provided with two layers of fur underlaid with blubber, polar bears are well
(10) adapted to resist heat loss. Also, their broad, snowshoe-like paws and sharp, curved claws enable them to traverse the ice with ease. They even possess the capacity to scent prey from a distance of 20 miles.

11. The author's attitude toward the polar bear's adaptation to its environment can best be characterized as one of

(A) ambivalence
(B) admiration
(C) bemusement
(D) indifference
(E) disapprobation

12. In line 13, "capacity" most nearly means

(A) ability
(B) stature
(C) quantity
(D) spaciousness
(E) intelligence

GO ON TO THE NEXT PAGE

2 2 2 2 2 2 2 2 2 2 2 2

Questions 13–24 are based on the following passage.

In this excerpt from an essay on the symbolic language of dreams, the writer Erich Fromm explores the nature of symbols.

One of the current definitions of a symbol is that it is "something that stands for something else." We can differentiate between three
Line kinds of symbols: the *conventional*, the *acci-*
(5) *dental*, and the *universal* symbol.

The *conventional* symbol is the best known of the three, since we employ it in everyday language. If we see the word "table" or hear the sound "table," the letters *t-a-b-l-e* stand for
(10) something else. They stand for the thing "table" that we see, touch, and use. What is the connection between the *word* "table" and the *thing* "table"? Is there any inherent relationship between them? Obviously not. The
(15) *thing* table has nothing to do with the *sound* table, and the only reason the word symbolizes the thing is the convention of calling this particular thing by a name. We learn this connection as children by the repeated experience
(20) of hearing the word in reference to the thing until a lasting association is formed so that we don't have to think to find the right word.

There are some words, however, in which the association is not only conventional. When
(25) we say "phooey," for instance, we make with our lips a movement of dispelling the air quickly. It is an expression of disgust in which our mouths participate. By this quick expulsion of air we imitate and thus express our
(30) intention to expel something, to get it out of our system. In this case, as in some others, the symbol has an inherent connection with the feeling it symbolizes. But even if we assume that originally many or even all words had
(35) their origins in some such inherent connection between symbol and the symbolized, most words no longer have this meaning for us when we learn a language.

Words are not the only illustration for con-
(40) ventional symbols, although they are the most frequent and best known ones. Pictures also can be conventional symbols. A flag, for instance, may stand for a specific country, and yet there is no intrinsic connection between
(45) the specific colors and the country for which they stand. They have been accepted as denoting that particular country, and we translate the visual impression of the flag into the concept of that country, again on conventional
(50) grounds.

The opposite to the conventional symbol is the *accidental* symbol, although they have one thing in common: there is no intrinsic relationship between the symbol and that which it
(55) symbolizes. Let us assume that someone has had a saddening experience in a certain city; when he hears the name of that city, he will easily connect the name with a mood of sadness, just as he would connect it with a mood
(60) of joy had his experience been a happy one. Quite obviously, there is nothing in the nature of the city that is either sad or joyful. It is the individual experience connected with the city that makes it a symbol of a mood.

(65) The same reaction could occur in connection with a house, a street, a certain dress, certain scenery, or anything once connected with a specific mood. We might find ourselves dreaming that we are in a certain city. We ask
(70) ourselves why we happened to think of that city in our sleep and may discover that we had fallen asleep in a mood similar to the one symbolized by the city. The picture in the dream represents this mood, the city "stands for" the
(75) mood once experienced in it. The connection between the symbol and the experience symbolized is entirely accidental.

GO ON TO THE NEXT PAGE

2 2 2 2 2 2 2 2 2 2 2

The *universal* symbol is one in which there is an intrinsic relationship between the symbol
(80) and that which it represents. Take, for instance, the symbol of fire. We are fascinated by certain qualities of fire in a fireplace. First of all, by its aliveness. It changes continuously, it moves all the time, and yet there is constancy
(85) in it. It remains the same without being the same. It gives the impression of power, of energy, of grace and lightness. It is as if it were dancing, and had an inexhaustible source of energy. When we use fire as a symbol, we
(90) describe the *inner experience* characterized by the same elements which we notice in the sensory experience of fire—the mood of energy, lightness, movement, grace, gaiety, sometimes one, sometimes another of these elements
(95) being predominant in the feeling.

The universal symbol is the only one in which the relationship between the symbol and that which is symbolized is not coincidental, but intrinsic. It is rooted in the experience
(100) of the affinity between an emotion or thought, on the one hand, and a sensory experience, on the other. It can be called universal because it is shared by all men, in contrast not only to the accidental symbol, which is by its very nature
(105) entirely personal, but also to the conventional symbol, which is restricted to a group of people sharing the same convention. The universal symbol is rooted in the properties of our body, our senses, and our mind, which
(110) are common to all men and, therefore, not restricted to individuals or to specific groups. Indeed, *the language of the universal symbol is the one common tongue developed by the human race, a language which it forgot before*
(115) *it succeeded in developing a universal conventional language.*

13. The passage is primarily concerned with

(A) refuting an argument
(B) illustrating an axiom
(C) describing a process
(D) proving a thesis
(E) refining a definition

14. The term "stand for" in line 9 means

(A) tolerate
(B) represent
(C) withstand
(D) endorse
(E) rise

15. According to lines 8–33, "table" and "phooey" differ in that

(A) only one is a conventional symbol
(B) "table" is a better known symbol than "phooey"
(C) "phooey" has an intrinsic natural link with its meaning
(D) children learn "phooey" more readily than they learn "table"
(E) only one is used exclusively by children

16. It can be inferred from the passage that another example of a word with both inherent and conventional associations to its meaning is

(A) hiss
(B) hike
(C) hold
(D) candle
(E) telephone

17. The author contends that conventional symbols

(A) are less meaningful than accidental ones
(B) necessarily have an innate connection with an emotion
(C) can be pictorial as well as linguistic
(D) are less familiar than universal symbols
(E) appeal chiefly to conventionally minded people

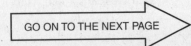
GO ON TO THE NEXT PAGE

2 2 2 2 2 2 2 2 2 2 2 2

18. Which of the following would the author be most likely to categorize as a conventional symbol?

(A) a country road
(B) a patchwork quilt
(C) a bonfire
(D) the city of London
(E) the Statue of Liberty

19. According to the author's argument, a relationship between the city of Paris and the mood of joy can best be described as

(A) innate
(B) dreamlike
(C) elemental
(D) coincidental
(E) immutable

20. A major factor distinguishing a universal symbol from conventional and accidental symbols is

(A) its origins in sensory experience
(B) its dependence on a specific occasion
(C) the intensity of the mood experienced
(D) its unmemorable nature
(E) its appeal to the individual

21. By saying "Take . . . the symbol of fire" (lines 80 and 81), the author is asking the reader to

(A) grasp it as an element
(B) consider it as an example
(C) accept it as a possibility
(D) prefer it as a category
(E) assume it as a standard

22. Which of the following would the author most likely categorize as a universal symbol?

(A) the letters f-i-r-e
(B) the letters p-h-o-o-e-y
(C) a red dress
(D) an American flag
(E) water in a stream

23. The word "properties" in line 108 means

(A) possessions
(B) attributes
(C) investments
(D) titles
(E) grounds

24. The author contends in lines 112–116 that the language of the universal symbol

(A) antedates the development of everyday conventional language
(B) restricts itself to those capable of comprehending symbolism
(C) should be adopted as the common tongue for the human race
(D) grew out of human efforts to create a universal conventional language
(E) developed accidentally from the human desire to communicate

STOP

IF YOU FINISH BEFORE TIME IS CALLED, YOU MAY CHECK YOUR WORK ON THIS SECTION ONLY. DO NOT WORK ON ANY OTHER SECTION IN THE TEST.

Section 3

TIME—25 MINUTES
35 QUESTIONS

For each of the following questions, choose the best answer and fill in the appropriate circle on the answer sheet.

Some or all parts of the following sentences are underlined. The first answer choice, (A), simply repeats the underlined part of the sentence. The other four choices present four alternative ways to phrase the underlined part. Select the answer that produces the most effective sentence, one that is clear and exact, and blacken the appropriate space on your answer sheet. In selecting your choice, be sure that it is standard written English, and that it expresses the meaning of the original sentence.

Example:
  The first biography of author Eudora Welty came out in 1998 and she was 89 years old at the time.

  (A) and she was 89 years old at the time
  (B) at the time she was 89
  (C) upon becoming an 89 year old
  (D) when she was 89
  (E) at the age of 89 years old

  Ⓐ Ⓑ Ⓒ ● Ⓔ

1. Her coach, along with her parents and friends, are confident she will win the tournament.

   (A) along with her parents and friends, are confident she
   (B) along with her parents and friends, are confident that she
   (C) along with her parents and friends, have been confident she
   (D) together with her parents and friends, are confident she
   (E) along with her parents and friends, is confident she

2. The referee would of stopped the fight even if the battered boxer would of risen to his feet.

   (A) would of stopped the fight even if the battered boxer would of risen
   (B) would have stopped the fight even if the battered boxer would of risen
   (C) would have stopped the fight even if the battered boxer had risen
   (D) would of stopped the fight even if the battered boxer would of rose
   (E) would have stopped the fight even if the battered boxer had rose

3. When the waitress told me I could have my choice of vanilla, chocolate, or pistachio ice cream, I selected the former even though I usually prefer the latter.

   (A) the former even though I usually prefer the latter
   (B) the first even though I usually prefer the latter
   (C) the former even though I usually prefer the last
   (D) the former even though it is the latter I usually prefer
   (E) the first even though I usually prefer the last

GO ON TO THE NEXT PAGE

3 3 3 3 3 3 3 3 3 3 3

4. <u>In visiting the Tower of London, Mrs. Pomeroy's hat was blown off her head into the river.</u>

   (A) In visiting the Tower of London, Mrs. Pomeroy's hat was blown off her head into the river.
   (B) Mrs. Pomeroy visited the Tower of London, her hat blew off her head into the river.
   (C) Mrs. Pomeroy, who was visiting the Tower of London when her hat blew off her head, saw it fall into the river.
   (D) When Mrs. Pomeroy visited the Tower of London, her hat was blown off her head and fell into the river.
   (E) Mrs. Pomeroy visited the Tower of London, suddenly her hat was blown off her head which fell into the river.

5. Wildly unscientific medical remedies, such as dosing people with mummy powder, were employed for <u>centuries, and they showed</u> no sign of doing the patients any good.

   (A) centuries, and they showed
   (B) centuries that showed
   (C) centuries, they showed
   (D) centuries, however, they showed
   (E) centuries though they showed

6. <u>The novelist Graham Greene is one of Britain's finest authors and the most important</u> collection of his manuscripts is located in Texas, not in England.

   (A) The novelist Graham Greene is one of Britain's finest authors and the most important
   (B) The novelist Graham Greene being one of Britain's finest authors and the most important
   (C) Although the novelist Graham Greene is one of Britain's finest authors, and the most important
   (D) Although the novelist Graham Greene is one of Britain's finest authors, the most important
   (E) The novelist Graham Greene is one of Britain's finest authors; furthermore, the most important

7. <u>Since all the tickets to the show had been sold,</u> we went instead to a concert at Carnegie Hall.

   (A) Since all the tickets to the show had been sold
   (B) Being that all the tickets to the show had been sold
   (C) All of the tickets to the show having since been sold
   (D) Because they have sold all the tickets to the show
   (E) Being that all the tickets to the show were sold

GO ON TO THE NEXT PAGE

8. If anyone asks for an application, send them to room 1134 to see the personnel director.

   (A) If anyone asks for an application, send them
   (B) Send anyone who asks for an application
   (C) When anyone asks for an application, send them
   (D) If anyone asks for an application, they should be sent
   (E) As soon as anyone asks for an application, send them

9. Celebrated for her clarity of prose and vividness of characterization, critics have been unanimous in their praises of Mary Renault for her peerless historical novels.

   (A) critics have been unanimous in their praises of Mary Renault for her peerless historical novels
   (B) critics have unanimously praised Mary Renault for her peerless historical novels
   (C) critics have been unanimously praising Mary Renault for her peerless historical novels
   (D) Mary Renault has received unanimous praise from critics for her peerless historical novels
   (E) Mary Renault because of her peerless historical novels has been receiving unanimous praise from the critics

10. A study in *The Journal of the American College of Nutrition* found that when young men drink only cola or caffeinated drinks, they became no more dehydrated than if they drank water.

    (A) drink only cola or caffeinated drinks, they
    (B) only drink cola or caffeinated drinks, they
    (C) drunk only cola or caffeinated drinks, they
    (D) drank only cola or caffeinated drinks, they
    (E) will only drink cola or caffeinated drinks, they

11. Edgar Bannister, a painter known primarily for his landscapes, reached a prominent position that was rare for black artists of his era.

    (A) reached a prominent position that was rare for black artists
    (B) reached a prominence, which was rare for black artists
    (C) reached a prominent position which rarely was for black artists
    (D) achieved a prominence rare for black artists
    (E) achieved a prominent position, a rarity for black artists

GO ON TO THE NEXT PAGE

3   3   3   3   3   3   3   3   3   3   3

The sentences in this section may contain errors in grammar, usage, choice of words, or idioms. Either there is just one error in a sentence or the sentence is correct. Some words or phrases are underlined and lettered; everything else in the sentence is correct.

If an underlined word or phrase is incorrect, choose that letter; if the sentence is correct, select <u>No error</u>. Then blacken the appropriate space on your answer sheet.

Example:

The region has a climate <u>so severe that</u> plants
                          A

<u>growing there</u> rarely <u>had been</u> more than twelve
     B   C

inches <u>high</u>. <u>No error</u>
        D   E

Ⓐ Ⓑ ● Ⓓ Ⓔ

12. <u>After having been</u> greeted at the front door by
          A

an elderly woman <u>which</u> he took to be a maid,
                   B

the reporter <u>realized with</u> embarrassment that
                   C

the "servant" was actually the person he

<u>was supposed</u> to interview. <u>No error</u>
     D   E

13. <u>Most of those</u> voting against the measure
          A

<u>were</u> legislators who, <u>by virtue of</u> their ties to
  B   C

big business, had a financial <u>stake in</u> the
                                  D

measure's defeat. <u>No error</u>
                     E

14. It is difficult for my fellow strikers <u>and I</u>
                                             A

<u>even to contemplate</u> returning to work for a
        B

company <u>that</u> has continually <u>reneged on</u>
           C   D

its promises to us. <u>No error</u>
                       E

15. The actors <u>came up with</u> a number of ideas to
                    A

improve the musical, including cutting some

unnecessary <u>exposition from</u> the opening scene
                  B

and inserting an additional song, <u>but</u> the
                                     C

director refused to <u>consider it</u>. <u>No error</u>
                          D   E

16. The artist has <u>drawn on</u> eclectic sources
                       A

<u>ranging from</u> the works of Paul Klee to
     B

Romanesque art and Chinese calligraphy and

has synthesized <u>them</u> into something <u>wholly</u>
                   C   D

his own. <u>No error</u>
            E

17. Our legal system has <u>ingrained for us</u> the
                              A

notion <u>that</u> somebody must be to <u>blame for</u>
          B   C

everything that <u>happens</u>. <u>No error</u>
                   D   E

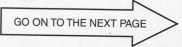
GO ON TO THE NEXT PAGE

3 3 3 3 3 3 3 3 3 3 3

18. <u>Like</u> America's own founding fathers,
    A
    Winston Churchill was an <u>enormously</u>
                              B
    complicated leader, simultaneously <u>capable of</u>
                                         C
    saving the Western world's freedoms

    <u>and he stifled</u> the aspirations of the enslaved
         D
    Indian people. <u>No error</u>
                       E

19. <u>For all</u> the book's length, the narrative is
    A
    <u>brisk, but only</u> as much background is included
         B
    <u>as is needed</u> to enable the reader to make
         C
    <u>sense of</u> a complex story. <u>No error</u>
         D   E

20. The author, born to Holocaust survivors in

    Poland in 1945, renders the catastrophe

    <u>as it is revealed</u> to members of a generation
         A
    <u>drastically effected</u> by events they cannot
         B
    <u>themselves</u> remember, <u>filtered through</u> the
         C   D
    memories of their elders. <u>No error</u>
                                   E

21. The museum is presenting an exhibition of

    <u>more than</u> sixty contemporary American
         A
    political cartoons <u>that</u> either were <u>censored by</u>
                          B   C
    newspaper editors or created a particularly

    strong public reaction because of <u>its</u> approach
                                          D
    to sensitive or controversial subject matter.

    <u>No error</u>
       E

22. The diverse utopias <u>that</u> filmmaker Bernardo
                          A
    Bertolucci <u>has tried to</u> depict on screen <u>has</u>
                   B   C
    sometimes been <u>Marxist, sometimes</u> Buddhist.
                        D
    <u>No error</u>
       E

23. What is <u>intriguing about</u> much of the research
                A
    <u>marked for</u> citation and discussion at the
         B
    economic forum is <u>how modest</u> a role
                          C
    technology plays in the gains in productivity

    <u>studied</u>. <u>No error</u>
       D   E

24. Chocolate, the drink restricted to Aztec kings,

    priests, warriors, and warrior merchants

    <u>until encountered</u> by sixteenth-century Spanish
         A
    warriors, remained <u>largely</u> unknown until the
                          B
    seventeenth century, when coffee, arriving

    <u>by way of</u> Greece and Turkey, became popular,
         C
    <u>as did</u> tea. <u>No error</u>
       D   E

25. In Chekhov's *The Seagull*, the symbolist

    playwright Treplev <u>complains to</u> his uncle
                          A
    about the <u>state of</u> the Russian theater, <u>that</u> he
                  B   C
    <u>describes as</u> moralistic, self-important, and
         D
    conservative. <u>No error</u>
                      E

GO ON TO THE NEXT PAGE

3 3 3 3 3 3 3 3 3 3 3

26. Although the rival mayoral candidates

    <u>have vowed</u> to drive special interests and
        A

    influence peddlers out of city hall, campaign

    financial figures <u>show that</u> several of the
                          B

    contenders have benefited <u>significantly</u> from
                                    C

    those <u>whom</u> they decry. <u>No error</u>
          D   E

27. Psychiatrists <u>who</u> spend many hours a day
                   A

    <u>devoting themselves to</u> the problems of their
         B

    patients often prove <u>sadly</u> <u>insensitive of</u> the
                            C   D

    needs of their spouses and children. <u>No error</u>
                                              E

28. If mortgage rates <u>raise sharply</u> during the next
                          A

    quarter, <u>prospective</u> home buyers may decide
                 B

    to <u>put off</u> any purchases until a <u>better</u> time.
        C   D

    <u>No error</u>
      E

29. *The New York Times* possesses <u>many sterling</u>
                                         A

    qualities, but <u>we cannot</u> hardly expect it or
                      B

    <u>any other</u> newspaper to be <u>free of</u> flaws.
      C   D

    <u>No error</u>
      E

The passage below is the unedited draft of a student's essay. Parts of the essay need to be rewritten to make the meaning clearer and more precise. Read the essay carefully.

The essay is followed by six questions about changes that might improve all or part of the organization, development, sentence structure, use of language, appropriateness to the audience, or use of standard written English. In each case, choose the answer that most clearly and effectively expresses the student's intended meaning. Indicate your choice by blackening the corresponding space on the answer sheet.

[1] From the colonial times until today, the appeal of the underdog has retained a hold on Americans. [2] It is a familiar sight today to see someone rooting for the underdog while watching a sports event on television. [3] Though that only happens if they don't already have a favorite team. [4] Variations of the David and Goliath story are popular in both fact and fiction. [5] Horatio Alger stories, wondrous tales of conquering the West, and the way that people have turned rags-to-riches stories such as Vanderbilt into national myths are three examples of America's fascination with the underdog.

[6] This appeal has been spurred by American tradition as well as an understandably selfish desire to feel good about oneself and life. [7] Part of the aura America has held since its creation is that the humblest and poorest person can make it here in America. [8] That dream is ingrained in the history of America. [9] America is made up of immigrants. [10] Most were poor when they came here. [11] They thought of America as the land of opportunity, where any little guy could succeed. [12] All it took was the desire to lift oneself up and some good honest work. [13] Millions succeeded on account of the American belief to honor and support the underdog in all its efforts.

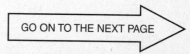
GO ON TO THE NEXT PAGE

3 3 3 3 3 3 3 3 3 3 3

[14] The underdog goes against all odds and defeats the stronger opponent with hope. [15] It makes people feel that maybe one day they too will triumph against the odds. [16] It changes their view of life's struggles because they trust that in the end all their hardships will amount to something. [17] Despair has no place in a society where everyone knows that they can succeed. [18] It's no wonder that the underdog has always had a tight hold upon American hopes and minds.

30. Which of the following is the best revision of the underlined sections of sentences 1 and 2 (below), so that the two sentences are combined into one?

    From the colonial times until today, the appeal of the underdog has retained a hold on Americans. It is a familiar sight today to see someone rooting for the underdog while watching a sports event on television.

    (A) the appeal of the underdog has retained a hold on Americans, and it is a familiar sight today to see underdogs being the one rooted for

    (B) the appeal of the underdog has retained a hold on Americans, but it is a familiar sight today to see someone rooting for the underdog

    (C) the underdog has retained a hold on Americans, who commonly root for the underdog, for example,

    (D) the underdog has retained a hold on Americans, commonly rooting for the underdog

    (E) the underdog's appeal has retained a hold on Americans, for example, they commonly root for the underdog

31. To improve the coherence of paragraph 1, which of the following sentences should be deleted?

    (A) Sentence 1
    (B) Sentence 2
    (C) Sentence 3
    (D) Sentence 4
    (E) Sentence 5

32. Considering the content of paragraph 2, which of the following is the best revision of the paragraph's topic sentence, sentence 6?

    (A) This appeal got spurred by American tradition as well as by an understandably selfish desire to feel good about oneself and one's life.

    (B) The appeal of the underdog has been spurred by American tradition.

    (C) The appeal has been spurred by Americans' traditional and selfish desire to feel good about themselves and life.

    (D) American tradition as well as Americans' desire to feel good about oneself and their life has spurred the appeal of underdogs.

    (E) American traditions include an understandably selfish desire to feel good about themselves and the appeal of the underdog.

GO ON TO THE NEXT PAGE ▷

3 3 3 3 3 3 3 3 3 3 3

33. In the context of paragraph 2, which of the following is the best way to combine sentences 8, 9, 10, and 11?

(A) That dream is ingrained in the experience of America, a country made up of poor immigrants who believed that in this land of opportunity any little guy had a chance to succeed.

(B) That dream was ingrained in our history, a country made up of immigrants, poor and hopeful that any little guy is able to succeed in America, the land of opportunity.

(C) That dream has been ingrained in America's history that poor immigrants look on America as a land of opportunity, which any little guy had been able to succeed in.

(D) The American experience has ingrained in it the dream that by immigrants coming to this country poorly could succeed because America is the land of opportunity.

(E) Ingrained in the American experience is the dream of poor immigrants that they could succeed here, after all, this is the land of opportunity.

34. In view of the sentences that precede and follow sentence 13, which of the following is the most effective revision of sentence 13?

(A) Americans believe that the underdog should be honored and supported, which led to their success.

(B) Because America believed in honoring and supporting the underdog, they succeed.

(C) And succeed they did because of America's commitment to honor and support the underdog.

(D) Honoring and supporting underdogs is a firmly held value in America, and it led to the success of underdogs.

(E) They succeeded with their efforts to be supported and honored by America.

35. Which of the following revisions of sentence 14 is the best transition between paragraphs 3 and 4?

(A) Underdogs, in addition, went against all odds and with hope defeat stronger opponents.

(B) The underdog, feeling hopeful, going against all odds, and defeating stronger opponents.

(C) It is the hope of the underdog who goes against the odds and defeats the stronger opponent.

(D) The triumph of the underdog over a strong opponent inspires hope.

(E) The underdog triumphs against all odds and defeats the stronger opponents.

STOP

IF YOU FINISH BEFORE TIME IS CALLED, YOU MAY CHECK YOUR WORK ON THIS SECTION ONLY. DO NOT WORK ON ANY OTHER SECTION IN THE TEST.

Section 4

TIME—25 MINUTES
24 QUESTIONS

For each of the following questions, select the best answer from the choices provided and fill in the appropriate circle on the answer sheet.

Each of the following sentences contains one or two blanks; each blank indicates that a word or set of words has been left out. Below the sentence are five words or phrases, lettered A through E. Select the word or set of words that best completes the sentence.

Example:

Fame is ----; today's rising star is all too soon tomorrow's washed-up has-been.

(A) rewarding   (B) gradual
 (C) essential   (D) spontaneous
  (E) transitory

Ⓐ Ⓑ Ⓒ Ⓓ ●

---

1. Though their lack of external ears might suggest otherwise, mole rats are able to use _____ to communicate.

    (A) gestures
    (B) touch
    (C) smells
    (D) sounds
    (E) symbols

2. The word *tephra*, from the Greek word meaning ash, has come into use among geologists to describe the assortment of fragments, ranging from blocks of material to dust, that is _____ into the air during a volcanic eruption.

    (A) amassed
    (B) ejected
    (C) repressed
    (D) wafted
    (E) absorbed

3. While most commentators' reaction to the candidate's acceptance speech was ____, a highly positive reaction came from columnist William Safire, who called it a rhetorical triumph.

    (A) enthusiastic
    (B) unrehearsed
    (C) tepid
    (D) groundless
    (E) immediate

4. Scientists are hard-line _____; only after failing to ____ a controversial theory do they accept the evidence.

    (A) militarists...exploit
    (B) optimists...believe
    (C) martinets...punish
    (D) innovators...refute
    (E) cynics...debunk

5. The founder of the Children's Defense Fund, Marian Wright Edelman, strongly _____ the lack of financial and moral support for children in America today.

    (A) advocates
    (B) condones
    (C) feigns
    (D) abets
    (E) decries

GO ON TO THE NEXT PAGE ➡

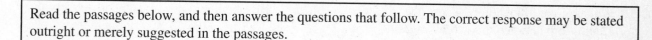

Read the passages below, and then answer the questions that follow. The correct response may be stated outright or merely suggested in the passages.

Questions 6–9 are based on the following passages.

Passage 1

Thomas Hobbes, who lived during the English Civil War (1642–1646), believed that a world without government would inevitably
Line be a war of every man against every man. His
(5) view of human nature was so fearful and bleak that he could not imagine people living in peace without an all-powerful government to constrain their actions. John Locke, writing nearly 40 years later, had a more optimistic
(10) impression of human nature. While he, like Hobbes, envisioned that a world without government would suffer disorder, he described this disorder as merely an "inconvenience."

Passage 2

Line What motivates a political philosopher? In
(15) the case of Thomas Hobbes, the driving force was fear. In his autobiography, Hobbes says as much, for it was fear that accompanied him into the world. On Good Friday of 1588, Hobbes's mother heard that the Spanish
(20) Armada had set sail for England. Hobbes relates what ensued: "the rumour went everywhere through our towns that the last day for our nation was coming by fleet. At that point my mother was filled with such fear that
(25) she bore twins, me together with fear." In Hobbes's philosophy, fear, especially fear of war, plays a central role.

6. The first two sentences of Passage 1 (lines 1–8) serve primarily to

(A) illustrate the physical damage done by the English Civil War to Thomas Hobbes
(B) demonstrate the need for government to function as a restraining influence
(C) present the thinking of a political theorist
(D) argue in favor of the world view held by John Locke
(E) emphasize the author's pacifist beliefs

7. The author of Passage 1 does all of the following EXCEPT

(A) establish a time frame
(B) contrast two differing viewpoints
(C) makes an assertion
(D) refute an argument
(E) quote a source

8. Both passages support which of the following conclusions about Hobbes's world view?

(A) It is more pragmatic than the world view expressed by John Locke.
(B) It provides an insightful perspective despite its evident inconsistencies.
(C) It met with little opposition in his lifetime.
(D) It cannot be easily ascertained, given its lack of documentation.
(E) It is inherently pessimistic in its outlook.

GO ON TO THE NEXT PAGE

9. Which of the following best describes the relationship between the two passages?

(A) Passage 1 draws a contrast that is weakened by examples in Passage 2.
(B) Passage 2 presents a hypothesis that is disproved by Passage 1.
(C) Passage 2 gives an anecdote that confirms a statement made in Passage 1.
(D) Passage 1 poses a question that is explicitly answered in Passage 2.
(E) Passage 2 attacks an opinion that is supported by Passage 1.

Questions 10–15 are based on the following passage.

In the following excerpt from Jane Austen's Pride and Prejudice, *the members of the Bennet family react to news of the marriage of Lydia, the youngest Bennet daughter, to Mr. Wickham. Elizabeth, oldest of the Bennet daughters and the novel's heroine, is in love with Mr. Darcy and worries how this unexpected marriage may affect her relationship with him.*

A long dispute followed this declaration;
but Mr. Bennet was firm: it soon led to
another; and Mrs. Bennet found, with amaze-
Line ment and horror, that her husband would not
(5) advance a guinea[1] to buy clothes for his
daughter. He protested that she should receive
from him no mark of affection whatever, on
the occasion of her marriage. Mrs. Bennet
could hardly comprehend it. That his anger
(10) could be carried to such a point of inconceiv-
able resentment, as to refuse his daughter a
privilege, without which her marriage would
scarcely seem valid, exceeded all that she
could believe possible. She was more alive to
(15) the disgrace, which the want of new clothes
must reflect on her daughter's nuptials, than to
any sense of shame at her eloping and living
with Wickham, a fortnight before they took
place.

(20)   Elizabeth was now most heartily sorry that
she had, from the distress of the moment, been
led to make Mr. Darcy acquainted with their
fears for her sister; for since her marriage
would so shortly give the proper termination
(25) to the elopement, they might hope to conceal
its unfavorable beginning, from all those who
were not immediately on the spot.

She had no fear of its spreading farther,
through his means. There were few people on
(30) whose secrecy she would have more confidently depended; but at the same time, there
was no one, whose knowledge of a sister's
frailty would have mortified her so much. Not,
however, from any fear of disadvantage from
(35) it, individually to herself; for at any rate, there
seemed a gulf impassable between them. Had
Lydia's marriage been concluded on the most
honorable terms, it was not to be supposed
that Mr. Darcy would connect himself with a
(40) family, where to every other objection would
now be added, an alliance and relationship of
the nearest kind with the man whom he so
justly scorned.

From such a connection she could not
(45) wonder that he should shrink. The wish of
procuring her regard, which she had assured
herself of his feeling in Derbyshire, could not
in rational expectation survive such a blow as
this. She was humbled, she was grieved; she
(50) repented, though she hardly knew of what.
She became jealous of his esteem, when she
could no longer hope to be benefitted by it.
She wanted to hear of him, when there seemed
the least chance of gaining intelligence. She
(55) was convinced that she could have been happy
with him, when it was no longer likely they
should meet.

---

[1] A British coin.

GO ON TO THE NEXT PAGE

10. All of the following statements about Mrs. Bennet may be inferred from the passage EXCEPT

    (A) She finds a lack of proper attire more shameful than a lack of proper conduct.
    (B) She is ready to welcome home her newly married daughter.
    (C) She is sensitive to the nature of her husband's scruples about the elopement.
    (D) She is unable to grasp the degree of emotion her daughter's conduct has aroused.
    (E) She is primarily concerned with external appearances.

11. The "privilege" that Mr. Bennet refuses to grant his daughter (line 12) is the privilege of

    (A) marrying Mr. Wickham
    (B) buying a new wardrobe
    (C) running away from home
    (D) seeing her mother and sisters
    (E) having a valid wedding ceremony

12. According to the passage, Elizabeth Bennet presently

    (A) has ceased to crave Darcy's affection
    (B) regrets having told Darcy of her sister's elopement
    (C) no longer desires to conceal Lydia's escapade
    (D) fears Darcy will spread the word about the sudden elopement
    (E) cares more for public opinion than for her family's welfare

13. The expression "a sister's frailty" (lines 32 and 33) refers to Elizabeth's sister's

    (A) delicate health since birth
    (B) embarrassing lack of proper wedding garments
    (C) reluctant marriage to a man whom she disdained
    (D) fear of being considered an old maid
    (E) moral weakness in running away with a man

14. According to lines 38–43, Mr. Darcy feels contempt for

    (A) Lydia's hasty marriage
    (B) secrets that are entrusted to him
    (C) Elizabeth's confession to him
    (D) Lydia's new husband
    (E) Mr. Bennet's harshness

15. The passage can best be described as

    (A) a description of the origins of a foolish and intemperate marriage
    (B) an account of one woman's reflections on the effects of her sister's runaway marriage
    (C) an analysis of the reasons underlying the separation of a young woman from her lover
    (D) a description of a conflict between a young woman and her temperamental parents
    (E) a discussion of the nature of sacred and profane love

Questions 16–24 are based on the following passage.

The following passage is taken from a classic study of tarantulas published in Scientific American *in 1952.*

   A fertilized female tarantula lays from 200 to 400 eggs at a time; thus it is possible for a single tarantula to produce several thousand
Line young. She takes no care of them beyond
 (5) weaving a cocoon of silk to enclose the eggs. After they hatch, the young walk away, find convenient places in which to dig their burrows and spend the rest of their lives in solitude. Tarantulas feed mostly on insects and
(10) millipedes. Once their appetite is appeased, they digest the food for several days before eating again. Their sight is poor, being limited to sensing a change in the intensity of light and to the perception of moving objects. They
(15) apparently have little or no sense of hearing,

GO ON TO THE NEXT PAGE

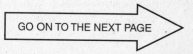

for a hungry tarantula will pay no attention to a loudly chirping cricket placed in its cage unless the insect happens to touch one of its legs.

(20)   But all spiders, and especially hairy ones, have an extremely delicate sense of touch. Laboratory experiments prove that tarantulas can distinguish three types of touch: pressure against the body wall, stroking of the body

(25) hair and riffling of certain very fine hairs on the legs called trichobothria. Pressure against the body, by a finger or the end of a pencil, causes the tarantula to move off slowly for a short distance. The touch excites no defensive

(30) response unless the approach is from above, where the spider can see the motion, in which case it rises on its hind legs, lifts its front legs, opens its fangs and holds this threatening posture as long as the object continues to move.

(35) When the motion stops, the spider drops back to the ground, remains quiet for a few seconds, and then moves slowly away.

The entire body of a tarantula, especially its legs, is thickly clothed with hair. Some of it

(40) is short and woolly, some long and stiff. Touching this body hair produces one of two distinct reactions. When the spider is hungry, it responds with an immediate and swift attack. At the touch of a cricket's antennae the

(45) tarantula seizes the insect so swiftly that a motion picture taken at the rate of 64 frames per second shows only the result and not the process of capture. But when the spider is not hungry, the stimulation of its hairs merely

(50) causes it to shake the touched limb. An insect can walk under its hairy belly unharmed.

The trichobothria, very fine hairs growing from disklike membranes on the legs, were once thought to be the spider's hearing organs,

(55) but we now know that they have nothing to do with sound. They are sensitive only to air movement. A light breeze makes them vibrate slowly without disturbing the common hair. When one blows gently on the trichobothria,

(60) the tarantula reacts with a quick jerk of its four front legs. If the front and hind legs are stimu-

lated at the same time, the spider makes a sudden jump. This reaction is quite independent of the state of its appetite.

(65)   These three tactile responses—to pressure on the body wall, to moving of the common hair, and to flexing of the trichobothria—are so different from one another that there is no possibility of confusing them. They serve the

(70) tarantula adequately for most of its needs and enable it to avoid most annoyances and dangers. But they fail the spider completely when it meets its deadly enemy, the digger wasp *Pepsis*.

16. According to the author, which of the following attributes is (are) characteristic of female tarantulas?

   I. Maternal instincts
   II. Visual acuity
   III. Fertility

   (A) I only
   (B) II only
   (C) III only
   (D) I and III only
   (E) II and III only

17. Lines 6–9 primarily suggest that the female tarantula

   (A) becomes apprehensive at sudden noises
   (B) is better able to discern pressure than stroking
   (C) must consume insects or millipedes daily
   (D) constructs a cocoon for her young
   (E) is reclusive by nature

18. The word "excites" in line 29 most nearly means

   (A) irritates
   (B) delights
   (C) stimulates
   (D) exhilarates
   (E) infuriates

GO ON TO THE NEXT PAGE

④ ④ ④ ④ ④ ④ ④ ④ ④

19. The author's attitude toward tarantulas would best be described as

    (A) fearful
    (B) sentimental
    (C) approving
    (D) objective
    (E) incredulous

20. The main purpose of the passage is to

    (A) report on controversial new discoveries about spider behavior
    (B) summarize what is known about the physical and social responses of tarantulas
    (C) challenge the findings of recent laboratory experiments involving tarantulas
    (D) explain the lack of social organization in the spider family
    (E) discuss the physical adaptations that make tarantulas unique

21. The description of what happens when one films a tarantula's reaction to the touch of a cricket (lines 44–48) chiefly is intended to convey a sense of the tarantula's

    (A) omnivorous appetite
    (B) photogenic appearance
    (C) graceful movement
    (D) quickness in attacking
    (E) lack of stimulation

22. The word "independent" in line 63 most nearly means

    (A) individualistic
    (B) self-governing
    (C) affluent
    (D) regardless
    (E) detached

23. In the passage, the author does all of the following EXCEPT

    (A) deny a possibility
    (B) describe a reaction
    (C) correct a misapprehension
    (D) define a term
    (E) pose a question

24. In the paragraphs immediately following this passage, the author most likely will

    (A) explain why scientists previously confused the tarantula's three tactile responses
    (B) demonstrate how the tarantula's three tactile responses enable it to meet its needs
    (C) point out the weaknesses of the digger wasp that enable the tarantula to subdue it
    (D) report on plans for experiments to explore the digger wasp's tactile sense
    (E) describe how the digger wasp goes about attacking tarantulas

STOP

IF YOU FINISH BEFORE TIME IS CALLED, YOU MAY CHECK YOUR WORK ON THIS SECTION ONLY. DO NOT WORK ON ANY OTHER SECTION IN THE TEST.

Section 5

TIME—20 MINUTES
19 QUESTIONS
For each of the following questions, select the best answer from the choices provided and fill in the appropriate circle on the answer sheet.

Each of the following sentences contains one or two blanks; each blank indicates that a word or set of words has been left out. Below the sentence are five words or phrases, lettered A through E. Select the word or set of words that best completes the sentence.

Example:

Fame is ----; today's rising star is all too soon tomorrow's washed-up has-been.

(A) rewarding   (B) gradual
(C) essential   (D) spontaneous
(E) transitory

Ⓐ Ⓑ Ⓒ Ⓓ ●

---

1. Excavation is, in essence, an act of _____: to clear a site down to the lowest level means that all the upper levels are completely obliterated.

(A) exploration
(B) destruction
(C) validation
(D) malice
(E) spontaneity

2. Hummingbirds use spider silk to strengthen nest walls to better _____ the weight and pressure of wriggling hatchlings.

(A) withstand
(B) discern
(C) expose
(D) transmute
(E) induce

3. A map purporting to show that Vikings charted North America long before Columbus, ____ as a fraud in 1974, could turn out to be ____ after all, according to California scientists.

(A) honored...questionable
(B) condemned...superficial
(C) branded...genuine
(D) labeled...fragmentary
(E) dismissed...extant

4. Although the poet Stevie Smith had a childhood that was far from ____, she always envied children, believing they alone had the ideal life.

(A) idyllic
(B) envious
(C) indifferent
(D) dubious
(E) neutral

5. A prudent, thrifty New Englander, DeWitt was naturally ____ of investing money in junk bonds, which he looked on as ____ ventures.

(A) enamored...worthless
(B) terrified...sound
(C) chary...risky
(D) tired...profitable
(E) cognizant...provincial

6. In Christopher's _____ family, _____ begun over dinner frequently carried over for days.

(A) contentious...arguments
(B) abstemious...accusations
(C) garrulous...doubts
(D) assiduous...conversations
(E) irreverent...rituals

GO ON TO THE NEXT PAGE

The questions that follow the next two passages relate to the content of both, and to their relationship. The correct response may be stated outright in the passage or merely suggested.

Questions 7–9 are based on the following passages.

The following passages describe the settling of the American West during the nineteenth century. The first was written by a social historian and scholar. The second comes from a widely used textbook in American history.

Passage 1

The populating of nearly one billion acres of empty land west of the Mississippi occurred in a series of peristaltic waves, beginning in
Line the 1840s and continuing for the rest of the
(5) century. First to arrive was the advance guard, the trailblazers—explorers, trappers, and mountain men, hide and tallow traders, free-lance adventurers, the military. Then the set-tlers in their wagon trains lumbering over the
(10) Oregon Trail to the lush meadows of the Oregon Territory and the inland valleys of California. Next, the gold-seekers, bowling across the plains and deserts pell-mell in 1848, working up and down the California mountain
(15) ranges, then backtracking to the gold and sil-ver country in the Rockies and the Southwest. And finally, a last great wave, first by wagons, then by railroads, to mop up the leapfrogged Great Plains. By 1890 the great movement
(20) west was over, ending in a final hurrahing stampede of boomers into Oklahoma Territory, a rush of humanity that created entire towns in an afternoon.

The vast, empty land demanded new tools,
(25) new social organizations, new men and women. And it produced a new canon of myths and heroes—the stuff of countless dime novels, Wild West shows, movies, and televi-sion series for later generations. The heroes
(30) are familiar enough—the cowboys, the law-men, the gamblers, the gold-hearted dance-hall girls, the bad men too, for heroes need evil to conquer. The western town played a part, too, mainly as backdrop and chorus,
(35) before which the central figures enacted their *agon* (struggle; contest). The fictional western town was as rigidly formalized as the set for a Japanese No play—the false-front stores on a dusty street lined with hitching rails, the
(40) saloons with bar, gambling tables, and stage for the dancers, the general store, the jail, and the church. The people of the chorus had a stereotypical form—women in crinolines and the men in frock coats and string ties, their
(45) striped pants tucked into boots. Their lives were projected as dim, ordinary, law-abiding shadows, against which were contrasted the bold-hued dramas of the principals. These were the "decent folk," whom the heroic law-
(50) men died for; they were the meek who would inherit the set after the leading actors left and the last wild cowboy was interred in Boot Hill. Colorless, sober, conservative, salt-of-the-earth, they represented the future—and a dull one it
(55) was. Occasionally, as in the film *High Noon*, their passive virtues were transmogrified into hypocrisy and timidity, mocking the lonely courage of the marshal they had hired to risk his life for them. The implication was: Are
(60) these dull, cautious folk really the worthy heirs of the noble cowboys? In Steven Crane's short story *The Bride Comes to Yellow Sky*, the last cowboy is a drunken anachronism, wear-ing his nobility in tatters, yet not to be
(65) scorned.

GO ON TO THE NEXT PAGE
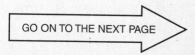

Passage 2

It was the miners who established the first
outposts of the Far West. The discovery of
gold in California had transformed that com-
Line monwealth from a pastoral outpost of New
(70) Spain to a thriving American state and had
opened up new and varied economic activities—farming, shipping, railroading, and manufacturing. That experience was to be repeated
again and again in the history of the mining
(75) kingdom; in the rush to Pike's Peak country in
1859, to Alder Gulch and Last Chance in
Montana and the banks of the Sweetwater in
Wyoming in the middle sixties, to the Black
Hills of the Dakota country in the seventies.
(80) Everywhere the miners opened up the country,
established political communities, and laid the
foundations for more permanent settlements.
As the gold and silver played out or fell into
the hands of eastern corporations and mining
(85) fever abated, the settlers would perceive the
farming and stock-raising possibilities around
them or find work on the railroads that were
pushing in from the East and West. Some
communities remained almost exclusively
(90) mining, but the real wealth of Montana and
Colorado, Wyoming and Idaho, as of
California, was in their grass and their soil.
Even in mineral wealth the value of the precious metals which had first lured adventurers
(95) was shortly exceeded by that of the copper
and coal and oil which were so abundant. . . .

Even while the miners were grubbing in
the hills of Nevada and Montana, a new and
more important chapter was being written in
(100) the history of the West. This was the rise of
the cattle kingdom. The physical basis of the
kingdom was the grasslands of the West,
stretching unbroken from the Rio Grande to
the northern frontier, from Kansas and
(105) Nebraska into the Rocky Mountain valleys.
Here millions of buffaloes had roamed at will,
but within two decades the buffalo was to
become almost extinct and its place taken by
even more millions of Texas longhorns and
(110) Wyoming and Montana steers. . . .

The cattle kingdom, like the mining, had
its romantic side, and the remembrance of this
has persisted in the American consciousness
after the cattle kingdom itself has vanished.
(115) The lonely life on the plain, the roundup, the
hieroglyphic brands, the long drive, the stampede, the war with cattle rustlers, the splendid
horsemanship, the picturesque costume
designed for usefulness, not effect—the wild
(120) life of the cow towns like Abilene and
Cheyenne, all have found their way into
American folklore and song. Children array
themselves now in imitation cowboy suits,
moving-picture ranchmen shoot down rustlers
(125) with unerring aim, and the whole country
sings what was reputed to be President
Franklin Roosevelt's favorite song:

Home, home on the range,
Where the deer and the antelope play
(130) Where seldom is heard, a discouraging word,
And the skies are not cloudy all day.

7. According to Passage 1, the settling of the
West took place

(A) during a steady migration that lasted for
60 years
(B) intermittently as people went farther and
farther west
(C) in two waves, the first during the 1840s,
the last in the 1890s
(D) in no discernible order
(E) sometimes slowly and sometimes rapidly
during a 50-year period

GO ON TO THE NEXT PAGE

8. Passage 1 implies that the settlers went to the West largely for

   (A) economic advancement
   (B) adventure
   (C) a desire for more space
   (D) free land
   (E) more individual liberty

9. The comparison between western towns and the set of a Japanese No play (line 38) is intended to make the point that

   (A) in the Old West, people mattered more than towns
   (B) all towns in the Old West looked alike
   (C) the towns looked good on the surface but not underneath
   (D) in books and films, western towns are all the same
   (E) towns were all show and no substance

10. The author of Passage 1 believes that after the westward migration the settlers were portrayed as people who

    (A) settled into routine lives
    (B) yearned for a return to the romantic days of the past
    (C) turned into hypocrites
    (D) failed to do what was expected of them
    (E) recreated their past in books, movies, and TV shows

11. The allusion to the cowboy in *The Bride Comes to Yellow Sky* (lines 62–65) is meant to show that

    (A) the people rejected the heroes of the Old West
    (B) many of the myths of the Old West were false
    (C) the legendary heroes of the Old West became obsolete
    (D) drunkenness and reckless behavior tarnished the image of the heroic cowboys of the Old West
    (E) all glamorous and romantic eras eventually die out

12. The center of the so-called "mining kingdom" (lines 67–82), as described in Passage 2,

    (A) was located in California
    (B) stretched from the Mississippi River to the western mountains
    (C) shifted from place to place
    (D) began in the Far West and then jumped to the East
    (E) drifted west throughout the second half of the nineteenth century

13. According to Passage 2, when the gold and silver ran out, the miners switched to

    (A) working on the land
    (B) searching for oil and other fuels
    (C) cattle rustling
    (D) their previous occupations
    (E) digging for other minerals

14. The author of Passage 2 believes that the defining event in the history of the West was

    (A) the founding of new cities and towns
    (B) the discovery of precious metals
    (C) the growth of the cattle industry
    (D) the development of the mining kingdom
    (E) the coming of the railroad

15. Passage 2 implies that the buffalo became almost extinct in the Great Plains because

    (A) they roamed westward
    (B) their land was fenced off for agriculture
    (C) the land could no longer support huge buffalo herds
    (D) they were killed to make room for cattle-grazing
    (E) they were driven north to Canada and south to Mexico

GO ON TO THE NEXT PAGE

16. According to Passage 2, the cowboy of the Old West is remembered today for all of the following EXCEPT his

(A) distinctive clothing
(B) ability to ride horses
(C) law-abiding nature
(D) fights with cattle thieves
(E) rugged individualism

17. Both passages suggest that settlers were attracted to California because of its

(A) gold
(B) mountains
(C) seacoast
(D) scenic splendor
(E) fertile valleys

18. The authors of Passage 1 and Passage 2 seem to have a common interest in

(A) defining the American dream
(B) political history
(C) mining
(D) American folklore and legend
(E) the social class structure in America

19. Compared to the account of the westward movement in Passage 1, Passage 2 pays more attention to the role of

(A) pioneer families
(B) miners
(C) politicians
(D) entrepreneurs
(E) outlaws discussion of the *miner*.

STOP

IF YOU FINISH BEFORE TIME IS CALLED, YOU MAY CHECK YOUR WORK ON THIS SECTION ONLY. DO NOT WORK ON ANY OTHER SECTION IN THE TEST.

⑥ ⑥ ⑥ ⑥ ⑥ ⑥ ⑥ ⑥ ⑥ ⑥ ⑥

Section 6

TIME—10 MINUTES
14 QUESTIONS

For each of the following questions, select the best answer from the choices provided and fill in the appropriate circle on the answer sheet.

Some or all parts of the following sentences are underlined. The first answer choice, (A), simply repeats the underlined part of the sentence. The other four choices present four alternative ways to phrase the underlined part. Select the answer that produces the most effective sentence, one that is clear and exact, and blacken the appropriate space on your answer sheet. In selecting your choice, be sure that it is standard written English, and that it expresses the meaning of the original sentence.

Example:

The first biography of author Eudora Welty came out in 1998 and she was 89 years old at the time.

(A) and she was 89 years old at the time
(B) at the time she was 89
(C) upon becoming an 89 year old
(D) when she was 89
(E) at the age of 89 years old

Ⓐ Ⓑ Ⓒ ● Ⓔ

1. Unfortunately, soul singer Anita Baker's voice has not weathered the years as well as other singers have.

(A) has not weathered the years as well as other singers have
(B) had not weathered the years as well as other singers have
(C) has not been weathered by the years as well asthe voices of other singers have been
(D) has not weathered the years as well as other singers' voices have
(E) has not weathered the years as good as other singers' voices have

2. The mathematics teacher drew a right triangle on the blackboard, he proceeded to demonstrate that we could determine the length of the longest side of the triangle if we knew the lengths of its two shorter sides.

(A) The mathematics teacher drew a right triangle on the blackboard, he
(B) The right triangle, which was drawn on the blackboard by the mathematics teacher, he
(C) After drawing a right triangle on the blackboard, the mathematics teacher
(D) A right triangle was first drawn on the blackboard by the mathematics teacher, then he
(E) Once a right triangle was drawn on the blackboard by the mathematics teacher, who then

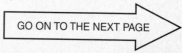
GO ON TO THE NEXT PAGE

3. An inside trader is <u>when a corporate officer who has access to "inside" or privileged information about a company's prospects uses that information</u> in buying or selling company shares.

(A) when a corporate officer who has access to "inside" or privileged information about a company's prospects uses that information

(B) when a corporate officer has access to "inside" or privileged information about a company's prospects and uses that information

(C) a corporate officer who has access to "inside" or privileged information about a company's prospects and uses that information

(D) a corporate officer who has accessed "inside" or privileged information about a company's prospects for use of that information

(E) that a corporate officer who has access to "inside" or privileged information about a company's prospects and he uses that information

4. Gymnastics students perform stretching <u>exercises to develop flexibility and to become a more agile tumbler</u>.

(A) exercises to develop flexibility and to become a more agile tumbler

(B) exercises for the development of flexibility and to become a more agile tumbler

(C) exercises so that they develop flexibility, becoming a more agile tumbler

(D) exercises to develop flexibility and to become more agile tumblers

(E) exercises because they want to develop flexibility in becoming a more agile tumbler

5. <u>Because the Ming vase is priceless plus being highly fragile,</u> it is kept safe in a sealed display case.

(A) Because the Ming vase is priceless plus being highly fragile,

(B) Being that the Ming vase is priceless and also it is highly fragile,

(C) Although the Ming vase is priceless and highly fragile,

(D) Because the Ming vase is priceless and highly fragile is why

(E) Because the Ming vase is both priceless and highly fragile,

6. The soft, pulpy flesh of the passion fruit possesses a flavor at once tart and <u>sweet and the flavor has captivated</u> many prominent chefs, among them Alice Waters.

(A) sweet and the flavor has captivated

(B) sweet that has captivated

(C) sweet that have captivated

(D) sweet and the flavors have captivated

(E) sweet and the favor captivates

7. Shakespeare's acting company performed in a relatively intimate setting, <u>appearing before smaller audiences than most theaters today</u>.

(A) appearing before smaller audiences than most theaters today

(B) they appeared before smaller audiences than most theaters today

(C) appearing before audiences smaller than most audiences today

(D) having appeared before smaller audiences than most theaters today

(E) and they appeared before audiences smaller than the ones at most theaters today

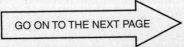
GO ON TO THE NEXT PAGE

8. <u>Observing the interactions of preschoolers in a playground setting, it can be seen</u> that the less adults relate to the children in their charge, the more these children relate to one another.

   (A) Observing the interactions of preschoolers in a playground setting, it can be seen
   (B) Having observed the interactions of preschoolers in a playground setting, it can be seen
   (C) If one observes the interactions of preschoolers in a playground setting, you can see
   (D) Observing the interactions of preschoolers in a playground setting, we can see
   (E) Observing the interactions of preschoolers in a playground setting can be seen

9. <u>Neither the Florida coast nor the Caribbean islands was prepared for</u> the series of hurricanes that devastated the region in 2004.

   (A) Neither the Florida coast nor the Caribbean islands was prepared for
   (B) Neither the Florida coast nor the Caribbean islands have been prepared for
   (C) Neither the Florida coast or the Caribbean islands were prepared for
   (D) Neither the Florida coast or the Caribbean islands was prepared for
   (E) Neither the Florida coast nor the Caribbean islands were prepared for

10. <u>Far from being mercenary ambulance chasers,</u> trial lawyers perform a public service by forcing corporations to consider the potential financial cost of pollution, unsafe products, and mistreatment of workers.

    (A) Far from being mercenary ambulance chasers
    (B) Despite them being mercenary ambulance chasers
    (C) Far from them being mercenary ambulance chasers
    (D) Far from having been mercenary ambulance chasers
    (E) Further from being mercenary ambulance chasers

11. *Unsafe at Any Speed* is Ralph Nader's detailed <u>portrait of how the auto industry willfully resisted safety innovations and thus contributed to</u> thousands of highway deaths a year.

    (A) portrait of how the auto industry willfully resisted safety innovations and thus contributed to
    (B) portrait of when the auto industry was willful about resisting safety innovations and thus contributing to
    (C) portrait of how the auto industry fully willed themselves to resist safety innovations and thus contributed to
    (D) portrait of how the auto industry willfully resisted safety innovations in order to contribute to
    (E) portrait showing how the auto industry willfully resisted safety innovations, and they thus contributed to

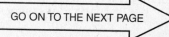
GO ON TO THE NEXT PAGE

12. In 1532, Francisco Pizarro and his troops arrived in Cuzco, took hostage the Incan king, <u>Atahualpa, and then they demanded ransom</u>.

   (A) Atahualpa, and then they demanded ransom
   (B) who was named Atahualpa, and then they demanded ransom
   (C) Atahualpa, it was so they could demand ransom
   (D) Atahualpa, and then there was a demand for ransom
   (E) Atahualpa, and demanded ransom

13. <u>Although demand for cars, motorcycles, and other consumer goods are booming</u>, the economy is growing only at roughly 4 percent a year, and the unemployment rate is about 10 percent.

   (A) Although demand for cars, motorcycles, and other consumer goods are booming
   (B) Because demand for cars, motorcycles, and other consumer goods are booming
   (C) Although demand for cars, motorcycles, and other consumer goods is booming
   (D) Although demand for cars, motorcycles, and other consumer goods have been booming
   (E) Although demand of cars, motorcycles, and other consumer goods is booming

14. <u>Samuel Sewall, who was a judge in the Salem witch trials but later repented his role and, in 1700,</u> wrote the first attack on the American slave trade.

   (A) Samuel Sewall, who was a judge in the Salem witch trials but later repented his role and, in 1700,
   (B) Samuel Sewall was a judge in the Salem witch trials but who later repented his role and, in 1700,
   (C) Samuel Sewall, a judge in the Salem witch trials, but later he repented his role and, in 1700,
   (D) Samuel Sewall, a judge in the Salem witch trials who later repented his role, in 1700
   (E) Samuel Sewall, who was a judge in the Salem witch trials but who later repented his role, and who, in 1700,

STOP

IF YOU FINISH BEFORE TIME IS CALLED, YOU MAY CHECK YOUR WORK ON THIS SECTION ONLY. DO NOT WORK ON ANY OTHER SECTION IN THE TEST.

ANSWER KEY

Section 2

1. **C**	5. **E**	9. **D**	13. **E**	17. **C**	21. **B**
2. **D**	6. **B**	10. **B**	14. **B**	18. **E**	22. **E**
3. **C**	7. **B**	11. **B**	15. **C**	19. **D**	23. **B**
4. **C**	8. **A**	12. **A**	16. **A**	20. **A**	24. **A**

Section 3

1. **E**	7. **A**	13. **E**	19. **B**	25. **C**	31. **C**
2. **C**	8. **B**	14. **A**	20. **B**	26. **E**	32. **B**
3. **E**	9. **D**	15. **D**	21. **D**	27. **D**	33. **A**
4. **D**	10. **D**	16. **E**	22. **C**	28. **A**	34. **C**
5. **E**	11. **D**	17. **A**	23. **E**	29. **B**	35. **D**
6. **D**	12. **B**	18. **D**	24. **E**	30. **C**	

Section 4

1. **D**	5. **E**	9. **C**	13. **E**	17. **E**	21. **D**
2. **B**	6. **C**	10. **C**	14. **D**	18. **C**	22. **D**
3. **C**	7. **D**	11. **B**	15. **B**	19. **D**	23. **E**
4. **E**	8. **E**	12. **B**	16. **C**	20. **B**	24. **E**

Section 5

1. **B**	5. **C**	9. **D**	13. **A**	17. **A**
2. **A**	6. **A**	10. **A**	14. **C**	18. **D**
3. **C**	7. **E**	11. **C**	15. **D**	19. **B**
4. **A**	8. **A**	12. **C**	16. **C**	

Section 6

1. **D**	5. **E**	9. **C**	13. **C**
2. **C**	6. **B**	10. **A**	14. **D**
3. **C**	7. **C**	11. **A**	
4. **D**	8. **D**	12. **E**	

ANALYSIS OF TEST RESULTS

I. Check your answers against the answer key.

II. Fill in the following chart.

						Total
Sentence Completion Number Correct	Section 1 (Questions 1–8) _____		Section 4 (Questions 1–5) _____	Section 5 (Questions 1–6) _____		_____
Reading Comprehension Number Correct	Section 2 (Questions 9–24) _____		Section 4 (Questions 6–24) _____	Section 5 (Questions 7–19) _____		_____
Sentence Improvement Number Correct		Section 3 (Questions 1–11) _____			Section 6 (Questions 1–14) _____	_____
Error Identification Number Correct		Section 3 (Questions 12–29) _____				_____
Paragraph Improvement Number Correct		Section 3 (Questions 30–35) _____				_____

III. Interpret your results.

Sentence Completion   Number Correct _____
Reading Comprehension   Number Correct _____
Sentence Improvement   Number Correct _____
Error Identification   Number Correct _____
Paragraph Improvement   Number Correct _____
                             Subtotal _____

Guessing Penalty: Subtract 1/4 point for each incorrect answer. _____
(Do not take off points for questions you left blank.)
                             TOTAL SCORE _____

	Sentence Completion Score	Reading Comprehension Score	Total
Excellent	18–19 Correct	43–48 Correct	60–67
Very Good	14–17 Correct	33–42 Correct	46–59
Good	11–13 Correct	25–32 Correct	35–45
Fair	9–10 Correct	20–24 Correct	28–34
Poor	6–8 Correct	12–19 Correct	17–27
Very Poor	0–5 Correct	0–11 Correct	0–16

	Sentence Improvement Score	Error Identification Score	Paragraph Improvement Score	Total
Excellent	21–25 Correct	13–18 Correct	6 Correct	38–49
Very Good	15–20 Correct	10–12 Correct	5 Correct	28–37
Good	8–14 Correct	7–9 Correct	4 Correct	17–27
Fair	5–7 Correct	5–6 Correct	2–3 Correct	11–16
Poor	3–4 Correct	3–4 Correct	1 Correct	5–10
Very Poor	0–2 Correct	0–2 Correct	0 Correct	0–4

SCORE YOUR OWN SAT ESSAY

Use this table as you rate your performance on the essay-writing section of this model test. Circle the phrase that most accurately describes your work. Enter the numbers in the scoring chart below. Add the numbers together and divide by 6 to determine your total score. The higher your total score, the better you are likely to do on the essay section of the SAT.

Note that on the actual SAT two readers will rate your essay; your essay score will be the sum of their two ratings and could range from 12 (highest) to 2 (lowest). Also, they will grade your essay holistically, rating it on the basis of their overall impression of its effectiveness. They will *not* analyze it piece by piece, giving separate grades for grammar, vocabulary level, and so on. Therefore, you cannot expect the score you give yourself on this model test to predict your eventual score on the SAT with any great degree of accuracy. Use this scoring guide instead to help you assess your writing strengths and weaknesses, so that you can decide which areas to focus on as you prepare for the SAT.

Like most people, you may find it difficult to rate your own writing objectively. Ask a teacher or fellow student to score your essay as well. With his or her help you should gain added insights into writing your 25-minute essay.

	6	5	4	3	2	1
POSITION ON THE TOPIC	Clear, convincing, & insightful	Fundamentally clear & coherent	Fairly clear & coherent	Insufficiently clear	Largely unclear	Extremely unclear
ORGANIZATION OF EVIDENCE	Well organized, with strong, relevant examples	Generally well organized, with apt examples	Adequately organized, with some examples	Sketchily developed, with weak examples	Lacking focus and evidence	Unfocused and disorganized
SENTENCE STRUCTURE	Varied, appealing sentences	Reasonably varied sentences	Some variety in sentences	Little variety in sentences	Errors in sentence structure	Severe errors in sentence structure
LEVEL OF VOCABULARY	Mature & apt word choice	Competent word choice	Adequate word choice	Inappropriate or weak vocabulary	Highly limited vocabulary	Rudimentary
GRAMMAR AND USAGE	Almost entirely free of errors	Relatively free of errors	Some technical errors	Minor errors and some major ones	Numerous major errors	Extensive severe errors
OVERALL EFFECT	Outstanding	Effective	Adequately competent	Inadequate, but shows some potential	Seriously flawed	Fundamentally deficient

Self-Scoring Chart

For each of the following categories, rate the essay from 1 (lowest) to 6 (highest)

Position on the Topic _____

Organization of Evidence _____

Sentence Structure _____

Level of Vocabulary _____

Grammar and Usage _____

Overall Effect _____

TOTAL _____

(To get a score, divide the total by 6) _____

Scoring Chart (Second Reader)

For each of the following categories, rate the essay from 1 (lowest) to 6 (highest)

Position on the Topic _____

Organization of Evidence _____

Sentence Structure _____

Level of Vocabulary _____

Grammar and Usage _____

Overall Effect _____

TOTAL _____

(To get a score, divide the total by 6) _____

You can get a rough idea of which areas you most need to work on by comparing your sentence completion, reading comprehension, and writing skills scores.

The College Board uses a guessing formula to compensate for the effect of wild guesses on people's scores. The formula is

$$\text{Raw score} = \underline{\qquad} - (\underline{\qquad} \text{ divided by 4})$$
$$\phantom{\text{Raw score} =} \text{no. correct} \quad \text{no. incorrect}$$

In calculating your raw score,* do not count any questions you left blank as incorrect.

> Raw scores of 60 to 67 (Critical Reading) and 38–49 (Writing Skills) are excellent.
> Raw scores of 46 to 59 (Critical Reading) and 28–37 (Writing Skills) are very good.
> Raw scores of 35 to 45 (Critical Reading) and 17–27 (Writing Skills) are above average.
> Raw scores of 23 to 34 (Critical Reading) and 5–16 (Writing Skills) are below average to average.

If your raw score differs from your total number of correct answers by more than 3 points, you should be very cautious about guessing on this test. Guess intelligently. Guess only when you can eliminate one or more of the five answer choices to the question.

IV. List any unfamiliar words you came across. Then look the words up in a dictionary and write down their definitions.

Word	Definition
_____	_____
_____	_____
_____	_____
_____	_____
_____	_____

V. Read the answer explanations and think about your performance.

Go over the questions you omitted as well as the ones you got wrong. Did you mark any answers in the wrong spot? Did you run out of time and have to leave out questions you could have answered correctly? Did you misread any questions, overlooking key words such as "except" and "best"? Were you too cautious about guessing, omitting questions that you had a chance of getting right if you had guessed? If necessary, reread the relevant sections in Part I. Then get to work on mastering the different question types.

*A very precise formula is used to convert raw scores to scaled scores for the SAT, and the results may vary slightly from test to test. This book uses a broad-range approximation to give you a ballpark estimate of how you will perform on an actual SAT.

ANSWER EXPLANATIONS

SECTION 2

1. **C**   If you *delegate* or assign a task to someone else, you do not have to attend to it yourself.

2. **D**   If you realize how very different caterpillars and spiders are, you will find it remarkable that they produce silks that are *similar*.

3. **C**   Like a sponge, concrete can soak up water because it is *porous*, or permeable to fluids.

4. **C**   Someone who flaunts or shows off his or her achievements or possessions is by definition a *braggart*, one who *boasts*.

5. **E**   We are now so used to Kandinsky's innovative designs that they can turn up anywhere without causing any widespread notice, or *stir*.

6. **B**   Just as the tip of the iceberg suggests or *hints at* the greater mass of the iceberg under the water, to Hemingway short stories *hint at* a *bulkier*, heavier tale underlying the small part of the story the reader gets to see.

7. **B**   To have so many advantages that one would have no *reason for* anger and yet to be angry all the same is clearly *paradoxical* (puzzling; contradictory).

8. **A**   The catastrophist theories hypothesized or *maintained* that mountains and species were created by sudden dramatic events or catastrophes. Darwin, however, theorized that nature was the result of cumulative, *gradual* change.

9. **D**   From its casual direction, "Flash back to 1937," to its quotes from computer users, the passage has a *chatty*, informal tone.

10. **B**   Given that SPAM was available for the soldier to eat three times a day, clearly it was *abundant* (plentiful).

11. **B**   The author describes the polar bear as "exquisitely adapted" to its bleak environment and calls it "a striking example of natural selection at work." His view of the polar bear is one of *admiration*.

12. **A**   The capacity in question is the bear's remarkable *ability* to smell its prey from a phenomenal distance away.

13. **E**   The author begins by giving a definition of the term *symbol* and proceeds to analyze three separate types of symbols. Thus, he is *refining* or further defining his somewhat rudimentary original definition.

14. **B**   For a group of letters to stand for an object, the letters must in some way *represent* that object to the people who accept the letters as a conventional symbol for the object.

15. **C**   In describing the associations of the word "phooey," the author states that "the symbol has an inherent connection with the feeling it symbolizes." In other words, there is an *intrinsic natural link* between the symbol and its meaning.

16. **A**   When we say "hiss," we expel air in a sibilant manner, making a sharp "s" sound as we thrust our tongue toward the tooth ridge and dispel the air quickly. Thus we express our disapproval of something, our desire to push it away from us, so that the meaning of "hiss" has both inherent and conventional associations.

17. **C**   The author gives the example of the flag as a conventional symbol that is *pictorial* rather than linguistic.

18. **E**   To the author, the *Statue of Liberty* would be a conventional symbol, one agreed upon by a group of people to stand for the abstract idea of freedom.

19. **D**   If by some accident you were to have a memorably joyful time in Paris, the city of Paris might come to have some symbolic value for you, bringing a mood of joy to your mind. However, the relationship between the city and the mood is not an inherent, built-in one; it is purely *coincidental*.

20. **A**   The author describes how one's inner experience of a universal symbol is rooted in or grows out of one's *sensory experience*.

21. **B**   The author offers fire as an *example* of a universal symbol and asks the reader to consider it.

22. **E**   Like fire, *water* is a universal symbol that we experience through our senses, feeling its fluidity, its movement, its power. The words *"fire"* and *"phooey"* are conventional symbols, as is the flag. A red dress, if it has any symbolic value at all, is an accidental symbol at best.

23. **B**   The *"properties"* mentioned here are our body's *attributes* or characteristics. To answer vocabulary-in-context questions, substitute each of the answer choices in the sentence in place of the word in quotes.

24. **A**   The closing sentence states that the human race forgot the language of universal symbols before it developed conventional language. Thus, the language of the universal symbol *antedates* or comes before the development of our everyday conventional tongues.

SECTION 3

1. **E**   Error in subject-verb agreement. Remember: the subject's grammatical number is not changed by the addition of a phrase that begins with *along with, together with,* or similar words. Here, the subject, *coach,* is singular. The verb should be singular as well. Only choice E corrects the error.

2. **C**   Error in usage. The phrase *would of* is nonstandard for *would have*. Only choice C corrects the error without adding new errors.

3. **E**   Error in usage. Remember: use *former* and *latter* to refer to two items; use *first* and *last* for three or more items.

4. **D**   Dangling participle. If you ask yourself who was visiting the Tower of London, Mrs. Pomeroy or her hat, you should be able to spot the correct answer.

5. **E**   Error in coordination and subordination. The relationship between the two clauses is one of contrast. The substitution of the conjunction *though* for *and* clarifies this relationship.

6. **D**   Error in coordination and subordination. The relationship between the two clauses is again one of contrast. It is made clear by the use of *although* at the start of the sentence

7. **A**   Sentence is correct.

8. **B**   Error in pronoun-antecedent agreement. Choices A, C, D, and E suffer from lack of agreement between the pronouns *they* and *them* (plural) and their antecedent *anyone* (singular).

9. **D**   Dangling past participle. Who has been celebrated for the clarity of her prose? Clearly, Mary Renault. Choice D neatly rearranges the sentence to eliminate the dangling participle. (While choice E also avoids the dangling participle, it does so awkwardly.)

10. **D**   Error in sequence of tenses. Replace *drink* with *drank*.

11. **D**   The suggested revision eliminates wordiness, cutting the unnecessary *that was* and substituting the strong noun *prominence* for the weaker phrase *prominent position*.

12. **B**   Error in pronoun choice. The general rule is to use *who* instead of *which* or *that* to refer to people. Substitute *whom* for *which*.

13. **E**   Sentence is correct.

14. **A**   Error in pronoun case. The pronoun here is the object of the preposition *for* and should be in the objective case. Change *and I* to *and me*.

15. **D** Error in pronoun-antecedent agreement. The actors came up with *a number of ideas* (plural). The director refused to consider these ideas. Change *it* to *them*.

16. **E** Sentence is correct.

17. **A** Error in idiomatic usage. The verb *ingrain* takes the preposition *in*. Change *ingrained for us* to *ingrained in us*.

18. **D** Lack of parallelism. Change *and he stifled* to *and of stifling* for parallel structure in the sentence.

19. **B** Error in subordination. The conjunction *but* makes no sense here. Change *brisk, but only* to *brisk; only*. The corrected sentence should read: "For all the book's length, the narrative is brisk; only as much background is included as is needed to enable the reader to make sense of a complex story."

20. **B** Error in usage. Substitute *affected* (influenced) for *effected* (achieved or brought about).

21. **D** Error in pronoun-antecedent agreement. The antecedent *cartoons* is plural; the pronoun should be plural as well. Change *its* to *their*.

22. **C** Error in subject-verb agreement. The subject, *utopias*, is plural; the verb should be plural as well. Change *has* to *have*.

23. **E** Sentence is correct.

24. **E** Sentence is correct.

25. **C** Error in pronoun choice. Change the restrictive *that* to the nonrestrictive *which*.

26. **E** Sentence is correct.

27. **D** Error in idiomatic usage. The adjective *insensitive* takes the preposition *to*. Change *insensitive of* to *insensitive to*.

28. **A** Error in usage. Substitute *rise sharply* for *raise sharply*.

29. **B** Error in usage. The phrase *cannot hardly* is a double negative. Change *we cannot* to *we can*.

30. **C** Choice A contains the extremely awkward phrase *to see underdogs being the one rooted for*. Choice B uses the coordinating conjunction *but*, which makes no sense in the context. It also contains the redundant phrase "sight . . . to see." Choice C clearly and concisely combines the thoughts contained in the two sentences. It is the best answer. Choice D contains a clause and a phrase that have no grammatical relationship. Choice E contains a comma splice between *Americans* and *for example*.

31. **C** All sentences except 3 contribute to the discussion of the underdog. Sentence 3 is an unnecessary digression. Therefore, choice C is the best answer.

32. **B** Choice A is grammatically correct, but it refers to Americans' desire to feel good, a topic not discussed in paragraph 2. Choice B accurately introduces the topic of the paragraph. It is the best answer. Choices C and D are similar to (A). Choice E is awkwardly expressed and contains the pronoun *themselves*, which refers grammatically to *traditions* instead of to *Americans*.

33. **A** Choice A clearly and accurately combines the sentences. It is the best answer. Choice B is awkward and cumbersome. Choice C contains an awkward shift in verb tense from present (*look*) to past perfect (*had been*). Choice D contains the adverb *poorly*, which should be an adjective and should modify *immigrants* instead of *coming*. Choice E contains a comma splice between *here* and *after*.

34. **C** Choice A is not an effective revision. It changes the focus of the discussion and contains the pronoun *their*, which refers grammatically to *Americans* instead of to *underdog*. Choice B contains an awkward shift in verb tense from past (*believed*) to present (*succeed*). Choice C follows naturally from the preceding sentence and is accurately and concisely expressed. It is the best answer. Choice D is grammatical, but it shifts the focus of the discussion. Choice E is confusing and contains the pronouns *they* and *their*, which lack a specific antecedent.

35. **D** Choice A contains some transitional material but shifts verb tenses from past (*went*) to present (*defeat*). Choice B, which lacks a main verb, is a sentence fragment. Choice C, although grammatically correct, seems incomplete because the pronoun *it* lacks a specific antecedent. Choice D provides a smooth transition between paragraphs and introduces the topic of paragraph 3. It is the best answer. Choice E lacks any meaningful transitional material.

SECTION 4

1. **D** Our experience suggests to us that a creature without visible ears would be unable to hear *sounds*.
2. **B** In a volcanic eruption, ash and other matter is *ejected* or forced out of the volcano.
3. **C** The opposite of a highly positive response is a *tepid* or lukewarm one. Note that *while* signals a contrast.
4. **E** *Cynics* distrust human nature and motives. Such persons would suspect the motives of anyone advancing a controversial theory and would accept evidence in favor of that theory only after having tried hard to *debunk* that evidence (expose it as a sham or false).
5. **E** As the founder of a fund for children, Edelman would be likely to *decry* (condemn) a lack of support for young people.
6. **C** The opening sentences simply present Hobbes's thoughts on the nature of government.
7. **D** You can answer this question by using the process of elimination.
   • Does the author establish a time frame? Yes. She states that the English Civil War took place between 1642 and 1646; she also states that Locke wrote 40 years after Hobbes did. You can eliminate (A).
   • Does the author contrast two differing viewpoints? Definitely. You can eliminate (B).
   • Does the author make an assertion? Yes. She asserts that Hobbes had a bleak view of human nature, that Locke had a more optimistic view, and so on. You can eliminate (C).
   • Does the author refute an argument? No. She merely states the arguments or beliefs of others. This is probably the correct answer. Just to be sure, check (E).
   • Does the author quote a source? Yes. She quotes Locke, citing his description of the disorder created by the absence of government. You can eliminate (E).
   Only (D) is left. It is the correct answer.
8. **E** Passage 1 describes Hobbes's view of human nature as "fearful and bleak." Passage 2 states that fear of war plays a central role in his philosophy. Both passages indicate that his world view *is inherently pessimistic*.
9. **C** The anecdote in Passage 2 about Hobbes's premature birth (which was brought on by his mother's fear of an attack by the Spanish fleet) *confirms the statement* in Passage 1 that his view of human nature was "fearful and bleak."
10. **C** Far from being *sensitive to the nature of her husband's scruples* or ethical considerations about his daughter's elopement, Mrs. Bennet can hardly comprehend them.
11. **B** The "privilege" Mr. Bennet refuses his daughter is *buying a new wardrobe*. In the opening sentence, we learn that Mr. Bennet would not come up with any money ("would not advance a guinea") to buy his daughter new clothes. To Mrs. Bennet, the purchase of new clothes on the occasion of a wedding was a privilege automatically granted the bride.
12. **B** The opening sentence of the second paragraph indicates Elizabeth's *regret*: she "was most heartily sorry."
13. **E** Frailty here is the *moral weakness* of giving way to temptation and running off to "live in sin" with a man.
14. **D** The concluding sentence of the third paragraph indicates that Darcy scorned or felt contempt for *Lydia's new husband*.
15. **B** Three of the four paragraphs trace Elizabeth's *reflections* or thoughts in detail.
16. **C** Neither maternal instincts nor visual acuity is characteristic of female tarantulas. Only *fertility* (the quality of being prolific) is.
17. **E** Since it is stated that young tarantulas go off to spend their lives in solitude, it follows that female tarantulas are *reclusive* or solitary by nature.
18. **C** To excite a defensive response is to *stimulate* that kind of reaction.
19. **D** The author's presentation of factual information about tarantulas is evidence of a scientifically *objective* (impartial) attitude toward them.

20. **B** Rather than covering new ground or challenging current theories, the passage *summarizes* general knowledge.

21. **D** The key words here are "seizes the insect so swiftly," which describe the spider's quickness in attacking.

22. **D** Under these conditions, the spider will jump whether or not it is hungry. Thus its reaction occurs quite *regardless* of the state of its appetite.

23. **E** Use the process of elimination to answer this question.
    - In lines 65–69 the author *denies the possibility* that the viewer could confuse the spider's three tactile responses. You can eliminate (A).
    - In the second, third, and fourth paragraphs the author *describes* the spider's three tactile responses or *reactions*. You can eliminate (B).
    - In lines 52–56 the author *corrects the misapprehension* that the trichobothria might be hearing organs. You can eliminate (C).
    - In lines 52 and 53, the author *defines* trichobothria as very fine hairs growing from disklike membranes on the spider's legs. You can eliminate (D).
    - Only (E) is left. At no time does the author *pose* or ask *a question.* By elimination, (E) is the correct answer.

24. **E** The concluding sentence of the passage states that the tarantula's tactile responses do not help it when it meets (that is, is attacked by) its deadly enemy, the digger wasp. It follows that subsequent paragraphs will discuss *digger wasp attacks* in more detail.

SECTION 5

1. **B** If, during an archeological excavation, a site's upper levels are obliterated or destroyed, then excavation is an act of *destruction*.

2. **A** If the silk makes the nest walls stronger, they will be more able to *withstand* or resist the weight and pressure of the small birds.

3. **C** Although once *branded* (stigmatized or discredited) as a fake, the map may turn out to be authentic or *genuine* after all.

4. **A** Despite Stevie Smith's belief in an ideal childhood, her childhood was not *idyllic* or charmingly simple.

5. **C** Someone prudent or cautious would look on junk bonds as *risky*, uncertain investments. Such a person would be *chary* of (cautiously hesitant about) investing in such poor risks.

6. **A** A *contentious* (quarrelsome, disputatious) family by definition is given to *arguments*.

7. **E** As described in the first paragraph of Passage 1, the settling of the West occurred in "peristaltic waves." In other words, it did not occur at a steady rate. Rather, it took place *sometimes slowly and sometimes rapidly during a 50-year period* from the 1840s to the 1890s. Nor did the settlers go farther and farther west. California was settled before the Rockies and the Great Plains.

8. **A** Those who went west were, among others, trappers and traders, gold- and oil-seekers, all hoping for *economic advancement* by cashing in on the rich resources of the area.

9. **D** The "fictional western town was as rigidly formalized (lines 36 and 37) as the set for a Japanese No play." It follows, therefore, *that in books and films, western towns are all the same*. In reality, of course, towns vary considerably.

10. **A** The passage describes a stereotype of townspeople frequently used in books, movies, and plays set in the period. The people seem always to be portrayed as "decent folk" (line 49) who had *settled into routine lives*.

11. **C** The cowboy in Crane's story is called a "drunken anachronism" (line 63), a label implying that he is a sad relic of a bygone era. In other words, he's a *hero of the Old West who became obsolete.*

12. **C**   The original center of the mining kingdom was California. Then, the center shifted to Colorado (Pike's Peak), to Montana, Wyoming, and the Black Hills of South Dakota. As new sources of precious metals were discovered throughout the nineteenth century, the center *shifted from place to place*.

13. **A**   Many ex-miners turned to farming and to raising cattle, occupations that required them to *work on the land*.

14. **C**   Passage 2 says that, although mining had been a major influence in shaping the history of the American West, *the growth of the cattle industry* was an even "more important chapter" (line 99).

15. **D**   The passage indicates that, before becoming "almost extinct" (line 108), millions of buffalo had "roamed at will" (line 106) throughout the Great Plains. Because ranchers needed the land to graze their "Texas longhorns and Wyoming and Montana steers," the buffalo *were killed to make room for cattle*.

16. **C**   The qualities of the cowboy mentioned in the passage are his "picturesque costume," his "splendid horsemanship," his "war with cattle rustlers," and his "lonely life on the plain." Only the cowboy's *law-abiding nature* is not mentioned.

17. **A**   Passage 1 tells of *gold*-seekers "working up and down the California mountain ranges" (lines 14 and 15). Passage 2 says that "the discovery of *gold* in California" (lines 67 and 68) triggered a rush of settlers to the area.

18. **D**   Both authors discuss the impact of the westward movement on American culture, *folklore and legend*. In particular, the cowboy epitomizes the romanticism of the westward movement.

19. **B**   In Passage 1 the *miner* is mentioned as one of several figures who participated in the settling of the West. On the other hand, almost half of Passage 2 is devoted to a discussion of the *miner*.

SECTION 6

1. **D**   Error in logical comparison. Compare voices with voices, not voices with singers.

2. **C**   Run-on sentence. Choice C corrects the error by turning the initial clause ("The … blackboard") into a participial phrase ("After … blackboard") and changing the subject of the main clause from *he* to *the mathematics instructor*.

3. **C**   Error in usage. Do not use *when* after *is* in making a definition.

4. **D**   Shift in number. The subject, *students,* is plural; the subject complement should be plural as well. Change *tumbler* to *tumblers*.

5. **E**   Lack of parallelism. The "both … and" construction provides parallel structure.

6. **B**   Wordiness. Choice B makes the writer's point simply and concisely.

7. **C**   Error in logical comparison. Compare audiences with audiences, not with theaters.

8. **D**   Dangling participle. Ask yourself who is observing the preschoolers' interactions.

9. **C**   Error in subject-verb agreement. In a "neither … nor" construction, if one subject is singular and the other is plural, the verb agrees with the nearer subject. Here, the subject nearer to the verb is *islands* (plural). The verb should be plural as well. Change *was prepared* to *were prepared*.

10. **A**   Sentence is correct.

11. **A**   Sentence is correct.

12. **E**   Lack of parallelism. Choice E has parallel structure.

13. **C**   Error in subject-verb agreement. The subject, *demand,* is singular; the verb should be singular as well. Change *are* to *is*.

14. **D**   Sentence fragment. Choice D economically corrects the fragment.

PART III

SENTENCE COMPLETION QUESTIONS

OVERVIEW

Sentence completion questions are the first critical reading questions you encounter as you take the SAT. These questions test your ability to use your vocabulary and to recognize how the different parts of a sentence fit together to make sense.

The sentence completion questions ask you to choose the best way to complete a sentence from which one or two words have been omitted. You must be able to recognize the logic, style, and tone of the sentence, so that you will be able to choose the answer that makes sense in this context. You must also be able to recognize the different ways in which words are normally defined. At some time or another, you have probably had a vocabulary assignment in which you were asked to define a word and use it in a sentence. In questions of this type, you have to *fit* words into sentences. Once you understand the implications of a sentence, you should be able to choose the answer that will make the sentence clear, logical, and consistent in style and tone.

The subject matter of these sentences comes from a wide variety of fields—music, art, science, literature, history. However, you are not being tested on your general knowledge. Though at times your knowledge of a particular fact may guide you in choosing the correct answer, you should be able to handle any of the sentences using your understanding of the English language.

TIPS ON HANDLING SENTENCE COMPLETION QUESTIONS

TIP 1

BEFORE YOU LOOK AT THE ANSWER CHOICES, THINK OF A WORD THAT MAKES SENSE

Your first step in answering a sentence completion question is, *without looking at the answer choices,* to try to come up with a word that fits in the blank. The word you think of may not be the exact word that appears in any of the answer choices, but it will probably be similar in meaning to the right answer. Then, when you turn to the answer choices, you'll have an idea of what you're looking for.

Try going through the sentence substituting the word *blank* for each missing word. Doing this will give you a feel for what the sentence means.

Example:

Unlike her gabby brother Bruce, Bea seldom _blanks_ .

Just from looking at the sentence, you know the answer must be *chatters, talks,* or a synonym.

At this point, look at the answer choices. If the word you thought of is one of the five choices, select it as your answer. If the word you thought of is *not* a choice, look for a synonym of that word.

See how the process works in dealing with a more complex sentence.

The psychologist set up the experiment to test the rat's ____; he wished to see how well the rat adjusted to the changing conditions it had to face.

Even before you look at the answer choices, you can figure out what the answer *should* be.

Look at the sentence. A psychologist is trying to test some particular quality or characteristic of a rat. What quality? How do you get the answer?

Note how the part of the sentence following the semicolon (the second clause, in technical terms) is being used to define or clarify what the psychologist is trying to test. He is trying to see how well the rat *adjusts*. What words does this suggest to you? Either *flexibility* or *adaptability* could complete the sentence's thought.

Here are the five answer choices given:

(A) reflexes
(B) communicability
(C) stamina
(D) sociability
(E) adaptability

The answer clearly is *adaptability*, (E).

Be sure to check out all five answer choices before you make your final choice. Don't leap at the first word that seems to fit. You are looking for the word that *best* fits the meaning of the sentence as a whole. In order to be sure you have not been hasty in making your decision, substitute each of the answer choices for the missing word. That way you can satisfy yourself that you have come up with the answer that best fits.

TIP 2 — SPOT CLUES IN THE SENTENCE: SIGNAL WORDS

Writers use transitions to link their ideas logically. These transitions or signal words are clues that can help you figure out what the sentence actually means.

Support Signals

Look for words or phrases that indicate that the omitted portion of the sentence continues a thought developed elsewhere in the sentence. Examples are *and*, *moreover*, *in addition*, and *furthermore*. In such cases, a synonym or near-synonym should provide the correct answer.

Here is an example of a sentence completion question in which a support signal provides a helpful clue.

He was habitually so docile and ____ that his friends could not understand his sudden outburst against his employers.

(A) submissive
(B) incorrigible

(C) contemptuous
(D) erratic
(E) hasty

The signal word *and* is your clue that the writer is trying to reinforce the notion of docility introduced in the sentence. Not only is this person docile, he is also ___blank___. Look through the answer choices for a synonym or near-synonym of *docile* or obedient. You find one immediately: (A), *submissive*. Check through the other answer choices. Nothing else makes sense. The correct answer is (A).

Contrast Signals

Look for words or phrases that indicate a contrast between one idea and another. Examples are *but*, *although*, *nevertheless*, *despite*, *however*, *even though*, and *on the other hand*. In such cases, an antonym or near-antonym for another word in the sentence should provide the correct answer.

Here is an example of a sentence completion question in which a contrast signal pinpoints the correct answer for you.

We expected her to be jubilant over her victory, but she was ____ instead.

(A) triumphant
(B) adult
(C) morose
(D) loquacious
(E) culpable

The signal word *but* suggests that the winner's expected reaction contrasts with her actual one. Instead of being "jubilant" (extremely joyful), she is sad. Look through the answer choices to find a word that is the *opposite* of jubilant. The correct answer is (C), *morose* or gloomy.

Cause and Effect Signals

Look for words or phrases that indicate that one thing causes another. Examples are *because*, *since*, *therefore*, *consequently*, *accordingly*, *hence*, *thus*, and *as a result*.

Here is an example of a sentence completion question in which a cause and effect signal should prove helpful to you.

Because his delivery was ____, the effect of his speech on the voters was nonexistent.

(A) plausible

(B) moving
(C) audible
(D) halting
(E) respectable

What sort of delivery would cause a speech to have no effect? A *plausible* (superficially pleasing and persuasive) delivery would probably have some effect on the voters. A *moving* or eloquent delivery certainly would. An *audible* delivery, one the audience could hear, would be more likely to have an effect than an inaudible one would. A *respectable*, appropriate delivery probably would have some impact as well. Only a *halting* or stumbling delivery would mar the voters' appreciation of the speech and cause it to have little or no effect on them. Thus, the correct answer is (D).

TIP 3   NOTICE NEGATIVES

Watch out for negative words and words with negative prefixes: *no, not, none; non-, un-, in-*. These negative words and word parts are killers, especially in combination.

Madison was not ____ person and thus made few public addresses; but those he made were memorable, filled with noble phrases.

(A) a reticent
(B) a stately
(C) an inspiring
(D) an introspective
(E) a communicative

The damage to the car was insignificant.
   ("Don't worry about it—it's just a scratch.")
The damage to the car was not insignificant.
   ("Oh, no, Bart! We totaled Mom's car!")

In particular, watch out for *not*: it's easy to overlook, but it's a key word, as the following sentence clearly illustrates.

What would happen if you overlooked *not* in this question? Probably you'd wind up choosing (A): Madison was a *reticent* (quiet; reserved) man. *For this reason* he made few public addresses.

Unfortunately, you'd have gotten things backward. The sentence isn't telling you what Madison was like. It's telling you what he was *not* like. And he was not a *communicative* person; he didn't

express himself freely. However, when he did get around to speaking, he had some good things to say.

TIP 4   TAKE ONE BLANK AT A TIME

Dealing with double-blank sentences can be tricky. Testing the first word of each answer pair helps you narrow things down.

Here's how to do it. Read through the entire sentence. Then insert the first word of each answer pair in the sentence's first blank. Ask yourself whether this particular word makes sense in this blank. If the initial word of an answer pair makes no sense in the sentence, you can eliminate the entire pair.

Next, check out the second word of each of the answer pairs that you haven't ruled out. Be careful. Remember: just as each word of the correct answer pair must make sense in its individual context, both words must make sense when used together.

Try this question to practice working with double-blank sentences.

The opossum is ____ the venom of snakes in the rattlesnake subfamily and thus views the reptiles not as ____ enemies but as a food source.

(A) vulnerable to...natural
(B) indicative of...mortal
(C) impervious to...lethal
(D) injurious to...deadly
(E) defenseless against...potential

Your first job is to eliminate any answer choices you can on the basis of their first word.
• Opossums might be *vulnerable to* snake poison. Keep (A).
• Opossums are unlikely to be *indicative* or suggestive *of* snake poison. Cross out (B).
• Opossums could be *impervious to* (unaffected by; immune to) snake poison. Keep (C).
• Opossums couldn't be *injurious* or harmful *to* snake poison. Cross out (D).
• Opossums could be *defenseless against* snake poison. Keep (E).

Now examine the second half of the sentence. Opossums look on rattlesnakes as a food source. They can eat rattlers for a reason. Why? Is it because opossums are *vulnerable to* or *defenseless against* the poison? No. It's because they're *impervious to* the poison (that is, unharmed by it). That's the reason they can treat the rattlesnake as a potential source of food and not as a *lethal*, or deadly, enemy. The correct answer is (C).

Note the cause-and-effect signal *thus*. The nature of the opossum's response to the venom explains *why* it can look on a dangerous snake as a possible prey.

SENTENCE COMPLETION EXERCISES

To develop your ability to handle sentence completion questions, work your way through the following three series of exercises. Warning: These series of exercises are graded in difficulty. The further you go, the harder the going gets, just as on a video game. Go all the way. Even if you do less well on Level C than you did on Level A, look on every error as an opportunity to learn. Study all the sentences that you found difficult. Review all the vocabulary words that you didn't know. Remember: these are all college-level sentences, set up to test your knowledge of college-level words.

After completing each exercise, see how many questions you answered correctly. (The correct answers are given on pages 92–93.) Then *read the answer explanations* for questions you answered incorrectly, questions you omitted, and questions you answered correctly but found difficult.

LEVEL A

Most high school students feel comfortable answering sentence completion questions on this level of difficulty. Consider the four practice exercises that follow to be a warm-up for the harder questions to come.

Each of the following sentences contains one or two blanks; each blank indicates that a word or set of words has been left out. Below the sentence are five words or phrases, lettered A through E. Select the word or set of words that best completes the sentence.

Example:

Fame is ----; today's rising star is all too soon tomorrow's washed-up has-been.

(A) rewarding   (B) gradual
(C) essential   (D) spontaneous
(E) transitory

Ⓐ Ⓑ Ⓒ Ⓓ ●

Exercise 1

1. The Cabinet member's resignation was not a total ____: rumors of his imminent departure had been making the rounds in Washington for a week.

   (A) withdrawal
   (B) success
   (C) shock
   (D) eclipse
   (E) pretense

2. The wagon train leaders chose to ____ their route when they realized that the heavy rains had made fording the river too ____ a task.

   (A) question...uncomplicated
   (B) disregard...common
   (C) abandon...legitimate
   (D) alter...impracticable
   (E) follow...elusive

3. It is possible to analyze a literary work to death, ____ what should be a living experience as if it were a laboratory specimen.

   (A) questioning
   (B) dissecting
   (C) amending
   (D) nurturing
   (E) reviving

4. Anthropologists traditionally argue that the male-female division of labor in hunter-gatherer societies arose because it ____ the nuclear family's joint interests and thereby represented a sound, ____ strategy.

   (A) impaired...collaborative
   (B) respected...divisive
   (C) ignored...disinterested
   (D) restricted...provisional
   (E) promoted...cooperative

5. Because of its strength, adhesiveness, and invaluable qualities as a nest-building material, many species of birds ____ silk into their nests.

   (A) smuggle
   (B) jettison
   (C) incorporate
   (D) entice
   (E) dissolve

6. The recruit was ____ by the sergeant's scathing rebuke; nobody had ever ____ him like that before.

   (A) flattered...honored
   (B) touched...noticed
   (C) stung...reprimanded
   (D) astonished...questioned
   (E) discouraged...intrigued

7. Her memoirs are quite unlike those of her predecessors, for she is bold and aggressive where they are ____ and comfortable.

   (A) audacious
   (B) vivid
   (C) bland
   (D) brazen
   (E) contentious

8. The report was relentlessly ____ to the scientist, interpreting one complex event after another to his ____.

   (A) magnanimous...dismay
   (B) disparaging...initiative
   (C) innocuous...indifference
   (D) hostile...discredit
   (E) obsequious...detriment

9. People who don't outgrow their colleges often don't grow in other ways; there remained in Forster's life and imagination a ____ of the undergraduate, clever but ____.

   (A) dislike...talented
   (B) touch...judicious
   (C) streak...immature
   (D) fear...dormant
   (E) trace...sincere

10. She ____ recognition and fame, yet she felt a deep suspicion and ____ for the world in which recognition and fame are granted, the world of money and opinion and power.

    (A) mistrusted...antagonism
    (B) worked for...respect
    (C) endured...veneration
    (D) shunned...enmity
    (E) yearned for...contempt

11. Unfortunately, excessive care in choosing one's words often results in a loss of ____.

    (A) precision
    (B) atmosphere
    (C) selectivity
    (D) spontaneity
    (E) credibility

12. Just as the earliest stone tools left by humans may seem nothing more than rock fragments to a layperson, so a lot of fossils require a trained eye to ____ them.

    (A) excavate
    (B) appreciate
    (C) disseminate
    (D) antedate
    (E) educate

13. According to a noted art critic, one would have to be completely immune to the sensuous pleasures of painting to be ____ Lucien Freud's mesmerizing art.

    (A) drawn to
    (B) overcome by
    (C) enamored of
    (D) unaffected by
    (E) consistent about

14. Most people who are color-blind actually can distinguish several colors; some, however, have a truly ____ view of a world all in shades of gray.

    (A) monochromatic
    (B) opalescent
    (C) translucent
    (D) astigmatic
    (E) roseate

15. For years no one could make this particular therapy work in animals larger than rodents, but now two research groups have demonstrated its ____ in dogs.

    (A) efficacy
    (B) defects
    (C) variability
    (D) origin
    (E) virulence

16. Thanks to the emerging technology of active noise control, automakers may soon be able to ____ noise inside a car and create the long-promised "quiet ride."

    (A) dampen
    (B) energize
    (C) undertake
    (D) concentrate
    (E) augment

17. Despite her father's ____ that "a woman's place is in the home" and a ____ reception from her professors and fellow graduate students, Marian Cleeves went on to become the first woman to receive a doctorate in anatomy from the University of California at Berkeley.

    (A) warning...gratifying
    (B) reprimand...lavish
    (C) encouragement...respectful
    (D) admonition...cool
    (E) maxim...hospitable

18. John Keats, Dylan Thomas, Arthur Rimbaud—all these were poets who *had* to be poets, whom no one or nothing short of death could have ____ their courses.

    (A) confirmed in
    (B) derailed from
    (C) lauded for
    (D) interested in
    (E) convinced of

19. By arguing that much of what scientists think they know about the focusing mechanism of the eye is untrue, this radical scholar has gained a reputation as ____ in the field.

    (A) a sycophant
    (B) a martinet
    (C) an opportunist
    (D) a maverick
    (E) a laggard

20. The philosopher Auguste Comte ____ the term *altruism* to ____ unselfish regard for the welfare of others.

    (A) avoided...rationalize
    (B) coined...denote
    (C) applied...lessen
    (D) explained...refute
    (E) understood...terminate

Exercise 2

1. Given the ability of modern technology to _____ the environment, it is clear that, if we are not careful, the human race may soon be as extinct as the dinosaur.

   (A) enhance
   (B) destroy
   (C) analyze
   (D) repair
   (E) nurture

2. As founder and president of the Children's Defense Fund, Marian Wright Edelman has ensured that, even though the young cannot vote or make campaign contributions, they are nevertheless not _____ in Washington.

   (A) represented
   (B) distrusted
   (C) ignored
   (D) committed
   (E) welcome

3. Using novel concepts and techniques previously unknown in commercial advertising, the _____ advertising campaign broke new ground in the field of marketing.

   (A) questionable
   (B) interminable
   (C) imitative
   (D) inadequate
   (E) innovative

4. The attorney's vibrant voice and _____ sense of timing were as useful to him as his prodigious preparation, attention to detail, and _____ of the law.

   (A) deficient...conception
   (B) excellent...ignorance
   (C) shaky...command
   (D) outstanding...mastery
   (E) impeccable...deprecation

5. Thomas Jefferson called *The Federalist* papers "the best commentaries on the principles of government ever written," and two centuries later they still _____ as the most _____ statements of American political philosophy.

   (A) stand...derivative
   (B) rate...abstruse
   (C) rank...impressive
   (D) fascinate...ambiguous
   (E) compete...underrated

6. Some spiderwebs are sheets or tangles of threads that delay the _____ of prey, allowing the spider, _____ by vibrations that travel through the threads, time to make its way over to the entangled victim.

   (A) escape...alerted
   (B) consumption...frightened
   (C) capture...thwarted
   (D) pursuit...soothed
   (E) sighting...irritated

7. Janet Malcolm depicts the biographer as a nosy, intrusive figure, _____ his subject's private papers.

   (A) annotating
   (B) restoring
   (C) invading
   (D) acknowledging
   (E) compiling

8. Because fruit juice fills babies' small stomachs and ruins their appetite for foods that contain nutrients they _____, consuming large quantities can actually prove _____ to babies less than 24 months old.

   (A) prefer...beneficial
   (B) choose...counterproductive
   (C) require...helpful
   (D) need...detrimental
   (E) ingest...advantageous

9. Telling gripping tales about a central character engaged in a mighty struggle with events, modern biographies satisfy the American appetite for _____ narratives.

   (A) lyrical
   (B) colloquial
   (C) digressive
   (D) undemanding
   (E) epic

10. A leading philosopher of our time, Ludwig Wittgenstein, laid down a _____ to which good historians _____: "Of that of which nothing is known nothing can be said."

    (A) burden...protest
    (B) law...amend
    (C) rule...adhere
    (D) maxim...succumb
    (E) weapon...surrender

11. Musk oxen survived in isolated arctic habitats, but in the nineteenth century they declined rapidly even there, their numbers _____ by the armed enthusiasm of explorers, whalers, fur traders, and Eskimo.

    (A) swelled
    (B) augmented
    (C) devastated
    (D) underestimated
    (E) calculated

12. The banquet had _____ effect on the overfed guests: they began to nod off in their seats.

    (A) a soporific
    (B) a cumulative
    (C) an immoderate
    (D) an invigorating
    (E) a negligible

13. He loved his friends, but he held people in general in _____ and maintained that human virtues were unworthy of comparison with a dog's devotion.

    (A) reverence
    (B) abeyance
    (C) contempt
    (D) affection
    (E) honor

14. Stunned by Professor Marian Diamond's work showing that rat-brain structure can increase by 5 to 7 percent, one _____ neuroanatomist stated flatly, "Young lady, that brain cannot _____!"

    (A) astounded...function
    (B) aghast...deteriorate
    (C) dumbfounded...think
    (D) skeptical...grow
    (E) finicky...die

15. For all his protestations of _____, Judge Learned Hand had been deeply _____ at being passed over for the United States Supreme Court, where Oliver Wendell Holmes, Jr., Benjamin Cardozo, and countless others said he belonged.

    (A) innocence...embarrassed
    (B) disbelief...enervated
    (C) indifference...disappointed
    (D) despondency...frustrated
    (E) affection...commiserated

16. Halls and audiences for *lieder* recitals tend to be smaller than those for opera and thus more _____ the intimacy and sense of close involvement, which is the recital's particular charm.

    (A) inauspicious for
    (B) destructive of
    (C) conducive to
    (D) compromised by
    (E) indifferent to

17. In this survey of Revolutionary America, the author finds a remarkable homogeneity of opinion from Massachusetts to Georgia; the differences between the sections are _____, almost always explainable by differences in climate or topography.

    (A) sharp
    (B) nonexistent
    (C) irreconcilable
    (D) superficial
    (E) enormous

18. According to Lionel Trilling, the paradox of liberalism is that in its quest for freedom it must move toward greater organization, stricter legislation, and increasing _____.

    (A) anarchy
    (B) self-realization
    (C) stagnation
    (D) control
    (E) levity

19. Our mood swings about the economy grow more extreme: when things go well, we become _____; when things go poorly, _____ descends.

    (A) restive...anxiety
    (B) euphoric...gloom
    (C) prudent...benevolence
    (D) ascetic...misery
    (E) ambivalence...optimism

20. Abandoning the moral principles of his youth, the aging emperor Tiberius led a _____, wanton life.

    (A) celibate
    (B) rudimentary
    (C) debauched
    (D) circumspect
    (E) peripatetic

Exercise 3

1. Although a few of her contemporaries _____ her book, most either ignored it or mocked it.

   (A) dismissed
   (B) disregarded
   (C) deprecated
   (D) misconstrued
   (E) appreciated

2. All critics have agreed that the opera's score is _____, but, curiously, no two critics have agreed which passages to praise and which to damn.

   (A) intolerable
   (B) melodious
   (C) unsurpassed
   (D) conventional
   (E) uneven

3. A man incapable of _____ action, he never had an opinion about something that he had not worked up beforehand, fashioning it with lengthy care.

   (A) premeditated
   (B) coherent
   (C) spontaneous
   (D) calculated
   (E) self-conscious

4. Even as the local climate changed from humid to arid and back—a change that caused other animals to become extinct—our almost-human ancestors _____ by learning how to use the new flora.

   (A) anticipated
   (B) survived
   (C) diverged
   (D) deteriorated
   (E) migrated

5. Marketing specialists have begun _____ what had once been a _____ audience into innumerable segments based on age, sex, income, and a host of pop sociological categories.

   (A) carving up...mass
   (B) bringing together...fragmented
   (C) tearing apart...sophisticated
   (D) unifying...distinct
   (E) transforming...responsive

6. Like a balloon that is _____, aneurysms (swellings in the walls of arteries) sometimes enlarge so much that they _____.

   (A) expanding...contract
   (B) punctured...dilate
   (C) elastic...stratify
   (D) weightless...stretch
   (E) overinflated...burst

7. Critics _____ the _____ in developing the new weather satellite to unexpected problems in manufacturing and testing its components.

   (A) credit...timeliness
   (B) impute...success
   (C) attribute...delay
   (D) assign...importance
   (E) deny...threat

8. As former Supreme Court Justice Warren Burger was fond of pointing out, many lawyers are not legal hotshots; they often come to court _____ and _____ professional skills.

   (A) ill prepared...lacking
   (B) hot-tempered...criticizing
   (C) reluctant...demonstrating
   (D) argumentative...manifesting
   (E) conservative...excelling

9. A hypothesis must not only account for what we already know, but must also be _____ by continued observation.

   (A) refuted
   (B) interrupted
   (C) verified
   (D) discredited
   (E) outmoded

10. *Elizabeth Gaskell: A Habit of Stories* is a considerable _____, superseding Winifred Gerin's learned biography of the English novelist.

    (A) failure
    (B) rationalization
    (C) accomplishment
    (D) recollection
    (E) muddle

11. Boccherini was a good and interesting composer whose reputation has not sufficiently ____ the decline into which it fell after his death.

   (A) contributed to
   (B) benefited from
   (C) recovered from
   (D) conflicted with
   (E) derived from

12. Having billed himself as "Mr. Clean," Hosokawa could not ____ the ____ of a major financial scandal.

   (A) survive...acclaim
   (B) withstand...notoriety
   (C) identify...exposure
   (D) resist...charms
   (E) censure...temptation

13. A curious ____ of Florence's history is that this great center of Italian ____ should time and again have been home to acts of appalling savagery and inhumanity.

   (A) example...conflict
   (B) paradox...civilization
   (C) result...brutality
   (D) convention...culture
   (E) distinction...quality

14. While some Southern writers see the past as a heavy burden, others see it as a subject for ____ reflection.

   (A) gloomy
   (B) wearisome
   (C) interminable
   (D) nostalgic
   (E) bleak

15. Lamenting that something horrid had recently befallen the craft of biography, biographer Arthur Schlesinger ____ the glut of gossipy new lives on the market.

   (A) deplored
   (B) forgot
   (C) acclaimed
   (D) composed
   (E) abridged

16. Instead of taking exaggerated precautions against touching or tipping or jarring the bottle of wine, the waitress handled it quite ____, being careful only to use a napkin to keep her hands from the cool bottle itself.

   (A) fastidiously
   (B) reverently
   (C) nonchalantly
   (D) tentatively
   (E) ambivalently

17. The eighteenth century was a kind of golden age in deaf history because, with the establishment of schools for the deaf, these people emerged from ____ and began to appear in positions of eminence and ____—as writers, engineers, philosophers, and intellectuals.

   (A) retirement...ambiguity
   (B) seclusion...compromise
   (C) obscurity...responsibility
   (D) hiding...ignominy
   (E) solicitude...disrepute

18. Left to endure a penniless old age, the ____ man lived to regret his ____ youth.

   (A) miserly...friendless
   (B) reclusive...affable
   (C) eccentric...fleeting
   (D) egotistical...frugal
   (E) improvident...prodigal

19. When Dorothy and her friends realized that, despite his claims, the Wizard of Oz didn't know how to get them back to Kansas, they were sure they'd been ____ by a ____.

   (A) befriended...philanthropist
   (B) succored...magician
   (C) captured...genius
   (D) duped...charlatan
   (E) delayed...miser

20. Egocentric, at times vindictive when he believed his authority was being questioned, White could also be kind, gracious, and even ____ when the circumstances seemed to require it.

   (A) self-deprecating
   (B) authoritarian
   (C) provocative
   (D) taciturn
   (E) disdainful

Exercise 4

1. Repeat offenders who continue to drive under the influence of alcohol face having their drivers' licenses permanently _____.

    (A) issued
    (B) recorded
    (C) authorized
    (D) revoked
    (E) disregarded

2. Excited and unafraid, the _____ child examined the stranger with bright-eyed curiosity.

    (A) apathetic
    (B) drowsy
    (C) timorous
    (D) inquisitive
    (E) hesitant

3. Though masterminded by the Metropolitan Museum's Guy Bauman, this survey of Flemish paintings in America was clearly a _____ operation, aided by scholars throughout North America.

    (A) marginal
    (B) derivative
    (C) worthwhile
    (D) circuitous
    (E) collective

4. I am seeking an _____ solution to this dispute, one that will be fair and acceptable to both sides.

    (A) equivocal
    (B) infamous
    (C) equitable
    (D) idiosyncratic
    (E) overrated

5. A New World lizard, the basilisk, occasionally does something that seems to _____ physics: it runs across the surface of water for distances of up to 30 feet.

    (A) defy
    (B) quantify
    (C) assess
    (D) exemplify
    (E) corroborate

6. The most consistent qualities of Forster's novels are the human isolation and passivity in them; his principal characters stand slightly apart and _____, but rarely _____.

    (A) sneer...collapse
    (B) interact...adapt
    (C) mourn...recollect
    (D) observe...act
    (E) domineer...participate

7. Far from being distracted or immobilized by his inner conflicts, Keynes was _____ by them into becoming one of the most productive, effective, and buoyant personalities of the twentieth century.

    (A) neutralized
    (B) energized
    (C) incapacitated
    (D) enervated
    (E) inhibited

8. A born teller of tales, Olsen used her impressive _____ skills to advantage in her story "I Stand Here Ironing."

    (A) domestic
    (B) metaphysical
    (C) narrative
    (D) diagnostic
    (E) argumentative

9. Waving broadly at the still-applauding crowd, the speaker was highly _____ by the _____ response to her talk.

    (A) exasperated...vehement
    (B) gratified...enthusiastic
    (C) bewildered...profound
    (D) intimidated...sincere
    (E) delighted....skeptical

10. As a scientific document, the book should stand for several years until further _____ again make revision _____.

    (A) developments...impossible
    (B) obstacles...optional
    (C) attempts...undesirable
    (D) failures...detrimental
    (E) advances...necessary

11. The jazz musician cannot play well if he is completely ____, as if lying half asleep in a Jacuzzi.

    (A) untruthful
    (B) autonomous
    (C) sincere
    (D) relaxed
    (E) talented

12. Why do some plant stems develop a protective bark that enables them to survive the winter, while others ____ at the first frost?

    (A) blossom
    (B) adapt
    (C) shrivel
    (D) mature
    (E) wake

13. Salvador Dali's tendency to fabricate events makes it difficult for the biographer to tell the story of his life with any degree of ____.

    (A) vividness
    (B) accuracy
    (C) solemnity
    (D) spontaneity
    (E) artistry

14. If Amelia Earhart's acceptance was by no means ____, her fame was unusually widespread and her popularity long-lived.

    (A) universal
    (B) ambiguous
    (C) expedient
    (D) partial
    (E) genuine

15. Throughout his career he demonstrated strong belief in individual faith but powerful ____ about the organized church.

    (A) modesty
    (B) skepticism
    (C) devotion
    (D) discernment
    (E) ambition

16. For a young person, Winston seems remarkably ____; you'd expect someone his age to show a little more life.

    (A) sophomoric
    (B) vigorous
    (C) stodgy
    (D) tidy
    (E) sensitive

17. The senator contended that, rather than being a ____ concern, global warming is a critical problem that imperils not just Americans but all life on Earth.

    (A) significant
    (B) hazardous
    (C) strategic
    (D) planetary
    (E) peripheral

18. It would be beneficial if someone so radical could be brought to believe that old customs need not necessarily be ____ and that change may possibly be ____.

    (A) defensible...premature
    (B) outdated...required
    (C) evil...salutary
    (D) invaluable...temporary
    (E) worthless...inadvisable

19. T. S. Eliot, famous for his ____, nevertheless accepted posterity's interest in his life, ____ that his correspondence with his lady friends eventually would be read.

    (A) reticence...assuming
    (B) modesty...prohibiting
    (C) boastfulness...remembering
    (D) vanity...intimating
    (E) curiosity...regretting

20. Waiting impatiently in line to see Santa Claus, even the best-behaved children grow ____ and start to fidget.

    (A) restive
    (B) noisome
    (C) sonorous
    (D) pungent
    (E) ambivalent

LEVEL B

Most high school students have some difficulty answering sentence completion questions on this level. Consider the four practice exercises that follow to be a good sample of the mid-range sentence completion questions you will face on the SAT.

Each of the following sentences contains one or two blanks; each blank indicates that a word or set of words has been left out. Below the sentence are five words or phrases, lettered A through E. Select the word or set of words that best completes the sentence.

Example:

Fame is ----; today's rising star is all too soon tomorrow's washed-up has-been.

(A) rewarding   (B) gradual
 (C) essential   (D) spontaneous
  (E) transitory

Ⓐ Ⓑ Ⓒ Ⓓ ●

Exercise 1

1. In the 1920s Hollywood became a magnet for men and women on the cutting edge—____ artists genuinely excited by the possibilities of the up-and-coming film medium.

    (A) irritable
    (B) innovative
    (C) untalented
    (D) outdated
    (E) inferior

2. According to poet John Berryman, there were so many ways to ____ a poem that it was quite amazing good ones ever got written.

    (A) dedicate
    (B) begin
    (C) ruin
    (D) recite
    (E) categorize

3. One by one, she ____ almost all of her supporters until, at the end, only a handful of her closest allies really wanted her to stay in office.

    (A) promoted
    (B) alienated
    (C) represented
    (D) exaggerated
    (E) liberated

4. The aorta is like a tree trunk from which other major arteries ____.

    (A) escape
    (B) subtract
    (C) clamber down
    (D) branch off
    (E) strip away

5. By putting the entire Woolf archive on microfilm, the project directors hope to make the contents of the manuscripts more ____ to scholars.

    (A) accessible
    (B) objective
    (C) appealing
    (D) implicit
    (E) relevant

6. The crisis is not ____; it will not affect us for years to come.

    (A) specious
    (B) fleeting
    (C) meaningless
    (D) minute
    (E) imminent

7. Peter has a bad habit of making _____ remarks that wander so far off topic that we forget the gist of what he is saying.

(A) awkward
(B) pertinent
(C) digressive
(D) telling
(E) tentative

8. Though set in a mythical South American country, Isabel Allende's novel is _____ the tragic history of Chile.

(A) irrelevant to
(B) rooted in
(C) inconsistent with
(D) exceeded by
(E) indifferent to

9. The marketers' _____ in donating the new basketball backboards to the school system are not solely _____; they plan to sell advertising space on the backboards, turning them into miniature billboards.

(A) losses...obvious
(B) expectations...peculiar
(C) aims...mercenary
(D) reasons...sensitive
(E) motivations...philanthropic

10. Justice Harry Blackmun's retirement, while unlikely to bring about a drastic change in the Supreme Court, will remove a distinctly _____ voice from the Court's often featureless mix.

(A) bland
(B) personal
(C) moderate
(D) neutral
(E) derivative

11. Having just published his fourth novel in an almost 40-year career, Gaddis describes himself, with some _____, as a writer who has never been in a _____ to get into print.

(A) expectation...mood
(B) impatience...technique
(C) understatement...rush
(D) indecision...position
(E) exaggeration...school

12. Actors fade out of view with depressing frequency; the theater is a _____ profession at best.

(A) romantic
(B) demanding
(C) chancy
(D) disinterested
(E) degenerate

13. Though Phil had expected to feel overawed when he met Joe Montana, he found the world-famous quarterback friendly and _____.

(A) querulous
(B) acerbic
(C) domineering
(D) unintimidating
(E) taciturn

14. Flying in the face of _____, the writer George Sand shocked her contemporaries by taking lovers and by wearing men's clothes.

(A) immodesty
(B) reconciliation
(C) emancipation
(D) convention
(E) modernism

15. In the poem "Annabel Lee," the speaker reveals that he is not _____ to the death of his beloved; on the contrary, he is _____.

(A) indifferent...apathetic
(B) reconciled...acquiescent
(C) resigned...inconsolable
(D) accustomed...inured
(E) relevant...responsive

16. The artists of the Chinese avant-garde have used Western styles _____ and meaningfully to accomplish artistic ends of their own.

(A) obsequiously
(B) shamefully
(C) cannily
(D) fortuitously
(E) problematically

17. Despite the poem's archaic and tortuous language, the thrust of the poet's argument is surprisingly _____.

(A) vapid
(B) dated
(C) blunted
(D) intelligible
(E) idiosyncratic

18. The biographer may not have _____ the depths of her subject's self-contradictory character, but she has traced its intriguingly complex _____.

    (A) plumbed...tedium
    (B) sounded...surface
    (C) thwarted...background
    (D) reached...insipidity
    (E) disregarded...psyche

19. Because of the trauma they have experienced, survivors of a major catastrophe are likely to exhibit _____ of behavior and may require the aid of competent therapists.

    (A) concessions
    (B) diminutions
    (C) aberrations
    (D) restrictions
    (E) altercations

20. The reader has the happy impression of watching an extraordinarily inventive and intellectually _____ novelist working at the _____ of her powers.

    (A) dishonest...apex
    (B) creative...eclipse
    (C) fecund...height
    (D) effete...limits
    (E) amenable...diminution

Exercise 2

1. Illness can be _____ as how disease *feels*, the experience of being sick: at once a physical or natural condition and a social and cultural one.

    (A) cured
    (B) survived
    (C) acclaimed
    (D) defined
    (E) deprecated

2. One of Detroit's great success stories was Lee Iacocca's revitalization of the moribund Chrysler Corporation, turning it into a _____ competitor.

    (A) vigorous
    (B) tentative
    (C) marginal
    (D) negligent
    (E) superficial

3. A journalist rather than a scholar, Mr. Cose seems nevertheless to be _____ most of the serious studies relevant to his topic.

    (A) overawed by
    (B) ignorant of
    (C) associated with
    (D) wearied by
    (E) familiar with

4. Now better known for its racetrack, Saratoga Springs first gained attention for the _____ qualities of its famous "healing waters."

    (A) diagnostic
    (B) commercial
    (C) therapeutic
    (D) overlooked
    (E) experimental

5. Far from being in the _____ condition promised by the realtor, the condo was shabby and dilapidated.

    (A) vacant
    (B) indifferent
    (C) pristine
    (D) marginal
    (E) euphoric

6. Polls indicate that many prospective voters in the next presidential election are _____ about the outcome; they do not seem to care who wins.

    (A) enthusiastic
    (B) inadequate
    (C) antagonistic
    (D) apathetic
    (E) suspicious

7. If you need car parts that the dealers no longer stock, try _____ for odd bits and pieces at the auto wreckers' yards.

    (A) waiting
    (B) bantering
    (C) scavenging
    (D) riveting
    (E) insuring

8. Grateful as we are for these splendid books, they remain isolated examples of excellence in a literature of _____.

    (A) competition
    (B) distinction
    (C) grandeur
    (D) mediocrity
    (E) affirmation

9. Despite the _____ discussions of recent months, observers say that the administration and the developer have made progress in their negotiations and are close to _____ on a purchase price.

   (A) amicable...haggling
   (B) acrimonious...defaulting
   (C) heated...agreeing
   (D) fruitful...settling
   (E) constructive...compromising

10. People expected Winston Churchill to take his painting lightly, but Churchill, no _____, regarded his artistic efforts most seriously indeed.

    (A) virtuoso
    (B) zealot
    (C) dilettante
    (D) altruist
    (E) renegade

11. Aimed at curbing European attempts to seize territory in the Americas, the Monroe Doctrine was a warning to _____ foreign powers.

    (A) magnanimous
    (B) credulous
    (C) reticent
    (D) predatory
    (E) allied

12. It is a spotty sort of book, with many pages that, if not exactly _____, are less than _____.

    (A) bland...tedious
    (B) pretentious...conventional
    (C) dull...exciting
    (D) eventful...newsworthy
    (E) murky...obscure

13. Unlike her sister the Widow Douglass, who _____ Huck's minor offenses, Miss Watson did nothing but scold the boy.

    (A) believed
    (B) rebuked
    (C) condoned
    (D) evaded
    (E) corroborated

14. In discussing Rothko's art, Breslin is _____ in keeping to the facts and resisting the _____ of fanciful interpretation.

    (A) scrupulous...temptation
    (B) meticulous...integrity
    (C) ungainly...reward
    (D) uninterested...echo
    (E) inept...bias

15. Burdened by debt, Lydgate abandons his dreams of reforming medicine to take a conventional but _____ practice in London.

    (A) lucrative
    (B) ordinary
    (C) innovative
    (D) intangible
    (E) exotic

16. The observers hope to find out how important _____ foraging is to these endangered shorebirds in order to _____ the importance of restricting nighttime human use of beaches to specific places or times.

    (A) nocturnal...ascertain
    (B) aerial...convey
    (C) underwater...rectify
    (D) sporadic...mitigate
    (E) desultory...mandate

17. When I listened to her cogent arguments, all my _____ were _____ and I was forced to agree with her point of view.

    (A) senses...stimulated
    (B) opinions...confirmed
    (C) preconceptions...substantiated
    (D) questions...interpolated
    (E) doubts...dispelled

18. The _____, by definition, possesses wisdom; the virtuoso, by definition, possesses _____.

    (A) scholar...morality
    (B) sage...expertise
    (C) zealot...sincerity
    (D) visionary...idealism
    (E) pedant...proficiency

19. Samuel Johnson gave more than ____ cooperation to his biographer, James Boswell; he made himself available to Boswell night after night, furnished Boswell with correspondence, even read his biographer's notes.

(A) innocuous
(B) collusive
(C) tacit
(D) edifying
(E) diplomatic

20. Where lesser scholars would have been ____ by the vast collection of unpublished letters, rough drafts, and journals left by Henry James, Leon Edel was emboldened by its discovery and began to plan an ambitious series of studies on the life and works of the novelist.

(A) intrigued
(B) encouraged
(C) incensed
(D) taxed
(E) daunted

Exercise 3

1. In their determination to discover ways to ____ human life, doctors fail to take into account that longer lives are not always happier ones.

(A) ease
(B) prolong
(C) eradicate
(D) recuperate
(E) dissect

2. The most crucial issue for wildlife in this arid land is unimpeded ____ water.

(A) passage through
(B) freedom from
(C) access to
(D) saturation in
(E) overflow of

3. Always trying to look on the bright side of every situation, she is a born ____.

(A) opportunist
(B) antagonist
(C) optimist
(D) maverick
(E) zealot

4. Despite their reputations as soothing love songs sung by mothers to lull fretful infants to sleep, many lullabies are of a dark, even ____ nature.

(A) soporific
(B) manipulative
(C) threatening
(D) auspicious
(E) innocuous

5. The mayor and school superintendent let their dispute over budget cuts ____ to ugly and destructive proportions.

(A) escalate
(B) automate
(C) stagnate
(D) condense
(E) dwindle

6. Wherever Lao Li travels, he makes slides of contemporary works of art; his archives ____ every meaningful artistic effort in modern China.

(A) deride
(B) ignore
(C) perpetrate
(D) document
(E) abridge

7. Contrary to her customary ____ behavior, Susan began leaving parties early to seek the solitude of her room.

(A) reclusive
(B) circumspect
(C) decorous
(D) gregarious
(E) altruistic

8. Science is always ____, expecting that modifications of its present theories will sooner or later be found necessary.

(A) conclusive
(B) irrefutable
(C) original
(D) tentative
(E) inflexible

9. One of the great killers until barely 50 years ago, tuberculosis ("consumption" as it was then named) seemed a scourge or _____ rather than the long-term _____ illness it was.

   (A) plague...chronic
   (B) detriment...ominous
   (C) antiseptic...prevalent
   (D) vestige...contemporary
   (E) epidemic...salutary

10. Gaddis is a formidably talented writer whose work has been, unhappily, more likely to intimidate or _____ his readers than to lure them into his fictional world.

    (A) entice
    (B) strengthen
    (C) invigorate
    (D) transform
    (E) repel

11. Compared with the ostentatious glamour of opera, classical song (increasingly called *lieder* everywhere) is a more _____ tradition.

    (A) articulate
    (B) unrepresentative
    (C) subdued
    (D) broad-minded
    (E) worldly

12. This well-documented book is _____ researched, fluently written, and unfailingly intelligent in tracing the _____ course of its subject's tormented career.

    (A) indifferently...triumphant
    (B) inadequately...unfortunate
    (C) painstakingly...tragic
    (D) carefully...auspicious
    (E) thoroughly...promising

13. Lexy's joy at finding the perfect Christmas gift for John was _____, for she still had to find presents for the cousins and Uncle Bob.

    (A) transient
    (B) antithetical
    (C) exuberant
    (D) exhaustive
    (E) incontrovertible

14. Life is a _____ of the sacred and the profane, of good and evil; to try to _____ them is futile.

    (A) rejection...embrace
    (B) commingling...separate
    (C) misalliance...endure
    (D) defamation...reform
    (E) confusion...promulgate

15. Under the rule of the foreign invaders, the land seemed asleep, save for a small group of rebels who sought to kindle the _____ nationalism of the people.

    (A) valid
    (B) blatant
    (C) dormant
    (D) pretentious
    (E) contemplated

16. Many of the early Hollywood moguls sought to _____ themselves and enhance their celluloid empires by snaring _____ writers and intellectuals as screenwriters.

    (A) advance...presumptuous
    (B) aggrandize...prestigious
    (C) intimidate...unsuspecting
    (D) glorify...superannuated
    (E) sabotage...distinguished

17. The Turner Network's production is an absorbing *Heart of Darkness*, watchful, surreptitious, almost _____ as it waits to _____ our emotions.

    (A) lighthearted...cater to
    (B) melancholy...cheer up
    (C) mercenary...pay for
    (D) predatory...pounce on
    (E) furtive...figure out

18. Helen valued people who behaved as if they respected themselves; nothing irritated her more than an excessively _____ waiter or a fawning salesclerk.

    (A) austere
    (B) domineering
    (C) grave
    (D) obsequious
    (E) contentious

19. Whereas most scholars have tended to regard Monteverdi's opera *L'Orfeo* as the beginning of a tradition, Mr. Pickett sensibly considers it the ____ of one.

(A) origin
(B) example
(C) presence
(D) culmination
(E) birthright

20. Though ostensibly teaching posture, Feher brings into play techniques of ballet, yoga, and vocal projection to come up with lessons that can best be described as ____.

(A) problematic
(B) eclectic
(C) homogeneous
(D) unpretentious
(E) doctrinaire

Exercise 4

1. During the troubles of 1750, the ____ of Scotland was terrible; many Scots could afford nothing to eat but oatmeal porridge.

(A) anarchy
(B) reputation
(C) punishment
(D) apathy
(E) poverty

2. The biographer of Tennyson is confronted with the problem, rarely solved, of how to make a basically ____ life interesting.

(A) dramatic
(B) bewildering
(C) intriguing
(D) controversial
(E) uneventful

3. If, like the mole rat, you could run backward as easily as forward but had weak eyes that could see only dim shadows of light and dark, you too might want touch-sensitive whiskers to help ____ you through the tunnels of your underground home.

(A) carry
(B) illuminate
(C) excavate
(D) distract
(E) guide

4. Getting into street brawls is no minor matter for professional boxers, who are required by law to restrict their ____ impulses to the ring.

(A) humorous
(B) aggressive
(C) obligatory
(D) amateurish
(E) legitimate

5. For all of his turn-of-the-century trappings, the novel's hero is basically a ____ voice; his values and cultural ____ are of the present more than the 1890s.

(A) derivative...antecedents
(B) modern...antiquity
(C) contemporary...sensibility
(D) familiar...descendants
(E) hollow...premises

6. She wondered whether triangles, which had only three sides, ____ as polygons, which she thought of as many-sided.

(A) theorized
(B) estimated
(C) qualified
(D) subsisted
(E) multiplied

7. Kepler's observations of the supernova would have been more ____ and valuable had they been made with a telescope; unfortunately, Kepler's supernova lighted the night skies five full years before Galileo made the first ____ telescopic scan of the heavens.

(A) remote...skeptical
(B) solemn...unseemly
(C) infamous...extraneous
(D) detailed...documented
(E) fortuitous...recorded

8. As a product of the Soviet literary establishment, the author was brave enough to ____ the hand that fed him, but not heroic enough to bite it.

(A) give up
(B) nibble at
(C) cringe from
(D) worship
(E) devour

9. It is a relief to see people who can be interested in the arts without being "arty"—collectors who collect for their own ____ rather than for ____.

   (A) enjoyment...satisfaction
   (B) interest...pleasure
   (C) reputation...amusement
   (D) delight...show
   (E) education...fulfillment

10. The periodic nature of her complaints began to concern us: alarmed by these ____ attacks, we decided to consult a doctor in spite of her opposition.

   (A) trivial
   (B) recurrent
   (C) superficial
   (D) spontaneous
   (E) tentative

11. Though critic John Simon seldom had a good word to say about most contemporary plays, his review of *All in the Timing* was a total ____.

   (A) mistake
   (B) dismissal
   (C) fraud
   (D) rave
   (E) farce

12. Traditional Chinese painters trained by copying their teachers; ____ was reserved for old age, when you might make changes so ____ that they were almost invisible.

   (A) imitation...ubiquitous
   (B) emulation...dramatic
   (C) novelty...marked
   (D) originality...slight
   (E) honor...petty

13. Satisfied that her name had been ____, she dropped her libel suit after the newspaper finally published a ____ of its original defamatory statement.

   (A) praised...summary
   (B) maligned...glossary
   (C) vindicated... repetition
   (D) enhanced...reaffirmation
   (E) cleared...retraction

14. Like Machiavelli before him, Henry Kissinger has a keen appreciation for the hard-headed, even ____, use of power, to the point of admiring some traits in leaders who were otherwise ____.

   (A) cynical...benevolent
   (B) gentle...insignificant
   (C) ruthless...detestable
   (D) resentful...charismatic
   (E) forceful...exemplary

15. Some thought Dali was a brilliant painter; others ____ him as a conceited poseur.

   (A) respected
   (B) venerated
   (C) dismissed
   (D) vindicated
   (E) exasperated

16. The late James Beard was ____ with his time and knowledge—a ____ trait in the narrow world of food writing, a milieu notorious for its pettiness and infighting.

   (A) unselfish...common
   (B) unconcerned...standard
   (C) stingy...remarkable
   (D) occupied...negative
   (E) generous...rare

17. *New Yorker* short stories often include ____ allusions to ____ people and events: the implication is, if you are in the in-crowd, you'll get the reference; if you come from Cleveland, you won't.

   (A) esoteric...obscure
   (B) redundant...celebrated
   (C) tedious...notorious
   (D) provincial...major
   (E) passing...common

18. Her growing bitterness was ____ by her professional rivalry with her sister, whose fortunes rose while her own ____.

   (A) represented...ascended
   (B) mitigated...dwindled
   (C) exemplified...soared
   (D) nurtured...multiplied
   (E) exacerbated...declined

19. Such was Brandon's _____ that he was frequently described as being honest as the day was long.

    (A) vigilance
    (B) munificence
    (C) probity
    (D) gravity
    (E) eminence

20. While the movie *Spellbound* is in many ways a glowing testimonial to the powers of psycho-analysis to overcome the evils of unreason, its portrait of the analytic profession is not entirely _____.

    (A) malignant
    (B) obscure
    (C) adulatory
    (D) vehement
    (E) derivative

LEVEL C

Most high school students have trouble answering many sentence completion questions on this level of difficulty. Consider the four practice exercises that follow to be a chance for you to acquaint yourself with the toughest sorts of sentence completion questions that occur on the SAT.

Each of the following sentences contains one or two blanks; each blank indicates that a word or set of words has been left out. Below the sentence are five words or phrases, lettered A through E. Select the word or set of words that best completes the sentence.

Example:

Fame is ----; today's rising star is all too soon tomorrow's washed-up has-been.

(A) rewarding   (B) gradual
(C) essential   (D) spontaneous
(E) transitory

Ⓐ Ⓑ Ⓒ Ⓓ ●

Exercise 1

1. The moon was hidden and the night had grown very dark; she had to _____ to see.

    (A) blink
    (B) strain
    (C) mask
    (D) remember
    (E) reflect

2. The Battle of Lexington was not, as most of us have been taught, a _____ rising of individual farmers, but was instead a tightly organized, well-planned event.

    (A) premeditated
    (B) cautionary
    (C) spontaneous
    (D) coordinated
    (E) theoretical

3. The book will arouse antagonism, disagreement, and animosity among theologians because it will _____ many _____ rituals and beliefs.

    (A) undermine...iconoclastic
    (B) tolerate...accepted
    (C) undermine...established
    (D) disregard...forgotten
    (E) observe...pious

4. What made Ann such a fine counselor was her
   ____, her ability to put herself in her client's place
   and feel his emotions as if they were her own.

   (A) integrity
   (B) empathy
   (C) tenacity
   (D) impartiality
   (E) aloofness

5. The text brims with details, but there are no
   overarching theses to ____ them.

   (A) specify
   (B) exaggerate
   (C) confound
   (D) unify
   (E) modify

6. The true historian finds the facts about
   Marlowe and Shakespeare far more interesting
   than people's unfounded ____.

   (A) complaints
   (B) evidence
   (C) conjectures
   (D) qualms
   (E) certainty

7. Even Cormac McCarthy, Don DeLillo, and
   William Gaddis—eminent novelists who are
   notoriously ____ when it comes to ____—have
   surrendered to the exigencies of modern publishing and agreed to be the subjects of magazine articles.

   (A) prolific...writing
   (B) egotistical...fame
   (C) overrated...style
   (D) irate...delays
   (E) shy...publicity

8. Tom prided himself on knowing the latest
   news, the secrets of the rich and the poor; it
   ____ him that there was something he did not
   know about his friend.

   (A) delighted
   (B) flattered
   (C) reminded
   (D) galled
   (E) reassured

9. Uncertain which suitor she ought to marry, the
   princess ____, saying now one, now the other.

   (A) improvised
   (B) vacillated
   (C) threatened
   (D) compromised
   (E) divulged

10. Factory trawlers, large fishing vessels that drag
    heavy nets over the seafloor, "vacuum" the
    North Pacific seas, trapping fish ____.

    (A) unintentionally
    (B) indiscriminately
    (C) paradoxically
    (D) collaboratively
    (E) temporarily

11. Elizabeth Barrett, whose ____ father would
    brook no interference or disagreement with his
    plans for his daughter, eloped in order to ____
    his autocratic rule.

    (A) attentive...underscore
    (B) vindictive...preserve
    (C) domineering...escape
    (D) idiosyncratic...accommodate
    (E) authoritarian...extend

12. Duke Ellington's jazz symphonies were
    attacked by classical critics who felt that the
    entire attempt to fuse jazz as a form with clas-
    sical music should be ____.

    (A) promoted
    (B) documented
    (C) discouraged
    (D) acclaimed
    (E) repeated

13. During the last four decades of Tennyson's
    long life, his creative powers never ____, some
    of his most remarkable work coming after the
    age of 70.

    (A) recovered
    (B) manifested
    (C) flagged
    (D) blossomed
    (E) broadened

14. The villagers fortified the town hall, hoping this improvised _____ could _____ them from the guerrilla raids.

(A) stronghold...alienate
(B) refuge...distinguish
(C) bastion...protect
(D) venture...intimidate
(E) disguise...safeguard

15. Lovejoy, the hero of Jonathan Gash's mystery novels, is an antiques dealer who gives the reader advice on how to tell _____ antiques from the real thing.

(A) priceless
(B) spurious
(C) classical
(D) authentic
(E) antiquated

16. The omniscient narrator stands above the story he is telling, _____ his knowledge of what will occur.

(A) disheartened by
(B) unlimited in
(C) ostracized for
(D) vindicated by
(E) uncertain of

17. Today employers no longer speak of firing or discharging employees; instead, according to the latest _____, they simply "effect a separation."

(A) digression
(B) overstatement
(C) euphemism
(D) paradox
(E) proverb

18. The TV news magazine sits precisely at the _____ of information and entertainment, for while it is not a silly sitcom, it is not a documentary either.

(A) foundation
(B) juncture
(C) cessation
(D) institution
(E) eclipse

19. Even though nonbreeding female mole rats are _____, when the queen mole rat dies, several females suddenly _____ their sexual and reproductive powers and battle one another to replace her.

(A) prolific...accept
(B) sterile...regain
(C) barren...relinquish
(D) fecund...recover
(E) fragile...lose

20. _____ by life's _____, the last emperor of China worked as a lowly gardener in the palace over which he had once ruled.

(A) Fortified...generosity
(B) Deluded...coincidences
(C) Humbled...vicissitudes
(D) Venerated...survivors
(E) Recognized...impostors

Exercise 2

1. Numerous studies have found that people who choose to represent themselves in court on the whole exercise pretty good judgment—they seem to have a _____ sense of when they need a lawyer and when they don't.

(A) faulty
(B) capricious
(C) reliable
(D) transient
(E) drastic

2. Skulls are the Rosetta stones of anthropology because they bear unique features that let scientists _____ whether two fossil samples come from the same type of creature.

(A) determine
(B) prophesy
(C) disregard
(D) initiate
(E) recollect

3. Even when being _____ in method, people can come up with incorrect answers by basing their arguments on false premises.

(A) original
(B) logical
(C) slipshod
(D) realistic
(E) careless

4. Was he so thin-skinned, then, to _____ any small _____ at his expense?

   (A) support...purchase
   (B) repeat...compliment
   (C) comprehend...mystery
   (D) resent...jest
   (E) disregard...insult

5. We look with pride at our new bridges and dams, for they are works of art as well as of _____.

   (A) leisure
   (B) aesthetics
   (C) drudgery
   (D) utility
   (E) anachronism

6. When clay dries out, it loses its plasticity and becomes less _____.

   (A) synthetic
   (B) expensive
   (C) malleable
   (D) tangible
   (E) brittle

7. For many years an unheralded researcher, Barbara McClintock gained international _____ when she won the Nobel Prize in Physiology and Medicine.

   (A) condemnation
   (B) notoriety
   (C) renown
   (D) affluence
   (E) camaraderie

8. In judging the degree of his guilt, the question remains whether he acted out of purely _____ motives or whether he acted with thoughts of his own _____ in mind.

   (A) benevolent...fame
   (B) disinterested...advantage
   (C) selfish...benefit
   (D) mercenary...profit
   (E) malicious...cleverness

9. Rosa was such a last-minute worker that she could never start writing a paper till the deadline was _____.

   (A) known
   (B) problematic
   (C) imminent
   (D) superseded
   (E) recent

10. Rather than feeling toward Miss Havisham the _____ due a benefactor, Estella became resentful and even _____ to her patron.

    (A) esteem...effusive
    (B) obligation...dutiful
    (C) altruism...quarrelsome
    (D) gratitude...hostile
    (E) condescension...benign

11. Trying to prove Hill a liar, Senator Specter repeatedly questioned her _____.

    (A) intelligence
    (B) veracity
    (C) optimism
    (D) autonomy
    (E) brevity

12. It was only the first day of summer vacation, but his nerves were already _____ by the constant clamor of the children.

    (A) eliminated
    (B) alleviated
    (C) replete
    (D) vacillated
    (E) frayed

13. Donald Trump's former casino in Atlantic City once was the most _____ gambling palace in the East, easily outglittering its competitors.

    (A) professional
    (B) speculative
    (C) ostentatious
    (D) lucrative
    (E) restrained

14. Mrs. Thatcher had a better eye for the weaknesses and _____ of her contemporaries than for their virtues.

    (A) responsibilities
    (B) foibles
    (C) merits
    (D) talents
    (E) attractions

15. American culture now stigmatizes, and some-
    times even heavily ____, behavior that was
    once taken for granted: overt racism, cigarette
    smoking, the use of sexual stereotypes.

    (A) advocates
    (B) penalizes
    (C) ignores
    (D) indoctrinates
    (E) advertises

16. Because we have completed our analysis of the
    major components of the proposed project, we
    are free to devote the remainder of this session
    to a study of the project's ____ details.

    (A) lurid
    (B) scrupulous
    (C) unquestionable
    (D) incidental
    (E) involuntary

17. When we encounter a tentative thought of our
    own in someone else's writings, any ____ we
    may have had of its validity is ____, and what
    we were hesitant to believe is confirmed as
    truth.

    (A) assurance...unfounded
    (B) intimation...imprudent
    (C) doubt...dispelled
    (D) proof...unjustified
    (E) suspicion...reinforced

18. Determined to hire employees on the basis of
    their merits rather than on the basis of their
    family connections, Johnson refused to ____
    nepotism and other forms of favoritism in the
    engagement of new workers.

    (A) obscure
    (B) proscribe
    (C) countenance
    (D) misrepresent
    (E) discern

19. Just as sloth is the mark of the idler, ____ is
    the mark of the ____.

    (A) grief...miser
    (B) obsequiousness...toady
    (C) wanderlust...trespasser
    (D) suspicion...tyrant
    (E) brevity...wit

20. Unlike Sartre, who was born into a cultivated
    environment, receiving culture in his feeding
    bottle, so to speak, the child Camus had to
    fight to ____ a culture that was not ____.

    (A) acquire...innate
    (B) encourage...barbarous
    (C) develop...frivolous
    (D) restrain...inferior
    (E) justify...conventional

Exercise 3

1. Because the damage to his car had been ____,
   Michael decided he wouldn't bother to report
   the matter to his insurance company.

   (A) intermittent
   (B) gratuitous
   (C) negligible
   (D) spontaneous
   (E) significant

2. Mr. Levi is ____ learned; he has read everything bearing on his subject and on poetry in
   general (in several languages), and he has
   forgotten little if anything.

   (A) moderately
   (B) spottily
   (C) inadvertently
   (D) formidably
   (E) inadequately

3. Because vast organizations are an inevitable
   element in modern life, it is ____ to aim at
   their abolition.

   (A) necessary
   (B) important
   (C) customary
   (D) realistic
   (E) futile

4. Hoping for a rave review of his new show, the
   playwright was ____ when the critics ____ it
   unanimously.

   (A) gloomy...condoned
   (B) incredulous...appraised
   (C) vexed...selected
   (D) miserable...panned
   (E) impressed...divulged

5. Because it had not been blasted into a stable orbit, the satellite moved ____ through space.

    (A) innocuously
    (B) gradually
    (C) erratically
    (D) effortlessly
    (E) routinely

6. When railroads first began to supplant rivers and canals as highways of commerce, they were regarded as blessings and their promoters were looked upon as ____.

    (A) hucksters
    (B) upstarts
    (C) atheists
    (D) benefactors
    (E) diehards

7. Though she tried to be happy living with Clara in the city, Heidi ____ for the mountains and for her gruff but loving grandfather.

    (A) pined
    (B) searched
    (C) cheered
    (D) labored
    (E) trembled

8. The discovery by George Poinar and Roberta Hess that amber can preserve intact tissue from million-year-old insects ____ the possibility, since proved correct, that it also can preserve intact DNA.

    (A) eliminated
    (B) distorted
    (C) raised
    (D) precluded
    (E) predestined

9. The new dance troupe's gravest problem, one that mars the current production, is a desire for correctness and technical accuracy that ____ both energy and musical response.

    (A) enhances
    (B) stifles
    (C) transforms
    (D) reflects
    (E) supplies

10. New judges often fear that the influence of their own backgrounds will ____ their verdicts, no matter how sincere they are in wanting to be ____.

    (A) contradict...revered
    (B) corroborate...silent
    (C) condition...impartial
    (D) disclose...secretive
    (E) falsify...humane

11. Because he had abandoned his post and joined forces with the Indians, his fellow officers considered the hero of *Dances with Wolves* a ____.

    (A) martinet
    (B) braggart
    (C) renegade
    (D) skinflint
    (E) laggard

12. To take a ____ attitude, looking down on others as one's inferiors, often is to ____ any chance of favorable relations with them.

    (A) promising...negate
    (B) patronizing...eliminate
    (C) modest...reduce
    (D) pertinent...violate
    (E) benign...deny

13. Contemporary critics often ____ the poet Longfellow as a simple sentimentalist who relied too much on poetic meters only suitable for light verse.

    (A) heed
    (B) endorse
    (C) dismiss
    (D) embellish
    (E) acclaim

14. On some occasions Monteverdi specifies the instruments he wishes to make up his orchestra, but more often he is ____ or silent on the issue.

    (A) enigmatic
    (B) precise
    (C) eloquent
    (D) resolute
    (E) vehement

15. Just as an ____ dish lacks flavor, an inane remark lacks ____.

   (A) intriguing...spice
   (B) insipid...sense
   (C) inedible...listeners
   (D) occasional...implications
   (E) offensive...taste

16. Deeply ____ by the insult to his dignity, he maintained that no true gentleman would accept such an ____ calmly.

   (A) mortified...opportunity
   (B) incensed...affront
   (C) puzzled...honor
   (D) shamed...iconoclasm
   (E) gratified...admonition

17. Isozaki's love for detail is apparent everywhere in the new museum, but happily the details are ____ to the building's larger formal composition, which is ____ by the unfortuante busyness of much recent architecture.

   (A) important...harmed
   (B) irrelevant...fragmented
   (C) subordinated...unencumbered
   (D) appropriate...echoed
   (E) incidental...nullified

18. Although most worthwhile criticism concentrates on the positive, one should not ____ praise everything.

   (A) argumentatively
   (B) constructively
   (C) derogatorily
   (D) analytically
   (E) indiscriminately

19. Splitting the country into conflicting factions, pitting brother against brother, the Civil War was ____ experience for the American people.

   (A) an ephemeral
   (B) a divisive
   (C) a peripheral
   (D) an illuminating
   (E) a salutary

20. Learned though she was, her ____ never degenerated into ____.

   (A) erudition...pedantry
   (B) knowledge...ignorance
   (C) scholarship...research
   (D) speculation...thought
   (E) education...inquiry

Exercise 4

1. Biologists categorize many of the world's environments as deserts: regions where the ____ availability of some key factor, such as water, sunlight, or an essential nutrient, places sharp constraints on the existence of living things.

   (A) ready
   (B) gradual
   (C) limited
   (D) nearby
   (E) unprecedented

2. The sea was so rough that the safest thing to do was to seize the railing of the ship and hang on; walking was too ____ a pastime.

   (A) leisurely
   (B) pleasant
   (C) tempting
   (D) precarious
   (E) prosaic

3. Though the ad writers had come up with a highly creative campaign to publicize the company's newest product, the head office rejected it for a more ____, down-to-earth approach.

   (A) innovative
   (B) drastic
   (C) prosaic
   (D) noteworthy
   (E) philosophic

4. The Americans and the British seem to have a dog-in-the-manger attitude toward the island of Malta, no longer needing it themselves but nevertheless wishing to ____ it to others.

   (A) interpret
   (B) offer
   (C) deny
   (D) praise
   (E) reveal

5. Increasingly silent and withdrawn, he changed from a fluent, articulate speaker to someone who gave only _____ answers to any questions asked of him.

   (A) bookish
   (B) effusive
   (C) idiomatic
   (D) pretentious
   (E) monosyllabic

6. When you learn archaeology solely from lectures, you get only _____ sense of the concepts presented, but when you hold a 5000-year-old artifact in your hands, you have a chance to involve your senses, not just your intellect.

   (A) an invalid
   (B) an anachronistic
   (C) an abstract
   (D) a specious
   (E) a tangential

7. Paradoxically, while it is relatively easy to prove a fraudulent work of art is a fraud, it is often virtually impossible to prove that an authentic one is _____.

   (A) unpretentious
   (B) objective
   (C) impartial
   (D) dubious
   (E) genuine

8. The humorist Mark Twain had a great _____ for history and historians, observing that each year the antiquarians shed new darkness on the past.

   (A) reverence
   (B) affinity
   (C) tolerance
   (D) contempt
   (E) empathy

9. Since novelty of presentation is apt to add to a performer's popularity, the most successful troubadours were those who were also the most _____ in their delivery.

   (A) spontaneous
   (B) lyrical
   (C) academic
   (D) practiced
   (E) repetitious

10. Unfortunately, in developing countries rapid economic growth often _____ the overexploitation of natural resources and _____ distribution of wealth.

    (A) halts...indiscriminate
    (B) holds off...inadequate
    (C) leads to...inequitable
    (D) continues...evenhanded
    (E) goes beyond...ungrateful

11. Untempered by any _____, she spread an ever more militant message to her followers.

    (A) conviction
    (B) enthusiasm
    (C) radicalism
    (D) hardship
    (E) discretion

12. The idea that people are basically economic creatures, intent only upon their own material advantage, induces disbelief in the _____ of any _____ motive.

    (A) purpose...natural
    (B) desirability...ulterior
    (C) stupidity...altruistic
    (D) seemliness...egoistic
    (E) integrity...unselfish

13. Leavening his decisions with humorous, down-to-earth anecdotes, Judge Wapner was not at all the _____ legal scholar.

    (A) considerate
    (B) pedantic
    (C) indecisive
    (D) competent
    (E) pragmatic

14. The Apache are a _____ society, where husbands typically move into wives' dwellings and women take the leadership role in family affairs.

    (A) sedentary
    (B) defunct
    (C) fragmented
    (D) matrilineal
    (E) xenophobic

15. _____ James Baldwin, who wrote of black Americans as being in a perpetual state of rage, Mr. Cose asserts that few human beings could _____ the psychic toll of uninterrupted anger.

(A) Corroborating...endure
(B) Refuting...enhance
(C) Dismissing...refine
(D) Challenging...survive
(E) Upholding...weather

16. Rather than allowing these dramatic exchanges between her characters to develop fully, Ms. Norman unfortunately tends to _____ the discussions involving the two women.

(A) exacerbate
(B) protract
(C) truncate
(D) augment
(E) elaborate

17. "The show must go on" is the oldest _____ of show business; every true performer lives by that creed.

(A) euphemism
(B) allegory
(C) precursor
(D) tenet
(E) corroboration

18. The _____ with which musicians and lovers of fine instruments _____ Paul Irvin's professional services attests to his great expertise and craftsmanship as a harpsichord maker.

(A) hesitation...acquire
(B) avidness...solicit
(C) persistence...supersede
(D) harmony...conjure
(E) vehemence...reject

19. From the critic's perspective, M. F. K. Fisher is a writer who _____ classification, for her food writing reads like love stories, her fiction like memoirs.

(A) remembered
(B) relished
(C) skirted
(D) complied with
(E) matured with

20. Because the apelike members of *Australopithecus afarensis* were capable both of walking and of swinging through trees, the anthropologist described them as a mosaic, bipedal from the waist down and _____ from the waist up.

(A) ethereal
(B) arboreal
(C) dysfunctional
(D) articulated
(E) pedestrian

ANSWERS TO SENTENCE COMPLETION EXERCISES

LEVEL A

Sentence Completion Exercise 1

1. C	3. B	5. C	7. C	9. C	11. D	13. D	15. A	17. D	19. D
2. D	4. E	6. C	8. D	10. E	12. B	14. A	16. A	18. B	20. B

Sentence Completion Exercise 2

1. B	3. E	5. C	7. C	9. E	11. C	13. C	15. C	17. D	19. B
2. C	4. D	6. A	8. D	10. C	12. A	14. D	16. C	18. D	20. C

Sentence Completion Exercise 3

1. E	3. C	5. A	7. C	9. C	11. C	13. B	15. A	17. C	19. D
2. E	4. B	6. E	8. A	10. C	12. B	14. D	16. C	18. E	20. A

Sentence Completion Exercise 4

1. D	3. E	5. A	7. B	9. B	11. D	13. B	15. B	17. E	19. A
2. D	4. C	6. D	8. C	10. E	12. C	14. A	16. C	18. E	20. A

LEVEL B

Sentence Completion Exercise 1

1. B	3. B	5. A	7. C	9. E	11. C	13. D	15. C	17. D	19. C
2. C	4. D	6. E	8. B	10. B	12. C	14. D	16. C	18. B	20. C

Sentence Completion Exercise 2

1. D	3. E	5. C	7. C	9. C	11. D	13. C	15. A	17. E	19. C
2. A	4. C	6. D	8. D	10. C	12. C	14. A	16. A	18. B	20. E

Sentence Completion Exercise 3

1. B	3. C	5. A	7. D	9. A	11. C	13. A	15. C	17. D	19. D
2. C	4. C	6. D	8. D	10. E	12. C	14. B	16. B	18. D	20. B

Sentence Completion Exercise 4

1. E	3. E	5. C	7. D	9. D	11. D	13. E	15. C	17. A	19. C
2. E	4. B	6. C	8. B	10. B	12. D	14. C	16. E	18. E	20. C

LEVEL C

Sentence Completion Exercise 1

1. **B**	3. **C**	5. **D**	7. **E**	9. **B**	11. **C**	13. **C**	15. **B**	17. **C**	19. **B**
2. **C**	4. **B**	6. **C**	8. **D**	10. **B**	12. **C**	14. **C**	16. **B**	18. **B**	20. **C**

Sentence Completion Exercise 2

1. **C**	3. **B**	5. **D**	7. **C**	9. **C**	11. **B**	13. **C**	15. **B**	17. **C**	19. **B**
2. **A**	4. **D**	6. **C**	8. **B**	10. **D**	12. **E**	14. **B**	16. **D**	18. **C**	20. **A**

Sentence Completion Exercise 3

1. **C**	3. **E**	5. **C**	7. **A**	9. **B**	11. **C**	13. **C**	15. **B**	17. **C**	19. **B**
2. **D**	4. **D**	6. **D**	8. **C**	10. **C**	12. **B**	14. **A**	16. **B**	18. **E**	20. **A**

Sentence Completion Exercise 4

1. **C**	3. **C**	5. **E**	7. **E**	9. **A**	11. **E**	13. **B**	15. **D**	17. **D**	19. **C**
2. **D**	4. **C**	6. **C**	8. **D**	10. **C**	12. **E**	14. **D**	16. **C**	18. **B**	20. **B**

ANSWER EXPLANATIONS

LEVEL A

Sentence Completion Exercise 1

1. **C** If Washington political circles had been aware for a week that the Cabinet member was on the way out, his resignation did not come as a *shock* or surprise to them.
2. **D** Because the heavy rains had made their original route *impracticable* or impassable, the leaders decided to *alter* their route.
3. **B** The key phrase "as if it were a laboratory specimen" signals you that excessive literary analysis is analogous to the *dissecting* or cutting apart of animals and plants done in a biology lab.
4. **E** Customs generally arise because they serve a function. In this case, the division of labor by gender probably came about because it *promoted* or furthered the interests of the family and in this way was a sensible *cooperative* strategy.
5. **C** Silk possesses qualities invaluable in nest building. Therefore birds *incorporate* or introduce silk into their nests, including it as a component.
6. **C** Because no one had ever rebuked or *reprimanded* the recruit so harshly, the sergeant's words particularly *stung* or smarted.
7. **C** The earlier writers' reminiscences differ from this writer's memoirs in being *bland* and unexciting.
8. **D** A report that constantly interpreted things to reflect badly on or *discredit* someone would clearly be unfriendly or *hostile* to that person.
9. **C** There remained in Foster, who had not grown up fully, a *streak* (trace) of the undergraduate; he was clever but in some ways *immature*.
10. **E** Although she felt *contempt* (scorn) for the world of money and opinion and power, she nevertheless desired or *yearned for* the fame that only that world could give.
11. **D** If you are excessively careful about what you say, you are not likely to be *spontaneous* or free in your choice of words.
12. **B** A layperson or nonexpert by definition lacks the training to *appreciate* or recognize the importance of fossils and ancient artifacts.
13. **D** It would be extremely hard to be *unaffected* or unmoved by truly mesmerizing, enchanting art.
14. **A** If you can see only shades of gray, your view is by definition *monochromatic* (made up of one color or hue).
15. **A** If the therapy has been shown to work in dogs (animals larger than rodents), then its *efficacy* or effectiveness in larger animals has been proven.
16. **A** To *dampen* or muffle the noise inside a car should make a trip in the car quieter.
17. **D** Neither her father's *admonition* (warning or counsel) nor her classmates' *cool* (unsociable; distant) reception stopped Cleeves from following her chosen path.
18. **B** To *derail* someone *from* his course is to throw him off track.
19. **D** By definition, a *maverick* (dissenter; nonconformist) is someone who takes a stand that differs from that of his or her associates.
20. **B** Comte *coined* (invented; created) a term to *denote* (stand for; mean) the concept of unselfishness.

Sentence Completion Exercise 2

1. **B** If we manage to *destroy* the environment, we will be well on the way to extinction as a species.
2. **C** "Even though" children cannot influence affairs in the usual ways, thanks to Edelman's work they are nevertheless not *ignored*.

3. **E**   A campaign that breaks new ground is by definition *innovative*.

4. **D**   Both an *outstanding* sense of timing and a *mastery* of the law would be helpful to an attorney.

5. **C**   The papers *rank* as (have the status or position of) the most *impressive* statements of American political philosophy.

6. **A**   The entangling threads that slow down the victim's *escape* vibrate from the prey's struggles. These vibrations *alert* (warn; inform) the spider that something is trapped in its web.

7. **C**   In poking through the subject's private papers, the biographer *invades* the subject's privacy.

8. **D**   If the babies drink so much fruit juice that they do not get the varied nourishment they *need*, then drinking large amounts of juice could be *detrimental* (harmful) to them.

9. **E**   An *epic* or account of heroic exploits by definition narrates the mighty struggles of a central character or protagonist.

10. **C**   Wittgenstein's comment is a *rule* to which good historians should *adhere* or stick. It says, "If you don't know anything about a subject, you can't say anything about it." In other words, write about what you know.

11. **C**   The musk oxen declined or grew fewer in number because the herds were *devastated* (destroyed; ravaged) by hunters.

12. **A**   A *soporific* effect by definition puts people to sleep, causing them to nod off.

13. **C**   Someone who looks on human virtues as less worthy than canine virtues clearly views people in general with *contempt* (scorn).

14. **D**   The dumbfounded neuroanatomist disbelieved Diamond's work. *Skeptical* of the results of her experiments, he maintained that a rat's brain could not increase or *grow*.

15. **C**   Though he maintained that he did not care (protested his *indifference*), Judge Hand was *disappointed* that he had not been nominated to the Supreme Court.

16. **C**   A small hall would tend to promote a sense of closeness appropriate to recitals. In other words, such a hall would be particularly *conducive to* the intimacy that is the recital's special charm.

17. **D**   If the colonies appeared remarkably homogeneous or uniform in opinion, then clearly there were only *superficial* or very minor differences among them.

18. **D**   One would expect that a liberal political movement advocating freedom would favor less authority, not more. However, Trilling asserts that, paradoxically, contrary to expectations, liberalism must move in the direction of increasing *control*.

19. **B**   The contrast here is between the extremes of *euphoria* (elation) and *gloom* (melancholy; depression).

20. **C**   By definition, to lead a lewd or wanton life is to be *debauched* (corrupted by sensuality).

Sentence Completion Exercise 3

1. **E**   Though most people disregarded or made fun of her book, some *appreciated* it (admired it; grasped its worth).

2. **E**   If the critics all say the opera's score has both praiseworthy and wretched sections, then they agree that the score varies in quality. In other words, it is *uneven*.

3. **C**   Someone who plans everything in advance is not *spontaneous*.

4. **B**   Our almost-human ancestors did not become extinct. Instead, they *survived*.

5. **A**   The marketing experts have divided or *carved up* the *mass* (whole) audience into segments.

6. **E**   Like an *overinflated* balloon, aneurysms *burst*.

7. **C**   Critics *attribute* the *delay* to unexpected problems, a common cause of slowdowns.

8. **A**   A hotshot is someone conspicuously talented and successful. Many lawyers are *not* legal hotshots. They are *ill prepared* and they *lack* professional skills.

9. **C**   Scientists continue to test hypotheses against experience, *verifying* them or establishing their accuracy by keeping on making observations.

10. **C**   To supersede or replace a learned, scholarly biography, this new life of Gaskell must be a very good book. In other words, it must be a considerable *accomplishment* or achievement for the author.

11. **C**   After Boccherini's death, the composer's reputation fell into a decline, or weakened. It has not yet *recovered* or improved enough to satisfy the writer of this sentence.

12. **B**   Because he had emphasized his scandal-free, virtuous reputation, Hosokawa could not *withstand* or successfully resist the *notoriety* (ill fame) of being connected with a scandal.

13. **B**   It is *paradoxical* (incongruous; puzzlingly contradictory) that a *civilized* center should have been the site of horribly uncivilized, inhumane acts.

14. **D**   The writers who are not negative about the past look on it positively, even *nostalgically* (sentimentally, with a sense of wistful longing).

15. **A**   If Schlesinger laments or mourns the state of biography, then he is unhappy about the gossipy new biographies currently on sale. Thus, he *deplores* (disapproves of) them.

16. **C**   The waitress handled the bottle *nonchalantly* or casually, without undue concern.

17. **C**   To begin to appear in prominent, *responsible* positions is to emerge from *obscurity* or anonymity into the public view.

18. **E**   Someone who has *improvidently* squandered his money without thinking about the future would regret his *prodigal*, wasteful ways.

19. **D**   A *charlatan* falsely pretends to know more than he actually does. When Dorothy finds out that the Wizard does not know how to get her home, she thinks he has *duped* or made a fool of her.

20. **A**   Despite his self-centeredness, White could be kind to others and even belittle or be modest about himself (be *self-deprecating*).

Sentence Completion Exercise 4

1. **D**   To *revoke* a license is to cancel it, to make it void.

2. **D**   A curious child is by definition *inquisitive*.

3. **E**   Since many scholars helped to put together the survey, it was a *collective* (combined; cooperative) effort, not an individual one.

4. **C**   A fair solution is by definition *equitable* or just.

5. **A**   It is physically impossible for most living creatures to walk on water. Thus, by running across the surface of water, the basilisk seems to *defy* or challenge the laws of physics.

6. **D**   Passive, inactive people tend to *observe* rather than to *act*.

7. **B**   Keynes was not immobilized. Instead, he was *energized* or invigorated.

8. **C**   The telling of tales is by definition *narrative*.

9. **B**   An *enthusiastic*, spirited response would be likely to please or *gratify* a speaker.

10. **E**   *Advances* or new developments in science would make it *necessary* to revise the book.

11. **D**   Someone lying half asleep in a hot tub is clearly *relaxed*.

12. **C**   Plants that do not survive *shrivel* (wither) and die.

13. **B**   To fabricate events is to make them up, to invent them. Dali's tendency to make things up makes it hard for biographers to portray his life with *accuracy*.

14. **A**   Many people accepted and liked Earhart ("her fame was unusually widespread and her popularity long-lived"). However, not everyone did: her acceptance was not *universal*.

15. **B**   His belief in individual faith contrasts with his doubts (*skepticism*) about the organized church.

16. **C**   Someone old for his years, slow and conservative, could well be called *stodgy*.

17. **E**   If global warming poses a threat to all life on Earth, then by definition it is not a *peripheral* (marginal; minor) issue.

18. **E**   Radicals tend to believe that old customs are nonsense and that change is always a good idea. This author thinks it would be good for radicals to rethink their beliefs. They need to realize that old customs are not always *worthless* and that change can sometimes be a bad idea (be *inadvisable*).

19. **A**   Though Eliot was personally *reticent* (reserved; uncommunicative about himself), he was realistic enough to *assume* that his private papers someday would be read.

20. **A**   To be *restive* by definition is to exhibit or be marked by impatience.

LEVEL B

Sentence Completion Exercise 1

1. **B**   People on the cutting edge—at the forefront of a new movement—are likely to be *innovative*.
2. **C**   If it is so amazing that good poems ever get written, there must be many ways to *ruin* poems.
3. **B**   If only a few of her allies stood by her, she must have *alienated* or estranged all the others.
4. **D**   Just as the limbs of a tree *branch off* from the trunk, the major arteries branch off from the aorta.
5. **A**   The goal of the project is to make Woolf's work more *accessible* or available to scholars.
6. **E**   If the crisis will not affect us for years, then by definition it is not *imminent* (immediately looming; near).
7. **C**   *Digressive* remarks that wander from the topic may make us forget the gist or main point of what's being said.
8. **B**   Allende's book is based on or *rooted in* actual Chilean history.
9. **E**   If they plan on selling ad space, their *motivations* in making the donation are at least partially financial and not solely charitable or *philanthropic*.
10. **B**   Blackmun's voice stood out from the featureless mix of the other Justices' voices: it was an individual, *personal* voice.
11. **C**   It is somewhat of an *understatement* for Gaddis to describe himself as never having been in a *rush* to get into print. At a rate of one book every 10 years, he's been markedly slow to publish.
12. **C**   *Chancy* means uncertain in prospects; risky. Acting as a career certainly is that.
13. **D**   Montana was *unintimidating*: he did not frighten or overawe those who met him.
14. **D**   In Sand's time, for a woman to take lovers or wear men's clothes was a shocking departure from *convention* (usual social custom).
15. **C**   The speaker is not *resigned* or reconciled to her death. Instead, he is *inconsolable* (heartbroken; unable to be comforted or consoled).
16. **C**   The Chinese artists have been clever. They have made *canny* (shrewd) use of Western styles.
17. **D**   One would expect the use of outmoded, archaic vocabulary and twisted, tortuous phrasing to make a poem unintelligible. However, contrary to expectations, the poet's argument is *intelligible*.
18. **B**   To *sound* the depths is to ascertain just how deep something is. This biographer has not reached the depths, but she has examined the *surface*.
19. **C**   Traumas or major shocks can lead to *aberrations* or abnormalities of behavior in survivors.
20. **C**   Someone intellectually *fecund* (fertile; prolific) is bursting with ideas. Clearly, this productive novelist is at the *height* of her powers.

Sentence Completion Exercise 2

1. **D**   The sentence serves to *define* the term *illness*.
2. **A**   By revitalizing Chrysler, Iacocca made it a *vigorous*, energetic company.
3. **E**   One expects a scholar to know the serious works on his subject. Though Cose is not a scholar, he nevertheless is *familiar with* the appropriate serious works.
4. **C**   Healing waters are by definition *therapeutic* (curative).
5. **C**   The contrast here is between the apartment's actual state ("shabby and dilapidated") and its promised condition: *pristine* (spotlessly clean).
6. **D**   By definition, someone *apathetic* does not care.
7. **C**   To *scavenge* is to hunt through discarded items to find useful bits.
8. **D**   Most of the books are not excellent, but are *mediocre* (of moderate or low quality) instead.
9. **C**   Angry, *heated* discussions suggest no settlement is near. However, the two sides actually are close to *agreeing*.
10. **C**   Churchill was not a *dilettante* or dabbler; he was a serious artist.
11. **D**   Foreign powers that look on territory in the Americas as prey to be seized are by definition *predatory*.

12. **C**   A spotty book is uneven in quality. This particular book suffers from sections that are relatively uninteresting, less than *exciting* though not precisely *dull*.

13. **C**   Widow Douglass did not always scold Huck. Instead, she *condoned* (voluntarily overlooked; forgave) his minor misdeeds.

14. **A**   To interpret art fancifully, inventing things, is a *temptation* to the critic. This critic resists the temptation; he is *scrupulous* (carefully painstaking) in sticking to the facts.

15. **A**   Because he owes money, Lydgate must take a *lucrative* (well-paying) position.

16. **A**   Before they can *ascertain* or figure out how important it is to limit the human use of the beaches at night, the observers must determine just how much the shorebirds depend on their *nocturnal* (nighttime) feeding.

17. **E**   For the listener to come to agree with the speaker, any *doubts* he might have had must have been *dispelled* (made to vanish).

18. **B**   By definition, a *sage* is a wise person. Likewise, a virtuoso is a skilled person, one who has *expertise*.

19. **C**   *Tacit* cooperation is implied but not expressed actively. Johnson's cooperation with Boswell went far beyond this.

20. **E**   Lesser scholars would have been intimidated or *daunted* by the amount of material to be explored.

Sentence Completion Exercise 3

1. **B**   The key phrase here is "longer lives." The doctors are trying to lengthen or *prolong* human life.

2. **C**   In an arid, extremely dry land, wildlife needs *access to* water.

3. **C**   Someone consistently hopeful is by definition an *optimist*.

4. **C**   "Even" intensifies what is being said. Lullabies not only have a dark side; many also have a *threatening*, menacing quality.

5. **A**   For a dispute to become ugly and destructive, the level of disagreement must *escalate* (intensify; increase).

6. **D**   Lao Li's archives *document* or record contemporary Chinese art.

7. **D**   Someone who leaves parties in order to go off alone clearly can no longer be described as *gregarious* (sociable).

8. **D**   If science is always ready to change or modify its theories, it clearly is *tentative* (provisional) rather than absolute in making its statements.

9. **A**   Because we today are able to cure tuberculosis, we think of it as simply another long-term *chronic* illness. In the past, however, people regarded it as a pestilence or *plague*.

10. **E**   Rather than lure or attract readers, Gaddis's work tends to *repel* or drive them away.

11. **C**   Instead of being showily glamorous like opera, classical song is more restrained or *subdued*.

12. **C**   The writer is uniformly positive about the book being reviewed, calling it *painstakingly* or carefully researched. The life the book describes, however, is not positive: the subject's tormented career was *tragic*.

13. **A**   Lexy's pleasure did not last long; it was *transient* or fleeting.

14. **B**   *Commingling* is a thorough combining of parts. It would be futile or pointless to try to *separate* elements that have been thoroughly mixed.

15. **C**   By describing the land as asleep, the writer means that the nation had yet to rouse itself to confront the foreign invaders. Clearly the people's sense of nationalism was *dormant* or sleeping.

16. **B**   In order to enhance or improve their empires, the moguls (cinema magnates) needed the services of *prestigious* writers whose eminence would rub off on them. In this way the moguls would *aggrandize* themselves, making themselves appear greater through their association with great intellectuals.

17. **D**   The production is described metaphorically as if it were a jungle creature, alert, stealthy, almost *predatory* (ready to seize its victim) as it waits to *pounce*.

18. **D**   *Obsequious* means servile or fawningly attentive.

19. **D** "Whereas" signals a contrast. *L'Orfeo* is not the beginning of a tradition. Instead, it is the *culmination* or highest achievement of one.

20. **B** In combining so many different approaches, Feher's lessons are clearly *eclectic* (composed of elements drawn from different sources).

Sentence Completion Exercise 4

1. **E** If you could afford only such meager nourishment, clearly you would be very poor—in other words, suffering from *poverty*.

2. **E** An *uneventful* life, one in which nothing much important or notable happened, would be difficult to make interesting.

3. **E** Unable to rely on its poor vision to help it move in the darkness, the mole rat depends on the sensitivity of its whiskers to what they touch to give it a feel for its surroundings. Thus, the whiskers help *guide* the mole rat.

4. **B** *Aggressive*, belligerent impulses push people to get into street brawls. However, professional boxers are allowed to fight only in professional competitions—that is, in the ring.

5. **C** The phrase "for all" as used here means "in spite of." It signals a contrast. The novel's hero does not really belong in the 1890s. He is a *contemporary* voice and has a contemporary cultural *sensibility* or capacity for appreciation.

6. **C** She wondered whether triangles *qualified* (demonstrated the required characteristics) to be called polygons.

7. **D** Telescopic observations are more *detailed* (complete) than ones made with the naked eye. However, the first *documented* or recorded use of the telescope came after Kepler saw the supernova.

8. **B** The author was not brave enough to attack the people who had the power to prevent his books from being published; he did not bite the hand that fed him. However, he was brave enough to make an occasional negative remark about these people; thus, he *nibbled at* the hand that fed him.

9. **D** People who are "arty" are showily or pretentiously artistic: they collect art in order to show off their belongings. True art lovers, however, collect for their own pleasure or *delight*, not for *show*.

10. **B** *Recurrent* (periodically reappearing) attacks or bouts of illness could well alarm someone's friends and family.

11. **D** "Though" signals a contrast. In this case, Simon's review of a contemporary play is a *rave* (extravagant praise).

12. **D** In their old age, Chinese painters no longer copied their teachers. However, their *originality* did not involve major changes; they made *slight*, barely visible ones.

13. **E** If you had your reputation damaged by a libelous statement, you would want your name *cleared* or freed of blame. Thus, you would welcome a *retraction* (disavowal; withdrawal) of the libel.

14. **C** Kissinger appreciates the hard-headed, realistic use of power. He even appreciates power when it is used *ruthlessly*, without compassion or remorse. For this reason, he is able to admire the ability to use power effectively even when he sees it in people who are otherwise *detestable* (odious).

15. **C** Poseurs by definition pretend to be something they are not. Some people thought Dali was a great artist. Others *dismissed* (slighted; made little of) him as a painter who pretended to be great.

16. **E** If the world of food writing is known for its pettiness (small-mindedness) and infighting (internal quarrels), then an author who was *generous* would be *rare* in this milieu.

17. **A** *Esoteric* allusions are by definition references that are understood by only a small, restricted group. References to *obscure*, little-known people and events clearly would not be understood by people in general.

18. **E** To see her sister's fortunes rise while her own *declined* or fell would be likely to *exacerbate* or intensify the subject's bitterness.

19. **C** *Probity* is by definition honesty or integrity.

20. **C** In calling *Spellbound* a glowing testimonial to (expression of the benefits received from) the powers of psychoanalysis to do good, the writer maintains that the movie presents a favorable picture of psychoanalysis. However, it is not an exclusively admiring, *adulatory* picture.

LEVEL C

Sentence Completion Exercise 1

1. **B** In the dark, one's eyes have to work hard or *strain* to be able to see.
2. **C** The uprising was organized and planned. Thus, it was not *spontaneous* or unpremeditated.
3. **C** Theologians (specialists in the study of religious faith and practices) would be upset by a book that *undermined* or weakened *established* rituals and beliefs.
4. **B** *Empathy* by definition is sensitivity to the feelings and thoughts of others.
5. **D** *Theses* is the plural form of *thesis*, which here means theory or contention. The details are disconnected; no overarching or encompassing theories bring them together or *unify* them.
6. **C** Preferring facts, the historian is uninterested in speculations or *conjectures*.
7. **E** By agreeing to be the subjects of magazine articles, these famously *shy* novelists have given in to their publishers' insistence on *publicity*.
8. **D** Caring so much about being in the know, Tom was vexed or *galled* by his ignorance.
9. **B** To waver between choices is by definition to *vacillate*.
10. **B** With their huge nets, the trawlers scoop up everything in their path. Thus, they trap fish *indiscriminately*, hauling them in without distinguishing among them.
11. **C** A father who rules autocratically and will brook or allow no disagreement is by definition *domineering* (overbearing; tyrannical). His daughter eloped to *escape* his control.
12. **C** The symphony is a classical music form. In writing jazz symphonies, Ellington was combining or fusing jazz with a classical form. He was attacked by critics who wished to *discourage* such fusions.
13. **C** If Tennyson managed to produce particularly impressive work in his last years, clearly his creative powers had not declined or *flagged*.
14. **C** A *bastion* (stronghold; fortified area) by definition is a place set up to *protect* people from attack.
15. **B** Lovejoy advises the reader how to avoid being fooled by fake or *spurious* antiques.
16. **B** Someone omniscient (all-knowing) would by definition be *unlimited in* knowledge.
17. **C** A *euphemism* is a mild expression used in place of a blunt, unpleasant one.
18. **B** By definition, a *juncture* is a point of convergence, here the point where televised information and entertainment are joined in a new format.
19. **B** For a nonbreeding female to be able to replace a queen, taking over her breeding functions, the female must *regain* her reproductive abilities. In other words, the nonbreeding female suddenly reverses her *sterility* (barrenness; inability to reproduce).
20. **C** *Vicissitudes* are the changes of fortune one experiences in the course of a lifetime. Going from ruling an empire to laboring in a garden, China's last emperor clearly would have been *humbled* or lowered in condition by these changes.

Sentence Completion Exercise 2

1. **C** The writer is relatively positive about people's decisions in choosing to represent themselves in court. He or she concludes that people have a *reliable* or dependable sense of when lawyers are and are not necessary.
2. **A** Anthropologists attempt to *determine* (discover; learn) the origins of the fossils they find.
3. **B** A faulty premise or underlying assumption can undermine the most *logically* reasoned argument.
4. **D** To be thin-skinned by definition is to be quick to *resent* any insult or joking remark (*jest*) that might reflect on one's dignity.
5. **D** Bridges and dams are built to serve useful functions: they are works of *utility*. However, this writer asserts that the new bridges and dams are works of art as well.
6. **C** By definition, something that loses its plasticity (capacity for being molded or shaped) is less *malleable* (capable of being shaped).

7. **C**   McClintock went from being unheralded (not celebrated or famous) to being *renowned* (celebrated; acclaimed).

8. **B**   A *disinterested* (unselfishly motivated) act would not be motivated by selfish thoughts of one's own *advantage*.

9. **C**   *Imminent* means near at hand, hanging threateningly over one's head. A procrastinator or last-minute worker often delays till the deadline is nearly upon her.

10. **D**   Conventionally, one owes a benefactor *gratitude*. Rather than feeling thankful, however, Estella felt resentful and even *hostile* (unfriendly; antagonistic).

11. **B**   *Veracity* means truthfulness. By questioning someone's truthfulness, you hope to prove he or she is a liar.

12. **E**   Nerves would be *frayed* or strained by constant clamor (noise).

13. **C**   Something that outglitters its rivals is more showy or *ostentatious* than they are.

14. **B**   *Foibles* by definition are minor flaws or weaknesses. The support signal *and* suggests that the missing word must be a synonym or near-synonym for "weaknesses."

15. **B**   To stigmatize behavior is to characterize or mark it as disgraceful or wicked. To *penalize* behavior is to go even further and punish it.

16. **D**   Now that they have dealt with the major items, they can move on to the minor or *incidental* ones.

17. **C**   If you now believe what you had been reluctant to believe, your *doubts* or uncertainties have been *dispelled* (dissipated; driven away).

18. **C**   Johnson would not *countenance* (tolerate; approve) such unfair hiring practices.

19. **B**   A *toady* (sycophant; flatterer in search of getting favors) is characterized by *obsequiousness* (servile attentiveness).

20. **A**   Camus had to fight to *acquire* or gain a culture that was not his by birth (in other words, was not *innate* or inborn).

Sentence Completion Exercise 3

1. **C**   One wouldn't bother to make an insurance claim for *negligible* (small; inconsequential) damage.

2. **D**   To have retained so much information is to be *formidably* or awe inspiringly learned.

3. **E**   It is *futile* or useless to try to abolish something whose existence is inevitable (unavoidable).

4. **D**   To have his work *panned* or harshly criticized would be likely to make a playwright *miserable*.

5. **C**   The satellite is off course and is moving *erratically* (irregularly or inconsistently) through space.

6. **D**   A *benefactor* by definition is someone who confers benefits or blessings on others.

7. **A**   "Though" signals a contrast. In spite of her attempts to be happy, Heidi was unhappy because she *pined* (fruitlessly longed) to be back home.

8. **C**   The couple's discovery *raised* or suggested a possibility that further investigation showed to be correct.

9. **B**   An overemphasis on correctness that *stifled* or repressed the performers' liveliness would mar or spoil a production.

10. **C**   Your background can *condition* or determine your thinking, subtly prejudicing you so that you cannot be truly *impartial* or fair.

11. **C**   A *renegade* by definition deserts one allegiance in favor of another.

12. **B**   A *patronizing* or condescending attitude may offend others and *eliminate* or rule out the possibility of good relations.

13. **C**   To *dismiss* Longfellow in this way is to reject him as unworthy of serious critical consideration.

14. **A**   By not specifically stating his wishes, Monteverdi leaves them a mystery. Thus, he is *enigmatic* (mysterious).

15. **B**   By definition, *insipid* means lacking flavor. By definition, inane means lacking *sense*.

16. **B**   An *affront* (deliberate offense or insult) would clearly *incense* or anger someone.

17. **C**   Because the details are *subordinated* or made less important than the building's total design, the building is *unencumbered* (unimpeded; unhampered) by a sense of busyness.

18. **E**   To praise things *indiscriminately*, making no distinctions between treasures and trash, is to fail to exercise proper critical selectivity.

19. **B**   By definition, an experience that splits a nation into factions or conflicting groups is *divisive* (dissension creating).

20. **A**   *Erudition* means great learning or scholarship. *Pedantry*, however, is a great show of learning, an excessive attention to petty details that lacks the true scholarly spirit.

Sentence Completion Exercise 4

1. **C**   A *limited* availability of necessities would put constraints or restrictions on the creatures needing them.

2. **D**   Under such rough conditions, it would be too risky or *precarious* to walk without holding on.

3. **C**   "Though" signals a contrast. Rather than being creative, the eventual publicity campaign was *prosaic* or unimaginative.

4. **C**   To *deny* or refuse to others something you yourself do not need or want is to behave like the proverbial dog-in-the-manger, who did not want to eat the hay in the manger but refused to let the hungry cattle get at it.

5. **E**   No longer fluent and prone to speech, he became *monosyllabic*, answering in words of one syllable.

6. **C**   Something understood only theoretically or intellectually is known only in the *abstract*.

7. **E**   It is incongruous that it is easier to prove something a fake than to prove it *genuine* or real.

8. **D**   When we say historians shed new light on or illuminate the past, we express respect for historians. When Twain observed that the antiquarians (students of ancient things) shed new darkness on the past, he expressed *contempt* or scorn for historians.

9. **A**   *Spontaneous* performances, performances arising from the impulse of the moment, tend to be fresh or *novel*.

10. **C**   The key word here is "unfortunately." To have rapid economic growth *lead to* the overexploitation or excessive, unjust use of resources and the unfair or *inequitable* sharing of wealth is truly unfortunate.

11. **E**   If she became increasingly militant (aggressively active), then she was not tempered (mellowed) by a spirit of *discretion* or caution.

12. **E**   If you think that people are motivated only by selfish thoughts of their own advantage, you will be unlikely to believe in the *integrity* or trustworthiness of any *unselfish* motive.

13. **B**   Wapner was not a *pedantic* scholar, fussing about minute points of law.

14. **D**   By definition, a *matrilineal* society, in which inheritance is determined through the female line, is one in which women have a significant role.

15. **D**   In remarking that few humans could *survive* living in a state of uninterrupted anger, Cose *challenges* or disputes Baldwin's statement about anger as a constant in black American life.

16. **C**   Instead of allowing the exchanges to develop fully, the playwright cuts short or *truncates* them.

17. **D**   By definition, a *tenet* is a belief generally held to be true. Here it is used as a synonym for guiding principle or "creed."

18. **B**   Musicians *solicit* or seek out Irvin's services with *avidness* (eagerness) because he is a highly skilled artisan.

19. **C**   Fisher's work evades or *skirts* classification because it does not fall neatly into set categories.

20. **B**   *Arboreal* means inhabiting or frequenting trees.

PART IV

READING COMPREHENSION QUESTIONS

OVERVIEW

SAT reading comprehension questions test your ability to understand what you read—both content and technique. Each critical reading section on the SAT will include one or two long reading passages of different length, followed by six to thirteen questions of assorted types. Two of the three critical reading sections will also include a pair of quite short reading passages—about 100 words in length—each followed by a couple of reading questions.

One passage on the test will be **narrative**: a passage from a novel, a short story, an autobiography, or a personal essay. One will deal with the **sciences** (including medicine, botany, zoology, chemistry, physics, geology, astronomy); another, with the **humanities** (including art, literature, music, philosophy, folklore); a third, with the **social sciences** (including history, economics, sociology, government). Some of the above passages may be what the College Board calls **argumentative**; these passages present definite points of view on the subjects. One passage most likely will be "**ethnic**" in content: whether it is a history passage, a personal narrative, or a passage on music, art, or literature, it will deal with concerns of a particular minority group.

The questions that follow each passage are not arranged in order of difficulty. Rather, they are arranged to suit the way the passage's content is organized. Thus, a question based on information presented at the beginning of the passage will come before a question based on information at the end.

TIPS ON HANDLING READING COMPREHENSION QUESTIONS

TIP 1
TRY TO ANTICIPATE WHAT THE PASSAGE IS ABOUT

As you read the italicized introductory material preceding the passage and tackle the passage's opening sentences, try to anticipate what the passage will be about. Ask yourself who or what the author is writing about. Recollect what else you may have read about the topic. You'll be in a better position to understand what you read.

TIP 2
PICK YOUR QUESTIONS TO ANSWER

On sections with both short and long reading passages, tackle the short passages first. Consider the paired short reading passages a warmup for the paired long reading passages that appear later in the test.

On sections with two long reading passages, head straight for the passage that appeals to you more. It is hard to concentrate when you read about something wholly unfamiliar to you. Give yourself a break. First tackle the reading passage that interests you or deals with topics in which you are well grounded. Then move on to the other passage. You'll do better that way.

Similarly, when you're ready to answer questions on a long passage, consider taking a quick glance at *all* the questions on that passage and starting off with answering the ones you feel you can handle easily. Check out the questions with answer choices that are only two or three words long. (Usually these are vocabulary-in-context questions, or questions on attitude or tone.) Answer them. Then focus on the longer, more difficult questions.

If you are stumped by a tough reading question, don't automatically skip the other questions on that passage. As stated on page 105, the reading comprehension questions following each passage are not arranged in order of difficulty. Instead, they tend to be arranged sequentially: questions on paragraph 1 come before questions on paragraph 2. Therefore, it pays to look over all the questions on

the passage. An essay question may be just one question away from a tough one.

Recognize the questions to bear down on as opposed to the questions to skip. Spot the most time-consuming questions; then, decide whether any given time-consumer is one you should skip. Questions containing the word EXCEPT in capital letters tend to be tricky; they may be ones to take a pass on. Questions using Roman numerals (I only, I and II only, and so on) that require you to use the process of elimination to reach your answer may be time-consuming. Similarly, the following sorts of questions may take a lot of time:

- ones that ask about the author's underlying assumptions;
- ones that ask what additional information would help to clarify points in the passage;
- ones that compare or contrast two passages in great detail;
- ones with extremely lengthy answer choices.

You may decide you want to skip one or more of them.

However...*try to answer all the questions* on one passage before you move on to the second. Often, working through one or two questions will provide you with information you can use in answering other questions on that passage.

Whenever you skip from question to question, or from passage to passage, *be sure you're filling in the right spaces on your answer sheet.*

TIP 3
READ PURPOSEFULLY: PASSAGE, QUESTIONS, AND ANSWER CHOICES

As you work through the passage, try to identify what *kind* of writing it represents, what *techniques* are being used, who the intended *audience* may be, and what *feeling* (if any) the author has toward this subject. Try to retain names, dates, and places for quick reference later. In particular, try to remember where in the passage the author makes *major* points. Underline key words, if you like, or indicate main ideas with a star (*) or arrow. Then, when you start looking for a phrase or sentence to justify your answer, you may be able to save time by going back to that section of the passage immediately without having to reread the whole thing.

Read as rapidly as you can with understanding, but do not force yourself. Do not worry about the time element. If you worry about not finishing the test, you will begin to take shortcuts and miss correct answers in your haste.

Figure out whether it ever helps you to read the questions before you read through the passage. For the long passages, our general advice is, to read the passage first; then read the questions. We find most students do better tackling reading exercises in this way. However, if you habitually read slowly and methodically, you may be better off reading an individual question and then scanning the passage to find its answer. Likewise, in dealing with an extra-long, 800-word reading passage, you may want to try skimming the questions *before* you read the passage to get a sense of what you should be on the lookout for. You have to know your strengths and weaknesses as a reader before you can select the approach that is right for you.

Use the practice exercises at the end of this chapter to find out whether or not the "questions first" approach works for you. Select an 800-word passage and skim the questions on it. Next, read the passage and answer the questions. Check your answers. Then think over your experience.

- Did you get through the passage and all 12 questions in 15 minutes or less?
- Did you answer a reasonable number of questions correctly?
- Did you feel in control as you started to read the passage, or did you feel as if you had a jumble of question words dancing around in your head?
- Did you feel that skimming the questions in advance slowed you down too much and wasted your time?

Try another 800-word passage, this time reading the passage first, and compare how you did on this passage with your result on the first one. Then decide what's right for you.

In answering questions, don't just settle for the first answer choice that looks good. Read each choice, and compare what it says to the actual words of the passage. When you come to an answer choice that contradicts information in the passage or that doesn't answer the question being asked, cross it out.

TIP 4 — GO BACK TO THE PASSAGE TO DOUBLE-CHECK YOUR ANSWER CHOICES

When you tackle the questions, *go back to the passage* to verify the answers you chose. Do not rely on your memory alone; above all, do not ignore the passage and just answer questions on the basis of other things you've read. Remember: the questions are asking you about what *this* author has to say about the subject, not about what some other author you once read said about it in another book.

Use the line references in the questions to be sure you've gone back to the correct spot in the passage. Most reading passages on the SAT tend to be long. Fortunately, all the lines are numbered, and the questions often refer you to specific lines in the passage by number. It takes less time to locate a line number than to spot a word or phrase. Use the line numbers to orient yourself in the text.

TIP 5 — TACKLE PAIRED PASSAGES ONE PASSAGE AT A TIME

If the double passage section has you worried, relax. It's not that formidable, especially if you deal with it our way. The double reading passage is usually found in a separate section. First you'll see a few lines in italics introducing both passages. Then will come the two passages. Their lines will be numbered as if they were one *enormous* passage: thus, if **Passage 1** ends on line 42, **Passage 2** will begin on line 43. However, they are two separate passages, and you should tackle them one at a time. Remember: the questions are organized sequentially: questions about **Passage 1** will come before questions about **Passage 2**. Therefore, do things in order. *First* read Passage 1; then jump straight to the questions and answer all those based on Passage 1. Most of the time, the Passage 1 questions will immediately follow the excerpts. Once in a great while, one or two questions that refer to both passages will precede the questions about Passage 1. In that case, don't get sidetracked. Skip the questions referring to both passages, and focus on those based on Passage 1. *Next* read Passage 2; then answer all the questions based on Passage 2. *Finally*, tackle the three or four questions that refer to *both* passages. Go back to both passages as needed.

READING COMPREHENSION EXERCISES

To develop your ability to handle reading comprehension questions, work your way through the following four exercises. Each exercise contains a full test's worth of long reading passages and questions: one 400-word passage followed by 6 questions, one 550-word passage followed by 9 questions, one 800-word passage followed by 12 questions, plus one pair of passages followed by 13 questions. The passages have been taken from published sources—the same sort of sources that are tapped by the makers of the SAT.

Warning: These exercises are graded in difficulty. Although the questions don't necessarily get harder the further you go, the reading passages definitely do. Go all the way. Even if you do less well on Level C than you did on Level A, look on every error as an opportunity to learn. Reread all the passages you found difficult. Review all the vocabulary words that you didn't know. Remember: these passages and questions are *all* comparable to the ones on the SAT.

After completing each exercise, see how many questions you answered correctly. (The correct answers are given on page 142.)

Then *read the answer explanations.*

LEVEL A

Most high school students feel comfortable interpreting reading passages on this level of difficulty. Consider the reading passages that follow to be a warm-up for the harder excerpts to come.

Exercise 1

Read each of the passages below, and then answer the questions that follow the passage. The correct response may be stated outright or merely suggested in the passage.

Questions 1–5 are based on the following passage.

The following passage is taken from a review of a general survey of the natural and physical sciences published in 1964.

"Idle speculation" has no place in science, but "speculation" is its very lifeblood, a well-known physicist believes.

Line
(5) "The more fundamental and far-reaching a scientific theory is, the more speculative it is likely to be," Dr. Michael W. Ovenden, author and lecturer at the University of Glasgow, Scotland, states in his book "Life in the Universe." Dr. Ovenden says it is erroneous to
(10) believe that science is only concerned with

"pure facts," for mere accumulation of facts is a primitive form of science. A mature science tries to arrange facts in significant patterns to see relationships between previously unrelated
(15) aspects of the universe.

A theory that does not suggest new ways of looking at the universe is not likely to make an important contribution to the development of science. However, it is also important that
(20) theories are checked by new experiments and observations.

Dr. Ovenden discusses recent discoveries in biology, chemistry and physics that give clues to the possibility of life in the solar sys-
(25) tem and other star systems. He discusses conditions on Mars, Venus, Jupiter and Saturn, and considers whether or not the same conditions

may be found on planets of other stars.

Only the planets Venus, Earth, and Mars
(30) lie within the temperature zone, about
75,000,000 miles wide, in which life can exist.
Venus is covered by a dense layer of clouds
which permits no observation of the surface,
and the surface temperature of the planet is
(35) not known.

Mars is colder than Earth, the average
temperature being about minus 40 degrees
Fahrenheit, compared with plus 59 degrees
Fahrenheit as the average for Earth. However,
(40) near the Mars poles during the summer season, temperatures may rise to as much as 70
degrees Fahrenheit, whereas winter temperatures may fall to minus 130 degrees
Fahrenheit.
(45) Because of the extreme difference in the
Martian seasons, the only life-forms expected
to exist, without a built-in temperature control
such as warm-blooded animals and humans
have, are those which would stay inactive
(50) most of the year. These life-forms may be a
kind of vegetation that opens its leaves to the
sun in the daytime, stores water and closes its
leaves in the night for protection against the
cold.
(55) Attempts have been made to detect in the
spectrum of the dark markings on Mars the
absorption lines due to chlorophyll. So far the
test has not succeeded. But the infrared spectrum of the Martian markings has been found
(60) to be very similar to the spectrum of Earth
vegetation when studied at high altitudes.

1. The word "idle" in line 1 most nearly means

(A) resting
(B) lazy
(C) empty
(D) lethargic
(E) leisurely

2. "Speculation is its [science's] very lifeblood"
(line 2) means that scientists

(A) are gamblers at heart
(B) must concern themselves with provable facts
(C) must understand all forms of science
(D) must form opinions about the data they gather
(E) must keep abreast of new developments

3. According to lines 12–15, a mature science

(A) concerns itself exclusively with gathering and recording facts
(B) dismisses speculative thinking as overly fanciful
(C) connects hitherto unlinked phenomena in meaningful ways
(D) subordinates speculative thought to the accumulation of facts
(E) differentiates between hypotheses and speculation

4. The similarity from high altitudes between the infrared spectrum of the Martian markings and the Earth spectrum suggests

(A) the value of speculative thinking
(B) the absence of chlorophyll on Mars
(C) a possibility that Mars has vegetation
(D) that Mars's surface has been cultivated
(E) the effect of cold on the color of the spectrum

5. The author does all of the following EXCEPT

(A) make an approximation
(B) use a metaphor
(C) state a resemblance
(D) make a conjecture
(E) deny a contradiction

Questions 6–15 are based on the following passage.

The following passage is taken from The Souls of Black Folk, *W. E. B. Du Bois's classic study of the African-American's struggle in this country.*

Once upon a time I taught school in the
hills of Tennessee, where the broad dark vale
of the Mississippi begins to roll and crumple
Line to greet the Alleghanies. I was a Fisk student
(5) then, and all Fisk men thought that Tennessee
was theirs alone, and in vacation time they sal-
lied forth in lusty bands to meet the county
school-commissioners. Young and happy, I too
went, and I shall not soon forget that summer,
(10) seventeen years ago.

First, there was a Teachers' Institute at the
county-seat; and there distinguished guests of
the superintendent taught the teachers frac-
tions and spelling and other mysteries—white

(15) teachers in the morning, Negroes at night. A
picnic now and then, and a supper, and the
rough world was softened by laughter and
song. I remember how—but I wander.

There came a day when all the teachers
(20) left the Institute and began the hunt for
schools. I learn from hearsay (for my mother
was mortally afraid of firearms) that the hunting of ducks and bears and men is wonderfully
interesting, but I am sure that the man who has
(25) never hunted a country school has something
to learn of the pleasures of the chase. I see
now the white, hot roads lazily rise and fall
and wind before me under the burning July
sun; I feel the deep weariness of heart and
(30) limb as ten, eight, six miles stretch relentlessly
ahead; I feel my heart sink heavily as I hear
again and again, "Got a teacher? Yes." So I
walked on and on—horses were too expensive—until I had wandered beyond railways,
(35) beyond stage lines, to a land of "varmints" and
rattlesnakes, where the coming of a stranger
was an event, and men lived and died in the
shadow of one blue hill.

Sprinkled over hill and dale lay cabins and
(40) farmhouses, shut out from the world by the
forests and the rolling hills toward the east.
There I found at last a little school. Josie told
me of it; she was a thin, homely girl of twenty,
with a dark-brown face and thick, hard hair. I
(45) had crossed the stream at Watertown, and rested under the great willows; then I had gone to
a little cabin where Josie was resting on her
way to town. The gaunt farmer made me welcome, and Josie, hearing my errand, told me
(50) anxiously that they wanted a school over the
hill; that but once since the war had a teacher
been there; that she herself longed to learn—
and thus she ran on, talking fast and loud, with
much earnestness and energy.
(55)   Next morning I crossed the tall, round hill,
plunged into the wood, and came out at Josie's
home. The father was a quiet, simple soul,
calmly ignorant, with no touch of vulgarity.
The mother was different—strong, bustling,
(60) and energetic, with a quick, restless tongue,
and an ambition to live "like folks." There was
a crowd of children. Two growing girls; a shy
midget of eight; John, tall, awkward, and eighteen; Jim, younger, quicker, and better-look-
(65) ing; and two babies of indefinite age. Then

there was Josie herself. She seemed to be the
center of the family: always busy at service, or
at home, or berry-picking; a little nervous and
inclined to scold, like her mother, yet faithful,
(70) too, like her father. I saw much of this family
afterwards, and grew to love them for their
honest efforts to be decent and comfortable,
and for their knowledge of their own ignorance. There was with them no affectation.
(75) The mother would scold the father for being
so "easy"; Josie would roundly berate the boys
for carelessness; and all knew that it was a
hard thing to dig a living out of a rocky side-
hill.

6. The passage as a whole is best characterized as
(A) an example of the harsh realities of searching for employment
(B) a description of the achievements of a
graduate of a prestigious school
(C) an analysis of teacher education in a rural
setting
(D) a reminiscence of a memorable time in one
man's life
(E) an illustration of the innocence and gullibility of youth

7. Lines 21–24 suggest that the author had no
firsthand knowledge of hunting living creatures
because
(A) he had too much sympathy for the hunter's
prey to become a hunter himself
(B) his studies had left him no time for recre-
ational activities
(C) small arms weapons had been forbidden in
his home
(D) hunting was an inappropriate activity for
teachers
(E) his mother had once been wounded by a
gunshot

8. To the author, his journey through the
Tennessee countryside seemed to be all of the
following EXCEPT
(A) gratifying
(B) interminable
(C) tiring
(D) carefree
(E) discouraging

9. The "stage lines" mentioned by the author in line 35 refer to

   (A) phases of personal growth
   (B) theatrical directions
   (C) horse-drawn transportation
   (D) cultural divisions
   (E) train stations

10. The author sets the word *varmints* in quotation marks (line 35) for which of the following reasons?

   (A) He wishes to indicate he is referring to an authority.
   (B) He is unsure of the correct spelling of the term.
   (C) He recognizes them as hunted creatures.
   (D) He is using the word colloquially.
   (E) He is defining it as a technical term.

11. The author's attitude toward his school-hunting days is predominantly one of

   (A) exasperation
   (B) nostalgia
   (C) bitterness
   (D) self-reproach
   (E) amusement

12. The passage suggests that Josie's interest on meeting the author was

   (A) magnified by her essentially gregarious nature
   (B) sufficiently strong to make her act uncharacteristically
   (C) prompted by her need for distractions on the long road to town
   (D) intensified by her desire to gain an education
   (E) motivated by her longing to escape her impoverished home

13. By saying she wished to live "like folks" (line 61), Josie's mother primarily emphasizes

   (A) apprehension about sinking to the level of mere brutes
   (B) an expanding greed for material possessions
   (C) impatience with people who think themselves too good for their fellows
   (D) a longing for her entire family to better themselves
   (E) an unfortunate inclination toward conformity

14. The word "roundly" in line 76 means

   (A) circuitously
   (B) bluntly
   (C) approximately
   (D) resonantly
   (E) fondly

15. The author most likely remembers Josie and her family primarily with feelings of

   (A) measured regret
   (B) grudging condescension
   (C) grateful veneration
   (D) outright curiosity
   (E) distinct affection

Questions 16–27 are based on the following passage.

The book from which the following passage was taken explains architectural methods both past and present.

The ancient Chinese believed that in the features of the natural landscape one could glimpse the mathematically precise order of
Line the universe and all the beneficial and harmful
(5) forces that were harmoniously connected according to the principle of the Tao—the Way. This was not a question of metaphor; the topography did not represent good or evil; it really *was* good or evil. Under these circum-
(10) stances, locating a building in the landscape became a decision of momentous proportions that could affect an individual and his family for generations to come. The result was *feng-shui*, which means "wind and water," and
(15) which was a kind of cosmic surveying tool. Its coherent, scientific practice dates from the Sung dynasty (960–1126), but its roots are much older than that. It was first used to locate grave sites—the Chinese worshiped their
(20) ancestors, who, they believed, influenced the good fortune of their descendants. Eventually it began to be used to locate the homes of the living; and, indeed, the earliest book on *feng-shui*, published during the Han dynasty (202
(25) B.C.–A.D. 220), was entitled *The Canon of the Dwellings*.

   Feng-shui combined an intricate set of related variables that reflected the three great

religions of China—Taoism, Buddhism, and
(30) Confucianism. First were the Taoist principles
of yang and yin—male and female. The five
Buddhist planets corresponded to the five elements, the five directions (north, south, west,
east, and center), and the five seasons (the
(35) usual four and midsummer). *Feng-shui*
employed the sixty-four epigrams of the *I-
Ching*, a classic manual of divination popular-
ized by Confucius, and also made use of the
astrological signs: the constellations were
(40) divided into four groups: the Azure Dragon
(east), the Black Tortoise (north), the White
Tiger (west), and the Red Bird (south).

The first task of the geomancer, who was
called *feng-shui hsien sheng*, or "doctor of the
(45) vital force," was to detect the presence of each
of these variables in the natural landscape.
Hilly ground represented the Dragon; low
ground was the Tiger: the ideal was to have
the Dragon on the left and the Tiger on the
(50) right (hence, to face south). In a predominantly hilly area, however, a low spot was a good
place to build; in flatter terrain, heights were
considered lucky. The best site was the junc-
tion between the Dragon and the Tiger, which
(55) is why the imperial tombs around Beijing are
so beautifully situated, just where the valley
floor begins to turn into mountain slopes.

The shape of mountain peaks, the presence of boulders, and the direction of streams
(60) all incorporated meanings that had to be
unraveled. Often simple observation did not
suffice, and the Chinese had to resort to external aids. The mariner compass was a Chinese
invention, but the *feng-shui* compass served a
(65) different purpose. It resembled a large, flat,
circular platter. In the center, like the bull's-
eye of a dartboard, was a magnetic needle,
surrounded by eighteen concentric circles.
Each ring represented a different factor and
(70) was inscribed with the constellations, odd and
even numbers, the planets and the elements,
the seasons, the hexagrams, the signs of the
zodiac, the solar orbit, and so on. With the aid
of the compass, the geomancer could discover
(75) the existence of these variables even when
they were not visible to the naked eye.

It might appear that *feng-shui* made man
the victim of fate, but this is not the case. For
one thing, there was a moral dimension to the
(80) belief; and to gain the full benefit of an auspi-

ciously placed home, the family itself had to
remain honest and upright. Moreover, the geomancer's job was not only to identify bad and
good sites but also to advise on how to miti-
(85) gate evil influences or to improve good ones.
Trees could be planted to camouflage undesir-
able views; streams could be rerouted;
mounds could be built up or cut down. It is no
accident that the greatest Chinese art of all is
(90) gardening.

Many villages in China have a grove of
trees or bamboo behind them, and a pond in
front. The function of these picturesque features is not as landscaping embellishment, or
(95) at least it is not only that; they are intended to
fend off evil influences. The pagodas that can
still be seen built on the tops of hills and
mounds serve the same purpose. When visiting some recently built farmhouses in the
(100) county of Wuqing, I noticed that the entrances
to some of the courtyards were screened by a
wall that forced the visitor to wind his way
around it, as in a maze or an obstacle course.
But the purpose of the *ying-pei*, as the Chinese
(105) walls are called, is not to prevent the passerby
from looking in. These are "spirit walls" and
are meant to keep out asomatous[1] trespassers.
The *ying-pei* is not an isolated superstition,
like lucky horseshoes in the West; it too is part
(110) of *feng-shui*.

---

[1]Lacking a body; ghostly; spirit-like.

16. The passage suggests that the ancient Chinese

(A) are not clearly understood by modern-day
thinkers
(B) were preoccupied with death
(C) did not understand the basic physical prin-
ciples that govern the universe
(D) behaved in a peaceful manner
(E) conducted their lives according to a
well-defined philosophy

17. As described in the passage, *feng-shui* is a
practice that

(A) has spread throughout the world
(B) is used to locate building sites
(C) is widely used near the water's edge
(D) most people consider a foolish superstition
(E) is used to determine the appearance of
buildings

18. According to the passage, the Tao apparently

    (A) originated about a thousand years ago
    (B) is a kind of metaphor
    (C) is a way of viewing the world
    (D) is a prescription for a happy life
    (E) is a moral code that guides human behavior

19. According to the passage, *feng-shui* seems to have developed as a practice mainly because the Chinese believed in

    (A) the sayings of Confucius
    (B) life after death
    (C) astrology
    (D) providing for future generations
    (E) original sin

20. The best definition of a "geomancer" (line 43) is one who

    (A) knew how to provide spiritual counsel
    (B) understood religion
    (C) could read and interpret the terrain
    (D) guided people in the wilderness
    (E) served as a medium between the living and the dead

21. The principles of *feng-shui* suggest that the best terrain on which to build a house is

    (A) partly flat and partly hilly
    (B) a river valley
    (C) mountainous
    (D) where mountains meet the sea
    (E) rugged with lots of trees

22. The author compares the center of a *feng-shui* compass to the bull's-eye of a dartboard (lines 66 and 67) in order to

    (A) suggest that *feng-shui* is like a game
    (B) clarify the appearance of the compass
    (C) indicate that *feng-shui* is a complex art
    (D) explain that it is extremely difficult to find ideal building sites
    (E) belittle the art of *feng-shui*

23. The author of the passage implies that the city of Beijing was deliberately built

    (A) near mountains
    (B) on a large bay
    (C) at the confluence of two rivers
    (D) to maximize the sun's light and warmth
    (E) close to ancient burial places

24. According to the passage, an ideally situated home

    (A) assures happiness to the family living there
    (B) is no guarantee of good fortune
    (C) empower families to ward off sickness and disease
    (D) helps a family establish financial security
    (E) keeps families together

25. The author calls gardening the "greatest" art in China (line 89) because

    (A) Chinese gardens are usually very beautiful
    (B) the best gardeners in the world come from China
    (C) gardening is a popular pastime in China
    (D) Chinese gardens contain symbolic meanings
    (E) the Chinese know how to grow exotic plants and flowers

26. Which of the following best describes the author's attitude toward *feng-shui*?

    (A) Mild skepticism
    (B) Surprise
    (C) Awe and wonder
    (D) Amused mockery
    (E) Intellectual curiosity

27. To repel evil spirits a family believing in *feng-shui* is likely to pay attention to all of the following EXCEPT

    (A) the distance from their home of large rock formations
    (B) the accessibility of the main entrance
    (C) the placement of trees around the house
    (D) the color of their house
    (E) the appearance of nearby mountains

Questions 28–40 are based on the following pair of passages.

The following passages discuss the problems of being poor in America. The first is an excerpt from a best-selling study of a Puerto Rican family, written by an anthropologist in the 1960s. The second is an excerpt from a speech given at a Florida school in 1965.

Passage 1

Low wages, chronic unemployment and underemployment lead to low income, lack of property ownership, absence of savings,
Line absence of food reserves in the home, and a
(5) chronic shortage of cash. These conditions reduce the possibility of effective participation in the larger economic system. And as a response to these conditions we find in the culture of poverty a high incidence of pawning
(10) personal goods, borrowing from local money-lenders at usurious rates of interest, sponta-neous informal credit devices organized by neighbors, the use of secondhand clothing and furniture, and the pattern of frequent buying of
(15) small quantities of food many times a day as the need arises.

People with a culture of poverty produce very little wealth and receive very little in return. They have a low level of literacy and
(20) education, usually do not belong to labor unions, are not members of political parties, generally do not participate in the national welfare agencies, and make very little use of banks, hospitals, department stores, museums
(25) or art galleries. They have a critical attitude toward some of the basic institutions of the dominant classes, hatred of the police, mis-trust of government and those in high position, and a cynicism which extends even to the
(30) church. This gives the culture of poverty a high potential for protest and for being used in political movements aimed against the exist-ing social order.

People with a culture of poverty are aware
(35) of middle-class values, talk about them and even claim some of them as their own, but on the whole they do not live by them. Thus it is important to distinguish between what they say and what they do. For example, many will
(40) tell you that marriage by law, by the church, or by both is the ideal form of marriage, but few

will marry. To men who have no steady jobs or other sources of income, who do not own property and have no wealth to pass on to their
(45) children, who are present-time oriented and who want to avoid the expense and legal diffi-culties involved in formal marriage and divorce, free unions or consensual marriages make a lot of sense. Women will often turn
(50) down offers of marriage because they feel it ties them down to men who are immature, punishing and generally unreliable. Women feel that consensual union gives them a better break; it gives them some of the freedom and
(55) flexibility that men have. By not giving the fathers of their children legal status as hus-bands, the women have a stronger claim on their children if they decide to leave their men. It [consensual union] also gives women exclu-
(60) sive rights to a house or any other property they may own.

Passage 2

You ask me what is poverty? Listen to me. Here I am, dirty, smelly, and with no "proper" underwear on and with the stench of my rot-
(65) ting teeth near you. I will tell you. Listen to me. Listen without pity. I cannot use your pity. Listen with understanding. Put yourself in my dirty, worn-out ill-fitting shoes, and hear me.

Poverty is getting up every morning from
(70) a dirt- and illness-stained mattress. The sheets have long since been used for diapers. Poverty is living in a smell that never leaves. This is a smell of urine, sour milk, and spoiling food sometimes joined with the strong smell of
(75) long-cooked onions. Onions are cheap. If you have smelled this smell, you did not know how it came. It is the smell of the outdoor privy. It is the smell of young children who cannot walk the long dark way in the night. It
(80) is the smell of the mattresses where years of "accidents" have happened. It is the smell of the milk which has gone sour because the refrigerator long has not worked, and it costs money to get it fixed. It is the smell of rotting
(85) garbage. I could bury it, but where is the shov-el? Shovels cost money.

Poverty is always being tired. I have always been tired. They told me at the hospital when the last baby came that I had chronic
(90) anemia caused from poor diet, a bad case of worms, and that I needed a corrective opera-

tion. I listened politely—the poor are always
polite. The poor always listen. They don't say
that there is no money for iron pills, or better
(95) food, or worm medicine. The idea of an operation is frightening and costs so much that, if I
had dared, I would have laughed. . . .
    Poverty is looking into a black future.
Your children won't play with my boys. They
(100) will turn to other boys who steal to get what
they want. I can already see them behind the
bars of their prison instead of behind the bars
of my poverty. Or they will turn to the freedom of alcohol or drugs, and find themselves
(105) enslaved. And my daughter? At best, there is
for her a life like mine. . . . Poverty is an acid
that drips on pride until all pride is worn away.
Poverty is a chisel that chips on honor until
honor is worn away. Some of you say that you
(110) would do *something* in my situation, and
maybe you would, for the first week or the
first month, but for year after year after year?
    I have come out of my despair to tell you
this. Remember I did not come from another
(115) place or another time. Others like me are all
around you. Look at us with an angry heart,
anger that will help you help me. Anger that
will let you tell of me. The poor are always
silent. Can you be silent too?

28. A defining characteristic of poverty, according
to the author of Passage 1, is that poor people

(A) lack the imagination to lift themselves out
of poverty
(B) lack the skills to find decent jobs
(C) are constantly in a state of crisis
(D) are somewhat responsible for their own
poverty
(E) are isolated from the mainstream of society

29. The author of Passage 1 uses the phrase "culture of poverty" (line 9) to suggest that

(A) causes of poverty have been carefully
studied and analyzed
(B) poor people often take pride in their
poverty
(C) for some people poverty has become a prevailing way of life
(D) poor people share a common background
(E) there are several levels and classifications
of poor people

30. By asserting that the culture of poverty can be
used by political movements (lines 30–33), the
author is

(A) predicting an uprising by the poor
(B) citing a reason for eliminating poverty
(C) cautioning the middle class to beware of
the poor
(D) criticizing the motives of politicians
(E) alluding to a particular historical event

31. The author's point about the need to "distinguish
between what they [poor people] say and what
they do" (lines 37–39) is meant to suggest that

(A) poor people are often hypocritical
(B) lying is part of the culture of poverty
(C) the poor are often unable to change the
conditions of their lives
(D) the poor are fooling themselves
(E) poverty causes people to have illusions

32. A conclusion to be drawn from the discussion of
marriage in Passage 1 is that men and women in
the culture of poverty

(A) avoid legalized marriages for practical and
economic reasons
(B) prefer to be independent
(C) cannot afford to marry and raise a family
(D) do not trust each other to be faithful hus-
bands and wives
(E) consider themselves unworthy of legal
marriage

33. The comparison between the "bars of their prison"
and the "bars of my poverty" (lines 102 and 103)
is meant to suggest that the speaker believes that

(A) her sons must choose between a life of
crime and a life of poverty
(B) escaping from poverty is more difficult
than escaping from prison
(C) her sons can escape from poverty but not
from prison
(D) crime results from poverty
(E) poverty and imprisonment are similar

34. Evidence in Passage 2 suggests that the
speaker lives

(A) on an isolated farm
(B) in an urban slum
(C) in a housing project
(D) in the country
(E) near a big city

35. The primary emotion conveyed by the speaker in Passage 2 is

    (A) jealousy
    (B) resentment
    (C) discouragement
    (D) hopelessness
    (E) resignation

36. When the speaker says "the poor always listen" (line 93) and "the poor are always silent" (lines 118 and 119) she is implying that poor people

    (A) feel intimidated by authority
    (B) cannot express themselves articulately
    (C) prefer to keep to themselves
    (D) suffer from powerlessness
    (E) don't want to antagonize other people

37. The main intent of the speaker in Passage 2 is to

    (A) convey information about poverty to the audience
    (B) enrage the audience
    (C) arouse the audience to action
    (D) define poverty
    (E) describe real differences between the rich and the poor

38. Compared to Passage 1, Passage 2 is more likely to evoke an emotional response from the reader because

    (A) it uses shocking language
    (B) it is written in first person singular
    (C) the speaker shows intense emotion
    (D) it repeatedly uses the word *poverty*
    (E) the audience is addressed as "you"

39. In discussing poverty, the authors of both passages seem to agree that poverty

    (A) cannot be clearly defined
    (B) means more than lack of money
    (C) is more widespread than most people think
    (D) cannot be eliminated
    (E) weakens the fabric of society

40. Passage 2 illustrates the contention in Passage 1 that the poor

    (A) suffer from a chronic shortage of cash
    (B) mistrust the government
    (C) have a low level of literacy and education
    (D) rely on neighbors to borrow money
    (E) make little use of banks, hospitals, and department stores

Exercise 2

Read each of the passages below, and then answer the questions that follow the passage. The correct response may be stated outright or merely suggested in the passage.

Questions 1–7 are based on the following passage.

The following passage, taken from a memoir by a Japanese-American writer, describes the conflicts she felt as she grew up living in two cultures and trying to meet two very different sets of expectations.

Whenever I succeeded in the *Hakujin* world, my brothers were supportive, whereas Papa would be disdainful, undermined by my
Line obvious capitulation to the ways of the West. I
(5) wanted to be like my Caucasian friends. Not only did I want to look like them, I wanted to act like them. I tried hard to be outgoing and socially aggressive and act confidently, like my girlfriends. At home I was careful not to
(10) show these personality traits to my father. For him it was bad enough that I did not even look Japanese: I was too big, and I walked too assertively. My behavior at home was never calm and serene, but around my father I still
(15) tried to be as Japanese as I could.

As I passed puberty and grew more interested in boys, I soon became aware that an Oriental female evoked a certain kind of interest from males. I was still too young to under-
(20) stand how or why an Oriental female fascinated Caucasian men, and of course, far too young to see then that it was a form of "not seeing." My brothers would warn me, "Don't trust the *Hakujin* boys. They only want one
(25) thing. They'll treat you like a servant and expect you to wait on them hand and foot. They don't even know how to be nice to you." My brothers never dated Caucasian girls. In fact, I never really dated Caucasian boys until
(30) I went to college. In high school, I used to sneak out to dances and parties where I would meet them. I wouldn't even dare to think what Papa would do if he knew.

What my brothers were saying was that I
(35) should not act toward Caucasian males as I did

toward them. I must not "wait on them" or allow them to think I would, because they wouldn't understand. In other words, be a Japanese female around Japanese men and act
(40) as a *Hakujin* around Caucasian men. The double identity within a "double standard" resulted not only in confusion for me of my role, or roles, as a female, but also in who or what I was racially. With the admonitions of my
(45) brothers lurking deep in my consciousness, I would try to be aggressive, assertive and "come on strong" toward Caucasian men. I mustn't let them think I was submissive, passive, and all-giving like Madame Butterfly.
(50) With Asian males I would tone down my natural enthusiasm and settle into patterns instilled in me through the models of my mother and sisters. I was not comfortable in either role.

1. The author's father reacted negatively to her successes in the Caucasian world because

   (A) he wanted her older sisters to be more successful than she was
   (B) his expectations were that she could do even better than he had done
   (C) he realized worldly success alone could not make her happy
   (D) he envied her for having opportunities that he had never known
   (E) he felt her Westernization was costing him his authority over her

2. The author most likely uses the Japanese word *Hakujin* to stand for Caucasians because

   (A) she knows no other word with that meaning
   (B) her brothers insisted that she address white boys in that way
   (C) she enjoys showing off her knowledge of exotic terminology
   (D) that is how her immediate family referred to them
   (E) it is a term that indicates deep respect

3. The father of the author expected her to be

   (A) tranquil and passive
   (B) subservient to Caucasian males
   (C) successful in the *Hakujin* way
   (D) increasingly independent and aggressive
   (E) open about going to school dances

4. By describing the white boys' fascination with Oriental women as "not seeing" (lines 22 and 23), the author primarily wishes to convey that

   (A) the white boys were reluctant to date their Oriental classmates or see them socially
   (B) they had no idea what she was like as an individual human being
   (C) the boys were too shy to look the girls in the eye
   (D) the boys could not see her attractions because she was too large to meet Japanese standards of beauty
   (E) love is nearsighted, if not blind

5. By a "double identity within a 'double standard'" (lines 40 and 41) the author primarily means that

   (A) she had one standard while her brothers had another
   (B) she had one standard while her mother had another
   (C) she was Japanese at home and *Hakujin* outside the home
   (D) she was too assertive at school to be passive at home
   (E) she felt like a double agent, betraying both sides

6. As used in lines 48 and 49, the figure of Madame Butterfly can best be described as

   (A) a model the author sought to emulate
   (B) the pattern the author's brothers wished her to follow
   (C) a particularly generous *Hakujin*
   (D) a role the author eventually found comfortable
   (E) an ethnic stereotype

7. The author's reaction to the roles she was required to adopt was primarily one of

   (A) indifference
   (B) despair
   (C) bemusement
   (D) outrage
   (E) unease

Questions 8–15 are based on the following passage.

The following excerpt is taken from a standard text on the history of Mexican art.

Pre-Spanish history in Mexico is riddled with lacunae or gaps. All that can be stated with certainty is that, quite independent of any
Line European or Oriental influence, peoples
(5) speaking different languages and at various stages of cultural development gradually created a civilization in Mexico which, by the tenth century, already knew the use of certain metals. This civilization has left us temples,
(10) palaces, tombs, ball-courts, images of its gods, ritual masks and funeral urns, mural paintings and codices, jewelry and personal ornaments, pottery for household and religious uses, weapons and primitive tools. All these do not
(15) belong to the same epoch, style, or culture, but together they form a rich and varied aggregation which is, nevertheless, homogeneous and comparable to Chinese art of the two thousand years from Confucius to the Ming dynasty.
(20)   Pre-Spanish art in Mexico served a religious function. It was not content to copy the external world, whose visible forms were for it no more than an outward testimony of great inner forces. It created original compositions,
(25) using real elements with an almost musical freedom. It is not a crude art; they are mistaken who see in its bold simplifications or wayward conceptions an inability to overcome technical difficulties. The ancient Mexican
(30) artist was deliberate and skillful, and, though never led by a merely descriptive aim, he often lingered over his subjects with realistic and minutely observant pleasure. One marvels at his plastic feeling and at his powers of dec-
(35) orative composition.
   The Mayas achieved in sculpture a placid and austere beauty of proportion and sensitiveness in modeling which has rarely been surpassed. The works of the Totonacs reveal a
(40) people of keen sensibility and varied means of expression. Their grace and tranquil, formal beauty, their plastic rhythm and interpretation of psychological values place their makers among the creators of purest art. Aztec works
(45) rival the sober and vigorous solidity of great Egyptian sculpture, which they surpass in

human intensity. The colossal statue of
Coatlicue shows that equilibrium between a
maximum richness of detail and an assertion
(50) of plastic structure which, centuries later, is
again to be found in the Mexican baroque.

In its finest works, Mexican sculpture
equals the masterpieces of any other period.
The plastic feeling of these mysterious people
(55) led them to solutions that are surprising in
their modernity. There are Tarascan statuettes
that anticipate the essential and drastic simplicity of Brancusi, and Totonac masks that
recall the poignant mortality which haunted
(60) Lehmbruck. The reclining figure of Chac-
mool seems to forecast the lines of "The
Mountains" by the English sculptor Henry
Moore. The ancient Mexicans tried sculptural
caricature also, and even sought to reproduce
(65) color effects plastically. These people have left
us, as Robert Fry affirms, "more masterpieces
of pure sculpture than the whole of
Mesopotamia, or than the majority of modern
European civilizations."

8. The word "riddled" in line 1 most nearly
   means

   (A) puzzled
   (B) questioned
   (C) interpreted
   (D) sifted
   (E) filled

9. The author stresses that our knowledge of pre-
   Spanish civilization in Mexico is

   (A) incomplete
   (B) homogeneous
   (C) academic
   (D) graphic
   (E) paradoxical

10. Which of the following statements best
    expresses the main idea of the passage?

    (A) Religion dominated early Mexican art.
    (B) The artists of ancient Mexico excelled
        chiefly in decoration.
    (C) Mexican art surpasses European and Asian
        art.
    (D) Many masterpieces exist among pre-
        Spanish Mexican art works.
    (E) Modern Mexican art cannot equal pre-
        Spanish Mexican art.

11. The author implies that distortions in ancient
    Mexican art were

    (A) reparable
    (B) deliberate
    (C) beautiful
    (D) caused by inferior tools
    (E) inflicted at a later date

12. The statement in lines 33–35 ("One marvels . . .
    decorative composition") is best interpreted as
    conveying

    (A) skepticism about the ancient Mexican
        artist's commitment to decorative art
    (B) distrust of the plastic, synthetic quality of
        purely decorative art
    (C) perplexity about how the pre-Spanish artist
        could have achieved his level of technical
        skill
    (D) admiration for both the artist's technical
        expertise and artistic sensibility
    (E) a desire to study the origins of Mexican art
        further

13. The word "modeling" in line 38 most nearly
    means

    (A) posing for artists
    (B) imitating the work of others
    (C) displaying fashions
    (D) being good examples
    (E) shaping objects

14. In the last paragraph, the author probably men-
    tions Brancusi, Lehmbruck, and Henry Moore
    in order to

    (A) prove that he is acquainted with the works
        of modern artists
    (B) show that their works were influenced by
        Mexican art
    (C) explain that good art has universal appeal
    (D) add a note of irony to his argument
    (E) relate Mexican art to more familiar works
        of art

15. It can be inferred from the passage that much
    of ancient Mexican art depicted

    (A) abstract patterns
    (B) landscapes
    (C) people
    (D) still life
    (E) pure color

Questions 16–27 are based on the following passage.

The following passage is an excerpt from a historical study, done in the 1980s, of the relationship between the press and each American president from George Washington to Ronald Reagan.

In the shifting relationship between the press and the presidency over nearly two centuries, there has remained one primary con-
Line stant—the dissatisfaction of one with the
(5) other. No president has escaped press criticism, and no president has considered himself fairly treated. The record of every administration has been the same, beginning with mutual protestations of goodwill, ending with recrimi-
(10) nations and mistrust.

This is the best proof we could have that the American concept of a free press in a free society is a viable idea, whatever defects the media may have. While the Founding Fathers
(15) and their constituencies did not always agree on the role the press should play, there was a basic consensus that the newspaper (the only medium of consequence at the time) should be the buffer state between the rulers and the ruled.
(20) The press could be expected to behave like a watchdog, and government at every level, dependent for its existence on the opinions of those it governed, could expect to resent being watched and having its shortcomings, real or
(25) imaginary, exposed to the public view.

Reduced to such simple terms, the relationship of the presidents to the press since George Washington's first term is understandable only as an underlying principle. But this
(30) basic concept has been increasingly complicated by the changing nature of the presidency, by the individual nature of presidents, by the rise of other media, especially television, and by the growing complexity of beliefs
(35) about the function of both press and government.

In surveying nearly two centuries of this relationship, it is wise to keep in mind an axiom of professional historians—that we
(40) should be careful not to view the past in terms of our own times, and make judgments accordingly. Certain parallels often become obvious, to be sure, but to assert what an individual president should or should not have

(45) done, by present standards, is to violate historical context. Historians occasionally castigate each other for this failing, and in the case of press and government, the danger becomes particularly great because the words them-
(50) selves—"press" and "government," even "presidency"—have changed in meaning so much during the past two hundred years.

Recent scholarship, for example, has emphasized that colonial Americans believed
(55) in a free press, but not at all in the sense that we understand it today. Basic to their belief was the understanding, which had prevailed since the invention of the printing press in the fifteenth century, that whoever controlled the
(60) printing press was in the best position to control the minds of men. The press was seen at once as an unprecedented instrument of power, and the struggle to control it began almost as soon as the Gutenberg (or Mazarin)
(65) Bible appeared at Mainz in 1456, an event which meant that, for the first time, books could be reproduced exactly and, more important, that they could be printed in quantity.

Two primary centers of social and politi-
(70) cal power—the state and the church—stood to benefit most from the invention of the printing press. In the beginning it was mutually advantageous for them to work together; consequently it was no accident that the first
(75) printing press on the North American continent was set up in Mexico City in 1539 by Fray Juan Zumarraga, first Catholic bishop of that country. It gave the church an unprecedented means of advancing conversion, along
(80) with the possibility of consolidating and extending its power, thus providing Catholic Spain with the same territorial advantages that would soon be extended elsewhere in the Americas.

(85) When British colonies were established in North America during the early part of the seventeenth century, it was once again a religious faith, this time Protestant, that brought the first printing press to what is now the
(90) United States. But while colonial printing in Central and South America remained the province of the Catholics for some time and was used primarily for religious purposes, in North America secular publishing became an
(95) adjunct of a church-dominated press almost at once and was soon dominant.

It is part of American mythology that the nation was "cradled in liberty" and that the colonists, seeking religious freedom, immedi-
(100) ately established a free society, but the facts are quite different. The danger of an uncontrolled press to those in power was well expressed by Sir William Berkeley, governor of Virginia, when he wrote home to his superi-
(105) ors in 1671: "I thank God there are no free schools nor printing, and I hope we shall not have these hundred years; for learning has brought disobedience, and heresy, and sects into the world, and printing has divulged
(110) them, and libels against the best government, God keep us from both." There are those in twentieth-century America who would say "Amen" to Berkeley's view of printing and "libels against the best government."

16. According to the passage, all American presidents have experienced

(A) disappointment with the quality of their press coverage
(B) goodwill from some reporters in the press corps
(C) alternating periods of antagonism and harmony with the press
(D) hostility between themselves and the press
(E) having untruthful reports published about themselves

17. Conflict between the president and the press indicates that

(A) the press publishes the truth even when it hurts the president
(B) freedom of the press is alive and well in the United States
(C) presidents have traditionally had little respect for the press
(D) the press is made up mostly of critics and cynics
(E) friendly reporters are rarely assigned to cover the president

18. In the early days of the country, the function of the press was to

(A) interpret the government's actions for the people
(B) carefully observe and report on the work of all elected officials

(C) serve as a conduit of information between the government and the people
(D) preserve, protect, and defend the Bill of Rights, especially freedom of the press
(E) mold public opinion

19. Since the early days the relationship between the president and the press has been altered by all of the following EXCEPT

(A) the president's term of office has remained four years
(B) the position of "Press Secretary" has been created
(C) presidents hold televised news conferences
(D) U.S presidents are expected to be world leaders
(E) an increasingly large number of news people cover the president

20. The author of the passage cautions the reader about judging presidents of the distant past because

(A) press reports of their day cannot be trusted
(B) modern scholars have revised history
(C) we can't fully grasp the context of the past
(D) second-guessing is unfair to former presidents
(E) history is an imprecise science

21. In colonial America, the phrase "free press" (line 55) meant that

(A) the same newspapers were published throughout the thirteen colonies
(B) the press influenced what people thought and did
(C) aside from the Bible, newspapers were the colonists' favorite reading material
(D) very few people could afford to own a printing press
(E) the government was less powerful than the press

22. The passage implies that before the invention of the printing press

(A) most people were illiterate
(B) people depended for their news on word-of-mouth
(C) governments played a less influential role in people's lives
(D) news about the government traveled more slowly
(E) the civil and church authorities were virtually the same

23. The notion that it was "no accident" (line 74) that Juan Zumarraga set up the first printing press in North America means that

    (A) the church ordered Zumarraga to set up a printing press
    (B) Zumarraga worked as an agent of the Spanish government
    (C) printing holy bibles raised funds for the church
    (D) the church quickly saw that the printing press could help spread the word of God
    (E) Zumarraga advocated the improvement of the printing press

24. In contrast to printing in South America, printing in North America

    (A) was less politically oriented
    (B) was founded by the Catholic church
    (C) was dominated by religion
    (D) began earlier in the history of the New World
    (E) quickly became less religious in nature

25. The author refers to Sir William Berkeley as an example of a colonist who

    (A) was loyal to the English crown
    (B) was appointed rather than elected to his office
    (C) held the church above other institutions
    (D) advocated religious tolerance
    (E) inspired confidence in the press

26. Americans who would say "Amen" to Berkeley's view (line 112 and 113) are likely to believe

    (A) that limits should be set on freedom of the press
    (B) in the exercise of complete religious freedom for all
    (C) in a *laissez-faire* type of government
    (D) in the separation of church and state
    (E) that extremism in defense of freedom is not justified

27. The passage suggests that issues of a free press

    (A) pertain only to the United States
    (B) have been intertwined with matters concerning the separation of church and state
    (C) still raise controversy in the United States
    (D) are clearly discussed in the Constitution of the United States
    (E) originated during George Washington's administration

Questions 28–40 are based on the following pair of passages.

The following passages are excerpts from the writings of two naturalists with a deep affection for the American wilderness. The first is about the Grand Canyon; the second, about the Sonoran Desert in the state of Arizona.

Passage 1

Those who have long and carefully studied the Grand Canyon of the Colorado do not hesitate for a moment to pronounce it by far

Line the most sublime of all earthly spectacles. If
(5) its sublimity consisted only in its dimensions, it could be sufficiently set forth in a single sentence. It is more than 200 miles long, from 5 to 12 miles wide, and from 5,000 to 6,000 feet deep. There are in the world valleys which
(10) are longer and a few which are deeper. There are valleys flanked by summits loftier than the palisades of the Kaibab. Still the Grand Canyon is the sublimest thing on earth. It is not so alone by virtue of its magnitudes, but
(15) by virtue of the whole—its *ensemble*.

The common notion of a canyon is that of a deep, narrow gash in the earth, with nearly vertical walls, like a great and neatly cut trench. There are hundreds of chasms in the
(20) Plateau Country which answer very well to this notion. Many of them are sunk to frightful depths and are fifty to a hundred miles in length. Some are exceedingly narrow, as the canyons of the forks of the Virgen, where the
(25) overhanging walls shut out the sky. Some are intricately sculptured, and illuminated with brilliant colors; others are picturesque by reason of their bold and striking sculpture. A few of them are most solemn and impressive by
(30) reason of their profundity and the majesty of their walls. But, as a rule, the common canyons are neither grand nor even attractive. Upon first acquaintance they are curious and awaken interest as a new sensation, but they
(35) soon grow tiresome for want of diversity, and become at last mere bores. The impressions they produce are very transient, because of their great simplicity, and the limited range of ideas they present.
(40) It is perhaps in some respects unfortunate that the stupendous pathway of the Colorado River through the Kaibabs was ever called a

canyon, for the name identifies it with a baser
conception. But the name presents as wide a
(45) range of signification as the word *house*. The
log cabin of the rancher, the painted and
vine-clad cottage of the mechanic, the home
of the millionaire, the places where parlia-
ments assemble, and the grandest temples of
(50) worship are all houses. Yet the contrast
between St. Mark's and the rude dwelling of
the frontiersman is not greater than that
between the chasm of the Colorado and the
trenches in the rocks which answer to the ordi-
(55) nary conception of a canyon. So is the chasm
an expansion of the simple type of drainage
channels peculiar to the Plateau Country. To
the conception of its vast proportions must be
added some notion of its intricate plan, the
(60) nobility of its architecture, its colossal buttes,
its wealth of ornamentation, the splendor of its
colors, and its wonderful atmosphere. All of
these attributes combine with infinite complexity to produce a whole which at first
(65) bewilders and at length overpowers.

Passage 2

Last Saturday before dusk, the summer's
114 degree heat broke to 79 within an hour. A
fury of wind whipped up, pelting houses with
dust, debris, and gravel. Then a scatter of rain
(70) came, as a froth of purplish clouds charged
across the skies. As the last of the sun's light
dissipated, we could see Baboquivari Peak sil-
houetted on a red horizon, lightning dancing
around its head.
(75)   The rains came that night—they changed
the world.
Crusty dry since April, the desert floor
softened under the rain's dance. Near the
rain-pocked surface, hundreds of thousands of
(80) bloodroot amaranth are popping off their seed-
coats and diving toward light. Barren places
will soon be shrouded in a veil of green.
Desert arroyos are running again, muddy
water swirling after a head of suds, dung, and
(85) detritus. Where sheetfloods pool, buried animals awake, or new broods hatch. At dawn,
dark egg-shaped clouds of flying ants hover
over ground, excited in the early morning light.
In newly filled waterholes, spadefoot
(90) toads suddenly congregate. The males bellow.
They seek out mates, then latch onto them
with their special nuptial pads. The females

spew out egg masses into the hot murky water.
For two nights, the toad ponds are wild with
(95) chanting while the Western spadefoot's
burnt-peanut-like smell looms thick in the air.
A yellow mud turtle crawls out of the
drenched bottom of an old adobe borrow pit
where he had been buried through the hot dry
(100) spell. He plods a hundred yards over to a
floodwater reservoir and dives in. He has no
memory of how many days it's been since his
last swim, but the pull of the water—*that* is
somehow familiar.
(105)   This is the time when the Papago Indians
of the Sonoran Desert celebrate the coming of
the rainy season moons, the *Jujkiabig
Mamsad,* and the beginning of a new year.
Fields lying fallow since the harvest of the
(110) winter crop are now ready for another planting.
If sown within a month after summer solstice,
they can produce a crop quick enough for harvest by the Feast of San Francisco, October 4.
When I went by the Madrugada home in
(115) Little Tucson on Monday, the family was
eagerly talking about planting the flashflood
field again. At the end of June, Julian wasn't
even sure if he would plant this year—no rain
yet, too hot to prepare the field, and hardly
(120) any water left in their *charco* catchment basin.
Now, a fortnight later, the pond is nearly
filled up to the brim. Runoff has fed into it
through four small washes. Sheetfloods have
swept across the field surface. Julian imagines
(125) big yellow squash blossoms in his field, just
another month or so away. It makes his mouth
water.
Once I asked a Papago youngster what the
desert smelled like to him. He answered with
(130) little hesitation:
"The desert smells like rain."
His reply is a contradiction in the minds of
most people. How could the desert smell like
rain, when deserts are, by definition, places
(135) which lack substantial rainfall?
The boy's response was a sort of Papago
shorthand. Hearing Papago can be like tasting a
delicious fruit, while sensing that the taste comes
from a tree with roots too deep to fathom.
(140)   The question had triggered a scent—cre-
osote bushes after a storm—their aromatic oils
released by the rains. His nose remembered
being out in the desert, overtaken: *the desert
smells like rain.*

28. Passage 1 indicates that the Grand Canyon is "the sublimest thing on earth" (line 13) because of its

   (A) size
   (B) geologic formations
   (C) mysterious beauty
   (D) overall appearance
   (E) stature among the world's natural wonders

29. Passage 1 implies that visitors to the Grand Canyon are most likely to be

   (A) enthusiastic at first but quick to seek fresh wonders
   (B) astonished by the Grand Canyon's incomparable size
   (C) overwhelmed by the canyon's variety of features
   (D) awestruck by the agelessness of the place
   (E) impressed by the mixture of colors and rock formations

30. The author thinks that the Grand Canyon should not have been called a "canyon" because

   (A) it is far too big for a canyon
   (B) most canyons have vertical walls
   (C) it is made up of several unconnected parts
   (D) the Grand Canyon transcends the common notion of the word
   (E) it was not formed the way most other canyons were

31. One can infer from the passage that St. Mark's (line 51) is:

   (A) a large church
   (B) an ornate structure
   (C) an archaeological ruin
   (D) a holy shrine
   (E) a tourist attraction

32. Relating the Grand Canyon to "drainage channels" (lines 56 and 57) helps the author make the point that

   (A) large canyons at one time were very small
   (B) flowing water is necessary in canyon formation
   (C) the Grand Canyon is in a class by itself
   (D) canyons change perpetually in Plateau Country
   (E) the canyons of Plateau Country are unique

33. According to Passage 2, rainshowers in the desert

   (A) soak instantly into the earth
   (B) are usually preceded by thunder
   (C) promote the growth of vegetation
   (D) force birds from their nests
   (E) keep the land cool enough for comfortable human habitation

34. The word "dissipated" (line 72) most nearly means

   (A) squandered
   (B) distributed
   (C) separated
   (D) vanished
   (E) indulged

35. The author's attitude toward the coming of the rains is best described as

   (A) respect for the rains' destructive powers
   (B) awe of their revitalizing effects
   (C) appreciation of the rains' practical utility
   (D) puzzlement at the rains' delayed arrival
   (E) skepticism of their ultimate influence

36. The author of Passage 2 identifies the spadefoot toad by all of the following characteristics EXCEPT

   (A) its relative size
   (B) the time of day it is particularly active
   (C) its manner of propagating offspring
   (D) the sound it makes as its mating call
   (E) its characteristic odor

37. According to the author, the Papago youngster's description of the desert's smell (line 131) would strike most readers as

   (A) incontrovertible
   (B) literal
   (C) tentative
   (D) paradoxical
   (E) hypothetical

38. In contrast to the author of Passage 2, the author of Passage 1 relies almost exclusively on his sense(s) of

   (A) sight and sound
   (B) sight and smell
   (C) sight only
   (D) smell only
   (E) sound only

39. The author of Passage 2 most obviously differs from the author of Passage 1 in that he

    (A) views nature more like a poet than a scientist
    (B) includes information about his personal experiences
    (C) uses figurative language
    (D) is more respectful of nature's wonders
    (E) includes more geological information

40. The two passages differ in that Passage 1 is

    (A) abstract, whereas Passage 2 is concrete
    (B) practical, whereas Passage 2 is speculative
    (C) analytical, whereas Passage 2 is didactic
    (D) cynical, whereas Passage 2 is earnest
    (E) resigned, whereas Passage 2 is argumentative

LEVEL B

Most high school students have some difficulty comprehending reading passages on this level. Consider the reading passages that follow to be a good sample of the mid-range prose excerpts you will face on the SAT.

Exercise 1

Read each of the passages below, and then answer the questions that follow the passage. The correct response may be stated outright or merely suggested in the passage.

Questions 1–6 are based on the following passage.

In the following passage, author Peter Matthiessen considers Native American spirituality.

We can no longer pretend—as we did for so long—that Indians are a primitive people: no, they are a traditional people, that is, a
Line "first" or "original" people, a primal people,
(5) the inheritors of a profound and exquisite wisdom distilled by long ages on this earth. The Indian concept of earth and spirit has been patronizingly dismissed as simple hearted "naturalism" or "animism," when in fact it
(10) derives from a holistic vision known to all mystics and great teachers of the most venerated religions of the world.

This universal and profound intuitive knowledge may have come to North America
(15) with the first peoples to arrive from Asia, although Indians say it was the other way around, that the assumption of white historians that a nomadic people made a one-way journey across the Bering Strait from Asia and
(20) down into America, and never attempted to travel the other way, makes little sense. Today most Indians believe that they originated on this continent: at the very least, there was travel in both directions. (In recent years, this the-
(25) ory has been given support by a young anthropologist who, on the basis of stone tools and skull measurements as well as pictographs and cave drawings, goes so far as to suggest that the Cro-Magnon—the first truly modern
(30) men—who came out of nowhere to displace the Neanderthals in Eurasia perhaps 40,000 years ago were a pre-Indian people from North America.) According to the Hopi, runners were sent west across the Bering Strait as
(35) messengers and couriers, and information was exchanged between North America and Eurasia in very early times, long before European history had begun.

The Old Way—what the Lakota call
(40) *wouncage*, "our way of doing"—is very consistent throughout the Indian nations, despite the great variety of cultures. The Indian cannot love the Creator and desecrate the earth, for Indian existence is not separable from Indian
(45) religion, which is not separable from the natural world. It is not a matter of "worshiping nature," as anthropologists suggest: to worship nature, one must stand apart from it and call it "nature" or the "human habitat" or "the envi-
(50) ronment." For the Indian, there is no separation. Man is an aspect of nature, and nature itself is a manifestation of primordial religion.

Even the word "religion" makes an unnecessary
separation, and there is no word for it in the
(55) Indian tongues. Nature is the "Great Mysterious,"
the "religion before religion," the profound intuitive apprehension of the true nature of existence
attained by sages of all epochs, everywhere on
earth: the whole universe is sacred, man is the
(60) whole universe, and the religious ceremony is life
itself, the miraculous common acts of every day.

1. To the author, the distinction between the
   words *primitive* and *primal* (lines 2–4) is that
   (A) whereas the former is excessively positive,
       the latter is neutral in significance
   (B) while the latter is often used metaphorical-
       ly, the former is not
   (C) the latter reinforces the notion of Indian
       barbarism that is implicit in the former
   (D) while the former has some negative connota-
       tions, the latter has neutral or positive ones
   (E) the former came into common use earlier
       than the latter did

2. The author most likely used quotation marks
   around certain words in the last sentence of the
   first paragraph (lines 6–12) because
   (A) they are quotations from another work
   (B) they are slang
   (C) they come from another language
   (D) he disagrees with their application here
   (E) he wishes to emphasize their appropriateness

3. Which of the following is the most accurate
   statement about the second paragraph of the
   passage?
   (A) It develops the idea of the first paragraph.
   (B) It is a digression from the author's argument.
   (C) It provides examples to illustrate the points
       made in the first paragraph.
   (D) It provides a logical introduction to the
       third paragraph.
   (E) It is full of totally unsupported assumptions.

4. The author's attitude toward Indian religion is
   one of
   (A) respect
   (B) idolatry
   (C) condemnation
   (D) pity
   (E) indifference

5. The word "apprehension" in line 57 means
   (A) capture
   (B) foreboding
   (C) understanding
   (D) achievement
   (E) approval

6. By calling the common acts of every day mirac-
   ulous (line 61), Matthiessen is being
   (A) paradoxical
   (B) allusive
   (C) sarcastic
   (D) analytical
   (E) apologetic

**Questions 7–15 are based on the following
passage.**

*The following passage, written by a zoological
anthropologist, is an excerpt from a field-research
study into the organization and behavior of chimpanzee society.*

Many primates live in an organized troop
in which all ages and both sexes are included,
and in which members always move compactly
Line together as a stable social unit. There is a
(5) ranking hierarchy among troop males,
although the strictness with which the hierarchy is enforced varies. The ranking relationship is recognized among them and the hierarchy functions to ameliorate conflict. The high-
(10) est-ranking male or males defend, control, and
lead the troop; the strong social bond among
members and their safety is maintained.
On the other hand, chimpanzees lack a
stable social troop. Even members of a region-
(15) al population, who are acquainted with each
other, rarely move en masse but move in temporarily formed parties that usually consist of
less than ten animals. Such parties maintain
associative and friendly contact through their
(20) rich vocal and behavioral communication.
Chimpanzee society ensures the free and independent movement of each individual based
on highly developed individuality without the
restriction of either territoriality or hierarchy.
(25) On the other hand, a chimpanzee enjoys the
benefits of group life in that it can avoid the
enemy and find fruits with less effort.

Although there is a loose dominant and subordinate relationship among individuals, (30) chimpanzees are rarely placed under the restraint of the ranking hierarchy. The rigidly organized troop characteristic of most primates must be an adaptation for avoiding enemies like man and carnivores and for defense (35) against these enemies. In this context, a group of monkeys is more likely to survive than a single individual. The group provides a social mechanism for survival. Females and young monkeys, especially a female with a baby, (40) must be protected by others. As their food, fruits, nuts, leaves, and some kinds of insects, is scattered in a wide area in the natural habitat, a dominant animal does not control the entire food source, nor does a subordinate animal (45) mal starve when the former is satiated. An important problem in the rigid hierarchical social organization is that each animal must adjust its movements and behaviors to those of the troop. A rigidly organized troop cannot be (50) maintained when individuals do not subordinate their personal desires for the good of troop unity or solidarity. The flexible social organization of the chimpanzee may be one resolution of this problem. This kind of social (55) organization may be one of the original factors raising individuality to the level of personality. Chimpanzees have not rejected group life, but they have rejected individual uniformity and the pressure of a dominance hierarchy. (60) That a number of experienced big males can serve as leader, appropriately coping with critical situations, and that followers can appropriately react to a leader's behavior, prove that chimpanzee society is not a simple (65) chaotic gathering but a developed society based on highly developed psychological processes and individuality. The identity of fellow chimpanzees is formed in the mind of those chimpanzees who utilize the same range. (70) The size of the regional population must be restricted by the upper limit of members that an animal can identify and have friendly relations with. Another factor restricting population size must be environmental conditions, (75) that is, the volume and the distribution of food and shelter and the geophysical condition of the habitat. The latter may influence the moving pattern, moving range, and the grouping

pattern of each individual and group of indi-(80) viduals. Chimpanzees form regional populations even in continuous habitats such as those found in the Budongo Forest.

7. In many primate troops, the social hierarchy consists of

   (A) females only
   (B) males only
   (C) males of all ages
   (D) females of all ages
   (E) both males and females of all ages

8. According to the passage, primate societies are
   (A) generally unstable
   (B) flexible
   (C) extremely competitive
   (D) dominated by adult males
   (E) frequently in conflict with each other

9. The author believes that primates establish strong bonds within a troop in order to
   (A) protect the members of the troop
   (B) facilitate food-gathering
   (C) establish loyalty to the group
   (D) keep other troops from encroaching on their territory
   (E) teach the youngest members how to survive

10. Unlike other primates, chimpanzees
    (A) are not bound to troops
    (B) lack a strict hierarchy within their troops
    (C) share the raising of their young
    (D) are hostile to chimpanzees from alien populations
    (E) form troops that consist of fewer than ten members

11. The author compares chimpanzees to other primates mainly to emphasize the point that
    (A) chimpanzees are more easily trained than other kinds of monkeys
    (B) great variations in behavior exist among primates of different species
    (C) chimpanzees are different
    (D) all primates have man as their common enemy
    (E) primate behavior is well understood

12. The passage implies that chimpanzees are more human-like than other primates because

   (A) the basic unit of chimpanzee society is the family
   (B) chimpanzees know how to express their emotions
   (C) each chimpanzee has a distinct personality
   (D) chimpanzees learn from their mistakes
   (E) loyalty to the group takes precedence over individuality

13. As described in the passage, the major difference between a rigid and a flexible social structure among primates is

   (A) the ability of each to withstand predators
   (B) the frequency of communication among members
   (C) the distances a member may travel from the main group
   (D) the amount of individual freedom afforded to members
   (E) the relative size of the main group

14. According to the passage, the chimpanzee population in a given area is partly determined by

   (A) dominant chimpanzee males
   (B) the proximity of humans
   (C) predators
   (D) the size of the food supply
   (E) the degree of compatibility between troops of chimpanzees

15. The author cites the Budongo Forest (line 82) as an example of a place where

   (A) chimpanzee troops have distinctive personalities
   (B) troops of chimpanzees have formed a melting pot
   (C) several species of primates coexist
   (D) geophysical conditions are conducive to large troops of chimpanzees
   (E) regional populations of chimpanzees have developed

Questions 16–27 are based on the following passage.

The following passage, taken from a historical study of war, discusses a research project undertaken to determine the real causes of war.

There has been no lack of theories on the cause of war. But we do lack theories that hold up when tested against the facts of history.
Line This deficiency of all existing theories has led
(5) a group of scholars to try to reverse the typical way of arriving at an explanation for war. Instead of coming up with a theory and then looking for the evidence, they have decided to look first at the evidence. Their first undertak-
(10) ing was to collect the most precise information possible about wars, their length, destructiveness, and participants. But before they could do even this they needed careful definitions of terms, so it would be clear which events
(15) belonged in the category of "war," when a state could be considered "participating in a war," what in fact a "state" was, and so on. Like all definitions, theirs were somewhat arbitrary, but they carefully justified their
(20) choices and, more important, they drew up their definitions first, before arriving at their conclusions so that they could not be accused of defining events in a way that would prove their presuppositions.
(25)   After agreeing on definitions, they set out to collect data. Even though they confined themselves to wars fought in the last 150 years, they encountered difficulties in getting precise information on items such as the number of
(30) casualties. Nevertheless, they argue, their results are better than any that preceded them. These basic facts about wars they published in a handbook, *The Wages of War 1865–1965*, edited by two leaders of the project, J. David
(35) Singer and Melvin Small. Even though this is only the beginning of the project, it already provides some answers to questions about wars. You might hear a street corner preacher tell you that the end of the world is at hand,
(40) because the number of wars is increasing just as the Bible prophesies. If you want to check the validity of such an assertion, you could turn to *The Wages of War* and answer the question using the best available data.

(45)   The next step in the project is to identify conditions or events that seem to be associated with wars. They are not looking for explanations, but just for correlations, that is, items that usually accompany each other. It is for *(50)* this reason that they have named their project "The Correlates of War." Starting with their collection of data on wars, they could examine the hypothesis of Woodrow Wilson that autocracies are the cause of wars. If this were true, *(55)* then autocracies would fight other autocracies and democracies might fight autocracies in defense but democracies would never fight democracies. After defining "democracy" in a way that could be measured (for example, the *(60)* frequency with which officeholders change office), they would see if any of the wars they had identified in the last 150 years had been fought between two countries clearly identifiable as democracies. If they could find no *(65)* such wars, they could say there was a *correlation* between democracy and peace. It would not yet be a *proof* that autocracies cause war. There could be other explanations—the world might contain only one or two democracies. *(70)* But a correlation would be an important first step.

The Correlates of War project is just entering this second stage. It will be some time before a full theory appears. Even when the *(75)* project does produce a theory of war (if it finds evidence to warrant such a theory), it may not provide the final word on the subject. Any such project must make decisions early in the research, such as what counts as a war and *(80)* what does not. These decisions can crucially affect the outcome, even though it might not be evident for a long time that they will. Here is an example of this problem. The Correlates of War project counts the wars fought by *(85)* Prussia under Bismarck as three separate wars because each stopped before the next one started. On the other hand, Hitler's belligerent moves against neighboring countries in 1939 and 1940 (Poland, Denmark, Belgium, France, *(90)* Norway) are counted as only one war because they took place in rapid succession. If these data are used in specific ways, they could "demonstrate" that Bismarck was more warlike than Hitler. For some purposes this might *(95)* be satisfactory but not for others.

Another problem is revealed by this example. Because the Danes capitulated to the Germans in 1940, that encounter is not listed as a war at all. Because the Belgians did resist, *(100)* that is counted as part of World War II. But the difference between these two situations was not the willingness of Germany to fight but the willingness of Germany's victim to resist. What is measured, then, is not so much the *(105)* willingness of states to go to war (which may be the most important phenomenon to explain) but the willingness of other states to resist aggression. In spite of such objections, however, the Correlates of War project is an *(110)* important effort, in many ways superior to earlier studies on the causes of war.

16. The goal of the research project described in the passage is to

(A) put an end to war once and for all
(B) develop a new theory about the causes of war
(C) correct errors in history books about the causes of war
(D) reverse the method customarily used to study wars
(E) compare and contrast several important wars

17. Historians participating in the study have devised new research methods because

(A) evidence becomes harder to find as time goes on
(B) past assumptions are being challenged by a new, younger generation of historians
(C) professional historians are divided into two groups—theoreticians and practitioners
(D) historians continually revise history as new evidence comes to light
(E) existing theories fail to coincide with facts

18. By calling the scholars' definitions of terms "somewhat arbitrary" (lines 18 and 19), the author of the passage is suggesting that

(A) the procedures used in the study were sloppy
(B) the scholars should have used dictionary definitions
(C) too much effort was wasted on defining terms
(D) the scholars had no better alternatives
(E) writing precise definitions was not important to the study

19. The author of the passage commends the researchers for

   (A) not being discouraged by the vast amount of factual information on war
   (B) devising a new theory about the causes of war
   (C) thoroughly surveying all the previous theories about the subject
   (D) defining their terms as objectively as possible
   (E) keeping personal bias out of their study

20. The author uses the example of the street corner preacher (line 38) in order to make the point that

   (A) many Americans are ignorant about history
   (B) you should not trust the word of people who speak on street corners
   (C) facts speak louder than opinions
   (D) ancient wars described in the Bible were not included in the study
   (E) the Bible is not a reliable source of historical information

21. After collecting factual data about wars, the scholars devoted themselves to studying

   (A) the political and social conditions that have often led to war
   (B) democracies and autocracies
   (C) the effectiveness of wartime propaganda
   (D) the important figures (e.g., Wilson, Hitler) associated with various wars
   (E) what caused the actual outbreak of hostilities

22. The study described in the passage has derived its name, "The Correlates of War," from

   (A) the name of the theory on which the study is based
   (B) a common explanation of the causes of war
   (C) the title of an important book on the subject
   (D) the researchers' expectations that they would find numerous correlations
   (E) the research method used by the participants

23. According to the author, a potential weakness of the study is that

   (A) the limits of the study are not clearly defined
   (B) the correlations may be misinterpreted
   (C) other historians will not accept the findings of the study
   (D) the present study ignores previous studies of the same subject
   (E) most correlations are unreliable

24. The author of the passage implies that research studies like "The Correlates of War"

   (A) are an essential function of the academic world
   (B) add immeasurably to the world's fund of knowledge
   (C) may fail to produce definitive results
   (D) inspire scholars to continue work in the field
   (E) serve as a valuable resource for policy makers

25. The author compares the warlike qualities of Bismarck and of Hitler in order to illustrate that

   (A) researchers generally prove whatever they want
   (B) research design and procedure may invalidate the findings
   (C) "The Correlates of War" project is notorious for its faulty research techniques
   (D) the preliminary findings of "The Correlates of War" project are invalid
   (E) evidence in historical research is subject to distortion and manipulation

26. The author seems to think that "The Correlates of War" project

   (A) is being carried out by hard-working researchers
   (B) is a formidable challenge for the researchers
   (C) has the potential to prevent future wars
   (D) will ultimately contribute to our understanding of war
   (E) is the best of its kind

27. Which pair of adjectives best describes the author's overall feelings about "The Correlates of War" project?

   (A) amazed and astonished
   (B) scornful and cynical
   (C) optimistic and hopeful
   (D) resentful and bitter
   (E) casual and indifferent

Questions 28–40 are based on the following pair of passages.

Pablo Picasso was probably the most influential painter of the twentieth century. In the first passage, written by Picasso himself, the artist explains his views on art. The second passage discusses Cubism, the type of modern art originated by Picasso.

Passage 1

I can hardly understand the importance
given to the word *research* in connection with
modern painting. In my opinion to search
Line means nothing in painting. To find, is the
(5) thing. Nobody is interested in following a man
who, with his eyes fixed on the ground, spends
his life looking for the pocketbook that fortune
should put in his path. The one who finds
something no matter what it might be, even if
(10) his intention were not to search for it, at least
arouses our curiosity, if not our admiration.

Among the several sins that I have been
accused of committing, none is more false
than the one that I have, as the principal objec-
(15) tive in my work, the spirit of research. When I
paint, my object is to show what I have found
and not what I am looking for. In art intentions
are not sufficient and, as we say in Spanish:
love must be proved by facts and not by rea-
(20) sons. What one does is what counts and not
what one had the intention of doing.

We all know that Art is not truth. Art is a
lie that makes us realize truth, at least the truth
that is given us to understand. The artist must
(25) know the manner whereby to convince others
of the truthfulness of his lies. If he only shows
in his work that he has searched, and
researched, for the way to put over lies, he
would never accomplish anything.

(30) The idea of research has often made painting go astray, and made the artist lose himself
in mental lucubrations.[1] Perhaps this has been
the principal fault of modern art. The spirit of
research had poisoned those who have not
(35) fully understood all the positive and conclusive elements in modern art and has made
them attempt to paint the invisible and, therefore, the unpaintable.

They speak of naturalism in opposition to
(40) modern painting. I would like to know if anyone has ever seen a natural work of art. Nature

and art, being two different things, cannot be
the same thing. Through art we express our
conception of what nature is not.

---

[1]Meditation; study.

Passage 2

(45) Cubism, with Picasso and Braque at its
head, rejected the conventional notions of
beauty. Discarding the world of perspectives
and naturalism, they put in their place a new
world obeying only the laws of the artist's
(50) inner vision. Picasso succeeded in freeing the
technique of painting from its slavish adherence to the description of nature, and he gave
it new laws of harmony and balance. This
break with the past had far-reaching conse-
(55) quences. From then on the painter became a
free creator, a poet.

Through the break in the wall, poetry
crept into painting, with all that is unusual,
miraculous, and disturbing. Things around us
(60) which do not seem worthy of the artist's
glance, things often considered ugly, were
revealed in Picasso's pictures in their most
ordinary essence but also in a new, extraordinary significance.

(65) "I put into my pictures all the things I
enjoy," said Picasso, and so he does, with his
pipe, glass, packet of tobacco, and guitar. He
is tireless in seeking to define the forms of
these objects and their essential volume, trans-
(70) forming them into poetic images, and treating
them freely and naturally as in daily life. In
this connection André Breton wrote of
Picasso: "It rested with a failure of the will of
this man, and what we are concerned about
(75) would have been at least postponed, if not
utterly lost." To which Paul Eluard added:
"Yes, for this man held in his hands the fragile
key to the problem of reality. He sought to see
what he sees, to set vision free, to attain sight.
(80) He achieved this."

Picasso considers art a process that is
never completed; he studies the problem that
interests him over and over again, from different angles. Thus he does not create pictures in
(85) the conventional, picture-gallery sense of the
word; he does not seek, but finds, in the words
of the aphorism attributed to him. The elemental side of his talent never allows him to rest
content with what he has achieved. He is

(90) always interested exclusively in the present, in the picture on which he is working. "Everything must be done anew, and not just patched up," he says, and these words sum up his programme.

(95) The constant creativity which has no regard for the nature of anything he has painted before gives Picasso the freedom to move at will in the boundless spaces of free expression. It gives him the freedom to draw on all

(100) sources of inspiration for the most varied motifs, opening up all spheres of culture, contemporary, distant, or historic.

Thus this restless, disturbing spirit, one of the most truthful witnesses to the conflict-torn

(105) century we live in, goes again and again into the attack on the gates of the unknown. Each new development in his art does more than merely increase the number of pictures he has painted: it turns against his very work itself,

(110) testing the foundations on which it rests. Picasso confounds his followers and turns inside out the aesthetic principles he himself has just established.

28. To Picasso, the author of Passage 1, the man who spends his life "with his eyes fixed on the ground" (lines 5 and 6) represents artists who

(A) don't appreciate modern art
(B) try hard but have no artistic talent
(C) contemplate their subjects too much before painting
(D) paint only to make money
(E) study the works of the great masters

29. The sentence "When I paint, my object is to show what I have found and not what I am looking for" (lines 15–17) is

(A) a digression from the main point of the passage
(B) a denial of an accusation
(C) an explanation of one of "several sins" (line 12)
(D) a paraphrase of what art critics have said about Picasso
(E) a false statement that the author intends to disprove

30. The statement "Art is not truth" (line 22) implies that

(A) artists are liars and are basically untrustworthy
(B) we should not take art too seriously
(C) art gives us more than truth; it gives us understanding
(D) we should be prepared to suspend our disbelief when we view art
(E) we must accept the idea that truth comes in many forms

31. To Picasso, the most successful art is that which

(A) shows what the artist has seen
(B) reveals what the artist has found
(C) arouses our curiosity but not our admiration
(D) accurately portrays the subject
(E) conceals the artist's techniques

32. As used in Passage 1, "naturalism" in art (line 39) refers to

(A) realism
(B) a school of contemporary art
(C) pre-twentieth-century painting
(D) outdoor paintings
(E) paintings using colors found only in nature

33. The aspect of Picasso's art that is emphasized in Passage 2 is his

(A) profundity
(B) enormous output of work
(C) innovations
(D) technical achievement
(E) appeal to art lovers

34. Passage 2 implies that, before Picasso, artists

(A) were held back by the social customs of the day
(B) were rarely encouraged to experiment
(C) were dependent on patrons for success
(D) adhered to strict rules of art
(E) restricted their paintings to one acceptable style

35. According to Passage 2, Picasso broke painting
tradition in all of the following ways EXCEPT by

(A) ignoring the need for harmony and balance
(B) expanding the subject matter of paintings
(C) throwing out the rules of perspective
(D) expressing himself more freely
(E) discarding the need for realistic painting

36. The statement "Everything must be done anew,
and not just patched up" (lines 92 and 93) suggests that Picasso believes that

(A) artists should practice leaving well enough
alone
(B) artists can benefit from their mistakes
(C) bad pictures need more than just patching up
(D) spontaneity is lost when artists start tinker-
ing with their pictures
(E) patching up a picture restricts artists' free-
dom of expression

37. The author of Passage 2 seems to believe that
Picasso is not only an energetic artist but also

(A) an observer of the politics of his time
(B) a social revolutionary
(C) a bold experimenter
(D) an inspiration to other artists
(E) an intellectual

38. Eluard's view that Picasso sought to "attain
sight" (line 79) coincides with Picasso's statement in Passage 1 that

(A) "to search means nothing" (lines 3 and 4)
(B) "my object is to show what I have found"
(line 16)
(C) "what one does is what counts" (line 20)
(D) "art is a lie" (lines 22 and 23)
(E) "Nature and art . . . cannot be the same
thing" (lines 41–43)

39. Both Passage 1 and Passage 2 describe Picasso
as an artist who

(A) transforms objects into "poetic images"
(line 70)
(B) "does not seek, but finds" (line 86)
(C) is never "content with what he has
achieved" (line 89)
(D) attacks the "gates of the unknown" (line 106)
(E) "confounds his followers" (line 111)

40. Compared to Passage 2, Passage 1 is

(A) less controversial
(B) more up-to-date
(C) more argumentative
(D) more historical
(E) less personal

LEVEL C

Most high school students have trouble following reading passages at this level of difficulty. Consider the
excerpts that follow as a chance for you to acquaint yourself with the toughest prose that occurs on the SAT.

Exercise 1

Read each of the passages below, and then answer the questions that follow the passage. The correct
response may be stated outright or merely suggested in the passage.

**Questions 1–7 are based on the following
passage.**

The following passage is taken from Cranford,
*Elizabeth Gaskell's nineteenth-century novel set in
a small English town.*

In the first place, in Cranford all the holders of houses, at least those above a certain
rent, are women. If a married couple come to
Line settle in the town, somehow the gentleman
(5) disappears; he is either fairly frightened to
death by being the only man in the Cranford
evening parties, or is accounted for by being

with his regiment, his ship, or closely engaged
in business all the week in the great neighbor-
(10) ing commercial town of Drumble, distant only
twenty miles on a railroad. In short, whatever
does become of the gentlemen, they are not at
Cranford. What could they do if they were
there? The surgeon has his round of thirty
(15) miles, and sleeps at Cranford; but every man
cannot be a surgeon. For keeping the trim gardens full of choice flowers without a weed to
speck them; for frightening away little boys
who look wistfully at the said flowers through
(20) the railings; for rushing out at the geese that
occasionally venture into the gardens if the
gates are left open; for deciding all questions
of literature and politics without troubling
themselves with unnecessary reasons or argu-
(25) ments; for obtaining clear and correct knowledge of everybody's affairs in the parish; for
keeping their neat maid-servants in admirable
order; for kindness (somewhat dictatorial) to
the poor, and real tender good offices to each
(30) other whenever they are in distress—the ladies
of Cranford are quite sufficient. "A man," as
one of them observed to me once, "is *so* in the
way in the house!" Although the ladies of
Cranford know all each other's proceedings,
(35) they are exceedingly indifferent to each
other's opinions. Indeed, as each has her own
individuality, not to say eccentricity, pretty
strongly developed, nothing is so easy as verbal retaliation; but, somehow, goodwill reigns
(40) among them to a considerable degree.
    The Cranford ladies have only an occa-
sional little quarrel, spurted out in a few pep-
pery words and angry jerks of the heads; just
enough to prevent the even tenor of their lives
(45) from becoming too flat. Their dress is very
independent of fashion; as they observe,
"What does it signify how we dress here at
Cranford, where everybody knows us?" And if
they go from home, their reasoning is equally
(50) cogent, "What does it signify how we dress
here, where nobody knows us?" The materials
of their clothes are, in general, good and plain,
and most of them are nearly as scrupulous as
Miss Tyler, of cleanly memory; but I will
(55) answer for it, the last gigot, the last tight and
scanty petticoat in wear in England, was seen
in Cranford—and seen without a smile.

1. The passage can best be described as
   (A) an argument in favor of the supremacy of
       women
   (B) a laudatory depiction of a vanishing way of
       life
   (C) an illustration of the virtues of female inde-
       pendence
   (D) an analysis of the reasons for the dearth of
       males
   (E) a humorous portrait of the residents of a town

2. According to the passage, the men of Cranford
   are primarily distinguished by their
   (A) docility
   (B) awkwardness
   (C) absence
   (D) cowardice
   (E) aloofness

3. The word "offices" in line 29 refers to
   (A) places of employment
   (B) daily religious ceremonies
   (C) rooms in which household work is performed
   (D) acts done on behalf of others
   (E) positions of authority

4. The narrator's attitude toward the ladies of
   Cranford is primarily one of
   (A) abiding suspicion
   (B) wistful nostalgia
   (C) bitter sarcasm
   (D) gentle mockery
   (E) fervent enthusiasm

5. The scrupulous Miss Tyler (lines 53 and 54)
   most likely was noted for her
   (A) chaste behavior
   (B) spotless attire
   (C) wholesome outlook
   (D) precise memory
   (E) humorless disposition

6. Lines 55 and 56 suggest that "the last gigot" is
   (A) a type of covered carriage
   (B) an outmoded article of apparel
   (C) a modish kind of fabric
   (D) a subject too grave to evoke a smile
   (E) a meticulous elderly woman

7. To the narrator, the ladies of Cranford seem to be all of the following EXCEPT

(A) idiosyncratic
(B) benevolent
(C) overbearing
(D) submissive
(E) inquisitive

Questions 8–15 are based on the following passage.

The following passage from a 1984 Scientific American *article reveals the ocean depths to be the home of strong, tumultuous currents. This theory challenges the once widely held view of the abyss as "a region as calm as it was dark."*

The notion of a tranquil abyss had been so generally held that many investigators were initially reluctant to accept the evidence for
Line strong currents and storms in the deep sea.
(5) The first argument for the existence of such currents came from theory. Cold water is denser than warm water, and models of ocean circulation showed that the sinking of cold water near the poles should generate strong,
(10) deep and steady currents flowing toward the Equator. Subsequent observations not only confirmed the presence of the deep currents but also disclosed the existence of eddies on the western side of ocean basins that can be
(15) some 300 times as energetic as the mean current. Photographs of the sea floor underlying the deep currents also revealed extensive graded beds indicative of the active transport of sediment. The final evidence for dynamic
(20) activity at great depths came from direct measurements of currents and sediments in the North Atlantic carried out in the HEBBLE[1] program.
Before we describe the HEBBLE find-
(25) ings in some detail let us briefly review the sources and sinks of deep-sea sediments and the forces that activate the global patterns of ocean circulation. The sediments that end up on the ocean floor are of two main types.

(30) One component is the detritus[2] whose source is the weathering of rocks on continents and islands. This detritus, together with decaying vegetable matter from land plants, is carried by rivers to the edge of the continent and out
(35) onto the continental shelf, where it is picked up by marine currents. Once the detritus reaches the edge of the shelf it is carried to the base of the continental rise by gravitational processes. A significant amount of ter-
(40) restrial material is also blown out to sea in subtropical regions by strong desert winds. Every year some 15 billion tons of continental material reaches the outlets of streams and rivers. Most of it is trapped there or on
(45) the continental shelves; only a few billion tons escapes into the deep sea.
The second major component arriving at the sea floor consists of the shells and skeletons of dead microscopic organisms that
(50) flourish and die in the sunlit waters of the top 100 meters of the world's oceans. Such biological material contributes to the total inventory at the bottom about three billion tons per year. Rates of accumulation are
(55) governed by rates of biological productivity, which are controlled in part by surface currents. Where surface currents meet they are said to converge, and where they part they are said to diverge. Zones of divergence of
(60) major water masses allow nutrient-rich deeper water to "outcrop" at the sunlit zone where photosynthesis and the resulting fixation of organic carbon take place. Such belts of high productivity and high rates of accu-
(65) mulation are normally around the major oceanic fronts (such as the region around the Antarctic) and along the edges of major currents (such as the Gulf Stream off New England and the Kuroshio currents off
(70) Japan). Nutrient-rich water also outcrops in a zone along the Equator, where there is a divergence of two major, wind-driven gyres.

---

[1] Naval research program known as the High-Energy Benthic Boundary-Layer Experiment.

[2] Debris; fragmented rock particles.

8. The primary purpose of the passage is to
   (A) contrast surface currents with marine currents
   (B) question the methods of earlier investigators
   (C) demonstrate the benefits of the HEBBLE program
   (D) describe a replicable laboratory experiment
   (E) summarize evidence supporting oceanic circulation

9. Which of the following best describes the attitude of many scientists when they first encountered the theory that strong currents are at work in the deeps?
   (A) Somber resignation
   (B) Measured approbation
   (C) Marked skepticism
   (D) Academic detachment
   (E) Active espousal

10. According to the passage, the earliest data supporting the idea that the sea depths are dynamic rather than placid came from theory based on
    (A) underwater photographic surveys
    (B) the activities of the HEBBLE program
    (C) analysis of North Atlantic sea-bed sediments
    (D) direct measurement of undersea currents
    (E) models showing how hot and cold water interact

11. The phrase "the weathering of rocks" (line 31) refers to their
    (A) moisture content
    (B) ability to withstand meteorological phenomena
    (C) wearing away from exposure to the elements
    (D) gradual hardening into geological strata
    (E) rugged foundation

12. As defined in the passage, the second type of deep-sea sediment consists of which of the following?
    I.   Minute particles of rock
    II. Fragmentary shells
    III. Wind-blown soil
    (A) I only
    (B) II only
    (C) I and II only
    (D) I and III only
    (E) I, II, and III

13. This passage most likely would be of particular interest to
    (A) navigators of sailing vessels
    (B) students of global weather patterns
    (C) current passengers on ocean liners
    (D) designers of sea-floor structures
    (E) researchers into photosynthesis

14. In the passage the authors do all of the following EXCEPT
    (A) approximate an amount
    (B) refer to a model
    (C) give an example
    (D) propose a solution
    (E) support a theory

15. The style of the passage can best be described as
    (A) oratorical
    (B) epigrammatic
    (C) expository
    (D) digressive
    (E) metaphorical

Questions 16–27 are based on the following passage.

The following passage, written by a university professor, is from a scholarly book describing how international monetary policy contributes to the world's problems.

What is money? That is not so simple a question as might appear. In fact, money can only be defined in terms of the functions it
Line performs—that is, by the need it fulfills. As
(5) Sir Ralph Hawtrey once noted, "Money is one of those concepts which, like a teaspoon or an umbrella, but unlike an earthquake or a butter-

cup, are definable primarily by the use or purpose which they serve." Money is anything,
(10) regardless of its physical or legal characteristics, that customarily and principally performs
certain functions.

Three such functions are usually specified,
corresponding to the three basic needs served
(15) by money—the need for a *medium of
exchange*, the need for a *unit of account*, and
the need for a *store of value*. Most familiar is
the first, the function of a medium of
exchange, whereby goods and services are
(20) paid for and contractual obligations dis-
charged. In performing this role the key
attribute of money is general acceptability in
the settlement of debt. The second function of
money, that of a unit of account, is to provide
(25) a medium of information—a common denom-
inator or *numeraire* in which goods and services may be valued and debts expressed. In
performing this role, money is said to be a
"standard of value" or "measure of value" in
(30) valuing goods and services and a "standard of
deferred payment" in expressing debts. The
third function of money, that of a store of
value, is to provide a means of holding wealth.

The development of money was one of the
(35) most important steps in the evolution of
human society, comparable, in the words of
one writer, "with the domestication of animals, the cultivation of the land, and the har-
nessing of power." Before money there was
(40) only barter, the archetypical economic transaction, which required an inverse double coincidence of wants in order for exchange to occur.
The two parties to any transaction each had to
desire what the other was prepared to offer.
(45) This was an obviously inefficient system of
exchange, since large amounts of time had to
be devoted to the necessary process of search
and bargaining. Under even the most elemental circumstances, barter was unlikely to
(50) exhaust all opportunities for advantageous
trade:

Bartering is costly in ways too numerous
to discuss. Among others, bartering
requires an expenditure of time and the
(55) use of specialized skills necessary for
judging the commodities that are being
exchanged. The more advanced the specialization in production and the more

complex the economy, the costlier it will
(60) be to undertake all the transactions necessary to make any given good reach its
ultimate user by using barter.

The introduction of generalized exchange
intermediaries cut the Gordian knot of barter
(65) by decomposing the single transaction of
barter into separate transactions of sale and
purchase, thereby obviating the need for a
double coincidence of wants. This served to
facilitate multilateral exchange; the costs of
(70) transactions reduced, exchange ratios could be
more efficiently equated with the demand and
supply of goods and services. Consequently,
specialization in production was promoted and
the advantages of economic division of labor
(75) became attainable—all because of the development of money.

The usefulness of money is inversely proportional to the number of currencies in circulation. The greater the number of currencies,
(80) the less is any single money able to perform
efficiently as a lubricant to improve resource
allocation and reduce transactions costs.
Diseconomies remain because of the need for
multiple price quotations (diminishing the
(85) information savings derived from money's
role as unit of account) and for frequent currency conversions (diminishing the stability
and predictability of purchasing power derived
from money's roles as medium of exchange
(90) and store of value). In all national societies,
there has been a clear historical tendency to
limit the number of currencies, and eventually
to standardize the domestic money on just a
single currency issued and managed by the
(95) national authorities. The result has been a
minimization of total transaction costs within
nation-states.

Between nation-states, however, costs of
transactions remain relatively high, because
(100) the number of currencies remains high. Does
this suggest that global efficiency would be
maximized if the number of currencies in the
world were minimized? Is this the optimal
organizational principle for international mon-
(105) etary relations? Not necessarily. It is true that
total transactions costs, other things being
equal, could be minimized by standardizing on
just a single global money. "On the basis of
the criterion of maximizing the usefulness of

(110) money, we should have a single world currency." But there are other criteria of judgment as
well; economic efficiency, as I have indicated,
is a multi-variate concept. And we shall soon
see that the costs of a single world currency or
(115) its equivalent, taking full account of both the
microeconomic and macroeconomic dimen-
sions of efficiency, could easily outweigh the
single microeconomic benefit of lower transaction costs. As Charles Kindleberger has
(120) written: "The case for international money is
the general case for money. [But] it may well
be that the costs of an international money are
so great that the world cannot afford it."

16. The author of the passage asks the reader,
"What is money?" in order to

(A) challenge the reader by asking an unan-
swerable question
(B) make the reader feel uncomfortable
(C) test the reader's intelligence
(D) introduce an unfamiliar definition of the
word
(E) feign ignorance

17. The explanation of the three functions of
money (lines 13–33)

(A) is a section of a controversial economic
theory
(B) is common knowledge among informed
people
(C) breaks new ground in economic thinking
(D) is a comprehensive analysis of monetary
policy
(E) is valid for only some kinds of money

18. According to the passage, money meets three
needs:

   I.   medium of exchange
   II. unit of account
   III. store of value
The sticker price of a new car in the dealer's
showroom is an example of

(A) II only
(B) III only
(C) I and III
(D) II and III
(E) I and II

19. By calling barter "the archetypical economic
transaction," the author is saying that barter

(A) is obsolete
(B) is both a theory and a real-life activity
(C) is a model for economic exchanges
(D) is a primitive form of exchange
(E) usually satisfies all the parties involved in
a deal

20. According to the passage, the chief shortcoming of barter is that

(A) making deals is too time-consuming
(B) three- or four-way deals are virtually
impossible
(C) down payments cannot be used
(D) neither party to a bartering agreement is
ever fully satisfied
(E) no one could ever make a profit

21. The reference to the "Gordian knot" (line 64)
suggests that the author thinks that

(A) barter was inherently too slow
(B) it was difficult to change the barter system
to a monetary system
(C) the economist Gordon deserves credit for
introducing the monetary system
(D) most people lack the skill to accurately
determine the value of commodities
(E) barter restricts the free exchange of goods
and services

22. Based on the passage, a monetary system has all
of the following advantages over barter EXCEPT

(A) a double coincidence of wants is eliminated
(B) the cost of doing business is lower
(C) supply and demand determine the cost of
goods and services
(D) a greater division of labor is possible
(E) opportunities of profitable trade are
reduced

23. The author believes that having a large number
of currencies in circulation

(A) leads to an unstable money supply
(B) reduces the efficiency of the international
economy
(C) makes international travel more complex
(D) requires the creation of a central monetary
authority
(E) widens the gap between rich nations and
poor nations

24. According to the passage, standardizing the currency of a nation is likely to result in

    (A) a reduction in the cost of monetary transactions
    (B) a short period of inflation
    (C) an increase of money in circulation
    (D) greater confidence in the banking system
    (E) increased international stature

25. By responding "Not necessarily" to the questions posed in lines 100–105, the author is suggesting that

    (A) a solution to the problem is still years away
    (B) advocates of minimizing the number of currencies are seriously mistaken
    (C) many nations resist the creation of a single world currency
    (D) the most obvious solution is not the best solution
    (E) the simplest solution is the one that will work

26. To improve the efficiency of the international monetary system, the author supports

    (A) increasing the world's gold supply
    (B) setting limits on the amount of money being exchanged
    (C) lowering tariffs between nations
    (D) creating a single worldwide currency
    (E) reducing transaction costs

27. The author of the passage draws which of the following conclusions about the creation of a worldwide currency?

    (A) It may cause more problems than it will solve.
    (B) Discussing it further is pointless.
    (C) Reducing transaction costs must precede the creation of a worldwide currency.
    (D) Proposals for such a currency must provide for a reduction of transaction costs.
    (E) It is an ideal never to be attained.

Questions 28–40 are based on the following pair of passages.

The following passages discuss This Side of Paradise, *F. Scott Fitzgerald's autobiographical first novel, written when the author was in his early twenties. Both passages are excerpts from essays by literary critics.*

Passage 1

    The defects of *This Side of Paradise* should not blind the reader to its importance in Fitzgerald's career. It marked his movement,
Line clumsy and pasted together as the novel often
(5) is, from a clever short-story writer and would-be poet to an ambitious novelist. All his life he was to think of himself primarily as a novelist, to save his best work for his novels, to plunder his published short stories for usable
(10) material for them. If he achieved nothing else in this first novel, he had at least taken his scattered literary effusions and his undescribed experiences, sifted them, shaped and reshaped them, often looked at them ironically, and fashioned
(15) them into a sustained narrative. Compared with the material he took directly from his *Nassau Lit* stories, the writing had improved greatly. In many rewritten passages, *This Side of Paradise* shows Fitzgerald moving to that freshness of
(20) language which became his identifying mark.
    The novel took the bold step that Fitzgerald needed: it confirmed his ideas about the importance of his feelings and about his ability to put them down. It helped Fitzgerald thrash out
(25) those "ideas still in riot" that he attributes to Amory [the novel's main character] at the close of the book: his ideas about love and women, about the Church, about his past, about the importance of *being* as contrasted with *doing*.
(30) Though it borrowed heavily from the many writers to whom he was attracted, the book still has Fitzgerald's own stamp: the naiveté and honesty that is part of "the stamp that goes into [each of] my books so that people can read it
(35) blind like Braille." If Amory is not as honest with himself as Fitzgerald's later characters can be, it is chiefly from a lack of perception rather than from a deliberate desire to deceive.
    Finally, though Fitzgerald placed his twin
(40) hopes of money and the girl in the book's great success, the book is not merely contrived to achieve these aims. The badness in it is not that of the professional who shrewdly calculates his effects; it is that of the ambitious amateur writer
(45) who produces what seems to him to be witty, fresh, and powerful prose. It is a much better book than *The Romantic Egotist*, the version he finished before he left Princeton. For Fitzgerald at twenty-three, it was the book he wanted to
(50) write, the book he could write, and the book

that did get written. Before it even reached its
audience, Fitzgerald had found his craft.

Passage 2

It has been said by a celebrated person that
to meet F. Scott Fitzgerald is to think of a stu-
(55) pid old woman with whom someone has left a
diamond; she is extremely proud of the diamond and shows it to everyone who comes by,
and everyone is surprised that such an ignorant
old woman should possess so valuable a jewel;
(60) for in nothing does she appear so inept as in
the remarks she makes about the diamond.

The person who invented this simile did
not know Fitzgerald very well and can only
have seen him, I think, in his more diffident or
(65) uninspired moods. The reader must not suppose that there is any literal truth in the image.
Scott Fitzgerald is, in fact, no old woman, but
a very good-looking young man, nor is he in
the least stupid, but, on the contrary, exhilarat-
(70) ingly clever. Yet there *is* a symbolic truth in
the description quoted above; it is true that
Fitzgerald has been left with a jewel which he
doesn't know quite what to do with. For he
has been given imagination without intellectu-
(75) al control of it; he has been given the desire
for beauty without an aesthetic ideal; and he
has been given a gift for expression without
very many ideas to express.

Consider, for example, the novel—*This*
(80) *Side of Paradise*—with which he founded his
reputation. It has almost every fault and deficiency that a novel can possibly have. It is not
only highly imitative but it imitates an inferior
model. Fitzgerald, when he wrote the book,
(85) was drunk with Compton Mackenzie, and it
sounds like an American attempt to rewrite
Sinister Street. Now, Mackenzie, in spite of his
gift for picturesque and comic invention and
the capacity for pretty writing that he says he
(90) learned from Keats, lacks both the intellectual
force and the emotional imagination to give
body and outline to the material which he
secretes in such enormous abundance. With the
seeds he took from Keats's garden, one of the
(95) best-arranged gardens in England, he enflore-
ated [generated flowers] so profusely that he
blotted out the path of his own. Michael Fane,
the hero of *Sinister Street*, was swamped in the
forest of descriptions; he was smothered by
(100) creepers and columbines. From the time he

went up to Oxford, his personality began to
grow dimmer, and, when he last turned up (in
Belgrade) he seemed quite to have lost his
identity. As a consequence, Amory Blaine, the
(105) hero of *This Side of Paradise*, had a very poor
chance of coherence: Fitzgerald did endow
him, to be sure, with a certain emotional life
which the phantom Michael Fane lacks; but he
was quite as much a wavering quantity in a
(110) phantasmagoria of incident that had no dominating intention to endow it with unity and
force. In short, one of the chief weaknesses of
This Side of Paradise is that it is really not
about anything: its intellectual and moral con-
(115) tent amounts to little more than a gesture—a
gesture of indefinite revolt. The story itself,
furthermore, is very immaturely imagined: it is
always just verging on the ludicrous. And
finally, *This Side of Paradise* is one of the most
(120) illiterate books of any merit ever published (a
fault which the publisher's proofreader seems
to have made no effort to remedy). Not only is
it ornamented with bogus ideas and faked literary references, but it is full of literary words
(125) tossed about with the most reckless inaccuracy.

28. The author of Passage 1 thinks that *This Side of
Paradise* demonstrates Fitzgerald's ability to

(A) compose both long stories and short novels
(B) write short stories
(C) include poetic language in his writing
(D) tell a long story
(E) edit his own writing

29. The author of Passage 1 believes that
Fitzgerald's reputation as a writer rests on

(A) his original use of words
(B) his compelling narratives
(C) the suspensefulness of his plots
(D) his use of irony
(E) using bits and pieces to create coherent
stories

30. Passage 1 suggests that Amory, the main character of *This Side of Paradise*,

(A) is a serious and responsible person
(B) is a thinly disguised version of Fitzgerald
(C) represents all that Fitzgerald admired
(D) symbolizes what Fitzgerald wanted to be
(E) is a composite of people that Fitzgerald
knew

31. By hoping that people could read his books "blind like Braille" (lines 34 and 35), Fitzgerald meant that his writing was

    (A) vivid and sensual
    (B) deep and full of meaning
    (C) sophisticated and subtle
    (D) plain and direct
    (E) truthful and innocent

32. Throughout Passage 1, the writing of Fitzgerald is characterized as

    (A) egotistical
    (B) immature
    (C) phony
    (D) optimistic
    (E) deceptively easy to read

33. The author of Passage 2 relates the anecdote of the old woman and the diamond in order to

    (A) disturb Fitzgerald's readers
    (B) belittle Fitzgerald as a writer
    (C) clarify a mistaken view of Fitzgerald
    (D) suggest that Fitzgerald is preoccupied with wealth
    (E) explain an aspect of Fitzgerald's personality

34. The author's assertion that "Fitzgerald has been left with a jewel which he doesn't know quite what to do with" (lines 72 and 73) most nearly means that

    (A) Fitzgerald's exceptional talent as a writer needs polishing
    (B) Fitzgerald should take more writing courses
    (C) Fitzgerald's writing needs better editing
    (D) Fitzgerald will probably become a best-selling author
    (E) Fitzgerald is destined to become one of the great American writers

35. According to the author of Passage 2, *Sinister Street* can best be described as

    (A) highly inferior to *This Side of Paradise*
    (B) more engrossing than *This Side of Paradise*
    (C) a pale imitation of *This Side of Paradise*
    (D) an unfortunate model for *This Side of Paradise*
    (E) more realistic than *This Side of Paradise*

36. The author of Passage 2 bases much of his criticism of *Sinister Street* on the grounds that

    (A) the book's hero is sadly overemotional
    (B) its flowery prose overshadows its hero's story
    (C) it deals with a conventional subject
    (D) the book lacks wit and inventiveness
    (E) the novel will fail to interest most readers

37. *This Side of Paradise* is called "illiterate" (line 120) because it

    (A) is incoherent
    (B) uses slang
    (C) lacks substance
    (D) contains many errors
    (E) is trite

38. The authors of Passage 1 and Passage 2 agree that *This Side of Paradise*

    (A) suggests that Fitzgerald is a talented writer
    (B) is the worst of Fitzgerald's novels
    (C) is a blot on Fitzgerald's career
    (D) should have been rewritten
    (E) will have a wide audience despite its flaws

39. According to both Passage 1 and Passage 2, a major flaw of *This Side of Paradise* is its

    (A) one-dimensional characters
    (B) long-winded descriptions
    (C) moralizing
    (D) excessive wordiness
    (E) lack of artistic focus

40. Based on evidence found in Passage 1 and Passage 2, when were the two passages apparently written?

    (A) Both passages were written at about the same time, immediately after the publication of *This Side of Paradise*.
    (B) Both passages were written long after the publication of *This Side of Paradise*.
    (C) Both passages were written sometime between the publication of *This Side of Paradise* and the publication of Fitzgerald's next novel.
    (D) Passage 1 was written long after the publication of *This Side of Paradise*; Passage 2 was written shortly afterward.
    (E) Passage 1 was written shortly after the publication of *This Side of Paradise*; Passage 2 was written long afterward.

ANSWERS TO READING COMPREHENSION EXERCISES

LEVEL A

Reading Comprehension Exercise 1

1. C	5. E	9. C	13. D	17. B	21. A	25. D	29. C	33. E	37. C
2. D	6. D	10. D	14. B	18. C	22. B	26. E	30. B	34. D	38. C
3. C	7. C	11. B	15. E	19. D	23. A	27. D	31. C	35. D	39. B
4. C	8. D	12. D	16. E	20. C	24. B	28. E	32. A	36. D	40. A

Reading Comprehension Exercise 2

1. E	5. C	9. A	13. E	17. B	21. B	25. C	29. B	33. C	37. D
2. D	6. E	10. D	14. E	18. B	22. C	26. A	30. D	34. D	38. C
3. A	7. E	11. B	15. C	19. A	23. D	27. C	31. B	35. B	39. B
4. B	8. E	12. D	16. D	20. C	24. E	28. D	32. A	36. A	40. A

LEVEL B

Reading Comprehension Exercise 1

1. D	5. C	9. A	13. D	17. E	21. A	25. B	29. B	33. C	37. C
2. D	6. A	10. A	14. D	18. D	22. E	26. E	30. C	34. D	38. B
3. B	7. B	11. C	15. E	19. D	23. B	27. C	31. B	35. A	39. B
4. A	8. D	12. C	16. B	20. C	24. C	28. C	32. A	36. E	40. C

LEVEL C

Reading Comprehension Exercise 1

1. E	5. B	9. C	13. D	17. B	21. B	25. D	29. A	33. C	37. D
2. C	6. B	10. E	14. D	18. A	22. E	26. E	30. B	34. A	38. A
3. D	7. D	11. C	15. C	19. C	23. B	27. A	31. E	35. D	39. E
4. D	8. E	12. B	16. D	20. A	24. A	28. D	32. B	36. B	40. D

ANSWER EXPLANATIONS

LEVEL A

Reading Comprehension Exercise 1

1. **C**   Ovenden clearly approves of speculation (pondering; evolving theories by taking a fresh look at a subject or concept). However, he approves of purposeful speculation, speculation that has as its goal the discovery of new ways of looking at the universe. Pointless, idle, *empty* speculation or woolgathering he finds unscientific.

2. **D**   By asserting that "Speculation is its [science's] very lifeblood," Ovenden says that science cannot exist without speculation. Scientists must speculate, must evolve theories, must *form opinions about the data they gather.*

3. **C**   A mature science tries "to see relationships between previously unrelated aspects of the universe," that is, to *connect hitherto unlinked phenomena* in significant patterns or *meaningful ways.*

4. **C**   The similarities of the spectrums suggest the *possibility of vegetation* on Mars.

5. **E**   Use the process of elimination to find the correct answer to this question.
    • The author *makes an approximation*: he indicates the temperature zone in which life can exist is "about [*approximately*] 75,000,000 miles wide." Therefore, you can eliminate (A).
    • The author *uses a metaphor*: he implicitly compares speculation to blood. Therefore, you can eliminate (B).
    • The author *states a resemblance*: in the last sentence of the passage, he says "the infrared spectrum of the Martian markings has been found to be very similar to the spectrum of Earth vegetation." Therefore, you can eliminate (C).
    • The author *makes a conjecture* about the sort of life-forms "without a built-in temperature control" that might exist on Mars: in the last sentence of the next-to-last paragraph, he conjectures (guesses; speculates) they "may be a form of vegetation" that closes its leaves at night. Therefore, you can eliminate (D).
    • Only (E) is left. At no time does the author *deny a contradiction*. The correct answer is (E).

6. **D**   As the comment "I shall not soon forget that summer" (line 9) suggests, in this passage Du Bois shares his memories or *reminiscences* of what was *a memorable time* in his life.

7. **C**   To "learn from hearsay" is to learn not from one's own personal experience but from the comments of others. Why did Du Bois have to learn about hunting from hearsay and not from experiences? The comment in parentheses suggests the reason: his mother was terrified of guns. Therefore, we can assume that he had no chance to learn about hunting because *small arms weapons had been forbidden in his home.*

8. **D**   Use the process of elimination to answer this question.
    • Is Du Bois's journey through the countryside *gratifying* to him? Yes; he enjoys "the pleasures of the chase." Therefore, you can eliminate (A).
    • Does his journey seem *interminable* to him? Yes; the "miles stretch relentlessly ahead," never letting up. Therefore, you can eliminate (B).
    • Is his journey *tiring* to him? Yes; he feels "deep weariness of heart and limb." Therefore, you can eliminate (C).
    • Does his hunt for a school feel *discouraging* to him? Yes; he feels "his heart sink heavily" as he hears there is no job opening. Therefore, you can eliminate (E).
    • Is his journey a *carefree* one? No; throughout his journey he has the ongoing anxiety about when and where he will find a job. The correct answer is (D).

9. **C** Note the context in which "stage lines" appears. Du Bois has "wandered beyond railways, beyond stage lines" to the back country. The parallel structure suggests that stage lines, like railways, has to do with *transportation*, in this case with the *horse-drawn* form of transportation that took over when travelers went beyond the railroad's extent.

10. **D** To indicate he finds himself way out in the back country, Du Bois adopts a *colloquial*, down-home manner of speech, referring to pests or vermin as *varmints*, a term he would not customarily use.

11. **B** Looking back on those memorable "pleasures of the chase" (line 26), Du Bois clearly feels *nostalgia* for days gone by.

12. **D** Immediately on learning why Du Bois is in the vicinity, Josie "anxiously," eagerly tells him all about a potential school, stressing how "she herself longed to learn." Living in the backwoods, Josie would have been interested in meeting any stranger. However, her interest in meeting this stranger was increased when she learned his errand; that is, it was *intensified by her desire to gain an education.*

13. **D** Making "honest efforts to be decent and comfortable," scolding her husband and children if they do not work to improve their lot and live "like folks," Josie's mother shows her *longing for her entire family to better themselves.*

14. **B** In scolding her brothers roundly, Josie is being *blunt* or plainspoken.

15. **E** The author "grew to love" this family. Clearly, he regards them with *distinct affection.*

16. **E** The ancient Chinese view of life is described in the opening lines of the passage. People believed in the "mathematically precise order of the universe" and in the "forces that were harmoniously connected." In other words, life was structured *according to a well-defined philosophy.*

17. **B** By defining *feng-shui* as a "kind of cosmic surveying tool" (line 15), the author is saying that it *is used to locate building sites.*

18. **C** As described in lines 1–9 of the passage, the Tao *is a way of viewing the world.*

19. **D** The main reason for the development of *feng-shui* is to "affect an individual and his family for generations to come" (lines 12 and 13). Evidently, the Chinese believed in *providing for future generations.*

20. **C** The function of a geomancer, according to lines 43–46, was to *read and interpret the terrain.*

21. **A** According to lines 47–57, the best building sites were located between the Dragon (hilly ground) and the Tiger (low ground), that is, on terrain that is *partly flat and partly hilly.*

22. **B** Because the *feng-shui* compass is an elaborate instrument with a complicated design, the author compares its center to the bull's-eye of a familiar dartboard in order to *clarify its appearance* for the reader.

23. **A** Lines 54–57 of the passage describe the setting of Beijing. The city is located where the valley floor begins to slope upward to the *mountains.*

24. **B** The use of *feng-shui* in selecting a homesite is intended to protect the residents from misfortune. However, the family, according to lines 77–83, must also be moral and upright because an ideally situated home *is no guarantee of good fortune.*

25. **D** Believers in *feng-shui* attentively care for the gardens surrounding their homes, since the various features of the gardens contribute to the well-being of the home and *contain symbolic meanings.*

26. **E** The author describes *feng-shui* objectively, as though the concept has aroused his *intellectual curiosity.*

27. **D** Adherents of *feng-shui* heed the presence of boulders (line 59), design proper access to the main entrance of the house (lines 100–108), consider the placement of trees (line 86) and the shape of nearby mountains (line 58). Only *the color of the house* is not mentioned.

28. **E** The passage states that the condition of poor people reduces the "possibility of . . . participation in the larger economic system," made up, for example, of labor unions, political parties, and welfare agencies. Nonparticipation *isolates* the poor *from the mainstream of society.*

29. **C** A "culture" may be defined as a group of people sharing a specific set of beliefs and values, customs, and traditions. The phrase "culture of poverty," therefore, signifies a group for whom poverty *has become a prevailing way of life.*

30. **B** By pointing out that the potential for protest and for being used in political movements resides in the culture of poverty, the author is indirectly citing *a reason for eliminating poverty* from our society.

31. **C** People in the culture of poverty, despite their intentions, cannot live up to the middle-class values they espouse mainly because they are *unable to change the conditions of their lives* as much as they may wish to.

32. **A** The discussion of marriage contains several *practical and economic* reasons why poor men and women avoid legal marriages. Men, for one, don't want "expense and legal difficulties." Women want to maintain "exclusive rights to a house or any other property."

33. **E** The metaphor suggests the similarity between *poverty and imprisonment.*

34. **D** Because the speaker talks about the smell of the outdoor privy and about burying the garbage in the ground, she appears to live *in the country.* However, she worries about her sons being influenced by bad companions. Thus, she is unlikely to live on an isolated farm (where her sons would not have other boys living nearby to influence them).

35. **D** Although all the listed emotions are evident in the passage, *hopelessness* and despair are prevalent. Near the end, the speaker actually says, "I have come out of my despair to tell you this."

36. **D** The silence of the poor reaffirms their sense of despair. They feel *powerless* to alter their condition. Therefore, they listen but don't say anything.

37. **C** The last paragraph summarizes the speaker's intent—to *arouse the audience into action:* "Look at us with an angry heart, anger that will help you help me."

38. **C** Each of the choices describes Passage 2. The quality of the passage to which the audience is most likely to respond, however, is that the speaker herself *shows intense emotion.*

39. **B** Both authors show that poverty *means more than lack of money.* Passage 1 stresses the whole "culture of poverty." Passage 2 highlights the smells, the weariness, and the hopelessness that accompany poverty.

40. **A** The speaker in Passage 2 says she has had no money to fix the refrigerator, to buy a shovel, to purchase iron pills, and so forth. Each of these examples indicate a *chronic shortage of cash.*

Reading Comprehension Exercise 2

1. **E** Her father scorned her successes in the world outside the home because he felt "undermined by" her clear surrender or "capitulation to the ways of the West." She had given in to Western ways, disobeying his wishes. Thus, *he felt her Westernization was costing him his authority over her.*

2. **D** In her Japanese home, *her immediate family* (including her Westernized brothers) customarily *referred to* Caucasians by using the Japanese term *Hakujin.* In explaining the conflicts she experienced as someone caught between two cultures, she uses the Japanese term for its authenticity.

3. **A** The author was careful not to show her aggressiveness and assertiveness to her father because these traits were unacceptable to him. Rather, he expected his daughter to be *tranquil* (calm; serene) *and passive* (submissive; not initiating action).

4. **B** "Not seeing" refers to the white boys' inability to see the author as she truly was. Instead of seeing the actual Japanese-American adolescent girl, with her worries about fitting in with her friends and her embarrassment about her father's conservatism, they saw a stereotypical Oriental *geisha,* someone straight out of a paperback fantasy. Clearly, *they had no idea what she was like as an individual human being.*

5. **C** The term "double standard" generally refers to male-female roles, and to the different expectations society has for male and female behavior. In referring to her "double identity within a 'double standard,'" the author indicates that she was *Japanese at home* and Hakujin *outside the home.*

6. **E** *Madame Butterfly,* the heroine of the opera of that name, is a classic example of submissive, obedient Japanese womanhood. Thus, over the years, she has grown from a simple literary figure to become (like Stowe's Uncle Tom or Puzo's Godfather) *an ethnic stereotype.*

7. **E** The last sentence of the passage states that the author "was not comfortable in either role" she had to play. In other words, her reaction to these roles was primarily one of discomfort or *unease.*

8. **E**   To be riddled with lacunae (that is, gaps or holes) is to be permeated with holes, *filled* with holes, the way a sieve is full of holes.

9. **A**   There are major gaps in our knowledge of pre-Spanish history in Mexico. Thus, our knowledge is *incomplete*.

10. **D**   Use the process of elimination to answer this question.
- While the passage states art in the period "served a religious function," the passage stresses the art itself, not the religious basis for the art. Therefore, you can eliminate (A).
- Though the early Mexican artists excelled in decorative composition, they created sculptures that went far beyond mere decoration. Therefore, you can eliminate (B).
- The author states that Mexican art "is comparable to" great Chinese art, rivals Egyptian art, foreshadows modern European art. He does not say it exceeds or surpasses European and Asian art. Therefore, you can eliminate (C).
- The author never discusses modern Mexican art. Therefore, you can eliminate (E).
- Throughout the passage, particularly in the final two paragraphs, the author cites masterpiece after masterpiece of pre-Spanish Mexican art. The correct answer is (D).

11. **B**   The author insists that the "bold simplifications or wayward conceptions" of early Mexican art were the result of creative decisions made by skilled artists and not the unfortunate consequences of sloppy technique. Thus, these supposed distortions were *deliberate* (intentional).

12. **D**   In marveling at the artist's plastic feeling, the author is awed by the sculptor's feel for carving and shaping works of art. In other words, the author feels *admiration for both the artist's technical expertise and artistic sensibility*.

13. **E**   The passage is discussing the Mexican artists' gift for sculpture, for fashioning or *shaping objects* into works or art. That is the sense in which "modeling" is used here.

14. **E**   The author refers to the "surprising . . . modernity" of early Mexican sculpture. He indicates these works "anticipate" more modern, and therefore *more familiar* to the reader, works by Brancusi, Lehmbruck, and Moore.

15. **C**   The emphasis on sculpture (masks, reclining figures, statuettes) suggests that much of Mexican art depicted *people*.

16. **D**   The first paragraph of the passage says that the administration of every president has ended with "recriminations and mistrust." Presidents, like everyone else, hate to be criticized in public. Therefore, they all have experienced *hostility between themselves and the press*.

17. **B**   Conflict between the president and the press is the "best proof" (line 11) that *freedom of the press is alive and well in the United States*.

18. **B**   In the days of the Founding Fathers, there was an expectation that the press would act "like a watchdog" (lines 20 and 21) that would *carefully observe and report on the work of all elected officials*.

19. **A**   The relationship between the press and the presidency has become increasingly complicated by changes in the nature of the presidency (lines 26–36), including the creation of the position of Press Secretary and the fact that the president is a world leader. The press itself now includes television, and reporters from all over the world cover the president. What hasn't altered the relationship between the press and the president is the fact that *the president's term of office has remained four years*.

20. **C**   The author advises the reader (lines 40 and 41) "not to view the past in terms of our own times" because to do so violates the historical context. In other words, *we can't fully grasp the context of the past*.

21. **B**   Basic to the beliefs of the colonists was that "whoever controlled the printing press was in the best position to control the minds of men" (lines 59–61), which meant that *the press influenced what people thought and did*.

22. **C**   The printing press endowed authorities of the church and state with unparalleled power to control the thoughts and actions of the people. Before Gutenberg's invention, then, *governments played a less influential role in people's lives*.

23. **D**   Early on, both the church and the state realized the power inherent in the printing press. It was to their mutual advantage to have a printing press set up in South America as quickly as possible. Using the printing press, the state gained control of territory, and the church *spread the word of God*.

24. **E** The passage says that in North America secular publishing "was soon dominant" (line 96). In other words, printing *quickly became less religious in nature.*

25. **C** The quotation by Berkeley suggests that the governor of Virginia took a dim view of antichurch activities, including printing anything that criticized the church. Evidently, he *held the church above other institutions,* including the government he served.

26. **A** Those who agree with Berkeley would support his general view *that limits should be set on freedom of the press.*

27. **C** The passage says that some twentieth-century people agree with Berkeley's sentiments about the free press. Issues of free press, even today *raise controversy in the United States.*

28. **D** In the last sentence of the first paragraph the author explains why the Grand Canyon is the "sublimest thing on earth." It is sublime "by virtue of the whole—its *ensemble,*" or its *overall appearance.*

29. **B** The first paragraph implies that the *Grand Canyon's incomparable size* is what is likely to impress a visitor. Only after long and careful study do observers begin to understand that the canyon has more to offer than magnitude. The distinctive quality of its overall appearance—its *ensemble,* in the author's words—lends it majesty.

30. **D** Lines 16–39 explain the author's view that *the Grand Canyon transcends the common notion of the word* canyon. The Grand Canyon is markedly different from other places we call *canyons.*

31. **B** To heighten the contrast between the Grand Canyon and ordinary canyons, the author makes a contrast between St. Mark's and a "rude (that is, crude) dwelling" on the frontier. Since a frontier dwelling is apt to be primitive and unadorned, this suggests that St. Mark's must be a refined, *ornate structure.*

32. **A** The passage calls the Grand Canyon an "expansion of the simple type of drainage channels peculiar to Plateau Country," implying that *large canyons at one time were very small.* Earlier in the passage the author cited the example of a huge building. It, too, is an expansion—an enlargement of a small house.

33. **C** As described in the third paragraph, the rain *promotes the growth of vegetation,* described as "a veil of green." The rain also prepares the ground "for another planting."

34. **D** The last of the sun's light dissipates or *vanishes* as darkness falls.

35. **B** To the author, the coming of the rains changes the world, transforming the desert into a *revitalized* landscape filled with creatures mating and giving birth. This transformation fills him with *awe.*

36. **A** Several distinctive qualities of the spadefoot toad are mentioned. The toads chant throughout the night. The female toads "spew out egg masses" as they reproduce. The male toads "bellow," in their characteristic mating call, and their "burnt-peanut-like" odor fills the air. Only the *relative size* of the toad is not mentioned in the passage.

37. **D** To most people, the youngster's reply "is a contradiction." In other words, it seems *paradoxical* to them that a desert could smell like rain.

38. **C** In describing the Grand Canyon, the author uses only his sense of *sight.*

39. **B** The author of Passage 2 writes in the first person. He recounts his *personal experiences* with rainshowers, with toads and turtles, and with members of the Papago tribe. The author of Passage 1, on the other hand, while equally passionate about his subject, removes himself from the writing. Both authors write poetically, using figures of speech, and both respect nature's wonders. The author of Passage 2 clearly includes far less geological data than does the author of Passage 1.

40. **A** Except for the facts and figures of the first paragraph, Passage 1 lacks the *concrete* details of Passage 2. The author of Passage 1 writes in more *abstract* language about the nature of canyons and the uniqueness of the Grand Canyon. Passage 2, in contrast, is filled with specific down-to-earth images of the sights and sounds of the desert, from the "veil of green" of nascent vegetation to the incessant chanting of the spadefoot toads.

LEVEL B

Reading Comprehension Exercise 1

1. **D**   To pretend that Indians are a primitive people is to choose to see them as unlettered and barbaric. To view them as a "first" or primal people is to choose to see them as linked to ancient truths. Thus, to the author, the distinction between "primitive" and "primal" is that, *while the former has some negative connotations, the latter has neutral or positive ones.*

2. **D**   Matthiessen rejects those who would patronizingly dismiss Indian spirituality as simple hearted (or simpleminded) in any way. Thus, he puts *animism* and *naturalism* in quotes because *he disagrees with their being applied* to something as profound as the Indian concept of earth and spirit.

3. **B**   In the first and third paragraphs, Matthiessen is making assertions about the nature of Indian spirituality. In the second paragraph, however, he moves away from the subject of religion to exploring various theories of Indian origins in North America. Thus, the second paragraph is a *digression from the argument* made in the opening and closing paragraphs of the passage.

4. **A**   Refusing to adopt a patronizing or condescending attitude toward Indian religion, comparing it to the most venerated or revered religions of the world, Matthiessen clearly views Indian religion with *respect.*
   (B) is incorrect. Though Matthiessen has great respect for Indian religion, his attachment to it is not so immoderate as to be termed *idolatry* (giving absolute religious devotion to something that is not actually God, for example, a physical object or man-made image).

5. **C**   Sages in their wisdom *understand* or apprehend the universe's true nature.

6. **A**   A miracle is by definition an act or event so extraordinary that it seems a manifestation of God's supernatural power. Thus, to call the ordinary, common acts of every day miraculous is to be self-contradictory or *paradoxical.*

7. **B**   Lines 4 and 5 of the passage say that the hierarchy consists of the troop's *males.*

8. **D**   Lines 9–11 of the passage say that, in primate troops, males "defend, control, and lead the troop." Therefore, the troops are *dominated by adult males.*

9. **A**   The passage says that the strong social bond in the troop is maintained for safety (line 12). Therefore, it is meant to *protect the members of the troop.*

10. **A**   According to lines 13 and 14, "chimpanzees lack a stable social troop." Rather, they form temporary groups (lines 16 and 17). Therefore, unlike other primates, chimpanzees *are not bound to troops.*

11. **C**   The second paragraph of the passage contrasts the social organization of chimpanzees and the social organization of other primates. Clearly, *chimpanzees are different.*

12. **C**   The discussion of chimpanzee social organization (lines 21–24) implies that each chimpanzee develops *a distinct personality.*

13. **D**   The two social structures differ markedly in *the amount of individual freedom afforded to members.* In a rigidly hierarchical society, individuals must adjust their behaviors to those of the troop. In a flexible society, individuals have more freedom to follow their personal desires.

14. **D**   Population size, according to lines 72–76, is partly controlled by *the size of the food supply.*

15. **E**   The Budongo Forest is called a "continuous habitat" (lines 80 and 81) in which several *regional populations of chimpanzees have developed.*

16. **B**   The opening paragraph of the passage describes the goal of the project. The project's objective is not to use a new research method but to use a different technique in order to *develop a new theory about the causes of war.*

17. **E**   The reason given in lines 2–6 for reversing the customary research method is that *existing theories fail to coincide with facts.*

18. **D**   Although the phrase has a negative ring, the author explains that all definitions are "somewhat arbitrary." Therefore, *the scholars had no better alternatives.*

19. **D**   The author takes pains to describe the care with which the researchers defined the terms of the study. Of particular note is that the researchers drew up their definitions "before arriving at their conclusions" (lines 21 and 22) so that they would keep *personal bias out of their study.*

20. **C**   By looking up the assertions of the street corner preacher in *The Wages of War,* one can check the facts. Ultimately, the author is suggesting, *facts speak louder than opinions.*

21. **A**   The next step taken by the researchers was "to identify conditions or events... associated with wars" (lines 45–47) because of the assumption that there have been certain *political and social conditions that have often led to war.*

22. **E**   The basic premise of the study is that there may be correlations of conditions or events that often lead to war. Seeking correlations is the basic *research method used by the participants* in the study.

23. **B**   The author argues that correlations do not necessarily constitute proof (lines 66–69). With so many variables at play in the conditions and events leading to war, *correlations may be misinterpreted.*

24. **C**   Lines 74–77 raise the possibility that the project may find that there is insufficient evidence to warrant a final theory of war. In other words, in spite of the participants' best intentions, the findings *may fail to produce definitive results.*

25. **B**   The discussion of Bismarck and Hitler (lines 83–94) is presented as an example of a potential problem. Because of faulty design (e.g., a definition of *war*), one or more conclusions can be dead wrong. Consequently, the *research design and procedure may invalidate the findings.*

26. **E**   Despite problems and flaws in "The Correlates of War" project, the author still maintains—in the last lines of the passage—that the study is *the best of its kind.*

27. **C**   Regardless of his doubts about some research techniques being used by the scholars engaged in the project, the author takes a generally positive position regarding the outcomes of the project. He is largely *optimistic and hopeful.*

28. **C**   The man "with his eyes fixed on the ground" is the artist who "searches." To Picasso, the search means nothing in painting. *Artists who contemplate their subjects too much* before painting may have good intentions, but they are likely to fail. After all, results, not intentions, count.

29. **B**   Picasso's statement is a *denial of the accusation* that the principal objective of his work is "the spirit of research," discussed in lines 12–15.

30. **C**   The idea that art *gives us more than truth; it gives us understanding* is made clear by the statement "Art is a lie that makes us realize truth, at least the truth that is given us to understand" (lines 22–24).

31. **B**   Picasso says that his object in art is to show what he has found, not what he was looking for. Therefore, in Picasso's opinion a successful piece of art *reveals what the artist has found.*

32. **A**   The word "naturalism" in this context means *realism.* Realists in art, as the name suggests, try to recreate as accurately as they can three-dimensional objects on a two-dimensional surface, an impossible undertaking in Picasso's view. As he writes, "Nature and art . . . cannot be the same thing."

33. **C**   Much of the passage describes Picasso's *innovations,* such as "freeing the technique of painting from its slavish adherence to the description of nature" and making the painter "a free creator, a poet."

34. **D**   The passage explains that, once Picasso burst onto the art scene, the *strict rules of art* no long applied. Among other things, Picasso broke with such past traditions as "obeying only the laws of the artist's inner vision" and painting with "slavish adherence to the description of nature."

35. **A**   Picasso gave painting "new laws of harmony and balance," but he was careful not to *ignore the need for harmony and balance.*

36. **E**   The notion that *patching up a picture restricts artists' freedom of expression* is supported by the paragraph beginning on line 95. When an artist has "no regard for the nature of anything he has painted before," he has the "freedom to move at will in the boundless spaces of free expression."

37. **C**   Throughout Passage 2, but particularly in the last paragraph, Picasso is portrayed as a *bold experimenter.* For example, the author says Picasso tested the foundations on which his own art rested.

38. **B**   Eluard's phrase reminds us of Picasso's statement in Passage 1 that "*my object is to show what I have found.*" In other words, Picasso wants to see objects anew, with fresh eyes, or to "attain sight."

39. **B**   Both passages allude to Picasso's "aphorism," that the artist "*does not seek, but finds*": In Passage 1, see the first paragraph; in Passage 2, see lines 86 and 87.

40. **C**   Passage 2 is an appreciation of Picasso as artist. Throughout Passage 1, Picasso defends himself from false accusations and clarifies misconceptions about art. The tone of Passage 1, therefore, is more contentious, *more argumentative* than the tone of Passage 2.

LEVEL C

Reading Comprehension Exercise 1

1. **E**   Both paragraphs *humorously portray the female residents* of Cranford, describing at length their idiosyncrasies of dress and behavior.

2. **C**   In stating that "whatever does become of the gentlemen, they are not at Cranford," the author indicates that the men are distinguished chiefly by their *absence*.

3. **D**   The "tender good offices [performed for] each other whenever they are in distress" are the kind *acts done* by the good ladies of Cranford *on behalf of others* needing their help.

4. **D**   In showing both the eccentricities and the virtues that characterize the ladies of Cranford, the author exhibits an attitude that is *mocking*, but only *gently* so.

5. **B**   Note the context in which the author refers to "Miss Tyler, of cleanly memory." The author has just been talking about the unfashionable attire of Cranford ladies, emphasizing that their clothes are made of good (that is, long-lasting) material. The Cranford ladies wear their clothes for years, but they are scrupulous about keeping them clean. In this they resemble Miss Tyler, known for her *spotless attire.*

6. **B**   Since the bulk of the last paragraph concerns the ladies' eccentricities of dress and indifference to current fashion, it can be inferred that "the last gigot" most likely is *an outmoded article of apparel* (leg-of-mutton sleeve) worn well after its time by the unfashionable ladies of Cranford.

7. **D**   Arbitrarily ready to decide issues "without troubling themselves with unnecessary reasons," dictatorial or overbearing to their dependents, and quite able to do without men, the ladies of Cranford do not seem in the least *submissive* (yielding).

8. **E**   By providing background on how the theory of a dynamic abyss came to take hold in the scientific community and on how the forces that activate the global patterns of ocean currents actually work, the passage serves to *summarize evidence supporting oceanic circulation.*

9. **C**   The opening sentence states that "many investigators were initially reluctant" to accept the evidence in favor of this controversial hypothesis. Committed to the belief that the depths of the ocean were calm ("the notion of a tranquil abyss"), these scientists at first viewed the idea that the abyss could be dynamic with *marked skepticism* (distinct doubt).

10. **E**   The passage states that the *first* argument for the existence of dynamic currents in the deeps came from theory, based on "*models* of ocean circulation" involving the tendency of cold water to sink.

11. **C**   The weathering of rocks is the source of detritus (debris; fragmented rock particles). These bits of debris are produced by the elements' gradual *wearing away* of the rocks, which disintegrates them over time.

12. **B**   Both minute particles of rock and grains of wind-blown soil belong to the first type of sediment discussed ("detritus whose source is the weathering of rocks on continents and islands"). Only the *fragmentary shells* of dead microscopic organisms belong to the second type.

13. **D**   Because they need to take into account the effects of strong sea-floor currents on the structures they plan to build, *designers of sea-floor structures* are most likely to be interested in this particular article.

14. **D**   The authors approximate an amount ("about three billion tons per year"), refer to a model of ocean circulation, give several examples ("such as the..."), and list evidence to support a theory. They never *propose a solution* to a problem.

15. **C**   The authors are objective and factual. Their style can best be described as *espository* (explanatory).

16. **D** The author asks this question, not because readers don't know what money is, but because he wishes them to consider a definition different from the usual one. By the end of the paragraph the author *introduces an unfamiliar* (to most readers) *definition of the word*.

17. **B** At the beginning of the second paragraph the author writes that "Three such functions are usually specified," which amounts to saying that these three functions are *common knowledge among informed people*.

18. **A** The sticker price on a car informs prospective buyers of the cost, or value, of the car. Therefore, the sticker price qualifies as *a unit of account*, as defined in lines 23–27.

19. **C** The definition of "archetype" is a pattern or model on which others are based. Consequently, barter *is a model for economic exchanges*.

20. **A** In line 46 the author says that bartering required "large amounts of time." The expenditure of time is reiterated in lines 53 and 54. Clearly, the chief shortcoming of barter is that *making deals is too time-consuming*.

21. **B** A Gordian knot, an allusion to an ancient Greek myth, has come to refer to anything that is difficult to untie or unravel. Hence, *it was difficult to change the barter system to a monetary system*.

22. **E** The passage cites several advantages of money over barter: the double coincidence of wants is eliminated by a monetary system (lines 63–68); when money is the medium of exchange, the cost of doing business is lower (lines 68–70); supply and demand determine the cost of goods and services (70–72)—a basic principle of economics; and in a monetary system a greater division of labor is possible (72–75), which increases efficiency.

   Only (E), *opportunities of advantageous trade are reduced,* is not mentioned in the passage.

23. **B** According the passage, "The usefulness of money is inversely proportional to the number of currencies in circulation" (lines 77–79). In other words, the presence of a large number of currencies *reduces the efficiency of the international economy*.

24. **A** Line 96 of the passage indicates that one of the benefits of a single national currency is a *reduction in the cost of monetary transactions*.

25. **D** After citing several reasons for streamlining the international economy by reducing the number of currencies, the next logical step is to create a single world currency. The author, however, demurs from proposing that step because, as the remainder of the passage explains, *the most obvious solution is not the best solution*.

26. **E** The one most desirable benefit to be derived from a single world currency, which the author reiterates throughout the discussion, is *reducing transaction costs*.

27. **A** The conclusion to be drawn from all the arguments about a single world currency, particularly the high cost of introducing a single standard, is that *it may cause more problems than it will solve*.

28. **D** Passage 1 says that in *This Side of Paradise*, Fitzgerald managed to turn a mass of diverse material "into a sustained narrative" (line 15), indicating that Fitzgerald knew how to *tell a long story*.

29. **A** Passage 1 says that "freshness of language" (lines 19 and 20) is Fitzgerald's "identifying mark." In other words, Fitzgerald built his reputation on *his original use of words*.

30. **B** The author of Passage 1 claims that *This Side of Paradise* helped "Fitzgerald thrash out those 'ideas still in riot' that he attributes to Amory" (lines 24–27). Amory, therefore, seems to be a *thinly disguised version of Fitzgerald* himself—a young man trying to find himself and make sense of life.

31. **E** In Passage 1, Fitzgerald's words are quoted in the context of a discussion of the "naiveté and honesty" of his work. The quotation confirms that Fitzgerald's writing is characteristically *truthful and innocent*.

32. **B** The entire passage describes the problems of Fitzgerald's *immature* writing. In comparison to the writing in Fitzgerald's earlier work, the writing in *This Side of Paradise* had "improved greatly" (line 17). Nevertheless, the author of the passage still regarded Fitzgerald as an "ambitious amateur" (line 44).

33. **C** The paragraph following the anecdote rebuts *a mistaken view of Fitzgerald*. Lines 63–70 portray Fitzgerald as anything but a "stupid old woman."

34. **A**   The "jewel" refers to Fitzgerald's exceptional talent with words. Talent is not enough, however. *Fitzgerald's talent needed polishing.*

35. **D**   Stating that *This Side of Paradise* "is not only highly imitative but…imitates an inferior model" (lines 82–84), the author indicates that *Sinister Street* was an *unfortunate* choice for a *model* on which Fitzgerald might base his book.

36. **B**   The author describes how the hero of *Sinister Street* is "swamped in the forest of descriptions" (lines 98 and 99). The author of the novel uses so many flowery descriptive phrases that the reader cannot keep track of the novel's plot. In other words, his pretty writing or *flowery prose overshadows* the *hero's story.*

37. **D**   One reason, among others explained in lines 121–125, that the author calls Fitzgerald's novel "illiterate" is that it *contains many errors* that should have been caught by the publisher's proofreader.

38. **A**   Despite the flaws of *This Side of Paradise*, the authors of both passages apparently recognize *Fitzgerald's talent as a writer.* More specifically, Passage 1 concludes with the words "Fitzgerald had found his craft." Passage 2 says that Fitzgerald has "imagination" (line 74) and a "gift for expression" (line 77).

39. **E**   Passage 1 describes *This Side of Paradise* as "clumsy and pasted together" (line 4). Passage 2 says the book has "no dominating intention to endow it with unity and force" (lines 110–112). Both criticisms refer to the book's *lack of artistic focus.*

40. **D**   Passage 1 was written long after Fitzgerald became an important literary figure, long after his death, in fact. The author speaks of Fitzgerald in the past tense: "All his life he was to think of himself . . ." (lines 6–10), etc. Passage 2 discusses Fitzgerald as a figure on the contemporary scene: "Scott Fitzgerald is, in fact, . . . a very good-looking young man . . ." (lines 67 and 68). It also suggests that *This Side of Paradise* illustrates Fitzgerald's talent as a writer, but that his work still needs improvement. The evidence in both passages shows that *Passage 1 was written long after the publication of* This Side of Paradise; *Passage 2 was written shortly afterward.*

PART V

BUILDING YOUR VOCABULARY

Overview
Tips on Building Your
  Vocabulary
SAT High-Frequency
  Word List

OVERVIEW

Recognizing the meaning of words is essential to comprehending what you read. The more you stumble over unfamiliar words in a text, the more you have to take time out to look up words in your dictionary, the more likely you are to wind up losing track of what the author has to say.

To succeed in college, you must develop a college-level vocabulary. You must familiarize yourself with technical words in a wide variety of fields, mastering each field's special vocabulary. You must learn to use these words, and re-use them until they become second nature to you. The time you put in now learning vocabulary-building techniques for this exam will pay off later on, and not just on the SAT.

This section provides you with a fundamental tool that will help you build your vocabulary: Barron's SAT High-Frequency Word List.

No matter how little time you have before you take the SAT, you can familiarize yourself with the sort of vocabulary you will be facing on the test.

Look over the words on our SAT High-Frequency Word List: each of these words, ranging from everyday words such as *abstract* and *objective* to less common ones such as *abstruse* and *iconoclast*, has appeared (as answer choices or as question words) from five to thirty times on SAT and SAT I tests published through 2003. Notice that the words have been divided into groups of ten so you won't be overwhelmed.

Not only will looking over the SAT High-Frequency Word List reassure you that you do know some SAT-type words, but also it will help you on the actual day of the test. These words have turned up on recent tests: some of them may turn up on the test you take. Look over these words. Review any of them that are unfamiliar to you. Try using these words on your parents and friends. Then, if the words do turn up on your test, feel confident: your knowledge of them will help you come up with the correct answers or eliminate incorrect answer choices.

TIPS ON BUILDING YOUR VOCABULARY

TIP 1
READ WIDELY TO DEVELOP YOUR FEELING FOR WORDS

There is only one effective long-range strategy for vocabulary building: READ.

Read—widely and well. Sample different fields—physics, art history, political science, geology—and different styles. Extensive reading is the one sure way to make your vocabulary grow and to develop your feeling for words.

The Sunday edition of *The New York Times* contains special sections on science, literature, and the arts. Tuesday's edition contains a special science section as well. *The Washington Post* and *The Christian Science Monitor* offer excellent coverage of the arts and sciences, as well as current events.

Try to develop an interest in as many fields as you can. Sample some of the quality magazines: *The New Yorker, Smithsonian, Scientific American, Natural History, Harper's, Newsweek, Time.* In these magazines, you'll find articles on the whole range of fields touched on by the SAT. If you take time to acquaint yourself with the contents of these magazines, you'll soon be in command of an expanding vocabulary.

USE MEMORY TRICKS TO KEEP NEW WORDS IN YOUR ACTIVE VOCABULARY

Reading widely does not always help you remember the words you read. You may have the words in your passive vocabulary and be able to recognize them when you see them in a particular context and yet be unable to define them clearly or think of additional contexts for them.

Remembering words takes work. It also takes wit. You can spend hours memorizing dictionary definitions and get no place. Try capitalizing on your native intelligence by thinking up mnemonic devices—memory tricks—to help you remember new words.

Consider the word *hovel*. A hovel is a dirty, mean house. How can you remember that? *Hovel* rhymes with *shovel*. You need to shovel out the hovel to live in it. Rhymes can help you remember what words mean.

Now consider the word *hover*. To hover is to hang fluttering in the air or to wait around. Can rhyme help you here? *Hover* rhymes with *cover*. That doesn't seem to work. However, take another look at *hover*. Cut off the letter *h* and you're left with the word *over*. If a helicopter hovers over an accident, it hangs in the air; if a mother hovers over a sick child, she waits around to care for it. Hidden little words can help you remember bigger words.

Try the hidden word trick with a less familiar word than hover. Take the word *credulous*, which means gullible or easily fooled. A credulous person will give money to someone who wants to sell him the Brooklyn Bridge. Now look closely at *credulous*. What little word is hidden within it? The hidden word is *red*. What happens when a person finds out he's been taken for a fool? Often, the poor fool turns red. *Credulous, red* in the face. There's your memory trick.

WORK THROUGH THE SAT HIGH-FREQUENCY WORD LIST TO EXPAND YOUR COLLEGE-LEVEL VOCABULARY

Take time to acquaint yourself specifically with the sorts of words you must know to do well on the SAT. Follow the procedures outlined below in order to work through the SAT High-Frequency List most profitably.

1. Select a list of ten words.
2. Allot a definite time each day to study the list.
3. Devote at least half an hour to the list.
4. First go through the list looking at the short, simple-looking words (7 letters at most). Mark those you don't know. In studying, pay particular attention to them.
5. Go through the list again, looking at the longer words. Pay particular attention to words with more than one meaning and to familiar-looking words that turn out to have unusual definitions that surprise you. Study these secondary definitions.
6. List unusual words on index cards that you can shuffle and review from time to time. (Study no more than 5 cards at a time.)
7. Use the illustrative sentences as models and make up new sentences of your own.
8. In making up new sentences, use familiar examples and be concrete: the junior high school band tuning up sounds *discordant*; in *Beauty and the Beast*, until Belle tames him, the Beast has a *volatile* temper.

For each word in the SAT High-Frequency List, the following is provided:

1. The word (printed in heavy type).
2. Its part of speech (abbreviated).
3. A brief definition.
4. A sentence illustrating the word's use.
5. Whenever appropriate, related words, together with their parts of speech.

The word list is arranged in alphabetical order.

SAT HIGH-FREQUENCY WORD LIST

Word List 1

abate   V. subside or moderate. Rather than leaving immediately, they waited for the storm to *abate*. abatement, N.

aberrant   ADJ. abnormal or deviant. Given the *aberrant* nature of the data, we came to doubt the validity of the entire experiment.

abrasive   ADJ. rubbing away; tending to grind down. Just as *abrasive* cleaning powders can wear away a shiny finish, *abrasive* remarks can wear away a listener's patience. abrade, V.

abridge   V. condense or shorten. Because the publishers felt the public wanted a shorter version of *War and Peace*, they proceeded to *abridge* the novel.

absolute   ADJ. complete; totally unlimited; certain. Although the King of Siam was an *absolute* monarch, he did not want to behead his unfaithful wife without *absolute* evidence of her infidelity.

abstemious   ADJ. sparing in eating and drinking; temperate. Concerned whether her vegetarian son's *abstemious* diet provided him with sufficient protein, the worried mother pressed food on him.

abstract   ADJ. theoretical; not concrete; nonrepresentational. To him, hunger was an *abstract* concept; he had never missed a meal.

abstruse   ADJ. obscure; profound; difficult to understand. She carried around *abstruse* works of philosophy, not because she understands them but because she wants her friends to think she does.

accessible   ADJ. easy to approach; obtainable. We asked our guide whether the ruins were *accessible* on foot.

acclaim   V. applaud; announce with great approval. The NBC sportscasters *acclaimed* every American victory in the Olympics and lamented every American defeat. acclamation, acclaim, N.

Word List 2

accolade   N. award of merit. In the world of public relations, a "Clio" is the highest *accolade* an advertising campaign can receive.

acknowledge   V. recognize; admit. Although I *acknowledge* that the Beatles' tunes sound pretty dated nowadays, I still prefer them to the "gangsta" rap songs my brothers play.

acquiesce   V. assent; agree without protesting. When we asked her to participate in the play, she immediately *acquiesced*. acquiescence, N.; acquiescent, ADJ.

acrimonious   ADJ. bitter in words or manner. The candidate attacked his opponent in highly *acrimonious* terms. acrimony, N.

acute   ADJ. quickly perceptive; keen; brief and severe. The *acute* young doctor realized immediately that the gradual deterioration of her patient's once-*acute* hearing was due to a chronic illness, not an *acute* one.

address   V. direct a speech to; deal with or discuss. Due to *address* the convention in July, Brown planned to *address* the issue of low-income housing in his speech.

adherent   N. supporter; follower. In the wake of the scandal, the senator's one-time *adherents* quietly deserted him.

adjacent   ADJ. neighboring; adjoining. You will find questions based on this reading passage located on the *adjacent* page.

adroit   ADJ. skillful; nimble. The juggler's admirers particularly enjoyed his *adroit* handling of difficult balancing tricks.

adulation   N. flattery; admiration. The rock star relished the *adulation* she received from her groupies and yes-men.

Word List 3

adversary   N. opponent. The young wrestler struggled to overcome his *adversary*.

adverse   ADJ. unfavorable; hostile. The recession had a highly *adverse* effect on Father's investment portfolio: he lost so much money that he could no longer afford the butler and the upstairs maid. adversity, N.

advocate   V. urge; plead for. Noted abolitionists such as Frederick Douglass and Sojourner Truth *advocated* the eradication of the Southern institution of slavery. also N.

aesthetic   ADJ. artistic; dealing with or capable of appreciation of the beautiful. The beauty of Tiffany's stained glass appealed to Esther's *aesthetic* sense. aesthete, N.

affable   ADJ. easily approachable; warmly friendly. Accustomed to cold, aloof supervisors, Nicholas was amazed at how *affable* his new employer was.

affinity   N. natural liking; kinship; similarity. Octavia felt an immediate *affinity* for the folk dancers she met; their love of dance was hers as well.

affirmation   N. positive assertion; confirmation; solemn pledge by one who refuses to take an oath. Despite Tom's *affirmations* of innocence, Aunt Polly still suspected he had eaten the pie.

aggressor   N. attacker. Before you punish both boys for fighting, see whether you can determine which one was the *aggressor*.

alienate   V. make hostile; separate. Heather's attempts to *alienate* Amy from Ellen failed because the two friends had complete faith in one another.

alleviate   V. relieve. The doctor's reassuring remarks *alleviated* June's fears for the baby; though he'd been born prematurely, he was rapidly gaining weight and could go home in a couple of weeks.

Word List 4

aloof   ADJ. apart; reserved; standoffish. His classmates thought James was a snob because, instead of joining in their conversations, he remained silent and *aloof*.

altruistic   ADJ. unselfishly generous; concerned for others. In providing tutorial assistance and college scholarships for hundreds of economically disadvantaged youths, Eugene Lang performed a truly *altruistic* deed. altruism, N.

ambiguous   ADJ. unclear or doubtful in meaning. The proctor's *ambiguous* instructions thoroughly confused us; we didn't know which columns we should mark and which we should leave blank. ambiguity, N.

ambivalence   N. the state of having contradictory or conflicting emotional attitudes. Torn between loving her parents one minute and hating them the next, she was confused by the *ambivalence* of her feelings. ambivalent, ADJ.

ameliorate   V. improve; make more satisfactory. Carl became a union organizer because he wanted to join the fight to *ameliorate* the working conditions in the factory.

amend   V. correct; change, generally for the better. Hoping to *amend* his circumstances, Luong left Vietnam for the United States.

amorphous   ADJ. formless; lacking shape or definition. As soon as we have decided on our itinerary, we shall send you a copy; right now, our plans are still *amorphous*.

ample   ADJ. abundant. Bond had *ample* opportunity to escape. Why did he let us catch him?

analogy   N. similarity; parallelism. A well-known *analogy* compares the body's immune system to an army whose defending troops are the lymphocytes or white blood cells. analogous, ADJ.

anarchist   N. person who seeks to overturn the established government; advocate of abolishing authority. Denying she was an *anarchist*, Katya maintained she wished only to make changes in our government, not to destroy it entirely. anarchy, N.

Word List 5

anecdote   N. short account of an amusing or interesting event. Rather than make concrete proposals for welfare reform, President Ronald Reagan told *anecdotes* about poor people who became wealthy despite their impoverished backgrounds. anecdotal, ADJ.

animosity   N. active enmity. By advocating cuts in campaign spending and limits on congressional powers, the reform candidate seemed almost to invite the *animosity* of the party's leaders.

antagonistic   ADJ. hostile; opposed. Despite his lawyers' best efforts to stop him, the angry prisoner continued to make *antagonistic* remarks to the judge. antagonism, N.

antidote   N. medicine to counteract a poison or disease. When Marge's child accidentally swallowed some cleaning fluid, the local poison control hotline told Marge how to administer the *antidote*.

antiquated   ADJ. old-fashioned; obsolete. Philip had grown so accustomed to editing his articles on word processors that he thought typewriters were too *antiquated* for him to use. antiquity, N.

antithesis N. contrast; direct opposite of or to. Good is the *antithesis* of evil, innocence the *antithesis* of guilt.

apathy N. lack of caring; indifference. A firm believer in democratic government, she could not understand the *apathy* of people who never bothered to vote. apathetic, ADJ.

apocryphal ADJ. untrue; made up. To impress his friends, Ted invented *apocryphal* tales of his adventures in the big city.

appease V. pacify or soothe; relieve. Tom and Jody tried to *appease* their crying baby by offering him one toy after another. However, they couldn't calm him down until they *appeased* his hunger by giving him a bottle.

appreciate V. be thankful for; increase in worth; be thoroughly conscious of. Little Orphan Annie truly *appreciated* the stocks Daddy Warbucks gave her, which *appreciated* in value considerably over the years.

Word List 6

apprehension N. fear; discernment; capture. The tourist refused to drive his rental car through downtown Miami because he felt some *apprehension* that he might be carjacked. apprehension, ADJ.

arable ADJ. fit for growing crops. The first settlers wrote home glowing reports of the New World, praising its vast acres of *arable* land ready for the plow.

arbitrary ADJ. unreasonable or capricious; randomly selected without any reason; based solely on one's unrestricted will or judgment. The coach claimed the team lost because the umpire made some *arbitrary* calls.

archaic ADJ. antiquated. "Methinks," "thee," and "thou" are *archaic* words that are no longer part of our standard vocabulary.

ardor N. heat; passion; zeal. Katya's *ardor* was catching; soon all her fellow demonstrators were busily making posters and handing out flyers, inspired by her enthusiasm for the cause. ardent, ADJ.

arid ADJ. dry; barren. The cactus has adapted to survive in an *arid* environment.

arrogance N. pride; haughtiness. Convinced that Emma thought she was better than anyone else in the class, Ed rebuked her for her *arrogance*. arrogant, ADJ.

articulate ADJ. effective; distinct. Her *articulate* presentation of the advertising campaign impressed her employers so much that they put her in charge of the project. also V.

artifact N. object made by human beings, either handmade or mass-produced. Archaeologists debated the significance of the *artifacts* discovered in the ruins of Asia Minor but came to no conclusion about the culture they represented.

artisan N. manually skilled worker; craftsman, as opposed to artist. Elderly *artisans* from Italy trained Harlem teenagers to carve the stone figures that would decorate the new wing of the cathedral.

Word List 7

ascendancy N. controlling influence. Leaders of religious cults maintain *ascendancy* over their followers by methods that can verge on brainwashing.

ascetic ADJ. practicing self-denial; austere. The wealthy, self-indulgent young man felt oddly drawn to the *ascetic* life led by members of some monastic orders. also N.

aspire V. seek to attain; long for. Because he *aspired* to a career in professional sports, Philip enrolled in a graduate program in sports management. aspiration, N.

assuage V. ease or lessen (pain); satisfy (hunger); soothe (anger). Jilted by Jane, Dick tried to *assuage* his heartache by indulging in ice cream. One gallon later, he had *assuaged* his appetite but not his grief.

astute ADJ. wise; shrewd. Expecting Miss Marple to be a woolly-headed old lady, Inspector Craddock was startled by the *astute* observations she made.

atrophy V. waste away. After three months in a cast, Stan's biceps had *atrophied* somewhat; however, he was sure that if he pumped iron for a while he would soon build them up. also, N.

attentive ADJ. considerate; thoughtful; paying attention. Thuy is very *attentive* to her Vietnamese-speaking parents, acting as their interpreter and helping them deal with American society.

attribute V. ascribe; explain. I *attribute* her success in science to the encouragement she received from her parents.

audacious ADJ. daring; bold. Audiences cheered as Luke Skywalker and Princess Leia made their *audacious*, death-defying leap to freedom, escaping Darth Vader's troops. audacity, N.

augment V. increase; add to. Beth *augmented* her inadequate salary by selling Tupperware at parties at friends' homes.

Word List 8

austerity N. sternness; severity; strict economy; lack of luxuries. The bishops charged with conducting the heresy inquiry were a solemn, somewhat forbidding group; their demeanor reflected their *austerity*. austere, ADJ.

authentic ADJ. genuine. The art expert was able to distinguish the *authentic* Van Gogh painting from the forged copy. authenticate, V.

authoritarian ADJ. favoring or exercising total control; nondemocratic. Forced to obey the dictates of the *authoritarian* regime, the people had no control over their own destiny. also N.

autonomous ADJ. self-governing. Although the University of California at Berkeley is just one part of the state university system, in many ways Cal Berkeley is *autonomous*, for it runs several programs that are not subject to outside control. autonomy, N.

aversion N. firm dislike. Their mutual *aversion* was so great that they refused to speak to one another.

banal ADJ. hackneyed; commonplace; trite. Was it Pendleton's stale plot or his cliché-ridden dialogue that made his play seem so *banal*? banality, N.

bane N. cause of ruin. Lack of public transportation is the *bane* of urban life.

belie V. contradict; give a false impression. His coarse, hard-bitten exterior *belied* his inner sensitivity.

belittle V. disparage; make fun of. Parents should not *belittle* their children's early attempts at drawing, but should encourage their efforts.

belligerent ADJ. quarrelsome. Whenever he had too much to drink, he became *belligerent* and tried to pick fights with strangers.

Word List 9

benevolent ADJ. generous; charitable. Mr. Fezziwig was a *benevolent* employer who wished to make Christmas merrier for young Scrooge and his other employees.

benign ADJ. kindly; favorable; not malignant.

Though her *benign* smile and gentle bearing made Miss Marple seem a sweet little old lady, in reality she was a tough-minded, shrewd observer of human nature.

bequeath V. leave to someone by a will; hand down. Although Maud had intended to *bequeath* the family home to her nephew, she died before changing her will. bequest, N.

biased ADJ. slanted; prejudiced. Because the judge played golf regularly with the district attorney's father, we feared he might be *biased* in the prosecution's favor. bias, N.

bland ADJ. soothing; mild; dull. Unless you want your stomach lining to be eaten away, stick to a *bland* diet. blandness, N.

blasphemy N. irreverence; sacrilege; cursing. In my father's house, the Dodgers were the holiest of holies; to cheer for another team was to utter words of *blasphemy*. blasphemous, ADJ.

bolster V. support; reinforce. The debaters amassed file boxes full of evidence to *bolster* their arguments.

braggart N. boastful person. I wouldn't mind Bob's being such a *braggart* if I felt he'd done anything worth bragging about.

brawn N. muscular strength; sturdiness. It takes *brawn* to become a champion weight-lifter. brawny, ADJ.

brevity N. conciseness; briefness. *Brevity* is essential when you send a telegram or cablegram; you are charged for every word.

Word List 10

buttress V. support; prop up. The attorney came up with several far-fetched arguments in a vain attempt to *buttress* his weak case. also N.

cacophonous ADJ. discordant; inharmonious. Do the students in the orchestra enjoy the *cacophonous* sounds they make when they're tuning up? I don't know how they can stand the racket. cacophony, N.

cajole V. coax; wheedle. Diane tried to *cajole* her father into letting her drive the family car. cajolery, N.

calculated ADJ. deliberately planned; likely. Lexy's choice of clothes to wear to the debate tournament was carefully *calculated*. Her conventional suit was one *calculated* to appeal to the conservative judges.

candor N. frankness. The *candor* with which Gene spoke during the job interview impressed us all; it was clear he held nothing back. can-did, ADJ.

capricious   ADJ. fickle; incalculable. The storm was *capricious*, changing its course constantly.

caricature   N. distortion; burlesque. The *caricatures* he drew always emphasized a personal weakness of the people he burlesqued. also V.

censorious   ADJ. critical. *Censorious* people delight in casting blame.

censure   V. blame; criticize. The senator was *censured* for his inappropriate behavior. also N.

certitude   N. certainty. Though there was no *certitude* of his getting the job, Lou thought he had a good chance of doing so.

Word List 11

charlatan   N. quack; pretender to knowledge. When they realized that the Wizard didn't know how to get them back to Kansas, Dorothy and her companions were indignant that they'd been duped by a *charlatan*.

chronicle   V. report; record (in chronological order). The gossip columnist was paid to *chronicle* the latest escapades of socially prominent celebrities. also N.

civil   ADJ. having to do with citizens or the state; courteous and polite. Although Internal Revenue Service agents are *civil* servants, they are not always *civil* to suspected tax cheats. civility, N.

clamor   N. noise. The *clamor* of the children at play outside made it impossible for her to take a nap. also V.

clemency   N. disposition to be lenient; mildness, as of the weather. Why did the defense lawyer look pleased when his case was sent to Judge Bland's chambers? Bland was known for her *clemency* toward first offenders. clement, ADJ.

coercion   N. use of force to get someone's compliance. They forced him to obey, but only by using great *coercion*. coerce, V.

commemorate   V. honor the memory of. The statue of the Minuteman *commemorates* the valiant soldiers who fought in the Revolutionary War.

compelling   ADJ. overpowering; irresistible in effect. The prosecutor presented a well-reasoned case, but the defense attorney's *compelling* arguments for leniency won over the jury.

compile   V. assemble; gather; accumulate. We planned to *compile* a list of the words most frequently used on the SAT examinations.

compliance   N. readiness to yield; conformity in fulfilling requirements. When I give an order, I expect *compliance*, not defiance. The design for the new school had to be in *compliance* with the local building code. comply, V.

Word List 12

composure   N. mental calmness. Even the latest crisis at work failed to shake Nancy's *composure*.

comprehensive   ADJ. thorough; inclusive. This book provides a *comprehensive* review of critical reading skills for the SAT.

concede   V. admit; yield. Despite all the evidence Monica had assembled, Mark refused to *concede* that she was right. concession, N.

conciliatory   ADJ. reconciling; appeasing; amiable. Hoping to end the coldness that had grown between them, he wrote a *conciliatory* note. conciliate, V.

concise   ADJ. brief and compact. When you define a new word, be *concise*: the shorter the definition, the easier it is to remember.

conclusive   ADJ. convincing; decisive. We have *conclusive* evidence that proves her innocence.

concur   V. agree in opinion. Justice O'Connor wrote a minority opinion because she did not *concur* with the reasoning of her fellow justices.

condone   V. overlook voluntarily; forgive. Although she had excused Huck for his earlier escapades, Widow Douglas refused to *condone* his latest prank.

confirm   V. corroborate; verify; support. I have several witnesses who will *confirm* my account of what happened.

conflagration   N. great fire. In the *conflagration* that followed the 1906 earthquake, much of San Francisco burned to the ground.

Word List 13

confound   V. confuse; puzzle. No mystery could *confound* Sherlock Holmes for long.

confront   V. face; challenge. All I ask is the chance to *confront* my accusers face to face.

conscientious   ADJ. scrupulous; careful. A *conscientious* editor, she checked every definition for its accuracy.

consensus   N. general agreement. After hours of debate, the *consensus* of the group was that we should approve the executive director's proposal.

consistency N. absence of contradictions; dependability; uniformity; degree of thickness. Holmes judged puddings and explanations on their *consistency*: he liked his puddings without lumps and his explanations without improbabilities.

constraint N. compulsion; repression of feelings. Because he trusted his therapist completely, he discussed his feelings openly with her without feeling the least *constraint*. constrain, V.

contagion N. infection. Fearing *contagion*, they took great steps to prevent the spread of the disease.

contemporary N. person belonging to the same period. Though Charlotte Bronte and George Eliot were *contemporaries*, the two novelists depicted their Victorian world in markedly different ways. also ADJ.

contend V. struggle; compete; assert earnestly. Sociologist Harry Edwards *contends* that young African-American athletes are exploited by some college recruiters. contention, N.

contentious ADJ. quarrelsome. Disagreeing violently with the referees' ruling, the coach became so *contentious* that they threw him out of the game.

Word List 14

contract V. compress or shrink; make a pledge; catch a disease. Warm metal expands; cold metal *contracts*.

converge V. approach; tend to meet; come together. African-American men from all over the United States *converged* on Washington to take part in the historic Million Man march.

conviction N. strongly held belief. Nothing could shake his *conviction* that she was innocent. (secondary meaning)

cordial ADJ. gracious; heartfelt. Our hosts greeted us at the airport with a *cordial* welcome and a hearty hug.

corroborate V. confirm; support. Though Huck was quite willing to *corroborate* Tom's story, Aunt Polly knew better than to believe either of them.

corrosion N. destruction by chemical action. The *corrosion* of the girders supporting the bridge took place so gradually that no one suspected any danger until the bridge suddenly collapsed. corrode, V.

credibility N. believability. Because the candidate had made some pretty unbelievable promises, we began to question the *credibility* of everything he said.

credulity N. belief on slight evidence; gullibility; naivete. Con artists take advantage of the *credulity* of inexperienced investors to swindle them out of their savings. credulous, ADJ.

criterion N. standard used in judging. What *criterion* did you use when you selected this essay as the prize winner? criteria, PL.

cryptic ADJ. mysterious; hidden; secret. Martin loved to act mysterious, making *cryptic* comments no one could understand.

Word List 15

cursory ADJ. casual; hastily done. Because a *cursory* examination of the ruins indicates the possibility of arson, we believe the insurance agency should undertake a more extensive investigation of the fire's cause.

curtail V. shorten; reduce. When Elton asked Cher for a date, she said she was really sorry she couldn't go out with him, but her dad had ordered her to *curtail* her social life.

cynic N. one who is skeptical or distrustful of human motives. A born *cynic*, Sidney was suspicious whenever anyone gave him a gift "with no strings attached." cynical, ADJ.

daunt V. intimidate; frighten. "Boast all you like of your prowess. Mere words cannot *daunt* me," the hero answered the villain.

dawdle V. loiter; waste time. We have to meet a deadline so don't *dawdle*; just get down to work.

debilitate V. weaken; enfeeble. Michael's severe bout of the flu *debilitated* him so much that he was too tired to go to work for a week.

debunk V. expose something as nonsensical or false. I have gathered enough evidence to *debunk* the legend that Billy the Kid was a heroic, Robin Hood-like figure.

decorum N. propriety; orderliness and good taste in manners. Even the best-mannered students have trouble behaving with *decorum* on the last day of school. decorous, ADJ.

defame V. harm someone's reputation; malign. If you try to *defame* my good name, my lawyers will see you in court. defamation, N.

deference N. courteous regard for another's wish. In *deference* to the minister's request, please do not take photographs during the wedding service.

Word List 16

defiance N. refusal to yield; resistance. When John reached the "terrible two's," he responded to every parental request with howls of *defiance*. defy, V. defiant, ADJ.

degenerate V. become worse; deteriorate. As the fight dragged on, the champion's stamina *degenerated* until he could barely keep on his feet.

degrade V. lower in rank or dignity; debase. Some secretaries object to fetching the boss a cup of coffee because they feel it *degrades* them to do such lowly tasks.

deliberate V. consider; ponder. Offered the new job, she asked for time to *deliberate* before she told them her decision.

delineate V. portray; depict; sketch. Using only a few descriptive phrases, Austen *delineates* the character of Mr. Collins so well that we can predict his every move. delineation, N.

denounce V. condemn; criticize. The reform candidate *denounced* the corrupt city officers for having betrayed the public's trust. denunciation, N.

deny V. contradict; refuse. Do you *deny* his story, or do you support what he says? denial, N.

depict V. portray; describe. Some newspaper accounts *depicted* the movie star as a reclusive prima donna; others portrayed her as a sensitive artist harassed by the media. depiction, N.

deplore V. regret strongly; express grief over. Although I *deplore* the disintegration of the modern family, I understand that not every marriage can be saved.

depravity N. corruption; wickedness. Even Romans who had grown accustomed to perversions and immorality during Tiberius's reign were shocked by the *depravity* of the emperor Caligula.

Word List 17

deprecate V. express disapproval of; protest against; belittle. A firm believer in old-fashioned courtesy, Miss Post *deprecated* the modern tendency to address new acquaintances by their first names. deprecatory, ADJ.

deride V. ridicule; make fun of. The critics *derided* his pretentious dialogue and refused to consider his play seriously. derision, N.

derivative ADJ. unoriginal; derived from another source. Although her early poetry was clearly *derivative* in nature, the critics felt she had promise and eventually would find her own voice.

despondent ADJ. depressed; gloomy. To the concern of his parents, William became seriously *despondent* after he broke up with Jan. despondency, N.

despot N. tyrant; harsh, authoritarian ruler. How could a benevolent king turn overnight into a *despot*?

detached ADJ. emotionally removed; calm and objective; indifferent. A psychoanalyst must maintain a *detached* point of view and stay uninvolved with her patients' personal lives. detachment, N. (secondary meaning)

deterrent N. something that discourages; hindrance. Does the threat of capital punishment serve as a *deterrent* to potential killers? deter, V.

detrimental ADJ. harmful; damaging. The candidate's acceptance of major financial contributions from a well-known racist ultimately proved *detrimental* to his campaign, for he lost the backing of many of his early grassroots supporters. detriment, N.

devious ADJ. roundabout; erratic; not straightforward. His plan was so *devious* that it was only with great difficulty we could follow its shifts and dodges.

devise V. think up; invent; plan. How clever he must be to have *devised* such a devious plan! What ingenious inventions might he have *devised* if he had turned his mind to science and not to crime!

Word List 18

didactic ADJ. teaching; instructional. Pope's lengthy poem *An Essay on Man* is too *didactic* for my taste: I dislike it when poets turn preachy and moralize.

diffuse ADJ. wordy; rambling; spread out. If you pay authors by the word, you tempt them to produce *diffuse* manuscripts rather than concise ones.

digression N. wandering away from the subject. Nobody minded when Professor Renoir's lectures wandered away from their official themes; his *digressions* were always more fascinating than the topic of the day. digress, V.

diligence N. steadiness of effort; persistent hard work. Her employers were greatly impressed by her *diligence* and offered her a partnership in the firm. diligent, ADJ.

diminution N. lessening; reduction in size. Old Jack was as sharp at eighty as he had been at fifty; increasing age led to no *diminution* of his mental acuity.

disband V. dissolve; disperse. The chess club *disbanded* after its disastrous initial season.

discerning ADJ. mentally quick and observant; having insight. Though no genius, the star was sufficiently *discerning* to tell her true friends from the countless phonies who flattered her. discernment, N.

disclose V. reveal. Although competitors offered him bribes, he refused to *disclose* any information about his company's forthcoming product. disclosure, N.

discordant ADJ. not harmonious; conflicting. Nothing is quite so *discordant* as the sound of a junior high school orchestra tuning up. discord, N.

discount V. disregard. Be prepared to *discount* what he has to say about his ex-wife; he is still very bitter about the divorce.

Word List 19

discredit V. defame; destroy confidence in; disbelieve. The campaign was highly negative in tone; each candidate tried to *discredit* the others.

discrepancy N. lack of consistency; difference. Noticing some *discrepancies* in his description of the crime, the police began to mistrust the witness's testimony.

discriminating ADJ. able to see differences; prejudiced. A superb interpreter of Picasso, she was sufficiently *discriminating* to judge the most complex works of modern art. (secondary meaning) discrimination, N.

discursive ADJ. digressing; rambling. As the lecturer wandered from topic to topic, we wondered what if any point there was to his *discursive* remarks.

disdain V. view with scorn or contempt. In the film *Funny Face*, the bookish heroine *disdained* fashion models for their lack of intellectual interests. also N.

disinclination N. unwillingness. Some mornings I feel a great *disinclination* to get out of bed.

disinterested ADJ. unprejudiced. In view of the judge's political ambitions and the lawyers' financial interest in the case, the only *disinterested* person in the courtroom may have been the court reporter.

dismantle V. take apart. When the show closed, they *dismantled* the scenery before storing it.

dismiss V. put away from consideration; reject. Believing in John's love for her, she *dismissed* the notion that he might be unfaithful. (secondary meaning)

disparage V. belittle. Do not *disparage* any donation, no matter how small it may be; every penny counts, and these little gifts mean a lot.

Word List 20

disparity N. difference; condition of inequality. Their *disparity* in rank made no difference at all to the prince and Cinderella.

dispassionate ADJ. calm; impartial. Known in the company for his cool judgment, Bill could impartially examine the causes of a problem, giving a *dispassionate* analysis of what had gone wrong, and go on to suggest how to correct the mess.

dispel V. drive away; scatter; cause to vanish. The bright sunlight eventually *dispelled* the morning mist.

disperse V. cause to break up; scatter. The police fired tear gas into the crowd to *disperse* the protesters.

disputatious ADJ. argumentative; fond of arguing. Convinced he knew more than his lawyers, Alan was a *disputatious* client, ready to argue about the best way to conduct the case.

disseminate V. distribute; spread; scatter (like seeds). By their use of the Internet, propagandists have been able to *disseminate* their pet doctrines to new audiences around the globe.

dissent V. disagree. In the recent Supreme Court decision, Justice O'Connor *dissented* from the majority opinion. also N.

dissipate V. squander; waste; scatter. He is a fine artist, but I fear he may *dissipate* his gifts if he keeps wasting his time on such trivial pursuits.

dissonance N. dissonance. Composer Charles Ives often used *dissonance*—clashing or unresolved chords—for special effects in his musical works.

dissuade V. advise against. Tom could not *dissuade* Huck from running away from home. dissuasion, N.

Word List 21

distant ADJ. reserved or aloof; cold in manner. His *distant* greeting made me feel unwelcome from the start. (secondary meaning)

divergent ADJ. differing; deviating. Since graduating from medical school, the two doctors have taken *divergent* paths, one going on to become a nationally prominent surgeon, the other dedicating himself to a small family practice in his home town. divergence, N.

diverse ADJ. differing in some characteristics; various. The professor suggested *diverse* ways of approaching the assignment and recommended that we choose one of them. diversity, N.

divulge V. reveal. No lover of gossip, Charlotte would never *divulge* anything that a friend told her in confidence.

doctrine N. teachings, in general; particular principle (religious, legal, and so on) taught. He was so committed to the *doctrines* of his faith that he was unable to evaluate them impartially.

document V. provide written evidence. She kept all the receipts from her business trip in order to *document* her expenses for the firm. also N.

dogmatic ADJ. opinionated; arbitrary; doctrinal. We tried to discourage Doug from being so *dogmatic*, but never could convince him that his opinions might be wrong.

dormant ADJ. sleeping; lethargic; latent. At fifty her long-*dormant* ambition to write flared up once more; within a year she had completed the first of her great historical novels.

dubious ADJ. doubtful; questionable. Many critics of the SAT contend the test is of *dubious* worth.

duplicity N. double-dealing; hypocrisy. When Tanya learned that Mark had been two-timing her, she was furious at his *duplicity*. duplicitous, ADJ.

Word List 22

duration N. length of time something lasts. Because she wanted the children to make a good impression on the dinner guests, Mother promised them a treat if they would behave for the *duration* of the meal.

dutiful ADJ. respectful; obedient. The *dutiful* child grew up to be a conscientious adult, aware of her civic obligations.

ebb V. recede; lessen. His fortunes began to *ebb* during the Recession. also, N.

eccentric ADJ. odd; whimsical; irregular. The comet passed close by Earth in its *eccentric* orbit.

eclectic ADJ. selective in choosing from a variety of sources. The reviewers praised the new restaurant's *eclectic* selection of dishes, which ranged from Oriental stir fries to French ragouts and stews.

eclipse V. darken; extinguish; surpass. The new stock market high *eclipsed* the previous record set in 1995.

effervescent ADJ. exuberant; bubbly and excited. Nothing depressed Amy for long; she was so naturally *effervescent* that she was soon as high-spirited as ever. effervesce, V.

egotistical ADJ. excessively self-centered; self-important; conceited. Typical *egotistical* remark: "But enough of this chit-chat about you and your little problems. Let's talk about what's really important: *me!*" egotism, N.

elated ADJ. overjoyed; in high spirits. Grinning from ear to ear, Bonnie Blair was clearly *elated* by her fifth Olympic gold medal. elation, N.

eloquence N. expressiveness; persuasive speech. The crowds were stirred by Martin Luther King's *eloquence*. eloquent, ADJ.

Word List 23

elusive ADJ. evasive; baffling; hard to grasp. Trying to pin down exactly when the contractors would be finished remodeling the house, Nancy was frustrated by their *elusive* replies. elude, V.

embellish V. adorn; ornament. The costume designer *embellished* the leading lady's ball gown with yards and yards of ribbon and lace.

emulate V. imitate; rival. In a brief essay, describe a person you admire, someone whose virtues you would like to *emulate*.

endorse V. approve; support. Everyone waited to see which one of the rival candidates for the city council the mayor would *endorse*. endorsement, N. (secondary meaning)

enduring ADJ. lasting; surviving. Keats believed in the *enduring* power of great art, which would outlast its creators' brief lives.

enervate V. weaken. She was slow to recover from her illness; even a short walk to the window would *enervate* her. enervation, N.

engender V. cause; produce. To receive praise for real accomplishments *engenders* self-confidence in a child.

enhance V. advance; improve. You can *enhance* your chances of being admitted to the college of your choice by learning to write well; an excellent essay can *enhance* any application.

enigma   N. puzzle; mystery. "What *do* women want?" asked Dr. Sigmund Freud. Their behavior was an *enigma* to him.

enmity   N. ill will; hatred. At Camp David President Carter labored to bring an end to the *enmity* that prevented Egypt and Israel from living in peace.

Word List 24

enumerate   V. list; mention one by one. Huck hung his head in shame as Miss Watson *enumerated* his many flaws.

ephemeral   ADJ. short-lived; fleeting. With its adult stage lasting less than two days, the mayfly is by definition an *ephemeral* creature.

epic   N. long heroic poem, or similar work of art. Kurosawa's film *Seven Samurai* is an *epic* that portrays the struggle of seven warriors to destroy a band of robbers. also ADJ.

epicure   N. connoisseur of food and drink. *Epicures* patronize this restaurant because it features exotic wines and dishes. epicurean, ADJ.

episodic   ADJ. loosely connected; divided into incidents; occurring at intervals. Though he tried to follow the plot of *Gravity's Rainbow*, John found the novel too *episodic*; he enjoyed individual passages, but had trouble following the work as a whole.

equanimity   N. calmness of temperament; composure. Even the inevitable strains of caring for an ailing mother did not disturb Bea's *equanimity*.

equivocal   ADJ. ambiguous; intentionally misleading. Rejecting the candidate's *equivocal* comments on tax reform, the reporters pressed him to say where he stood on the issue. equivocate, V.

erratic   ADJ. odd; unpredictable; wandering. Investors become anxious when the stock market appears *erratic*.

erroneous   ADJ. mistaken; wrong. I thought my answer was correct, but it was *erroneous*.

erudite   ADJ. learned; scholarly. Though his fellow students thought him *erudite*, Paul knew he would have to spend many years in serious study before he could consider himself a scholar.

Word List 25

esoteric   ADJ. hard to understand; known only to the chosen few. *New Yorker* short stories often include *esoteric* allusions to obscure people and events: the implication is, if you are in the in-crowd, you'll get the reference; if you come from Cleveland, you won't.

espouse   V. adopt; support. She was always ready to *espouse* a worthy cause.

esteem   V. respect; value; judge. Though I reject Ezra Pound's politics, I *esteem* him for his superb poetry and his acute literary criticism.

ethereal   ADJ. light; heavenly; unusually refined. In Shakespeare's *The Tempest*, the spirit Ariel is an *ethereal* creature, too airy and unearthly for our mortal world.

eulogy   N. expression of praise, often on the occasion of someone's death. Instead of delivering a spoken *eulogy* at Genny's memorial service, Jeff sang a song he had written in her honor.

euphemism   N. mild expression used in place of an unpleasant one. Until recently, many Southern Americans avoided the word *bull* in polite speech, replacing it by a *euphemism*, such as *he-cow* or *male beast*.

euphonious   ADJ. pleasing in sound. *Euphonious* even when spoken, the Italian language is particularly pleasing to the ear when sung. euphony, N.

euphoria   N. feeling of great happiness and well-being (sometimes exaggerated). Delighted with her SAT scores, sure that the university would accept her, Allison was filled with *euphoria*. euphoric, ADJ.

evanescent   ADJ. fleeting; vanishing. Brandon's satisfaction in his new job was *evanescent*, for he immediately began to notice its many drawbacks. evanescence, N.

exacerbate   V. worsen; embitter. The latest bombing *exacerbated* England's already existing bitterness against the IRA, causing the prime minister to break off the peace talks abruptly.

Word List 26

exacting   ADJ. extremely demanding. Cleaning the ceiling of the Sistine Chapel was an *exacting* task, one that demanded extremely meticulous care on the part of the restorers. exaction, N.

exalt   V. raise in rank or dignity; praise. The actor Alec Guinness was *exalted* to the rank of knighthood by the queen.

execute   V. put into effect; carry out. The choreographer wanted to see how well Margaret could *execute* a pirouette. (secondary meaning) execution, N.

exemplary ADJ. serving as a model; outstanding. At commencement the dean praised Ellen for her *exemplary* behavior as class president.

exemplify V. serve as an example of; embody. For a generation of balletgoers, Rudolf Nureyev *exemplified* the ideal of masculine grace.

exhaustive ADJ. thorough; comprehensive. We have made an *exhaustive* study of all published SAT tests and are happy to share our research with you.

exhilarating ADJ. invigorating and refreshing; cheering. Though some of the hikers found tramping through the snow tiring, Jeffrey found the walk on the cold, crisp day *exhilarating*.

exonerate V. acquit; exculpate. The defense team feverishly sought fresh evidence that might *exonerate* their client.

expedient ADJ. suitable to achieve a particular end; practical; politic. A pragmatic politician, he was guided by what was *expedient* rather than by what was ethical. expediency, N.

expedite V. hasten. Because we are on a tight schedule, we hope you will be able to *expedite* the delivery of our order.

Word List 27

expertise N. specialized knowledge; expert skill. Although she is knowledgeable in a number of fields, she was hired for her special *expertise* in computer programming.

explicit ADJ. totally clear; definite; outspoken. Don't just hint around that you're dissatisfied: be *explicit* about what's bothering you.

exploit N. deed or action, particularly a brave deed. Raoul Wallenberg was noted for his *exploits* in rescuing Jews from Hitler's forces.

exploit V. make use of, sometimes unjustly. Cesar Chavez fought attempts to *exploit* migrant farmworkers in California. exploitation, N.

expository ADJ. explanatory; intended to explain. The manual that came with my VCR was no masterpiece of *expository* prose: its explanations were so garbled that I couldn't even figure out how to rewind a tape. exposition, N.

extant ADJ. still in existence. I'd hoped to buy a copy of Margaret Dean Smith's facsimile of *The Dancing Master*. Unfortunately, all the copies *extant* are in libraries or private collections; none is for sale.

extol V. praise; glorified. The president *extolled* the astronauts, calling them the pioneers of the Space Age.

extraneous ADJ. not essential; superfluous. No wonder Ted can't think straight! His mind is so cluttered up with *extraneous* trivia that he can't concentrate on the essentials.

extricate V. free; disentangle. The fox could not *extricate* itself from the trap.

exuberance N. overflowing abundance; joyful enthusiasm; flamboyance; lavishness. I was bowled over by the *exuberance* of Amy's welcome. What an enthusiastic greeting!

Word List 28

facile ADJ. easily accomplished; ready or fluent; superficial. Words came easily to Jonathan: he was a *facile* speaker and prided himself on being ready to make a speech at a moment's notice.

facilitate V. help bring about; make less difficult. Rest and proper nourishment should *facilitate* the patient's recovery.

fallacious ADJ. false; misleading. Paradoxically, *fallacious* reasoning does not always yield erroneous results: even though your logic may be faulty, the answer you get may nevertheless be correct. fallacy, N.

fanaticism N. excessive zeal; extreme devotion to a belief or cause. When Islamic fundamentalists demanded the death of Salman Rushdie because his novel questioned their faith, world opinion condemned them for their *fanaticism*.

fastidious ADJ. difficult to please; squeamish. Bobby was such a *fastidious* eater that he would eat a sandwich only if his mother first cut off every scrap of crust.

feasible ADJ. practical. Was it *feasible* to build a new stadium for the Yankees on New York's West Side? Without additional funding, the project was clearly unrealistic.

fervor N. glowing ardor; intensity of feeling. At the protest rally, the students cheered the strikers and booed the dean with equal *fervor*.

fickle ADJ. changeable; faithless. As soon as Romeo saw Juliet, he forgot all about his old girlfriend Rosaline. Was Romeo *fickle*?

figurative ADJ. not literal, but metaphorical; using a figure of speech. "To lose one's marbles" is a *figurative* expression; if you're told that Jack has lost his marbles, no one expects you to rush out to buy him a replacement set.

flagrant ADJ. conspicuously wicked; blatant; outrageous. The governor's appointment of his brother-in-law to the State Supreme Court was a *flagrant* violation of the state laws against nepotism (favoritism based on kinship).

Word List 29

flippant ADJ. lacking proper seriousness. When Mark told Mona he loved her, she dismissed his earnest declaration with a *flippant* "Oh, you say that to all the girls!" flippancy, N.

florid ADJ. ruddy; reddish; flowery. If you go to Florida and get a sunburn, your complexion will look *florid*.

fluctuate V. waver; shift. The water pressure in our shower *fluctuates* wildly; you start rinsing yourself off with a trickle, and two minutes later, you think you're going to drown.

foolhardy ADJ. rash; heedless. Don't be *foolhardy*. Get some advice from experienced people before you strike out on your own.

foresight N. ability to foresee future happenings; prudence. A wise investor, she had the *foresight* to buy land just before the current real estate boom.

forestall V. prevent by taking action in advance. By setting up a prenuptial agreement, the prospective bride and groom hoped to *forestall* any potential arguments about money in the event of a divorce.

forsake V. desert; abandon; renounce. No one expected Gauguin to *forsake* his wife and children and run off to Tahiti.

forthright ADJ. outspoken; frank. Never afraid to call a spade a spade, she was perhaps too *forthright* to be a successful party politician.

fortuitous ADJ. accidental; by chance. Though he pretended their encounter was *fortuitous*, he'd actually been hanging around her usual haunts for the past two weeks.

foster V. rear; encourage; nurture. According to the legend, Romulus and Remus were *fostered* by a she-wolf who raised them as if they were her cubs. also ADJ.

Word List 30

founder V. fail completely; sink. After hitting the submerged iceberg, the *Titanic* started taking in water rapidly and soon *foundered*.

founder N. person who establishes (an organiza-tion, business). Among those drowned when the *Titanic* sank was the *founder* of the Abraham & Straus department store.

frail ADJ. weak. The sickly child seemed too *frail* to lift the heavy carton.

frivolous ADJ. lacking in seriousness; self-indul-gently carefree; relatively unimportant. Though Nancy enjoyed Bill's *frivolous*, lighthearted companionship, she sometimes wondered whether he could ever be serious. frivolity, N.

frugality N. thrift; economy. In economically hard times, those who do not learn to practice *frugality* risk bankruptcy. frugal, ADJ.

fundamental V. basic; primary; essential. The committee discussed all sorts of side issues without ever getting down to addressing the *fundamental* problem.

furtive ADJ. stealthy; sneaky. Noticing the *furtive* glance the customer gave the diamond bracelet on the counter, the jeweler wondered whether he had a potential shoplifter on his hands.

futile ADJ. ineffective; fruitless. Why waste your time on *futile* pursuits?

galvanize V. stimulate by shock; stir up; revital-ize. News that the prince was almost at their door *galvanized* the ugly stepsisters into a fren-zy of combing and primping.

garbled ADJ. mixed up; jumbled; distorted. A favorite party game involves passing a whis-pered message from one person to another, till, by the time it reaches the last player, the mes-sage is totally *garbled*.

Word List 31

garrulous ADJ. loquacious; wordy; talkative. My Uncle Henry can out-talk any three people I know. He is the most *garrulous* person in Cayuga County.

genre N. particular variety of art or literature. Both a short-story writer and a poet, Langston Hughes proved himself equally skilled in either *genre*.

germane ADJ. pertinent; bearing upon the case at hand. The judge would not allow the testi-mony to be heard by the jury because it was not *germane* to the case.

glacial ADJ. like a glacier; extremely cold. Never a warm person, John, when offended, could seem positively *glacial*.

glib ADJ. fluent; facile; slick. Keeping up a steady patter to entertain his customers, the kitchen gadget salesman was a *glib* speaker, never at a loss for a word.

glutton   N. someone who eats too much; greedy person. Who is the *glutton* who ate up all the chocolate chip cookies I made for dessert? gluttonous, ADJ.

gorge   N. small, steep-walled canyon. The white-water rafting guide warned us about the rapids farther downstream, where the river cut through a narrow *gorge*.

grandiose   ADJ. pretentious; high-flown; ridiculously exaggerated; impressive. The aged matinee idol still had *grandiose* notions of his supposed importance in the theatrical world.

gratify   V. please. Amy's success in her new job *gratified* her parents.

gratuitous   ADJ. given freely; unwarranted; unprovoked. Who asked you to comment? We don't need any *gratuitous* criticism from someone who has no business dissing us.

Word List 32

gravity   N. seriousness. We could tell we were in serious trouble from the *gravity* of the principal's expression. (secondary meaning) grave, ADJ.

gregarious   ADJ. sociable. Typically, partygoers are *gregarious*; hermits are not.

grievance   N. cause of complaint. When her supervisor ignored her complaint, she took her *grievance* to the union.

grudging   ADJ. unwilling; reluctant; stingy. We received only *grudging* support from the mayor despite his earlier promises of aid.

guile   N. deceit; duplicity; wiliness; cunning. Iago uses considerable *guile* to trick Othello into believing that Desdemona has been unfaithful.

gullible   ADJ. easily deceived. *Gullible* people have only themselves to blame if they fall for scams repeatedly. As the saying goes, "Fool me once, shame on you. Fool me twice, shame on *me*."

hackneyed   ADJ. commonplace; trite. When the reviewer criticized the movie for its *hackneyed* plot, we agreed; we had seen similar stories hundreds of times before.

hallowed   ADJ. blessed; consecrated. Although the dead girl's parents had never been active churchgoers, they insisted that their daughter be buried in *hallowed* ground.

hamper   V. obstruct. The new mother didn't realize how much the effort of caring for an infant would *hamper* her ability to keep an immaculate house.

harass   V. annoy by repeated attacks; torment. When he could not pay his bills as quickly as he had promised, he was *harassed* by his creditors.

Word List 33

hardy   ADJ. sturdy; robust; able to stand inclement weather. We asked the gardening expert to recommend particularly *hardy* plants that could withstand our harsh New England winters.

haughtiness   N. pride; arrogance. When she realized that Darcy believed himself too good to dance with his inferiors, Elizabeth took great offense at his *haughtiness*.

hedonist   N. one who believes that pleasure is the sole aim in life. A thoroughgoing *hedonist*, he considered only his own pleasure and ignored any claims others had on his money or time.

heed   V. pay attention to; consider. We hope you *heed* our advice and get a good night's sleep before the test. also N.

heresy   N. opinion contrary to popular belief; opinion contrary to accepted religion. Galileo's assertion that Earth moves around the sun directly contradicted the religious teachings of his day; as a result, he was tried for *heresy*. heretic, N.

heterodox   ADJ. unorthodox; unconventional. To those who upheld the belief that Earth did not move, Galileo's theory that Earth circles the sun was disturbingly *heterodox*.

heterogeneous   ADJ. dissimilar; mixed. This year's entering class is a remarkably *heterogeneous* body: it includes students from 40 different states and 26 foreign countries, some the children of billionaires, others the offspring of welfare families.

heyday   N. time of greatest success; prime. In their *heyday*, the San Francisco Forty-Niners won the Super Bowl two years running.

hiatus   N. gap; interruption in duration or continuity; pause. During the summer *hiatus*, many students try to earn enough money to pay their tuition for the next school year.

hierarchy   N. arrangement by rank or standing; authoritarian body divided into ranks. To be low man on the totem pole is to have an inferior place in the *hierarchy*.

Word List 34

hindrance   N. block; obstacle. Stalled cars along the highway present a *hindrance* to traffic that tow trucks should remove without delay. hinder, V.

hoard   V. stockpile; accumulate for future use. Whenever there are rumors of a food shortage, many people are tempted to *hoard* food. also N.

homogeneous   ADJ. of the same kind. Because the student body at Elite Prep was so *homogeneous*, Sara and James decided to send their daughter to a school that offered greater cultural diversity.

hone   V. sharpen. Determined to get a good shave, Ed *honed* his razor with great care.

hostility   N. unfriendliness; hatred. Children often feel *hostility* toward the new baby in the family.

humane   ADJ. marked by kindness or consideration. It is ironic that the *Humane* Society sometimes must show its compassion toward mistreated animals by killing them to put them out of their misery.

husband   V. use sparingly; conserve; save. Marathon runners must *husband* their energy so that they can keep going for the entire distance.

hyperbole   N. exaggeration; overstatement. As far as I'm concerned, Apple's claims about the new computer are pure *hyperbole*: no machine is that good!

hypocritical   ADJ. pretending to be virtuous; deceiving. Believing Eddie to be interested only in his own advancement, Greg resented his *hypocritical* posing as a friend. hypocrisy, N.

hypothetical   ADJ. based on assumptions or hypotheses; supposed. Suppose you are accepted by Harvard, Stanford, and Brown. Which one would you choose to attend? Remember: this is only a *hypothetical* situation. hypothesis, N.

Word List 35

iconoclast   N. one who attacks cherished traditions. A born *iconoclast*, Jean Genet deliberately set out to shock conventional theatergoers with his radical plays.

idiosyncrasy   N. individual trait, usually odd in nature; eccentricity. One of Richard Nixon's little *idiosyncracies* was his liking for ketchup on cottage cheese. One of Hannibal Lecter's little *idiosyncrasies* was his liking for human flesh.

ignominy   N. deep disgrace; shame or dishonor. To lose the Ping-Pong match to a trained chimpanzee! How could Rollo stand the *ignominy* of his defeat?

illicit   ADJ. illegal. The defense attorney maintained that her client had never performed any *illicit* action.

illuminate   V. brighten; clear up or make understandable; enlighten. Just as a lamp can *illuminate* a dark room, a perceptive comment can *illuminate* a knotty problem.

illusory   ADJ. deceptive; not real. Unfortunately, the costs of running the lemonade stand were so high that Tom's profits proved *illusory*.

imbalance   N. lack of balance or symmetry; disproportion. Because of the great *imbalance* between the number of males and females invited, the dance was unsuccessful.

immaculate   ADJ. spotless; flawless; absolutely clean. Ken and Jessica were wonderful tenants and left the apartment in *immaculate* condition when they moved out.

immune   ADJ. resistant to; free or exempt from. Fortunately, Florence had contracted chicken pox as a child and was *immune* to it when her baby broke out in spots. immunity, N.

immutable   ADJ. unchangeable. All things change over time; nothing is *immutable*.

Word List 36

impair   V. injure; hurt. Drinking alcohol can *impair* your ability to drive safely; if you're going to drink, don't drive.

impartial   ADJ. not biased; fair. As members of the jury, you must be *impartial*, showing no favoritism to either party but judging the case on its merits.

impassive   ADJ. without feeling; imperturbable; stoical. Refusing to let the enemy see how deeply shaken he was by his capture, the prisoner kept his face *impassive*.

impeccable   ADJ. faultless. The uncrowned queen of the fashion industry, Diana was acclaimed for her *impeccable* taste.

impecunious   ADJ. without money. Though Scrooge claimed he was too *impecunious* to give alms, he easily could have afforded to be charitable.

impede   V. hinder; block; delay. A series of accidents *impeded* the launching of the space shuttle.

impel V. drive or force onward. A strong feeling of urgency *impelled* her; if she failed to finish the project right then, she knew that she would never get it done.

imperceptible ADJ. unnoticeable; undetectable. Fortunately, the stain on the blouse was *imperceptible* after the blouse had gone through the wash.

imperious ADJ. domineering; haughty. Jane rather liked a man to be masterful, but Mr. Rochester seemed so bent on getting his own way that he was actually *imperious*!

impervious ADJ. impenetrable; incapable of being damaged or distressed. The carpet salesman told Simone that his most expensive brand of floor covering was warranted to be *impervious* to ordinary wear and tear.

Word List 37

impetuous ADJ. violent; hasty; rash. "Leap before you look" was the motto suggested by one particularly *impetuous* young man.

implausible ADJ. unlikely; unbelievable. Though her alibi seemed *implausible*, it in fact turned out to be true.

implement V. put into effect; supply with tools. The mayor was unwilling to *implement* the plan until she was sure it had the governor's backing. implementation N.

implication N. something hinted at or suggested. When Miss Watson said she hadn't seen her purse since the last time Jim was in the house, the *implication* was that she suspected Jim had taken it. imply, V.

implicit ADJ. understood but not stated. Jack never told Jill he adored her; he believed his love was *implicit* in his actions.

impoverished ADJ. poor. The loss of their ancestral farm left the family *impoverished* and without hope.

impromptu ADJ. without previous preparation; off the cuff; on the spur of the moment. The judges were amazed that she could make such a thorough, well-supported presentation in an *impromptu* speech.

impudence N. impertinence; insolence. When kissed on the cheek by a perfect stranger, Lady Catherine exclaimed, "Of all the nerve! Young man, I should have you horsewhipped for your *impudence*."

inadvertently ADV. by oversight; carelessly or unintentionally. He *inadvertently* failed to answer two questions on the examination.

inane ADJ. silly; senseless. There's no point to what you're saying. Why are you bothering to make such *inane* remarks?

Word List 38

inaugurate V. start; initiate; install in office. The airline decided to *inaugurate* its new route to the Far East with a special reduced fare offer. inaugural, ADJ.

incense V. enrage; infuriate. Cruelty to defenseless animals *incensed* Kit.

incentive N. spur; motive. Mike's strong desire to outshine his big sister was all the *incentive* he needed to do well in school.

incessant ADJ. uninterrupted; unceasing. In a famous TV commercial, the frogs' *incessant* croaking goes on and on until eventually it turns into a single word: "Bud-weis-er."

incidental ADJ. not essential; minor. The scholarship covered his major expenses at college and some of his *incidental* expenses as well.

incisive ADJ. cutting; sharp. Her *incisive* commentary cut through the tangle of arguments, exposing fallacies and logical flaws.

incite V. arouse to action; goad; motivate; induce to exist. In a fiery speech, Mario *incited* his fellow students to go out on strike to protest the university's anti-affirmative-action stand.

incline N. slope; slant. The architect recommended that the nursing home's ramp be rebuilt because its *incline* was too steep for wheelchairs.

inclined ADJ. tending or leaning toward; bent. Though I am *inclined* to be skeptical, the witness's manner *inclines* me to believe his story. also V.

inclusive ADJ. tending to include all. The comedian turned down the invitation to join the Players' Club, saying any club that would let him in was too *inclusive* for him.

Word List 39

incoherent ADJ. unintelligible; muddled; illogical. The bereaved father sobbed and stammered, his words becoming almost *incoherent* in his grief. incoherence, N.

incongruous ADJ. not fitting; absurd. Dave saw nothing *incongruous* about wearing sneakers with his tuxedo; he couldn't understand why his date took one look at him and started to laugh. incongruity, N.

inconsequential   ADJ. insignificant; unimportant. Brushing off Ali's apologies for having broken the wineglass, Tamara said, "Don't worry about it; it's *inconsequential*."

incontrovertible   ADJ. indisputable; not open to question. Unless you find the evidence against my client absolutely *incontrovertible*, you must declare her not guilty of this charge.

incorrigible   ADJ. uncorrectable. Though Widow Douglass hoped to reform Huck, Miss Watson called him *incorrigible* and said he would come to no good end.

indefatigable   ADJ. tireless. Although the effort of taking out the garbage tired Wayne out for the entire morning, when it came to partying, he was *indefatigable*.

indict   V. charge. The district attorney didn't want to *indict* the suspect until she was sure she had a strong enough case to convince a jury. indictment, N.

indifferent   ADJ. unmoved; lacking concern. Because she felt no desire to marry, she was *indifferent* to his constant proposals.

indigenous   ADJ. native. Cigarettes are made of tobacco, one of the *indigenous* plants the early explorers found in the New World.

indigent   ADJ. poor; destitute. Someone who is truly *indigent* can't even afford to buy a pack of cigarettes. (Don't mix up *indigent* and *indigenous*. See preceding example.)

Word List 40

indiscriminate   ADJ. choosing at random; confused. Disapproving of her son's *indiscriminate* television viewing, Shirley decided to restrict him to watching educational programs.

indolent   ADJ. lazy. Couch potatoes lead an *indolent* life lying back in their Lazyboy recliners to watch TV. indolence, N.

indomitable   ADJ. unconquerable; unyielding. Focusing on her game despite all her personal problems, tennis champion Steffi Graf proved she had an *indomitable* will to win.

indubitable   ADJ. unable to be doubted; unquestionable. Auditioning for the chorus line, Molly was an *indubitable* hit: the director fired the leading lady and hired Molly in her place!

induce   V. persuade; bring about. After the quarrel, Tina said nothing could *induce* her to talk to Tony again. inducement, N.

indulge   V. humor; treat leniently. Parents who constantly *indulge* their children by giving in to their every whim may thoroughly spoil them.

industrious   ADJ. diligent; hard-working. If you are *industrious* and apply yourself to your assignments, you will do well in college. industry, N.

ineffectual   ADJ. not effective; weak. Because the candidate failed to get across his message to the public, his campaign was *ineffectual*.

inept   ADJ. unsuited; absurd; incompetent. The *inept* glovemaker was all thumbs.

inequity   N. unfairness. In demanding equal pay for equal work, women protest the basic *inequity* of a system that gives greater financial rewards to men.

Word List 41

inert   ADJ. inactive; lacking power to move. "Get up, you lazybones," Tina cried to Tony, who lay in bed *inert*.

inexorable   ADJ. relentless; unyielding; implacable. Ignoring the defense attorney's pleas for clemency, the judge was *inexorable*, giving the convicted felon the maximum punishment allowed by law.

infamous   ADJ. notoriously bad. Charles Manson and Jeffrey Dahmer are both *infamous* killers.

infer   V. deduce; conclude. From the students' glazed looks, it was easy for me to *infer* that they were bored out of their minds.

infiltrate   V. pass into or through; penetrate (an organization) sneakily. In order to be able to *infiltrate* enemy lines at night without being seen, the scouts darkened their faces and wore black coveralls. infiltrator, N.

infinitesimal   ADJ. exceedingly small; so small as to be almost nonexistent. Making sure everyone was aware she was on an extremely strict diet, Melanie said she would have only an *infinitesimal* sliver of pie.

infraction   N. violation (of a rule or regulation); breach. When Dennis Rodman butted heads with a referee, he committed a clear *infraction* of NBA rules.

ingenious   ADJ. clever; resourceful. Kit admired the *ingenious* way that her computer keyboard opened up to reveal the built-in CD-ROM below. ingenuity, N.

ingrate N. ungrateful person. That *ingrate* Bob sneered at the tie I gave him.

inherent ADJ. firmly established by nature or habit; intrinsic. Elaine's *inherent* love of justice caused her to champion people whom she thought society had treated unfairly.

Word List 42

inimical ADJ. unfriendly; hostile; harmful; detrimental. I've always been friendly to Martha. Why is she so *inimical* to me?

initiate V. begin; originate; receive into a group. The college is about to *initiate* a program to reduce math anxiety among students.

injurious ADJ. harmful. Smoking cigarettes can be *injurious* to your health.

innate ADJ. inborn. Mozart's parents soon recognized young Wolfgang's *innate* talent for music.

innocuous ADJ. harmless. An occasional glass of wine with dinner is relatively *innocuous* and should have no ill effect.

innovation N. change; introduction of something new. Although Richard liked to keep up with all the latest technological *innovations*, he didn't always abandon tried and true techniques in favor of something new. innovate, V.

inopportune ADJ. untimely; poorly chosen. A rock concert is an *inopportune* setting for a quiet conversation.

insatiable ADJ. not easily satisfied; greedy. Lexy's passion for new clothes is *insatiable*; she can shop till she literally drops.

insightful ADJ. discerning; perceptive. Sol thought he was very *insightful* about human behavior, but he hadn't a clue why people acted the way they did.

insinuate V. hint; imply; creep in. When you said I looked robust, were you trying to *insinuate* I'm getting fat?

Word List 43

insipid ADJ. lacking in flavor; dull. Flat prose and flat ginger ale are equally *insipid*: both lack sparkle.

insolvent ADJ. bankrupt; unable to repay one's debts. Although young Lord Widgeon was *insolvent*, he had no fear of being thrown into debtors' prison; he was sure that, if his creditors pressed him for payment, his wealthy parents would repay what he owed.

instigate V. urge; start; provoke. Rumors of police corruption led the mayor to *instigate* an investigation into the department's activities.

insularity N. narrow-mindedness; isolation. The *insularity* of the islanders manifested itself in their suspicion of anything foreign. insular, ADJ.

insuperable ADJ. insurmountable; unbeatable. Faced by almost *insuperable* obstacles, the members of the underground maintained their courage and will to resist.

insurgent ADJ. rebellious. Because the *insurgent* forces had occupied the capital and had gained control of the railway lines, several of the war correspondents covering the uprising predicted a rebel victory.

intangible ADJ. not material; not able to be perceived by touch; vague; elusive. Emotions are *intangible*, and yet we know that we feel love and hate, though we cannot grasp these feelings in our hands.

integral ADJ. complete; necessary for completeness. Physical education is an *integral* part of our curriculum; a sound mind and a sound body are complementary.

integrity N. uprightness; wholeness. Lincoln, whose personal *integrity* has inspired millions, fought a civil war to maintain the *integrity* of the republic, that these United States might remain undivided for all time.

intermittent ADJ. periodic; on and off. The outdoor wedding reception had to be moved indoors to avoid the *intermittent* showers that fell on and off all afternoon.

Word List 44

intervene V. come between. Rachel tried to *intervene* in the quarrel between her two sons.

intimidate V. frighten. I'll learn karate and then those big bullies won't be able to *intimidate* me any more.

intractable ADJ. unruly; stubborn; unyielding. Charlie Brown's friend Pigpen was *intractable*: he absolutely refused to take a bath.

intransigence N. refusal of any compromise; stubbornness. When I predicted that the strike would be over in a week, I didn't expect to encounter such *intransigence* from both sides. intransigent, ADJ.

intrepid   ADJ. fearless. For her *intrepid* conduct in nursing the wounded during the war, Florence Nightingale was honored by Queen Victoria.

intricate   ADJ. complex; knotty; tangled. Eric spent many hours designing mazes so *intricate* that none of his classmates could solve them. intricacy, N.

intrinsic   ADJ. essential; inherent; built-in; natural. Although my grandmother's china has little *intrinsic* value, I shall always treasure it for the memories it evokes.

introspective   ADJ. looking within oneself. Though young Francis of Assisi led a wild and worldly life, even he had *introspective* moments during which he examined his soul.

intuition   N. immediate insight; power of knowing without reasoning. Even though Tony denied that anything was wrong, Tina trusted her *intuition* that something was bothering him. intuitive, ADJ.

inundate   V. overwhelm; flood; submerge. This semester I am *inundated* with work. You should see the piles of paperwork flooding my desk.

Word List 45

invert   V. turn upside down or inside out. When he *inverted* his body in a handstand, he felt the blood rush to his head.

irascible   ADJ. irritable; easily angered. Miss Minchin's *irascible* temper intimidated the younger schoolgirls, who feared she'd burst into a rage at any moment.

ironic   ADJ. relating to a contradiction between an event's expected result and its actual outcome; sarcastic. It is *ironic* that his success came when he least wanted it. irony, N.

irrational   ADJ. illogical; lacking reason; insane. Many people have such an *irrational* fear of snakes that they panic at the sight of a harmless garter snake.

irrelevant   ADJ. not applicable; unrelated. No matter how *irrelevant* the patient's mumblings may seem, they give us some indications of what he has on his mind.

irreproachable   ADJ. blameless; impeccable. Homer's conduct at the office party was *irreproachable*; even Marge didn't have anything bad to say about how he behaved.

irresolute   ADJ. uncertain how to act; weak. She had no respect for him because he seemed weak-willed and *irresolute*.

irreverence   N. lack of proper respect. Some audience members were amused by the *irreverence* of the comedian's jokes about the Pope; others felt offended by his lack of respect for their faith. irreverent, ADJ.

jargon   N. language used by a special group; technical terminology; gibberish. The computer salesmen at the store used a *jargon* of their own that we simply couldn't follow; we had no idea what they were jabbering about.

jocular   ADJ. said or done in jest; joking. Please do not take my *jocular* remarks seriously.

Word List 46

judicious   ADJ. sound in judgment; wise. At a key moment in his life, Tom made a *judicious* investment that was the foundation of his later wealth.

justification   N. good or just reason; defense; excuse. The jury found him guilty of the more serious charge because they could see no possible *justification* for his actions.

kindle   V. start a fire; inspire. Her teacher's praise *kindled* a spark of hope inside Maya.

labyrinth   N. maze. Hiding from Indian Joe, Tom and Becky soon lost themselves in the *labyrinth* of secret underground caves.

laconic   ADJ. brief and to the point. Many of the characters portrayed by Clint Eastwood are *laconic* types: strong men of few words.

lament   V. grieve; express sorrow. Even advocates of the war *lamented* the loss of so many lives in combat. also N. lamentation, N.

lassitude   N. languor; weariness. After a massage and a long soak in the hot tub, I gave in to my growing *lassitude* and lay down for a nap.

laud   V. praise. The NFL *lauded* Boomer Esiason's efforts to raise money to combat cystic fibrosis. laudable, laudatory, ADJ.

lavish   ADJ. liberal; wasteful. The prince's *lavish* gifts delighted the showgirl. also V.

legacy   N. a gift made by a will. Part of my *legacy* from my parents is an album of family photographs.

Word List 47

lethargic   ADJ. drowsy; dull. The stifling classroom made Sarah *lethargic*: she felt as if she were about to nod off. lethargy, N.

levity N. lack of seriousness; lightness. Stop giggling and wriggling around in your seats: such *levity* is inappropriate in church.

linger V. loiter or dawdle; continue or persist. Hoping to see Juliet pass by, Romeo *lingered* outside the Capulet house for hours. Though Mother made stuffed cabbage on Monday, the smell *lingered* around the house for days.

list V. tilt; lean over. That flagpole should be absolutely vertical; instead, it *lists* to one side. (secondary meaning)

listlessness N. lack in spirit or energy. We had expected him to be full of enthusiasm and were surprised by his *listlessness*.

loathe V. detest. Booing and hissing, the audience showed how much they *loathed* the wicked villain.

lofty ADJ. very high. Barbara Jordan's fellow students used to tease her about her *lofty* ambitions.

loquacious ADJ. talkative. Though our daughter barely says a word to us these days, put a phone in her hand and you'll see how *loquacious* she really is: our phone bills are out of sight!

lucid ADJ. easily understood; clear; intelligible. Ellen made an excellent teacher: her explanations of technical points were *lucid* enough for a child to grasp. lucidity, N.

lurid ADJ. wild; sensational; graphic; gruesome. Do the *lurid* cover stories in the *Enquirer* actually attract people to buy that trashy tabloid?

Word List 48

magnanimous ADJ. generous. Philanthropists by definition are *magnanimous*; misers, by definition, are not. magnanimity, N.

magnate N. person of prominence or influence. Growing up in Pittsburgh, Annie Dillard was surrounded by the mansions of the great steel and coal *magnates* who set their mark on that city.

maladroit ADJ. clumsy; bungling. How *maladroit* it was of me to mention seeing you out partying last night! From the look on his face, I take it that your boyfriend thought you were otherwise occupied.

malevolent ADJ. wishing evil. Iago is a *malevolent* villain who takes pleasure in ruining Othello.

malice N. hatred; spite. Jealous of Cinderella's beauty, her wicked stepsisters expressed their *malice* by forcing her to do menial tasks. malicious, ADJ.

malign V. speak evil of; bad-mouth; defame. Her hatred of her ex-husband ran so deep that she *maligned* anyone who even casually dated him.

marred ADJ. damaged; disfigured. She had to refinish the *marred* surface of the table. mar, V.

martinet N. rigid disciplinarian; strict military officer. No talking at meals! No mingling with the servants! Miss Minchin was a *martinet* who insisted that the schoolgirls in her charge observe each regulation to the letter.

materialism N. preoccupation with physical comforts and things. By its nature, *materialism* is opposed to idealism, for where the materialist emphasizes the needs of the body, the idealist emphasizes the needs of the soul.

meager ADJ. scanty; inadequate. His salary was far too *meager* for him to afford to buy a new car.

Word List 49

meander V. wind or turn in a course. Needing to stay close to a source of water, he followed every twist and turn of the stream as it *meandered* through the countryside.

medley N. mixture. The band played a *medley* of Gershwin tunes.

meek ADJ. quiet and obedient; spiritless. Can Lois Lane see through Superman's disguise and spot the superhero hiding behind the guise of *meek*, timorous Clark Kent?

melancholy ADJ. gloomy; morose; blue. To Eugene, stuck in his small town, a train whistle was a *melancholy* sound, for it made him think of all the places he would never get to see.

mercenary ADJ. interested in money or gain. Andy's every act was prompted by *mercenary* motives: his first question was always "What's in it for me?" also N.

mercurial ADJ. capricious; changing; fickle. Quick as quicksilver to change, he was *mercurial* in nature and therefore erratic.

merger N. combination (of two business corporations). When the firm's president married the director of financial planning, the office joke was that it wasn't a marriage, it was a *merger*.

methodical ADJ. systematic. An accountant must be *methodical* and maintain order among his financial records.

meticulous ADJ. excessively careful; painstaking; scrupulous. Martha Stewart was a *meticulous* housekeeper, fussing about each and every detail that went into making up her perfect home.

minute ADJ. extremely small. The twins resembled one another closely; only *minute* differences set them apart.

Word List 50

misanthrope N. one who hates mankind. In *Gulliver's Travels*, Swift portrays an image of humanity as vile, degraded beasts; for this reason, some critics consider him a *misanthrope*.

miserly ADJ. stingy; mean. The *miserly* old man greedily counted the gold coins he had hoarded over the years.

misnomer N. wrong name; incorrect designation. His tyrannical conduct proved to us all that his nickname, King Eric the Just, was a *misnomer*.

mitigate V. appease; moderate. Nothing Jason did could *mitigate* Medea's anger; she refused to forgive him for betraying her.

mock V. ridicule; imitate, often in derision. It is unkind to mock anyone; it is stupid to *mock* anyone significantly bigger than you. mockery, N.

mollify V. soothe. The airline customer service representative tried to *mollify* the angry passenger by offering her a seat in first class.

momentous ADJ. very important. When Marie and Pierre Curie discovered radium, they had no idea of the *momentous* impact their discovery would have upon society.

monotony N. sameness leading to boredom. He took a clerical job, but soon grew to hate the *monotony* of his daily routine. monotonous, ADJ.

morbid ADJ. given to unwholesome thought; moody; characteristic of disease. This *morbid* dwelling on cancer is unhealthy; quit sitting around brooding and think of more pleasant topics.

morose ADJ. ill-humored; sullen; melancholy. Forced to take early retirement, Bill acted *morose* for months; then, all of a sudden, he shook off his sullen mood and was his usual cheerful self.

Word List 51

mundane ADJ. worldly as opposed to spiritual. Uninterested in philosophical or spiritual discussions, Tom talked only of *mundane* matters such as the daily weather forecast or the latest basketball results.

munificent ADJ. very generous. The Annenberg Trust made a *munificent* gift that supported art programs in the public schools. munificence, N.

mutability N. ability to change in form; fickleness. Going from rags to riches, and then back to rags again, the bankrupt financier was a victim of the *mutability* of fortune.

muted ADJ. silent; muffled; toned down. In the funeral parlor, the mourners' voices had a *muted* quality. mute, V.

naivete N. quality of being unsophisticated; simplicity; artlessness; gullibility. Touched by the *naivete* of sweet, convent-trained Cosette, Marius pledges himself to protect her innocence. naive, ADJ.

nefarious ADJ. very wicked. The villain's crimes, though various, were one and all *nefarious*.

negate V. cancel out; nullify; deny. A sudden surge of adrenaline can *negate* the effects of fatigue; there's nothing like a good shock to wake you up.

nonchalance N. indifference; lack of concern; composure. The first time they performed at the club, all the guys tried to look cool and unconcerned, but none of them could match Dale's *nonchalance*; you would have thought he'd been onstage for years. nonchalant, ADJ.

nonentity N. person of no importance; nonexistence. Don't dismiss William as a *nonentity*; in his quiet way, he's very important to the firm.

nostalgia N. homesickness; longing for the past. My grandfather seldom spoke of life in the old country; he had little patience with *nostalgia*. nostalgic, ADJ.

Word List 52

notoriety N. disrepute; ill fame. To the starlet, any publicity was good publicity: if she couldn't have a good reputation, she'd settle for *notoriety*. notorious, ADJ.

novelty N. something new; newness. The computer is no longer a *novelty* around the office. novel, ADJ.

novice N. beginner. Even a *novice* at word processing can start writing letters right away by following these simple directions.

nuance N. shade of difference in meaning or color. Jody has an extraordinary eye for color. She can look at a painting and see *nuances* in the paint that are indistinguishable to me.

nullify V. to make invalid; void; abolish. Once the contract was *nullified*, it no longer had any legal force.

nurture V. nourish; educate; foster. The Head Start program attempts to *nurture* pre-kindergarten children so that they will do well when they enter public school. also N.

obdurate ADJ. stubborn. The manager was *obdurate* in refusing to discuss the workers' grievances.

objective ADJ. not influenced by emotions; fair. Even though he was her son, she tried to be *objective* about his behavior. objectivity, N.

objective N. goal; aim. A degree in medicine was her ultimate *objective*.

obliterate V. destroy completely. The explosion *obliterated* the facade of the Federal Building, gutting it completely.

Word List 53

oblivion N. obscurity; forgetfulness. After a brief period of popularity, Hurston's works fell into *oblivion*; no one bothered to reprint them, or even to read them any more.

oblivious ADJ. inattentive or unmindful; wholly absorbed. Deep in her book, Nancy was *oblivious* to the noisy squabbles of her brother and his friends.

obscure ADJ. dark; vague; unclear. Even after I read the poem a fourth time, its meaning was still *obscure*. obscurity, N.

obscure V. darken; make unclear. At times he seemed purposely to *obscure* his meaning, preferring mystery to clarity.

obsequious ADJ. slavishly attentive; servile; fawning; sycophantic. Why are some waiters in fancy restaurants so *obsequious*? What makes them think I want people fawning all over me?

obsessive ADJ. related to thinking about something constantly; preoccupying. Ballet, which had been a hobby, began to dominate his life; his love of dancing became *obsessive*. obsession, N.

obstinate ADJ. stubborn; hard to control or treat. We tried to persuade him to give up smoking, but he was *obstinate* and refused to change. obstinacy, N.

obtuse ADJ. blunt; stupid. What can you do with somebody who's so *obtuse* that he can't even tell that you're insulting him?

officious ADJ. meddlesome; excessively pushy in offering one's services. After the long flight, Jill just wanted to nap, but the *officious* bellboy was intent on showing her all the special features of the deluxe suite.

ominous ADJ. threatening. Those clouds are *ominous*; they suggest a severe storm is on the way.

Word List 54

opaque ADJ. dark; not transparent. The *opaque* window shade kept the sunlight out of the room. opacity, N.

opportunist N. individual who sacrifices principles for expediency by taking advantage of circumstances. Forget about ethics! He's such an *opportunist* that he'll vote in favor of any deal that will give him a break.

optimist N. person who looks on the good side. The pessimist says the glass is half-empty; the *optimist* says it is half-full.

optional ADJ. not compulsory; left to one's choice. I was impressed by the range of *optional* accessories for my laptop computer that were available. option, N.

opulence N. extreme wealth; luxuriousness; abundance. The glitter and *opulence* of the ballroom took Cinderella's breath away. opulent, ADJ.

orator N. public speaker. The abolitionist Frederick Douglass was a brilliant *orator* whose speeches brought home to his audience the evils of slavery.

ornate ADJ. excessively or elaborately decorated. The furnishings of homes shown on *Lifestyles of the Rich and Famous* tend to be highly *ornate*.

ostentatious ADJ. showy; pretentious; trying to attract attention. Trump's latest casino in Atlantic City is the most *ostentatious* gambling palace in the East: it easily outglitters its competitors. ostentation, N.

pacifist N. one opposed to force; antimilitarist. During the war, *pacifists*, though they refused to bear arms, nevertheless served in the front lines as ambulance drivers and medical corpsmen.

painstaking ADJ. showing hard work; taking great care. The new high-frequency word list is the result of *painstaking* efforts on the part of our research staff.

Word List 55

paltry ADJ. insignificant; petty; trifling. One hundred dollars for a genuine imitation Rolex watch! Lady, this is a *paltry* sum to pay for such a high-class piece of jewelry.

paradigm N. model; example; pattern. Pavlov's experiment in which he trains a dog to salivate on hearing a bell is a *paradigm* of the conditioned-response experiment in behavioral psychology.

paradox N. something apparently contradictory in nature; statement that looks false but is actually correct. Richard presents a bit of a *paradox*, for he is a card-carrying member of both the National Rifle Association and the relatively pacifist American Civil Liberties Union. paradoxical, ADJ.

paragon N. model of perfection. Her fellow students disliked Lavinia because Miss Minchin always pointed her out as a *paragon* of virtue.

parochial ADJ. narrow in outlook; provincial; related to parishes. Although Jane Austen's novels are set in small rural communities, her concerns are universal, not *parochial*.

parody N. humorous imitation; spoof; takeoff; travesty. The show *Forbidden Broadway* presents *parodies* spoofing the year's new productions playing on Broadway.

parry V. ward off a blow; deflect. Unwilling to injure his opponent in such a pointless clash, Dartagnan simply tried to *parry* his rival's thrusts.

parsimony N. stinginess; excessive frugality. Silas Marner's *parsimony* did not allow him to indulge himself in any luxuries.

partial ADJ. incomplete. In this issue we have published only a *partial* list of contributors because we lack space to acknowledge everyone.

partial ADJ. biased; having a liking for something. I am extremely *partial* to chocolate eclairs. partiality, N.

partisan ADJ. one-sided; prejudiced; committed to a party. On certain issues of conscience, she refused to take a *partisan* stand. also N.

Word List 56

passive ADJ. not active; acted upon. Mahatma Gandhi urged his followers to pursue a program of *passive* resistance rather than resorting to violence and acts of terrorism.

paucity N. scarcity; lack. They closed the restaurant because the *paucity* of customers meant that it was a losing proposition to operate.

pedantic ADJ. showing off learning; bookish. Leavening his decisions with humorous, down-to-earth anecdotes, Judge Wapner was a pleasant contrast to the typical *pedantic* legal scholar. pedant, pedantry, N.

penchant N. strong inclination; liking. Dave has a *penchant* for taking risks: one semester he went steady with three girls, two of whom were stars on the school karate team.

pensive ADJ. dreamily thoughtful; thoughtful with a hint of sadness; contemplative. The *pensive* lover gazed at the portrait of his beloved and deeply sighed.

perceptive ADJ. insightful; aware; wise. Although Maud was a generally *perceptive* critic, she had her blind spots: she could never see flaws in the work of her friends.

perfunctory ADJ. superficial; not thorough; lacking interest, care, or enthusiasm. The auditor's *perfunctory* inspection of the books failed to spot many obvious errors.

peripheral ADJ. marginal; outer. We lived, not in central London, but in one of those *peripheral* suburbs that spring up on the outskirts of a great city. periphery, N.

perjury N. false testimony while under oath. Rather than lie under oath and perhaps be indicted for *perjury*, the witness chose to take the Fifth Amendment, refusing to answer any questions on the grounds that he might incriminate himself.

pernicious ADJ. very destructive. The Athenians argued that Socrates's teachings had a *pernicious* effect on young and susceptible minds; therefore, they condemned him to death.

Word List 57

perpetuate V. make something last; preserve from extinction. Some critics attack *The Adventures of Huckleberry Finn* because they believe Twain's book *perpetuates* a false image of African-Americans in this country.

perturb V. disturb greatly. The thought that electricity might be leaking out of the empty light bulb sockets *perturbed* my aunt so much that at night she crept about the house screwing fresh bulbs in the vacant spots.

pervasive ADJ. pervading; spread throughout

every part. Despite airing them for several hours, Martha could not rid her clothes of the *pervasive* odor of mothballs that clung to them. pervade, V.

pessimism N. belief that life is basically bad or evil; gloominess. Considering how well you have done in the course so far, you have no real reason for such *pessimism* about your final grade.

petty ADJ. trivial; unimportant; very small. She had no major complaints about his work, only a few *petty* quibbles that were almost too minor to state.

petulant ADJ. touchy; peevish. If you'd had hardly any sleep for three nights and people kept phoning and waking you up, you'd sound *petulant*, too.

phenomena N. PL. observable facts; subjects of scientific investigation. We kept careful records of the *phenomena* we noted in the course of these experiments. phenomenon, SING.

philanthropist N. lover of mankind; doer of good. In his role as *philanthropist* and public benefactor, John D. Rockefeller, Sr., donated millions to charity; as an individual, however, he was a tight-fisted old man.

pious ADJ. devout; religious. The challenge for church people today is how to be *pious* in the best sense, that is, to be devout without becoming hypocritical or sanctimonious. piety, N.

pitfall N. hidden danger; concealed trap. Her parents warned young Sophie against the many *pitfalls* that lay in wait for her in the dangerous big city.

Word List 58

pithy ADJ. concise; meaningful; substantial; meaty. Some of Whoopi Goldberg's one-liners at the Oscar Awards were *pithy* and to the point: they packed a wallop, but were short and sweet.

pivotal ADJ. crucial; key; vital. The new "smart weapons" technology played a *pivotal* role in the quick resolution of the war.

placate V. pacify; conciliate. The store manager tried to *placate* the angry customer, offering to replace the damaged merchandise or to give back her money right away.

plagiarize V. steal another's ideas and pass them off as one's own. The teacher could tell that the student had *plagiarized* parts of his essay; she recognized whole paragraphs straight from *Barron's Book Notes*.

platitude N. trite remark; commonplace statement. In giving advice to his son, old Polonius expressed himself only *in platitudes*; every word out of his mouth was a commonplace.

plausible ADJ. having a show of truth but open to doubt; specious. Your mother made you stay home from school because she needed you to program the VCR? I'm sorry, you'll have to come up with a more *plausible* excuse than that.

pliant ADJ. flexible; easily influenced. Pinocchio's disposition was *pliant*; he was like putty in his tempters' hands.

plight N. condition, state (especially a bad state or condition); predicament. Many people feel that the federal government should do more to alleviate the *plight* of the homeless.

poignancy N. quality of being deeply moving; keenness of emotion. Watching the tearful reunion of the long-separated mother and child, the social worker was touched by the *poignancy* of the scene. poignant, ADJ.

polemical ADJ. aggressive in verbal attack; disputatious. Alexis was a master of *polemical* rhetoric; she should have worn a T-shirt with the slogan "Born to Debate." polemic, N.

Word List 59

pomposity N. self-important behavior; acting like a stuffed shirt. Although the commencement speaker had some good things to say, we had to laugh at his *pomposity* and general air of parading his own dignity. pompous, ADJ.

ponderous ADJ. weighty; unwieldy. Sol's humor lacked the light touch; his jokes were always *ponderous*.

porous ADJ. full of pores; like a sieve. Dancers like to wear *porous* clothing because it allows the ready passage of water and air.

potent ADJ. powerful; persuasive; greatly influential. The jury was swayed by the highly *potent* testimony of the crime's sole eyewitness. potency, N.

pragmatic ADJ. practical (as opposed to idealistic); concerned with the practical worth or impact of something. This coming trip to France should provide me with a *pragmatic* test of the value of my conversational French class.

prattle V. babble. Baby John *prattled* endlessly about his cats and his ball and his bottle of juice.

precarious   ADJ. uncertain; risky. Saying the stock would be a *precarious* investment, Tom advised me against purchasing it.

precedent   N. something preceding in time that may be used as an authority or guide for future action. If I buy you a car for your sixteenth birthday, your brothers will want me to buy them cars when they turn sixteen, too; I can't afford to set such an expensive *precedent*.

precipitate   ADJ. rash; premature; hasty; sudden. Though I was angry enough to resign on the spot, I had enough sense to keep myself from quitting a job in such a *precipitate* fashion.

precipitous   ADJ. steep; overhasty. This hill is difficult to climb because it is so *precipitous*; one slip, and our descent will be *precipitous* as well.

Word List 60

preclude   V. make impossible; eliminate. The fact that the band was already booked to play in Hollywood on New Year's Eve *precluded* its accepting the New Year's Eve gig in London.

precocious   ADJ. advanced in development. Listening to the grown-up way the child discussed serious topics, we couldn't help remarking how *precocious* she was. precocity, N.

predator   N. creature that seizes and devours another animal; person who robs or exploits others. Not just cats, but a wide variety of *predators*—owls, hawks, weasels, foxes—catch mice for dinner. A carnivore is by definition *predatory*, for it *preys* on weaker creatures. prey, V.

predecessor   N. former occupant of a post. I hope I can live up to the fine example set by my late *predecessor* in this office.

predilection   N. partiality; preference. Although I have written all sorts of poetry over the years, I have a definite *predilection* for occasional verse.

preposterous   ADJ. absurd; ridiculous. When he tried to downplay his youthful experiments with marijuana by saying he hadn't inhaled, we all thought, "What a *preposterous* excuse!"

prestige   N. impression produced by achievements or reputation. Did Rockefeller become a philanthropist because he was innately generous or because he hoped to gain social *prestige* by donating to popular causes?

presumptuous   ADJ. overconfident; impertinently bold; taking liberties. Matilda thought it was somewhat *presumptuous* of the young man to have addressed her without first having been introduced. Perhaps manners were freer here in the New World.

pretentious   ADJ. ostentatious; pompous; making unjustified claims; overambitious. None of the other prize winners is wearing her medal; isn't it a bit *pretentious* of you to wear yours?

prevalent   ADJ. widespread; generally accepted. A radical committed to social change, Reed had no patience with the conservative views *prevalent* in the America of his day.

Word List 61

problematic   ADJ. doubtful; unsettled; questionable; perplexing. Given the many areas of conflict still awaiting resolution, the outcome of the peace talks remains *problematic*.

proclivity   N. inclination; natural tendency. Watching the two-year-old voluntarily put away his toys, I was amazed by his *proclivity* for neatness.

procrastinate   V. postpone; delay or put off. Looking at four years of receipts and checks he still had to sort through, Bob was truly sorry he had *procrastinated* for so long and not finished filing his taxes long ago.

prodigal   ADJ. wasteful; reckless with money. Don't be so *prodigal* spending my money; when you've earned some money, you can waste it as much as you want! also N.

prodigious   ADJ. marvelous; enormous. Watching the champion weight lifter heave the weighty barbell to shoulder height and then boost it overhead, we marveled at his *prodigious* strength.

prodigy   N. marvel; highly gifted child. Menuhin was a *prodigy*, performing wonders on his violin when he was barely eight years old.

profane   V. violate; desecrate; treat unworthily. The members of the mysterious Far Eastern cult sought to kill the British explorer because he had *profaned* the sanctity of their holy goblet by using it as an ashtray. also ADJ.

profligate   ADJ. dissipated; wasteful; wildly immoral. Although surrounded by wild and *profligate* companions, she nevertheless managed to retain some sense of decency. also N.

profound ADJ. deep; not superficial; complete. Freud's remarkable insights into human behavior caused his fellow scientists to honor him as a *profound* thinker. profundity, N.

profusion N. overabundance; lavish expenditure; excess. At the wedding feast, food and drink were served in such *profusion* that the goodies piled on the tables almost overflowed onto the floor.

Word List 62

proliferation N. rapid growth; spread; multiplication. Times of economic hardship inevitably encourage the *proliferation* of countless get-rich-quick schemes. proliferate, V.

prolific ADJ. abundantly fruitful. My editors must assume I'm a *prolific* writer: they expect me to revise six books this year!

prologue N. introduction (to a poem or play). In the *prologue* to *Romeo and Juliet*, Shakespeare introduces the audience to the feud between the Montagues and the Capulets.

prophetic ADJ. foretelling the future. I have no magical *prophetic* powers; when I predict what will happen, I base my predictions on common sense. prophesy, V.

propitious ADJ. favorable; fortunate; advantageous. Chloe consulted her horoscope to see whether Tuesday would be a *propitious* time to dump her boyfriend.

propriety N. fitness; correct conduct. Miss Manners counsels her readers so that they may behave with due *propriety* in any social situation and not embarrass themselves.

prosaic ADJ. dull and unimaginative; matter-of-fact; factual. Though the ad writers had come up with a wildly imaginative campaign to publicize the new product, the head office rejected it for a more *prosaic*, ordinary approach.

protract V. prolong. Seeking to delay the union members' vote, the management team tried to *protract* the negotiations endlessly.

provincial ADJ. pertaining to a province; limited in outlook; unsophisticated. As *provincial* governor, Sir Henry administered the Queen's law in his remote corner of Canada. Caught up in local problems, out of touch with London news, he became sadly *provincial*.

provisional ADJ. tentative. Edward's appointment was *provisional*; he needed the approval of the board of directors before it would be made permanent.

Word List 63

provocative ADJ. arousing anger or interest; annoying. In a typically *provocative* act, the bully kicked sand into the weaker man's face.

proximity N. nearness. Blind people sometimes develop a compensatory ability to sense the *proximity* of objects around them.

prudent ADJ. cautious; careful. A miser hoards money not because he is *prudent* but because he is greedy. prudence, N.

pugnacity N. combativeness; disposition to fight. "Put up your dukes!" he cried, making a fist to show his *pugnacity*. pugnacious, ADJ.

pungent ADJ. stinging; sharp in taste or smell; caustic. The *pungent* odor of ripe Limburger cheese appealed to Simone but made Stanley gag.

purse V. pucker; contract into wrinkles. Miss Watson *pursed* her lips to show her disapproval of Huck's bedraggled appearance.

qualified ADJ. limited; restricted. Unable to give the candidate full support, the mayor gave him only a *qualified* endorsement. (secondary meaning)

quandary N. dilemma. When both Harvard and Stanford accepted Laura, she was in a *quandary* as to which school she should attend.

quell V. extinguish; put down; quiet. Miss Minchin's demeanor was so stern and forbidding that she could *quell* any unrest among her students with one intimidating glance.

querulous ADJ. fretful; whining. Even the most agreeable toddlers can begin to act *querulous* if they miss their nap.

Word List 64

quiescent ADJ. at rest; dormant; temporarily inactive. After the great eruption, fear of Mount Etna was great; people did not return to cultivate its rich hillside lands until the volcano had been *quiescent* for a full two years.

ramble V. wander aimlessly (physically or mentally). Listening to the teacher *ramble*, Judy wondered whether he'd ever make his point.

rancor N. bitterness; hatred. Let us forget our *rancor* and join together in a new spirit of friendship and cooperation.

rant V. rave; talk excitedly; scold; make a grandiloquent speech. When he heard that I'd totaled the family car, Dad began to *rant* at me like a complete madman.

ratify V. approve formally; verify. Before the treaty could go into effect, it had to be *ratified* by the president.

raucous ADJ. harsh and shrill; disorderly and boisterous. The *raucous* crowd of New Year's Eve revelers got progressively noisier as midnight drew near.

raze V. destroy completely. Spelling is important: to raise a building is to put it up; to *raze* a building is to tear it down.

rebuttal N. refutation; response with contrary evidence. The defense lawyer confidently listened to the prosecutor sum up his case, sure that she could answer his arguments in her *rebuttal*.

recalcitrant ADJ. obstinately stubborn; determined to resist authority; unruly. Which animal do you think is more *recalcitrant*, a pig or a mule?

recant V. disclaim or disavow; retract a previous statement; openly confess error. Those who can, keep true to their faith; those who can't, *recant*.

Word List 65

receptive ADJ. quick or willing to receive ideas, suggestions, etc. Adventure-loving Huck Finn proved a *receptive* audience for Tom's tales of buried treasure and piracy.

recluse N. hermit; loner. Disappointed in love, Miss Emily became a *recluse*; she shut herself away in her empty mansion and refused to see another living soul. reclusive, ADJ.

recount V. narrate or tell; count over again. A born storyteller, my father loved to *recount* anecdotes about his early years in New York.

rectify V. set right; correct. You had better send a check to *rectify* your account before American Express cancels your credit card.

redundant ADJ. superfluous; repetitious; excessively wordy. In your essay, you unnecessarily repeat several points; try to be less *redundant* in future. redundancy, N.

refute V. disprove. The defense called several respectable witnesses who were able to *refute* the false testimony of the prosecution's sole witness.

relegate V. banish to an inferior position; delegate; assign. After Ralph dropped his second tray of drinks that week, the manager swiftly *relegated* him to a minor post cleaning up behind the bar.

relevant ADJ. pertinent; referring to the case in hand. How *relevant* Virginia Woolf's essays are to women writers today! It's as if Woolf in the 1930s foresaw their current literary struggles. relevance, N. relevancy, N.

relinquish V. give up something with reluctance; yield. Denise never realized how hard it would be for her to *relinquish* her newborn son to the care of his adoptive parents.

relish V. savor; enjoy. Watching Peter enthusiastically chow down, I thought, "Now there's a man who *relishes* a good dinner!" also N.

Word List 66

remorse N. guilt; self-reproach. The murderer felt no *remorse* for his crime.

renegade N. deserter; traitor. Because he had abandoned his post and joined forces with the Indians, his fellow officers considered the hero of *Dancing with Wolves* a *renegade*. also ADJ.

renounce V. forswear; repudiate; abandon; discontinue. Joan of Arc refused to *renounce* her testimony even though she knew she would be burned at the stake as a witch.

repel V. drive away; disgust. At first, the Beast's ferocious appearance *repelled* Beauty, but she came to love the tender heart hidden behind that beastly exterior.

replete ADJ. filled to the brim or to the point of being stuffed; abundantly supplied. The movie star's memoir was *replete* with juicy details about the love life of half of Hollywood.

reprehensible ADJ. deserving blame. Shocked by the viciousness of the bombing, politicians of every party uniformly condemned the terrorists' *reprehensible* deed.

repress V. restrain; hold back; crush; suppress. Anne's parents tried to curb her impetuosity without *repressing* her boundless high spirits.

reprimand V. reprove severely; rebuke. Every time Ermengarde made a mistake in class, she was afraid that Miss Minchin would *reprimand* her and tell her father how badly she was doing in school. also N.

reproach V. express disapproval. He never could do anything wrong without imagining how the look on his mother's face would *reproach* him afterwards. also N. reproachful, ADJ.

reprove V. censure; rebuke. The principal severely *reproved* the students whenever they talked in the halls.

Word List 67

repudiate   V. disown; disavow. On separating from Tony, Tina announced that she would *repudiate* all debts incurred by her soon-to-be ex-husband.

rescind   V. cancel. Because of the public outcry against the new taxes, the senator proposed a bill to *rescind* the unpopular financial measure.

reserve   N. self-control; formal but distant manner. Although some girls were attracted by Mark's air of *reserve*, Judy was put off by it, for she felt his aloofness indicated a lack of openness. reserved, ADJ.

resigned   ADJ. unresisting; patiently submissive. *Resigned* to his downtrodden existence, Bob Cratchit was too meek to protest Scrooge's bullying.

resolution   N. determination; resolve. Nothing could shake his *resolution* that his children would get the best education that money could buy. resolute, ADJ.

resolve   N. determination; firmness of purpose. How dare you question my *resolve* to take up skydiving! Of course I haven't changed my mind!

resolve   V. decide; settle; solve. Holmes *resolved* to travel to Bohemia to *resolve* the dispute between Irene Adler and the king.

respite   N. interval of relief; time for rest; delay in punishment. After working nonstop on this project for three straight months, I need a *respite*!

resplendent   ADJ. dazzling; glorious; brilliant. While all the adults were commenting how glorious the emperor looked in his *resplendent* new clothes, one little boy was heard to say, "But he's naked!"

restraint   N. controlling force; control over one's emotions. Amanda dreamed of living an independent life, free of all parental *restraints*.

Word List 68

reticent   ADJ. reserved; uncommunicative; inclined to be silent. Fearing his competitors might get advance word about his plans from talkative staff members, Hughes preferred *reticent* employees to loquacious ones. reticence, N.

retiring   ADJ. modest; shy. Given Susan's *retiring* personality, no one expected her to take up public speaking; surprisingly enough, she became a star of the school debate team.

retract   V. withdraw; take back. When I saw how Fred and his fraternity brothers had trashed the frat house, I decided to *retract* my offer to let them use our summer cottage for the weekend. retraction, N.

reverent   ADJ. respectful. The young acolyte's *reverent* attitude was appropriate in a house of worship.

rhetorical   ADJ. pertaining to effective communication; insincere in language. To win his audience, the speaker used every *rhetorical* trick in the book.

rigorous   ADJ. severe; harsh; demanding; exact. Disliked by his superiors, the officer candidate in *An Officer and a Gentleman* went through an extremely *rigorous* training program.

robust   ADJ. vigorous; strong. After pumping iron and taking karate for six months, the little old lady was far more *robust* in health and could break a plank with her fist.

rudimentary   ADJ. not developed; elementary; crude. Although my grandmother's English vocabulary was limited to a few *rudimentary* phrases, she always could make herself understood.

ruthless   ADJ. pitiless; cruel. Captain Hook was a dangerous, *ruthless* villain who would stop at nothing to destroy Peter Pan.

sagacious   ADJ. perceptive; shrewd; having insight. Mr. Bond, that was not a particularly *sagacious* move on your part. I had not expected such a foolish trick from a smart fellow like you. sagacity, N.

Word List 69

sage   N. person celebrated for wisdom. Hearing tales of a mysterious Master of All Knowledge who lived in the hills of Tibet, Sandy was possessed with a burning desire to consult the legendary *sage*. also ADJ.

sanction   V. approve; ratify. Nothing will convince me to *sanction* the engagement of my daughter to such a worthless young man.

sanctuary   N. refuge; shelter; shrine; holy place. The tiny attic was Helen's *sanctuary* to which she fled when she had to get away from the rest of her family.

sarcasm   N. scornful remarks; stinging rebuke. Though Ralph tried to ignore the mocking comments of his supposed friends, their *sarcasm* wounded him deeply.

satirical ADJ. mocking. The humor of cartoonist Gary Trudeau often is *satirical*; through the comments of the Doonesbury characters, Trudeau ridicules political corruption and folly.

saturate V. soak thoroughly. *Saturate* your sponge with water until it can't hold any more.

savory ADJ. tasty; pleasing, attractive, or agreeable. Julia Child's recipes enable amateur chefs to create *savory* delicacies for their guests.

scanty ADJ. meager; insufficient. Thinking his helping of food was *scanty*, Oliver Twist asked for more.

scrupulous ADJ. conscientious; extremely thorough. I'm very happy to recommend Adam as an employee because he's always been highly *scrupulous* about doing a good job whenever he's worked for me.

scrutinize V. examine closely and critically. Searching for flaws, the sergeant *scrutinized* every detail of the private's uniform.

Word List 70

seclusion N. isolation; solitude. One moment she loved crowds; the next, she sought *seclusion*. secluded, ADJ.

sectarian ADJ. relating to a religious faction or subgroup; narrow-minded; limited. Far from being broad-minded, the religious leader was intolerant of new ideas, paying attention only to purely *sectarian* interests. sect, N.

sedentary ADJ. requiring sitting. Disliking the effect of her *sedentary* occupation on her figure, Stacy decided to work out at the gym every other day.

sequester V. isolate; retire from public life; segregate; seclude. Banished from his kingdom, the wizard Prospero *sequestered* himself on a desert island.

serenity N. calmness; placidity. The sound of air raid sirens pierced the *serenity* of the quiet village of Pearl Harbor.

servile ADJ. slavishly submissive; fawning; cringing. Constantly fawning on his employer, Uriah Heep was a *servile* creature.

sever V. cut; separate. The released prisoner wanted to begin a new life and *sever* all connections with his criminal past. reverance, N.

severity N. harshness; intensity; austerity; rigidity. The newspaper editorials disapproved of the *severity* of the sentence.

shrewd ADJ. clever; astute. A *shrewd* investor,

he took clever advantage of the fluctuations of the stock market.

singular ADJ. unique; extraordinary; odd. Though the young man tried to understand Father William's *singular* behavior, he still found it odd that the old man incessantly stood on his head. singularity, N.

Word List 71

skeptical ADJ. doubting; suspending judgment until one has examined the evidence supporting a point of view. I am *skeptical* about the new health plan; I want some proof that it can work. skepticism, N.

slacken V. slow up; loosen. As they passed the finish line, the runners *slackened* their pace.

slander N. defamation; utterance of false and malicious statements. Considering the negative comments politicians make about each other, it's a wonder that more of them aren't sued for *slander*. also V.

slothful ADJ. lazy. The British word "layabout" is a splendid descriptive term for someone *slothful*: What did the lazy bum do? He lay about the house all day. sloth, N.

sluggish ADJ. slow; lazy; lethargic. After two nights without sleep, she felt *sluggish* and incapable of exertion.

solemnity N. seriousness; gravity. The minister was concerned that nothing should disturb the *solemnity* of the marriage service.

solicit V. request earnestly; seek. Knowing she needed to have a solid majority for the budget to pass, the mayor telephoned all the members of the city council to *solicit* their votes.

solitude N. state of being alone; seclusion. Much depends on how much you like your own company. What to one person seems fearful isolation, to another is blessed *solitude*.

soluble ADJ. able to be dissolved; able to be explained. Sherlock Holmes took the *soluble* powder and dissolved it into a seven percent solution.

somber ADJ. gloomy; depressing; dark; drab. From the doctor's grim expression, I could tell he had *somber* news.

Word List 72

sparse ADJ. not thick; thinly scattered; scanty. He had moved from the densely populated city to the remote countryside where the population was *sparse*.

spendthrift N. someone who wastes money. Easy access to credit encourages people to turn into *spendthrifts* who shop till they drop.

spontaneity N. lack of premeditation; naturalness; freedom from constraint. When Betty and Amy met, Amy impulsively hugged her roommate-to-be, but Betty drew back, unprepared for such *spontaneity*. spontaneous, ADJ.

sporadic ADJ. occurring irregularly. Although you can still hear *sporadic* outbursts of laughter and singing outside, the big Halloween parade has passed; the party's over till next year.

spurious ADJ. false; counterfeit. Unaccustomed to the design of the new hundred-dollar bills, many storekeepers rejected them as *spurious*.

spurn V. reject; scorn. The heroine *spurned* the villain's advances.

squalor N. filth; degradation; dirty, neglected state. Rusted, broken-down cars in the yard, trash piled up on the porch, tar paper peeling from the roof, the shack was the picture of *squalor*.

squander V. waste. If you *squander* your allowance on candy and comic books, you won't have any money left to buy the new box of crayons you want.

stagnant ADJ. motionless; stale; dull. Mosquitoes commonly breed in ponds of *stagnant* water. stagnate, V.

stanza N. division of a poem. Do you know the last *stanza* of "The Star-Spangled Banner"?

Word List 73

static ADJ. unchanging; lacking development. Nothing had changed at home; life was *static*. stasis, N.

steadfast ADJ. loyal; unswerving. Penelope was *steadfast* in her affections, faithfully waiting for Ulysses to return from his wanderings.

stoic ADJ. impassive; unmoved by joy or grief. I wasn't particularly *stoic* when I had my flu shot; I squealed like a stuck pig. also N.

strident ADJ. loud and harsh; insistent. We could barely hear the speaker over the *strident* cries of the hecklers.

strut N. pompous walk; swagger. Colonel Blimp's *strut* as he marched about the parade ground revealed him for what he was: a pompous buffoon. also V.

stupefy V. make numb; stun; amaze. Disapproving of drugs in general, Laura refused to take sleeping pills or any other medicine that might *stupefy* her.

subdued ADJ. less intense; quieter. In the hospital visitors spoke in a *subdued* tone of voice for fear of disturbing the patients.

submissive ADJ. yielding; timid. Crushed by his authoritarian father, Will had no defiance left in him; he was totally *submissive* in the face of authority.

subordinate ADJ. occupying a lower rank; inferior; submissive. Bishop Proudie's wife expected all the *subordinate* clergy to behave with great deference to the wife of their superior. alos N., V.

subside V. settle down; descend; grow quiet. The doctor assured us that the fever would eventually *subside*.

Word List 74

substantial ADJ. ample; solid. The scholarship represented a *substantial* sum of money.

substantiate V. establish by evidence; verify; support. These endorsements from satisfied customers *substantiate* our claim that Barron's *How to Prepare for the SAT* is the best SAT-prep book on the market.

subtlety N. perceptiveness; ingenuity; delicacy. Never obvious, she expressed herself with such *subtlety* that her remarks went right over the heads of most of her audience. subtle, ADJ.

succinct ADJ. brief; terse; compact. Don't bore your audience with excess verbiage: be *succinct*.

supercilious ADJ. arrogant; condescending; patronizing. The *supercilious* headwaiter sneered at customers who he thought did not fit in at a restaurant catering to an ultrafashionable crowd.

superficial ADJ. trivial; shallow. Since your report gave only a *superficial* analysis of the problem, I cannot give you more than a passing grade.

superfluous ADJ. excessive; overabundant; unnecessary. Please try not to include so many *superfluous* details in your report; just give me the facts. superfluity, N.

supplant V. replace; usurp. Did the other woman actually *supplant* Princess Diana in Prince Charles's affections, or did Charles never love Diana at all?

suppress   V. crush; subdue; inhibit. After the armed troops had *suppressed* the rebellion, the city was placed under martial law.

surmount   V. overcome. I know you can *surmount* any difficulties that may stand in the way of your getting an education.

Word List 75

surpass   V. exceed. Her SAT scores *surpassed* our expectations.

surreptitious   ADJ. secret; furtive; sneaky; hidden. Hoping to discover where his mom had hidden the Christmas presents, Timmy took a *surreptitious* peek into the master bedroom closet.

susceptible   ADJ. impressionable; easily influenced; having little resistance, as to a disease; receptive to. Said the patent medicine man to the extremely *susceptible* customer: "Buy this new miracle drug, and you will no longer be *susceptible* to the common cold."

sustain   V. experience; support; nourish. Stuart *sustained* such a severe injury that the doctors feared he would be unable to work to *sustain* his growing family.

swindler   N. cheat. She was gullible and trusting, an easy victim for the first *swindler* who came along.

sycophant   N. servile flatterer; bootlicker; yes man. Fed up with the toadies and brownnosers who made up his entourage, the star cried, "Get out, all of you! I'm sick to death of *sycophants*!"

symmetry   N. arrangement of parts so that balance is obtained; congruity. Something lopsided by definition lacks *symmetry*.

taciturn   ADJ. habitually silent; talking little. The stereotypical cowboy is a *taciturn* soul, answering lengthy questions with "Yep" or "Nope."

taint   V. contaminate; cause to lose purity; modify with a trace of something bad. Fighting to preserve her good name, Desdemona wondered what had occurred to *taint* her reputation. also N.

tangential   ADJ. peripheral; only slightly connected; digressing. Despite Clark's attempts to distract her with *tangential* remarks, Lois kept on coming back to her main question: why couldn't he come out to dinner with Superman and her?

Word List 76

tangible   ADJ. able to be touched; real; palpable. Although Tom did not own a house, he had several *tangible* assets—a car, a television, a PC—that he could sell if he needed cash.

tantamount   ADJ. equivalent in effect or value. Though Rudy claimed his wife was off visiting friends, his shriek of horror when she walked into the room was *tantamount* to a confession that he believed she was dead.

tedious   ADJ. boring; tiring. The repetitious nature of work on the assembly line made Martin's job very *tedious*. tedium, N.

temper   V. moderate; tone down or restrain; toughen (steel). Not even her supervisor's grumpiness could *temper* Nancy's enthusiasm for her new job.

tenacity   N. firmness; persistence. Jean Valjean could not believe the *tenacity* of Inspector Javert. All Valjean had done was to steal a loaf of bread, and the inspector had pursued him doggedly for twenty years! tenacious, ADJ.

tentative   ADJ. provisional; experimental; doubtful. Your *tentative* proposal sounds feasible; let me know when the final details are worked out.

termination   N. end. Because of the unexpected *termination* of his contract, he urgently needed a new job.

terse   ADJ. concise; abrupt; pithy. There is a fine line between speech that is *terse* and to the point and speech that is too abrupt.

threadbare   ADJ. worn through till the threads show; shabby and poor. The poor adjunct professor hid the *threadbare* spots on his jacket by sewing leather patches on his sleeves.

thrive   V. prosper; flourish. Despite the impact of the recession on the restaurant trade, Philip's cafe *thrived*.

Word List 77

tirade   N. extended scolding; denunciation; harangue. The cigar smoker went into a bitter *tirade* denouncing the antismoking forces that had succeeded in banning smoking from most planes and restaurants.

torpor   N. lethargy; sluggishness; dormancy. Throughout the winter, nothing aroused the bear from his *torpor*: he would not emerge from hibernation until spring.

tractable   ADJ. docile; easily managed. Although Susan seemed a *tractable* young woman, she had a stubborn streak of independence that occasionally led her to defy the powers-that-be when she felt they were in the wrong.

tranquillity   N. calmness; peace. After the commotion and excitement of the city, I appreciate the *tranquillity* of these fields and forests.

transcendent   ADJ. surpassing; exceeding ordinary limits; superior. For the amateur chef, dining at the four-star restaurant was a *transcendent* experience: the meal surpassed his wildest dreams.

transient   ADJ. momentary; temporary; staying for a short time. Lexy's joy at finding the perfect Christmas gift for Phil was *transient*; she still had to find presents for Roger, Laura, Allison, and Uncle Bob.

transparent   ADJ. easily detected; permitting light to pass through freely. Bobby managed to put an innocent look on his face; to his mother, however, his guilt was *transparent*.

trepidation   N. fear; nervous apprehension. If you've never seen an SAT test, it's natural for you to feel some *trepidation* when you take the exam; if you're familiar with the test, however, you've got a much better chance of staying calm.

trifling   ADJ. trivial; unimportant. Why bother going to see a doctor for such a *trifling*, everyday cold?

trite   ADJ. hackneyed; commonplace. The *trite* and predictable situations in many television programs turn off many viewers, who respond by turning off their sets.

Word List 78

trivial   ADJ. unimportant; trifling. Too many magazines ignore newsworthy subjects and feature *trivial* affairs. trivia, N.

turbulence   N. state of violent agitation. Warned of approaching *turbulence* in the atmosphere, the pilot told the passengers to fasten their seat belts.

turmoil   N. great commotion and confusion. Lydia running off with a soldier! Mother fainting at the news! The Bennet household was in *turmoil*.

tyranny   N. oppression; cruel government. Frederick Douglass fought against the *tyranny* of slavery throughout his entire life.

undermine   V. weaken; sap. The recent corruption scandals have *undermined* many people's faith in the city government.

uniformity   N. sameness; monotony. After a while, the *uniformity* of TV situation comedies becomes boring. uniform, ADJ.

universal   ADJ. characterizing or affecting all; present everywhere. At first, no one shared Christopher's opinions; his theory that the world was round was met with *universal* disdain.

unkempt   ADJ. disheveled; uncared for in appearance. Jeremy hated his neighbor's *unkempt* lawn: he thought its neglected appearance had a detrimental effect on neighborhood property values.

unprecedented   ADJ. novel; unparalleled. For a first novel, Margaret Mitchell's novel *Gone with the Wind* was an *unprecedented* success.

unwarranted   ADJ. unjustified; groundless; undeserved. We could not understand Martin's *unwarranted* rudeness to his mother's guests.

Word List 79

usurp   V. seize another's power or rank. The revolution ended when the victorious rebel general succeeded in his attempt to *usurp* the throne.

vacillate   V. waver; fluctuate. Uncertain which suitor she ought to marry, the princess *vacillated*, saying now one, now the other. vacillation, N.

venerate   V. revere. In Tibet today, the common people still *venerate* their traditional spiritual leader, the Dalai Lama.

veracity   N. truthfulness. Trying to prove Anita Hill a liar, Senator Specter repeatedly questioned her *veracity*.

verbose   ADJ. wordy. We had to make some major cuts in Senator Foghorn's speech because it was far too *verbose*. verbosity, N.

viable   ADJ. practical or workable; capable of maintaining life. The plan to build a new baseball stadium, though missing a few details, is *viable* and stands a good chance of winning popular support.

vigor   N. active strength. Although he was over seventy years old, Jack had the *vigor* of a man in his prime. vigorous, ADJ.

vilify   V. slander. Waging a highly negative campaign, the candidate attempted to *vilify* his opponent's reputation.

vindicate V. clear from blame; exonerate; justify or support. The lawyer's goal was to *vindicate* her client and prove him innocent on all charges. The critics' extremely favorable reviews *vindicate* my opinion that *The Madness of King George* is a brilliant movie.

vindictive ADJ. out for revenge; malicious. Divorce sometimes brings out a *vindictive* streak in people; when Tony told Tina he was getting a divorce, she poured green Jello into his aquarium and turned his tropical fish into dessert.

Word List 80

virtuoso N. highly skilled artist. The child prodigy Yehudi Menuhin grew into a *virtuoso* whose violin performances thrilled millions. virtuosity, N.

virulent ADJ. extremely poisonous; hostile; bitter. Laid up with an extremely *virulent* case of measles, he blamed his doctors because his recovery took so long. In fact, he became quite *virulent* on the subject of the quality of modern medical care. virulence, N.

volatile ADJ. changeable; explosive; evaporating rapidly. The political climate today is extremely *volatile*: no one can predict what the electorate will do next. Maria Callas's temper was extremely *volatile*: the only thing you could predict was that she would blow up. Acetone is an extremely *volatile* liquid: it evaporates instantly.

voluble ADJ. fluent; glib; talkative. An excessively *voluble* speaker suffers from logorrhea: he runs off at the mouth a lot!

voluminous ADJ. bulky; large. Despite her family burdens, she kept up a *voluminous* correspondence with her friends.

vulnerable ADJ. susceptible to wounds. His opponents could not harm Achilles, who was *vulnerable* only in his heel.

whimsical ADJ. capricious; fanciful. He dismissed his generous gift to his college as a sentimental fancy, an old man's *whimsical* gesture. whimsy, N.

willful ADJ. intentional; headstrong; stubbornly set on getting one's way. Donald had planned to kill his wife for months; clearly, her death was a case of deliberate, *willful* murder, not a crime of passion committed by a hasty, *willful* youth unable to foresee the consequences of his deeds.

withhold V. refuse to give; hold back. The NCAA may *withhold* permission for academically underprepared athletes to participate in intercollegiate sports as freshmen.

zealot N. fanatic; person who shows excessive zeal. Though Glenn was devout, he was no *zealot*; he never tried to force his beliefs on his friends.

PART VI

WRITING SKILLS QUESTIONS

OVERVIEW

The questions in the writing skills section test your ability to recognize clear, correct standard written English, the kind of writing your college professors will expect on the papers you write for them. You'll be expected to know basic grammar, such as subject-verb agreement, pronoun-antecedent agreement, correct verb tense, correct sentence structure, and correct diction. You'll need to know how to recognize a dangling participle and how to spot when two parts of a sentence are not clearly connected. You'll also need to know when a paragraph is (or isn't) properly developed and organized.

GRAMMAR, PLAIN AND FANCIFUL[1]

Plain grammar gives us the horrors. Our eyes glaze over when we read "Nouns are words that name or designate persons, places, things, states, or qualities." Nevertheless, we need to have some understanding of grammar to survive the writing sections on the SAT. That brings us to fanciful grammar, the rules of grammar illustrated in ways to keep both the reader and the writer awake.

First, we need to be sure we understand what a sentence is. A sentence consists of at least two parts: a subject or topic (the someone or something we are talking about) and a predicate or comment (what we are saying about that someone or something). It may have other parts, but these two are essential.

Let's look at a few sentences.

The witch is bending over the cauldron.

The witch bending over the cauldron is a student.

The cauldron bubbled.

The pot overflowed.

She was scalded.

Her long, thin, elegant fingers writhed with the agony of her burns.

The professor of herbology concocted a healing salve.

The witch's blistered digits twitched as the infirmarian slathered dollops of ointment on the irritated skin.

In each of the sentences above, the complete subject appears in **boldface.** Within each complete subject, there is a simple subject, the heart of the matter, a noun or pronoun.

In each of the sentences below, the simple subject appears in **boldface** also.

The **wizard** wavered.

The **troll** pounced.

It bounced off the bannister.

The **incantations** chanted by the enchanter were consistently off-key.

A **spoonful** of sugar makes the elixir go down.

(*Wizard, troll, incantations,* and *spoonful* all are nouns. *It* is a pronoun, of course.)

Now let's look at the predicate, the comment about the subject.

The witch **is bending over the cauldron.**

---

[1]With thanks and/or apologies to J. K. Rowling, J. R. R. Tolkien, C. S. Lewis, William Butler Yeats, Diana Wynne Jones, Homer (the Great), Homer (the Simpson), and of course the ever-popular Anon.

Berenice and Benedick **hid under the cloak of invisibility.**

The professor of herbology **concocted a healing salve.**

The troll **pounced.**

The mandrake **began to scream.**

In each of the sentences above, the part in **boldface** is the complete predicate, or everything the sentence has to say about its subject. Just as within each complete subject lies a simple subject, within each complete predicate lies a simple predicate, or verb. The simple predicate (the verb) appears in **boldface** in each of the sentences below.

The witch **is bending** over the cauldron.

The mandrake **began** to scream.

Berenice and Benedick **hid** under the cloak of invisibility.

The troll **pounced.**

The subject usually precedes the predicate. However, exceptions do occur.

Over the parapets and into the sky flew **a silver and gold Rolls Royce.**

There were **twenty-nine would-be wizards** practicing their potions.

Simple subjects can be compound (that means you're talking about more than one someone or something). A compound subject consists of at least two subjects, linked by *and*, *or*, or *nor*. These subjects have something in common: they may or may not enjoy doing things together, but they do share the same verb.

A witch and **an apprentice** are bending over the cauldron.

Berenice or **Benedick** lurked beneath the balustrade.

Either **the lion** or **the witch** escaped from the wardrobe.

The Greeks and **the Trojans** ran down to the sea higgledy-piggledy.

Neither **the mandrake** nor **the mummy** enjoyed being dug up.

Simple predicates can be compound as well (that means the schizophrenic subject gets to do more than one thing at a time). A compound predicate consists of at least two verbs—linked by *and*, *or*, *nor*, *yet*, or *but*—that have a common subject.

The cauldron **bubbled** and **overflowed.**

Her long, thin, elegant fingers **writhed** with the agony of her burns or **flexed** in evidence of her dexterity.

The glum troll neither **bustled** nor **bounced.**

I **will arise** and **go** now, and **go** to Innisfree.

The Greeks and the Trojans **ran** down to the sea higgledy-piggledy yet never **got** their armor wet.

The walrus **wept** but **ate** the oysters, every one.

Completing this discussion of the basic sentence pattern and completing the predicate as well is the complement. The complement is the part of the predicate that lets us know just what (or whom) the verb has been up to. It completes the verb. Often it answers the question "What?"

Witches want. (This could be an existential comment on the nature of witches, but it's simply an incomplete predicate.)

What do witches want?

Witches want **equal rites.**

Witches want **some enchanted evenings.**

Witches want **a chicken in every cauldron.**

Witches want **not to be hassled by wizards.**

Witches want **to sit down for a spell.**

Now we know. The complement clues us in, satisfying our curiosity as it helps the verb tell its tale. Complements come in several guises. There is the direct object. Direct objects are directly affected by the actions of verbs. They are like punching bags: they feel the effect of the blow.

In the following examples, the direct object is underlined.

The troll holds **several <u>captives</u>.**

The troll holds **his <u>tongue</u> with difficulty.**

The troll holds **<u>him</u> in a headlock.**

The troll holds **<u>her</u> in shackles and suspense.**

Some verbs may have both a direct object and an indirect object. Examples include *assign, award, bake, bring, buy, furnish, give, grant, issue, lend, mail, offer, present, sell, send, ship, show,* and *take.* These verbs raise a fresh question: *To whom* or *for whom* (*to what* or *for what*) is the subject performing this action? The indirect object is the person (or place or thing) to whom or for whom the subject performs the action.

The troll sends his compliments.
[The subject is *troll*; the verb, *sends*; the direct object, *compliments*.]

To whom does the troll send his compliments?
The troll sends the **chef** his compliments.
[The indirect object is *chef*.]

The owl bought new sails.
[The subject is *owl*; the verb, *bought*; the direct object, *sails*.]

For what did the owl buy new sails?
The owl bought the pea-green **boat** new sails.
[The indirect object is *boat*.]

The Greeks showed no mercy.
[The subject is *Greeks*; the verb, *showed*; the direct object, *mercy*.]

To whom (or to what) did the Greeks show no mercy?
The Greeks showed the **Trojans** no mercy.
The Greeks showed **Troy** no mercy.

Yet another form of complement is the subject (or subjective) complement. Just as transitive verbs[2] by definition must have direct objects to be complete, linking verbs (*be, become, feel, look, seem, smell, sound, taste,* etc.) must hook up with a noun, adjective, or pronoun to avoid going through an identity crisis.

The troll is. (Yet another existential comment on the "is-ness" of trolls? No, just an example of a linking verb looking for its missing link.)

The troll is *what?*

The troll is a born **storyteller.** [The noun *storyteller*, the subject complement, identifies or explains *troll*, the subject.]

The troll is *what?*

The troll is so **droll.** [The adjective *droll*, meaning whimsically humorous, describes or qualifies *troll*.]

Only certain verbs take subject complements: *to be*, in all its forms (*am, are, is, was, were,* etc.); sensory verbs (*feel, look, smell, sound, taste*); and other state of being verbs (*appear, become, grow, prove, remain, seem, stay, turn*).

Imogen looks a **fright.**

The potion proved **palatable.** In other words, it tasted **good.**

The troll grows **bold,** but Sybilla remains **cold.** (The troll's emotions seem **palpable,** though perhaps less palpable than his enlarged spleen.)

Our final group of complements consists of the object (or objective) complements. These tagalongs follow the direct object, identifying it or qualifying it. We find them in the vicinity of such verbs as *appoint, call, consider, designate, elect, find, label, make, name, nominate, render,* and *term.*

The walrus found the oysters. [The subject is *walrus;* the verb, *found;* the direct object, *oysters.*]

The walrus found the oysters **yummy.** [Direct object is *oysters.* Object complement is *yummy.*]

---

[2] Transitive verbs *must* have a direct object to complete their meaning. For example, take the verb *hate.* It's a typical transitive verb: without a direct object it feels incomplete. Only a refugee from a bad horror movie would wander around proclaiming, "I hate, I hate...." The subject hates *something.* "I hate spinach." "I hate Donald Trump." "I hate MTV."

Verbs that do not have direct objects are called intransitive verbs. These verbs tell you all you need to know about the subject. No direct objects are needed at all. Think of the seven dwarfs. Doc *blusters.* Grumpy *frowns.* Bashful *stammers.* Sleepy *dozes* and *snores.* Happy *chuckles.* Sneezy...you guessed it. Linking verbs (forms of *be, seem, feel,* etc., that relate the subject to the subject complement) are by definition intransitive verbs.

Some verbs can be transitive in one sentence and intransitive in another:

"Auntie Em," cried Dorothy, "I *missed* you so much!" (Transitive)

"Oops!" said the knife-thrower. "I *missed*." (Intransitive)

Do not worry about these labels. What's important is that you understand how the words are being used.

Sybilla considers the troll an uncouth **brute.** [Direct object is *troll*. Object complement is *brute*. Sybilla is not being very complimentary about the troll.]

Sybilla's scorn makes the troll **melancholy. In** fact, it renders him downright **glum.**

On this note, we leave the basic sentence. In the following section we, together with the troll, the walrus, and several junior witches, will explore some common problems in grammar and usage that are likely to turn up on the SAT.

COMMON PROBLEMS IN GRAMMAR AND USAGE

COMMON PROBLEMS IN GRAMMAR

Sentence Fragments

What is a sentence fragment? A sentence fragment is a broken chunk of sentence in need of fixing. The poor fractured thing can't stand alone. In this section, we'll look at some broken sentences and fix them, too.

Here are the fragments. Let's examine them one at a time.

When the troll bounced off the bannister.

Muttering over the cauldron.

To harvest mandrakes nocturnally.

In our preparation of the purple potion.

Or lurk beneath the balustrade.

Say the first sentence fragment aloud: "When the troll bounced off the bannister." Say it again. Do you feel as if something is missing? Do the words trigger questions in your mind? "What?" "What happened?" That's great. You are reacting to a dependent clause that is being treated as if it were a sentence. But it isn't.

Here are a couple of ways to correct this fragment. You can simply chop off the subordinating conjunction *when*, leaving yourself with a simple sentence:

The troll bounced off the bannister.

You can also provide the dependent clause with an independent clause to lean on:

When the troll bounced off the bannister, **he bowled over the professor of herbology.**

The little wizards laughed to see such sport when the troll bounced off the bannister.

Now for the second fragment, "Muttering over the cauldron." Again, something feels incomplete. This is either a participial phrase or a gerund phrase. It needs a subject; it also needs a complete verb. Here's the simplest way to repair the fragment:

The witch is muttering over the cauldron.

Here's another:

Muttering over the cauldron **is a bad habit that good witches should avoid.**

Here's a third:

Muttering over the cauldron, **the witch failed to enunciate the incantation clearly.**

The third fragment again has several fixes. You can turn the infinitive phrase "To harvest mandrakes nocturnally" into a command:

Harvest mandrakes nocturnally! (The professor of herbology does not recommend that you harvest them by day.)

You can provide a simple subject and complete the verb:

We will harvest mandrakes nocturnally.

COMMON PROBLEMS IN GRAMMAR AND USAGE 195

You can treat "To harvest mandrakes nocturnally" as the subject of your sentence and add a predicate:

To harvest mandrakes nocturnally **is a task that only a fearless junior wizard would undertake.**

You can also keep "To harvest mandrakes nocturnally" as an infinitive phrase and attach it to an independent clause:

To harvest mandrakes nocturnally, **you must wait for a completely moonless night.**

The next to last sentence fragment, "In our preparation of the purple potion," is a phrase.

To fix it, you can provide a simple subject and create a verb:

We prepared the purple potion.

You can assume an implicit subject (*you*) and turn it into a command:

Prepare the purple potion!

You can also attach it to an independent clause:

We miscalculated the proportions in our preparation of the purple potion.

The final sentence fragment, "Or lurk beneath the balustrade," is part of a compound predicate. Take away the initial *Or* and you have a command:

Lurk beneath the balustrade!

Provide a simple subject and you have a straightforward declarative sentence:

Orcs lurk beneath the balustrade.

Combine the fragment with the other part or parts of the compound predicate, and you have a complete sentence:

Orcs slink around the cellarage or lurk beneath the balustrade.

Here is a question involving a sentence fragment. See whether you can select the correct answer.

Some parts of the following sentence are underlined. The first answer choice, (A), simply repeats the underlined part of the sentence. The other four choices present four alternative ways to phrase the underlined part. Select the answer that produces the most effective sentence, one that is clear and exact. In selecting your choice, be sure that it is standard written English, and that it expresses the meaning of the original sentence.

J. K. Rowling, a British novelist, whose fame as an innovator in the field of fantasy may come to equal that of J. R. R. Tolkien.

(A) J. K. Rowling, a British novelist, whose fame as an innovator
(B) A British novelist who is famous as an innovator, J. K. Rowling
(C) J. K. Rowling, who is a British novelist and whose fame as an innovator
(D) J. K. Rowling is a British novelist whose fame as an innovator
(E) A British novelist, J. K. Rowling, who is a famous innovator

Did you spot that the original sentence was missing its verb? The sentence's subject is J. K. Rowling. She *is* a British novelist. That is the core of the sentence. Everything else in the sentence simply serves to clarify what kind of novelist Rowling is. She is a novelist whose fame may come to equal Tolkien's fame. The correct answer is choice D.

Try this second question, also involving a sentence fragment.

The new vacation resort, featuring tropical gardens and man-made lagoons, and overlooks a magnificent white sand beach.

(A) resort, featuring tropical gardens and man-made lagoons and overlooks a magnificent white sand beach
(B) resort overlooks a magnificent white sand beach, it features tropical gardens and man-made lagoons
(C) resort, featuring tropical gardens and man-made lagoons and overlooking a magnificent white sand beach
(D) resort, featuring tropical gardens and man-made lagoons, overlooks a magnificent white sand beach
(E) resort to feature tropical gardens and man-made lagoons and to overlook a magnificent white sand beach

What makes this a sentence fragment? Note the presence of *and* just before the verb *overlooks*. The presence of *and* immediately before a verb is a sign of a compound predicate, as in the sentence "The cauldron bubbled and overflowed." (*Definition*: A compound predicate consists of at least two verbs, linked by *and*, *or*, *nor*, *yet*, or *but*, that have a common subject.) But there is only one verb here, not two.

How can you fix this fragment? You can rewrite the sentence, substituting the verb *features* for the participle *featuring* so that the sentence has two verbs:

The new vacation resort **features** tropical gardens and man-made lagoons and **overlooks** a magnificent white sand beach.

Or, you can simply take away the *and*. The sentence then would read:

The new vacation resort, featuring tropical gardens and man-made lagoons, **overlooks** a magnificent white sand beach.

This sentence is grammatically complete. It has a subject, *resort*, and a verb, *overlooks*. The bit between the commas ("featuring...lagoons") simply

describes the subject. (It's called a participial phrase.) The correct answer is choice D.

The Run-On Sentence

The run-on sentence is a criminal connection operating under several aliases: the *comma fault sentence*, the *comma splice sentence*, the *fused sentence*. Fortunately, there's no need for you to learn the grammar teachers' names for these flawed sentences. You just need to know they are flawed.

Here are two run-on sentences. It's easy to spot the comma fault or comma splice: it's the example that contains the comma.

EXAMPLE 1:

The wizards tasted the potion, they found the mixture tasty.

EXAMPLE 2:

The troll is very hungry I think he is going to pounce.

The *comma splice* or *comma fault* sentence is a sentence in which two independent, self-supporting clauses are improperly connected by a comma. Clearly, the two are in need of a separation if not a divorce. Example 1 above illustrates a comma splice or comma fault. The *fused sentence* (Example 2) consists of two sentences that run together without benefit of any punctuation at all. Such sentences are definitely *not* PG (Properly Grammatical).

You can correct run-on sentences in at least four different ways.

1. Use a period, not a comma, at the end of the first independent clause. Begin the second independent clause with a capital letter.

The wizards tasted the potion. They found the mixture tasty.

The troll is very hungry. I think he is going to pounce.

2. Connect the two independent clauses by using a coordinating conjunction.

The wizards tasted the potion, and they found the mixture tasty.

The troll is very hungry, so I think he is going to pounce.

3. Insert a semicolon between two main clauses.

The wizards tasted the <u>potion; they</u> found the mixture tasty.

The troll is very <u>hungry; I</u> think he is going to pounce.

4. Use a subordinating conjunction to indicate that one of the independent clauses is dependent on the other.

<u>When</u> the wizards tasted the potion, they found the mixture tasty.

<u>Because</u> the troll is very hungry, I think he is going to pounce.

Here is a question involving a run-on sentence. See whether you can select the correct answer.

Some parts of the following sentence are underlined. The first answer choice, (A), simply repeats the underlined part of the sentence. The other four choices present four alternative ways to phrase the underlined part. Select the answer that produces the most effective sentence, one that is clear and exact. In selecting your choice, be sure that it is standard written English, and that it expresses the meaning of the original sentence.

Many students work after school and on <u>weekends, consequently they do not have</u> much time for doing their homework.

(A) weekends, consequently they do not have
(B) weekends, they do not have
(C) weekends, as a consequence they do not have
(D) weekends, therefore they do not have
(E) weekends; consequently, they do not have

What makes this a run-on sentence? There are two main clauses here, separated by a comma. The rule is: use a comma between main clauses only when they are linked by a coordinating conjunction (*and, but, for, or, nor, so, yet*). There's no coordinating conjunction here, so you know the sentence as it stands is wrong. The main clauses here are linked by *consequently*, which is what grammar teachers call a conjunctive adverb. A rule also covers conjunctive adverbs. That rule is: use a semicolon before a conjunctive adverb set between two main

clauses. Only one answer choice uses a semicolon before *consequently*: the correct answer, choice E.

PROBLEMS WITH AGREEMENT

Subject-Verb Agreement

The verb and its subject must get along; otherwise, things turn nasty. The rule is that a verb and its subject must agree in person and number. A singular verb must have a singular subject; a plural verb must have a plural subject.

Here are some singular subjects, properly agreeing with their singular verbs:

I conjure	You lurk	She undulates
I am conjuring	You are lurking	He is ogling
I have conjured	You have lurked	It has levitated

Here are the corresponding plural subjects with their plural verbs:

We pirouette	You pillage	They sulk
We are pirouetting	You are pillaging	They are sulking
We have pirouetted	You have pillaged	They have sulked

Normally, it's simple to match a singular subject with an appropriate singular verb, or a plural subject with a plural verb. However, problems can arise, especially when phrases or parenthetical expressions separate the subject from the verb. Even the rudest intrusion is no reason for the subject and the verb to disagree.

A **cluster** of grapes **was** hanging just out of the fox's reach.

The **elixir** in these bottles **is** brewed from honey and rue.

The **dexterity** of her long, thin, elegant fingers **has** improved immeasurably since she began playing the vielle.

The **cabin** of clay and wattles **was** built by William Butler Yeats.

Parenthetical expressions are introduced by *as well as*, *with*, *along with*, *together with*, *in addition to*, *no less than*, *rather than*, *like*, and similar phrases. Although they come between the subject and the verb, they do not interfere with the subject and verb's agreement.

The **owl** together with the pussycat **has** gone to sea in a beautiful pea-green boat.

The **walrus** with the carpenter **is** eating all the oysters.

Dorothy along with the lion, the scarecrow, the woodman, and her little dog Toto **is** following the yellow brick road.

Berenice as well as Benedick **was** hidden under the cloak.

The Trojan **horse,** including the Greek soldiers hidden within it, **was** hauled through the gates of Troy.

Henbane, rather than hellebore or rue, **is** the secret ingredient in this potion.

Henbane, in addition to hops, **gives** the potion a real kick.

I, like the mandrake, **am** ready to scream.

Likewise, if a clause comes between the subject and its verb, it should not cause them to disagree. A singular subject still takes a singular verb.

The **troll** who lurched along the corridors **was** looking for the loo.

The **phoenix** that arose from the ashes **has** scattered cinders everywhere.

The **way** you're wrestling those alligators **is** causing them some distress.

A compound subject (two or more nouns or pronouns connected by *and*) traditionally takes a plural verb.

The walrus and the carpenter were strolling on the strand.

"The King and I," said Alice, "are on our way to tea."

However, there are exceptions. If the compound subject refers to a single person or thing, don't worry that it is made up of multiple nouns. Simply regard it as singular and follow it with a singular verb.

The Lion, the Witch, and the Wardrobe, written by C.S. Lewis, is an admirable tale.

The Eagle and Child is a pub in Oxford where Lewis and Tolkien regularly sampled the admirable ale.

Green eggs and ham was our family's favorite breakfast every St. Patrick's Day.

The King and I is a musical comedy.

Frodo's guide and betrayer literally bites the hand that feeds him. (Both *guide* and *betrayer* refer to the same creature, Gollum.)

(Note that the title of a work of art—a novel, poem, painting, play, opera, ballet, statue—*always* takes a singular verb, even if the title contains a plural subject. *The Burghers of Calais* is a statue by Rodin. The burgers of Burger King are whoppers.)

Some words are inherently singular. In American English, collective nouns like *team, community, jury, swarm, entourage,* and so on are customarily treated as singular.

The croquet team is playing brilliantly, don't you think?

The community of swamp dwellers has elected Pogo president.

The jury was convinced that Alice should be decapitated.

A swarm of bees is dive-bombing Willie Yeats.

My entourage of sycophants fawns on me in a most satisfying fashion.

However, when a collective noun is used to refer to *individual members* of a group, it is considered a plural noun.

The jury were unable to reach a verdict. (The individual jurors could not come to a decision.)

I hate it when my entourage of sycophants compete with one another for my attention. (This sentence is technically correct. However, it calls excessive attention to its correctness. In real life, you'd want to rewrite it. Here's one possible revision: I hate it when my hangers-on compete with one another for my attention.)

Sometimes the article used with a collective noun is a clue to whether the verb is singular or plural. The expressions *the number* and *the variety* generally are regarded as singular and take a singular verb. The expressions *a number* and *a variety* generally are regarded as plural and take a plural verb.

The number of angels able to dance on the head of a pin is limited by Fire Department regulations.

A number of angels able to dance on the head of a pin have been booked to perform at Radio City Music Hall.

The variety of potions concocted by the junior wizards is indescribable.

A variety of noises in the night have alarmed the palace guard. (Has Imogen been serenading Peregrine again?)

Some nouns look plural but refer to something singular. These nouns take singular verbs. Consider *billiards, checkers,* and *dominoes* (the game, not the pieces). Each is an individual game. What about *astrophysics, economics, ethics, linguistics, mathematics, politics, statistics* (the field as a whole, not any specific figures), and *thermodynamics?* Each is an individual discipline or organized body of knowledge. What about *measles, mumps,* and *rickets?* Each is an individual disease. Other camouflaged singular nouns are *customs* (as in baggage inspections at borders), *molasses, news,* and *summons.*

While dominoes is Dominick's favorite pastime, billiards is Benedick's.

The molasses in the potion disguises the taste of garlic and hellebore.

Rickets is endemic in trolls because of their inadequate exposure to sunlight. (Trolls who get adequate exposure to sunlight suffer instead from petrification.)

This summons to a midnight assignation was from Sybilla, not from Berenice.

Some plural nouns actually name single things that are made of two connected parts: *eyeglasses, knickers, pliers, scissors, sunglasses, tights, tongs, trousers, tweezers.* Don't let this confuse you. Just match them up with plural verbs.

Imogen's knickers are in a twist.

Peregrine's sunglasses are in the Lost and Found.

Watch out, however, when these plural nouns crop up in the phrase "a pair of...." The scissors are on the escritoire, but a *pair* of scissors is on the writing desk.

Watch out, also, when a sentence begins with *here* or *there.* In such cases, the subject of the verb *follows* the verb in the sentence.

There are many angels dancing on the head of this pin. [*Angels* is the subject of the verb *are.*]

Here is the pellet with the poison. [*Pellet* is the subject of the verb *is.*]

In the wizard's library there exist many unusual spelling books. [*Books* is the subject of the verb *exist.*]

Somewhere over the rainbow there lies the land of Oz. [*Land* is the subject of the verb *lies.*]

Likewise, watch out for sentences whose word order is inverted, so that the verb precedes the subject. In such cases, your mission is to find the actual subject.

Among the greatest treasures of all the realms is the cloak of invisibility.

Beyond the reckoning of man are the workings of a wizard's mind.

(Of even greater mystery to men are the workings of a woman's mind....)

Here is a question involving subject-verb agreement.

The following sentence may contain an error in grammar, usage, choice of words, or idioms. Either there is just one error in a sentence or the sentence is correct. Some words or phrases are underlined and lettered; everything else in the sentence is correct.

If an underlined word or phrase is incorrect, choose that letter; if the sentence is correct, select No error.

Proficiency in mathematics and language skills
   A
are tested in third grade and eighth grade
B C
as well as in high school. No error
D   E

Do not let yourself be fooled by nouns or pronouns that come between the subject and the verb. The subject of this sentence is *not* the plural noun *skills*. It is the singular noun *proficiency*. The verb should be singular as well. The subject-verb agreement error is choice B. To correct the error, substitute *is* for *are*.

Pronoun-Verb Agreement

Watch out for errors in agreement between pronouns and verbs. (A pronoun is *not* a noun that has lost its amateur standing. Instead, it's a last-minute substitute, called upon to stand in for a noun that's overworked.) You already know the basic pronouns: *I, you, he, she, it, we, they* and their various forms. Here is an additional bunch of singular pronouns that, when used as subjects, typically team up with singular verbs.

Each of the songs Imogen sang was off-key. (Was that why her knickers were in a twist?)

Either of the potions packs a punch.

Neither of the orcs packs a lunch. (But, then, neither of the orcs is a vegetarian.)

Someone in my entourage has been nibbling my chocolates.

Does anyone who is anyone go to Innisfree nowadays?

Everything is up to date in Kansas City.

Somebody loves Imogen; she wonders who.

Nobody loves the troll. (At least, no one admits to loving the troll. Everybody is much too shy.)

Does everyone really love Raymond?

Exception: Although singular subjects linked by *either...or* or *neither...nor* typically team up with singular verbs, a different rule applies when one subject is singular and one is plural. In such cases, proximity matters: the verb agrees with the subject nearer to it. (This rule also holds true when singular and plural subjects are linked by the correlative conjunctions *not only...but also* and *not...but*.)

Either the troll or the orcs have broken the balustrade.

Either the hobbits or the elf has hidden the wizard's pipe.

Neither the junior witches nor the professor of herbology has come up with a cure for warts.

Neither Dorothy nor her three companions were happy about carrying Toto everywhere.

Not only the oysters but also the walrus was eager to go for a stroll.

Not only Berenice but also Benedick and the troll have hidden under the cloak of invisibility.

Oddly enough, not the carpenter but the oysters were consumed by a desire to go for a stroll.

Not the elves but the dwarf enjoys messing about in caves.

The words *few, many,* and *several* are plural; they take plural verbs.

Many are cold, but few are frozen.

Several are decidedly lukewarm.

Here is a question involving pronoun-verb agreement.

The following sentence may contain an error in grammar, usage, choice of words, or idioms. Either there is just one error in a sentence or the sentence is correct. Some words or phrases are underlined and lettered; everything else in the sentence is correct.

If an underlined word or phrase is incorrect, choose that letter; if the sentence is correct, select No error.

Neither the President nor the members of his
A
Cabinet was happy with the reporter's account
B   C
of dissension within their ranks. No error
D   E

Here we have one subject that is singular (*President*) and one that is plural (*members*). In such cases, the verb agrees with the subject nearer to it. *Members* is plural; therefore, the verb should be plural as well. Substitute *were* for *was*. The correct answer is choice B.

Pronoun-Antecedent Agreement

A pronoun must agree with its antecedent in person, number, and gender. (The antecedent is the noun or pronoun to which the pronoun refers, or possibly defers.) Such a degree of agreement is unlikely, but in grammar (almost) all things are possible.

The munchkins welcomed <u>Dorothy</u> as <u>she</u> arrived in Munchkinland. (The antecedent *Dorothy* is a third person singular feminine noun; *she* is the third person singular feminine pronoun.)

Sometimes the antecedent is an indefinite singular pronoun: *any, anybody, anyone, each, either, every, everybody, everyone, neither, nobody, no one, somebody,* or *someone.* If so, the pronoun should be singular.

<u>Neither</u> of the twins is wearing <u>his</u> propeller beanie.

<u>Each</u> of the bronco-busters was assigned <u>his or her</u> own horse.

<u>Anybody</u> with any sense would refrain from serenading <u>his</u> inamorata on television.

When the antecedent is compound (two or more nouns or pronouns connected by *and*), the pronoun should be plural.

The <u>walrus</u> <u>and</u> <u>the carpenter</u> relished <u>their</u> outing with the oysters.

<u>The walrus</u> always takes salt in <u>his</u> tea.

<u>Christopher Robin</u> <u>and</u> <u>I</u> always have honey in <u>ours</u>.

<u>You</u> <u>and</u> <u>your nasty little dog</u> will get <u>yours</u> someday!

When the antecedent is part of an *either...or* or *neither...nor* statement, the pronoun will find it most politic to agree with the nearer antecedent.

Either Sybilla or <u>Berenice</u> always has the troll on <u>her</u> mind. (Actually, they both do, but in different ways.)

[Given the *either...or* construction, you need to check which antecedent is nearer to the pronoun. The ever-feminine, highly singular *Berenice* is; therefore, the correct pronoun is *her* rather than *their*.]

Neither the professor of herbology nor the junior <u>wizards</u> have finished digging up <u>their</u> mandrake roots. [*Wizards* is closer to *their*.]

Neither the hobbits nor the <u>wizard</u> has eaten all <u>his</u> mushrooms. [*Wizard* is closer to *his*.]

Here is a question involving pronoun-antecedent agreement.

> The following sentence may contain an error in grammar, usage, choice of words, or idioms. Either there is just one error in a sentence or the sentence is correct. Some words or phrases are underlined and lettered; everything else in the sentence is correct.
>
> If an underlined word or phrase is incorrect, choose that letter; if the sentence is correct, select <u>No error</u>.

Admirers of the vocal ensemble *Chanticleer*

<u>have come to wonder</u> over the years whether the
      A

group, known for <u>their</u> mastery of Gregorian
         B

chant, might have abandoned its <u>roots in</u> early
             C

music <u>to explore</u> new musical paths. <u>No error</u>
    D   E

The error here is in choice B. The sentence is talking about a group. Is the group known for *their* mastery or for *its* mastery? *Group* is a collective noun. In American English collective nouns are usually treated as singular and take singular pronouns. Is that the case here? Yes. How can you be sure? Later in the sentence, a second pronoun appears: *its*. This pronoun refers to the same noun: *group*. *Its* is *not* underlined. Therefore, by definition, the singular pronoun must be correct.

In solving error identification questions, remember that anything *not* underlined in the sentence is correct.

PROBLEMS WITH CASE

Now let's get down to cases. In the English language, there are three: nominative (sometimes called subjective), possessive, and objective. Cases are special forms of words that signal how these words function in sentences. Most nouns, many indefinite pronouns, and a couple of personal pronouns reveal little about themselves: they have special case forms only for the possessive case (*Berenice's* cauldron, the *potion's* pungency, *its* flavor, *your* tastebuds, *anyone's* guess, *nobody's* sweetheart). Several pronouns, however, reveal much more, as the following chart demonstrates.

Case Study

Nominative	Possessive	Objective
I	my/mine	me
we	our/ours	us
you	your/yours	you
he	his/his	him
she	her/hers	her
it	its/its	it
they	their/theirs	them
who	whose/whose	whom

The Nominative Case: *I, we, he, she, it, they, you, who*

The nominative case signals that the pronoun involved is functioning as the subject of a verb or as a subject complement.

Ludovic and *I* purloined the Grey Poupon. [subject of verb]

The only contestants still tossing gnomes were Berenice and *he*. [subject complement]

The eventual winners—*he* and *she*—each received a keg of ale. [appositives identifying the subject]

Sir Bedivere unhorsed the knight *who* had debagged Sir Caradoc. [subject in clause]

The Possessive Case: *mine, ours, his, hers, theirs, yours; my, our, his, her, its, their, your, whose*

The possessive case signals ownership. Two-year-olds have an inherent understanding of the possessive: *Mine!*

Drink to me only with *thine* eyes, and I will pledge with *mine*.

Please remember that the walrus takes only salt in *his* tea, while Christopher Robin and I prefer honey in *ours*, and the Duchess enjoys a drop of Drambuie in *hers*.

Ludovic put henbane in *whose* tea?

The possessive case also serves to indicate that a quality belongs to or is characteristic of someone or something.

Her long, thin, elegant fingers once again demonstrated *their* dexterity.

The troll rebounded at Berenice but failed to shake *her* composure.

A noun or pronoun immediately preceding a gerund (that is, a verbal that ends in *-ing* and acts like a noun) is in the possessive case.

The *troll's* bouncing into the bannister creates problems for passersby on the staircase. [*Troll's* immediately precedes the gerund *bouncing*.]

The troll would enjoy *his* bouncing more if Sybilla rather than Berenice caught him on the rebound. [*His* immediately precedes the gerund *bouncing*.]

The Objective Case

Traditionally, the objective case indicates that a noun or pronoun receives whatever action is taking place. A pronoun in the objective case can serve as a direct object of a transitive verb, as an indirect object, as an object of a preposition, or, oddly enough, as the subject or object of an infinitive.

Berenice bounced *him* off the bannister again. [direct object]

The walrus gave *them* no chance to refuse his invitation to go for a stroll. [indirect object]

William Yeats, by *whom* the small cabin was built, was a better poet than carpenter. [object of preposition within a clause]

Peregrine expected *her* to serenade *him*. [subject and object of the infinitive *to serenade*.]

Be careful to use objective pronouns as objects of prepositions.

Everyone loves Raymond except Berenice and *me*.

Between you and *me,* I'm becoming suspicious of Sybilla and *him*.

Here are a couple of questions with problems involving case.

The following sentences may contain an error in grammar, usage, choice of words, or idioms. Either there is just one error in a sentence or the sentence is correct. Some words or phrases are underlined and lettered; everything else in the sentence is correct.

If an underlined word or phrase is incorrect, choose that letter; if the sentence is correct, select No error.

All of the flood victims except Lloyd and I
                                          A
have decided to accept the settlement
     B   C
proposed by the insurance company. No error
     D   E

The object of the preposition *except* should be in the objective case. Change *I* to *me*. The correct answer is choice A.

Because the other jurors and her differed in their
          A   B   C   D
interpretation of the judge's instructions, they

asked for a clarification. No error
                            E

Here we have a compound subject. The subject of the initial clause ("Because...instructions") should be in the nominative case. Change *her* to *she*. The correct answer is choice B.

Many confusions about case involve compound subjects ("the other jurors and she") or compound objects of prepositions ("except Lloyd and me"). If you are having trouble recognizing which form of a pronoun to use, try reversing the noun-pronoun word order, or even dropping the noun. For example, instead of saying "Because the other jurors and her differed," try saying "Because her and the other jurors differed." Or simply say, "Because her differed." Does the pronoun sound odd to you? It should. When that happens, check whether the pronoun is in the right case.

PROBLEMS INVOLVING MODIFIERS

Unclear Placement of Modifiers

Location, location, location. In general, adjectives, adverbs, adjective phrases, adverbial phrases, adjective clauses, and adverbial clauses need to be close to the words they modify. If these modifiers are separated from the words they modify, confusion may set in.

Some specific rules to apply:

1. Place the adverbs *only, almost, even, ever, just, merely,* and *scarcely* right next to the words they modify.

   Ambiguous: The walrus *almost* ate all the oysters. (Did he just chew them up and spit them out without swallowing?)

   Clear: The walrus ate *almost* all the oysters. (He left a few for the carpenter.)

   Ambiguous: This elephant *only* costs peanuts.

   Clear: *Only* this elephant costs peanuts. (The other elephants are traded for papayas and pomegranates.)

   Clear: This elephant costs *only* peanuts. (What a cheap price for such a princely pachyderm!)

2. Place phrases close to the words they modify.

Unclear: The advertisement stated that a used cauldron was wanted by an elderly witch *with stubby legs*. (Obviously, the advertisement was not written to reveal the lady's physical oddity.)

Clear: The advertisement stated that a used cauldron *with stubby legs* was wanted by an elderly witch.

3. Place adjective clauses near the words they modify.

Misplaced: The owl and the pussycat bought a wedding ring from the pig *that cost one shilling*.

Clear: The owl and the pussycat bought a wedding ring *that cost one shilling* from the pig.

4. A word that may modify either a preceding or following word is called a *squinting modifier*. (It looks both ways at once; no wonder it's walleyed.) To correct the ambiguity, move the modifier so that its relationship to one word is clear.

Squinting: Peregrine said that if Imogen refused to quit caterwauling beneath his balcony *in two minutes* he would send for the troll.

Clear: Peregrine said that he would send for the troll if Imogen refused to quit caterwauling beneath his balcony *in two minutes*.

Clear: Peregrine said that he would send for the troll *in two minutes* if Imogen refused to quit caterwauling beneath his balcony.

Squinting: The oysters agreed *on Sunday* to go for a stroll with the walrus.

Clear: *On Sunday*, the oysters agreed to go for a stroll with the walrus.

Clear: The oysters agreed to go for a stroll with the walrus *on Sunday*.

Dangling Modifiers

When modifying phrases or clauses precede the main clause of a sentence, position is everything. These modifiers should come directly before the subject of the main clause and should clearly refer to that subject. If the modifiers foolishly hang out in the wrong part of the sentence, they may wind up dangling there making no sense at all.

To correct a dangling modifier, rearrange the words of the sentence to bring together the subject and its wayward modifier. You may need to add a few words to the sentence to clarify its meaning.

Dangling Participle: Walking down the Yellow Brick Road, the Castle of Great Oz was seen. (Did you ever see a castle walking? Well, I didn't.)

Corrected: Walking down the Yellow Brick Road, Dorothy and her companions saw the Castle of Great Oz. (The participle *walking* immediately precedes the subject of the main clause *Dorothy and her companions*.)

In the preceding example, the participial phrase comes at the beginning of the sentence. In the example below, the participial phrase follows the sentence base.

Dangling Participle: The time passed very enjoyably, singing songs and romping with Toto. (Who's that romping with Toto?)

Corrected: They passed the time very enjoyably, singing songs and romping with Toto.

Watch out for dangling phrases containing gerunds or infinitives.

Dangling Phrase Containing Gerund: Upon hearing the report that a troll had been found in the cellars, the building was cleared. (Again, ask yourself who heard the report. Even though the building was a school for wizards, its walls did *not* have ears.)

Corrected: Upon hearing the report that a troll had been found in the cellars, the headmaster cleared the building.

Dangling Phrase Containing Infinitive: Unable to defeat the Trojans in open battle, a trick was resorted to by the Greeks.

Corrected: Unable to defeat the Trojans in open battle, the Greeks resorted to a trick.

Be careful when you create elliptical constructions (ones in which some words are implied rather than explicitly stated) that you don't cut out so many words that you wind up with a dangling elliptical adverb clause.

Dangling Elliptical Construction: *When presented with the potion*, not one drop was drunk.

Corrected: *When presented with the potion, nobody* drank a drop.

Corrected: *When they were presented with the potion*, not one drop was drunk.

Yet Another Dangling Elliptical Construction: *Although only a small dog*, Dorothy found Toto a big responsibility.

Corrected: *Although Toto was only a small dog*, Dorothy found him a big responsibility.

Here are a couple of questions involving misplaced modifiers:

Some parts of the following sentences are underlined. The first answer choice, (A), simply repeats the underlined part of the sentence. The other four choices present four alternative ways to phrase the underlined part. Select the answer that produces the most effective sentence, one that is clear and exact. In selecting your choice, be sure that it is standard written English, and that it expresses the meaning of the original sentence.

<u>Returning to Harvard after three decades, the campus seemed much less cheery to Sharon</u> than it had been when she was studying there.

(A) Returning to Harvard after three decades, the campus seemed much less cheery to Sharon
(B) After Sharon returned to Harvard in three decades, it seemed a much less cheery campus to her
(C) Having returned to Harvard after three decades, it seemed a much less cheery campus to Sharon
(D) When Sharon returned to Harvard after three decades, she thought the campus much less cheery
(E) Sharon returned to Harvard after three decades, and then she thought the campus much less cheery

Did you recognize that the original sentence contains a dangling modifier? Clearly, the campus did not return to Harvard; Sharon returned to Harvard. By replacing the participial phrase with a subordinate clause ("When...decades") and by making *she* the subject of the sentence, choice D corrects the error in the original sentence.

Try this second question, also involving a dangling modifier.

Having drafted the museum floor plan with exceptional care, <u>that the planning commission rejected his design upset the architect greatly.</u>

(A) that the planning commission rejected his design upset the architect greatly
(B) the planning commission's rejection of his design caused the architect a great upset
(C) the architect found the planning commission's rejection of his design greatly upsetting
(D) the architect was greatly upset about the planning commission rejecting his design
(E) the architect's upset at the planning commission's rejection of his design was great.

Again, ask yourself who drafted the museum floor plan. Clearly, it was the architect. *Architect*, therefore, must be the sentence's subject. The correct answer must be either choice C or choice D. Choice D, however, introduces a fresh error. The phrase "rejecting his design" is a gerund. As a rule, you should use the possessive case before a gerund: to be correct, the sentence would have to read "the architect was greatly upset about the planning com<u>mission's</u> rejecting his design. Choice D, therefore, is incorrect. The correct answer is choice C.

COMMON PROBLEMS IN USAGE

Words Often Misused or Confused

Errors in *diction*—that is, choice of words—have frequently been tested on the SAT II Writing Test and the writing section of the PSAT. You can be sure they'll crop up on the writing skills section of the new SAT. Here are some of the most common diction errors to watch for:

accept/except. These two words are often confused. *Accept* means to take or receive; to give a favorable response to something; to regard as proper. *Except*, when used as a verb, means to preclude or exclude. (*Except* may also be used as a preposition or a conjunction.)

> Benedick will *accept* the gnome-tossing award on Berenice's behalf.

> The necromancer's deeds were so nefarious that he was *excepted* from the general pardon. In other words, they pardoned everyone *except* him.

affect/effect. *Affect*, used as a verb, means to influence or impress, and to feign or assume. *Effect*, used as a verb, means to cause or bring about.

> When Berenice bounced the troll against the balustrade, she *effected* a major change in his behavior.

> The blow *affected* him conspicuously, denting his skull and his complacency.

> To cover her embarrassment about the brawl, Berenice *affected* an air of nonchalance.

Effect and *affect* are also used as nouns. *Effect* as a noun means result, purpose, or influence. *Affect*, a much less common noun, is a psychological term referring to an observed emotional response.

> Did being bounced against the balustrade have a beneficial *effect* on the troll?

> The troll's *affect* was flat. So was his skull.

aggravate. *Aggravate* means to worsen or exacerbate. Do not use it as a synonym for *annoy* or *irritate*.

> The orc will *aggravate* his condition if he tries to toss any gnomes so soon after his operation.

> The professor of herbology was *irritated* [not *aggravated*] by the mandrakes' screams.

ain't. *Ain't* is nonstandard. Avoid it.

already/all ready. These expressions are frequently confused. *Already* means previously; *all ready* means completely prepared.

> The mandrakes have *already* been dug up.

> Now the mandrakes are *all ready* to be replanted.

alright. Use *all right* instead of the misspelling *alright*. (Is that *all right* with you?)

all together/altogether. *All together* means as a group. *Altogether* means entirely, completely.

> The walrus waited until the oysters were *all together* on the beach before he ate them.

> There was *altogether* too much sand in those oysters.

among/between. Use *among* when you are discussing more than two persons or things; *between*, when you are limiting yourself to only two persons or things.

> The oysters were divided *among* the walrus, the carpenter, and the troll.

> The relationship *between* Berenice and Benedick has always been a bit kinky.

amount/number. Use *amount* when you are referring to mass, bulk, or quantity. Use *number* when the quantity can be counted.

> We were amazed by the *amount* of henbane the troll could eat without getting sick.

> We were amazed by the *number* of hens the troll could eat without getting sick.

and etc. The *and* is unnecessary. Cut it.

being as/being that. These phrases are nonstandard; avoid them. Use *since* or *that*.

beside/besides. These words are often confused. *Beside* is always a preposition. It means "next to" or, sometimes, "apart from." Watch out for possible ambiguities or ambiguous possibilities. "No one was seated at the Round Table *beside* Sir Bedivere" has two possible meanings.

> No one was seated at the Round Table *beside* Sir Bedivere. [There were empty seats on either side of Bedivere; however, Sir Kay, Sir Gawain, and Sir Galahad were sitting across from him on the other side of the table.]

> No one was seated at the Round Table *beside* Sir Bedivere. [Poor Bedivere was all alone.]

Besides, when used as a preposition, means "in addition to" or "other than."

Besides oysters, the walrus and the carpenter have eaten countless cockles and mussels and clams.

Who will go to the bear-baiting *besides* Berenice and Benedick?

Besides also is used as an adverb. At such times, it means moreover or also.

The troll broke the balustrade—and the newel post *besides*.

between. See *among*.

but what. Avoid this phrase. Use *that* instead.

Wrong: Imogen could not believe *but what* Peregrine would overlook their assignation.

Better: Imogen could not believe *that* Peregrine would overlook their assignation.

can't hardly/can't scarcely. You have just encountered the dreaded double negative. (I *can hardly* believe anyone writes that way, can you?) Use *can hardly* or *can scarcely*.

conscious/conscience. Do not confuse these words. *Conscious*, an adjective, means aware and alert; it also means deliberate.

Don't talk to Berenice before she's had her morning cup of coffee; she isn't really *conscious* until she has some caffeine in her system.

When Ludovic laced the professor's potion with strychnine, was he making a *conscious* attempt to kill the prof?

Conscience, a noun, means one's sense of right and wrong.

Don't bother appealing to the orc's *conscience*: he has none.

could of. This phrase is nonstandard. Substitute *could have*.

different from/different than. Current usage accepts both forms; however, a Google check indicates that *different from* is the more popular usage.

effect. See *affect*.

farther/further. Some writers use the adverb *farther* when discussing physical or spatial distances; *further*, when discussing quantities. Most use them interchangeably. The adjective *further* is a synonym for *additional*.

Benedick has given up gnome-tossing contests because Berenice always tosses her gnomes yards *farther* than Benedick can toss his. [adverb]

This elixir is *further* enriched by abundant infusions of henbane and hellebore. [adverb]

Stay tuned for *further* announcements of the latest results in today's gnome-tossing state finals. [adjective]

fewer/less. Use *fewer* with things that you can count (one hippogriff, two hippogriffs,...); *less*, with things that you cannot count but can measure in other ways.

"There are *fewer* oysters on the beach today than yesterday, I fear. How sad!" said the carpenter, and brushed away a tear.

Berenice should pay *less* attention to troll tossing and more to divination and elementary herbology.

former/latter. Use *former* and *latter* only when you discuss two items. (*Former* refers to the first item in a pair of two; *latter*, to the second.) When you discuss a series of three or more items, use *first* and *last*.

Who was madder, the March Hare or the Hatter? Was it the *former*, or was it the *latter* (the Hatter)?

Though the spoon, the knife, and the fork each asked the dish to elope, everyone knows the dish ran away with the *first*.

further. See *farther*.

had of/had have. These phrases are nonstandard. Substitute *had*.

Do Not Write:	If Benedick had of [nonstandard] tossed the gnome a foot farther, he could of [also nonstandard] won the contest.
Write:	If Benedick *had* tossed the gnome a foot farther, he *could have* won the contest.

hanged/hung. Both words are the past participle of the verb *hang*. However, in writing formal English, use *hanged* when you are discussing someone's execution; use *hung* when you are talking about the suspension of an object.

Ludovic objected to being *hanged* at dawn, saying he wouldn't get up that early for anybody's execution, much less his own.

The stockings were *hung* from the chimney with care.

hardly/scarcely. These words are sufficiently negative on their own that you don't need any extra negatives (such as *not, nothing,* or *without*) to get your point across. In fact, if you do add that extra *not* or *nothing,* you've perpetrated the dreaded double negative.

Do Not Write:	The walrus couldn't hardly eat another bite.
Write:	The walrus *could hardly* eat another bite.
Do Not Write:	Compared to the walrus, the carpenter ate hardly nothing.
Write:	Compared to the walrus, the carpenter ate *hardly anything* (or anyone).
Do Not Write:	The troll pounced without scarcely a moment's hesitation.
Write:	The troll pounced *with scarcely* a moment's hesitation.

imply/infer. People often use these words interchangeably to mean hint at or suggest. However, *imply* and *infer* have precise meanings that you need to tell apart. *Imply* means to suggest something without coming right out and saying it. *Infer* means to draw a conclusion, basing it on some sort of evidence.

When Auntie Em said, "My! That's a big piece of pie, young lady," did she mean to *imply* that Dorothy was being a glutton in taking such a huge slice?

Dorothy *inferred* from Auntie Em's comment that she'd better not ask for a second piece.

Imogen *inferred* from the fresh dent in the troll's skull that Berenice had been bouncing him off the balustrade again.

in back of. Avoid this expression. Use *behind* instead.

incredible/incredulous. *Incredible* means unbelievable, too improbable to be believed. *Incredulous* means doubtful or skeptical, unwilling to believe.

When Ludovic saw Berenice juggling three trolls in the air, he was amazed at her *incredible* strength.

Do you believe all this jabber about Berenice's strength, or are you *incredulous?*

irregardless. This nonstandard usage particularly irritates graders. Use *regardless* instead.

kind of/sort of. In writing formal prose, avoid using these phrases adverbially (that is, with the meaning of *somewhat* or *to a degree,* as in "kind of bashful" or "sort of infatuated"). Use words like *quite, rather,* or *somewhat* instead.

Informal:	Dorothy was kind of annoyed by the wizard's obfuscations.
Approved:	Dorothy was *quite* annoyed by the wizard's obfuscations.

kind of a/sort of a. In writing formal prose, cut out the *a.*

Do Not Write:	Sybilla seldom brews this kind of a potion.
Write:	Sybilla seldom brews this *kind of* potion.

last/latter. See *former.*

later/latter. Use *later* when you're talking about time (you'll do it sooner or later). Use *latter* when you're talking about the second one of a pair of two (not the former—that comes first—but the latter).

Every night Imogen stays up *later* and *later* serenading Peregrine.

Berenice tossed both the troll and a gnome. The *latter* bounced farther.

lay/lie. *Lay,* a transitive verb, means to put or place. *Lie,* an intransitive verb, means to rest or recline. One way to tell whether to use *lay* (*laying, laid*) or *lie* (*lying, lay, lain*) is to examine the sentence. If the verb has an object, use the correct form of *lay.* If the verb has no object, use *lie.*

Toto, *lie* down and roll over!

Toto *lay* down on the floor. [*Lay* is past tense of *lie.*]

Auntie Em, Toto's just *lying* there. He's not rolling over!

How long *has* he *lain* there, Dorothy? Maybe he's taking a nap. [The verb has no object. *Has lain* is the present perfect tense of *lie*.]

Berenice, please *lay* the troll down gently. [Object is *troll*.]

Instead of *laying* the troll down, Berenice bounced him off the bannister.

Ludovic *laid* the loot on the escritoire. [Object is *loot*. *Laid* is past tense of *lay*.]

learn/teach. *Learn* means to get knowledge; *teach* means to instruct, to give knowledge or information. Don't confuse the two.

Incorrect: I'll learn you, you stupid troll!

Correct: I'll *teach* you, you obtuse orc!

leave/let. *Leave* primarily means to depart; *let,* to permit. Don't confuse them. (*Leave*, when followed by an object and an infinitive or a prepositional phrase, as in "Leave him to do his worst" or "Leave it to Beaver," has other meanings. Consult an unabridged dictionary.)

Incorrect: Leave me go, Berenice.

Correct: *Let* me go, Berenice. Please *let* me leave.

less. See *fewer.*

liable to/likely to. *Likely to* refers simply to probability. When speaking informally, people are likely to use *liable to* in place of *likely to*. However, in formal writing, *liable to* conveys a sense of possible harm or misfortune.

Informal: The owl and the pussycat are liable to go for a sail. [This is a simple statement of probability. More formally, you would write "The owl and the pussycat are likely to go for a sail."]

Preferable: The beautiful but leaky pea-green boat is *liable to* sink. [This conveys a sense of likely danger.]

lie. See *lay.*

loose/lose. These are not synonyms. *Loose* is primarily an adjective meaning free or inexact or not firmly fastened ("a *loose* prisoner," "a *loose* translation," "a *loose* tooth." As a verb, *loose* means to set free or let fly.

   Loose the elephants!

   The elf *loosed* his arrows at the orcs.

Lose is always a verb.

   If the elf *loses* any more arrows in the bushes, he won't have any left to loose at the orcs.

   Hey, baby, *lose* the sidekick, and you and I can have a good time.

me and. Unacceptable as part of a compound subject.

Nonstandard: Me and Berenice can beat any three trolls in the house.

Preferred: Berenice *and I* can beat any three trolls in the house. (Actually, Berenice can beat them perfectly well without any help from me.)

number. See *amount.*

of. Don't write *of* in place of *have* in the expressions *could have, would have, should have, must have,* and so on.

off of. In formal writing, the *of* is superfluous. Cut it.

Incorrect: The troll bounced off of the bannister.

Correct: The troll bounced *off* the bannister.

principal/principle. Do not confuse the adjective *principal*, meaning chief, with the noun *principle*, a rule or law.

   Berenice's *principal principle* (that is, her chief rule of conduct) is "The bigger they are, the harder they bounce."

In a few cases, *principal* is used as a noun: the *principal* of a loan (the main sum you borrowed); the *principal* in a transaction (the chief person involved in the deal); the *principal* of a school (originally the head teacher). Don't worry about these instances. If you can substitute the word *rule* for the noun in your sentence, then the word you want is *principle*.

raise/rise. Do not confuse the verb *raise (raised, raising)* with *rise (rose, risen, rising)*. *Raise* means to increase, to lift up, to collect, or to nurture. It is transitive (it takes an object). *Rise* means to ascend, to get up, or to grow. It is intransitive (no objects need apply).

Incorrect: They are rising the portcullis.

Correct: They are *raising* the portcullis. [The object is portcullis, a most heavy object indeed.]

Incorrect: The sun raised over the battlements.

Correct: The sun *rose* over the battlements.

real. This word is an adjective meaning genuine or concrete. Do not use it as an adverb meaning very or extremely.

Too Informal: This is a real weird list of illustrative sentences.

Preferable: This is a *really* weird list of illustrative sentences.

Even Better: This is an *extremely* weird list of illustrative sentences.

the reason is because. This expression is ungrammatical. If you decide to use the phrase *the reason is*, follow it with a concise statement of the reason, not with a *because* clause.

Incorrect: *The reason* the oysters failed to answer *is because* the walrus and the carpenter had eaten every one.

Correct but Wordy: *The reason* the oysters failed to answer *is that* the walrus and the carpenter had eaten every one.

Correct and Concise: The oysters failed to answer *because* the walrus and the carpenter had eaten every one.

same. Lawyers and writers of commercial documents sometimes use *same* as a pronoun. In writing essays, use the pronouns *it, them, this, that* in its place.

Incorrect: I have received your billet-doux and will answer same once my messenger owl returns home.

Correct: I have received your billet-doux and will answer *it* once my messenger owl returns home.

scarcely. See *hardly.*

sort of. See *kind of.*

teach. See *learn.*

try and.   Avoid this phrase. Use *try to* in its place.

Incorrect: We must try and destroy the Ring of the Enemy.

Correct: We must *try to* destroy the Ring of the Enemy.

unique. The adjective *unique* describes something that is the only one of its kind. Don't qualify this adjective by *more, most, less, least, slightly,* or *a little bit.* It's just as illogical to label something a little bit unique as it is to describe someone as a little bit pregnant.

Incorrect: Only the One Ring has the power to rule elves, dwarfs, and mortal men. It is most unique.

Correct: Only the One Ring has the power to rule elves, dwarfs, and mortal men. It is *unique.*

PICKING PROPER PREPOSITIONS

Occasionally, you may get back papers from your teachers with certain expressions labeled "unidiomatic." Often these errors involve prepositions. When you are in doubt about what preposition to use after a particular word, look up that word in an unabridged dictionary. Meanwhile, look over the list below to see which preposition customarily accompanies each of the following words.

accede to

Sybilla graciously *acceded to* Peregrine's request to compose a villanelle.

according to

According to Abelard, Esperanto is the language of love.

accuse of

Berenice vociferously *accused* the troll *of* borrowing her leotard.

addicted to

The professor of herbology is reputedly *addicted to* comfrey tea.

adhere to

Muttering the conjunction spell under his breath, the wizard *adhered* the brigand *to* the bottom of the balcony.

adverse to

Imogen is *adverse to* Peregrine's writing verse to other women.

afflict with

The wizard *afflicted* the brigand *with* borborygmus and boils.

agree on (come to terms)

The owl and the pussycat could not *agree on* what color to repaint their pea-green boat.

agree with (suit; be similar to; be consistent with)

Burping miserably, the carpenter confessed that a diet of oysters did not *agree with* him.

agreeable to

The troll found tiddlywinks an occupation most *agreeable to* his tastes.

amazement at

Imagine Imogen's *amazement at* discovering the brigand dangling from the bottom of the balcony!

amenable to

Excessively *amenable to* persuasion, Imogen is the archetypal girl who can't say no.

appetite for

The walrus had an insatiable *appetite for* oysters.

appreciation of

The troll's *appreciation of* the fine points of pillaging was sadly limited.

aside from

The professor of potions had run out of ingredients, *aside from* a few sprigs of dried hellebore.

associate with

Dorothy's Auntie Em warned her not to *associate with* lions and tigers and bears.

blame for, blame on

Orcs never *blame* themselves *for* ravaging the environment; instead, they *blame* the damage *on* the trolls.

capable of

Who knows what vile and abhorrent deeds trolls are *capable of?*

chary of

Snow White was insufficiently *chary of* accepting apples from strange old women.

compatible with

Is Peregrine *compatible with* Imogen? I doubt it!

comply with

Sybilla was reluctant to *comply with* the troll's incessant importuning.

conform to (occasionally **conform with**)

Apprentice wizards are expected to obey their masters and *conform to* proper wizardly practices.

conversant with

Anyone *conversant with* trolls' table manners knows better than to invite one to tea.

desire for

Even Sybilla's *desire for* new experiences could not tempt her to elope with the troll.

desirous of

Being *desirous of* a salad for dinner, Gargantua cut some heads of lettuce as large as walnut trees.

desist from

If the troll does not *desist from* importuning Sybilla, she's going to sic Berenice on him.

die of

When Homer's belching drowned out her saxophone solo, Lisa nearly *died of* embarrassment.

different from

In what way is Tweedledum *different from* Tweedledee? I thought they were exactly alike.

disagree with

Hellebore *disagreed with* the pygmy, causing his stomach to rumble. (The pygmy had borborygmi.)

disdain for

The immaculate elves were too polite to show their *disdain for* the unkempt orcs.

enamored of

The troll is *enamored of* Sybilla, who in turn is *enamored of* Benedick.

indulge in

Berenice *indulges in* the curious hobby of tossing trolls.

inferior to

The orcs' perfunctory grooming was *inferior to* the elves' more meticulous toilette.

oblivious to

Imogen is *oblivious to* Peregrine's flaws and all too aware of his perfection.

partial to

The walrus is extremely *partial to* oysters; he likes them too much for their own good.

peculiar to

A total aversion to sunlight is a condition *peculiar to* vampires and trolls.

preoccupation with

The troll could not comprehend Sybilla's *preoccupation with* Benedick.

prevent from

There is nothing we can do to *prevent* Berenice *from* bouncing the troll off the balustrade. We'll have to catch him on the rebound.

prior to

Prior to eating the oysters, the walrus and the carpenter took them for a stroll.

prone to

Imogen is *prone to* infatuations. Just ask Peregrine.

separate from

No wicked witch could *separate* Dorothy *from* her little dog Toto.

tamper with

Do not *tamper with* the purple potion.

weary of

Will Berenice ever *weary of* bouncing the troll off the balustrade?

willing to

I'm *willing to* bet that she won't.

IMPROVING SENTENCES

There are three different kinds of questions on the writing skills sections of the SAT: improving sentences, identifying sentence errors, and improving paragraphs. The most numerous questions in these sections involve spotting the form of a sentence that works best. In these improving sentence questions, you will be presented with five different versions of the same sentence; you must choose the best one. Here are the directions:

Some or all parts of the following sentences are underlined. The first answer choice, (A), simply repeats the underlined part of the sentence. The other four choices present four alternative ways to phrase the underlined part. Select the answer that produces the most effective sentence, one that is clear and exact, and blacken the appropriate space on your answer sheet. In selecting your choice, be sure that it is standard written English, and that it expresses the meaning of the original sentence.

Example:

The first biography of author Eudora Welty came out in 1998 and she was 89 years old at the time.

(A) and she was 89 years old at the time
(B) at the time when she was 89
(C) upon becoming an 89 year old
(D) when she was 89
(E) at the age of 89 years old

Ⓐ Ⓑ Ⓒ ● Ⓔ

TIPS ON HANDLING SENTENCE IMPROVEMENT QUESTIONS

TIP 1

IF YOU SPOT AN ERROR IN THE UNDERLINED SECTION, ELIMINATE ANY ANSWER THAT REPEATS IT.

If something in the underlined section of a sentence correction question strikes you as an obvious error, you can immediately ignore any answer choices that repeat it. Remember: you still don't have to be able to explain what is wrong. You just need to find a correct equivalent. If the error you found in the underlined section is absent from more than one of

the answer choices, look over those choices again to see if they add any new errors.

Example:

Being as I had studied for the test with a tutor, I was confident.

(A) Being as I had studied for the test
(B) Being as I studied for the test
(C) Since I studied for the test
(D) Since I had studied for the test
(E) Because I studied for the test

Since you immediately recognize that *Being as* is not acceptable as a conjunction in standard written English, you can eliminate choices A and B right away. But you also know that both *Since* and *Because* are perfectly acceptable conjunctions, so you have to look more closely at choices C, D, and E. The only other changes these choices make are in the tense of the verb. Since the studying occurred before the taking of the test, the past perfect tense, *had studied*, is correct, so the answer is choice D. Even if you hadn't known that, you could have figured it out. Since *Because* and *Since* are both acceptable conjunctions, and since choices C and E both use the same verb, *studied,* in the simple past tense, those two choices must be wrong. Otherwise, they would both be right, and the SAT doesn't have questions with two right answers.

IF YOU DON'T SPOT THE ERROR IN THE UNDERLINED SECTION, LOOK AT THE ANSWER CHOICES TO SEE WHAT IS CHANGED.

Sometimes it's hard to spot what's wrong with the underlined section in a sentence correction question. When that happens, turn to the answer choices. Find the changes in the answers. The changes will tell you what kind of error is being tested. When you substitute the answer choices in the original sentence, ask yourself which of these choices makes the sentence seem clearest to you. The answer may well be the correct answer choice.

Example:

Even the play's most minor characters work together with extraordinary skill, their interplay creates a moving theatrical experience.

(A) their interplay creates a moving theatrical experience
(B) a moving theatrical experience is created by their interplay
(C) and their interplay creates a moving theatrical experience
(D) and a moving theatrical experience being the creation of their interplay
(E) with their interplay they create a moving theatrical experience

Look at the underlined section of the sentence. Nothing seems wrong with it. It could stand on its own as an independent sentence: *Their interplay creates a moving theatrical experience*. Choices B and E are similar to it, for both could stand as independent sentences. Choices C and D, however, are not independent sentences; both begin with the linking word *and*. The error needing correction here is the common comma splice, in which two sentences are carelessly linked with only a comma. Choice C corrects this error in the simplest way possible, adding the word *and* to tie these sentences together.

TIP 3

MAKE SURE THAT ALL PARTS OF THE SENTENCE ARE LOGICALLY CONNECTED.

Not all parts of a sentence are created equal. Some parts should be subordinated to the rest, connected with subordinating conjunctions or relative pronouns, not just added on with *and*. Overuse of *and* frequently makes sentences sound babyish. Compare "We had dinner at the Hard Rock Cafe, and we went to a concert" with "After we had dinner at the Hard Rock Cafe, we went to a concert."

Example:

The rock star always had enthusiastic fans and they loved him.

(A) and they loved him
(B) and they loving him
(C) what loved him
(D) who loved him
(E) which loved him

The original version of this sentence doesn't have any grammatical errors, but it is a poor sentence because it doesn't connect its two clauses logically. The second clause ("and they loved him") is merely adding information about the fans, so it should be turned into an adjective clause, introduced by a relative pronoun. Choices D and E both seem to fit, but you know that *which* should never be used to refer to people, so choice D is obviously the correct answer.

TIP 4

MAKE SURE THAT ALL PARTS OF A SENTENCE GIVEN IN A SERIES ARE SIMILAR IN FORM.

If they are not, the sentence suffers from a lack of parallel structure. The sentence "I'm taking classes in algebra, history, and how to speak French" lacks parallel structure. *Algebra* and *history* are nouns, names of subjects. The third subject should also be a noun: *conversational French*.

Example:

In this chapter we'll analyze both types of questions, suggest useful techniques for tackling them, providing some sample items for you to try.

(A) suggest useful techniques for tackling them, providing some sample items for you to try
(B) suggest useful techniques for tackling them, providing some sample items which you can try
(C) suggest useful tactics for tackling them, and provide some sample items for you to try
(D) and suggest useful techniques for tackling them by providing some sample items for you to try
(E) having suggested useful techniques for tackling them and provided some sample items for you to try

To answer questions like this correctly, you must pay particular attention to what the sentence means. You must first decide whether *analyzing, suggesting,* and *providing* are logically equal in importance here. Since they are—all are activities that "we" will do—they should be given equal emphasis. Only choice C provides the proper parallel structure.

TIP 5

PAY PARTICULAR ATTENTION TO THE SHORTER ANSWER CHOICES.

(This tactic also applies to certain paragraph correction questions.) Good prose is economical. Often the correct answer choice will be the shortest, most direct way of making a point. If you spot no grammatical errors or errors in logic in a concise answer choice, it may well be right.

Example:

The turning point in the battle of Waterloo probably was Blucher, who was arriving in time to save the day.

(A) Blucher, who was arriving
(B) Blucher, in that he arrived
(C) Blucher's arrival
(D) when Blucher was arriving
(E) that Blucher had arrived

Which answer choice uses the fewest words? Choice C, *Blucher's arrival.* It also happens to be the right answer.

Choice C is both concise in style and correct in grammar. Look back at the original sentence. Strip it of its modifiers, and what is left? "The turning point . . . was Blucher." A turning point is not a person; it is a *thing.* The turning point in the battle was not Blucher, but Blucher's *action,* the thing he did. The correct answer is choice C, *Blucher's arrival.* Pay particular attention to such concise answer choices. If a concise choice sounds natural when you substitute it for the original underlined phrase, it's a reasonable guess.

IDENTIFYING SENTENCE ERRORS

Approximately one-third of the questions in the writing skills sections are identifying sentence errors questions in which you have to find an error in the underlined section of a sentence. You do not have to correct the sentence or explain what is wrong. Here are the directions.

The sentences in this section may contain errors in grammar, usage, choice of words, or idioms. Either there is just one error in a sentence or the sentence is correct. Some words or phrases are underlined and lettered; everything else in the sentence is correct.

If an underlined word or phrase is incorrect, choose that letter; if the sentence is correct, select <u>No error</u>. Then blacken the appropriate space on your answer sheet.

Example:

The region has a climate <u>so severe that</u> plants
A

<u>growing there</u> rarely <u>had been</u> more than twelve
B   C

inches <u>high</u>. <u>No error</u>
D   E

ⒶⒷ●ⒹⒺ

TIPS ON HANDLING ERROR IDENTIFICATION QUESTIONS

TIP 1

REMEMBER THAT THE ERROR, IF THERE IS ONE, MUST BE IN THE UNDERLINED PART OF THE SENTENCE.

You don't have to worry about making improvements that could be made in the rest of the sentence. For example, if you have a sentence in which the subject is plural and the verb is singular, you could call either one the error. But if only the verb is underlined, the error for that sentence is the verb.

Example:

Mr. Brown <u>is</u> one of the commuters who <u>takes</u>
A   B

the 7:30 train <u>from</u> Brooktown <u>every</u> morning.
C   D

<u>No error</u>
E

Since *who* refers to *commuters*, it is plural, and needs a plural verb. Therefore, the error is choice B. If you were writing this sentence yourself, you could correct it in any number of other ways. You could say, "Mr. Brown is a commuter who takes . . ." or "Mr. Brown, a commuter, takes . . ." or "Mr. Brown, who is one of the commuters, takes . . .". However, the actual question doesn't offer you any of these possibilities. You have to choose from the underlined choices. Don't waste your time considering other ways to fix the sentence.

TIP 2

USE YOUR EAR FOR THE LANGUAGE.

Remember: you don't have to name the error, or be able to explain why it is wrong. All you have to do is recognize that something *is* wrong. On the early, easy questions in the set, if a word or phrase sounds wrong to you, it probably is, even if you don't know why.

See if your ear helps you with this question.

In my history class learned why the
    A   B
American colonies opposed the British,
                     C
how they organized the militia, and

the work of the Continental Congress. No error
            D   E

The last part of this sentence probably sounds funny to you—awkward, strange, wooden. You may not know exactly what it is, but something sounds wrong here. If you followed your instincts and chose choice D as the error, you would be right. The error is a lack of parallel structure. The sentence is listing three things you learned, and they should all be in the same form. Your ear expects the pattern to be the same. Since the first two items listed are clauses, the third should be too: "In my history class I learned why the American colonies opposed the British, how they organized the militia, and how the Continental Congress worked."

TIP 3

LOOK FIRST FOR THE MOST COMMON ERRORS.

Most of the sentences will have errors. If you are having trouble finding mistakes, check for some of the more common ones: subject-verb agreement, pronoun-antecedent problems, misuse of adjectives and adverbs, dangling modifiers. But look for errors only in the underlined parts of the sentence.

Marilyn and I ran as fast as we could, but
           A   B
we missed our train, which made us late for
                 C   D

work. No error
        E

Imagine that you have this sentence, and you can't see what is wrong with it. Start at the beginning and check each answer choice. *I* is part of the subject, so it is the right case: after all, you wouldn't say "Me ran fast." *Fast* can be an adverb, so it is being used correctly here. *Which* is a pronoun, and needs a noun for its antecedent. The only available noun is *train*, but that doesn't make sense (the train didn't make us late—*missing* the train made us late). There is your error, choice C.

Once you have checked each answer choice, if you still can't find an error, choose choice E, "No error." A certain number of questions have no errors.

TIP 4

REMEMBER THAT NOT EVERY SENTENCE CONTAINS AN ERROR.

Ten to twenty percent of the time, the sentence is correct as it stands. Do not get so caught up in hunting for errors that you start seeing errors that aren't there. If no obvious errors strike your eye and the sentence sounds natural to your ear, go with choice E: No error.

IMPROVING PARAGRAPHS

In the improving paragraph questions, you will confront a flawed student essay followed by six questions. In some cases, you must select the answer choice that best rewrites and combines portions of two separate sentences. In others, you must decide where in the essay a sentence best fits. In still others, you must choose what sort of additional information would most strengthen the writer's argument. Here are the directions.

> The passage below is the unedited draft of a student's essay. Parts of the essay need to be rewritten to make the meaning clearer and more precise. Read the essay carefully.
>
> The essay is followed by six questions about changes that might improve all or part of the organization, development, sentence structure, use of language, appropriateness to the audience, or use of standard written English. In each case, choose the answer that most clearly and effectively expresses the student's intended meaning. Indicate your choice by blackening the corresponding space on the answer sheet.

[1] *Nowadays the average cost of a new home in San Francisco is over $500,000.* [2] *For this reason it is not surprising that people are talking about a cheaper new type of home called a Glidehouse.* [3] *The Glidehouse is a type of factory-built housing.* [4] *It was designed by a young woman architect named Michelle Kaufmann.* [5] *Michelle was disgusted by having to pay $600,000 for a fixer-upper.* [6] *So she designed a kind of a modular house with walls that glide.*

Example:

Sentences 3, 4, and 5 (reproduced below) could best be written in which of the following ways?

The Glidehouse is a type of factory-built housing. It was designed by a young woman architect named Michelle Kaufmann. Michelle was disgusted by having to pay $600,000 for a fixer-upper.

(A) (Exactly as shown above)
(B) The Glidehouse typifies factory-built housing. A young woman architect named Michelle Kaufmann designed it, having been disgusted at having to pay $600,000 for a fixer-upper.
(C) The Glidehouse is a type of factory-built home, it was a young woman architect named Michelle Kaufmann who designed it because she resented having to pay $600,000 for a fixer-upper.
(D) An example of housing that has been built in a factory, the Glidehouse was the design of a young woman architect named Michelle Kaufmann whom having to pay $600,000 for a fixer-upper resented.
(E) The Glidehouse, a factory-built home, was designed by the young architect Michelle Kaufmann, who resented having to pay $600,000 for a fixer-upper.

In the original essay, sentences 3, 4, and 5 are wordy and rely heavily on passive voice constructions. Read aloud, they sound choppy. Choice E combines these three simple sentences into a single sentence that is both coherent and grammatically correct.

TIPS ON HANDLING PARAGRAPH IMPROVEMENT QUESTIONS

TIP 1
FIRST READ THE PASSAGE; THEN READ THE QUESTIONS.

Whether you choose to skim the student essay quickly or to read it closely, you need to have a reasonable idea of what the student author is trying to say before you set out to correct this rough first draft.

TIP 2
FIRST TACKLE THE QUESTIONS THAT ASK YOU TO IMPROVE INDIVIDUAL SENTENCES; THEN TACKLE THE ONES THAT ASK YOU TO STRENGTHEN THE PASSAGE AS A WHOLE.

In the sentence correction questions, you've just been weeding out ineffective sentences and selecting effective ones. Here you're doing more of the same. It generally takes less time to spot an effective sentence than it does to figure out a way to strengthen an argument or link up two paragraphs.

TIP 3
CONSIDER WHETHER THE ADDITION OF SIGNAL WORDS OR PHRASES—TRANSITIONS—WOULD STRENGTHEN THE PASSAGE OR PARTICULAR SENTENCES WITHIN IT.

If the essay is trying to contrast two ideas, it might benefit from the addition of a contrast signal.

Contrast Signals: *although, despite, however, in contrast, nevertheless, on the contrary, on the other hand.*

If one portion of the essay is trying to support or continue a thought developed elsewhere in the passage, it might benefit from the addition of a support signal.

Support Signals: *additionally, furthermore, in addition, likewise, moreover.*

If the essay is trying to indicate that one thing causes another, it might benefit from the addition of a cause and effect signal.

Cause and Effect Signals: *accordingly, as a result of, because, consequently, hence, therefore, thus.*

Pay particular attention to answer choices that contain such signal words.

TIP 4
WHEN YOU TACKLE THE QUESTIONS, GO BACK TO THE PASSAGE TO VERIFY EACH ANSWER CHOICE.

See whether your revised version of a particular sentence sounds right in its context. Ask yourself whether your choice follows naturally from the sentence before.

COMMON GRAMMAR AND USAGE ERRORS

The writing skills section tests certain errors again and again. Here are several that appear frequently on the examination. Watch out for them when you do the practice exercises and when you take the SAT.

THE RUN-ON SENTENCE

Mary's party was very exciting, it lasted until 2 A.M.

It is raining today, I need a raincoat.

You may also have heard this error called a comma splice. It can be corrected by making two sentences instead of one:

Mary's party was very exciting. It lasted until 2 A.M.

or by using a semicolon in place of the comma:

Mary's party was very exciting; it lasted until 2 A.M.

or by proper compounding:

Mary's party was very exciting and lasted until 2 A.M.

You can also correct this error with proper subordination. The second example above could be corrected:

Since it is raining today, I need a raincoat.

It is raining today, so I need a raincoat.

THE SENTENCE FRAGMENT

Since John was talking during the entire class, making it impossible for anyone to concentrate.

This is the opposite of the first error. Instead of too much in one sentence, here you have too little. Do not be misled by the length of the fragment. It must have a main clause before it can be a complete sentence. All you have in this example is the cause. You still need a result. For example, the sentence could be corrected:

Since John was talking during the entire class, making it impossible for anyone to concentrate, the teacher made him stay after school.

ERROR IN THE CASE OF A NOUN OR PRONOUN

Between you and I, this test is not really very difficult.

Case problems usually involve personal pronouns, which are in the nominative case (*I, he, she, we, they, who*) when they are used as subjects or predicate nominatives, and in the objective case (*me, him, her, us, them, whom*) when they are used as direct objects, indirect objects, and objects of prepositions. In this example, if you realize that *between* is a preposition, you know that *I* should be changed to the objective *me* because it is the object of a preposition.

ERROR IN SUBJECT-VERB AGREEMENT

Harvard College, along with several other Ivy League schools, are sending students to the conference.

Phrases starting with *along with* or *as well as* or *in addition to* that are placed in between the subject and the verb do not affect the verb. The subject of this sentence is *Harvard College,* so the verb should be *is sending.*

There is three bears living in that house.

Sentences that begin with *there* almost always have the subject after the verb. The subject of this sentence is *bears,* so the verb should be *are.*

ERROR IN PRONOUN-NUMBER AGREEMENT

Every one of the girls on the team is trying to do their best.

Every pronoun must have a specific noun or noun substitute for an antecedent, and it must agree with that antecedent in number (singular or plural). In this example, *their* refers to *one* and must be singular:

Every one of the girls on the team is trying to do her best.

ERROR IN THE TENSE OR FORM OF A VERB

After the sun set behind the mountain, a cool breeze sprang up and brought relief from the heat.

Make sure the verbs in a sentence appear in the proper sequence of tenses, so that it is clear what happened when. Since, according to the sentence, the breeze did not appear until after the sun had finished setting, the setting belongs in the past perfect tense:

After the sun had set behind the mountain, a cool breeze sprang up and brought relief from the heat.

ERROR IN LOGICAL COMPARISON

I can go to California or Florida. I wonder which is best.

When you are comparing only two things, you should use the comparative form of the adjective, not the superlative:

I wonder which is better.

Comparisons must also be complete and logical.

The rooms on the second floor are larger than the first floor.

It would be a strange building that had rooms larger than an entire floor. Logically, this sentence should be corrected to:

The rooms on the second floor are larger than those on the first floor.

ADJECTIVE AND ADVERB CONFUSION

She did good on the test.

They felt badly about leaving their friends.

These are the two most common ways that adjectives and adverbs are misused. In the first example, when you are talking about how someone did, you want the adverb *well*, not the adjective *good:*

She did well on the test.

In the second example, after the linking verb *feel* you want a predicate adjective to describe the subject:

They felt bad about leaving their friends.

ERROR IN MODIFICATION AND WORD ORDER

Reaching for the book, the ladder slipped out from under him.

A participial phrase at the beginning of the sentence should describe the subject of the sentence. Since it doesn't make sense to think of a ladder reaching for a book, this participle is left dangling with nothing to modify. The sentence needs some rewriting:

When he reached for the book, the ladder slipped out from under him.

ERROR IN PARALLELISM

In his book on winter sports, the author discusses ice-skating, skiing, hockey, and how to fish in an ice-covered lake.

Logically, equal and similar ideas belong in similar form. This shows that they are equal. In this sentence, the author discusses four sports, and all four should be presented the same way:

In his book on winter sports, the author discusses ice skating, skiing, hockey, and fishing in an ice-covered lake.

ERROR IN DICTION OR IDIOM

The affects of the storm could be seen everywhere.

Your ear for the language will help you handle these errors, especially if you are accustomed to reading standard English. These questions test you on words that are frequently misused, on levels of usage (informal versus formal), and on standard English idioms. In this example, the verb *affect*, meaning "to influence," has been confused with the noun *effect*, meaning "result."

The effects of the storm could be seen everywhere.

The exercises that follow will give you practice in answering the three types of questions you'll find on identifying sentence errors, improving sentences, and improving paragraphs. When you have completed each exercise, check your answers against the answer key. Then, read the answer explanations for any questions you either answered incorrectly or omitted.

WRITING SKILLS EXERCISES

The sentences in this section may contain errors in grammar, usage, choice of words, or idioms. Either there is just one error in a sentence or the sentence is correct. Some words or phrases are underlined and lettered; everything else in the sentence is correct.

If an underlined word or phrase is incorrect, choose that letter; if the sentence is correct, select <u>No error</u>. Then blacken the appropriate space on your answer sheet.

Example:

The region has a climate <u>so severe that</u> plants
                A

<u>growing there</u> rarely <u>had been</u> more than twelve
  B   C

inches <u>high</u>. <u>No error</u>
     D   E

Ⓐ Ⓑ ● Ⓓ Ⓔ

1. The exhibit now in progress at the Academy of

Sciences <u>feature</u> six colonies of live ants,
       A
<u>each of which</u> <u>displays</u> <u>distinctive</u> nest-building
    B   C   D
and food-collecting behaviors. <u>No error</u>
                      E

2. <u>Although</u> the artist Frida Kahlo <u>suffered from</u>
   A   B
severe health problems that prevented her

<u>ever</u> painting a mural, she is often <u>associated in</u>
 C   D
the mural movement. <u>No error</u>
               E

3. <u>In</u> botanical terms, a hothouse is a
 A
<u>high-temperature</u> greenhouse <u>for</u> the
      B   C
<u>cultivation of</u> tropical plants.
    D
<u>No error</u>
 E

4. One of Confucius's <u>principal</u> legacies
              A
<u>will have been</u> the notion of the enlightened
     B
civil servant, a concept that centuries later

<u>would spawn</u> the <u>system of</u> all-powerful
  C   D
mandarins. <u>No error</u>
          E

5. Recent <u>advances in</u> <u>basic</u> neurobiological
         A   B
research <u>has established</u> a close <u>link between</u>
          C   D
the brain's hearing and emotional centers.

<u>No error</u>
 E

6. If we <u>are going</u> to send human beings into
    A
space, <u>one must recognize</u> that we are doing it
        B
<u>primarily</u> to fulfill the human <u>yearning for</u>
  C   D
adventure. <u>No error</u>
          E

7. A new survey <u>released by</u> the National
                      A
    Endowment for the Arts <u>that describes</u> a steep
                                    B
    <u>downward</u> trend in book <u>consumption by</u>
         C   D
    Americans. <u>No error</u>
                     E

8. <u>As</u> a living species, the coelacanth <u>is believed</u>
    A   B
    to hold <u>a most unique place</u> in the evolutionary
                      C
    chain <u>from</u> fish to land vertebrates. <u>No error</u>
           D   E

9. <u>One's</u> <u>initial</u> impression of the novels of
      A   B
    William Faulkner <u>gives</u> little inkling of the
                          C
    writer's <u>capacity toward</u> humor. <u>No error</u>
                    D   E

10. <u>All of the members</u> of the debate team except
         A
    <u>Philip and I</u> <u>expect</u> to compete in the state
         B   C
    tournament <u>to be held</u> during spring break.
                     D
    <u>No error</u>
        E

11. <u>When</u> Marie Curie <u>realized that</u> both thorium
      A   B
    and uranium compounds <u>emit</u> Becquerel rays,
                                C
    she invented the word "radioactivity" to

    describe <u>their</u> behavior. <u>No error</u>
                 D   E

12. Although Confucianism has a <u>strong</u> following
                                      A
    in South Korea, Japan, and Vietnam, it <u>has had</u>
                                                B
    its ups and downs in its homeland, China,

    <u>not least</u> early in the twentieth century, when
        C
    it was <u>blamed about</u> China's cultural
                 D
    backwardness. <u>No error</u>
                        E

13. <u>When one drives</u> along the <u>winding</u> roads
         A   B
    of the Mendocino coastline, fresh beauties

    <u>await</u> you <u>at each new turn</u> in the road.
        C   D
    <u>No error</u>
        E

14. <u>Although</u> Jody Lee <u>primarily illustrates</u>
         A   B
    fantasy novels, art critics <u>have found</u> her
                                      C
    drawings to be <u>surprising</u> realistic. <u>No error</u>
                         D   E

15. Some people <u>look on</u> the cell phone <u>as</u> a
                      A   B
    pointless luxury; countless others, however,

    <u>rely on</u> <u>them</u> as a lifeline in emergencies.
        C   D
    <u>No error</u>
        E

16. <u>Attempting</u> to maximize the income-
         A
    producing <u>potential</u> of her pension plan by
                     B
    <u>investing in</u> <u>so-called</u> junk bonds. <u>No error</u>
         C   D   E

17. Noting that Homer's *Iliad* was written five
    A
centuries after the Trojan War was supposed
                                    B
to have taken place, the lecturer expressed

some doubts about the reliability of the poet's
        C
account for the conflict. No error
    D   E

18. Even more than the cancellation of last
    A
summer's art festivals, any disruption of
                            B
the Cannes Festival would be a blemish on
                        C   D
France's image of itself as a land of culture.

No error
E

19. Life on earth has taken a tremendous range
                    A
of forms, but all species arise from the same
    B
molecular ingredients, these ingredients limit
                    C
the chemical reactions that can happen inside

cells and so constrain what life can do.
        D
No error
E

Some or all parts of the following sentences are underlined. The first answer choice, (A), simply repeats the underlined part of the sentence. The other four choices present four alternative ways to phrase the underlined part. Select the answer that produces the most effective sentence, one that is clear and exact, and blacken the appropriate space on your answer sheet. In selecting your choice, be sure that it is standard written English, and that it expresses the meaning of the original sentence.

Example:

The first biography of author Eudora Welty came out in 1998 and she was 89 years old at the time.

(A) and she was 89 years old at the time
(B) at the time she was 89
(C) upon becoming an 89 year old
(D) when she was 89
(E) at the age of 89 years old

Ⓐ Ⓑ Ⓒ ● Ⓔ

20. Basking in the afternoon sun, a feeling of complete relaxation came over her.

(A) Basking in the afternoon sun,
(B) While basking in the afternoon sun,
(C) As she basked in the afternoon sun,
(D) After basking in the afternoon sun,
(E) She was basking in the afternoon sun,

21. The popular author visited our local bookstore and she would sign copies of her latest novel.

(A) bookstore and she would sign
(B) bookstore; where she would sign
(C) bookstore, and then she could sign
(D) bookstore to sign
(E) bookstore, with her signing

22. When trying to distinguish alligators from crocodiles, the alligator has the broader snout.

(A) When trying to distinguish alligators from crocodiles,
(B) In an attempt to distinguish alligators from crocodiles,
(C) While trying to distinguish alligators from crocodiles, however,
(D) When trying to distinguish alligators from crocodiles, it is true that
(E) When trying to distinguish alligators from crocodiles, remember that

23. To understand trees or ferns or mushrooms, you must master certain aspects of biology, such as what a fungus is, how it reproduces, and the real nature of those delicious fiddleheads.

(A) how it reproduces, and the real nature of those delicious fiddleheads
(B) its method of reproduction, and the real nature of those delicious fiddleheads
(C) how it reproduces, and what those delicious fiddleheads really are
(D) their method of reproduction, and the real nature of those delicious fiddleheads
(E) how it reproduces, and what is the real nature of those delicious fiddleheads

24. The doctor instructed the nurse to change the patient's sheets who was running a high fever.

(A) patient's sheets who was running
(B) sheets of the running patient with
(C) sheets of the patient who was running
(D) patient's sheets when he was running
(E) patient's sheets, being that he was running

25. Richard Feynman's wit and good humor made a great impression on many of the young physicists who studied under him.

(A) made a great impression on many of the young physicists who studied under him
(B) were what made him greatly impressive to many of the young physicists who studied under him.
(C) greatly impressed many of his young physics students
(D) greatly made an impression on many of his young physics students
(E) were great at making an impression on many of the young physicists studying under him

26. I wish there were a few honest politicians who I thought would represent my views in Congress.

(A) who I thought
(B) whom I thought
(C) which I thought
(D) of whom I thought
(E) who I was thinking

27. Familiar with the route from her driving lessons, the student driver's road test was simplicity itself.

(A) the student driver's road test was simplicity itself
(B) the student driver's road test was itself simple
(C) the student driver was simply testing the road
(D) the student driver found the road test simplicity itself
(E) the student driver simplified the road test herself

28. A born dancer who mastered a wide variety of styles, Gregory Hines's superb performances brought him international fame as the leading tap dancer of his generation.

(A) A born dancer who mastered a wide variety of styles, Gregory Hines's superb performances brought him
(B) A born dancer, he mastered a wide variety of styles, and Gregory Hines's superb performances brought him
(C) A born dancer who mastered a wide variety of styles, Gregory Hines put on superb performances that brought him
(D) Born a dancer and master of a wide variety of styles, Gregory Hines performed superbly and his performances brought him
(E) Gregory Hines was a born dancer and mastered a wide variety of styles, and his superb performances brought him

29. Many student procrastinators try to cram a whole term's worth of studying into a single night, but inevitably failing to master their coursework.

   (A) but inevitably failing to master their coursework
   (B) but they inevitably fail to master their coursework
   (C) but inevitably failing to master the work in their course
   (D) who inevitably fail to master their coursework
   (E) whose is the inevitable failure at mastering their coursework

30. Security regulations demand not only presenting a photo ID but also to submit to a metal detector test whenever we wish to travel by air.

   (A) not only presenting a photo ID but also to submit
   (B) we not only present a photo ID but also submit
   (C) to not only present a photo ID but also to submit
   (D) not only the presentation of a photo ID but also we should submit
   (E) not only to present a photo ID but also to submit

31. Upon weighing the evidence, the verdict was obvious; the jurors needed less than half an hour for their deliberations.

   (A) Upon weighing
   (B) When weighing
   (C) From weighing
   (D) When they weighed
   (E) Considering the weight of

32. It is typical of the computer industry for a skilled programmer to be hired and then you spend your whole career filling out forms and supervising trainees.

   (A) then you spend your whole career filling out forms and supervising trainees
   (B) to spend your whole career
   (C) then they spend their whole career
   (D) then spend his whole career
   (E) then spending his whole career

33. Colleagues of the world-famous diva have called her at once daunting because of her temperament but her talent is nonetheless an inspiration.

   (A) but her talent is nonetheless an inspiration
   (B) although she is inspiringly talented
   (C) and inspiring because of her talent
   (D) while being so talented as to inspire them
   (E) but being so talented as to inspire them nonetheless

The passage below is the unedited draft of a student's essay. Parts of the essay need to be rewritten to make the meaning clearer and more precise. Read the essay carefully.

The essay is followed by six questions about changes that might improve all or part of the organization, development, sentence structure, use of language, appropriateness to the audience, or use of standard written English. In each case, choose the answer that most clearly and effectively expresses the student's intended meaning. Indicate your choice by blackening the corresponding space on the answer sheet.

[1] Throughout history, people have speculated about the future. [2] Will it be a utopia? they wondered. [3] Will injustice and poverty be eliminated? [4] Will people accept ethnic diversity, learning to live in peace? [5] Will the world be clean and unpolluted? [6] Or will technology aid us in creating a trap for ourselves we cannot escape, for example such as the world in 1984? [7] With the turn of the millennium just around the corner these questions are in the back of our minds.

[8] Science fiction often portrays the future as a technological Garden of Eden. [9] With interactive computers, TVs and robots at our command, we barely need to lift a finger to go to school, to work, to go shopping, and education is also easy and convenient. [10] Yet, the problems of the real twentieth century seem to point in another direction. [11] The environment, far from improving, keeps deteriorating. [12] Wars and other civil conflicts breakout regularly. [13] The world's population is growing out of control. [14] The majority of people on earth live in poverty. [15] Many of them are starving. [16] Illiteracy is a problem in most poor countries. [17] Diseases and malnourishment is

very common. [18] Rich countries like the U.S.A. don't have the resources to help the "have-not" countries.

[19] Instead, think instead of all the silly inventions such as tablets you put in your toilet tank to make the water blue, or electric toothbrushes. [20] More money is spent on space and defense than on education and health care. [21] Advancements in agriculture can produce enough food to feed the whole country, yet people in the U.S. are starving.

[22] Although the USSR is gone, the nuclear threat continues from small countries like Iraq. [23] Until the world puts its priorities straight, we can't look for a bright future in the twenty-first century, despite the rosy picture painted for us by the science fiction writers.

34. In the context of paragraph 1, which of the following is the best revision of sentence 6?

    (A) Or will technology create a trap for ourselves from which we cannot escape, for example the world in *1984*?
    (B) Or will technology aid people in creating a trap for themselves that they cannot escape; for example, the world in *1984*?
    (C) Or will technology create a trap from which there is no escape, as it did in the world in *1984*?
    (D) Or will technology trap us in an inescapable world, for example, it did so in the world of *1984*?
    (E) Perhaps technology will aid people in creating a trap for themselves from which they cannot escape, just as they did it in the world of *1984*.

35. With regard to the essay as a whole, which of the following best describes the writer's intention in paragraph 1?

    (A) To announce the purpose of the essay
    (B) To compare two ideas discussed later in the essay
    (C) To take a position on the essay's main issue
    (D) To reveal the organization of the essay
    (E) To raise questions that will be answered in the essay

36. Which of the following is the best revision of the underlined segment of sentence 9 below?

    [9] With interactive computers, TVs and robots at our command, we barely need to lift a finger to go to school, to work, to go shopping, and education is also easy and convenient.

    (A) and to go shopping, while education is also easy and convenient
    (B) to go shopping, and getting an education is also easy and convenient
    (C) to go shopping as well as educating ourselves are all easy and convenient
    (D) to shop, and an easy and convenient education
    (E) to shop, and to get an easy and convenient education

37. Which of the following is the most effective way to combine sentences 14, 15, 16, and 17?

    (A) The majority of people on Earth are living in poverty and are starving, with illiteracy, and disease and being malnourished are also a common problems.
    (B) Common problems for the majority of people on Earth are poverty, illiteracy, diseases, malnourishment, and many are illiterate.
    (C) The majority of people on Earth are poor, starving, sick, malnourished and illiterate.
    (D) Common among the poor majority on Earth is poverty, starvation, disease, malnourishment, and illiteracy.
    (E) The majority of the Earth's people living in poverty with starvation, disease, malnourishment and illiteracy a constant threat.

38. In the context of the sentences that precede and follow sentence 19, which of the following is the most effective revision of sentence 19 ?

(A) Instead they are devoting resources on silly inventions such as tablets to make toilet tank water blue or electric toothbrushes.

(B) Instead, they waste their resources on producing silly inventions like electric toothbrushes and tablets for bluing toilet tank water.

(C) Think of all the silly inventions: tablets you put in your toilet tank to make the water blue and electric toothbrushes.

(D) Instead, tablets you put in your toilet tank to make the water blue or electric toothbrushes are examples of useless products on the market today.

(E) Instead of spending on useful things, think of all the silly inventions such as tablets you put in your toilet tank to make the water blue or electric toothbrushes.

39. Which of the following revisions would most improve the overall coherence of the essay?

(A) Move sentence 7 to paragraph 2
(B) Move sentence 10 to paragraph 1
(C) Move sentence 22 to paragraph 2
(D) Delete sentence 8
(E) Delete sentence 23

ANSWERS TO WRITING SKILLS EXERCISES

1. A	9. D	17. D	25. C	33. C
2. D	10. B	18. E	26. A	34. C
3. E	11. E	19. C	27. D	35. E
4. B	12. D	20. C	28. C	36. E
5. C	13. A	21. D	29. B	37. C
6. B	14. D	22. E	30. B	38. B
7. B	15. D	23. C	31. D	39. C
8. C	16. A	24. C	32. D	

ANSWER EXPLANATIONS

1. **A**   Error in subject-verb agreement. The subject of the sentence is *exhibit* (singular); the verb should be singular as well. Change *feature* to *features*.

2. **D**   Error in idiomatic usage. Although Kahlo never participated *in* the mural movement, she is associated *with* that movement. Change *associated in* to *associated with*.

3. **E**   Sentence is correct.

4. **B**   Error in sequence of tenses. Change *will have been* to *was*.

5. **C**   Error in subject-verb agreement. The subject of the sentence is *advances* (plural); the verb should be plural as well. Change *has established* to *have established*.

6. **B**   Error in pronoun choice. Avoid shifting from one pronoun to another within a single sentence. Change *one must recognize* to *we must recognize*.

7. **B**   Sentence fragment. Delete *that* to create a correct sentence.

8. **C**   Error in usage. Most writers still consider *unique* an absolute adjective, one without degrees of comparison. Change *a most unique place* to *a unique place*.

9. **D**   Error in idiomatic usage. Change *capacity toward* to *capacity for*.

10. **B**   Error in pronoun case. The preposition *except* requires the objective case. Change *Philip and I* to *Philip and me*.

11. **E**   Sentence is correct.

12. **D**   Error in idiomatic usage. Change *blamed about* to *blamed for*.

13. **A**   Error in pronoun choice. Avoid shifting from one pronoun to another within a single sentence. Change *When one drives* to *When you drive*.

14. **D**   Adjective-adverb confusion. Change *surprising realistic* to *surprisingly realistic*.

15. **D**   Error in pronoun-antecedent agreement. *Cell phone* is singular. The pronoun referring to cell phone should be singular as well. Change *them* to *it*.

16. **A**   Sentence fragment. You can correct this error most easily by replacing *Attempting* with *She attempted*.

17. **D**   Error in idiomatic usage. What is intended here is not the *account* that refers to a financial or banking arrangement, but the *account* that means a narrative or tale. Change *account for* to *account of*.

18. **E**   Sentence is correct.

19. **C**   Run-on sentence. Change *ingredients, these ingredients* to *ingredients, which*.

20. **C**   Dangling modifier. Ask yourself who or what was basking in the sun. Only choice C corrects the error in modification without introducing a fresh error.

21. **D**   Choice D tightens the original loose sentence by clarifying why the author visited the bookstore: she did so *to sign* copies of her novel.

22. **E**   Dangling modifier. Who is trying to distinguish alligators from crocodiles? Clearly, a person is. In choice E, that person, though not stated explicitly, is implied: the subject of the sentence is *you*.

23. **C**   Lack of parallelism. Choice C observes parallel structure by balancing the three parallel clauses.

24. **C**   Misplaced modifier. Who was running a high fever? Not the sheets, but the patient! Choice C makes this clear.

25. **C**   Wordiness. Choice C deftly cuts the unnecessary words.

26. **A**   Sentence is correct. In the subordinate clause, *who* is the subject of the verb *would represent*. Therefore the pronoun is in the nominative case.

27. **D**   Error in modification. Who was familiar with the route from her driving lessons? Clearly, the student driver was. Choice D corrects the error in modification without changing the sentence's basic meaning. (Although choices C and E also correct the error in modification, both change the sentence's meaning drastically.)

28. **C** Again, an error in modification. Ask yourself who was a born dancer who mastered a wide variety of styles. Clearly it was Gregory Hines, not his performances. Although choice D corrects the error in modification, it changes the sentence's meaning. Likewise, although choice E corrects the error in modification, it lacks conciseness.

29. **B** Error in coordination. The coordinating conjunction *but* connects sentence elements that are equal in grammatical rank. What precedes the conjunction *but*? A main clause: "Many student procrastinators try to cram a whole term's worth of studying into a single night." You must follow *but* with another main clause. Choice B corrects the error in coordination.

30. **B** Error in parallelism. Only choice B observes parallel structure by balancing sentence elements of equal grammatical rank. Here the verb *present* parallels the verb *submit*.

31. **D** Dangling modifier. Who weighed the evidence? The jurors did. In other words, *they* weighed or assessed it, as stated in Choice D.

32. **D** Shift in pronoun person. Do not switch from the third person singular ("a skilled programmer," that is, *he* or *she*) to the second person (*you*). Only choice D uses an appropriate possessive form of the third person pronoun (*his*) without introducing any new errors.

33. **C** Error in parallelism. The diva is *daunting* (adjective) *because of her temperament* (prepositional phrase). The correct answer should follow the same form. Only choice C does so: the diva is *inspiring* (adjective) *because of her talent* (prepositional phrase).

34. **C** Choice A is awkward and, like sentence 6, shifts the pronoun usage in the paragraph from third to first person. Choice B is awkward and contains a semicolon error. A semicolon is used to separate two independent clauses; in (B) the material after the semicolon is a sentence fragment. Choice C is succinctly and accurately expressed. It is the best answer. Choice D contains a comma splice between *world* and *for*. A comma may not be used to join two independent clauses. Choice E is awkwardly expressed and contains the pronoun *it*, which lacks a clear antecedent.

35. **E** Choice A indirectly describes the purpose of paragraph 1 but does not identify the writer's main intention. Choices B, C, and D fail to describe the writer's main intention. Choice E accurately describes the writer's main intention. It is the best answer.

36. **E** Choice A is grammatically correct but cumbersome. Choice B contains an error in parallel construction. The clause that begins *and getting* is not grammatically parallel to the preceding items on the list. Choice C contains a mixed construction. The first and last parts of the sentence are grammatically unrelated. Choice D contains faulty parallel structure. Choice E is correct and accurately expressed. It is the best answer.

37. **C** Choice A is wordy and awkwardly expressed. Choice B contains an error in parallel structure. The clause *and many are illiterate* is not grammatically parallel to the preceding items on the list of problems. Choice C is concise and accurately expressed. It is the best answer. Choice D is concise, but it contains an error in subject-verb agreement. The subject is *poverty, starvation, . . ., etc.,* so a plural verb is required; the verb *is* is singular. Choice E is a sentence fragment; it has no main verb.

38. **B** Choice A contains an error in idiom. The standard phrase is *devoting to,* not *devoting on.* Choice B ties sentence 19 to the preceding sentence and is accurately expressed. It is the best answer. Choice C fails to improve the coherence of the paragraph. Choice D is wordy and awkwardly phrased. Choice E is ambiguously worded.

39. **C** Sentence 7 (A) should stay put because it provides a transition between the questions in paragraph 1 and the beginning of paragraph 2. Sentence 10 (B) is a pivotal sentence in paragraph 2 and should not be moved. Sentence 22 (C) fits the topics of paragraph 2 and, therefore should be moved to paragraph 2. Choice C is the best answer. Sentence 8 (D) is needed as an introductory sentence in paragraph 2. It should not be deleted. Sentence 23 (E) provides the essay with a meaningful conclusion and should not be deleted.

PART VII

WRITING A 25-MINUTE ESSAY

In this part you will find basic guidelines for writing an essay, plus tips on dealing with the pressures inherent in writing a timed essay on an unfamiliar topic. You'll also become acquainted with a host of resources that will help you develop your essay-writing skills.

SCORING

First, a few words about how your SAT essay will be scored, and about what the readers expect of you. Two readers will grade your essay in about two minutes, reading it very quickly to judge it as a whole. (The College Board calls this process *holistic scoring*.) Each reader will assign your essay a score of 1 to 6, with 6 the highest possible score. If both readers give your essay a 4, your combined score will be 8. If one reader gives your essay a 3 and the other assigns it a 4, your combined score will be 7. If the two readers seriously disagree about your score—for example, if one reader considers your essay a 3 and the other judges it a 5—a third reader will look over your essay and determine your score.

What characteristics distinguish essays at the various scoring levels? Here's what the test makers say:

SCORING LEVEL 6

Essays on this level demonstrate a clear command of writing and thinking skills, despite an occasional, infrequent, minor error. Characteristics of essays on this level include:

1. intelligent, convincing development of a position on the issue
2. selection of relevant examples and other evidence to support its position
3. smooth, well-orchestrated progression from idea to idea
4. use of varied sentence types and appropriate vocabulary
5. freedom from most technical flaws (mistakes in grammar, usage, diction)

These essays are *insightful*.

SCORING LEVEL 5

Essays on this level exhibit a generally dependable command of writing and thinking skills, despite some mistakes along the way. Characteristics of essays on this level include:

1. proficient, coherent development of a position on the issue
2. selection of basically relevant evidence to support its position
3. relatively well-ordered progression from idea to idea
4. reasonably varied sentence structure
5. relative freedom from technical flaws

These essays are *effective*.

SCORING LEVEL 4

Essays on this level exhibit a generally adequate command of writing and thinking skills, although they are typically inconsistent in quality. Characteristics of essays on this level include:

1. workmanlike development of a position on the issue
2. selection of reasonably appropriate evidence to support its position
3. acceptable progression from idea to idea
4. somewhat varied sentence structure
5. some flaws in mechanics, usage, and grammar

These essays are *competent*.

SCORING LEVEL 3

Essays on this level exhibit an insufficient command of writing and thinking skills, although they do show some signs of developing proficiency. Characteristics of essays on this level include:

1. sketchy development of a position on the issue
2. selection of weak or inappropriate evidence to support its position
3. erratic progression from idea to idea
4. somewhat limited vocabulary
5. inadequately varied sentence structure
6. multiple flaws in mechanics, usage, and grammar

These essays are *inadequate*.

SCORING LEVEL 2

Essays on this level exhibit a quite flawed command of writing and thinking skills. Characteristics of essays on this level include:

1. limited development of a position on the issue
2. selection of weak or inappropriate evidence to support its position
3. tendency toward incoherence
4. highly limited vocabulary

5. numerous problems with sentence structure
6. errors in mechanics, usage, and grammar serious enough to interfere with the reader's comprehension

These essays are *seriously flawed*.

SCORING LEVEL 1

Essays on this level exhibit an acutely flawed command of writing and thinking skills. Characteristics of an essay on this level include:

1. absence of evidence to support a point of view
2. lack of a position on the issue
3. absence of focus and organization
4. rudimentary vocabulary
5. severe problems with sentence structure
6. extensive flaws in mechanics, usage, and grammar severe enough to block the reader's comprehension.

These essays are *fundamentally deficient*.

Scored sample essays appear at the end of this part.

Your essay subscore (that is, your combined score of 2 to 12) and your multiple-choice writing subscore from Part VI will determine your eventual writing skills score, with the essay subscore counting as one-third of your total writing score.

BEFORE THE TEST

GEARING UP FOR WRITING A TIMED ESSAY

Five minutes remaining!? I can't possibly have only five minutes left. I haven't even started my third paragraph...and I'm not sure what to say next. I guess I should just write a conclusion...summarize what I already wrote. What did I write? What was the question? Whoa...did I even answer the question?

"Two minutes remaining."

TWO MINUTES?! Okay, here goes...

Your first impulse in embarking on a timed writing assignment may be to begin writing immediately. This is understandable, given the time pressure you are feeling and the natural fear of being unable to complete your essay in the allotted time. It is, however, a big mistake. Taking the time to brainstorm and outline is the best way to ensure that you write a complete essay, with a strong thesis and clear organization. The test taker's nightmare depicted above often results from poor planning; you can best avoid it by investing a portion of your allowed time in developing a thumbnail outline of your essay.

Although planning your essay is essential, you should also avoid devoting too much time to planning. Your first instinct, to start writing ASAP because time is short, is not entirely wrong. Time *is* short, and the key to successful timed essay writing is the ability to plan your essay quickly. For a 25-minute essay, you should plan to spend no more than five minutes on brainstorming and outlining. If this sounds like a daunting task, you are correct. Thinking clearly on the fly and responding well under extreme time pressure are difficult, but are skills that you can develop with practice.

TIPS ON PREPARING FOR THE ESSAY TEST

TIP 1

FAMILIARIZE YOURSELF WITH THE MOST COMMON TYPES OF ESSAY QUESTIONS.

In past years, ETS has used three types of essay questions on the SAT II Writing Test; it is likely to use a similar formula for the new SAT writing prompts.

The first type of essay question asks you to **respond to a statement**. A good example of this type of prompt is:

Genius is one percent inspiration, and ninety-nine percent perspiration. – Thomas Alva Edison

Assignment: The statement above implies that effort is of greater importance than creativity in achieving success. Write an essay supporting, disputing, or qualifying the statement. You may use examples from history, literature, popular culture, current events, or personal experience to support your position.

The second type of prompt asks you to **choose between contrasting statements**. For example:

1. *Education is a kind of continuing dialogue, and a dialogue assumes … different points of view.*
   – Robert M. Hutchins

2. *What does education often do? It makes a straight-cut ditch of a free, meandering brook.*
   – Henry David Thoreau

Assignment: Consider the statements above. Choose the one that best represents your beliefs, and write an essay explaining your choice. You may use examples from history, literature, popular culture, current events, or personal experience to support your position.

The third type of prompt asks you to **complete a statement**.

A great work of fiction can allow us to see truths that may be hidden from us in real life. A good example of the ability of fiction to teach important truths is _____.

Assignment: Complete the sentence above with the title of a fictional work from literature, film, or television and write an essay demonstrating how that story teaches an important truth.

Though the three question types may appear different on the surface, they have much in common. Each question demands that you take a position and provide evidence (examples) to support that position. The third question type is in some ways the simplest, because it dictates your thesis. You are not asked to agree or disagree with the statement. Instead, the prompt takes your agreement for granted and requires you to focus your energies on supporting the statement with a well-chosen example. The first type of question provides you with more latitude, allowing you to agree or disagree with the statement, in whole or in part. The second question type appears more complicated than the first, but it is really no different. Rather than choosing to agree or disagree with a single statement, you choose between two statements that disagree, selecting the one that better represents your beliefs.

You do not need to practice brainstorming and creating outlines for all three question types. If you can handle **responding to a statement**, you can handle the other question types as well. If you get a **contrasting statements** topic, once you have chosen the statement with which you basically agree, your essay will be a **response to statement** essay in which you indicate your agreement with that statement. If you are assigned a **complete a statement** essay, your essay essentially will also be a **response to statement** essay in which you support the statement.

TIP 2

CREATE A POOL OF PRACTICE ESSAY TOPICS.

To practice brainstorming and outlining, you will need a good supply of potential essay topics. Most test prep books give you a few, but you can generate a nearly limitless supply by leafing through good books of quotations. The two books listed below are especially good, but you can use any quotation book that is organized by subject. Avoid books that are organized by author or (even worse) that are in no particular order at all. They are much harder to use.

Suggested Quotation Books:

The Harper Book of Quotations, Revised Edition by Robert I. Fitzhenry

Peter's Quotations: Ideas for Our Times by Laurence J. Peter

An additional (and free) resource for quotations can be found on the Web at: *http://www.bartleby.com/ quotations/*

What sorts of topics should you choose? ETS tends to use topics that are relevant to young adults about to enter college. Common topic areas include education, success, challenges, risk taking, individuality, and self-knowledge. ETS appears to avoid topics that may be emotionally charged (such as family relationships) or relevant to a limited audience (such as sports). With this information in mind and a quotation book in hand, you should be able to come up with dozens (perhaps even hundreds) of practice topics.

Here are some sample topics to get you started:

> Each of the excerpts appearing below makes a point about a particular topic. Read the passage carefully, and think about the assignment that follows.

"I have never in my life learned anything from any man who agreed with me."
—Dudley Field Malone

Assignment: What is your view on the idea that we learn the most from those with whom we disagree? Plan and write an essay in which you develop your point of view on this topic. Support your position with reasoning and examples taken from your reading, studies, experience, or observations.

"Bluntness is a virtue."
—Allison Ling

Assignment: What is your view on the idea that one cannot be too frank or honest? Plan and write an essay in which you develop your point of view on this issue. Support your position with reasoning and examples taken from your reading, studies, experience, or observations.

"If you don't like something, change it. If you can't change it, change your attitude. Don't complain."
—Maya Angelou

Assignment: What is your view on the idea that we should be satisfied with that which we cannot change? Plan and write an essay in which you develop your point of view on this issue. Support your position with reasoning and examples taken from your reading, studies, experience, or observations.

It has been said that the end does not justify the means—that an immoral act cannot be justified by a desirable outcome. Mahatma Gandhi, the father of nonviolent protest, supports the belief that ends and means must be consistent when he writes, "You must be the change you wish to see in the world."

Assignment: What is your view on the idea that our actions must be consistent with our goals? Plan and write an essay in which you develop your point of view on this issue. Support your position with reasoning and examples taken from your reading, studies, experience, or observations.

"Advice is like snow—the softer it falls, the longer it dwells upon, and the deeper in sinks into the mind."
—Samuel Taylor Coleridge

Assignment: What is your view on the idea that the most effective advice is that which is offered gently? Plan and write an essay in which you develop your point of view on this issue. Support your position with reasoning and examples taken from your reading, studies, experience, or observations.

Dreamers hope to change the world, while pessimists doubt that change is possible. Neither group accomplishes much. Instead, according to Jonathan Kozol, those who hope to make real change should "Pick battles big enough to matter, small enough to win."

Assignment: What is your view on the idea that one should avoid setting goals that are unrealistically large? Plan and write an essay in which you develop your point of view on this issue. Support your position with reasoning and examples taken from your reading, studies, experience, or observations.

"Whenever you find yourself on the side of the majority, it's time to pause and reflect."
—Mark Twain

Assignment: What is your view on the idea that there is something suspect about beliefs that are held by the majority? Plan and write an essay in which you develop your point of view on this issue. Support your position with reasoning and examples taken from your reading, studies, experience, or observations.

"In a democracy dissent is an act of faith. Like medicine, the test of its value is not in its taste, but in its effects."
—J. W. Fulbright

Assignment: What is your view on the idea that dissent is beneficial? Plan and write an essay in which you develop your point of view on this issue. Support your position with reasoning and examples taken from your reading, studies, experience, or observations.

"When you make the finding yourself—even if you're the last person on Earth to see the light—you'll never forget it."
—Carl Sagan

Assignment: What is your view on the idea that we learn best when we are allowed to discover things for ourselves? Plan and write an essay in which you develop your point of view on this issue. Support your position with reasoning and examples taken from your reading, studies, experience, or observations.

"History is a vast early warning system."
—Norman Cousins

Assignment: What is your view on the idea that history can help us to avoid repeating our mistakes? Plan and write an essay in which you develop your point of view on this issue. Support your position with reasoning and examples taken from your reading, studies, experience, or observations.

"There are no mistakes, no coincidences. All events are blessings given to us to learn from."
—Elizabeth Kubler-Ross

Assignment: What is your view on the idea that we should learn from, rather than regret, our failures? Plan and write an essay in which you develop your point of view on this issue. Support your position with reasoning and examples taken from your reading, studies, experience, or observations.

"Only those who dare to fail greatly can ever achieve greatly."
—Robert Francis Kennedy

Assignment: What is your view on the idea that great success requires substantial risk? Plan and write an essay in which you develop your point of view on this issue. Support your position with reasoning and examples taken from your reading, studies, experience, or observations.

TIP 3

FIND OUT HOW MUCH YOU CAN WRITE IN 25 MINUTES.

Now that you have topics, what should you do with them? Although you could write many practice essays, you do not need to go to this extreme. Write a few (two or three) practice essays in the allotted 25-minute time span to get a clear idea of how much you can produce in that period. This information is critical to outlining your essay, because you do not want to plan an essay that you cannot execute within the time limit. For your essay to earn a top score, it is more important that the essay be complete and well organized than that it be very long, so try to get a sense of what you can reasonably accomplish in 25 minutes. Anything in the neighborhood of three to five solid paragraphs is fine.

Note: Length *is* important. Top-scoring SAT II essays published by ETS have averaged about 400 to 500 words. These essays were written in only 20 minutes. For your *25-minute* essay to earn a top score of 5 or 6, it should be *at least* 400 words long.

TIP 4

PRACTICE BRAINSTORMING AND OUTLINING.

Once you have a good idea of the essay length at which you should aim, you can begin practicing brainstorming and outlining. Though outlining may seem like a waste of time, it is the best way to ensure that you both answer the question and reach the conclusion you intend. The outline is a map of the essay—without it, you may end up anywhere. However, you do not need a detailed outline (like the ones you prepare before writing major research papers); all that is called for is a simple, thumbnail sketch of your essay. A few words per paragraph will be fine.

There are two approaches to the initial brainstorming part of planning your essay. You should choose the approach that works better for you. Some students like to begin with the thesis. They read the topic, ponder its meaning, and go with their gut reaction to it. In other words, they agree or they disagree. From this point they begin to look for evidence to support their positions. Evidence can take the form of examples from history, science, literature, popular culture, and even anecdotes and stories from personal experience. Others prefer to begin brainstorming by looking for evidence. They first figure out what the topic means and then brainstorm examples related to it. After examining the examples, they develop positions based on the evidence. You may find that your choice of approach is dictated by your familiarity with the topic and the strength of your beliefs about it. The second approach is likely to work best when the topic is relatively unfamiliar or when you have no preexisting opinion on it.

Here is an example of the thought process you might go through in developing an essay with the first approach.

If you rest, you rust.
—Helen Hayes

Assignment: The statement above argues that those who fail to strive regress. Write an essay supporting, disputing, or qualifying the statement. You may use examples from history, literature, popular culture, current events, or personal experience to support your position.

The Thesis-First Approach:

1. What does the quote mean? If you aren't working hard, you don't make progress. Resting is bad. It leads to failure.
2. Gut reaction? It isn't true. When you are busy and caught up in doing things, it's hard to have perspective on what you are doing. You need to rest to see clearly, set priorities, and achieve.
3. Now gather evidence. Think about rest: its importance to moving forward. Consider what you know about sleep. "I know studies have found that sleep deprivation lowers IQ and harms performance." What about perspective? "My older brother worked hard all through high school, but he figured out what he wanted to study only after he took a year off to travel before he went to college."

The Examples-First Approach:

1. What does the quote mean? If you aren't working hard, you don't make progress. Resting is bad. It leads to failure.
2. Examples. Do you know of any physical examples? "What about when you don't use a muscle and it atrophies, the way it does when you wear a cast?" Mental examples? "I read in the paper that older people can do memory exercises to improve their memory." Examples from daily life? "In business, if you don't keep improving your product, other companies move ahead of you—just as the Japanese auto industry surpassed U.S. car makers. And there's foreign language fluency: people always say use it or lose it."
3. Thesis. What great examples! I think I definitely have to agree with Helen Hayes: "If you rest, you rust!"

Now that you have a thesis and examples, all that remains is organizing them into an essay. You have two simple options for beginning your essay. The first is to introduce the topic directly, as in this outline of a four-paragraph essay:

1. Introduction

   A. Topic: If you rest, you rust.

   B. Thesis: Our negative attitude toward rest is harmful.

   C. Roadmap: Rest is critical to progress because it allows us to function well and it helps us set appropriate goals.

2. Rest is critical to progress.

   A. Sleep deprivation lowers IQ.

   B. Sleep-deprived drivers are as dangerous as drunk drivers.

3. Rest allows us to develop perspective and set goals.

   A. Working too hard doesn't allow us time to question what we are doing and why.

   B. My brother's year off.

4. Conclusion

   A. Summarize arguments and examples.

   B. Move beyond the thesis—still need to work hard, but without rest that work is ineffective.

Here is the essay, based on the preceding outline:

    Helen Hayes takes a firm stand against indolence when she says, "If you rest, you rust." Though indolence is commonly considered a sin at worst and a waste at best, our negative attitude toward rest is detrimental. Rest is critical to progress because it enables us to function well and it helps us set appropriate goals.

    Rest is vital to our ability to function at our best. Recent news stories report that scientists are learning surprising things about the importance of sleep. Lack of adequate rest impairs brain function, so much so that sleep experts have been able to measure drops in IQ in patients who are deprived of sleep. Other studies have demonstrated a negative impact on brain function and coordination in sleep-deprived subjects. It should not, therefore, be a surprise that the California Highway Patrol has stated that sleep-deprived drivers are as great a threat to road safety as are drunk drivers.

    Rest is important for more than just brain function. Those who are caught up in extremely busy lives lack the time to think about what they are doing and gain perspective. Busyness may prevent "rust," but it does not encourage us to maximize our potential. My older brother learned this lesson when he took a year off from school before college. In high school he had been a straight-A student, staying up late into the night in search of perfect grades. It was only when he took a year off from school to travel that he had the time to think about what he really wanted to do, to consider goals beyond grades. In that year off, my brother had a chance to figure out what he genuinely enjoyed. He returned to school knowing that he wants to be a writer, and this knowledge is helping him achieve something of real value.

    Time off to sleep and think is critical to our ability to recognize what is important, and our ability to achieve it. It does not, however, follow from this that we would be better off on a permanent vacation. Rest is critical because it allows us to perform well when we work. It is not an end in itself.

The second approach, introducing the topic with an example, works best when you have several examples. Here is a sample outline.

1. Introduction

    A. Example: I was bilingual in Spanish in elementary school, but I can't even read a burrito shop menu now.

    B. Topic: If you rest, you rust.

    C. Thesis: If you stop moving you will fall behind.

    D. Roadmap: You have to keep moving both to keep up with others and to maintain your own abilities.

2. You have to keep improving to avoid falling behind.

    A. Example: American auto industry.

3. You have to keep moving to avoid atrophy.

    A. Example: Muscles

    B. Example: Memory

4. Conclusion

    A. Summarize.

    B. Return to Spanish anecdote.

Here is the student essay, based on the preceding outline:

I was, according to my mother, bilingual in English and Spanish before I entered kindergarten. Now my mother, like most, enjoys bragging about my accomplishments, including some that border on the implausible, but I think she may be right about this particular one. I remember walking to the park and eating helado (ice cream) with my Salvadoran babysitter, and I remember being rocked to sleep as she sang "Dormite Ninito." Today, however, I can scarcely navigate the menu at a Mexican restaurant. What happened to my fluent Spanish? I went off to "big boy" school. My babysitter moved on to another family with a pre-school-aged child, and I basically had no more opportunities to speak or to hear Spanish.

Helen Hayes was right when she observed, "If you rest, you rust." As I stopped using Spanish, I not only failed to progress in that language, I also fell behind, ultimately losing the ability that I had once possessed. This lesson, that one must strive and exercise in order to keep up with others, and in order to maintain what one has, is an important one because it holds true in every aspect of our lives.

The collapse of the U.S. auto industry is a perfect example of the risk inherent in failing to keep moving forward. For decades, Detroit had dominated the industry, and it felt no need to innovate. Ultimately, Japanese auto makers began to threaten Detroit's dominance because they developed more efficient business practices and better engineered products. When Detroit rested on its laurels, it rusted, and the U.S. auto industry has yet to achieve a full recovery.

The problem with resting is not, however, limited to allowing others to pass you. Sometimes one actually loses one's ability, as I lost my fluency in Spanish. Muscles, for example, atrophy when they are not used—a lesson learned by everyone who has ever worn a cast for any period of time. Even the human brain loses its ability if it is not used. Conversely, recent studies of elderly people have shown that doing memory exercises can improve memory and brain function. The lesson is simple: use it or lose it.

Our lives abound with examples of the importance of remaining active. It is the key to economic success, good health, and, even, speaking Spanish. I think I'll start my exercise by walking to the park and ordering helado for old times' sake.

TIP 5

STOCKPILE EXAMPLES FOR FUTURE USE.

If you are having trouble generating examples, try either of the following approaches. The first approach is chronological. Think of one example from the past and another from the present. This approach lays the foundation for a *simple* organization, and even suggests a conclusion (in which you speculate on the future). See how this approach works with the following prompt.

Success is somebody else's failure.
—Ursula K. Le Guin

Assignment: The statement above argues that success and failure trade off, that there can be no "win-win" situation. Write an essay supporting, disputing, or qualifying the statement. You may use examples from history, literature, popular culture, current events, or personal experience to support your position.

Example from the Past: U.S. westward expansion and the treatment of Native Americans.

Example from the Present: Control of fossil fuel resources.

The second approach focuses on two examples, one a personal, or individual, example and the other a societal example. See how this approach works with the prompt below.

Progress is not an illusion; it happens, but it is slow and invariably disappointing.
—George Orwell

Assignment: The statement above argues that rapid progress is not possible. Write an essay supporting, disputing, or qualifying the statement. You may use examples from history, literature, popular culture, current events, or personal experience to support your position.

Personal Example: Learning to play an instrument.

Societal Example: Equal opportunity for women and minorities.

Keep on the lookout for potential examples that you can use on the SAT. As you read books for your English class or watch the news on television, consider how these stories relate to the topics that occur over and over again in SAT prompts: self-discovery ("In *Great Expectations*, Pip achieves self-understanding only after going through great pain and disillusionment."); the necessity of censorship (prison photos from Iraq); the nature of success, both positive and negative; the deceptiveness of appearances; the cost of making choices.

TIP 6

WRITE WHAT YOU KNOW.

Avoid the temptation to use examples about which you are uncertain. It is far better to use material from your own experience or popular culture than it is to fake knowledge that you lack. Although readers may be impressed that you have read Chaucer and Goethe, they are not evaluating your essay based on the sophistication or obscurity of your examples. It is far more important that your examples prove your point than that they prove your erudition. If you have studied Chaucer and Goethe, feel free to use them. But if you have not, do not reveal your ignorance—or even dishonesty—by pretending to be familiar with texts that you have not read. Similarly, if you are drawing an example from the film version of a great book, be sure to make that clear. Often the two differ significantly; if you fail to be clear about which one you are discussing, you may wind up looking like a poor reader. (Did you know that the most recent film version of the *Scarlet Letter* has a happy ending? That isn't the way the novel ends!) The best examples that you can use are the ones that you know in greatest detail, because you can write about them with authority.

DURING THE TEST

Here are some basic guidelines that will keep you stress-free and focused during the essay section.

TIPS ON WRITING THE ESSAY

TIP 1

KEEP CAREFUL TRACK OF YOUR TIME.

Writing an essay on an unfamiliar subject is pressure enough. You don't need the added pressure that you'll feel if you lose track of the time and discover you have only 60 seconds left to write the two final paragraphs that are critical to your argument.

TIP 2

PACE YOURSELF: KEEP TO YOUR ESSAY-WRITING PLAN.

You have only 25 minutes. Allow yourself 5 minutes for prewriting. Read the essay topic or prompt with care. If you haven't a clue where to begin, jot down words and ideas that pop into your mind when you look at the prompt (brainstorming). Generate questions about the topic until you come up with a point you want to make. If you have found outlining to be helpful, briefly outline what you plan to say. Then devote the remaining 20 minutes to writing your essay, reserving a minute or two at the end to clean up your draft.

TIP 3

REMEMBER THAT YOU DON'T HAVE TO WRITE A PERFECT ESSAY TO EARN A HIGH SCORE.

The readers are instructed to overlook false starts ("beginning stutters," some readers call them) and incomplete conclusions in determining your score. It's all too easy to psych yourself out about the essay-writing assignment and wind up so blocked that you can barely write a paragraph, much less a fully developed essay. Relax. Loosen your grip on your pen. Shake out your fingers if that helps. Your job is to turn out a promising first draft in 25 minutes, not to create a finished work of prose.

TIP 4

WRITE AS LEGIBLY AS YOU POSSIBLY CAN.

Neatness helps. If your printing is neater than your cursive and you can print rapidly, by all means print. Keep within the margins on the page. The easier you make the readers' job, the more kindly disposed they will be toward your essay.

TIP 5

FOLLOW TRADITIONAL ESSAY-WRITING CONVENTIONS.

Make a point of showing the readers you know the "right" way to set up an essay. Indent each new paragraph clearly. Use transitions—signal words and phrases, such as "consequently" and "for this reason"—to indicate your progress from idea to idea.

TIP 6

DON'T ALTER YOUR ESSAY CAPRICIOUSLY.

Change what you have written only if you have a solid reason for doing so. If you have time to read over your paper and spot a grammatical error or a spelling mistake, by all means correct it, making sure your correction is legible. However, try to avoid making major alterations in your text. Last-minute changes can create more problems than they solve. You may run out of time and wind up with a muddle instead of a coherent argument. Or, in your haste to finish your revision, you may scribble sentences that not even a cryptologist could decipher.

TIP 7

UPGRADE YOUR VOCABULARY JUDICIOUSLY.

Top-scoring essays typically include a sprinkling of "college-level" words. (See our High-Frequency Word List in Part V.) The readers like your using big words, words like *theoretical* and *allusion*, but **only if you use them correctly**. Don't try to bluff: it's too risky. If you have a minute or two to spare and are absolutely sure of the meaning of a college-level word that you can substitute for a simple one, go for it. But use your judgment.

Look over the changes in the paragraph below to see how the student writer replaced a couple of easy words with more impressive ones:

> Helen Hayes takes a firm stand against ~~laziness~~ indolence when she says, "If you rest, you rust." Though ~~laziness~~ indolence is commonly considered a sin at worst and a waste at best, our negative attitude toward rest is ~~harmful~~ detrimental. Rest is critical to progress because it enables us to function well and it helps us set appropriate goals.

TIP 8

DON'T SECOND-GUESS YOURSELF.

Once you have finished writing your essay, let it go. You have been concentrating on a single topic for almost half an hour, and you may find it difficult to refocus on a fresh set of multiple-choice questions when you are still worrying about your essay. Avoid the temptation to criticize yourself for any grammatical and spelling errors you may have made or to brood over all the clever arguments you *might* have made. Take a deep breath, loosen up your shoulders, and move on.

RESOURCES TO HELP YOU BECOME A BETTER WRITER

RECOMMENDED BOOKS

The Elements of Style, Strunk and White (Strunk's original *Elements of Style*, without E. B. White's revisions and added chapter, is available on the Web at *www.bartleby.com/141/*)

The Careful Writer, Theodore M. Bernstein

The Practical Stylist, Sheridan Baker

On Writing Well, William K. Zinsser

Line by Line: How to Edit Your Own Writing, Claire Kehrwald Cook

A Dictionary of Modern English Usage, H. W. Fowler (Fowler's classic *The King's English* is available on the Web at *www.bartleby.com/116/*)

ADDITIONAL SOURCES OF HELP

You learn to write by writing and rewriting, preferably with lots of feedback from your teachers and classmates. If you are not getting enough opportunities to write in high school, create fresh opportunities for yourself.

Find writing help through after-school tutorials, public library programs, and other sources.

Join your high school forensics team, and consider specializing in impromptu debate.

Set up writing cooperatives with your fellow students and practice critiquing one another's drafts.

Volunteer as a reporter for your local neighborhood newspaper.

Keep a folder of your old book reports and compositions, and review it periodically to see whether you are still making the same old mistakes.

Find writing help through the Internet. Potentially useful websites are:

http://writingcenter.gmu.edu/
The George Mason University Writing Center site contains useful material on grammar, punctuation, and the writing process.

http://rwc.hunter.cuny.edu/writing/index.html
The Hunter College Writing Center site is a source of handouts on grammar and mechanics, the writing demands of different disciplines, and the writing process in general.

www.lynchburg.edu/writcntr/guide/
The Lynchburg College Writing Center provides online guides to grammar and to general writing techniques.

www.nutsandboltsguide.com
Author Michael Harvey offers extracts from his reader-friendly *Nuts and Bolts of College Writing*.

www.powa.org
The Paradigm Online Writing Assistant provides advice on writing and revising various types of essays.

www.scholastic.com/writewit/index.htm
The Scholastic site features an excellent section, Writing with Writers, offering workshops on writing news articles, speeches, and book reviews.

www.teenwriting.about.com
In addition to providing advice on the writing process and on fine-tuning your grammar, the Teenwriting Forum enables teens to discuss writing problems and critique one another's poetry and prose.

SAMPLE SCORED ESSAYS

Look over the following scored sample essays to see the characteristic strengths and weaknesses of compositions on each of the six scoring levels.

SAMPLE ESSAY U—SCORE 6

Those who have overcome great adversity in life can take satisfaction from Thomas Paine's assertion, "The harder the conflict, the more glorious the triumph." For people truly to appreciate their victories, they must be able to contrast these victories with the hardships they have undergone. To value their good fortune, they must suffer ill fortune as well.

In Charlotte Bronte's Jane Eyre, the theme of overcoming adversity occurs again and again. At each stage of Jane's life she struggles to overcome adversity and, succeeding, values her victory against the odds. In the novel's opening chapters, the orphaned Jane is at the mercy of her wealthy, uncaring Aunt Reed and her bullying cousin John. When she is sent away to Lowood School, she is overjoyed, because she is free from their cruelties. Yet Jane soon finds that her life at Lowood School is not as idylic as she had hoped it would be. Though she finds a friend in Helen Burns, Jane and the other students face adversity in the form of Mr. Brocklehurst, the headmaster, who deprives the girls of proper clothing and nourishment and spends school funds on his own family. Only after an epidemic hits the school, killing Helen, do the authorities step in to remove Mr. Brocklehurst and restore the school.

Jane survives this adversity and grows up to become a teacher at Lowood School. Facing a dull existence, she desires new experiences and accepts a position as governess at an estate owned by a man named Rochester. She wins his love and they are to be married when she discovers on their wedding day that

Sample Essay U—Score 6 (continued)

he is already married to a madwoman, Bertha Mason, whom he cannot divorce. Jane is torn between her love for Rochester and her conscience. She struggles with herself and wins a hard victory: she runs away from Rochester, and, penniless and ill, lives on the streets until she is taken in by the Rivers family. Once again, she has survived adversity, and she rejoices as she regains her peace of mind and begins to do good works teaching in the local charity school.

Jane has survived, and in time she wins her greatest victory. St. John Rivers urges Jane to join him in missionary work in India and offers to marry her. Still loving Rochester, she does not wish to marry Rivers; however, she feels drawn to a life of service as a missionary. She struggles with herself, and one night she mysteriously hears Rochester's voice calling her name. Jane immediately hurries back to Rochester's estate and finds it has been burned to the ground by Bertha Mason, who died in the fire. Rochester also has suffered adversity: trying to save Bertha and the servant from the flames, he has lost his eyesight and one of his hands and needs Jane's help to keep him from giving in to despair. This is Jane's greatest victory and Rochester's as well, for they marry and live happily. Having struggled with their consciences and fought temptation, they value all the more their glorious victory.

SAMPLE ESSAY V—SCORE 5

When Thomas Paine wrote "The harder the conflict, the more glorious the triumph," he was writing in a time of war. The American colonies were still struggling to win their independance against the English. It was a hard and bloody conflict that pitted brother against brother. Paine wrote to inspire his fellow countrymen to persist in the fight. He promised them they would value their freedom even more because it had been so hard to attain. Paine's words inspired the people then and they can inspire us today.

Today Americans are fighting a terrible war, a war against terrorism. This war has taken reservists from jobs and families to face danger and death in the Middle East. These soldiers have been doing their job fighting our country's battles. They have been walking in harm's way. By fighting hard against the evils of terrorism and to bring democracy to the Middle East they are demonstrating to the world that "the harder the conflict, the more glorious the triumph."

In addition to our soldiers overseas today, the civil rights workers who protested in the South during the fifties and sixties also fought a great fight and won glorious victories. Students sat in at lunch counters and marched to integrate all-white schools. They faced fire hoses and police dogs singing "We shall overcome" and showed they were willing to fight and die for the principle of equal rights and equal opportunity. Freedom riders came to the South; some of them even died there. They paid with their lives so that others might be free. Without their attempts to break down the barriers, injustice and racial prejudice might still prevale.

Many times people who are engaged in a great conflict may feel like giving up, but our soldiers today and the civil rights workers of yesterday teach us a different lesson. The most important fights to fight are the hardest ones, the ones that cost some people everything they have. Only by fighting such a hard fight will you truly value your victory. That was true in Thomas Paine's time and in Martin Luther King's time and in our time today.

I partly agree with Thomas Paine's idea that "The harder the conflict, the more glorious the triumph." When you struggle hard for something, you can appreciate it more than if ~~you~~ it comes to you easily, however you can also decide it wasn't worth the fight. There are times when keeping on fighting is the best thing to do, while other times giving up the fight makes the most sence. You need to choose whether or not to keep fighting depending on what the situation is.

In ordinary life young people face many conflicts, especially when they have to decide about education and careers. There are many colleges in the ~~world~~ United States where the students have to fight hard to get accepted. They also can cost alot of money. There are in addition many ~~care~~ careers that take hard work and persistence before you can get a good job. An example of this is medicine, where people who want to become doctors have to pass course after course just to get into medical school and

Sample Essay W—Score 4 (continued)

then have to complete medical school and pass their boards before they can practice medicine. Another example of struggling hard to get an education was in the south during the Civil Rights movement when Black people fought to integrate the schools.

Many people today still have to fight to get a good education or a job. One example problem is outsourcing. Outsourcing is when American jobs go to peoples overseas, for example in India. The American people who lose their jobs are struggling to get new ones, but sometime there are no new jobs in their home town or they have to find a job in a different field. This is also true for young people just coming out of college. The struggle is hard but the reward is great.

Just as Thomas Paine wrote in his quote, "the harder the conflict, the more glorious the triumph." It costs a lot of money and effort to get a good education. It takes a lot of searching to find a good job. But when you get that job or the degree, you will know how special it can be.

SAMPLE ESSAY X—SCORE 3

People often think that they would like an easy life. They think conflict and fighting are always bad. However it seems when they have to fight for what they want they are happier with what they get.

The phrase "easy come, easy go" shows how people do not value things they can get easily. They have low esteem. At least some struggle is necessary in making the victories feel more meaningfull. There are some fights that are too hard to win and then no one is happy, but if someone can fight and win they are better off.

Some conflicts are simply too much to handle, for various reasons. Often times a fight cannot be won because one side is too strong. Conflicts can bring out the best in people, they can bring out the worst in people too. There is just no way of avoiding conflicts, so if you have to fight do your best to win and let yourself feel good about the victory.

SAMPLE ESSAY Y—SCORE 2

Fighting a hard conflict is a difficult thing. There are always wars and no one can predicts which side is going to win. If you look back at all the wars the United States has gotten in to over the years, many have ended up with a withdrawl and not a victory. In some cases the goverment tells the public that it is a victory but that is not necesarly true. They only tell the public about the fights they win or sometimes they make it sound like they won even if they have not.

To feel realy victorious about a conflict you have to actually win it. Thomas Paine once said "The harder the conflict, the more glorious the triumph. What we obtain too cheaply, we esteem too lightly." But it is realy cheap to pretend to win a victory.

THomas Pain once said" The harder the conflict, the more glorious the triumph" If a conflict is hard it is not all bad because when u win you are happier then befor. A hard conflict can be very bad dangerous for a community and its people. When things are bad the people can be discouraged phcysologicly and even give up. Many times they need to fight hard and things get better they will have a triumph.

PART VIII

TESTS FOR PRACTICE

ANSWER SHEET FOR CRITICAL READING AND WRITING SKILLS TEST 1

Section 1   **ESSAY**   Time allowed: 25 minutes

Essay (continued)

Section 2

1. Ⓐ Ⓑ Ⓒ Ⓓ Ⓔ　　9. Ⓐ Ⓑ Ⓒ Ⓓ Ⓔ　　17. Ⓐ Ⓑ Ⓒ Ⓓ Ⓔ　　25. Ⓐ Ⓑ Ⓒ Ⓓ Ⓔ
2. Ⓐ Ⓑ Ⓒ Ⓓ Ⓔ　　10. Ⓐ Ⓑ Ⓒ Ⓓ Ⓔ　　18. Ⓐ Ⓑ Ⓒ Ⓓ Ⓔ　　26. Ⓐ Ⓑ Ⓒ Ⓓ Ⓔ
3. Ⓐ Ⓑ Ⓒ Ⓓ Ⓔ　　11. Ⓐ Ⓑ Ⓒ Ⓓ Ⓔ　　19. Ⓐ Ⓑ Ⓒ Ⓓ Ⓔ　　27. Ⓐ Ⓑ Ⓒ Ⓓ Ⓔ
4. Ⓐ Ⓑ Ⓒ Ⓓ Ⓔ　　12. Ⓐ Ⓑ Ⓒ Ⓓ Ⓔ　　20. Ⓐ Ⓑ Ⓒ Ⓓ Ⓔ　　28. Ⓐ Ⓑ Ⓒ Ⓓ Ⓔ
5. Ⓐ Ⓑ Ⓒ Ⓓ Ⓔ　　13. Ⓐ Ⓑ Ⓒ Ⓓ Ⓔ　　21. Ⓐ Ⓑ Ⓒ Ⓓ Ⓔ　　29. Ⓐ Ⓑ Ⓒ Ⓓ Ⓔ
6. Ⓐ Ⓑ Ⓒ Ⓓ Ⓔ　　14. Ⓐ Ⓑ Ⓒ Ⓓ Ⓔ　　22. Ⓐ Ⓑ Ⓒ Ⓓ Ⓔ　　30. Ⓐ Ⓑ Ⓒ Ⓓ Ⓔ
7. Ⓐ Ⓑ Ⓒ Ⓓ Ⓔ　　15. Ⓐ Ⓑ Ⓒ Ⓓ Ⓔ　　23. Ⓐ Ⓑ Ⓒ Ⓓ Ⓔ
8. Ⓐ Ⓑ Ⓒ Ⓓ Ⓔ　　16. Ⓐ Ⓑ Ⓒ Ⓓ Ⓔ　　24. Ⓐ Ⓑ Ⓒ Ⓓ Ⓔ

Section 3

1. Ⓐ Ⓑ Ⓒ Ⓓ Ⓔ　　10. Ⓐ Ⓑ Ⓒ Ⓓ Ⓔ　　19. Ⓐ Ⓑ Ⓒ Ⓓ Ⓔ　　28. Ⓐ Ⓑ Ⓒ Ⓓ Ⓔ
2. Ⓐ Ⓑ Ⓒ Ⓓ Ⓔ　　11. Ⓐ Ⓑ Ⓒ Ⓓ Ⓔ　　20. Ⓐ Ⓑ Ⓒ Ⓓ Ⓔ　　29. Ⓐ Ⓑ Ⓒ Ⓓ Ⓔ
3. Ⓐ Ⓑ Ⓒ Ⓓ Ⓔ　　12. Ⓐ Ⓑ Ⓒ Ⓓ Ⓔ　　21. Ⓐ Ⓑ Ⓒ Ⓓ Ⓔ　　30. Ⓐ Ⓑ Ⓒ Ⓓ Ⓔ
4. Ⓐ Ⓑ Ⓒ Ⓓ Ⓔ　　13. Ⓐ Ⓑ Ⓒ Ⓓ Ⓔ　　22. Ⓐ Ⓑ Ⓒ Ⓓ Ⓔ　　31. Ⓐ Ⓑ Ⓒ Ⓓ Ⓔ
5. Ⓐ Ⓑ Ⓒ Ⓓ Ⓔ　　14. Ⓐ Ⓑ Ⓒ Ⓓ Ⓔ　　23. Ⓐ Ⓑ Ⓒ Ⓓ Ⓔ　　32. Ⓐ Ⓑ Ⓒ Ⓓ Ⓔ
6. Ⓐ Ⓑ Ⓒ Ⓓ Ⓔ　　15. Ⓐ Ⓑ Ⓒ Ⓓ Ⓔ　　24. Ⓐ Ⓑ Ⓒ Ⓓ Ⓔ　　33. Ⓐ Ⓑ Ⓒ Ⓓ Ⓔ
7. Ⓐ Ⓑ Ⓒ Ⓓ Ⓔ　　16. Ⓐ Ⓑ Ⓒ Ⓓ Ⓔ　　25. Ⓐ Ⓑ Ⓒ Ⓓ Ⓔ　　34. Ⓐ Ⓑ Ⓒ Ⓓ Ⓔ
8. Ⓐ Ⓑ Ⓒ Ⓓ Ⓔ　　17. Ⓐ Ⓑ Ⓒ Ⓓ Ⓔ　　26. Ⓐ Ⓑ Ⓒ Ⓓ Ⓔ　　35. Ⓐ Ⓑ Ⓒ Ⓓ Ⓔ
9. Ⓐ Ⓑ Ⓒ Ⓓ Ⓔ　　18. Ⓐ Ⓑ Ⓒ Ⓓ Ⓔ　　27. Ⓐ Ⓑ Ⓒ Ⓓ Ⓔ

Section 4

1. Ⓐ Ⓑ Ⓒ Ⓓ Ⓔ　　9. Ⓐ Ⓑ Ⓒ Ⓓ Ⓔ　　17. Ⓐ Ⓑ Ⓒ Ⓓ Ⓔ　　25. Ⓐ Ⓑ Ⓒ Ⓓ Ⓔ
2. Ⓐ Ⓑ Ⓒ Ⓓ Ⓔ　　10. Ⓐ Ⓑ Ⓒ Ⓓ Ⓔ　　18. Ⓐ Ⓑ Ⓒ Ⓓ Ⓔ　　26. Ⓐ Ⓑ Ⓒ Ⓓ Ⓔ
3. Ⓐ Ⓑ Ⓒ Ⓓ Ⓔ　　11. Ⓐ Ⓑ Ⓒ Ⓓ Ⓔ　　19. Ⓐ Ⓑ Ⓒ Ⓓ Ⓔ　　27. Ⓐ Ⓑ Ⓒ Ⓓ Ⓔ
4. Ⓐ Ⓑ Ⓒ Ⓓ Ⓔ　　12. Ⓐ Ⓑ Ⓒ Ⓓ Ⓔ　　20. Ⓐ Ⓑ Ⓒ Ⓓ Ⓔ　　28. Ⓐ Ⓑ Ⓒ Ⓓ Ⓔ
5. Ⓐ Ⓑ Ⓒ Ⓓ Ⓔ　　13. Ⓐ Ⓑ Ⓒ Ⓓ Ⓔ　　21. Ⓐ Ⓑ Ⓒ Ⓓ Ⓔ　　29. Ⓐ Ⓑ Ⓒ Ⓓ Ⓔ
6. Ⓐ Ⓑ Ⓒ Ⓓ Ⓔ　　14. Ⓐ Ⓑ Ⓒ Ⓓ Ⓔ　　22. Ⓐ Ⓑ Ⓒ Ⓓ Ⓔ　　30. Ⓐ Ⓑ Ⓒ Ⓓ Ⓔ
7. Ⓐ Ⓑ Ⓒ Ⓓ Ⓔ　　15. Ⓐ Ⓑ Ⓒ Ⓓ Ⓔ　　23. Ⓐ Ⓑ Ⓒ Ⓓ Ⓔ
8. Ⓐ Ⓑ Ⓒ Ⓓ Ⓔ　　16. Ⓐ Ⓑ Ⓒ Ⓓ Ⓔ　　24. Ⓐ Ⓑ Ⓒ Ⓓ Ⓔ

Section 5

1. Ⓐ Ⓑ Ⓒ Ⓓ Ⓔ
2. Ⓐ Ⓑ Ⓒ Ⓓ Ⓔ
3. Ⓐ Ⓑ Ⓒ Ⓓ Ⓔ
4. Ⓐ Ⓑ Ⓒ Ⓓ Ⓔ
5. Ⓐ Ⓑ Ⓒ Ⓓ Ⓔ
6. Ⓐ Ⓑ Ⓒ Ⓓ Ⓔ
7. Ⓐ Ⓑ Ⓒ Ⓓ Ⓔ
8. Ⓐ Ⓑ Ⓒ Ⓓ Ⓔ

9. Ⓐ Ⓑ Ⓒ Ⓓ Ⓔ
10. Ⓐ Ⓑ Ⓒ Ⓓ Ⓔ
11. Ⓐ Ⓑ Ⓒ Ⓓ Ⓔ
12. Ⓐ Ⓑ Ⓒ Ⓓ Ⓔ
13. Ⓐ Ⓑ Ⓒ Ⓓ Ⓔ
14. Ⓐ Ⓑ Ⓒ Ⓓ Ⓔ
15. Ⓐ Ⓑ Ⓒ Ⓓ Ⓔ
16. Ⓐ Ⓑ Ⓒ Ⓓ Ⓔ

17. Ⓐ Ⓑ Ⓒ Ⓓ Ⓔ
18. Ⓐ Ⓑ Ⓒ Ⓓ Ⓔ
19. Ⓐ Ⓑ Ⓒ Ⓓ Ⓔ
20. Ⓐ Ⓑ Ⓒ Ⓓ Ⓔ
21. Ⓐ Ⓑ Ⓒ Ⓓ Ⓔ
22. Ⓐ Ⓑ Ⓒ Ⓓ Ⓔ
23. Ⓐ Ⓑ Ⓒ Ⓓ Ⓔ
24. Ⓐ Ⓑ Ⓒ Ⓓ Ⓔ

25. Ⓐ Ⓑ Ⓒ Ⓓ Ⓔ
26. Ⓐ Ⓑ Ⓒ Ⓓ Ⓔ
27. Ⓐ Ⓑ Ⓒ Ⓓ Ⓔ
28. Ⓐ Ⓑ Ⓒ Ⓓ Ⓔ
29. Ⓐ Ⓑ Ⓒ Ⓓ Ⓔ
30. Ⓐ Ⓑ Ⓒ Ⓓ Ⓔ

Section 6

1. Ⓐ Ⓑ Ⓒ Ⓓ Ⓔ
2. Ⓐ Ⓑ Ⓒ Ⓓ Ⓔ
3. Ⓐ Ⓑ Ⓒ Ⓓ Ⓔ
4. Ⓐ Ⓑ Ⓒ Ⓓ Ⓔ
5. Ⓐ Ⓑ Ⓒ Ⓓ Ⓔ
6. Ⓐ Ⓑ Ⓒ Ⓓ Ⓔ
7. Ⓐ Ⓑ Ⓒ Ⓓ Ⓔ
8. Ⓐ Ⓑ Ⓒ Ⓓ Ⓔ

9. Ⓐ Ⓑ Ⓒ Ⓓ Ⓔ
10. Ⓐ Ⓑ Ⓒ Ⓓ Ⓔ
11. Ⓐ Ⓑ Ⓒ Ⓓ Ⓔ
12. Ⓐ Ⓑ Ⓒ Ⓓ Ⓔ
13. Ⓐ Ⓑ Ⓒ Ⓓ Ⓔ
14. Ⓐ Ⓑ Ⓒ Ⓓ Ⓔ
15. Ⓐ Ⓑ Ⓒ Ⓓ Ⓔ
16. Ⓐ Ⓑ Ⓒ Ⓓ Ⓔ

17. Ⓐ Ⓑ Ⓒ Ⓓ Ⓔ
18. Ⓐ Ⓑ Ⓒ Ⓓ Ⓔ
19. Ⓐ Ⓑ Ⓒ Ⓓ Ⓔ
20. Ⓐ Ⓑ Ⓒ Ⓓ Ⓔ
21. Ⓐ Ⓑ Ⓒ Ⓓ Ⓔ
22. Ⓐ Ⓑ Ⓒ Ⓓ Ⓔ
23. Ⓐ Ⓑ Ⓒ Ⓓ Ⓔ
24. Ⓐ Ⓑ Ⓒ Ⓓ Ⓔ

25. Ⓐ Ⓑ Ⓒ Ⓓ Ⓔ
26. Ⓐ Ⓑ Ⓒ Ⓓ Ⓔ
27. Ⓐ Ⓑ Ⓒ Ⓓ Ⓔ
28. Ⓐ Ⓑ Ⓒ Ⓓ Ⓔ
29. Ⓐ Ⓑ Ⓒ Ⓓ Ⓔ
30. Ⓐ Ⓑ Ⓒ Ⓓ Ⓔ

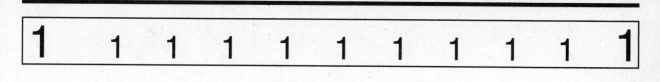

TIME—25 MINUTES

MODEL TEST 1
Section 1
Essay

Turn to your answer sheet and write your essay on the lined portion of the page. To receive credit, you must write your essay in the area provided.

Write on the assigned topic below. If you write on any other topic, your essay will be given a score of zero.

Write or print legibly: your readers will be unfamiliar with your handwriting, and you want them to be able to read what you write.

The excerpt below makes a point about a particular topic. Read the passage carefully, and think about the assignment that follows.

We can succeed only by concert. It is not "Can any of us imagine better?" but "Can we all do better?"
—Abraham Lincoln

Assignment: The excerpt above argues that we can achieve only through collective effort, not as individuals. Write an essay supporting, disputing, or qualifying this thesis. You may use examples from history, literature, popular culture, current events, or personal experience to support your position.

BEGIN WRITING YOUR ESSAY ON THE ANSWER SHEET

STOP
IF YOU FINISH BEFORE TIME IS CALLED, YOU MAY CHECK YOUR WORK ON THIS SECTION ONLY. DO NOT WORK ON ANY OTHER SECTION IN THE TEST.

2 2 2 2 2 2 2 2 2 2 2

Section 2

TIME—25 MINUTES
24 QUESTIONS

For each of the following questions, select the best answer from the choices provided and fill in the appropriate circle on the answer sheet.

Each of the following sentences contains one or two blanks; each blank indicates that a word or set of words has been left out. Below the sentence are five words or phrases, lettered A through E. Select the word or set of words that best completes the sentence.

Example:

Fame is ----; today's rising star is all too soon tomorrow's washed-up has-been.

(A) rewarding   (B) gradual
(C) essential   (D) spontaneous
(E) transitory

Ⓐ Ⓑ Ⓒ Ⓓ ●

---

1. Despite careful restoration and cleaning of the murals in the 1960s, the colors slowly but steadily ____.
   (A) persisted
   (B) embellished
   (C) saturated
   (D) deteriorated
   (E) stabilized

2. After the lonely rigors of writing, Mr. Doyle enjoys the ____ aspects of filmmaking.
   (A) impersonal
   (B) transitory
   (C) narrative
   (D) social
   (E) profitable

3. So ____ was the textile trade between England and America—vast quantities of indigo and raw-ginned cotton a year going in one direction, millions of yards of printed cotton fabrics in the other—that it ____ right through the American War of Independence.
   (A) negligible...endured
   (B) important...continued
   (C) illicit...collaborated
   (D) inappropriate...persisted
   (E) pervasive...ceased

4. Like doctors exploring the mysteries concealed within the human body, astronomers are finding that X rays offer an invaluable means for examining otherwise ____ structures.
   (A) inconsequential
   (B) hidden
   (C) ambivalent
   (D) diseased
   (E) ephemeral

5. When trees go dormant in winter, the procedure is anything but ____: it is an active metabolic process that changes the plant ____.
   (A) sleepy...radically
   (B) pleasant...intermittently
   (C) dynamic...majestically
   (D) overt...openly
   (E) organic...thoroughly

GO ON TO THE NEXT PAGE ⇨

2   2   2   2   2   2   2   2   2   2   2

6. As Reginald Machell's lavishly carved throne clearly illustrates, California craftsmen were not afraid of ____.

(A) competition
(B) embellishment
(C) imitation
(D) expediency
(E) antiquity

7. One might dispute the author's handling of particular points of Kandinsky's interaction with his artistic environment, but her main theses are ____.

(A) unaesthetic
(B) incongruous
(C) untenable
(D) undecipherable
(E) irreproachable

8. After reading numbers of biographies recounting dysfunctions and disasters, failed marriages and failed careers, Joyce Carol Oates ____ a word to ____ the genre: *pathography*, the story of diseased lives.

(A) invented...curtail
(B) reiterated...criticize
(C) hypothesized...indict
(D) dismissed...obscure
(E) coined...describe

GO ON TO THE NEXT PAGE

2 2 2 2 2 2 2 2 2 2 2

Read each of the passages below, and then answer the questions that follow the passage. The correct response may be stated outright or merely suggested in the passage.

Questions 9 and 10 are based on the following passage.

Did she or didn't she? From the 1950s popular song lyrics proclaiming that
Captain Smith and Pocahontas
Line   *Had a very mad affair*
(5) to the 1995 Walt Disney animated film, the legend of Pocahontas has been widely popular in American culture. But the romance between John Smith and the Indian chieftain's daughter appears to have been a total fabrication. True,
(10) young Matoaka, whose pet name was Pocahontas ("favorite daughter") interceded to save Smith's life, but she was only 11 at the time, and though she eventually married an Englishman named John, his surname was
(15) Rolfe, not Smith.

9. The author's primary purpose in this paragraph is to
   (A) debunk a common myth
   (B) refute a challenge to an argument
   (C) encourage us to identify with historical figures
   (D) celebrate a legendary romance
   (E) distinguish between history and drama

10. The word "True" in line 9 serves primarily to acknowledge the
   (A) existence of a relationship between Pocahontas and Smith
   (B) high esteem in which Pocahontas was held by her father
   (C) lack of information about Matoaka's actual emotions
   (D) authoritative nature of the Disney animated version
   (E) enduring popularity of legendary heroic figures

Questions 11 and 12 are based on the following passage.

Today more than ever Hollywood depends on adaptations rather than original screenplays for its story material. This is a far cry from
Line years ago when studio writers created most of
(5) a producer's scripts. To filmmakers, a best-selling novel has a peculiar advantage over an original script: already popular with the public, it *must* be a potential box-office success. Furthermore, it is usually easier and less time-
(10) consuming for a script writer to adapt a major work than to write one. The rub for producers is that they pay such extravagant prices for these properties that the excess load on the budget often puts the movie in the red.

11. The word "peculiar" (line 6) most nearly means
   (A) quaint
   (B) bizarre
   (C) unfortunate
   (D) particular
   (E) artistic

12. The primary drawback to basing a screenplay on a best-selling novel is
   (A) the amount of time it takes to create a script based on a novel
   (B) the public's resentment of changes the script writer makes to the novel's story
   (C) the degree of difficulty involved in faithfully adapting a novel for the screen
   (D) the desire of studio writers to create their own original scripts
   (E) the financial impact of purchasing rights to adapt the novel

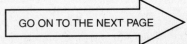
GO ON TO THE NEXT PAGE

2 2 2 2 2 2 2 2 2 2 2 2

Questions 13–24 are based on the following passage.

The following passage is an excerpt from Henry James's short story "The Pupil." In this section, Pemberton, the young British tutor, describes some of the hasty trips around Europe during which he came to know his pupil, Morgan Moreen, and Morgan's family.

A year after he had come to live with them Mr. and Mrs. Moreen suddenly gave up the villa at Nice. Pemberton had got used to sud-
Line denness, having seen it practiced on a consid-
(5) erable scale during two jerky little tours—one in Switzerland the first summer, and the other late in the winter, when they all ran down to Florence and then, at the end of ten days, lik-ing it much less than they had intended, strag-
(10) gled back in mysterious depression. They had returned to Nice "for ever," as they said; but this didn't prevent their squeezing, one rainy muggy May night, into a second-class railway-carriage—you could never tell by
(15) which class they would travel—where Pemberton helped them to stow away a won-derful collection of bundles and bags. The explanation of this manoeuvre was that they had determined to spend the summer "in some
(20) bracing place"; but in Paris they dropped into a small furnished apartment—a fourth floor in a third-rate avenue, where there was a smell on the staircase and the *portier*[1] was hateful—and passed the next four months in blank
(25) indigence.

The better part of this forced temporary stay belonged to the tutor and his pupil, who, visiting the Invalides[2] and Notre Dame, the Conciergerie and all the museums, took a hun-
(30) dred rewarding rambles. They learned to know their Paris, which was useful, for they came back another year for a longer stay, the general character of which in Pemberton's memory today mixes pitiably and confusedly with that
(35) of the first. He sees Morgan's shabby knicker-bockers—the everlasting pair that didn't match his blouse and that as he grew longer

could only grow faded. He remembers the particular holes in his three or four pairs of
(40) colored stockings.

Morgan was dear to his mother, but he never was better dressed than was absolutely necessary—partly, no doubt, by his own fault, for he was as indifferent to his appearance as a
(45) German philosopher. "My dear fellow, so are you! I don't want to cast you in the shade." Pemberton could have no rejoinder for this—the assertion so closely represented the fact. If however the deficiencies of his own wardrobe
(50) were a chapter by themselves he didn't like his little charge to look too poor. Later he used to say "Well, if we're poor, why, after all, shouldn't we look it?" and he consoled him-self with thinking there was something rather
(55) elderly and gentlemanly in Morgan's disre-pair—it differed from the untidiness of the urchin who plays and spoils his things. He could trace perfectly the degrees by which, in proportion as her little son confined himself to
(60) his tutor for society, Mrs. Moreen shrewdly forbore to renew his garments. She did noth-ing that didn't show, neglected him because he escaped notice, and then, as he illustrated this clever policy, discouraged at home his public
(65) appearances. Her position was logical enough—those members of her family who did show had to be showy.

During this period and several others Pemberton was quite aware of how he and his
(70) comrade might strike people; wandering lan-guidly through the Jardin des Plantes[3] as if they had nowhere to go, sitting on the winter days in the galleries of the Louvre, so splen-didly ironical to the homeless, as if for the
(75) advantage of the steam radiators. They joked about it sometimes: it was the sort of joke that was perfectly within the boy's compass. They figured themselves as part of the vast vague hand-to-mouth multitude of the enormous
(80) city and pretended they were proud of their

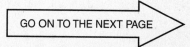

GO ON TO THE NEXT PAGE

2   2   2   2   2   2   2   2   2   2   2

position in it—it showed them "such a lot of life" and made them conscious of a democratic brotherhood. If Pemberton couldn't feel a sympathy in destitution with his small com-
(85) panion—for after all Morgan's fond parents would never have let him really suffer—the boy would at least feel it with him, so it came to the same thing. He used sometimes to wonder what people would think they were—to
(90) fancy they were looked askance at, as if it might be a suspected case of kidnapping. Morgan wouldn't be taken for a young patrician with a tutor—he wasn't smart enough—though he might pass for his companion's
(95) sickly little brother. Now and then he had a five-franc piece, and except once, when they bought a couple of lovely neckties, one of which he made Pemberton accept, they laid it out scientifically in old books. This was sure
(100) to be a great day, always spent at the used book stands on the quays, in a rummage of the dusty boxes that garnish the parapets. Such occasions helped them to live, for their books ran low very soon after the beginning of their
(105) acquaintance. Pemberton had a good many in England, but he was obliged to write to a friend and ask him kindly to get some fellow to give him something for them.

---

[1] Hall porter or custodian.

[2] Famous Paris monument; site of the tomb of Napoleon.

[3] Botanical garden.

13. The primary purpose of the passage is to

(A) denounce the ill treatment of an exceptional child
(B) describe a boy's reactions to his irresponsible parents
(C) portray a selfish and unfeeling mother and son
(D) recount an outsider's impressions of an odd family
(E) advocate an unusual educational experiment

14. It can be inferred from lines 10–25 that the reason for the Moreens' sudden departure from Nice had to do with

(A) ill health
(B) changes in climate
(C) educational opportunities
(D) financial problems
(E) shifts of mood

15. According to lines 17–25, Pemberton's visit to Paris can be described as all of the following EXCEPT

(A) gratifying
(B) sudden
(C) instructive
(D) elegant
(E) frugal

16. Lines 30–35 suggest that the narrator is making these comments about Pemberton's travels with the Moreen family

(A) on Pemberton's return with the Moreens to Nice
(B) in response to visiting Paris for the first time
(C) some time after Pemberton's wanderings with the Moreens
(D) in answer to Morgan's questions about his childhood
(E) in an effort to write down his memoirs

17. The tone of Morgan's speech to his tutor (lines 45 and 46) can best be described as

(A) apathetic
(B) bitter
(C) teasing
(D) exasperated
(E) self-righteous

GO ON TO THE NEXT PAGE →

2 2 2 2 2 2 2 2 2 2 2

18. The statement that "the deficiencies of his own wardrobe were a chapter by themselves" (lines 49 and 50) serves to

(A) indicate the author's intention to cover this topic in a separate chapter
(B) separate Pemberton's problems from those of Morgan and the rest of the Moreens
(C) suggest that Pemberton was allotted insufficient closet space by the Moreens
(D) establish Pemberton's inability to learn to dress himself appropriately
(E) convey Pemberton's sensitivity about the disreputable state of his clothes

19. According to lines 61–67, Mrs. Moreen most likely ceases to spend money on new clothing for Morgan because

(A) she and her husband have grown increasingly miserly with the passage of time
(B) the child is so small for his age that he needs little in the way of clothing
(C) she is unwilling to offend Pemberton by dressing his pupil in finer garments than Pemberton can afford
(D) she resents the child and intentionally neglects him, spending money on herself that should be his
(E) she has only enough money to buy clothes for the family members who must appear in polite society

20. As described in lines 41–67, Mrs. Moreen's approach toward Morgan can best be described as

(A) stern but nurturing
(B) fond but pragmatic
(C) cruel and unfeeling
(D) tentative but loving
(E) doting and overprotective

21. The author most likely describes the galleries of the Louvre as "so splendidly ironical to the homeless" (lines 73 and 74) because

(A) homeless and other destitute people are not allowed within the museum
(B) people in the galleries make sarcastic comments about poorly dressed museum goers
(C) the Louvre originated as a shelter for the homeless of Paris
(D) their opulence contrasts so markedly with the poverty of those who lack homes
(E) the museum does an excellent job of teaching poor people about different styles of life

22. Morgan and Pemberton regard the "hand-to-mouth multitude" of Paris (lines 77–83) with a sense of

(A) amusement
(B) condescension
(C) indifference
(D) identification
(E) resentment

23. The word "smart" in line 93 means

(A) intelligent
(B) painful
(C) fashionable
(D) impudent
(E) resourceful

24. An aspect of Pemberton's character that is made particularly clear in the final paragraph is his

(A) tendency to joke about serious matters
(B) longing to have a younger brother
(C) concern for how he appears to others
(D) reluctance to accept gifts from Morgan
(E) pride in his identification with the poor

STOP

IF YOU FINISH BEFORE TIME IS CALLED, YOU MAY CHECK YOUR WORK ON THIS SECTION ONLY. DO NOT WORK ON ANY OTHER SECTION IN THE TEST.

Section 3

TIME—25 MINUTES
35 QUESTIONS

For each of the following questions, choose the best answer and fill in the appropriate circle on the answer sheet.

Some or all parts of the following sentences are underlined. The first answer choice, (A), simply repeats the underlined part of the sentence. The other four choices present four alternative ways to phrase the underlined part. Select the answer that produces the most effective sentence, one that is clear and exact, and blacken the appropriate space on your answer sheet. In selecting your choice, be sure that it is standard written English, and that it expresses the meaning of the original sentence.

Example:
The first biography of author Eudora Welty came out in 1998 and she was 89 years old at the time.

(A) and she was 89 years old at the time
(B) at the time she was 89
(C) upon becoming an 89 year old
(D) when she was 89
(E) at the age of 89 years old

Ⓐ Ⓑ Ⓒ ● Ⓔ

---

1. Jane Austen wrote novels and they depicted the courtships and eventual marriages of members of the middle classes.

(A) novels and they depicted
(B) novels, being depictions of
(C) novels, they depicted
(D) novels that depict
(E) novels, and depictions in them

2. The princess, together with the members of her retinue, are scheduled to attend the opening ceremonies.

(A) together with the members of her retinue, are scheduled
(B) together with the members of her retinue, were scheduled
(C) along with the members of the retinue, are scheduled
(D) together with the members of her retinue, is scheduled
(E) being together with the members of her retinue, is scheduled

3. Dog experts describe the chihuahua as the smallest dog, and also the most truculent of them.

(A) the smallest dog, and also the most truculent of them
(B) the smallest and yet the most truculent of dogs
(C) the smallest dog at the same time it is the most truculent dog
(D) not only the smallest dog, but also more truculent than any
(E) the smallest of dogs in spite of being the most truculent of them

GO ON TO THE NEXT PAGE ⟩

3 3 3 3 3 3 3 3 3 3 3

4. Painters of the Art Deco period took motifs from the art of Africa, South America, and the Far East <u>as well as incorporating</u> them with the sleek lines of modern industry.

   (A) as well as incorporating
   (B) they also incorporated
   (C) and incorporated
   (D) likewise they incorporated
   (E) furthermore incorporating

5. The university reserves the right to sublet <u>students' rooms who are</u> away on leave.

   (A) students' rooms who are
   (B) students whose rooms are
   (C) the rooms of students who are
   (D) the rooms of students which are
   (E) students' rooms which are

6. High school students at the beginning of the twenty-first century ate more fast food <u>than</u> the middle of the twentieth century.

   (A) than
   (B) than the high schools during
   (C) than occurred in
   (D) than did students in
   (E) than did

7. Her thesis explained what motivated Stiller and Meara to give up their separate theatrical careers <u>to become comedy duos</u> in the late 1960s.

   (A) to become comedy duos
   (B) when they will become comedy duos
   (C) that they had become a comedy duo
   (D) in favor of becoming comedy duos
   (E) to become a comedy duo

8. <u>Writing a review of opening night, the production was panned by the *Chronicle*'s theater critic</u>.

   (A) Writing a review of opening night, the production was panned by the *Chronicle*'s theater critic.
   (B) Because he was writing a review of opening night, the production was panned by the *Chronicle*'s theater critic.
   (C) Writing a review of opening night, the *Chronicle*'s theater critic panned the production.
   (D) In a written review of opening night, the production by the *Chronicle*'s theater critic was being panned.
   (E) Having written a review of opening night, the production was panned by the *Chronicle*'s theater critic.

9. Frightened of meeting anyone outside her immediate family circle, <u>it was only after Elizabeth Barrett had eloped with Robert Browning that she grew to enjoy herself in society</u>.

   (A) it was only after Elizabeth Barrett had eloped with Robert Browning that she grew to enjoy herself in society.
   (B) it was only after eloping with Robert Browning that Elizabeth Barrett grew to enjoy herself in society.
   (C) Elizabeth Barrett grew to enjoy herself in society only after she had eloped with Robert Browning.
   (D) it was only after Elizabeth Barrett had eloped with Robert Browning that she had grown to enjoy herself in society.
   (E) Elizabeth Barrett grew to enjoy herself in society, however it was only after her eloping with Robert Browning.

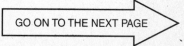
GO ON TO THE NEXT PAGE

3 3 3 3 3 3 3 3 3 3 3

10. Many of the students found the visiting professor the greatest lecturer they had ever heard, but for others they found him a deadly bore with little of interest to impart.

   (A) but for others they found him
   (B) except others that found him
   (C) however, others found him
   (D) but others found him
   (E) others they found him

11. Visitors to Yosemite National Park encounter a landscape of great ruggedness and majesty and the landscape has inspired many photographers, above all Ansel Adams.

   (A) majesty and the landscape has
   (B) majesty, the reason being that the landscape has
   (C) majesty, but the landscape has
   (D) majesty, a landscape that has
   (E) majesty, it has

The sentences in this section may contain errors in grammar, usage, choice of words, or idioms. Either there is just one error in a sentence or the sentence is correct. Some words or phrases are underlined and lettered; everything else in the sentence is correct.

If an underlined word or phrase is incorrect, choose that letter; if the sentence is correct, select No error. Then blacken the appropriate space on your answer sheet.

Example:

The region has a climate so severe that plants
                                  A

growing there rarely had been more than twelve
       B   C

inches high. No error
       D   E

Ⓐ Ⓑ ● Ⓓ Ⓔ

12. Despite the countless hours that astronomers
    A
    have spent observing the solar system,

    surprising little is known about the mass and
        B
    density of Pluto, the planet that lies farthest
                                       C   D
    from the sun. No error
                     E

13. In the novel *Pollyanna*, the orphaned heroine
                                    A
    had suffered many hardships, but she never
        B   C
    loses her fundamental optimism. No error
               D   E

GO ON TO THE NEXT PAGE

3 3 3 3 3 3 3 3 3 3 **3**

14. Some scientists speculate that an early

    exposure to common allergens such as pollen
    A
    and animal hair may prevent children
                    B
    from developing severe allergies later in life.
    C   D
    No error
    E

15. Of the four plays that the Drama Club
                      A
    had considered, the comedy was

    the more appropriate for them to perform
        B   C   D
    at the festival. No error
                      E

16. In many states, facility in mathematics and
        A
    language skills are tested in third grade and
                      B   C
    eighth grade as well as in high school.
                      D
    No error
    E

17. Stephen King's novel *Pet Sematary* was

    inspired by a misspelled sign on a real pet
    A   B
    cemetery near Orrington, where the Kings
                              C
    once are living. No error
          D   E

18. We cannot hardly believe how rapidly the
        A   B
    population of Columbia County has grown in
                                      C
    just the past two decades. No error
    D   E

19. In the movie *Quiz Show,* the winning

    contestants, which ranged
                  A
    from Columbia University professor
    B
    Charles Van Doren to former G.I. Herbert

    Stempel, became national celebrities before

    they were exposed as cheaters. No error
        C   D   E

20. Down the face of the cliff flows the silvery
                              A
    waterfalls that make Yosemite Valley such a
              B   C
    mecca for tourists throughout the year.
          D
    No error
    E

21. Employment statistics indicate that the
                          A
    percentage of workers who found jobs in the
                          B
    fall quarter is lower than the spring. No error
              C   D   E

22. Journalists whose job is to interview
                A
    entrepreneurs about their careers often
                  B
    focus on dramatic turning points, such
    C
    as the start of a new company or

    how it eventually failed. No error
    D   E

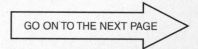
GO ON TO THE NEXT PAGE

3 3 3 3 3 3 3 3 3 3 3

23. <u>Most of</u> the free libraries founded by Andrew
    A
Carnegie <u>were located</u> in communities where
        B
there were <u>hardly no</u> other cultural institutions
        C
<u>available to</u> members of the working classes.
  D
<u>No error</u>
  E

24. Writers <u>from</u> Thomas Hardy to D.H. Lawrence
      A
<u>whose works</u> <u>were banned</u> in Boston survived
  B   C
nonetheless with reputations intact and <u>even</u>
                             D
enhanced. <u>No error</u>
        E

25. There <u>has been</u> <u>striking</u> improvements in the
       A   B
<u>training of</u> gymnasts since the first modern
  C
Olympic Games <u>were held</u> in Athens in 1896.
             D
<u>No error</u>
  E

26. When we learned that our parents planned to

    send <u>my brother and I</u> to boarding school in
           A
    France, we wondered <u>whether</u> the two of us
               B
    <u>ever</u> would become <u>fluent in</u> French. <u>No error</u>
    C   D   E

27. The graduate student had focused his research

on the <u>study of</u> one aspect of a single minor
      A
poem by a particular Romantic poet and thus

<u>gaining</u> little <u>feeling for</u> Romantic verse
  B   C
<u>as a whole.</u> <u>No error</u>
  D   E

28. <u>Concerned about</u> the <u>extent of</u> Daniel's
    A   B
<u>preoccupation in</u> his academic standing, the
    C
counselor suggested that he <u>take advantage</u>
                         D
of some of the opportunities for extracurricular

activity available in the city. <u>No error</u>
                               E

29. <u>Just as</u> elderly people differ in their
    A
willingness to <u>retire from</u> work, so young
          B
people differ in <u>his or her</u> willingness <u>to get</u>
           C   D
a job. <u>No error</u>
    E

GO ON TO THE NEXT PAGE

3 3 3 3 3 3 3 3 3 3 3

The passage below is the unedited draft of a student's essay. Parts of the essay need to be rewritten to make the meaning clearer and more precise. Read the essay carefully.

The essay is followed by six questions about changes that might improve all or part of the organization, development, sentence structure, use of language, appropriateness to the audience, or use of standard written English. In each case, choose the answer that most clearly and effectively expresses the student's intended meaning. Indicate your choice by blackening the corresponding space on the answer sheet.

[1] Although some people believe that certain celebrations have no point, celebrations are one of the few things that all people have in common. [2] They take place everywhere. [3] Listing all of them would be an impossible task. [4] People of all kinds look forward to celebrations for keeping traditions alive for generation after generation. [5] Those who criticize celebrations do not understand the human need to preserve tradition and culture.

[6] In the Muslim religion, the Ead is a celebration. [7] It begins as soon as Ramadan (the fasting month) is over. [8] During the Ead, families gather together. [9] New clothes are bought for children, and they receive money from both family and friends. [10] Also, each family, if they can afford it, slaughters a sheep or a cow. [11] They keep a small fraction of the meat, and the rest must give to the poor. [12] They also donate money to a mosque.

[14] Many celebrations involve eating meals. [15] In the United States, people gather together on Thanksgiving to say thank you for their blessings by having a huge feast with turkey, sweet potatoes, and cranberry sauce. [16] Christmas and Easter holiday dinners are a custom in the Christian religion. [17] They have a roast at Christmas. [18] At Easter they serve ham. [19] The Jewish people celebrate Passover with a big meal called a seder. [20] They say prayers, drink wine, and sing songs to remember how Jews suffered centuries ago when they escaped from slavery in Egypt.

[21] A celebration is held each year to honor great people like Dr. Martin Luther King. [22] His birthday is celebrated because of this man's noble belief in equality of all races. [23] People wish to remember not only his famous speeches, including "I Have A Dream," but also about him being assassinated in Memphis in 1968. [24] He died while fighting for the equality of minorities. [25] Unlike religious celebrations, celebrations for great heroes like Martin Luther King are for all people everywhere in the world. [26] He is a world-class hero and he deserved the Nobel Prize for Peace that he won.

30. To improve the unity of the first paragraph, which of the following is the best sentence to delete?

(A) Sentence 1
(B) Sentence 2
(C) Sentence 3
(D) Sentence 4
(E) Sentence 5

31. Which is the best revision of sentence 9 below?

New clothes are bought for children, and they receive money from both family and friends.

(A) New clothes are bought for children, and they receive money from both family and friends.
(B) The children receive new clothes and gifts of money from family and friends.
(C) Receiving new clothes, money is also given by family and friends.
(D) Gifts are given to the children of new clothes and money by family and friends.
(E) Parents buy new clothes for their children, and family and friends also give money to them.

GO ON TO THE NEXT PAGE

3 3 3 3 3 3 3 3 3 3 3

32. In the context of the third paragraph, which is the best way to combine sentences 16, 17, and 18?

(A) A roast at Christmas, ham at Easter—that's what Christians eat.

(B) Christians customarily serve a roast for Christmas dinner, at Easter ham is eaten.

(C) At customary holiday dinners, Christians eat a roast at Christmas and ham is for Easter dinner.

(D) Christians often celebrate the Christmas holiday with a roast for dinner and Easter with a traditional ham.

(E) Christmas and Easter dinners are the custom in the Christian religion, where they have a roast at Christmas and ham at Easter.

33. In an effort to provide a more effective transition between paragraphs 3 and 4, which of the following would be the best revision of sentence 21 below?

A celebration is held each year to honor great people like Dr. Martin Luther King.

(A) There are also some celebrations to honor great people like Dr. Martin Luther King.

(B) Martin Luther King is also celebrated in the United States.

(C) In the United States, celebrating to honor great people like Dr. Martin Luther King has become a tradition.

(D) In addition to observing religious holidays, people hold celebrations to honor great leaders like Dr. Martin Luther King.

(E) Besides holding religion-type celebrations, celebrations to honor great people like Dr. Martin Luther King are also held.

34. Which is the best revision of the underlined segment of sentence 23 below?

People wish to remember not only his famous speeches, including "I Have A Dream," but also about him being assassinated in Memphis in 1968.

(A) that his assassination occurred

(B) about his being assassinated

(C) the fact that he was assassinated

(D) about the assassination, too,

(E) his assassination

35. In the context of the essay as a whole, which one of the following best explains the main function of the last paragraph?

(A) To summarize the main idea of the essay

(B) To refute a previous argument stated in the essay

(C) To give an example

(D) To provide a solution to a problem

(E) To evaluate the validity of the essay's main idea

STOP

IF YOU FINISH BEFORE TIME IS CALLED, YOU MAY CHECK YOUR WORK ON THIS SECTION ONLY. DO NOT WORK ON ANY OTHER SECTION IN THE TEST.

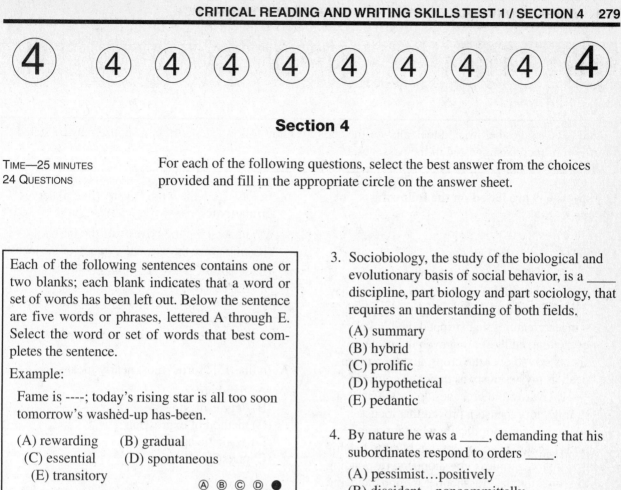

Section 4

TIME—25 MINUTES
24 QUESTIONS

For each of the following questions, select the best answer from the choices provided and fill in the appropriate circle on the answer sheet.

Each of the following sentences contains one or two blanks; each blank indicates that a word or set of words has been left out. Below the sentence are five words or phrases, lettered A through E. Select the word or set of words that best completes the sentence.

Example:

Fame is ----; today's rising star is all too soon tomorrow's washed-up has-been.

(A) rewarding   (B) gradual
(C) essential   (D) spontaneous
(E) transitory

Ⓐ Ⓑ Ⓒ Ⓓ ●

---

1. Because the salt used to deice highways in snowbelt states is highly _____ , it can turn the reinforcing bars in the concrete on highways, bridges, and parking garages into rusty mush.

(A) adhesive
(B) obvious
(C) diluted
(D) corrosive
(E) profitable

2. Although the book might satisfy Bloom's hard-core fans, it is _____ by its monotonous citations and its _____ style.

(A) marred…slipshod
(B) warped…elegant
(C) enhanced…impeccable
(D) unified…laconic
(E) annotated…exhaustive

3. Sociobiology, the study of the biological and evolutionary basis of social behavior, is a _____ discipline, part biology and part sociology, that requires an understanding of both fields.

(A) summary
(B) hybrid
(C) prolific
(D) hypothetical
(E) pedantic

4. By nature he was a _____, demanding that his subordinates respond to orders _____.

(A) pessimist…positively
(B) dissident…noncommittally
(C) martinet…promptly
(D) despot…magnanimously
(E) virtuoso…obsequiously

5. Publishers have discovered that Black America is not a _____ of attitudes and opinions but a rich mixture lending itself to numerous expressions in print.

(A) concoction
(B) medley
(C) monolith
(D) paradox
(E) controversy

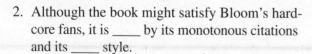
GO ON TO THE NEXT PAGE

Read the passages below, and then answer the questions that follow. The correct response may be stated outright or merely suggested in the passages.

Questions 6–9 are based on the following passages.

Passage 1

Since biblical times, plagues of locusts have devastated the earth. From nowhere they would come, dark clouds of glittering, long-
Line winged creatures that stripped the land of
(5) everything edible, eating even the protective sheets spread over the crops, and then disappear, as mysteriously as they had come. In 1921, Uvarov, the great acridologist (student of migratory locusts), proved that locust
(10) swarms occur periodically when favorable rains encourage an exceptionally large hatch of solitary, harmless grasshoppers; responding to crowding, the grasshopper nymphs undergo a metamorphosis into their gregarious, migra-
(15) tory phase. They change color and form, developing longer wings, broader shoulders, a ravenous appetite. Then they swarm.

Passage 2

To what extent can desert locust plagues be
Line controlled? More important, to what extent
(20) should they be controlled? These are issues that directly confront the developing countries of Africa. In the 1950s, the use of chemical pesticides appeared to promise a locust-free future, one in which plagues could be con-
(25) trolled by spraying breeding areas or by spraying attacking swarms. However, these organochlorine pesticides proved both environmentally hazardous and economically costly. Moreover, pesticides contributed little
(30) to wiping out the last major locust outbreak in Northern Africa. Instead, chance eradicated the 1988–1989 plague: rather than heading inland, the swarm turned out to sea and ran out of food in the Atlantic.

6. In Passage 1 the word "even" (line 5) serves primarily to
   (A) underscore the poverty of the farmers
   (B) emphasize the extreme voracity of the locusts
   (C) illustrate the effectiveness of the sheets as protection
   (D) demonstrate the rapidity of the swarm's approach
   (E) stress the care taken to safeguard the crops

7. In line 15, "form" most nearly means
   (A) fixed order
   (B) degree of fitness
   (C) method of expression
   (D) aesthetic appearance
   (E) physical shape

8. The primary purpose of Passage 1 is to
   (A) correct a misconception
   (B) describe a scientific experiment
   (C) explain a natural phenomenon
   (D) challenge a scientific theory
   (E) prescribe new directions for research

GO ON TO THE NEXT PAGE

9. How do the authors of the two passages differ in their approach to locust plagues?

(A) The author of Passage 1 views locust plagues as a natural phenomenon to be observed, whereas the author of Passage 2 treats them as a natural phenomenon to be controlled.

(B) The author of Passage 1 believes that locust plagues are inherently dangerous, whereas the author of Passage 2 believes they serve a higher purpose.

(C) The author of Passage 1 suggests that locust plagues can be kept in check, whereas the author of Passage 2 argues that they can merely be endured.

(D) The author of Passage 1 considers locust plagues relatively unimportant, whereas the author of Passage 2 shows that they have significant economic impact.

(E) The author of Passage 1 views locust plagues with indignation, whereas the author of Passage 2 looks on them with curiosity.

Questions 10–15 are based on the following passage.

The style of the renowned modern artist Pablo Picasso changed radically in the course of his long career, as he reacted to new artistic stimuli and fresh ways of seeing the world. In this excerpt from a survey of Picasso's art, the critic Alfred Barr considers the impact of Black African art on Picasso's work, in particular on his painting Les Demoiselles d'Avignon (The Girls of Avignon).

Traditionally, *Les Demoiselles d'Avignon* was indeed supposed to have been influenced by African Negro sculpture, but Picasso has since
Line denied this, affirming that although he was
(5) much interested in Iberian[1] sculpture he had no knowledge of Negro art while he was working on *Les Demoiselles*. Only later in 1907, he states, did he discover Negro sculpture.

Quite recently however, Picasso has
(10) assured us that the two right-hand figures of *Les Demoiselles* were completed some time after the rest of the composition. It seems pos-

sible therefore that Picasso's memory is incomplete and that he may well have painted
(15) or repainted the astonishing heads of these fig- ures *after* his discovery of African sculpture, just as only a year before, stimulated by Iberian sculpture, he had repainted the head of Gertrude Stein's portrait months after he had
(20) completed the rest of the picture . . . .

The discovery and appreciation of African Negro sculpture among the artists of Paris in the early 1900s is still a somewhat confused story. It seems probable that as early as 1904
(25) Vlaminck began to take an interest in this hitherto neglected art. Shortly afterwards he introduced Derain to his new enthusiasm, and before long Derain and his fellow *fauve*[2] Matisse began to form collections. Vlaminck's
(30) admiration lay more in the romantic and exotic values of the masks and fetishes but Derain and Matisse found in them unhack- neyed aesthetic values involving the bold dis- tortion and structural reorganization of natural
(35) forms.

It is strange that Picasso, who had met Matisse by 1906, should have been unaware of African art until the middle of 1907 when, as he says, he discovered it for himself almost
(40) accidentally while leaving the gallery of his- toric sculpture in the Trocadero. However, the discovery, he affirms, was a "revelation" to him and he began immediately to make use of it. Whatever general stimulation the *fauves*
(45) had got from African art there is little specific trace of it in their painting. But several of Picasso's works of 1907–08 incorporate African forms and possibly colors to such an extent that the title "Negro Period" has hith-
(50) erto been applied to his art of this time, including *Les Demoiselles d'Avignon*. Actually, Iberian sculpture continued to inter- est him and often its forms were fused (and by critics confused) with those of the Congo and
(55) the Guinea Coast.

GO ON TO THE NEXT PAGE

For instance the *Woman in Yellow* has long been considered one of the important paintings of Picasso's Negro Period but it now seems clear that this hieratically impressive
(60) figure is related to Iberian bronzes even more closely than are the three earlier figures of *Les Demoiselles d'Avignon* which it resembles in style. As Sweeney has pointed out, the face and pose are remarkably similar to an archaic
(65) votive figure from Despenaperros. The ocher color and striated patterns, however, may have been suggested by Negro art. More African in form is the *Head*, which may have been inspired by the almond-shaped masks of the
(70) Ivory Coast or French Congo.

----

[1] The term Iberian refers to the peninsula in southwest Europe that is made up of Spain and Portugal.

[2] The *fauves* were a group of twentieth-century French artists noted for vivid colors and striking contrasts.

10. The opening paragraph suggests that Picasso would have agreed with which of the following statements?

(A) In painting *Les Demoiselles d'Avignon*, he was directly inspired by black art.
(B) In painting *Les Demoiselles d'Avignon*, he may have been indirectly influenced by African sculpture.
(C) In painting *Les Demoiselles d'Avignon*, he explicitly copied Iberian models.
(D) In painting *Les Demoiselles d'Avignon*, he may have been influenced by ancient Spanish art.
(E) In painting *Les Demoiselles d'Avignon*, he lost interest in Iberian sculpture.

11. As shown in lines 12–20, Picasso reacted to new artistic stimuli by

(A) attempting to reproduce them faithfully
(B) deciding to come back to his artistic roots
(C) rethinking already completed works of art
(D) beginning to collect inspiring examples
(E) forgetting his earlier influences

12. In the second paragraph, the author

(A) poses a question
(B) refutes a misapprehension
(C) makes a hypothesis
(D) cites the testimony of authorities
(E) contrasts two unlike situations

13. According to lines 36–41, Picasso first became acquainted with African art

(A) through another artist
(B) on a trip to Africa
(C) through an art historian
(D) in an art gallery
(E) in a book of reproductions

24. The term "applied to" (line 50) most likely means

(A) spread on
(B) credited to
(C) placed in contact with
(D) used to designate
(E) requested as

15. We can infer from lines 63–65 that Despenaperros is most likely

(A) a town on the Ivory Coast of Africa
(B) the name of a young French girl from Avignon
(C) a contemporary artist known to Picasso
(D) a location on the Iberian peninsula
(E) the name of a village near Avignon

GO ON TO THE NEXT PAGE

Questions 16–24 are based on the following passage.

Taken from the writings of Benjamin Franklin, the following excerpt, published in 1784, demonstrates Franklin's attitude toward the so-called savages of North America and reveals something of what these Native Americans thought about the white men and women who had come to their land.

Savages we call them, because their manners differ from ours, which we think the perfection of civility; they think the same of
Line theirs.
(5)   Perhaps, if we could examine the manners of different nations with impartiality, we should find no people so rude as to be without rules of politeness, nor any so polite as not to have some remains of rudeness.
(10)   The Indian men, when young, are hunters and warriors; when old, counselors, for all their government is by counsel of the sages; there is no force, there are no prisons, no officers to compel obedience or inflict punish-
(15) ment. Hence they generally study oratory, the best speaker having the most influence. The Indian women till the ground, dress the food, nurse and bring up the children, and preserve and hand down to posterity the memory of
(20) public transactions. These employments of men and women are accounted natural and honorable. Having few artificial wants, they have abundance of leisure for improvement by conversation. Our laborious manner of life,
(25) compared with theirs, they esteem slavish and base; and the learning, on which we value ourselves, they regard as frivolous and useless.
An instance of this occurred at the treaty of Lancaster, in Pennsylvania, in the year
(30) 1744, between the government of Virginia and the Six Nations. After the principal business was settled, the commissioners from Virginia acquainted the Indians by a speech that there was at Williamsburg a college, with a fund for
(35) educating Indian youth; and that, if the Six Nations would send down half a dozen of their

young lads to that college, the government would take care that they should be well provided for, and instructed in all the learning of
(40) the white people. It is one of the Indian rules of politeness not to answer a public proposition the same day that it is made; they think that it would be treating it as a light matter, and that they show it respect by taking time to
(45) consider it, as of a matter important. They therefore deferred their answer till the day following; when their speaker began by expressing their deep sense of the kindness of the Virginia government in making them that
(50) offer, saying:
"We know that you highly esteem the kind of learning taught in those colleges, and that the maintenance of our young men, while with you, would be very expensive to you. We are
(55) convinced, therefore, that you mean to do us good by your proposal, and we thank you heartily. But you, who are wise, must know that different nations have different conceptions of things; and you will therefore not take
(60) it amiss, if our ideas of this kind of education happen not to be the same as yours. We have had some experience of it. Several of our young people were formerly brought up at the colleges of the northern provinces: they were
(65) instructed in all your sciences; but when they came back to us they were bad runners, ignorant of every means of living in the woods, unable to bear cold or hunger. They knew neither how to build a cabin, take a deer, nor kill
(70) an enemy, spoke our language imperfectly, were therefore neither fit for hunters, warriors, nor counselors; they were totally good for nothing.
We are, however, not the less obliged by
(75) your kind offer, though we decline accepting it; and, to show our grateful sense of it, if the gentlemen of Virginia will send us a dozen of their sons, we will take care of their education, instruct them in all we know, and make *men* of
(80) them."

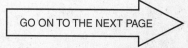
GO ON TO THE NEXT PAGE

16. According to Franklin, Indian leaders maintain their authority by means of their

    (A) warlike ability
    (B) skill as hunters
    (C) verbal prowess
    (D) personal wealth
    (E) punitive capacity

17. The word "dress" in line 17 means

    (A) clothe
    (B) adorn
    (C) medicate
    (D) straighten
    (E) prepare

18. To which of the following does Franklin attribute the amount of leisure time for conversing available to the Indians?

    I.   Their greater efficiency and productivity
    II. Their simpler, more natural lifestyle
    III. Their distinctive set of values

    (A) I only
    (B) II only
    (C) I and II only
    (D) II and III only
    (E) I, II, and III

19. Franklin's purpose in quoting the speech that concludes the excerpt is primarily to

    (A) demonstrate the natural oratorical abilities of Indians
    (B) condemn the Virginians' failure to recruit Indian students for their schools
    (C) give an example of the Indian viewpoint on the benefits of white civilization
    (D) describe a breakdown in communications between Indians and whites
    (E) advocate the adoption of Indian educational techniques

20. The Indians' chief purpose in making the speech seems to be to

    (A) tactfully refuse a friendly gesture
    (B) express their opinions on equality
    (C) gratify their intended audience
    (D) describe native American customs
    (E) request funds to start their own school

21. According to this passage, the Indians' idea of education differs from that of the gentlemen of Virginia in that the Indians

    (A) also believe in the education of young women
    (B) have different educational goals
    (C) teach different branches of science
    (D) include different aspects of nature
    (E) speak a different language

GO ON TO THE NEXT PAGE

4 4 4 4 4 4 4 4 4 4

22. The word "take" in line 69 means

(A) endure
(B) transport
(C) confiscate
(D) capture
(E) accept

23. The Indians responsible for the speech would probably agree that they

(A) have no right to deny Indian boys the opportunity for schooling
(B) are being insulted by the offer of the commissioners
(C) know more about the various branches of science than the commissioners do
(D) have a better way of educating young men than the commissioners do
(E) should not offer to educate the sons of the gentlemen of Virginia

24. The tone of the speech as a whole is best described as

(A) aloof but angry
(B) insistently demanding
(C) grudgingly admiring
(D) eager and inquiring
(E) courteous but ironic

STOP

IF YOU FINISH BEFORE TIME IS CALLED, YOU MAY CHECK YOUR WORK ON THIS SECTION ONLY. DO NOT WORK ON ANY OTHER SECTION IN THE TEST.

Section 5

TIME—20 MINUTES
19 QUESTIONS

For each of the following questions, select the best answer from the choices provided and fill in the appropriate circle on the answer sheet.

Each of the following sentences contains one or two blanks; each blank indicates that a word or set of words has been left out. Below the sentence are five words or phrases, lettered A through E. Select the word or set of words that best completes the sentence.

Example:

Fame is ----; today's rising star is all too soon tomorrow's washed-up has-been.

(A) rewarding   (B) gradual
  (C) essential   (D) spontaneous
    (E) transitory

Ⓐ Ⓑ Ⓒ Ⓓ ●

---

1. Before the 1960s, African-American cartoonists labored mostly without mainstream recognition, their work _____ African-American magazines, journals, and newspapers.

   (A) confined to
   (B) unconscious of
   (C) irrelevant to
   (D) unacceptable to
   (E) derided by

2. Calculation and planning informed the actress's every word and gesture: there was not a _____ moment in her entire performance.

   (A) spontaneous
   (B) tasteful
   (C) histrionic
   (D) lethargic
   (E) poignant

3. None of her students minded when Professor Rivera's lectures wandered away from their official theme; her _____ were always more fascinating than the topic of the day.

   (A) summaries
   (B) digressions
   (C) intimations
   (D) metaphors
   (E) imprecations

4. Though Widow Douglass hoped to reform Huck, her sister Miss Watson _____ him _____ and said he would come to no good end.

   (A) called...amendable
   (B) declared...qualified
   (C) pronounced...incorrigible
   (D) proclaimed...optimistic
   (E) professed...cured

5. Critics point out that, far from moving _____ closer to its goals, the field of behavioral genetics is _____ the same problems that have always plagued it.

   (A) intermittently...composed of
   (B) dramatically...divorced from
   (C) inexorably...mired in
   (D) steadily...acclaimed for
   (E) uniformly...enhanced by

6. Rebuffed by his colleagues, the initially _____ young researcher became increasingly _____.

   (A) outgoing...withdrawn
   (B) boisterous...excitable
   (C) diligent...tolerant
   (D) theoretical...pragmatic
   (E) tedious...polished

GO ON TO THE NEXT PAGE ⟹

The questions that follow the next two passages relate to the content of both, and to their relationship. The correct response may be stated outright in the passage or merely suggested.

Questions 7–19 are based on the following passages.

The following passages concern the learning and behavior of infants during the first months of life. The first passage comes from a popular guide for new parents, the second from a textbook on child development.

Passage 1

The two-month-old baby has hardly roused himself from the long night of his first weeks in this world when he is confronted
Line with some of the profound problems of the
(5) race. We invite him to study the nature of reality, to differentiate self and non-self, and to establish useful criteria in each of these categories. A project of such magnitude in academic research would require extensive laboratory
(10) equipment and personnel; to be fair about it, it has taken just that to reconstruct the experiments of the infant. And there are few grown and fully accredited scientists who can equal the infant for zeal and energy in sorting out
(15) the raw data in this project. His equipment is limited to his sensory organs, his hands, his mouth, and a primitive memory apparatus.

At two months, as we have seen, he recognizes an object that *we* know to be a human
(20) face and we know to be an object outside himself. But to the baby this is just an image, an image incidentally that he can't differentiate from the mental image, the picture in memory. But this face is one piece in the jigsaw puz-
(25) zle—a key piece, we think. Then gradually in the weeks to come the association of breast or bottle, of hands, voice, a multitude of pleasurable sense experiences begin to cluster around this face and to form the crude image of a
(30) person.

Meantime the infant is conducting a series of complicated experiments in sensory discrimination. We must remember that in the early months he does not discriminate
(35) between his body and other bodies. When he clutches the finger of his mother or his father he doesn't see it as someone else's finger and his behavior indicates that he treats it exactly the same as he does his own finger. It takes
(40) him some time, in fact, to recognize his own hand at sight and to acquire even a rudimentary feeling that this is part of his own body. In the first group of experiments he discovers that the object that passes occasionally in front
(45) of his eyes (which *we* know to be his hand) is the same as the object with visual and taste qualities that he can identify. In another experimental series he discovers that the sensations that accompany the introduction of *this* object
(50) into his mouth are different from those experienced when he takes a nipple into his mouth, or a toy, or his mother's or father's finger.

Passage 2

Very soon after birth, environmental forces, or response contingencies, begin to
(55) operate in conjunction with the infant's built-in response repertoire to produce learned changes in behavior. It will not be long before the baby, instead of awaiting a touch near the mouth to open it, will do so when the bottle or
(60) nipple is seen approaching it. Or the head may be turned in the appropriate direction when the baby is placed in the accustomed feeding posture. Such anticipatory gestures symbolize the essence of learning. Such response systems
(65) are the classically conditioned or Pavlovian variety, because they involve elicited behavior.

GO ON TO THE NEXT PAGE

Operant conditioning is in a sense also anticipatory; the infant makes a response pre-sumably in anticipation of receiving a reward.
(70) Response consequences serve as reinforcers of the behavior, then, and tend to perpetuate the behavior. Thus an infant who spontaneously makes a sound, which is then followed by an attractive consequence such as sweet fluid or
(75) the smiling presence of the mother, will very likely repeat the act with increasing frequency as time (and reinforcement) goes on. Similarly, a response which is followed by an aversive consequence, such as a frightening
(80) noise, will tend not to be repeated in the future. The infant thus behaves in accordance with expectations about the availability of positive reinforcers or punishments, based upon past experience.
(85)   It must be clear by now that thought begins at birth. There are psychologists who would not want to term the anticipatory ges-tures just spoken of as thought. Even they, however, would have difficulty pinpointing
(90) the stage of development or learning at which the onset of thought occurs. It is perhaps more meaningful to speak of increasing levels of symbolization.
    A number of developmental theorists have
(95) postulated stages of thought development. While no two systems or theories of cognition or thought development are exactly the same, most are agreed that the baby begins with a primitive appreciation of what is there and
(100) what is not, and most agree that early in life what is not there is unimportant to the child. Only with increasing cortical development, cognitive complexity, and experience in sens-ing, perceiving, and storing information does
(105) the child begin to take into consideration the current absence of past stimulation and to consider how things are different or might be different than they are. Such "mental manipu-lations" occur later and set the stage for very
(110) symbolic higher thought processes of which mature persons are capable.

7. By stating that a two-month-old baby confronts "some of the profound problems of the race" (lines 1–5), the author means that the infant

(A) will start to figure out what is real and what is imaginary
(B) is far more intelligent that we may think
(C) begins to understand that dreams are not real
(D) begins to locate his physical boundaries
(E) soon learns to communicate with the world outside itself.

8. The author of Passage 1 compares a baby with a scientist (lines 12–15) in order to make the point that

(A) infants are tireless in their efforts to understand their environments
(B) infants use a form of the scientific method
(C) scientific experimentation is very time-consuming
(D) an infant is a human laboratory
(E) many scientific studies have been done on how infants learn

9. The author of Passage 1 apparently believes that during infancy learning begins with

(A) feeling loved
(B) the baby's senses
(C) images that the infant sees
(D) ideas stored in the infant's memory
(E) repetition of certain sights and sounds

10. The account in Passage 1 of how an infant learns to discriminate between has own body and the body of others suggests that

(A) all babies follow one of several well-defined patterns
(B) the sequence is highly structured and precise
(C) some babies learn more quickly than others
(D) there are several different theories about how the process works
(E) male babies learn differently from female babies

GO ON TO THE NEXT PAGE ⇨

11. According to Passage 1, an important milestone in infant development apparently occurs when a baby learns

    (A) to grasp someone else's finger with his hand
    (B) to remember objects like a mother's face even when the object is out of sight
    (C) that his mother and father have different faces
    (D) that his own hand has a distinctive smell and taste
    (E) that his own hand is different from another person's hand

12. The behavior of infants discussed in the first paragraph of Passage 2 occurs because

    (A) infants feel emotions just as adults do
    (B) every baby responds to the environment in certain predictable ways
    (C) every baby is born with certain instincts
    (D) infants naturally learn to respond to certain stimuli in the environment
    (E) healthy babies do not need to be taught to ingest food

13. The author uses the phrase "classically conditioned" response system (lines 64–66) to mean that infants

    (A) use built-in response contingencies to satisfy their basic needs
    (B) cry when they are hungry
    (C) respond to their environments early in life
    (D) can be trained to learn from their environments
    (E) learn to elicit certain behaviors from their caregivers

14. With regard to an infant's capacity to think, the author of Passage 2 believes that

    (A) newborns are capable of thought
    (B) thought develops even without external stimulation
    (C) real thought does not occur until an infant has had some experience
    (D) the development of memory triggers thought
    (E) all newborns have the same thoughts

15. The author suggests that the term "symbolization" (line 93) be used to refer to

    (A) fright that infants feel after hearing a loud noise
    (B) vivid images in an infant's mind
    (C) the difference between positive and negative reinforcement
    (D) a form of mental activity occurring in an infant
    (E) an infant's memory

16. Passage 2 implies that one can determine the maturity of people's thought processes by

    (A) observing their capacities to think abstractly
    (B) measuring the speeds at which their minds work
    (C) checking their rates of intellectual growth
    (D) assessing the sizes of their memory banks
    (E) evaluating their abilities to retain information

GO ON TO THE NEXT PAGE

17. The authors of both passages agree that early in life newborns learn

   (A) to manipulate ideas in a primitive form
   (B) to differentiate between things that are not there and things that are
   (C) what to do when they feel discomfort
   (D) to distinguish between behaviors that provide pleasure and behaviors that don't
   (E) to influence the immediate environment

18. Compared to Passage 1, Passage 2 places more emphasis on the

   (A) research being done to understand newborn infants
   (B) parents' role in helping an infant develop
   (C) external indications of an infant's thought patterns
   (D) emotional growth of infants
   (E) psychology of thought development

19. In contrast to the author of Passage 2, the author of Passage 1 describes the development of an infant's thought with greater

   (A) attention to theory
   (B) authority
   (C) seriousness of purpose
   (D) scientific evidence
   (E) accuracy

STOP

IF YOU FINISH BEFORE TIME IS CALLED, YOU MAY CHECK YOUR WORK ON THIS SECTION ONLY. DO NOT WORK ON ANY OTHER SECTION IN THE TEST.

Section 6

For each of the following questions, select the best answer from the choices provided and fill in the appropriate circle on the answer sheet.

Some or all parts of the following sentences are underlined. The first answer choice, (A), simply repeats the underlined part of the sentence. The other four choices present four alternative ways to phrase the underlined part. Select the answer that produces the most effective sentence, one that is clear and exact, and blacken the appropriate space on your answer sheet. In selecting your choice, be sure that it is standard written English, and that it expresses the meaning of the original sentence.

Example:

The first biography of author Eudora Welty came out in 1998 and she was 89 years old at the time.

(A) and she was 89 years old at the time
(B) at the time she was 89
(C) upon becoming an 89 year old
(D) when she was 89
(E) at the age of 89 years old

Ⓐ Ⓑ Ⓒ ● Ⓔ

---

1. Because each year our children are spending increasingly more time in front of computer monitors and television screens, you need to limit their viewing hours and encourage them to go outdoors and play.

   (A) you need to limit their viewing hours and encourage them to go outdoors and play
   (B) one needs to limit our viewing hours and encourage ourselves to go outdoors and play
   (C) it is necessary that their viewing hours should be limited and they themselves be encouraged to go outdoors and play
   (D) we need to limit their viewing hours and encourage them to go outdoors and play
   (E) you need to limit their viewing hours and encourage them to go outside and play

2. To the painter Frida Kahlo, life was as intricate tangled as the intertwined figures on an antique Mexican votive painting.

   (A) life was as intricate tangled as the intertwined figures
   (B) life was as intricately tangled as the intertwined figures
   (C) life was as intricate tangled such as the intertwined figures
   (D) life was as much intricate as tangled as the intertwined figures
   (E) life was intricately a tangle of the intertwined figures

GO ON TO THE NEXT PAGE

3. Asthma is caused by narrowing and clogging of the small <u>tubes called bronchi, they carry air</u> in and out of the lungs.

   (A) tubes called bronchi, they carry air
   (B) tubes that are called bronchi, they carry air
   (C) tubes called bronchi that carry air
   (D) tubes which are called bronchi, and they carry air
   (E) tubes called bronchi; as they carry air

4. Most conservationists <u>agree that only a 1989 ban on poaching saved the elephant</u> from extinction.

   (A) agree that only a 1989 ban on poaching saved the elephant
   (B) agree that a 1989 ban on poaching which only saved the elephant
   (C) agree that a 1989 ban on poaching which saved only the elephant
   (D) agree with the fact that only a 1989 ban on poaching saved the elephant
   (E) are in agreement that it was only a 1989 ban on poaching saving the elephant

5. At Civil War reenactments, participants dress in period uniforms <u>as if they were a Union or Confederate soldier</u>.

   (A) as if they were a Union or Confederate soldier
   (B) as if you were a Union or Confederate soldier
   (C) like they were Union or Confederate soldiers
   (D) as if one was a Union or Confederate soldier
   (E) as if they were Union or Confederate soldiers

6. <u>An advocate is when a person argues for something</u> he or she believes in.

   (A) An advocate is when a person argues for something
   (B) An advocate is if a person argues for something
   (C) Advocates are when a person argues for something
   (D) An advocate was when a person argues for something
   (E) An advocate is a person who argues for something

7. <u>The Debate Club host lunchtime debates on current issues</u> ranging from affirmative action to nuclear proliferation.

   (A) The Debate Club host lunchtime debates on current issues
   (B) The Debate Club host lunchtime debates on current issues,
   (C) The Debate Club hosts lunchtime debates on current issues
   (D) Lunchtime debates on current issues being hosted by the Debate Club,
   (E) Lunchtime debates on current issues hosted by the Debate Club,

8. Many educators maintain that standardized tests <u>are unfair to students which are culturally biased</u>.

   (A) are unfair to students which are culturally biased
   (B) being that they are culturally biased are unfair to students
   (C) are unfair to students that are culturally biased
   (D) that are culturally biased are unfair to students
   (E) are unfair to students; the reason is because they are culturally biased

GO ON TO THE NEXT PAGE

9. Pulp fiction, <u>some of which was initially published in hardcover editions, got its name</u> from the cheap paper it was printed on.

   (A) some of which was initially published in hardcover editions, got its name
   (B) some of which were initially published in hardcover editions, got its name
   (C) some of which were initially published in a hardcover edition, got their name
   (D) some of which was initial published in hardcover editions, got named
   (E) some that were initially being published in hardcover editions, got its name

10. E. B. White once said that dissecting <u>humor was like dissecting a frog: nobody is much interested, and the frog dies</u>.

    (A) humor was like dissecting a frog: nobody is much interested, and the frog dies
    (B) humor was like the dissection of a frog: nobody has much interest in it because the frog dies
    (C) humor, like dissecting a frog, was of hardly no interest to anybody, and then the frog dies
    (D) humor was like dissecting a frog, and that nobody was much interested, and the frog dies
    (E) humor is similar to the experience of dissecting a frog in that nobody is greatly interested, and the frog dies

11. Medical studies are providing increasing evidence that alternative therapies <u>are beneficial, and patients are gradually demanding it</u>.

    (A) are beneficial, and patients are gradually demanding it
    (B) have benefits, and patients are gradually demanding it
    (C) are beneficial; and that patients are gradually demanding it
    (D) are beneficial, and patients are gradually demanding them
    (E) benefit patients, and they are gradually demanding it

12. <u>The cratered surface of the moon, Earth's sole natural satellite, seen</u> through the telescopes mounted at Lick Observatory on Mount Hamilton.

    (A) The cratered surface of the moon, Earth's sole natural satellite, seen
    (B) The cratered surface of the moon, which is Earth's sole natural satellite, seen
    (C) The cratered surface of the moon, Earth's sole natural satellite, is seen
    (D) The cratered surface of the moon, Earth's solely natural satellite, seen
    (E) The cratered surface of the moon, Earth's sole natural satellite, are seen

13. <u>Although most celebrated for his performance as the Jedi knight Obi Wan Kenobi, Alec Guinness also won acclaim</u> for his skill in portraying a wide range of character roles, most notably in *Kind Hearts and Coronets*, in which he played twelve separate characters.

    (A) Although most celebrated for his performance as the Jedi knight Obi Wan Kenobi, Alec Guinness also won acclaim
    (B) Besides being celebrated mostly for his performance as the Jedi knight Obi Wan Kenobi, Alec Guinness also won acclaim
    (C) Alec Guinness is most celebrated for his performance as the Jedi knight Obi Wan Kenobi, nonetheless he also was acclaimed
    (D) Alec Guinness is celebrated most for his performance as the Jedi knight Obi Wan Kenobi, and he also won acclaim
    (E) While celebrated most for his performance as the Jedi knight Obi Wan Kenobi, Alec Guinness, winning acclaim

GO ON TO THE NEXT PAGE

14. Rarely has a funeral procession been as moving to the public as was the cortège that accompanied John F. Kennedy to his final resting place.

(A) Rarely has a funeral procession been as moving to the public as was the cortège that accompanied John F. Kennedy to his final resting place.

(B) It was rare that there was a funeral procession that was as moving to the public as the cortège that accompanied John F. Kennedy to his final resting place.

(C) A funeral procession was very rare as the cortège that moved the public as it accompanied John F. Kennedy to his final resting place.

(D) Rarely has there ever been any funeral procession moving the public that finally accompanied John F. Kennedy to his resting place.

(E) Rarely has a funeral procession been so publicly moving as the cortège that had been accompanying John F. Kennedy to his final resting place.

STOP

IF YOU FINISH BEFORE TIME IS CALLED, YOU MAY CHECK YOUR WORK ON THIS SECTION ONLY. DO NOT WORK ON ANY OTHER SECTION IN THE TEST.

ANSWER KEY

Section 2

1. **D**	5. **A**	9. **A**	13. **D**	17. **C**	21. **D**
2. **D**	6. **B**	10. **A**	14. **D**	18. **E**	22. **D**
3. **B**	7. **E**	11. **D**	15. **D**	19. **E**	23. **C**
4. **B**	8. **E**	12. **E**	16. **C**	20. **B**	24. **C**

Section 3

1. **D**	7. **E**	13. **B**	19. **A**	25. **A**	31. **B**
2. **D**	8. **C**	14. **E**	20. **A**	26. **A**	32. **D**
3. **B**	9. **C**	15. **B**	21. **D**	27. **B**	33. **D**
4. **C**	10. **D**	16. **B**	22. **D**	28. **C**	34. **E**
5. **C**	11. **D**	17. **D**	23. **C**	29. **C**	35. **C**
6. **D**	12. **B**	18. **A**	24. **E**	30. **C**	

Section 4

1. **D**	5. **C**	9. **A**	13. **D**	17. **E**	21. **B**
2. **A**	6. **B**	10. **D**	14. **D**	18. **D**	22. **D**
3. **B**	7. **E**	11. **C**	15. **D**	19. **C**	23. **D**
4. **C**	8. **C**	12. **C**	16. **C**	20. **A**	24. **E**

Section 5

1. **A**	5. **C**	9. **B**	13. **C**	17. **B**
2. **A**	6. **A**	10. **B**	14. **A**	18. **E**
3. **B**	7. **D**	11. **E**	15. **D**	19. **B**
4. **C**	8. **A**	12. **D**	16. **A**	

Section 6

1. **D**	5. **E**	9. **A**	13. **A**
2. **B**	6. **E**	10. **A**	14. **A**
3. **C**	7. **C**	11. **D**	
4. **A**	8. **D**	12. **C**	

ANALYSIS OF TEST RESULTS

I. Check your answers against the answer key.

II. Fill in the following chart.

Sentence Completion Number Correct _____	Section 1 (Questions 1–8) _____		Section 4 (Questions 1–5) _____	Section 5 (Questions 1–6) _____		Total _____
Reading Comprehension Number Correct _____	Section 2 (Questions 9–24) _____		Section 4 (Questions 6–24) _____	Section 5 (Questions 7–19) _____		Total _____
Sentence Improvement Number Correct _____		Section 3 (Questions 1–11) _____			Section 6 (Questions 1–14) _____	Total _____
Error Identification Number Correct _____		Section 3 (Questions 12–29) _____				Total _____
Paragraph Improvement Number Correct _____		Section 3 (Questions 30–35) _____				Total _____

III. Interpret your results.

Sentence Completion	Number Correct	_____
Reading Comprehension	Number Correct	_____
Sentence Improvement	Number Correct	_____
Error Identification	Number Correct	_____
Paragraph Improvement	Number Correct	_____
	Subtotal	_____

Guessing Penalty: Subtract 1/4 point for each incorrect answer.   _____
(Do not take off points for questions you left blank.)

TOTAL SCORE _____

	Sentence Completion Score	Reading Comprehension Score	Total
Excellent	18–19 Correct	43–48 Correct	60–67
Very Good	14–17 Correct	33–42 Correct	46–59
Good	11–13 Correct	25–32 Correct	35–45
Fair	9–10 Correct	20–24 Correct	28–34
Poor	6–8 Correct	12–19 Correct	17–27
Very Poor	0–5 Correct	0–11 Correct	0–16

	Sentence Improvement Score	Error Identification Score	Paragraph Improvement Score	Total
Excellent	21–25 Correct	13–18 Correct	6 Correct	38–49
Very Good	15–20 Correct	10–12 Correct	5 Correct	28–37
Good	8–14 Correct	7–9 Correct	4 Correct	17–27
Fair	5–7 Correct	5–6 Correct	2–3 Correct	11–16
Poor	3–4 Correct	3–4 Correct	1 Correct	5–10
Very Poor	0–2 Correct	0–2 Correct	0 Correct	0–4

SCORE YOUR OWN SAT ESSAY

Use this table as you rate your performance on the essay-writing section of this model test. Circle the phrase that most accurately describes your work. Enter the numbers in the scoring chart below. Add the numbers together and divide by 6 to determine your total score. The higher your total score, the better you are likely to do on the essay section of the SAT.

Note that on the actual SAT two readers will rate your essay; your essay score will be the sum of their two ratings and could range from 12 (highest) to 2 (lowest). Also, they will grade your essay holistically, rating it on the basis of their overall impression of its effectiveness. They will *not* analyze it piece by piece, giving separate grades for grammar, vocabulary level, and so on. Therefore, you cannot expect the score you give yourself on this model test to predict your eventual score on the SAT with any great degree of accuracy. Use this scoring guide instead to help you assess your writing strengths and weaknesses, so that you can decide which areas to focus on as you prepare for the SAT.

Like most people, you may find it difficult to rate your own writing objectively. Ask a teacher or fellow student to score your essay as well. With his or her help you should gain added insights into writing your 25-minute essay.

	6	5	4	3	2	1
POSITION ON THE TOPIC	Clear, convincing, & insightful	Fundamentally clear & coherent	Fairly clear & coherent	Insufficiently clear	Largely unclear	Extremely unclear
ORGANIZATION OF EVIDENCE	Well organized, with strong, relevant examples	Generally well organized, with apt examples	Adequately organized, with some examples	Sketchily developed, with weak examples	Lacking focus and evidence	Unfocused and disorganized
SENTENCE STRUCTURE	Varied, appealing sentences	Reasonably varied sentences	Some variety in sentences	Little variety in sentences	Errors in sentence structure	Severe errors in sentence structure
LEVEL OF VOCABULARY	Mature & apt word choice	Competent word choice	Adequate word choice	Inappropriate or weak vocabulary	Highly limited vocabulary	Rudimentary
GRAMMAR AND USAGE	Almost entirely free of errors	Relatively free of errors	Some technical errors	Minor errors and some major ones	Numerous major errors	Extensive severe errors
OVERALL EFFECT	Outstanding	Effective	Adequately competent	Inadequate, but shows some potential	Seriously flawed	Fundamentally deficient

Self-Scoring Chart

For each of the following categories, rate the essay from 1 (lowest) to 6 (highest)

Position on the Topic _____

Organization of Evidence _____

Sentence Structure _____

Level of Vocabulary _____

Grammar and Usage _____

Overall Effect _____

TOTAL _____

(To get a score, divide the total by 6) _____

Scoring Chart (Second Reader)

For each of the following categories, rate the essay from 1 (lowest) to 6 (highest)

Position on the Topic _____

Organization of Evidence _____

Sentence Structure _____

Level of Vocabulary _____

Grammar and Usage _____

Overall Effect _____

TOTAL _____

(To get a score, divide the total by 6) _____

ANSWER EXPLANATIONS

SECTION 2

1. **D**   One would expect restoration and cleaning to enhance or improve the murals' colors. Instead, the colors *deteriorated* or grew worse.
2. **D**   In contrast to the loneliness of writing, Mr. Doyle appreciates the *sociability* of working with others on films.
3. **B**   This *important* trade involving vast quantities of textiles was so vital to the economy that not even a war could stop it. Thus, it *continued* or kept on taking place through the Revolutionary War.
4. **B**   The astronomers resemble the doctors in their use of X rays to examine things that are concealed or *hidden*.
5. **A**   The phrase "anything but" signals an extreme degree of contrast. When trees go dormant, the process is decidedly not *sleepy* or sluggish, and the change is extreme or *radical*.
6. **B**   Lavish carvings decorating a throne are a form of *embellishment* (decoration; ornamentation).
7. **E**   "But" signals a contrast. Though one can dispute the way the author treats certain details, one cannot find fault with her main arguments or theses. They are *irreproachable* (flawless; blameless).
8. **E**   Oates has invented or *coined* a new word to *describe* a particular genre.
9. **A**   By denying the existence of a love affair between Pocahontas and John Smith, the author is *debunking* or exposing the falseness of *a common myth*.
10. **A**   By saying "True," the author admits that there was some sort of relationship between Pocahontas and Smith, even if it was not the passionate relationship that lovers of romantic tales would prefer.
11. **D**   The peculiar advantage that a best-selling novel has over an original script is its *particular,* special advantage: its popularity with a substantial segment of the population is guaranteed.
12. **E**   The final sentence of the passage explains that the "rub" or difficulty involved in working with best-selling novels is that producers have to pay so much money to get the screen rights that they often wind up losing money on the movie. In other words, the problem is the *financial impact of purchasing rights to adapt the novel.*
13. **D**   The tutor, who is not related to the Moreens and is therefore an outsider to the group, is telling the story of his relationship to this unusual family.
14. **D**   The Moreens' sudden shifts are apparently motivated by financial problems, for the class they travel in and the apartment they stay in vary with their financial state.
15. **D**   Living as he did in a small, uncomfortable apartment and dressing shabbily in threadbare clothes, Pemberton did not lead an *elegant* life during his visit to Paris. Use the process of elimination to answer this question.
    - Pemberton's visit to Paris was *gratifying*; he found his rambles with Morgan rewarding. You can eliminate (A).
    - Pemberton's visit to Paris was *sudden*; the Moreens suddenly gave up their villa in Nice and headed for Paris. You can eliminate (B).
    - Pemberton's visit to Paris was *instructive*; he and Morgan "learned to know their Paris." You can eliminate (C).
    - Pemberton's visit to Paris was *frugal*; he and Morgan seldom had any money, and when they did have some, they were very careful about what they spent it on. You can eliminate (E).
16. **C**   Lines 30–35 state that the Moreens "came back another year for a longer stay, the general character of which in Pemberton's memory today mixes pitiably and confusedly with that of the first." The narrator's reference to "Pemberton's memory *today*" indicates that he is speaking *some time after* the

events recounted in this tale. The narrator is telling the story of events his friend Pemberton remembers from years past.

17. **C** In telling his tutor that he does not wish to outshine him or cast him in the shade by dressing better than he does, Morgan is affectionately *teasing* Pemberton.

18. **E** To say that something is a chapter by itself is a way of saying that it would take an entire chapter of a book to deal with that subject fully. Thus, Pemberton is asserting that his wardrobe's shortcomings are major. Clearly, he is *sensitive about the disreputable state of his clothes*.

19. **E** Mrs. Moreen does not spend money for new clothes for Morgan because he does not make public appearances, that is, does not appear in "polite society." She does spend money on new clothes for the family members who move in polite circles. She loves Morgan and does not neglect him intentionally. This suggests that *she has only enough money to buy clothes for the family members who must appear in polite society*.

20. **B** Mrs. Moreen loves Morgan ("Morgan was dear to his mother"), but she shrewdly refrains from buying him new clothes when she realizes that nobody "important" will see how he is dressed. Her attitude is *fond* (loving) *but pragmatic* (practical).

21. **D** Morgan and Pemberton consider themselves "part of the vast vague hand-to-mouth multitude of" Paris and feel conscious of being part of a "democratic brotherhood." Thus, on some levels, even if partly in jest, they *identify* with the poor.

22. **D** Here the irony lies in the *contrast* between the splendors of the great museum and the shabbiness of the poor and homeless who flock to it for shelter and a bit of warmth.

23. **C** A young patrician is the child of an aristocratic family. Given Morgan's shabby clothing, he does not look smart or *fashionable* enough for people to consider him a member of the aristocracy.

24. **C** The opening sentence of the final paragraph states that Pemberton was "quite aware of how he and his comrade might strike people." The paragraph then proceeds to give examples of Pemberton's self-consciousness about appearances, as he wonders "what people would think they were" and fancies or imagines they are getting odd looks from people because they are such a mismatched pair. Clearly, the paragraph particularly brings home Pemberton's *concern for how he appears to others*.

SECTION 3

1. **D** Wordiness. Choice D makes the writer's point simply and concisely.

2. **D** Error in subject-verb agreement. Remember: the subject's grammatical number is not changed by the addition of a phrase that begins with *along with, together with,* or a similar expression. The subject, *princess,* is singular. The verb should be singular as well. Only choice D corrects the error without introducing fresh errors.

3. **B** Lack of parallelism. Choice B tightens the original loose sentence, neatly linking its similar elements (*the smallest* and *the most truculent*) with the connective *yet* to produce a balanced sentence.

4. **C** Lack of parallelism. Choice C balances the past tense verb *took* with a similar verb in the past tense (*incorporated*), linking them with the connective *and*.

5. **C** Misplaced modifier. Who are away on leave? Not the rooms, but the students!

6. **D** Error in logical comparison. Compare students with students, not students with a time period ("the middle of the twentieth century").

7. **E** Error in usage. A comedy duo by definition consists of two comedians.

8. **C** Error in modification. Ask yourself who was writing the review. Was it the production? No, the production was *being* reviewed: the reviewer was the paper's theater critic. Only choice C rewrites the sentence so that the phrase *Writing a review of opening night* correctly modifies *critic*.

9. **C** Dangling modifier. Who was afraid of meeting strangers? Obviously, Elizabeth Barrett. Choice C rearranges the sentence to eliminate the dangling modifier. (While choice E also rearranges the sentence so that the opening phrase modifies Barrett, it introduces a comma splice.)

10. **D**   Wordiness. Choice D eliminates the unnecessary words *for* and *they*.

11. **D**   The suggested revision tightens this ineffective compound sentence in two ways: first, it eliminates the connective *and;* second, it repeats the phrase *a landscape* to emphasize its importance.

12. **B**   Adjective-adverb confusion. Change *surprising* to *surprisingly*.

13. **B**   Error in sequence of tenses. Change *had suffered* to *suffers*.

14. **E**   Sentence is correct.

15. **B**   Error in comparison. Change *the more appropriate* to *the most appropriate*.

16. **B**   Error in subject-verb agreement. Change *are tested* to *is tested*.

17. **D**   Error in sequence of tenses. Change *are living* to *lived*.

18. **A**   Error in usage. The nonstandard phrase *cannot hardly* is a double negative. Change *cannot hardly believe* to *can hardly believe*.

19. **A**   Error in pronoun choice. Change *which ranged* to *who ranged*.

20. **A**   Error in subject-verb agreement. Be on the lookout for sentences in which the subject follows the verb. Here, the subject is *waterfalls* (plural); the verb should be plural as well. Change *flows* to *flow*.

21. **D**   Error in logical comparison. Compare percentages with percentages, not percentages with seasons. Change *the spring* to *the percentage in the spring*.

22. **D**   Lack of parallelism. Change *how it eventually failed* to *its eventual failure*.

23. **C**   Error in usage. The nonstandard phrase *hardly no* is a double negative. Change *hardly no* to *hardly any*.

24. **E**   Sentence is correct.

25. **A**   Error in subject-verb agreement. Be on the lookout for sentences in which the subject follows the verb. Here, the subject is *improvements* (plural); the verb should be plural as well. Change *has been* to *have been*.

26. **A**   Error in pronoun case. Change *my brother and I* to *my brother and me*.

27. **B**   Error in verb usage. Change *gaining* to *had gained*.

28. **C**   Error in idiomatic usage. Change *preoccupation in* to *preoccupation with*.

29. **C**   Error in pronoun-antecedent agreement. Young people differ in *their* willingness to get a job. Change *his or her* to *their*.

30. **C**   All sentences except sentence 3 contribute to the paragraph's main point, that celebrations help to unite people and keep traditions alive. Therefore, choice C is the best answer.

31. **B**   Choice A is grammatically correct, but the first clause is awkwardly expressed in the passive voice. Choice B is clearly written and to the point. It is the best answer. Choice C contains a dangling participle. The phrase *Receiving new clothes* should modify *children*, not *money*. Choice D is awkwardly expressed. Choice E is wordy and awkward.

32. **D**   Choice A is succinct, but its tone is not consistent with the rest of the essay. Choice B contains a comma splice between *dinner* and *at*. Choice C emphasizes the idea properly, but lacks parallel construction. Choice D places the emphasis where it belongs and expresses the idea effectively. It is the best answer. Choice E is repetitious, and it contains an error in pronoun reference. *They* has no specific antecedent.

33. **D**   Choice A does not provide a significantly better transition. Choice B does nothing to improve the relationship between paragraphs 3 and 4. Choice C is awkwardly worded and does not include transitional material. Choice D provides an effective transition between paragraphs. It is the best answer. Choice E tries to provide a transition, but it is wordy and it contains a dangling participle.

34. **E**   Choice A places emphasis on the location of the assassination instead of on the event itself, an emphasis that the writer did not intend. Choice B contains a nonstandard usage: the phrase *to remember about*. Choice C is grammatically correct but wordy.

Choice D is the same as B.

Choice E is a succinct and proper revision. It is the best answer.

35. **C** The main purpose of the last paragraph is to provide an example of a celebration that unites people and preserves tradition. Therefore, choice C is the best answer.

SECTION 4

1. **D** Salt eats away iron bars, turning them into rusty mush, by the process known as corrosion; salt is a highly *corrosive* substance.

2. **A** The writer is criticizing Bloom's book, which is *marred* (damaged) by its *slipshod* or sloppy style. *Although* is a contrast signal. Its use signals that the writer is *not* satisfied by Bloom's book.

3. **B** Because sociobiology combines aspects of two fields it is a *hybrid* or combined discipline (just as a mule, the offspring of a horse and an ass, is a hybrid animal).

4. **C** By definition, a *martinet* (stickler for discipline) would want his subordinates to follow orders *promptly*.

5. **C** By definition, a *monolith* is something solidly uniform, an undifferentiated whole. Black America, however, is a mixture of different attitudes and opinions; it is not monolithic at all.

6. **B** We expect insects to eat crops. We do not expect them to eat inedible items like sheets. That the locusts would eat the very sheets with which the farmers tried to protect their crops underscores or *emphasizes the extreme voracity* (ravenous hunger) *of the locusts*.

7. **E** Note the physical description of the grasshopper nymphs after their metamorphosis into gregarious migratory locusts. They have longer wings and broader shoulders. These are changes in form or *physical shape*.

8. **C** The metamorphosis of the locust from its harmless, solitary phase to its ravenous, migratory phase is *a natural phenomenon* that the passage attempts to *explain*.

9. **A** The author of Passage 1 describes locust plagues and discusses the factors that create them. To him, they are *a natural phenomenon to be observed*. In contrast, the author of Passage 2 analyzes the effectiveness of methods used to control locust plagues. To him, they are *a natural phenomenon to be controlled*.

10. **D** Picasso admitted that at the time he was working on *Les Demoiselles* "he was much interested in Iberian" or ancient Spanish sculpture. Thus, *he may have been influenced by ancient Spanish art*.

11. **C** Picasso had been moved in the past to *rethink completed works*. "Only a year before, stimulated by Iberian sculpture, he had repainted the head of Gertrude Stein's portrait months after he had completed the rest of the picture."

12. **C** In asserting that Picasso's memory might have been inaccurate and that he might have repainted the heads after his discovery of African sculpture, the author is *making a hypothesis* about what actually took place.

13. **D** Picasso was in the sculpture galleries of the Trocadero when he ran across African carvings.

14. **D** The title "Negro Period" has been given to this period or *used to designate* it, distinguishing it from Picasso's art of earlier times.

15. **D** The author asserts that experts today agree the *Woman in Yellow* is quite closely related to Iberian bronze statues. To back up this assertion, he cites Sweeney's observation that the *Woman in Yellow* looks remarkably similar to an ancient votive figure from Despenaperros. Thus, it seems most likely that Despenaperros is *a location on the Iberian peninsula* associated with ancient Iberian bronzes.

16. **C** If "the best speaker" has the most influence in the Indians' counsels, clearly the Indian leaders maintain their authority by means of their *verbal prowess* or skill.

17. **E** To dress food is to *prepare* it so that it can be cooked.

18. **D** You can answer this question by using the process of elimination.

- Statement I is untrue. Franklin never states that the Indians are more productive than the whites. Therefore, you can eliminate (A), (C), and (E).
- Statement II is true. According to Franklin, the Indians have abundance of leisure because they have "few artificial wants." They work only to satisfy their simple physical needs. When compared with the whites' laborious manner of life, theirs is a *simpler, more natural lifestyle*.
- Statement III is also true. The Indians do not value the time-consuming learning valued by the whites because they have a different, *distinctive set of values*. Therefore, you can eliminate (B).
- Only (D) is left. It is the correct answer.

19. **C** Just before he quotes the speech, Franklin states that the Indians look on the learning of the whites as useless. In recounting this instance of Indian diplomacy, he is *giving an example of the Indian viewpoint on the benefits of white civilization*.

20. **A** In assuring the commissioners that they recognize both the commissioners' good intentions and wisdom, the Indians are being most diplomatic. However, they are not agreeing to the commissioners' offer. Instead, they are declining or *tactfully refusing* it.

21. **B** While the education provided the Indians in the colleges of the northern provinces included all the white men's sciences, it did not prepare these young men for life in the woods. Thus, it did not meet the Indian elders' educational goals. It is clear that the Indians and the gentlemen of Virginia *have different educational goals*.

22. **D** To "take" a deer in this context is to kill or *capture* it; the speaker is describing how the white man's education fails to prepare young men to become hunters.

23. **D** The Indians state that a white college education made worthless good-for-nothings out of young Indians. They also assert that they can make men out of the Virginian commissioners' sons. Thus, it seems likely that the Indians would agree that they *have a better way of educating young men than the commissioners do*.

24. **E** In expressing their gratitude for the offer and thanking the Virginians for their intent, the Indians are being most *courteous*. In making the Virginians an offer they realize the Virginians are unlikely to accept, they are somewhat *ironic* as well.

SECTION 5

1. **A** Until the 1960s, the work of African-American cartoonists was largely limited or *confined* to African-American publications; their cartoons generally did not appear in the mainstream, general press.

2. **A** The actress thinks out every move she makes. Consequently, her performance is not *spontaneous* (unplanned, impulsive).

3. **B** To wander away from one's subject is to *digress*; the students enjoyed the professor's *digressions* or departures from the assigned topic.

4. **C** Miss Watson *pronounces* (asserts) that Huck cannot be reformed; she calls him *incorrigible* (uncorrectable). *Though* is a contrast signal. Its use signals that, unlike her widowed sister, Miss Watson has *no* hope of being able to reform Huck.

5. **C** Rather than moving *inexorably* (relentlessly, unstoppably) closer to its goals, the field is stuck or *mired in* its usual problems. The phrase "far from" is a contrast signal. Its use signals that the second missing word means the opposite of "moving *inexorably* closer."

6. **A** To be rebuffed is to be rejected or slighted. Being ignored by one's co-workers could make an *outgoing*, sociable person become unsociable and *withdrawn*.

7. **D** The phrase refers to the task of differentiating "self and nonself." In other words, the infant *begins to locate his physical boundaries*, learning where his own body ends and the rest of the world begins.

8. **A** The passage says that few scientists "can equal the infant for zeal and energy." An infant, therefore, is *tireless in his efforts* to figure things out.

9. **B** Throughout the passage, the author points out the vital role of the *baby's senses* in learning. See, for example, "sensory organs" (lines 15–17), "sense experiences" (lines 25–30), and "sensory discrimination" (lines 31–33).

10. **B** The infant conducts a step-by-step "series of complicated experiments," which can be described only as *highly structured and precise*.

11. **E** In lines 47–52 the passage describes the infant's discovery that *his own hand is different from another person's hand*.

12. **D** The fundamental principle of stimulus-response behavior, which is discussed in the passage, is that organisms, including infants, *naturally learn to respond to certain stimuli in the environment*.

13. **C** Stimulus-response conditioning is a "classical," universally acknowledged principle of behavioral psychology. We see evidence of it in newborns when they *respond to their environments early in life*. Pavlov, whose experiments with dogs is widely known, was one of the first scientists to describe the principle.

14. **A** The author states that *newborns are capable of thought* in lines 85 and 86.

15. **D** Because psychologists cannot agree on a precise definition of "thought," the author suggests "symbolization" as an alternative word to describe *the activity that takes place in an infant's mind*.

16. **A** Mature thought is that which allows the mind to consider "how things are different or might be different than they are." Such speculation demonstrates *a capacity to think abstractly*.

17. **B** Much of Passage 1 discusses how newborns begin *to differentiate between things that are not there and things that are*. In Passage 2 the author states that "the baby begins with a primitive appreciation of what is there and what is not."

18. **E** Passage 1 stresses the behavior that a parent might observe as a newborn infant learns to think. Passage 2, on the other hand, focuses on behavior in terms of the *psychology of thought development*.

19. **B** Passage 2 is written more tentatively; that is, the author recognizes that many assertions regarding infant thought are theoretical and that not all psychologists agree on every theory. In comparison, Passage 1 sounds like the voice of *authority*. This is probably as it should be, for nervous parents want to be told exactly what is going on with their newborns.

SECTION 6

1. **D** Error in pronoun choice. Avoid shifting from one pronoun to another within a single sentence. Change *you need* to *we need*.

2. **B** Adjective-adverb confusion. Change *intricate tangled* to *intricately tangled*.

3. **C** Run-on sentence. Do not link two independent clauses with a comma.

4. **A** Sentence is correct.

5. **E** Shift in number. The subject of the subordinate clause, *they*, is plural; the subject complement should be plural as well. Change *soldier* to *soldiers*.

6. **E** Error in usage. Do not use *when* after *is* in making a definition.

7. **C** Error in subject-verb agreement. *Club* is a collective noun. It takes a singular verb when it refers to the group as a unit. Change *host* to *hosts*.

8. **D** Errors in modification and in pronoun choice. The educators assert, not that the students are culturally biased, but that the standardized tests the students take may be, and that such biased tests are unfair to students. Here the restrictive pronoun *that*, not the nonrestrictive *which*, is required.

9. **A** Sentence is correct.

10. **A** Sentence is correct.

11. **D** Error in pronoun-antecedent agreement. The antecedent, *therapies*, is plural; the pronoun should be plural as well. Change *it* to *them*.

12. **C** Sentence fragment. Choice C completes the missing verb.

13. **A** Sentence is correct.

14. **A** Sentence is correct. Remember: a sentence in which the subject follows the verb may well be correct.

ANSWER SHEET FOR CRITICAL READING AND WRITING SKILLS TEST 2

Section 1   **ESSAY**   Time allowed: 25 minutes

Essay (continued)

Section 2

1. Ⓐ Ⓑ Ⓒ Ⓓ Ⓔ
2. Ⓐ Ⓑ Ⓒ Ⓓ Ⓔ
3. Ⓐ Ⓑ Ⓒ Ⓓ Ⓔ
4. Ⓐ Ⓑ Ⓒ Ⓓ Ⓔ
5. Ⓐ Ⓑ Ⓒ Ⓓ Ⓔ
6. Ⓐ Ⓑ Ⓒ Ⓓ Ⓔ
7. Ⓐ Ⓑ Ⓒ Ⓓ Ⓔ
8. Ⓐ Ⓑ Ⓒ Ⓓ Ⓔ

9. Ⓐ Ⓑ Ⓒ Ⓓ Ⓔ
10. Ⓐ Ⓑ Ⓒ Ⓓ Ⓔ
11. Ⓐ Ⓑ Ⓒ Ⓓ Ⓔ
12. Ⓐ Ⓑ Ⓒ Ⓓ Ⓔ
13. Ⓐ Ⓑ Ⓒ Ⓓ Ⓔ
14. Ⓐ Ⓑ Ⓒ Ⓓ Ⓔ
15. Ⓐ Ⓑ Ⓒ Ⓓ Ⓔ
16. Ⓐ Ⓑ Ⓒ Ⓓ Ⓔ

17. Ⓐ Ⓑ Ⓒ Ⓓ Ⓔ
18. Ⓐ Ⓑ Ⓒ Ⓓ Ⓔ
19. Ⓐ Ⓑ Ⓒ Ⓓ Ⓔ
20. Ⓐ Ⓑ Ⓒ Ⓓ Ⓔ
21. Ⓐ Ⓑ Ⓒ Ⓓ Ⓔ
22. Ⓐ Ⓑ Ⓒ Ⓓ Ⓔ
23. Ⓐ Ⓑ Ⓒ Ⓓ Ⓔ
24. Ⓐ Ⓑ Ⓒ Ⓓ Ⓔ

25. Ⓐ Ⓑ Ⓒ Ⓓ Ⓔ
26. Ⓐ Ⓑ Ⓒ Ⓓ Ⓔ
27. Ⓐ Ⓑ Ⓒ Ⓓ Ⓔ
28. Ⓐ Ⓑ Ⓒ Ⓓ Ⓔ
29. Ⓐ Ⓑ Ⓒ Ⓓ Ⓔ
30. Ⓐ Ⓑ Ⓒ Ⓓ Ⓔ

Section 3

1. Ⓐ Ⓑ Ⓒ Ⓓ Ⓔ
2. Ⓐ Ⓑ Ⓒ Ⓓ Ⓔ
3. Ⓐ Ⓑ Ⓒ Ⓓ Ⓔ
4. Ⓐ Ⓑ Ⓒ Ⓓ Ⓔ
5. Ⓐ Ⓑ Ⓒ Ⓓ Ⓔ
6. Ⓐ Ⓑ Ⓒ Ⓓ Ⓔ
7. Ⓐ Ⓑ Ⓒ Ⓓ Ⓔ
8. Ⓐ Ⓑ Ⓒ Ⓓ Ⓔ
9. Ⓐ Ⓑ Ⓒ Ⓓ Ⓔ

10. Ⓐ Ⓑ Ⓒ Ⓓ Ⓔ
11. Ⓐ Ⓑ Ⓒ Ⓓ Ⓔ
12. Ⓐ Ⓑ Ⓒ Ⓓ Ⓔ
13. Ⓐ Ⓑ Ⓒ Ⓓ Ⓔ
14. Ⓐ Ⓑ Ⓒ Ⓓ Ⓔ
15. Ⓐ Ⓑ Ⓒ Ⓓ Ⓔ
16. Ⓐ Ⓑ Ⓒ Ⓓ Ⓔ
17. Ⓐ Ⓑ Ⓒ Ⓓ Ⓔ
18. Ⓐ Ⓑ Ⓒ Ⓓ Ⓔ

19. Ⓐ Ⓑ Ⓒ Ⓓ Ⓔ
20. Ⓐ Ⓑ Ⓒ Ⓓ Ⓔ
21. Ⓐ Ⓑ Ⓒ Ⓓ Ⓔ
22. Ⓐ Ⓑ Ⓒ Ⓓ Ⓔ
23. Ⓐ Ⓑ Ⓒ Ⓓ Ⓔ
24. Ⓐ Ⓑ Ⓒ Ⓓ Ⓔ
25. Ⓐ Ⓑ Ⓒ Ⓓ Ⓔ
26. Ⓐ Ⓑ Ⓒ Ⓓ Ⓔ
27. Ⓐ Ⓑ Ⓒ Ⓓ Ⓔ

28. Ⓐ Ⓑ Ⓒ Ⓓ Ⓔ
29. Ⓐ Ⓑ Ⓒ Ⓓ Ⓔ
30. Ⓐ Ⓑ Ⓒ Ⓓ Ⓔ
31. Ⓐ Ⓑ Ⓒ Ⓓ Ⓔ
32. Ⓐ Ⓑ Ⓒ Ⓓ Ⓔ
33. Ⓐ Ⓑ Ⓒ Ⓓ Ⓔ
34. Ⓐ Ⓑ Ⓒ Ⓓ Ⓔ
35. Ⓐ Ⓑ Ⓒ Ⓓ Ⓔ

Section 4

1. Ⓐ Ⓑ Ⓒ Ⓓ Ⓔ
2. Ⓐ Ⓑ Ⓒ Ⓓ Ⓔ
3. Ⓐ Ⓑ Ⓒ Ⓓ Ⓔ
4. Ⓐ Ⓑ Ⓒ Ⓓ Ⓔ
5. Ⓐ Ⓑ Ⓒ Ⓓ Ⓔ
6. Ⓐ Ⓑ Ⓒ Ⓓ Ⓔ
7. Ⓐ Ⓑ Ⓒ Ⓓ Ⓔ
8. Ⓐ Ⓑ Ⓒ Ⓓ Ⓔ

9. Ⓐ Ⓑ Ⓒ Ⓓ Ⓔ
10. Ⓐ Ⓑ Ⓒ Ⓓ Ⓔ
11. Ⓐ Ⓑ Ⓒ Ⓓ Ⓔ
12. Ⓐ Ⓑ Ⓒ Ⓓ Ⓔ
13. Ⓐ Ⓑ Ⓒ Ⓓ Ⓔ
14. Ⓐ Ⓑ Ⓒ Ⓓ Ⓔ
15. Ⓐ Ⓑ Ⓒ Ⓓ Ⓔ
16. Ⓐ Ⓑ Ⓒ Ⓓ Ⓔ

17. Ⓐ Ⓑ Ⓒ Ⓓ Ⓔ
18. Ⓐ Ⓑ Ⓒ Ⓓ Ⓔ
19. Ⓐ Ⓑ Ⓒ Ⓓ Ⓔ
20. Ⓐ Ⓑ Ⓒ Ⓓ Ⓔ
21. Ⓐ Ⓑ Ⓒ Ⓓ Ⓔ
22. Ⓐ Ⓑ Ⓒ Ⓓ Ⓔ
23. Ⓐ Ⓑ Ⓒ Ⓓ Ⓔ
24. Ⓐ Ⓑ Ⓒ Ⓓ Ⓔ

25. Ⓐ Ⓑ Ⓒ Ⓓ Ⓔ
26. Ⓐ Ⓑ Ⓒ Ⓓ Ⓔ
27. Ⓐ Ⓑ Ⓒ Ⓓ Ⓔ
28. Ⓐ Ⓑ Ⓒ Ⓓ Ⓔ
29. Ⓐ Ⓑ Ⓒ Ⓓ Ⓔ
30. Ⓐ Ⓑ Ⓒ Ⓓ Ⓔ

Section 5

1. Ⓐ Ⓑ Ⓒ Ⓓ Ⓔ
2. Ⓐ Ⓑ Ⓒ Ⓓ Ⓔ
3. Ⓐ Ⓑ Ⓒ Ⓓ Ⓔ
4. Ⓐ Ⓑ Ⓒ Ⓓ Ⓔ
5. Ⓐ Ⓑ Ⓒ Ⓓ Ⓔ
6 Ⓐ Ⓑ Ⓒ Ⓓ Ⓔ
7. Ⓐ Ⓑ Ⓒ Ⓓ Ⓔ
8. Ⓐ Ⓑ Ⓒ Ⓓ Ⓔ

9. Ⓐ Ⓑ Ⓒ Ⓓ Ⓔ
10. Ⓐ Ⓑ Ⓒ Ⓓ Ⓔ
11. Ⓐ Ⓑ Ⓒ Ⓓ Ⓔ
12. Ⓐ Ⓑ Ⓒ Ⓓ Ⓔ
13. Ⓐ Ⓑ Ⓒ Ⓓ Ⓔ
14. Ⓐ Ⓑ Ⓒ Ⓓ Ⓔ
15. Ⓐ Ⓑ Ⓒ Ⓓ Ⓔ
16. Ⓐ Ⓑ Ⓒ Ⓓ Ⓔ

17. Ⓐ Ⓑ Ⓒ Ⓓ Ⓔ
18. Ⓐ Ⓑ Ⓒ Ⓓ Ⓔ
19. Ⓐ Ⓑ Ⓒ Ⓓ Ⓔ
20. Ⓐ Ⓑ Ⓒ Ⓓ Ⓔ
21. Ⓐ Ⓑ Ⓒ Ⓓ Ⓔ
22. Ⓐ Ⓑ Ⓒ Ⓓ Ⓔ
23. Ⓐ Ⓑ Ⓒ Ⓓ Ⓔ
24. Ⓐ Ⓑ Ⓒ Ⓓ Ⓔ

25. Ⓐ Ⓑ Ⓒ Ⓓ Ⓔ
26. Ⓐ Ⓑ Ⓒ Ⓓ Ⓔ
27. Ⓐ Ⓑ Ⓒ Ⓓ Ⓔ
28. Ⓐ Ⓑ Ⓒ Ⓓ Ⓔ
29. Ⓐ Ⓑ Ⓒ Ⓓ Ⓔ
30. Ⓐ Ⓑ Ⓒ Ⓓ Ⓔ

Section 6

1. Ⓐ Ⓑ Ⓒ Ⓓ Ⓔ
2. Ⓐ Ⓑ Ⓒ Ⓓ Ⓔ
3. Ⓐ Ⓑ Ⓒ Ⓓ Ⓔ
4. Ⓐ Ⓑ Ⓒ Ⓓ Ⓔ
5. Ⓐ Ⓑ Ⓒ Ⓓ Ⓔ
6 Ⓐ Ⓑ Ⓒ Ⓓ Ⓔ
7. Ⓐ Ⓑ Ⓒ Ⓓ Ⓔ
8. Ⓐ Ⓑ Ⓒ Ⓓ Ⓔ

9. Ⓐ Ⓑ Ⓒ Ⓓ Ⓔ
10. Ⓐ Ⓑ Ⓒ Ⓓ Ⓔ
11. Ⓐ Ⓑ Ⓒ Ⓓ Ⓔ
12. Ⓐ Ⓑ Ⓒ Ⓓ Ⓔ
13. Ⓐ Ⓑ Ⓒ Ⓓ Ⓔ
14. Ⓐ Ⓑ Ⓒ Ⓓ Ⓔ
15. Ⓐ Ⓑ Ⓒ Ⓓ Ⓔ
16. Ⓐ Ⓑ Ⓒ Ⓓ Ⓔ

17. Ⓐ Ⓑ Ⓒ Ⓓ Ⓔ
18. Ⓐ Ⓑ Ⓒ Ⓓ Ⓔ
19. Ⓐ Ⓑ Ⓒ Ⓓ Ⓔ
20. Ⓐ Ⓑ Ⓒ Ⓓ Ⓔ
21. Ⓐ Ⓑ Ⓒ Ⓓ Ⓔ
22. Ⓐ Ⓑ Ⓒ Ⓓ Ⓔ
23. Ⓐ Ⓑ Ⓒ Ⓓ Ⓔ
24. Ⓐ Ⓑ Ⓒ Ⓓ Ⓔ

25. Ⓐ Ⓑ Ⓒ Ⓓ Ⓔ
26. Ⓐ Ⓑ Ⓒ Ⓓ Ⓔ
27. Ⓐ Ⓑ Ⓒ Ⓓ Ⓔ
28. Ⓐ Ⓑ Ⓒ Ⓓ Ⓔ
29. Ⓐ Ⓑ Ⓒ Ⓓ Ⓔ
30. Ⓐ Ⓑ Ⓒ Ⓓ Ⓔ

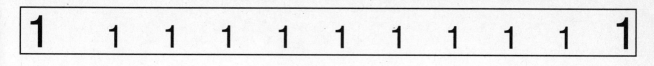

MODEL TEST 2
Section 1
Essay

Turn to your answer sheet and write your essay on the lined portion of the page. To receive credit, you must write your essay in the area provided.

Write on the assigned topic below. If you write on any other topic, your essay will be given a score of zero.

Write or print legibly: your readers will be unfamiliar with your handwriting, and you want them to be able to read what you write.

The excerpt appearing below makes a point about a particular topic. Read the statement carefully, and think about the assignment that follows.

Learning starts with failure; the first failure is the beginning of education.
—John Hersey

Assignment: The statement above implies that failure is educational. Write an essay supporting, disputing, or qualifying this thesis. You may use examples from history, literature, popular culture, current events, or personal experience to support your position.

BEGIN WRITING YOUR ESSAY ON THE ANSWER SHEET

STOP
IF YOU FINISH BEFORE TIME IS CALLED, YOU MAY CHECK YOUR WORK ON THIS SECTION ONLY. DO NOT WORK ON ANY OTHER SECTION IN THE TEST.

2 2 2 2 2 2 2 2 2 2 2 2

Section 2

TIME—25 MINUTES
24 QUESTIONS

For each of the following questions, select the best answer from the choices provided and fill in the appropriate circle on the answer sheet.

Each of the following sentences contains one or two blanks; each blank indicates that a word or set of words has been left out. Below the sentence are five words or phrases, lettered A through E. Select the word or set of words that best completes the sentence.

Example:

Fame is ----; today's rising star is all too soon tomorrow's washed-up has-been.

(A) rewarding   (B) gradual
(C) essential   (D) spontaneous
(E) transitory

Ⓐ Ⓑ Ⓒ Ⓓ ●

---

1. The museum administration appears to be singularly ____ the comforts of its employees, providing an employee health club, a lending library, and a part-time social worker to help staff members with financial or domestic problems.

    (A) ignorant of
    (B) indifferent to
    (C) attentive to
    (D) exploited by
    (E) uninvolved in

2. The assemblyman instructed his staff to be courteous in responding to requests from his ____, the voters belonging to the district he represented.

    (A) collaborators
    (B) interviewers
    (C) adversaries
    (D) constituents
    (E) predecessors

3. Trees native to warmer climates are genetically programmed for shorter, milder winters and are therefore ____ to both cold snaps and sudden thaws.

    (A) indifferent
    (B) restricted
    (C) vulnerable
    (D) accessible
    (E) attributed

4. Although, as wife of President John Adams, Abigail Adams sought a greater voice for women, she was not a feminist in the modern sense; she ____ the ____ view of women as "beings placed by providence" under male protection.

    (A) anticipated…current
    (B) regretted…heretical
    (C) distorted…outmoded
    (D) repudiated…radical
    (E) accepted…traditional

5. An unattractive feature of this memoir is the casually dismissive, often downright ____, comments the author makes about almost all of her former colleagues.

    (A) elegiac
    (B) euphemistic
    (C) objective
    (D) contemptuous
    (E) laudatory

GO ON TO THE NEXT PAGE ⇨

2 2 2 2 2 2 2 2 2 2 2 **2**

6. There was some stagecraft behind the supposedly ____ moments photographed by Doisneau; in a legal dispute last year, Doisneau ____ that he had paid two models to pose for his famous *The Kiss at the Hotel de Ville*.

   (A) innocent…disproved
   (B) candid…acknowledged
   (C) theatrical…regretted
   (D) affected…intimated
   (E) spontaneous…urged

7. The protagonist of the poem "Richard Cory" appears ____ but has no real joy in his gifts and possessions; he ____ his feelings with a mask of lightheartedness.

   (A) talented…manifests
   (B) nonchalant…adapts
   (C) jovial…camouflages
   (D) affluent…suppresses
   (E) acquisitive…unburdens

8. Always less secure in herself than she liked to admit, she too often ____ disagreement as ____ and opposition as treachery.

   (A) rewarded…virtue
   (B) construed…betrayal
   (C) condemned…detachment
   (D) invited…provocation
   (E) interpreted…drollery

GO ON TO THE NEXT PAGE

2   2   2   2   2   2   2   2   2   2   2

Read each of the passages below, and then answer the questions that follow the passage. The correct response may be stated outright or merely suggested in the passage.

Questions 9 and 10 are based on the following passage.

The Rosetta Stone! What a providential find that was! And what a remarkable set of circumstances it took for people to be able to
Line read Egyptian hieroglyphics after a hiatus of
(5) some 1400 years. It even took a military campaign. In 1798, Napoleon Bonaparte's army attacked British-held Egypt, seeking to cut off England from the riches of the Middle East. Rebuilding a fortress, a French soldier uncov-
(10) ered a block of basalt inscribed with writing in three distinct scripts, one Greek, one demotic script (an everyday cursive form of Egyptian), and one Egyptian hieroglyphs. At that moment, modern Egyptology began.

9. The primary purpose of the opening sentences of the passage (lines 1–6) is to

(A) describe the physical attributes of an artifact
(B) underscore the difficulty of translating ancient texts
(C) indicate a new direction for linguistic research
(D) qualify an excessively sweeping generalization
(E) emphasize the unusual background of a discovery

10. The author's tone in writing of the discovery of the Rosetta Stone can best be characterized as

(A) ironic
(B) enthusiastic
(C) condescending
(D) nostalgic
(E) objective

Questions 11 and 12 are based on the following passage.

The faculty for myth is innate in the human race. It seizes with avidity upon any incidents, surprising or mysterious, in the
Line careers of those who have at all distinguished
(5) themselves from their fellows, and invents a legend. It is the protest of romance against the commonplace of life. The incidents of the legend become the hero's surest passport to immortality. The ironic philosopher reflects
(10) with a smile that Sir Walter Raleigh is more safely enshrined in the memory of mankind because he set his cloak for the Virgin Queen to walk on than because he carried the English name to undiscovered countries.

11. As used in the passage, the word "faculty" (line 1) most nearly means

(A) capacity
(B) distinction
(C) authority
(D) teaching staff
(E) branch of learning

12. In lines 9–14, the author mentions Sir Walter Raleigh primarily to

(A) demonstrate the importance of Raleigh's voyages of discovery
(B) mock Raleigh's behavior in casting down his cloak to protect the queen's feet from the mud
(C) illustrate how legendary events outshine historical achievements in the public's mind
(D) distinguish between Raleigh the courtier and Raleigh the seafarer
(E) remind us that historical figures may act in idiosyncratic ways

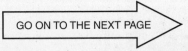
GO ON TO THE NEXT PAGE

Questions 13–24 are based on the following passage.

In this excerpt from The Joy of Music, *the composer and conductor Leonard Bernstein describes the characteristics of the ideal conductor.*

For the qualities that distinguish *great*
conductors lie far beyond and above what we
have spoken of. We now begin to deal with the
Line intangibles, the deep magical aspect of con-
(5) ducting. It is the mystery of relationships—
conductor and orchestra bound together by the
tiny but powerful split second. How can I
describe to you the magic of the moment of
beginning a piece of music? There is only one
(10) possible fraction of a second that feels exactly
right for starting. There is a wait while the
orchestra readies itself and collects its powers;
while the conductor concentrates his whole
will and force toward the work in hand; while
(15) the audience quiets down, and the last cough
has died away. There is no slight rustle of a
program book; the instruments are poised
and—bang! That's it. One second later, it is
too late, and the magic has vanished.
(20)   This psychological timing is constantly in
play throughout the performance of music. It
means that a great conductor is one who has
great sensitivity to the flow of time; who
makes one note move to the next in exactly the
(25) right way and at the right instant. For music,
as we said, exists in the medium of time. It is
time itself that must be carved up, molded and
remolded until it becomes, like a statue, an
existing shape and form. This is the hardest to
(30) do. For a symphony is not like a statue, which
can be viewed all at once, or bit by bit at
leisure, in one's own chosen time. With music,
we are trapped in time. Each note is gone as
soon as it has sounded, and it never can be
(35) recontemplated or heard again at the particular
instant of rightness. It is always too late for a
second look.
So the conductor is a kind of sculptor
whose element is time instead of marble; and
(40) in sculpting it, he must have a superior sense

of proportion and relationship. He must judge
the largest rhythms, the whole phraseology of
a work. He must conquer the form of a piece
not only in the sense of form as a mold, but
(45) form in its deepest sense, knowing and controlling where the music relaxes, where it
begins to accumulate tension, where the greatest tension is reached, where it must ease up to
gather strength for the next lap, where it
(50) unloads that strength.
These are the intangibles of conducting,
the mysteries that no conductor can learn or
acquire. If he has a natural faculty for deep
perception, it will increase and deepen as he
(55) matures. If he hasn't, he will always be a
pretty good conductor. But even the pretty
good conductor must have one more attribute
in his personality, without which all the
mechanics and knowledge and perception are
(60) useless; and that is the power to *communicate*
all this to his orchestra—through his arms,
face, eyes, fingers, and whatever vibrations
may flow from him. If he uses a baton, the
baton itself must be a living thing, charged
(65) with a kind of electricity, which makes it an
instrument of meaning in its tiniest movement.
If he does not use a baton, his hands must do
the job with equal clarity. But baton or no
baton, his gestures must be first and always
(70) meaningful in terms of the music.
The chief element in the conductor's technique of communication is the preparation.
Everything must be shown to the orchestra
before it happens. Once the player is playing
(75) the note, it is too late. So the conductor always
has to be a beat or two ahead of the orchestra
. . . . And he must hear two things at the same
time: what the players are doing at any
moment, and what they are about to do a
(80) moment later. Therefore, the basic trick is in
the preparatory upbeat. If our conductor is
back again on page one of Brahms's *First
Symphony*, he must show, in his silent upbeat,

GO ON TO THE NEXT PAGE

the character of the music which is about to (85) sound. Whether he thinks of it as tense and agitated, or weighty and doom-ridden, his upbeat should show this, in order to enable the orchestra players to respond in kind. It is exactly like breathing: the preparation is like (90) an inhalation, and the music sounds as an exhalation. We all have to inhale in order to speak, for example; all verbal expression is exhaled. So it is with music: we inhale on the upbeat and sing out a phrase of music, then (95) inhale again and breathe out the next phrase. A conductor who breathes with the music has gone far in acquiring a technique.

But the conductor must not only make his orchestra play; he must make them want to (100) play. He must exalt them, lift them, start their adrenaline pouring, either through cajoling or demanding or raging. But however he does it, he must make the orchestra love the music as he loves it. It is not so much imposing his will (105) on them like a dictator; it is more like projecting his feelings around him so that they reach the last player in the second violin section. And when this happens—when one hundred players share his feelings, exactly, simultane- (110) ously, responding as one to each rise and fall of the music, to each point of arrival and departure, to each little inner pulse—then there is a human identity of feeling that has no equal elsewhere. It is the closest thing I know (115) to love itself. On this current of love the conductor can communicate at the deepest levels with his players, and ultimately with his audience. He may shout and rant and curse and insult his players at rehearsal—as some of our (120) greatest conductors are famous for doing—but if there is this love, the conductor and his orchestra will remain knit together through it all and function as one.

Well, there is our ideal conductor. And (125) perhaps the chief requirement of all this is that he be humble before the composer; that he never interpose himself between the music and the audience; that all his efforts, however

strenuous or glamorous, be made in the ser- (130) vice of the composer's meaning—the music itself, which, after all, is the whole reason for the conductor's existence.

13. In the first paragraph, in creating an initial impression of the qualities of the ideal conductor for the reader, the author makes use of

(A) reference to musical notation
(B) contrast to the musicians
(C) comparison with other leaders of ensembles
(D) narration of a sequence of events
(E) allusion to psychological studies

14. The passage is most likely to have been preceded by a discussion of

(A) the deficiencies of conductors whom the author has known
(B) how the conductor relates to the composer
(C) ways in which the orchestra complements the conductor
(D) the technical skills needed to be a reasonably competent conductor
(E) the qualities that transform a conductor into a superior musician

15. The conductor's decision as to the moment when to begin a piece of music can best be described as

(A) tentative
(B) imperceptible
(C) intuitive
(D) trivial
(E) hypothetical

16. In stating that "with music, we are trapped in time" (lines 32 and 33), the author is being

(A) resigned
(B) wistful
(C) ironic
(D) figurative
(E) resentful

GO ON TO THE NEXT PAGE

2 2 2 2 2 2 2 2 2 2 2

17. The author mentions sculpting chiefly in order to

    (A) place conducting in perspective as one of the fine arts

    (B) contrast it informally with conducting

    (C) help the reader get an image of the conductor's work

    (D) illustrate the difficulties of the sculptor's task

    (E) show how the study of sculpture can benefit the conductor

18. In line 44, "mold" most nearly means

    (A) decaying surface

    (B) fixed pattern

    (C) decorative strip

    (D) organic growth

    (E) cooking utensil

19. Lines 51–55 indicate that the author believes that the ideal conductor's most important attributes are

    (A) innate

    (B) transient

    (C) technical

    (D) symbolic

    (E) unclear

20. The author regards the conductor's baton primarily as

    (A) a necessary evil

    (B) a symbol of strength

    (C) an electrical implement

    (D) an improvement over hand gestures

    (E) a tool for transmitting meaning

21. In dealing with musicians, the author believes conductors

    (A) must do whatever it takes to motivate them to perform

    (B) should never resort to pleading with their subordinates

    (C) must maintain their composure under trying circumstances

    (D) work best if they love the musicians with whom they work

    (E) must assert dominance over the musicians autocratically

22. In lines 105–107, the author mentions "the last player in the second violin section" primarily to emphasize

    (A) the number of musicians necessary in an orchestra

    (B) the particular importance of violins in ensemble work

    (C) how sensitive secondary musicians can be

    (D) how the role of the conductor differs from that of the musician

    (E) the distance across which the conductor must communicate

23. The author regards temperamental behavior during rehearsals on the part of conductors with

    (A) disapprobation

    (B) tolerance

    (C) bemusement

    (D) regret

    (E) awe

24. To the author, the conductor's primary concern is to maintain

    (A) rapport with the audience

    (B) authority over the orchestra

    (C) the respect of the musicians

    (D) the tempo of the music

    (E) the integrity of the musical piece

STOP

IF YOU FINISH BEFORE TIME IS CALLED, YOU MAY CHECK YOUR WORK ON THIS SECTION ONLY. DO NOT WORK ON ANY OTHER SECTION IN THE TEST.

Section 3

For each of the following questions, choose the best answer and fill in the appropriate circle on the answer sheet.

Some or all parts of the following sentences are underlined. The first answer choice, (A), simply repeats the underlined part of the sentence. The other four choices present four alternative ways to phrase the underlined part. Select the answer that produces the most effective sentence, one that is clear and exact, and blacken the appropriate space on your answer sheet. In selecting your choice, be sure that it is standard written English, and that it expresses the meaning of the original sentence.

Example:
The first biography of author Eudora Welty came out in 1998 and she was 89 years old at the time.

(A) and she was 89 years old at the time
(B) at the time she was 89
(C) upon becoming an 89 year old
(D) when she was 89
(E) at the age of 89 years old

Ⓐ Ⓑ Ⓒ ● Ⓔ

---

1. In the four chapels of Santa Croce, Giotto painted <u>frescoes and they portrayed</u> the lives of the saints.

   (A) frescoes and they portrayed
   (B) frescoes, being portrayals of
   (C) frescoes, they portrayed
   (D) frescoes that portrayed
   (E) frescoes because they portrayed

2. The debate coach, <u>together with the members of the winning team, is traveling</u> to Washington for the awards ceremony.

   (A) together with the members of the winning team, is traveling
   (B) along with the members of the winning team, they are traveling
   (C) along with the members of the winning team, are traveling
   (D) together with the members of the winning team, are traveling
   (E) together with the members of the winning team, are to travel

3. By establishing strict rules of hygiene in maternity wards, Ignaz Semmelweis saved many women from dying of childbed <u>fever, this was a fate that many expectant mothers feared</u>.

   (A) fever, this was a fate that many expectant mothers feared
   (B) fever, since many expectant mothers feared this was their fate
   (C) fever, it was a fate of which many expectant mothers were afraid
   (D) fever, because many expectant mothers feared this fate
   (E) fever, a fate that many expectant mothers feared

GO ON TO THE NEXT PAGE ⇨

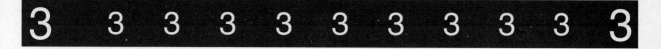

4. Veterans of World War II received greater support from the public <u>than</u> the Korean and Vietnam Wars.

   (A) than
   (B) than did
   (C) than did veterans of
   (D) than from the support of
   (E) than from the

5. Nowadays airport security guards have the right to search <u>people's bags who act</u> in a suspicious manner.

   (A) people's bags who act
   (B) persons' bags who act
   (C) the bags of people who act
   (D) the bags of persons that act
   (E) personal bags which act

6. The clipper ship was the fastest ocean-going vessel of its <u>time; it ruled the waves only briefly, however,</u> before the faster and more reliable steamship took its place.

   (A) time; it ruled the waves only briefly, however,
   (B) time, for it ruled the waves only briefly
   (C) time; however, ruling the waves only briefly
   (D) time, having ruled the waves only briefly, however,
   (E) time, but was ruling the waves only briefly, however,

7. The real estate reporter maintained that housing prices in San Francisco were <u>higher than any other city</u> in the country.

   (A) higher than any other city
   (B) higher than every other city
   (C) the highest of those of any other city
   (D) higher than those in any other city
   (E) higher than any city

8. During the eighteenth century, inoculations against smallpox became increasingly popular among the English upper classes <u>although to the lower classes it</u> remained mysterious and therefore threatening.

   (A) although to the lower classes it
   (B) because to the lower classes it
   (C) although to the lower classes such inoculations
   (D) however, to the lower classes the inoculations
   (E) although among the lower classes it

9. With the rift between the two sides apparently widening, analysts said that they <u>considered the likelihood of a merger between the two corporations to be negligible</u>.

   (A) considered the likelihood of a merger between the two corporations to be negligible
   (B) considered it was likely a merger between the two corporations being negligible
   (C) considered the two corporations' merger likely to be negligible
   (D) considered the likelihood of the two corporations merging between them to have been negligible
   (E) considered between the two corporations such a merger to be negligible

GO ON TO THE NEXT PAGE

3 3 3 3 3 3 3 3 3 3 3

10. <u>Gold was discovered at Sutter's Mill in 1848, and</u> the prospectors who flocked to the gold fields are known not as the forty-eighters but as the forty-niners.

(A) Gold was discovered at Sutter's Mill in 1848, and

(B) They discovered gold at Sutter's Mill in 1848, and

(C) Although gold was discovered at Sutter's Mill in 1848,

(D) Upon the discovery of gold at Sutter's Mill in 1848,

(E) Because gold was discovered at Sutter's Mill in 1848,

11. Once a leading light of the Harlem Renaissance, <u>the revived interest in African-American literary pioneers rescued Zora Neale Hurston from decades of obscurity</u>.

(A) the revived interest in African-American literary pioneers rescued Zora Neale Hurston from decades of obscurity

(B) through the revived interest in African-American literary pioneers, Zora Neale Hurston was rescued from decades of obscurity

(C) Zora Neale Hurston's rescue from decades of literary obscurity was due to the revived interest in African-American literary pioneers

(D) Zora Neale Hurston was rescued from decades of literary obscurity by the revived interest in African-American literary pioneers

(E) Zora Neale Hurston was rescued from decades of literary obscurity by reviving the interest in African-American literary pioneers

The sentences in this section may contain errors in grammar, usage, choice of words, or idioms. Either there is just one error in a sentence or the sentence is correct. Some words or phrases are underlined and lettered; everything else in the sentence is correct.

If an underlined word or phrase is incorrect, choose that letter; if the sentence is correct, select <u>No error</u>. Then blacken the appropriate space on your answer sheet.

Example:
The region has a climate <u>so severe that</u> plants
                          A
growing there rarely <u>had been</u> more than twelve
       B   C
inches <u>high.</u> <u>No error</u>
        D   E

Ⓐ Ⓑ ● Ⓓ Ⓔ

12. All of the candidates except Mr. Nader and

<u>I</u> <u>have begun</u> <u>to engage in</u> negative
 A   B   C
<u>campaigning.</u> <u>No error</u>
      D   E

13. The historians of geography and cartography

seem <u>more</u> interested in their maps than in the
      A
explorers who went into the field, <u>often</u>
                                      B
<u>at great risk</u>, to get the information that these
      C
maps <u>contain.</u> <u>No error</u>
        D   E

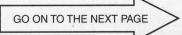
GO ON TO THE NEXT PAGE

3   3   3   3   3   3   3   3   3   3   3

14. Although scientists know <u>surprising</u> little
                          A
    about Americans' favorite stimulant, coffee,

    they <u>do know</u> that most people do not use
          B
    <u>it</u> <u>efficiently</u>. <u>No error</u>
    C   D   E

15. <u>Irregardless of</u> studies that <u>have shown</u>
       A   B
    echinacea to have no <u>effect against</u> the
                         C
    common cold, Americans spend about $300

    million every year <u>for</u> echinacea-based cold
                  D
    remedies. <u>No error</u>
            E

16. Because most <u>species of</u> frogs live <u>both</u> on
             A   B
    land and in water, they are <u>vulnerable for</u>
                      C
    more than the usual <u>threats to</u> survival in
                  D
    modern times. <u>No error</u>
            E

17. Although many ten-year-olds are <u>quite</u> mature
                      A
    for <u>their</u> age, we <u>cannot hardly</u> expect them to
      B   C
    act <u>like</u> adults. <u>No error</u>
       D   E

18. The tapeworm is an <u>example of</u> a parasitic
                  A
    organism, <u>one that</u> lives within or on another
            B
    creature, <u>deriving some</u> or all of its nutriment
             C
    from <u>its</u> host. <u>No error</u>
        D   E

19. <u>In the course of</u> his <u>varied</u> musical career,
       A   B
    Wayne Hankin <u>has been</u> a composer, a circus
                C
    performer, and <u>arranged music for</u> Meredith
                D
    Monk. <u>No error</u>
          E

20. It is <u>important for</u> graders <u>to remember when</u>
        A   B
    these student essay writers <u>have been allowed</u>
                      C
    only a short span of time <u>in which to compose</u>
                    D
    their essays. <u>No error</u>
             E

21. The sighting of several <u>previously</u> unknown
                  A
    astral bodies <u>in orbit</u> beyond Pluto
             B
    <u>have thrilled</u> astronomers and science fiction
        C
    writers <u>alike</u>. <u>No error</u>
        D   E

GO ON TO THE NEXT PAGE

3 3 3 3 3 3 3 3 3 3 3

22. Friends of the family <u>constantly</u> <u>remark on</u>
                  A   B
    the <u>striking</u> resemblance between my
        C
    <u>daughter and I</u>. <u>No error</u>
        D   E

23. <u>Although</u> J. R. R. Tolkien and J. K. Rowling
     A
    are <u>superficially</u> similar authors, Tolkien
           B
    <u>possesses</u> the <u>greatest</u> range and sense of
     C   D
    history. <u>No error</u>
          E

24. A new and <u>rapid changing</u> field, nanotechnology
          A
    involves the <u>manipulation of</u> matter at the
           B
    molecular level <u>to create</u> computer chips
           C
    and other devices that are thousands of times
    <u>smaller than</u> current technologies permit.
      D
    <u>No error</u>
     E

25. Police reports <u>indicate that</u> the <u>percentage of</u>
           A   B
    teenagers <u>involved in</u> automobile accidents is
          C
    similar <u>to senior citizens</u>. <u>No error</u>
          D   E

26. <u>Featuring</u> more than three hundred stunning
     A
    objects, the Art Deco exhibition <u>investigates</u>
                    B
    the period between the two world wars and
    provides <u>insights into</u> the social and cultural
           C
    <u>contexts for</u> the production of decorative
        D
    artifacts. <u>No error</u>
          E

27. Whether one chooses <u>to visit</u> Hawaii or New
                A
    Zealand, <u>you are</u> sure to find innumerable
          B
    <u>opportunities for</u> swimming, sailing, surfing,
        C
    and <u>other</u> water sports. <u>No error</u>
        D   E

28. The dances that Alvin Ailey <u>choreographed</u>
                   A
    for his company <u>were</u> <u>less stylized</u> and more
          B   C
    energetic than <u>George Balanchine</u>. <u>No error</u>
          D   E

29. Once <u>thought to be</u> the <u>earliest</u> Americans,
        A   B
    the nomadic Clovis hunters left their <u>finely</u>
                C
    worked flint arrowheads across the United
    States <u>over</u> a period of five centuries,
         D
    beginning 13,000 years ago. <u>No error</u>
                 E

GO ON TO THE NEXT PAGE

3 3 3 3 3 3 3 3 3 3 3

The passage below is the unedited draft of a student's essay. Parts of the essay need to be rewritten to make the meaning clearer and more precise. Read the essay carefully.

The essay is followed by six questions about changes that might improve all or part of the organization, development, sentence structure, use of language, appropriateness to the audience, or use of standard written English. In each case, choose the answer that most clearly and effectively expresses the student's intended meaning. Indicate your choice by blackening the corresponding space on the answer sheet.

[1] Members of our community have objected to the inclusion of various pieces of art in the local art exhibit. [2] They say that these pieces offend community values. [3] The exhibit in its entirety should be presented.

[4] The reason for this is that people have varied tastes, and those who like this form of art have a right to see the complete exhibit. [5] An exhibit like this one gives the community a rare chance to see the latest modern art nearby, and many people have looked forward to it with great anticipation. [6] It would be an unfortunate blow to those people for it not to be shown.

[7] The exhibit may contain pieces of art that tend to be slightly erotic, but what is being shown that most people haven't already seen? [8] So, give it an R or an X rating and don't let small children in. [9] But how many small children voluntarily go to see an art exhibit? [10] The exhibit includes examples of a new style of modern art. [11] The paintings show crowds of nude people. [12] The exhibit is at the library's new art gallery. [13] For centuries artists have been painting and sculpting people in the nude. [14] Why are these works of art different? [15] Perhaps they are more graphic in some respects, but we live in an entirely different society than from the past. [16] It is strange indeed for people in this day and age to be offended by the sight of the human anatomy.

[17] If people don't agree with these pieces, they simply should just not go. [18] But they should not be allowed to prevent others from seeing it.

30. With regard to the sentences that precede and follow sentence 3, which of the following is the best revision of sentence 3?

(A) On the other hand, the whole exhibit should be presented.
(B) The exhibit, however, should be presented in its entirety.
(C) The exhibit should be entirely presented regardless of what the critics say.
(D) But another point of view is that the exhibit should be presented in its entirety.
(E) Still other members also say the whole exhibit should be presented in its entirety.

31. In the context of paragraph 3, which of the following is the best revision of sentence 8?

(A) So, an R or X rating will warn people with small children to keep them out.
(B) Therefore, giving it an R or an X rating and not letting small children in.
(C) To satisfy everyone objecting to the exhibit, perhaps the exhibit could be given an R or an X rating to advise parents that some of the art on exhibit may not be suitable for young children.
(D) Let an R or an X rating caution the public that some of the art may be offensive and be unsuitable for young children.
(E) In conclusion, small children will be kept out by giving it an R or an X rating.

GO ON TO THE NEXT PAGE

3   3   3   3   3   3   3   3   3   3   3

32. In the context of paragraph 3, which of the following is the best revision of sentences 10, 11, and 12?

(A) Paintings on exhibit at the library showing crowds of nude people and done in a new style of modern art.

(B) The exhibit, on display at the library, includes paintings of crowds of nude people done in a new style of modern art.

(C) The exhibit includes paintings in a new style of modern art, which shows crowds of nude people at the library.

(D) The library is the site of the exhibit which shows a new style of modern art, with paintings showing crowds of nude people.

(E) The new style of modern art includes examples of paintings showing crowds of nude people on exhibit in the library.

33. To improve the clarity and coherence of the whole essay, where is the best place to relocate the ideas contained in sentences 10, 11, and 12?

(A) Before sentence 1
(B) Between sentences 1 and 2
(C) Between sentences 8 and 9
(D) Between sentences 15 and 16
(E) After sentence 18

34. Which of the following is the best revision of the underlined segment of sentence 15 below?

Perhaps they are more graphic in some respects, but we live in an entirely different society than from the past.

(A) an entirely different society than of the past
(B) a completely different society than the past
(C) a society completely different than from past societies
(D) a society that is entirely different from the way societies have been in the past
(E) an entirely different society from that of the past

35. Which of the following revisions of sentence 17 provides the best transition between paragraphs 3 and 4?

(A) If anyone doesn't approve of these pieces, they simply should not go to the exhibit.
(B) Anyone disagreeing with the pieces in the exhibit shouldn't go to it.
(C) Anyone who disapproves of nudity in art simply shouldn't go to the exhibit.
(D) If anyone dislikes the sight of nudes in art, this show isn't for them.
(E) Don't go if you disapprove of nudity in art.

STOP

IF YOU FINISH BEFORE TIME IS CALLED, YOU MAY CHECK YOUR WORK ON THIS SECTION ONLY. DO NOT WORK ON ANY OTHER SECTION IN THE TEST.

(4) (4) (4) (4) (4) (4) (4) (4) (4) (4)

Section 4

TIME—25 MINUTES
24 QUESTIONS

For each of the following questions, select the best answer from the choices provided and fill in the appropriate circle on the answer sheet.

Each of the following sentences contains one or two blanks; each blank indicates that a word or set of words has been left out. Below the sentence are five words or phrases, lettered A through E. Select the word or set of words that best completes the sentence.

Example:

Fame is ----; today's rising star is all too soon tomorrow's washed-up has-been.

(A) rewarding   (B) gradual
(C) essential   (D) spontaneous
(E) transitory   Ⓐ Ⓑ Ⓒ Ⓓ ●

1. Just as all roads once led to Rome, all blood vessels in the human body ultimately _____ the heart.

    (A) detour around
    (B) shut off
    (C) empty into
    (D) look after
    (E) beat back

2. One of photography's most basic and powerful traits is its ability to give substance to _____, to present precise visual details of a time gone by.

    (A) romance
    (B) premonition
    (C) mysticism
    (D) invisibility
    (E) history

3. Michael purchased a season subscription to the symphony in order to gratify his _____ classical music.

    (A) predilection for
    (B) subservience to
    (C) impatience with
    (D) divergence from
    (E) reservations about

4. The president was _____ about farm subsidies, nor did he say much about the even more _____ topic of unemployment.

    (A) expansive…interesting
    (B) wordy…important
    (C) uncommunicative…academic
    (D) noncommittal…vital
    (E) enthusiastic…stimulating

5. As more people try to navigate the legal system by themselves, representing themselves in court and drawing up their own wills and contracts, the question arises whether they will be able to _____ judicial _____ without lawyers to guide them.

    (A) await…decisions
    (B) overturn…stipulations
    (C) avoid…quagmires
    (D) forfeit…penalties
    (E) arouse…enmity

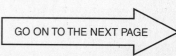

GO ON TO THE NEXT PAGE

Read the passages below, and then answer the questions that follow them. The correct response may be stated outright or merely suggested in the passages.

Questions 6–9 are based on the following passages.

Passage 1

In 1979, when the World Health Organization declared smallpox had finally been eradicated, few, if any, people recollected
Line the efforts of an eighteenth-century English
(5) aristocrat to combat the then-fatal disease. As a young woman, Lady Mary Wortley Montagu had suffered severely from smallpox. In Turkey, she observed the Eastern custom of inoculating people with a mild form of the
(10) pox, thereby immunizing them, a practice she later championed in England. The Turks, she wrote home, even held house parties during which inoculated youngsters played together happily until they came down with the pox,
(15) after which they convalesced together.

Passage 2

Who was Onesimus? New Testament students say that Onesimus was a slave converted to Christianity by the apostle Paul. In doing
Line so, they ignore the claims of another slave
(20) named Onesimus, an African, who in 1721 helped stem a smallpox epidemic threatening the city of Boston. Asked by his owner, Cotton Mather, whether he had ever had smallpox, Onesimus responded, "Yes, and no," for as a
(25) child he had been intentionally infected with smallpox in a process called inoculation and had become immune to the disease. Emboldened by Onesimus's account, Mather led a successful campaign to inoculate
(30) Bostonians against the dread disease.

6. The primary purpose of both passages is to
   (A) celebrate the total eradication of smallpox
   (B) challenge the achievements of Lady Mary Wortley Montagu
   (C) remind us that we can learn from foreign cultures
   (D) show that smallpox was a serious problem in the eighteenth century
   (E) call attention to neglected historical figures

7. According to Passage 1, Lady Mary's efforts to combat smallpox in England came about
   (A) as a direct result of her childhood exposure to the disease
   (B) as part of a World Health Organization campaign against the epidemic
   (C) in response to the migration of Turks to England
   (D) as a consequence of her travels in the East
   (E) in the face of opposition from the medical profession

8. In Passage 1, the author uses the word "even" (line 12) primarily to
   (A) exaggerate the duration of the house parties
   (B) emphasize the widespread acceptance of the procedure
   (C) indicate the most appropriate setting for treatment
   (D) encourage her readers to travel to Turkey
   (E) underscore the dangers of English methods for treating the disease

GO ON TO THE NEXT PAGE

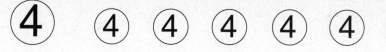

9. Lady Mary Wortley Montagu (lines 5–11, Passage 1) and Cotton Mather (lines 28–30, Passage 2) serve as examples of

(A) scientists who were authorities on epidemiology
(B) individuals who advocated a foreign medical practice
(C) travelers who brought back word of new therapeutic techniques
(D) slave owners who had the wisdom to learn from their slaves
(E) writers whose works reveal an ignorance of current medical traditions

Questions 10–15 are based on the following passage.

Largely unexplored, the canopy or treetop region of the tropical rain forest is one of the most diverse plant and animal communities on Earth. In this excerpt from a 1984 article on the rain forest canopy, the naturalist Donald R. Perry shares his research team's observations of epiphytes, unusual plants that flourish in this treetop environment.

The upper story of the rain forest, which we investigated, incorporates two-thirds of its volume. This region can be divided arbitrarily
Line into a lower canopy, extending from 10 to 25
(5) meters above the ground, an upper canopy, reaching a height of 35 meters, and an emergent zone that encompasses the tops of the tallest trees, which commonly grow to heights of more than 50 meters. The canopy is well
(10) lighted, in contrast to the forest understory, which because of thick vegetation above receives only about 1 percent of the sunlight that falls on the treetops. In the canopy all but the smallest of the rain forest trees put forth
(15) their leaves, flowers and fruit. It also contains many plants that exist entirely within its compass, forming vegetative communities that in number of species and complexity of interactions surpass any others on the earth.
(20) Among the most conspicuous features of vegetation in the canopy of the tropical rain forest are epiphytes. About 28,000 species in

65 families are known worldwide, 15,500 of them in Central and South America; they
(25) include species of orchids, bromeliads, and arboreal cacti as well as lower plants such as lichens, mosses, and ferns. Thousands more epiphyte varieties remain unidentified.

The Greek meaning of the word epiphyte
(30) is "plant that grows on a plant," and they carpet tree trunks and branches. Epiphytes sprout from seeds borne by the wind or deposited by animals, their roots holding tight to the interstices of the bark. Yet they are nonparasitic;
(35) their hosts provide them with nothing more than a favorable position in the brightly lighted canopy. For nourishment epiphytes depend on soil particles and dissolved minerals carried in rainwater, and on aerial deposits of humus. The
(40) deposits are the product of organic debris, such as dead leaves from epiphytes and other plants, that lodges among epiphyte roots.

Water is directly available to epiphytes only when it rains; other plants have continuous
(45) access to moisture trapped in the soil. As a result many epiphytes have developed features that collect and retain rainwater. Some, including orchids and arboreal cacti, have succulent stems and leaves, with spongy tissues that store
(50) water, as well as waxy leaf coatings that reduce the loss of moisture through transpiration.[1] Many orchids have bulbous stem bases; other families of epiphytes impound water in tanks formed by tight rosettes of leaves or in cups
(55) shaped by the junctions of broadened petioles[2] and stems. Some species possess absorbent, spongelike root masses that soak up and hold water. Bromeliads, a Central and South American family, can hold reserves of several
(60) gallons within their cisternlike bases, forming "arboreal swamps" that attract insects of many species, earthworms, spiders, sow bugs, scorpions, tree frogs, and insect-eating birds.

---

[1] Passage of water through a plant to the atmosphere.

[2] Slender stalks that attach a leaf to the stem.

GO ON TO THE NEXT PAGE

10. In lines 9–13, the author characterizes the floor or understory of the rain forest as relatively

   (A) insignificant
   (B) windy
   (C) thick
   (D) obscure
   (E) voluminous

11. In lines 16 and 17, "compass" most nearly means

   (A) a curved arc
   (B) an instrument for determining direction
   (C) passageway
   (D) boundaries
   (E) specifications

12. It can be inferred that which of the following is true of epiphytes?

   (A) They lack an adequate root system.
   (B) They cannot draw moisture from tree trunks.
   (C) They are incapable of transpiration.
   (D) They are hard to perceive in the dense rain forest canopy.
   (E) They originated in the Southern Hemisphere.

13. According to lines 46–48, epiphytes are particularly adapted to

   (A) independent growth
   (B) a cloudless environment
   (C) the dissipation of rainwater
   (D) drawing sustenance from a host
   (E) the retention of liquid

14. Epiphytes have direct access to water only when it rains because

   (A) they lack the ability to collect moisture
   (B) the frequency of rain keeps them excessively wet
   (C) the thick canopy protects them from rainstorms
   (D) they lack connections to water in the ground
   (E) dead leaves and other organic debris cover their roots

15. Desert cacti are likely to resemble arboreal cacti most in their

   (A) tolerance of extremes of heat and cold
   (B) dependence on tree trunks for support rather than nourishment
   (C) development of features to cut down the loss of moisture
   (D) lack of roots connecting them to the ground
   (E) absence of variations in size

Questions 16–24 are based on the following passage.

In this excerpt from the novel A Tale of Two Cities, *Charles Dickens describes the journey of a coach carrying mail and passengers to the seaport town of Dover.*

It was the Dover road that lay, on a Friday night late in November, before the first of the persons with whom this history has business.
Line The Dover road lay, as to him, beyond the
(5) Dover mail, as it lumbered up Shooter's Hill. He walked uphill in the mire by the side of the mail, as the rest of the passengers did; not because they had the least relish for walking exercise, under the circumstances, but because
(10) the hill, and the harness, and the mud, and the mail, were all so heavy, that the horses had three times already come to a stop, besides once drawing the coach across the road, with the mutinous intent of taking it back to
(15) Blackheath.
   With drooping heads and tremulous tails, the horses mashed their way through the thick mud, floundering and stumbling between whiles as if they were falling to pieces at the
(20) larger joints. As often as the driver rested them and brought them to a stand, with a wary "Wo-ho! so-ho then!" the near leader violently

GO ON TO THE NEXT PAGE

shook his head and everything upon it—like
an unusually emphatic horse, denying that the
(25) coach could be got up the hill. Whenever the
leader made this rattle, the passenger started,
as a nervous passenger might, and was dis-
turbed in mind.

There was a steaming mist in all the hol-
(30) lows, and it had roamed in its forlornness up
the hill, like an evil spirit, seeking rest and
finding none. A clammy and intensely cold
mist, it made its slow way through the air in
ripples that visibly followed and overspread
(35) one another, as the waves of an unwholesome
sea might do. It was dense enough to shut out
everything from the light of the coachlamps
but these its own workings, and a few yards of
road; and the reek of the laboring horses
(40) steamed into it, as if they had made it all.

Two other passengers, besides the one,
were plodding up the hill by the side of the
mail. All three were wrapped to the cheek-
bones and over the ears, and wore jack-boots.
(45) Not one of the three could have said, from
anything he saw, what either of the other two
was like; and each was hidden under almost as
many wrappers from the eyes of the mind, as
from the eyes of the body, of his two compan-
(50) ions. In those days, travelers were very shy of
being confidential on a short notice, for anyone on the road might be a robber or in league
with robbers. As to the latter, when every post-
ing-house and ale-house could produce some-
(55) body in "the Captain's" pay, ranging from the
landlord to the lowest stable nondescript, it
was the likeliest thing upon the cards. So the
guard of the Dover mail thought to himself,
that Friday night in November, one thousand
(60) seven hundred and seventy-five, lumbering up
Shooter's Hill, as he stood on his own particular perch behind the mail, beating his feet, and
keeping an eye and a hand on the arm-chest
before him, where a loaded blunderbuss lay at
(65) the top of six or eight loaded horse-pistols,
deposited on a substratum of cutlass.

The Dover mail was in its usual genial
position that the guard suspected the passengers, the passengers suspected one another and
(70) the guard, they all suspected everybody else,
and the coachman was sure of nothing but the
horses; as to which cattle he could with a clear
conscience have taken his oath on the two
Testaments that they were not fit for the journey.

16. It can be inferred that the passengers are
walking because

(A) they need fresh air and exercise
(B) they are afraid of being robbed
(C) their trip is over
(D) the guard is suspicious of them
(E) the coach cannot carry them uphill

17. In creating an impression of the mail coach's
uphill progress for the reader, the author uses
all of the following devices EXCEPT

(A) description of its surroundings
(B) humorous turns of phrase
(C) contrast with more attractive areas
(D) exaggerated comparisons
(E) references to geographic locations

18. The purpose cited as supporting the argument
that some brute animals are endowed with
reason most likely is

(A) the driver's intent to use the whip to moti-
vate the horses
(B) the passengers' willingness to walk by the
side of the coach
(C) the horses' determination to turn back to
Blackheath
(D) the traveler's resolve to undertake such a
rugged journey
(E) the guard's aim to quell any manifestations
of mutiny

GO ON TO THE NEXT PAGE
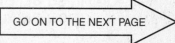

19. The passage suggests that the rattle referred to in line 26 most likely was

(A) the call of the driver to the horses to halt
(B) the clatter of the wooden wheels upon the cobblestones
(C) the jangle of the harness when the horse shook his head
(D) the creaking of the wagon's joints under the strain
(E) the sound of the coachman using his whip

20. In line 26, the word "started" most nearly means

(A) began
(B) jumped
(C) set out
(D) went first
(E) activated

21. In lines 31–36, the author includes the description of the mist primarily to emphasize the

(A) nearness of the sea
(B) weariness of the travelers
(C) gloominess of the surroundings
(D) transience of the journey
(E) lateness of the hour

22. The term "the Captain" in line 55 most likely refers to

(A) the master of a sailing ship
(B) a police officer
(C) a highwayman
(D) an innkeeper or hotel employee
(E) a town official

23. The attitude of the passengers toward one another shown in lines 67–70 can best be described as

(A) conspiratorial
(B) guarded
(C) benevolent
(D) resentful
(E) pugnacious

24. The use of the word "genial" in line 67 is an example of

(A) understatement
(B) archaism
(C) simile
(D) digression
(E) irony

STOP

IF YOU FINISH BEFORE TIME IS CALLED, YOU MAY CHECK YOUR WORK ON THIS SECTION ONLY. DO NOT WORK ON ANY OTHER SECTION IN THE TEST.

Section 5

TIME—20 MINUTES
19 QUESTIONS

For each of the following questions, select the best answer from the choices provided and fill in the appropriate circle on the answer sheet.

Each of the following sentences contains one or two blanks; each blank indicates that a word or set of words has been left out. Below the sentence are five words or phrases, lettered A through E. Select the word or set of words that best completes the sentence.

Example:

Fame is ----; today's rising star is all too soon tomorrow's washed-up has-been.

(A) rewarding   (B) gradual
(C) essential   (D) spontaneous
(E) transitory
Ⓐ Ⓑ Ⓒ Ⓓ ●

---

1. Supporters of the proposed waterway argue that it will ____ rather than ____ railroad facilities, since the waterway will be icebound during the only months when the railroads can absorb much traffic.

   (A) limit…extend
   (B) build…destroy
   (C) weaken…help
   (D) surpass…equal
   (E) supplement…threaten

2. Although he was widely celebrated as a radio and motion picture star in the 1940s, George Burns enjoyed his greatest ____ after his return to the screen in the "Oh God" films of the 1980s.

   (A) respite
   (B) collaboration
   (C) renown
   (D) disappointment
   (E) inducement

3. Despite some personal habits that most people would find repulsive, naked mole rats are ____ housekeepers.

   (A) slovenly
   (B) indifferent
   (C) meticulous
   (D) perfunctory
   (E) repugnant

4. Biography is a literary genre whose primary ____ is an ability to ____ imaginatively the inner life of a subject on the basis of all the knowable external evidence.

   (A) requisite…reconstruct
   (B) consequence…disregard
   (C) peculiarity…envision
   (D) weapon…undermine
   (E) claim…counteract

5. Many scientific discoveries are a matter of ____ : Newton was not sitting on the ground thinking about gravity when the apple dropped on his head.

   (A) serendipity
   (B) experimentation
   (C) casuistry
   (D) technology
   (E) principle

6. In prison Malcolm X set himself the task of reading straight through the dictionary; to him, reading was purposeful, not ____.

   (A) deliberate
   (B) retentive
   (C) critical
   (D) desultory
   (E) exhaustive

GO ON TO THE NEXT PAGE ⟹

The questions that follow the next two passages relate to the content of both, and to their relationship. The correct response may be stated outright in the passage or merely suggested.

Questions 7–19 are based on the following passages.

The following passages, written in the 1960s, explore the roots of anti-Japanese and anti-Jewish feelings in America during the first half of the twentieth century.

Passage 1

Prejudice, the sociologists tell us, is learned behavior. Twentieth-century Californians learned the lesson well. Although
Line racial prejudice, directed at various ethnic
(5) groups, flourished throughout the United States during the period under discussion, nowhere north of the Mason-Dixon line did any single group encounter the sustained nativist assault that was directed against
(10) California's Japanese. There seem to be four chief reasons for this. First, the Japanese were of a distinct racial group; no amount of acculturation could mask their foreignness. Second, unlike the Chinese, they rapidly began to chal-
(15) lenge whites in many businesses and professions—as a group, Japanese in the United States became very quickly imbued with what, in Europeans, would be called the Protestant ethic. Third, the growing unpopularity of their
(20) homeland . . . further served to make immigrants from Japan special objects of suspicion. These three conditions would have made any large group of Japanese a particularly despised minority anywhere in the United States.
(25) Finally, the fact that most of the Japanese were in California probably made things worse, for California probably had a lower boiling point than did the country at large.

California, by virtue of its anti-Chinese
(30) tradition and frontier psychology, was already conditioned to anti-Orientalism before the Japanese arrived. Other special California characteristics abetted the success of the agitation. In the prewar years, the extraordinary
(35) power of organized labor in northern California gave the anti-Japanese movement a much stronger base than it would have enjoyed elsewhere; in the postwar years, open-shop southern California proved almost
(40) equally hospitable to an agitation pitched to middle-class white Protestants. In the two periods anti-Japanese sentiment flourished among completely disparate populations: the first- and second-generation immigrants who
(45) were the backbone of California's labor movement, and the Midwestern émigrés who came to dominate the southern California scene. For most of these Californians, opposition to the Japanese was based upon fears which were
(50) largely nonrational.

Passage 2

To say that anti-Semitism in America sprang chiefly from the difficulties of integrating large numbers of first- and second-generation immigrants is, inferentially, to stress its
(55) similarity to other kinds of anti-immigrant sentiment—to put it in the same class with dislike of the Irish, Italians, Japanese, Mexicans and other transplanted minorities, while making allowances for the differential
(60) characteristics of each group. Likewise, this approach minimizes distinctions often made between different kinds of anti-Semitism, in that it relates all of them to a common root. Yet we must also consider the role of irrational
(65) anti-Semitic fantasies that had no direct connection with real problems of ethnic integration. The ideological hatreds spread by the agitator and the fanatic have had a place in American history, too.

GO ON TO THE NEXT PAGE

(70)   Unlike . . . more ordinary social prejudices
. . . , ideological anti-Semitism condemns the
Jews as incapable of assimilation and disloyal
to the basic institutions of the country. In its
more extreme forms, it portrays them as
(75) leagued together in a vast international con-
spiracy. The alleged plot usually centers on
gaining control of the money supply and
wrecking the financial system; sometimes it
extends to polluting the nation's morals
(80) through control of communications and entertainment. The supposed eventual aim is to
overthrow the government and establish a
superstate. In America, anti-Semitism of this
kind has not been so well organized or so pro-
(85) ductive of violence as other racial and religious phobias. But it has enjoyed an unusually
rich and complex imagery.
      Religious motifs, by and large, have not
figured prominently in American anti-Semitic
(90) thought. Except among certain preachers
spawned by the Fundamentalist movement of
the 1920s (notably Gerald Winrod and Gerald
L. K. Smith), one looks in vain for a clearly
religious animus. Though not entirely lacking
(95) in references to the treachery of Judas, ideological anti-Semitism has always dwelled
mainly on the power of Shylock. Whether the
Jew appears in his traditional role as exploiter
or in his later incarnation as Bolshevik, his
(100) subversive influence supposedly flows from
an unwillingness or inability to abide by the
existing economic morality.

7. The author of Passage 1 makes the point that
prejudice against the Japanese in the twentieth
century

(A) began in California
(B) was comparable to racial prejudice in the
South
(C) was taught in the schools of California
(D) often bred violence
(E) was a shameful chapter in the history of
California

8. Passage 1 implies that the Japanese would not
have faced such intense prejudice if

(A) their physical appearance had been different
(B) they had arrived in California via New York
(C) they had emigrated to California a century
earlier
(D) they had settled in southern California
(E) Californians had themselves been recent
immigrants

9. Passage 1 suggests that, after Japanese immigrants arrived in California, they

(A) joined unions
(B) often went on welfare until they got jobs
(C) created Japanese ghettos in several cities
(D) worked hard to be successful
(E) contributed technical skills to the state's
work force.

10. According to information in Passage 1, World
War II

(A) provided California's Japanese population
temporary relief from prejudice
(B) caused prejudice against the Japanese to
intensify
(C) had little impact on prejudice against the
Japanese
(D) diverted the hatred from Japanese civilians
to the Japanese military
(E) shifted the center of anti-Japanese feeling
in California

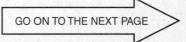 GO ON TO THE NEXT PAGE

11. One can infer from Passage 1 that hostility toward the Japanese flourished in California because

(A) California was closer to Pearl Harbor than any other state
(B) Californians are more intolerant than other Americans
(C) Japan-bashing was an official policy of the labor unions in the state
(D) Japanese were quickly buying up buildings, land, and other property throughout the state
(E) American workers felt threatened by Japanese workers

12. The author of Passage 2 believes that anti-Semitism in America differs from other forms of prejudice because

(A) it is based on a long tradition
(B) anti-Semites tend to be more hateful than other types of bigots
(C) most anti-Semites are fanatics
(D) it comes in many forms and guises
(E) each ethnic minority experiences prejudice in a different way

13. The term "ideological hatreds" (line 67–69) refers to prejudice

(A) only against Jews
(B) that is openly declared in public
(C) that existed in an earlier era
(D) that is inspired by the victims' beliefs and values
(E) that has gone out of control

14. The author of Passage 2 implies that violence against Jews in the United States has been

(A) fed by social anti-Semitism rather than ideological anti-Semitism
(B) has been directed mostly at first-generation Jewish immigrants
(C) has helped other minorities to cope with violence against them
(D) has been more verbal and psychological than physical
(E) has been less severe than violence against other minorities

15. Passage 2 indicates that avid anti-Semites fear Jews for all of the following reasons EXCEPT that

(A) it is hard to tell a Jew from a non-Jew
(B) Jews crave power
(C) Jews are immoral
(D) the media are controlled by Jews
(E) Jews do not value democracy

16. Gerald Winrod and Gerald L. K. Smith (lines 92 and 93) are cited as anti-Semites

(A) who advocated the violent treatment of Jews
(B) whose hatred of Jews was based largely on religion
(C) who sought to convert Jews to Christianity
(D) who alleged that Jews were a danger to the United States
(E) who founded the Christian Fundamentalist movement in the United States

GO ON TO THE NEXT PAGE

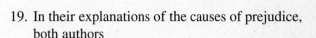

17. Based on the two passages, it is fair to say that prejudice against the Jews in the United States compared to prejudice against the Japanese

 (A) has been more violent
 (B) has been more strenuously opposed by fair-minded people
 (C) is more complex and diffuse
 (D) has a longer history
 (E) has increased at a greater rate since World War II

18. The authors of both passages appear to agree that

 (A) prejudice in the United States is gradually diminishing
 (B) prejudice in the United States is gradually increasing
 (C) prejudice is based on irrational thinking
 (D) physical appearance is a major cause of prejudice against both Jews and Japanese
 (E) stereotypes are hard to break

19. In their explanations of the causes of prejudice, both authors

 (A) stress economic reasons
 (B) focus on the historical roots of prejudice in America
 (C) are hopeful that justice will eventually prevail
 (D) agree that the Japanese and the Jews have been scapegoats
 (E) think that extreme nationalism may lie at the heart of bigotry

STOP

IF YOU FINISH BEFORE TIME IS CALLED, YOU MAY CHECK YOUR WORK ON THIS SECTION ONLY. DO NOT WORK ON ANY OTHER SECTION IN THE TEST.

Section 6

TIME—10 MINUTES
14 QUESTIONS
For each of the following questions, select the best answer from the choices provided and fill in the appropriate circle on the answer sheet.

Some or all parts of the following sentences are underlined. The first answer choice, (A), simply repeats the underlined part of the sentence. The other four choices present four alternative ways to phrase the underlined part. Select the answer that produces the most effective sentence, one that is clear and exact, and blacken the appropriate space on your answer sheet. In selecting your choice, be sure that it is standard written English, and that it expresses the meaning of the original sentence.

Example:

The first biography of author Eudora Welty came out in 1998 and she was 89 years old at the time.

(A) and she was 89 years old at the time
(B) at the time she was 89
(C) upon becoming an 89 year old
(D) when she was 89
(E) at the age of 89 years old

Ⓐ Ⓑ Ⓒ ● Ⓔ

1. Into her shopping basket she placed her favorite vegetables, an assortment of fresh fruit, and she included a loaf of French bread.

(A) and she included a loaf of French bread
(B) and a loaf of French bread
(C) and she also included a loaf of French bread
(D) a loaf of French bread as well
(E) and she includes a loaf of French bread

2. Heather Hurst's paintings and architectural renderings of the pre-Columbian Americas not only recover records that were previously lost, but these are works of art in their own right.

(A) not only recover records that were previously lost, but these are works of art
(B) not only recover records that had been previously lost, but these are works of art
(C) not only recover previously lost records but also are works of art
(D) do not recover only records that were previously lost, but these are works of art
(E) not only recovers records that were previously lost, but they are works of art

3. Today, among twentieth-century artists, Salvador Dali's renown is probably exceeded only by Picasso.

(A) artists, Salvador Dali's renown is probably exceeded only by Picasso
(B) artists, Salvador Dali is probably exceeded in renown only by Picasso's
(C) artists, Salvador Dali's renown is probably exceeded only by Picasso's
(D) artists, Salvador Dali is only exceeded in renown probably by only Picasso
(E) artists, Salvador Dali's renown is only probably exceeded by Picasso's

GO ON TO THE NEXT PAGE ⟹

4. So many of the internal workings of the lungs change at night that lung diseases, particularly <u>asthma, has become the best studied of the nighttime illnesses</u>.

   (A) asthma, has become the best studied of the nighttime illnesses
   (B) asthma, has become the best studied nighttime illnesses
   (C) asthma, has become the better studied of the nighttime illnesses
   (D) asthma, have become the best studied of the nighttime illnesses
   (E) asthma, have been becoming the better studied out of all the nighttime illness

5. <u>There are a long list of causes of air pollution,</u> ranging from automobile exhaust to methane emissions from livestock.

   (A) There are a long list of causes of air pollution,
   (B) There were a long list of things causing air pollution,
   (C) There are a lengthy list of causes of air pollution,
   (D) There have been a long list of causes of air pollution,
   (E) There is a long list of causes of air pollution,

6. <u>Acupuncture has been widely used for years to ease chronic pain conditions, studies</u> have repeatedly endorsed its usefulness.

   (A) Acupuncture has been widely used for years to ease chronic pain conditions, studies
   (B) Although acupuncture having been been widely used for years to ease chronic pain conditions, studies
   (C) Acupuncture has been widely used for years to ease chronic pain conditions, and studies
   (D) Due to the fact that acupuncture has been widely used for years to ease chronic pain conditions, studies
   (E) Because acupuncture has been widely used for years to ease chronic pain conditions is the reason why studies

7. Lower Manhattan was a seasonal home for the Lenni Lenape <u>Indians, who granted the Dutch settlers land-use rights to Manhattan, but</u> did not actually sell it for $24 in trinkets.

   (A) Indians, who granted the Dutch settlers land-use rights to Manhattan, but
   (B) Indians, which granted the Dutch settlers land-use rights to Manhattan, but
   (C) Indians, who granted the Dutch settlers land-use rights to Manhattan, however they
   (D) Indians, and they granted the Dutch settlers land-use rights to Manhattan, but
   (E) Indians, where they granted the Dutch settlers land-use rights to Manhattan; but they

8. From papayas in Hawaii to canola in Canada, the spread of pollen or seeds from genetically engineered <u>plants are evolving from an abstract scientific worry into</u> a significant practical problem.

   (A) plants are evolving from an abstract scientific worry into
   (B) plants are evolving from an abstractly scientific worry into
   (C) plants are in process of evolving from an abstract scientific worry into
   (D) plants is evolving from an abstract scientific worry into
   (E) plants having evolved from an abstract scientific worry into

9. <u>After removing their skins,</u> the children sliced the carrots into sticks for dipping.

   (A) After removing their skins,
   (B) After they removed their skins,
   (C) After they had removed their skins,
   (D) After removing the carrots' skins,
   (E) After they had removed the skins from the carrots,

GO ON TO THE NEXT PAGE

⑥   ⑥ ⑥ ⑥ ⑥ ⑥ ⑥ ⑥ ⑥ ⑥ ⑥

10. Opinion polls show the public <u>has about as dim a view of pharmaceutical companies as tobacco companies</u>.

 (A) has about as dim a view of pharmaceutical companies as tobacco companies
 (B) have about as dim a view of pharmaceutical companies as tobacco companies
 (C) has about as dim a view of pharmaceutical companies as it does of tobacco companies
 (D) has almost so dim a view of pharmaceutical companies as of tobacco companies
 (E) has approximately as dim a view of pharmaceutical companies as tobacco companies

11. The adjacent homes were dissimilar enough <u>to justify their radically different prices</u>.

 (A) to justify their radically different prices
 (B) to justify its radically different prices
 (C) to be justified by their radically different prices
 (D) to justify there radically different prices
 (E) to be a justification for their radically different prices

12. The pale white petals of the gardenia possess a scent of great sweetness and <u>subtlety and the scent has</u> intrigued many perfume-makers.

 (A) subtlety and the scent has
 (B) subtlety, that being the reason why the scent has
 (C) subtlety, but the scent has
 (D) subtlety, a scent that has
 (E) subtlety, it has

13. <u>Attempting to maximize the income-producing potential of her pension plan by investing a substantial amount</u> in so-called junk bonds.

 (A) Attempting to maximize the income-producing potential of her pension plan by investing a substantial amount
 (B) Attempting to maximize the income-producing potential of her pension plan by substantially investing an amount
 (C) She made an attempt to produce the maximum potentiality in income out of her pension plan and she invested a substantial amount
 (D) In an attempt to produce the maximum income-producing potential from her pension plan by investing a substantial amount
 (E) She attempted to maximize the income-producing potential of her pension plan by investing a substantial amount

14. <u>Seldom do the barriers between the races seem less in evidence than on this league-leading high school football team</u>.

 (A) Seldom do the barriers between the races seem less in evidence than on this league-leading high school football team
 (B) More so than on other teams, they seem to be less evident barriers between the races on this league-leading high school football team
 (C) On this league-leading high school football team, more so than on other teams, the barriers between the races are less in evidence, it seems
 (D) The barriers between the races do seem fewer in evidence seldom on this league-leading high school football team
 (E) Seldom less than on this league-leading high school football team does the barriers between the races seem less in evidence

STOP

IF YOU FINISH BEFORE TIME IS CALLED, YOU MAY CHECK YOUR WORK ON THIS SECTION ONLY. DO NOT WORK ON ANY OTHER SECTION IN THE TEST.

ANSWER KEY

Section 2

1.	C	5.	D	9.	E	13.	D	17.	C
2.	D	6.	B	10.	B	14.	D	18.	B
3.	C	7.	C	11.	A	15.	C	19.	A
4.	E	8.	B	12.	C	16.	D	20.	E

21.	A
22.	E
23.	B
24.	E

Section 3

1.	D	7.	D	13.	E	19.	D	25.	D	31.	D
2.	A	8.	C	14.	A	20.	B	26.	E	32.	B
3.	E	9.	A	15.	A	21.	C	27.	B	33.	A
4.	C	10.	C	16.	C	22.	D	28.	D	34.	E
5.	C	11.	D	17.	C	23.	D	29.	E	35.	C
6.	A	12.	A	18.	E	24.	A	30.	D		

Section 4

1.	C	5.	C	9.	B	13.	E	17.	C	21.	C
2.	E	6.	E	10.	D	14.	D	18.	C	22.	C
3.	A	7.	D	11.	D	15.	C	19.	C	23.	B
4.	D	8.	B	12.	B	16.	E	20.	B	24.	E

Section 5

1.	E	5.	A	9.	D	13.	D	17.	C
2.	C	6.	D	10.	E	14.	A	18.	C
3.	C	7.	B	11.	E	15.	A	19.	A
4.	A	8.	A	12.	D	16.	B		

Section 6

1.	B	5.	E	9.	D	13.	E
2.	C	6.	C	10.	C	14.	A
3.	C	7.	A	11.	A		
4.	D	8.	D	12.	D		

ANALYSIS OF TEST RESULTS

I. Check your answers against the answer key.

II. Fill in the following chart.

Sentence Completion Number Correct _____	Section 1 (Questions 1–8) _____			Section 4 (Questions 1–5) _____	Section 5 (Questions 1–6) _____		Total _____
Reading Comprehension Number Correct _____	Section 2 (Questions 9–24) _____			Section 4 (Questions 6–24) _____	Section 5 (Questions 7–19) _____		Total _____
Sentence Improvement Number Correct _____		Section 3 (Questions 1–11) _____				Section 6 (Questions 1–14) _____	Total _____
Error Identification Number Correct _____		Section 3 (Questions 12–29) _____					Total _____
Paragraph Improvement Number Correct _____		Section 3 (Questions 30–35) _____					Total _____

III. Interpret your results.

Sentence Completion   Number Correct _____

Reading Comprehension   Number Correct _____

Sentence Improvement   Number Correct _____

Error Identification   Number Correct _____

Paragraph Improvement   Number Correct _____

Subtotal _____

Guessing Penalty: Subtract 1/4 point for each incorrect answer. _____
(Do not take off points for questions you left blank.)

TOTAL SCORE _____

	Sentence Completion Score	Reading Comprehension Score	Total
Excellent	18–19 Correct	43–48 Correct	60–67
Very Good	14–17 Correct	33–42 Correct	46–59
Good	11–13 Correct	25–32 Correct	35–45
Fair	9–10 Correct	20–24 Correct	28–34
Poor	6–8 Correct	12–19 Correct	17–27
Very Poor	0–5 Correct	0–11 Correct	0–16

	Sentence Improvement Score	Error Identification Score	Paragraph Improvement Score	Total
Excellent	21–25 Correct	13–18 Correct	6 Correct	38–49
Very Good	15–20 Correct	10–12 Correct	5 Correct	28–37
Good	8–14 Correct	7–9 Correct	4 Correct	17–27
Fair	5–7 Correct	5–6 Correct	2–3 Correct	11–16
Poor	3–4 Correct	3–4 Correct	1 Correct	5–10
Very Poor	0–2 Correct	0–2 Correct	0 Correct	0–4

SCORE YOUR OWN SAT ESSAY

Use this table as you rate your performance on the essay-writing section of this model test. Circle the phrase that most accurately describes your work. Enter the numbers in the scoring chart below. Add the numbers together and divide by 6 to determine your total score. The higher your total score, the better you are likely to do on the essay section of the SAT.

Note that on the actual SAT two readers will rate your essay; your essay score will be the sum of their two ratings and could range from 12 (highest) to 2 (lowest). Also, they will grade your essay holistically, rating it on the basis of their overall impression of its effectiveness. They will *not* analyze it piece by piece, giving separate grades for grammar, vocabulary level, and so on. Therefore, you cannot expect the score you give yourself on this model test to predict your eventual score on the SAT with any great degree of accuracy. Use this scoring guide instead to help you assess your writing strengths and weaknesses, so that you can decide which areas to focus on as you prepare for the SAT.

Like most people, you may find it difficult to rate your own writing objectively. Ask a teacher or fellow student to score your essay as well. With his or her help you should gain added insights into writing your 25-minute essay.

	6	5	4	3	2	1
POSITION ON THE TOPIC	Clear, convincing, & insightful	Fundamentally clear & coherent	Fairly clear & coherent	Insufficiently clear	Largely unclear	Extremely unclear
ORGANIZATION OF EVIDENCE	Well organized, with strong, relevant examples	Generally well organized, with apt examples	Adequately organized, with some examples	Sketchily developed, with weak examples	Lacking focus and evidence	Unfocused and disorganized
SENTENCE STRUCTURE	Varied, appealing sentences	Reasonably varied sentences	Some variety in sentences	Little variety in sentences	Errors in sentence structure	Severe errors in sentence structure
LEVEL OF VOCABULARY	Mature & apt word choice	Competent word choice	Adequate word choice	Inappropriate or weak vocabulary	Highly limited vocabulary	Rudimentary
GRAMMAR AND USAGE	Almost entirely free of errors	Relatively free of errors	Some technical errors	Minor errors and some major ones	Numerous major errors	Extensive severe errors
OVERALL EFFECT	Outstanding	Effective	Adequately competent	Inadequate, but shows some potential	Seriously flawed	Fundamentally deficient

Self-Scoring Chart

For each of the following categories, rate the essay from 1 (lowest) to 6 (highest)

Position on the Topic   _____

Organization of Evidence   _____

Sentence Structure   _____

Level of Vocabulary   _____

Grammar and Usage   _____

Overall Effect   _____

TOTAL   _____

(To get a score, divide the total by 6)   _____

Scoring Chart (Second Reader)

For each of the following categories, rate the essay from 1 (lowest) to 6 (highest)

Position on the Topic   _____

Organization of Evidence   _____

Sentence Structure   _____

Level of Vocabulary   _____

Grammar and Usage   _____

Overall Effect   _____

TOTAL   _____

(To get a score, divide the total by 6)   _____

ANSWER EXPLANATIONS

SECTION 2

1. **C**   Given the examples listed, the administration seems unusually considerate of or *attentive to* the well-being of its employees.

2. **D**   By definition, an assemblyman's *constituents* are the voters who belong to the district he represents.

3. **C**   If trees have adapted to survive short, mild winters, then they're not likely to do well in harsh winters with extreme temperature changes. In fact, they will prove *vulnerable to* (defenseless against) cold snaps and sudden thaws.

4. **E**   Unlike a contemporary feminist, Abigail Adams *accepted* the then-*traditional* view of the roles of women and men.
      The second clause of the sentence serves to explain in what way Abigail Adams was unlike feminists today.

5. **D**   The author is making highly negative comments, ones that go beyond being casually dismissive (indifferent or disapproving) to being bluntly *contemptuous* (scornful).

6. **B**   Though people assumed Doisneau's pictures were unposed, he *acknowledged* (admitted) he had staged some shots that were supposed to have been *candid* (informal, unposed).

7. **C**   The *jovial*-appearing Cory used a mask of lightheartedness to *camouflage* or disguise his underlying depression.

8. **B**   Someone insecure would be likely to *construe* (interpret) disagreement as *betrayal* (disloyalty).

9. **E**   In stating that it took a *remarkable* set of circumstances, even a war, for people to be able to read Egyptian hieroglyphs, the passage emphasizes or underscores the discovery's *unusual background*.

10. **B**   Using exclamation points and terming the discovery *providential* (highly opportune or miraculous), the author clearly conveys her excitement about the topic. Her tone is *enthusiastic*.

11. **A**   The human faculty for myth is our *capacity* or ability to invent legends.

12. **C**   The fact that we remember Raleigh more for a romantic, perhaps apocryphal gesture than for his military victories and voyages of exploration serves to *illustrate how legendary events outshine historical achievements in the public's mind*.

13. **D**   The author tells or *narrates* what happens during the period of time just before the conductor gives the upbeat to signal the orchestra to begin.

14. **D**   The opening of the first paragraph states that "the qualities that distinguish *great* conductors," the qualities about which the author is going to speak, "lie far beyond and above what we have spoken of." Clearly, he has just been speaking of other qualities that conductors must possess. However, these are not the high, artistic skills that one needs to be a great conductor. They are merely *the technical skills needed to be a reasonably competent conductor*.

15. **C**   The magic moment for beginning a piece of music is the moment that "feels exactly right" (lines 10 and 11). The conductor's decision is based on instinct, on feelings, not on logic; it is *intuitive*.

16. **D**   The author does not mean we are literally trapped or captive; he is being *figurative* or metaphorical.

17. **C**   Throughout the passage, the author uses different approaches to give the reader an idea of the nature of just what a conductor does. Here, he compares a conductor's working with time to a sculptor's working with physical blocks of stone. He does this to *help the reader get an image of the conductor's work*.

18. **B**   "Mold" here is a *fixed pattern* or shape.

19. **A**   The author states that "no conductor can learn or acquire" the mysteries or most important attributes of conducting. The "natural faculty for deep perception" is inborn or *innate*.

20. **E** The author looks on the baton as a tool he uses to help him communicate with the orchestra, in other words, as *a tool for transmitting meaning*.

(A) is incorrect. The author does not consider the baton either necessary (he can gesture equally clearly with his hands) or evil.

(B) is incorrect. The author is not talking about the baton as a symbol; he is talking about it as an instrument that gets used.

(C) is incorrect. In talking of the baton's being "charged with a kind of electricity," the author is being figurative, not literal. He does not literally look on the baton as an electrical appliance or tool.

(D) is incorrect. The author never states a preference for one means of communication over the other.

21. **A** The author suggests a variety of things the conductor can do to get a performance out of the musicians—cajoling (coaxing), demanding, raging. Clearly he believes conductors *must do whatever it takes to motivate* the musicians to want to perform.

22. **E** The author is talking about projecting his feelings, conveying his emotions so vividly and intensely that they reach each and every one of his hundred musicians, no matter where in the orchestra they are. Thus, in singling out the "last" player, the one farthest back, in the "second" violin section, the section behind the first violins, he is emphasizing *the distance across which the conductor must communicate*.

23. **B** The author's concern is for the orchestra to learn to function as a whole. He views the temperamental behavior of conductors—ranting, cursing, insulting musicians—with *tolerance*, accepting these actions as either unimportant personal quirks on the part of the conductor or tactical moves in the conductor's grand design to stimulate the musicians to play at their best.

24. **E** In dedicating himself to "the service of the composer's meaning" (lines 129–132), the conductor is laboring to maintain *the integrity of the musical piece* in accordance with the composer's design.

SECTION 3

1. **D** Wordiness. Choice D makes the writer's point simply and concisely.
2. **A** Sentence is correct. Remember: the subject's grammatical number is not changed by the addition of a phrase that begins with *along with, together with,* or a similar expression. The subject, *coach,* is singular. The verb should be singular as well.
3. **E** Run-on sentence. Choice E eliminates the original comma splice to produce a balanced sentence.
4. **C** Error in logical comparison. Compare veterans with veterans, not veterans with wars.
5. **C** Misplaced modifier. Who are acting suspiciously? Not the bags, but the people who packed them!
6. **A** Sentence is correct.
7. **D** Error in logical comparison. Compare prices with prices, not prices with cities.
8. **C** Error in pronoun-antecedent agreement. The subject of the sentence is *inoculations* (plural). The pronoun should be plural as well. In this particular instance, the plural pronoun *they* has been replaced by the noun phrase *such inoculations*.
9. **A** Sentence is correct.
10. **C** Error in subordination. The use of the conjunction *Although* in choice C signals the contrast between what one might have expected (i.e., that the prospectors, who arrived in 1848, would become known as the forty-eighters) and what actually took place (they became known as the forty-niners instead).
11. **D** Misplaced appositional phrase. Who was once a leading light of the Harlem Renaissance? Clearly, Hurston was. Choice D correctly positions the word being described (Hurston) closer to the descriptive phrase.
12. **A** Error in pronoun case. Change *I* to *me*.
13. **E** Sentence is correct.
14. **A** Adjective-adverb confusion. Change *surprising* to *surprisingly*.

15. **A**   Error in usage. *Irregardless* is nonstandard. Replace it with *Regardless*.

16. **C**   Error in idiomatic usage. Change *vulnerable for* to *vulnerable to*.

17. **C**   Error in usage. The phrase *cannot hardly* is a double negative. Replace it with *can hardly*.

18. **E**   Sentence is correct.

19. **D**   Lack of parallelism. Change *arranged music for* to *a musical arranger for*.

20. **B**   Error in usage. The graders must remember *that* the students have little time in which to write.

21. **C**   Error in subject-verb agreement. Do not be distracted by nouns or pronouns coming between subjects and verbs. The subject is *sighting* (singular); the verb should be singular as well. Change *have thrilled* to *has thrilled*.

22. **D**   Error in pronoun case. The object of the preposition b*etween* should be in the objective case. Change *daughter and I* to *daughter and me*.

23. **D**   Error in comparison. Use the comparative degree for two persons or things. Change *greatest* to *greater*.

24. **A**   Adjective-adverb confusion. Use adverbs to modify adjectives. Change *rapid changing* to *rapidly changing*.

25. **D**   Error in logical comparison. Compare percentages with percentages, not percentages with senior citizens. Change *to senior citizens* to *to that of senior citizens*.

26. **E**   Sentence is correct.

27. **B**   Error in pronoun choice. Avoid shifting from one pronoun to another within a single sentence. Change *you are* to *one is*.

28. **D**   Error in logical comparison. Compare dances with dances, not dances with Balanchine. Change *George Balanchine* to *those of George Balanchine*.

29. **E**   Sentence is correct.

30. **D**   Choices A, B, and C abruptly state the contrasting point of view without regard to the context. Choice D takes the context into account and provides for a smooth progression of thought. It is the best answer.
Choice E is confusing. It is unclear until the end of the sentence whether the *other members* support or oppose the exhibit.

31. **D**   Choice A is not consistent in style and mood with the rest of the paragraph.
Choice B is a sentence fragment.
Choice C is excessively wordy.
Choice D fits the context of the paragraph and expresses the idea correctly. It is the best answer.
Choice E inappropriately uses *in conclusion* and contains the pronoun *it*, which lacks a specific antecedent.

32. **B**   Choice A lacks a main verb; therefore, it is a sentence fragment.
Choice B accurately combines the sentences. It is the best answer.
Choice C expresses the idea in a way that the writer could not have intended.
Choice D subordinates important ideas and emphasizes a lesser one.
Choice E restates the idea in a manner that changes the writer's intended meaning.

33. **A**   Choice A is the best answer because sentences 10–12 contain basic information about the topic. Readers are left in the dark unless the information appears as early as possible in the essay.

34. **E**   Choice A contains a faulty idiom; the phrase *than of the past* is nonstandard usage.
Choice B contains a faulty comparison; *society* and *the past* cannot be logically compared.
Choice C contains an error in idiom; *than from* is redundant.
Choice D is correct but excessively wordy.
Choice E is the best answer.

35. **C**   Choice A provides a reasonable transition, but it contains an error in pronoun-antecedent agreement. The pronoun *they* is plural; its antecedent *anyone* is singular.
Choice B contains an error in diction. One can *disapprove of* but not *disagree with* a piece of art.
Choice C alludes to the content of the preceding paragraph and is clearly and succinctly expressed. It is the best answer.

Choice D contains an error in pronoun-antecedent agreement. The pronoun *them* is plural; the antecedent *anyone* is singular.

Choice E is inconsistent in tone and mood with the rest of the essay.

SECTION 4

1. **C** To complete the comparison, in the same way that the roads all led to the city of Rome, the heart of the Roman Empire, the blood vessels all lead to or *empty into* the heart.

2. **E** To give the visual details of past events is to make *history* real to people.

3. **A** A *predilection* or fondness *for* classical music could well lead someone to subscribe to the symphony for a season.

4. **D** The president did not say much about farm subsidies: he was *noncommittal*, taking no clear position on this important issue. He also did not say much about the more important or *vital* issue of unemployment.

    (C) is incorrect. While it would be possible in this context to describe the president as *uncommunicative* about farm subsidies, it would be inaccurate to describe the critical issue of unemployment as merely *academic* (theoretical; of no practical significance).

5. **C** In navigating tricky legal waters, one hopes to be able to *avoid* judicial *quagmires* (marshes; swamps) in which one might bog down.

6. **E** The opening sentence of Passage 1 states that few, if any, people recalled Lady Mary's efforts to fight smallpox. Her efforts have largely been forgotten. Likewise, the opening sentences of Passage 2 assert that some people "ignore the claims" of the African slave Onesimus, who played a small but important part in the battle against the deadly disease. Thus, both passages attempt to *call attention to neglected historical figures*.

7. **D** Without her travels in the East, where she encountered the Eastern custom of inoculation, Lady Mary would not have been inspired to bring back this custom to England. Thus, her smallpox-fighting efforts in England came about *as a consequence of her travels in the East*.

8. **B** Not only did the Turks practice the custom of inoculation, they "even" held house parties so that inoculated youngsters could convalesce in company and in comfort. Clearly the procedure enjoyed *widespread acceptance*.

9. **B** Both Montagu and Mather *advocated* inoculation, a *foreign medical practice* well-known in Turkey and in parts of Africa.

10. **D** The shadowy, gloomy understory is dimly lit or *obscure*.

11. **D** The plants that exist only within the compass of the canopy live within its *boundaries*.

12. **B** The tree trunks provide the epiphytes only with a good location up in the canopy. Being nonparasitic, epiphytes *cannot draw moisture* (or any nourishment whatsoever) *from tree trunks*.

13. **E** Having developed features that collect and retain rainwater, epiphytes clearly are particularly well suited to the *retention* (holding; storing up) *of liquid*.

14. **D** Because epiphytes do not sink their roots into the earth, *they lack connections* to the earth and thus do not have direct access *to water in the ground*. They have direct access to water only when it rains.

15. **C** Both desert cacti and arboreal cacti grow in environments in which access to moisture is difficult to achieve. The desert cacti lack access to moisture because the amount of rainfall in desert regions is minimal and little moisture exists in the soil. The arboreal cacti lack access to moisture because they grow high up in the canopy with no root connections to the soil. Thus, both kinds of cacti have had to develop *features to cut down* or reduce *the loss of moisture*.

16. **E** The passengers are walking because the coach cannot carry them uphill. Note that the horses have already come to a stop three times.

17. **C** The author describes the immediate, rather unwholesome area. However, he never *contrasts it with more attractive areas*.

18. **C**   Given the inclement weather, the muddy footing, and the uphill struggle, the fact that *the horses* (brute animals) *strongly attempted to turn back to Blackheath* suggests that they were more reasonable creatures than the humans who forced them to struggle on.

19. **C**   The lead horse *shook his head* and everything upon it, that is, his head and his harness, which made a rattling noise.

20. **B**   It is not surprising that, at the sudden, emphatic noise the nervous passenger started or *jumped*.

21. **C**   All the descriptive terms in the paragraph—mist "like an evil spirit," "waves of an unwholesome sea," fog "dense enough to shut out everything from the light"—emphasize the *gloominess* and dark melancholy of the scene.

22. **C**   The sentence that immediately precedes the reference to the Captain maintains that anyone on the road might be in league with robbers, that is, might be a robber's accomplice or confederate. Thus, to be in the Captain's pay means to be a robber's paid accomplice, and the Captain is clearly a highway robber or *highwayman*.

23. **B**   Viewing one another with suspicion, the passengers maintain a *guarded* or wary stance.

24. **E**   By definition, *genial* means cordial or friendly. However, the situation shown here is grim and unfriendly rather than genial. Thus, the word is being used in an *ironic*, unexpected way.

SECTION 5

1. **E**   Currently, the railroads can take on additional shipping only during the winter; at other times of the year, they can't absorb any more traffic. During the winter months the waterway could not take traffic away from the railroads (an icebound waterway is useless as a route for traffic). Thus, those in favor of the waterway argue that it will *supplement* or be a desirable addition to railroad facilities and will not *threaten* or endanger the railroads.

2. **C**   George Burns had even greater celebrity or *renown* in the 1980s than he had known in the 1940s.

3. **C**   "Despite" signals the contrast between the mole rat's repulsive, disgusting habits and its *meticulous*, painstakingly careful cleaning of its burrow.

4. **A**   It is a major *requisite* (requirement or necessity) of the genre that the biographer be able to *reconstruct* or mentally build up again his or her subject's inner life.

5. **A**   The dictionary defines *serendipity* as good luck, and aptitude for making valuable discoveries by accident. Newton's discovery of the law of gravity is a classic example of serendipity at work.

6. **D**   The opposite of a purposeful, determined action is a *desultory*, aimless one.
         "Not" is a contrast signal. The missing word must be an antonym or near-antonym for "purposeful."

7. **B**   In the first paragraph the author, by likening the prejudice against the Japanese to the prejudice below the Mason-Dixon line, argues that anti-Japanese feeling *was comparable to racial prejudice in the South*.

8. **A**   The intensity of anti-Japanese feeling is explained in part by the fact that the Japanese "were of a distinct racial group; no amount of acculturation could mask their foreignness" (lines 11–13). Logically, then, had *their physical appearance been different*, they might not have experienced such intense hatred.

9. **D**   Among the causes of prejudice against the Japanese was the rapidity with which the Japanese immigrants adopted the so-called Protestant ethic, which includes the notion that you must *work hard to be successful*.

10. **E**   Before the war, anti-Japanese feelings were most intense in northern California. Afterward, southern California became the locus of prejudice. World War II, then, *shifted the center of anti-Japanese feeling*.

11. **E**   The passage explains that labor unions provided the base of the anti-Japanese movement. Presumably, labor unions voiced their opposition because members felt that their jobs were being *threatened by Japanese workers*.

12. **D**   The author of Passage 2 cautions readers not to confuse anti-Semitism with other forms of anti-immigrant sentiment, but to be mindful of "different kinds of anti-Semitism." The passage then describes *many forms and guises* (appearances) of anti-Semitism.

13. **D**   The author refers to ideological anti-Semitism as that which has "no direct connection with . . . ethnic integration." In other words, it is hatred of others' assumed *beliefs and values*, such as the anti-Semitic notion cited in the passage that Jews want to take control of the United States.

14. **A**   According to the passage, ideological anti-Semitism has not been as "productive of violence as other racial and religious phobias." When violence has occurred, therefore, it has been inspired or *fed by social anti-Semitism.*

15. **A**   The second paragraph of the passage lists several explanations for hatred of Jews, but not that *it is hard to tell a Jew from a non-Jew.*

16. **B**   In the third paragraph Winrod and Smith are cited as examples of anti-Semites *whose hatred of Jews was based largely on religion.* As the passage says, except for Winrod and Smith, "one looks in vain for a clearly religious animus" to explain anti-Semitic feelings.

17. **C**   The first passage pinpoints California as the center of anti-Japanese feeling and gives several precise explanations for its growth in that state. In contrast, Passage 2 portrays anti-Semitism as a *more complex and diffuse* (widespread) form of bigotry. It describes various reasons for anti-Semitism and fails to identify a place or region where it is concentrated.

18. **C**   Both authors cite *irrational thinking* as the cause of prejudice. The first says the "opposition to the Japanese was based upon fears which were largely nonrational" (lines 47–50), while the second refers to the role played by "irrational anti-Semitic fantasies" (lines 64–67).

19. **A**   *Economic reasons* dominate both authors' explanations of prejudice. The Japanese were hated for challenging whites in many businesses and professions, for working hard, and for competing with American workers for jobs. Jews were accused of plotting to take control of America's money supply, wrecking the financial system, and taking over the communications and entertainment industries.

SECTION 6

1. **B**   Lack of parallelism. Choice B demonstrates proper parallel structure.

2. **C**   Lack of parallelism. The correlatives, *not only ... but also*, typically connect parallel structures. Choice C reflects the appropriate parallel construction.

3. **C**   Error in logical comparison. Compare renown with renown, not with a renowned painter.

4. **D**   Error in subject-verb agreement. The subject, *diseases*, is plural. The verb should be plural as well. Change *has become* to *have become.*

5. **E**   Error in subject-verb agreement. Do not be misled by sentences in which the subject follows the verb. Here, the subject, *list*, is singular; the verb should be singular as well. Change *There are* to *There is.*

6. **C**   Run-on sentence. Do not link two independent clauses with a comma. The addition of the connective *and* in choice C corrects the error.

7. **A**   Sentence is correct.

8. **D**   Error in subject-verb agreement. The subject, *spread*, is singular; the verb should be singular as well. Change *are evolving* to *is evolving.*

9. **D**   Ambiguous reference. The children were removing the carrots' skins, not their own skins.

10. **C**   Lack of parallelism. Choice C supplies the appropriate parallel structure.

11. **A**   Sentence is correct.

12. **D**   Wordiness. The suggested revision tightens this ineffective compound sentence in two ways: first, it eliminates the connective *and;* second, it repeats the phrase *a scent* to emphasize its importance.

13. **E**   Sentence fragment. The introduction of a subject (*She*) and change of the participle (*Attempting*) into a main verb (*attempted*) completes the sentence.

14. **A**   Sentence is correct.

ANSWER SHEET FOR CRITICAL READING AND WRITING SKILLS TEST 3

Section 1　　　　　　　　**ESSAY**　　　　　　　Time allowed: 25 minutes

Essay (continued)

Section 2

1. Ⓐ Ⓑ Ⓒ Ⓓ Ⓔ
2. Ⓐ Ⓑ Ⓒ Ⓓ Ⓔ
3. Ⓐ Ⓑ Ⓒ Ⓓ Ⓔ
4. Ⓐ Ⓑ Ⓒ Ⓓ Ⓔ
5. Ⓐ Ⓑ Ⓒ Ⓓ Ⓔ
6. Ⓐ Ⓑ Ⓒ Ⓓ Ⓔ
7. Ⓐ Ⓑ Ⓒ Ⓓ Ⓔ
8. Ⓐ Ⓑ Ⓒ Ⓓ Ⓔ

9. Ⓐ Ⓑ Ⓒ Ⓓ Ⓔ
10. Ⓐ Ⓑ Ⓒ Ⓓ Ⓔ
11. Ⓐ Ⓑ Ⓒ Ⓓ Ⓔ
12. Ⓐ Ⓑ Ⓒ Ⓓ Ⓔ
13. Ⓐ Ⓑ Ⓒ Ⓓ Ⓔ
14. Ⓐ Ⓑ Ⓒ Ⓓ Ⓔ
15. Ⓐ Ⓑ Ⓒ Ⓓ Ⓔ
16. Ⓐ Ⓑ Ⓒ Ⓓ Ⓔ

17. Ⓐ Ⓑ Ⓒ Ⓓ Ⓔ
18. Ⓐ Ⓑ Ⓒ Ⓓ Ⓔ
19. Ⓐ Ⓑ Ⓒ Ⓓ Ⓔ
20. Ⓐ Ⓑ Ⓒ Ⓓ Ⓔ
21. Ⓐ Ⓑ Ⓒ Ⓓ Ⓔ
22. Ⓐ Ⓑ Ⓒ Ⓓ Ⓔ
23. Ⓐ Ⓑ Ⓒ Ⓓ Ⓔ
24. Ⓐ Ⓑ Ⓒ Ⓓ Ⓔ

25. Ⓐ Ⓑ Ⓒ Ⓓ Ⓔ
26. Ⓐ Ⓑ Ⓒ Ⓓ Ⓔ
27. Ⓐ Ⓑ Ⓒ Ⓓ Ⓔ
28. Ⓐ Ⓑ Ⓒ Ⓓ Ⓔ
29. Ⓐ Ⓑ Ⓒ Ⓓ Ⓔ
30. Ⓐ Ⓑ Ⓒ Ⓓ Ⓔ

Section 3

1. Ⓐ Ⓑ Ⓒ Ⓓ Ⓔ
2. Ⓐ Ⓑ Ⓒ Ⓓ Ⓔ
3. Ⓐ Ⓑ Ⓒ Ⓓ Ⓔ
4. Ⓐ Ⓑ Ⓒ Ⓓ Ⓔ
5. Ⓐ Ⓑ Ⓒ Ⓓ Ⓔ
6. Ⓐ Ⓑ Ⓒ Ⓓ Ⓔ
7. Ⓐ Ⓑ Ⓒ Ⓓ Ⓔ
8. Ⓐ Ⓑ Ⓒ Ⓓ Ⓔ
9. Ⓐ Ⓑ Ⓒ Ⓓ Ⓔ

10. Ⓐ Ⓑ Ⓒ Ⓓ Ⓔ
11. Ⓐ Ⓑ Ⓒ Ⓓ Ⓔ
12. Ⓐ Ⓑ Ⓒ Ⓓ Ⓔ
13. Ⓐ Ⓑ Ⓒ Ⓓ Ⓔ
14. Ⓐ Ⓑ Ⓒ Ⓓ Ⓔ
15. Ⓐ Ⓑ Ⓒ Ⓓ Ⓔ
16. Ⓐ Ⓑ Ⓒ Ⓓ Ⓔ
17. Ⓐ Ⓑ Ⓒ Ⓓ Ⓔ
18. Ⓐ Ⓑ Ⓒ Ⓓ Ⓔ

19. Ⓐ Ⓑ Ⓒ Ⓓ Ⓔ
20. Ⓐ Ⓑ Ⓒ Ⓓ Ⓔ
21. Ⓐ Ⓑ Ⓒ Ⓓ Ⓔ
22. Ⓐ Ⓑ Ⓒ Ⓓ Ⓔ
23. Ⓐ Ⓑ Ⓒ Ⓓ Ⓔ
24. Ⓐ Ⓑ Ⓒ Ⓓ Ⓔ
25. Ⓐ Ⓑ Ⓒ Ⓓ Ⓔ
26. Ⓐ Ⓑ Ⓒ Ⓓ Ⓔ
27. Ⓐ Ⓑ Ⓒ Ⓓ Ⓔ

28. Ⓐ Ⓑ Ⓒ Ⓓ Ⓔ
29. Ⓐ Ⓑ Ⓒ Ⓓ Ⓔ
30. Ⓐ Ⓑ Ⓒ Ⓓ Ⓔ
31. Ⓐ Ⓑ Ⓒ Ⓓ Ⓔ
32. Ⓐ Ⓑ Ⓒ Ⓓ Ⓔ
33. Ⓐ Ⓑ Ⓒ Ⓓ Ⓔ
34. Ⓐ Ⓑ Ⓒ Ⓓ Ⓔ
35. Ⓐ Ⓑ Ⓒ Ⓓ Ⓔ

Section 4

1. Ⓐ Ⓑ Ⓒ Ⓓ Ⓔ
2. Ⓐ Ⓑ Ⓒ Ⓓ Ⓔ
3. Ⓐ Ⓑ Ⓒ Ⓓ Ⓔ
4. Ⓐ Ⓑ Ⓒ Ⓓ Ⓔ
5. Ⓐ Ⓑ Ⓒ Ⓓ Ⓔ
6. Ⓐ Ⓑ Ⓒ Ⓓ Ⓔ
7. Ⓐ Ⓑ Ⓒ Ⓓ Ⓔ
8. Ⓐ Ⓑ Ⓒ Ⓓ Ⓔ

9. Ⓐ Ⓑ Ⓒ Ⓓ Ⓔ
10. Ⓐ Ⓑ Ⓒ Ⓓ Ⓔ
11. Ⓐ Ⓑ Ⓒ Ⓓ Ⓔ
12. Ⓐ Ⓑ Ⓒ Ⓓ Ⓔ
13. Ⓐ Ⓑ Ⓒ Ⓓ Ⓔ
14. Ⓐ Ⓑ Ⓒ Ⓓ Ⓔ
15. Ⓐ Ⓑ Ⓒ Ⓓ Ⓔ
16. Ⓐ Ⓑ Ⓒ Ⓓ Ⓔ

17. Ⓐ Ⓑ Ⓒ Ⓓ Ⓔ
18. Ⓐ Ⓑ Ⓒ Ⓓ Ⓔ
19. Ⓐ Ⓑ Ⓒ Ⓓ Ⓔ
20. Ⓐ Ⓑ Ⓒ Ⓓ Ⓔ
21. Ⓐ Ⓑ Ⓒ Ⓓ Ⓔ
22. Ⓐ Ⓑ Ⓒ Ⓓ Ⓔ
23. Ⓐ Ⓑ Ⓒ Ⓓ Ⓔ
24. Ⓐ Ⓑ Ⓒ Ⓓ Ⓔ

25. Ⓐ Ⓑ Ⓒ Ⓓ Ⓔ
26. Ⓐ Ⓑ Ⓒ Ⓓ Ⓔ
27. Ⓐ Ⓑ Ⓒ Ⓓ Ⓔ
28. Ⓐ Ⓑ Ⓒ Ⓓ Ⓔ
29. Ⓐ Ⓑ Ⓒ Ⓓ Ⓔ
30. Ⓐ Ⓑ Ⓒ Ⓓ Ⓔ

Section 5

1. Ⓐ Ⓑ Ⓒ Ⓓ Ⓔ   9. Ⓐ Ⓑ Ⓒ Ⓓ Ⓔ   17. Ⓐ Ⓑ Ⓒ Ⓓ Ⓔ   25. Ⓐ Ⓑ Ⓒ Ⓓ Ⓔ
2. Ⓐ Ⓑ Ⓒ Ⓓ Ⓔ   10. Ⓐ Ⓑ Ⓒ Ⓓ Ⓔ   18. Ⓐ Ⓑ Ⓒ Ⓓ Ⓔ   26. Ⓐ Ⓑ Ⓒ Ⓓ Ⓔ
3. Ⓐ Ⓑ Ⓒ Ⓓ Ⓔ   11. Ⓐ Ⓑ Ⓒ Ⓓ Ⓔ   19. Ⓐ Ⓑ Ⓒ Ⓓ Ⓔ   27. Ⓐ Ⓑ Ⓒ Ⓓ Ⓔ
4. Ⓐ Ⓑ Ⓒ Ⓓ Ⓔ   12. Ⓐ Ⓑ Ⓒ Ⓓ Ⓔ   20. Ⓐ Ⓑ Ⓒ Ⓓ Ⓔ   28. Ⓐ Ⓑ Ⓒ Ⓓ Ⓔ
5. Ⓐ Ⓑ Ⓒ Ⓓ Ⓔ   13. Ⓐ Ⓑ Ⓒ Ⓓ Ⓔ   21. Ⓐ Ⓑ Ⓒ Ⓓ Ⓔ   29. Ⓐ Ⓑ Ⓒ Ⓓ Ⓔ
6 Ⓐ Ⓑ Ⓒ Ⓓ Ⓔ   14. Ⓐ Ⓑ Ⓒ Ⓓ Ⓔ   22. Ⓐ Ⓑ Ⓒ Ⓓ Ⓔ   30. Ⓐ Ⓑ Ⓒ Ⓓ Ⓔ
7. Ⓐ Ⓑ Ⓒ Ⓓ Ⓔ   15. Ⓐ Ⓑ Ⓒ Ⓓ Ⓔ   23. Ⓐ Ⓑ Ⓒ Ⓓ Ⓔ
8. Ⓐ Ⓑ Ⓒ Ⓓ Ⓔ   16. Ⓐ Ⓑ Ⓒ Ⓓ Ⓔ   24. Ⓐ Ⓑ Ⓒ Ⓓ Ⓔ

Section 6

1. Ⓐ Ⓑ Ⓒ Ⓓ Ⓔ   9. Ⓐ Ⓑ Ⓒ Ⓓ Ⓔ   17. Ⓐ Ⓑ Ⓒ Ⓓ Ⓔ   25. Ⓐ Ⓑ Ⓒ Ⓓ Ⓔ
2. Ⓐ Ⓑ Ⓒ Ⓓ Ⓔ   10. Ⓐ Ⓑ Ⓒ Ⓓ Ⓔ   18. Ⓐ Ⓑ Ⓒ Ⓓ Ⓔ   26. Ⓐ Ⓑ Ⓒ Ⓓ Ⓔ
3. Ⓐ Ⓑ Ⓒ Ⓓ Ⓔ   11. Ⓐ Ⓑ Ⓒ Ⓓ Ⓔ   19. Ⓐ Ⓑ Ⓒ Ⓓ Ⓔ   27. Ⓐ Ⓑ Ⓒ Ⓓ Ⓔ
4. Ⓐ Ⓑ Ⓒ Ⓓ Ⓔ   12. Ⓐ Ⓑ Ⓒ Ⓓ Ⓔ   20. Ⓐ Ⓑ Ⓒ Ⓓ Ⓔ   28. Ⓐ Ⓑ Ⓒ Ⓓ Ⓔ
5. Ⓐ Ⓑ Ⓒ Ⓓ Ⓔ   13. Ⓐ Ⓑ Ⓒ Ⓓ Ⓔ   21. Ⓐ Ⓑ Ⓒ Ⓓ Ⓔ   29. Ⓐ Ⓑ Ⓒ Ⓓ Ⓔ
6 Ⓐ Ⓑ Ⓒ Ⓓ Ⓔ   14. Ⓐ Ⓑ Ⓒ Ⓓ Ⓔ   22. Ⓐ Ⓑ Ⓒ Ⓓ Ⓔ   30. Ⓐ Ⓑ Ⓒ Ⓓ Ⓔ
7. Ⓐ Ⓑ Ⓒ Ⓓ Ⓔ   15. Ⓐ Ⓑ Ⓒ Ⓓ Ⓔ   23. Ⓐ Ⓑ Ⓒ Ⓓ Ⓔ
8. Ⓐ Ⓑ Ⓒ Ⓓ Ⓔ   16. Ⓐ Ⓑ Ⓒ Ⓓ Ⓔ   24. Ⓐ Ⓑ Ⓒ Ⓓ Ⓔ

1   1   1   1   1   1   1   1   1   1   **1**

TIME—25 MINUTES

MODEL TEST 3
Section 1
Essay

Turn to your answer sheet and write your essay on the lined portion of the page. To receive credit, you must write your essay in the area provided.

    Write on the assigned topic below. If you write on any other topic, your essay will be given a score of zero.

    Write or print legibly: your readers will be unfamiliar with your handwriting, and you want them to be able to read what you write.

The excerpt appearing below makes a point about a particular topic. Read the statement carefully, and think about the assignment that follows.

In crisis is cleverness born.
—Chinese Proverb

Assignment: The statement above implies that crises can benefit us by fostering creativity. Write an essay supporting, disputing, or qualifying this statement. You may use examples from history, literature, popular culture, current events, or personal experience to support your position.

BEGIN WRITING YOUR ESSAY ON THE ANSWER SHEET

STOP
**IF YOU FINISH BEFORE TIME IS CALLED, YOU MAY CHECK YOUR WORK ON THIS
SECTION ONLY. DO NOT WORK ON ANY OTHER SECTION IN THE TEST.**

2 2 2 2 2 2 2 2 2 2 2

Section 2

TIME—25 MINUTES
24 QUESTIONS

For each of the following questions, select the best answer from the choices provided and fill in the appropriate circle.

Each of the following sentences contains one or two blanks; each blank indicates that a word or set of words has been left out. Below the sentence are five words or phrases, lettered A through E. Select the word or set of words that best completes the sentence.

Example:

Fame is ----; today's rising star is all too soon tomorrow's washed-up has-been.

(A) rewarding   (B) gradual
 (C) essential   (D) spontaneous
  (E) transitory

Ⓐ Ⓑ Ⓒ Ⓓ ●

1. Though financially successful, the theater season, once again, is more noted for its ____ than for its original productions.

(A) musicals
(B) revivals
(C) failures
(D) rehearsals
(E) commercials

2. During the Ice Ages, musk oxen ranged as far south as Iowa, in North America, and Spain, in Europe, but in recent centuries the species has been ____ arctic tundra habitats, such as Greenland and the arctic islands of Canada.

(A) barred from
(B) confined to
(C) dissatisfied with
(D) enervated by
(E) unknown in

3. Just as an orchestra cannot consist only of violins, a society cannot consist only of managers, for society is an ____ in which different parts have different ____.

(A) anarchy…powers
(B) edifice…complaints
(C) organism…functions
(D) institution…results
(E) urbanity…ambitions

4. A ____ person is one who will ____ something on the slightest of evidence.

(A) restive…forget
(B) garrulous…criticize
(C) maudlin…censure
(D) phlegmatic…condemn
(E) credulous…believe

5. That the brain physically changes when stimulated, instead of remaining ____ from infancy to death, as previously thought, was Dr. Marian Diamond's first, and perhaps most far-reaching discovery.

(A) mutable
(B) static
(C) sensory
(D) vigorous
(E) fluid

GO ON TO THE NEXT PAGE

2 2 2 2 2 2 2 2 2 2 2 **2**

6. There were ____ in her nature that made her seem an ____ enigma: she was severe and gentle; she was modest and disdainful; she longed for affection and was cold.

    (A) aspirations…irreducible
    (B) contradictions…inexplicable
    (C) distortions…impetuous
    (D) disparities…interminable
    (E) incongruities…irrelevant

7. At a time when biographies that debunk their subjects are all the rage, it is refreshing to have one idol who not only lives up to her legend but also ____ it.

    (A) complicates
    (B) surpasses
    (C) compromises
    (D) rejects
    (E) subverts

8. *Morphing* is a term ____ for the metamorphosis of one shape into another, such as the smooth formation of a live actor from a silvery puddle as seen in *Terminator 2*.

    (A) coined
    (B) denigrated
    (C) simulated
    (D) mistaken
    (E) repudiated

GO ON TO THE NEXT PAGE

2 2 2 2 2 2 2 2 2 2 2

Read each of the passages below, and then answer the questions that follow the passage. The correct response may be stated outright or merely suggested in the passage.

Questions 9 and 10 are based on the following passage.

The Mayans and Aztecs considered chocolate the food of the gods, but today's lovers of sweets would not find the earliest
Line chocolate heavenly. Chocolate is made from
(5) the roasted and ground seeds of the cacao tree. Until the sixteenth century, ground chocolate was mixed with water and spices, including chili peppers, to make a bitter, frothy beverage that Spanish explorers termed fitter for hogs
(10) than men. Not until Cortez brought chocolate back to Spain in 1526 was sugar added to the mix, but once it was, European royalty prized hot chocolate drinks. Over the next two centuries, hot chocolate became fashionable;
(15) chocolate houses (like coffeehouses) sprang up throughout Europe.

9. The opening sentence of the passage makes use primarily of which of the following?

   (A) Humorous understatement
   (B) Classical allusion
   (C) Personification
   (D) Allegory
   (E) Simile

10. The initial attitude of the Spaniards toward the Aztec chocolate beverage can best be characterized as

   (A) appreciative
   (B) indifferent
   (C) objective
   (D) derisive
   (E) nostalgic

Questions 11 and 12 are based on the following passage.

On receiving the Congressional Medal for Distinguished Civilian Achievement, Dr. Jonas Salk declared, "I feel that the greatest
Line reward for doing is the opportunity to do
(5) more." People worldwide would agree that, in his forty-year medical career, Salk did a stunning amount for humanity. His work developing the first polio vaccine was the opening shot in a war that has led to the disease's vir-
(10) tual eradication. (In 2001, polio, which once paralyzed hundreds of thousands of children annually, claimed only 600 new victims worldwide.) Though Salk's vaccine has been superseded by Albert Sabin's cheaper oral
(15) vaccine, Salk's legacy and name live on.

11. In the course of the passage, the author does all of the following EXCEPT

   (A) use a metaphor
   (B) cite a statistic
   (C) quote a historic figure
   (D) describe a process
   (E) make an assertion

12. The word "stunning" (lines 6 and 7) most nearly means

   (A) gorgeous
   (B) perplexing
   (C) amazing
   (D) critical
   (E) unique

GO ON TO THE NEXT PAGE

2 2 2 2 2 2 2 2 2 2 2 **2**

Questions 13–24 are based on the following passage.

The following passage is taken from an article by a contemporary poet about Clement Clarke Moore, the nineteenth-century writer best known as the author of "A Visit From Saint Nicholas."

If he wasn't a myth maker himself, at least Clement Clarke Moore was a great myth refiner. He started with St. Nicholas, giver of
Line presents, whom the Dutch settlers had brought
(5) over to New York. Moore's portrait of the good saint is as fleshy and real as some Frans Hals painting of a burgher:

The stump of a pipe he held tight in his teeth,
(10) *And the smoke it encircled his head like a wreath.*

But with American efficiency, Moore combines the figure of St. Nicholas with that of Kris Kringle, who (in Norwegian lore)
(15) helped the saint by driving a reindeer-drawn sleigh. Moore fires Kris, leaving St. Nick to do his own driving. The result is our own American Santa Claus. Moore removes St. Nick's bishop's miter, decks him out in fur,
(20) gives him a ruddy face and a pot belly, hands him a sack of toys and calls him an elf—suggesting a pointed cap. Thomas Nast, our most authoritative Santa Claus delineator, stuck closely to Moore's description, and ever since,
(25) few artists have dared depart from it.

To see how good Moore's imagination is, you have only to compare his version of St. Nicholas with Washington Irving's of a few years earlier. In 1809, in "Knickerbocker's
(30) History of New York," Irving makes St. Nick a friendly Dutch-American deity "riding jollily among the tree-tops" in (of all things) a wagon, not only on Christmas but also on any old holiday afternoon. What pulled that silly
(35) wagon Irving doesn't say, or why it didn't snag itself on a branch and bust both axles.

But Moore in his genius provides St. Nick with reindeer power. And by laying marvelous names on those obedient steeds, he makes
(40) each one an individual. Though ruminants may be poorly designed for flight, Moore doesn't worry his head about aerodynamics; he just sidesteps the whole problem. Dasher, Dancer, Prancer, and the rest of the crew sim-
(45) ply whiz up to the rooftop by pure magic. It never occurs to us to question such a feat. We are one with Moore's protagonist, a man with "wondering eyes."

Delving into John Hollander's recent
(50) Library of America anthology "American Poetry: The Nineteenth Century," I was glad to find "A Visit From St. Nicholas" right there along with works by Whitman, Emily Dickinson and Jones Very. Professional decon-
(55) structionists may sneer, but popular demand has fixed the poem securely in our national heritage. If Mr. Hollander had left it out, it would have been missed. Statistics are scarce, but it seems likely that Moore's masterwork
(60) has been reprinted, recited and learned by heart more often than any other American poem—and that goes for "The Raven," "Casey at the Bat," and Sylvia Plath's "Daddy."

To be sure, mere popularity doesn't make
(65) a work of art great. If it did, then "September Morn," that delicate tribute to skinny-dipping once reproduced on calendars hung in barbershops and pool halls galore, would be a better

GO ON TO THE NEXT PAGE

painting than "Nude Descending a Staircase"
(70) any day. And yet a poem like Moore's that has
stuck around for 171 years has to have something going for it.

Well then, what? I submit that the poem's
immortality may be due not only to Moore's
(75) perfecting a great myth, but also to his skill in
music-making. It is a moribund reader who
doesn't feel the spell of its bounding anapests,
as hard to ignore as a herd of reindeer on your
roof. Poets today tend to shy away from such
(80) obvious rhythms. They shrink too from alliteration, which, applied badly, seems bric-a-brac.
But Moore lays it on thick, and makes it work
like a charm: the "fl" sounds in "Away to the
window I flew like a flash," the hard "c"
(85) sounds in "More rapid than eagles his coursers
they came." As for his rhymes, most clunk
along unsurprisingly (like "house" and
"mouse"), but a few sound Muse-inspired. If
any later versifier ever hits upon another pair
(90) of rhyming words as fresh and precise as
these, let him die smug:

He sprang to his sleigh, to his team gave a
whistle,
And away they all flew like the down of
(95) *a thistle.*

History doesn't tell us whether Moore's
daughters, who first received the poem as a
Christmas present in 1822, were disappointed
at not getting dolls instead. Anyhow, it is a
(100) safe bet that, a hundred years from now, many
a more serious and respectable poem will have
departed from human memory like the down
of a thistle, while Moore's vision of that won-
derful eight-deer sleigh will go thundering on.
(105) "A Visit From St. Nicholas" may be only a
sweet confection, yet how well it lasts. On a
cold winter night, it can warm you to the
quick: a homemade verbal cookie dipped in
Ovaltine.

13. The passage serves primarily to
(A) inform the reader of a new anthology fea-
turing "A Visit from St. Nicholas"
(B) encourage contemporary poets to adopt the
literary techniques used by Clement Clarke
Moore
(C) give an instance of a great work of art that
has won universal renown
(D) correct a misconception about the origins
of Santa Claus
(E) explain the enduring appeal of a classic
example of light verse

14. By calling Clement Clarke Moore "a great
myth refiner," the author intends to convey that
Moore
(A) was skillful at explaining myths
(B) created brand new legends
(C) studied the origins of myths
(D) transformed old myths into something new
(E) disdained the crudity of early mythology

15. Moore's sources for his Saint Nicholas can best
be described as
(A) eclectic
(B) pagan
(C) meager
(D) illusory
(E) authoritative

16. We can infer from lines 22–25 that Thomas
Nast most likely was
(A) an imitator of Moore's verse
(B) a critic of Moore's changes to traditional
figures
(C) an illustrator of Moore's poem
(D) an iconoclastic artist
(E) a competitor of Moore's

GO ON TO THE NEXT PAGE

2 2 2 2 2 2 2 2 2 2 2

17. Which statement best summarizes the point made in lines 26–48?

(A) Moore's portrait of Saint Nicholas antedates Washington Irving's interpretation.
(B) Irving's version of Saint Nicholas surpasses the one created by Moore.
(C) Moore's interpretation of Saint Nicholas is less friendly than Irving's interpretation.
(D) Moore preferred his version of Saint Nicholas to Irving's variant.
(E) Moore showed greater creativity than Irving in constructing his picture of Saint Nicholas.

18. The statement in lines 46–48 ("We are one . . . eyes'") is best interpreted as conveying the idea that

(A) we share the identity of the protagonist
(B) we too view the proceedings with astonishment and awe
(C) we do not understand the attraction of what takes place
(D) we question the events as they occur
(E) we also resemble Saint Nicholas in nature

19. The author's attitude toward "professional deconstructionists" (lines 54–57) can best be described as

(A) respectful
(B) dismissive
(C) adulatory
(D) timorous
(E) perplexed

20. In line 62, the phrase "goes for" most nearly means

(A) aims at
(B) passes for
(C) holds true for
(D) gives approval to
(E) attacks physically

21. The word "mere" in line 64 means

(A) insignificant
(B) involuntary
(C) momentary
(D) simple
(E) problematic

22. In line 76, the author uses the word "moribund" to emphasize the reader's

(A) immortality
(B) fear of dying
(C) ignorance of mythology
(D) reservations about magic
(E) insensitivity to verse

23. The author regards Moore's use of the rhyming words "whistle" and "thistle" with

(A) self-satisfaction and complacency
(B) amusement and condescension
(C) delight and admiration
(D) interest yet envy
(E) derision and disdain

24. One aspect of the passage that might make it difficult to appreciate is the author's apparent assumption that readers will

(A) prefer the realistic paintings of Hals to later artworks
(B) have read Hollander's anthology of American poetry
(C) be acquainted with statistics about the memorization of verse
(D) understand the author's childhood associations with Saint Nicholas
(E) already be familiar in great detail with Moore's poem

STOP

IF YOU FINISH BEFORE TIME IS CALLED, YOU MAY CHECK YOUR WORK ON THIS SECTION ONLY. DO NOT WORK ON ANY OTHER SECTION IN THE TEST.

3 3 3 3 3 3 3 3 3 3 3

Section 3

TIME—25 MINUTES
35 QUESTIONS

For each of the following questions, choose the best answer and fill in the appropriate circle on the answer sheet.

Some or all parts of the following sentences are underlined. The first answer choice, (A), simply repeats the underlined part of the sentence. The other four choices present four alternative ways to phrase the underlined part. Select the answer that produces the most effective sentence, one that is clear and exact, and blacken the appropriate space on your answer sheet. In selecting your choice, be sure that it is standard written English, and that it expresses the meaning of the original sentence.

Example:
  The first biography of author Eudora Welty came out in 1998 <u>and she was 89 years old at the time</u>.

  (A) and she was 89 years old at the time
  (B) at the time she was 89
  (C) upon becoming an 89 year old
  (D) when she was 89
  (E) at the age of 89 years old

          Ⓐ Ⓑ Ⓒ ● Ⓔ

---

1. In his seminal novel *Ulysses*, James Joyce wrote a <u>masterpiece and it captured</u> a single day in the life of Dublin.

  (A) masterpiece and it captured
  (B) masterpiece that captured
  (C) masterpiece although it captured
  (D) masterpiece and he captured
  (E) masterpiece and capturing

2. The prominent theater critic agreed to come to the <u>campus and he would lead</u> a series of discussions on new trends in contemporary American drama.

  (A) campus and he would lead
  (B) campus; where he would lead
  (C) campus and he could lead
  (D) campus, with his leading
  (E) campus to lead

3. Efficiency experts have developed methods that, if properly applied, can <u>cause an office's total workload to become a great deal simpler</u>.

  (A) cause an office's total workload to become a great deal simpler
  (B) cause an office's total workload to become greatly simpler
  (C) greatly simplify an office's total workload
  (D) cause an office's workload to totally become a great deal simpler
  (E) make an office's total workload a lot more simple

4. For nearly seventy years, *The New Yorker* contained no <u>photographs; its stories were told solely</u> through words and drawings.

  (A) photographs; its stories were told solely
  (B) photographs; it told its sole stories
  (C) photographs; and it told its stories solely
  (D) photographs; they told their stories solely
  (E) photographs; their stories were told solely

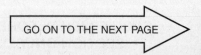
GO ON TO THE NEXT PAGE

3   3   3   3   3   3   3   3   3   3   3

5. The judge refused to allow the jurors to hear the <u>defendant's confession who was coerced</u> by the police.

   (A) defendant's confession who was coerced
   (B) confession that was coerced out of the defendant
   (C) confession of the defendant who was coerced
   (D) defendant's confession when he was coerced
   (E) defendant's confession, being that he was coerced

6. The invention of movable type enabled printers to copy texts inexpensively <u>and they could produce books quickly</u> without needing the efforts of innumerable scribes.

   (A) and they could produce books quickly
   (B) and it could produce books quickly
   (C) and to produce books quickly
   (D) and producing books quickly
   (E) and the quick production of books

7. Reading the epigrams of Alexander Pope, <u>the economy of his verse impresses me</u>: in just a few words he conveys worlds of meaning.

   (A) the economy of his verse impresses me
   (B) the economy of his verse is what is impressive to me
   (C) I had been impressed by the economy of his verse
   (D) I find the economy of his verse impressive
   (E) the economy of his verse is my impression

8. <u>J. R. R. Tolkien is best known for his trilogy of fantasy novels, and</u> his actual academic specialty was Anglo-Saxon literature.

   (A) J. R. R. Tolkien is best known for his trilogy of fantasy novels, and
   (B) Because J. R. R. Tolkien is best known for his trilogy of fantasy novels,
   (C) J. R. R. Tolkien is best known for his trilogy of fantasy novels, however,
   (D) Although J. R. R. Tolkien is best known for his trilogy of fantasy novels,
   (E) J. R. R. Tolkien was best known for his trilogy of fantasy novels, and

9. The chef Alice Waters had extremely high culinary standards and consequently <u>only the freshest seasonal ingredients were used</u> in her dishes.

   (A) only the freshest seasonal ingredients were used
   (B) the freshest seasonal ingredients only were used
   (C) the freshest seasonal ingredients were used only
   (D) used only the freshest seasonal ingredients
   (E) only the freshest of seasonal ingredients were used

10. An immense and complex system of dams and tunnels, aqueducts and <u>reservoirs, by which water was brought</u> from the mountains to the cities.

   (A) reservoirs, by which water was brought
   (B) reservoirs brought water
   (C) reservoirs which brought water
   (D) reservoirs, through which water was brought
   (E) reservoirs bringing water

GO ON TO THE NEXT PAGE

3 3 3 3 3 3 3 3 3 3 3

11. <u>Because the federal government has drastically reduced its support for the arts is the reason why</u> many performing arts companies have had to curtail their projected seasons.

   (A) Because the federal government has drastically reduced its support for the arts is the reason why
   (B) As a result of the federal government drastically reducing its support for the arts,
   (C) Because the federal government has drastically reduced its support for the arts,
   (D) The fact that the federal government has drastically reduced its support for the arts is why
   (E) Support for the arts having been drastically reduced by the federal government is the reason why

---

The sentences in this section may contain errors in grammar, usage, choice of words, or idioms. Either there is just one error in a sentence or the sentence is correct. Some words or phrases are underlined and lettered; everything else in the sentence is correct.

If an underlined word or phrase is incorrect, choose that letter; if the sentence is correct, select <u>No error</u>. Then blacken the appropriate space on your answer sheet.

Example:

The region has a climate <u>so severe that</u> plants
                              A
<u>growing there</u> rarely <u>had been</u> more than twelve
      B   C
inches <u>high.</u> <u>No error</u>
        D   E

Ⓐ Ⓑ ● Ⓓ Ⓔ

---

12. George <u>never understood</u> that he
                    A
gained <u>promotions</u> in the company <u>through</u>
        B   C
his family connections <u>and not in</u> his native
                            D
ability. <u>No error</u>
          E

13. Although electronic voting technology may

appear a <u>quick and efficient</u> way for the federal
              A
government <u>to hold</u> elections, <u>they</u> may have
              B   C
drawbacks <u>that</u> could undermine the
              D
democratic process. <u>No error</u>
                        E

GO ON TO THE NEXT PAGE

3 3 3 3 3 3 3 3 3 3 3

14. In the novel *Madame Bovary*, the heroine

    has <u>scarcely no</u> <u>comprehension of</u> her <u>own</u>
         A   B   C
    motivations in developing a <u>relationship with</u>
                                   D
    the young lawyer Dupuis. <u>No error</u>
                             E

15. <u>Just as</u> some people are <u>exceeding</u> fond of the
     A   B
    taste of cilantro, so others <u>detest</u> <u>it</u>. <u>No error</u>
                          C D   E

16. The limerick, in contrast to <u>various more</u>
                               A
    demanding verse forms, <u>are</u> so simple that
                        B
    <u>even</u> a child <u>can write</u> one. <u>No error</u>
     C   D   E

17. When a highway is <u>under construction,</u>
                        A
    <u>and drivers</u> find themselves <u>taking</u> significant
       B   C
    detours to avoid the <u>almost certain</u> bottlenecks
                     D
    in their way. <u>No error</u>
              E

18. Little League programs introduce young

    people <u>to</u> the <u>concept of</u> team play, teach them
        A   B
    sportsmanship, and give them the <u>chance to</u>
                               C
    learn fielding, hitting, and <u>how to pitch</u>.
                           D
    <u>No error</u>
     E

10. Many of the students <u>which</u> were studying
                       A
    for the final examination found the questions
    so difficult that they <u>were discouraged</u> about
                        B
    <u>their</u> <u>prospects for</u> a good grade. <u>No error</u>
     C   D   E

20. <u>Deep within</u> the forest there <u>lurks</u> the fierce
     A   B
    bandits <u>who</u> make these roads <u>so dangerous</u>
            C   D
    to travelers. <u>No error</u>
               E

21. The painter John James Audubon,

    <u>who portrayed</u> birds not in clinical isolation
       A
    <u>but</u> in <u>their</u> natural habitats, differed in this
     B   C
    respect <u>from other</u> artists of his era. <u>No error</u>
             D   E

22. <u>Upon dressing, you</u> should refrigerate the
           A
    potato salad immediately <u>to prevent</u> <u>its</u>
                          B   C
    ingredients <u>from spoiling</u>. <u>No error</u>
             D   E

23. <u>In devoting herself</u> to the study of gorillas,
          A
    Dian Fossey <u>embarked on</u> a course of action
                   B
    that <u>was to</u> <u>result in</u> her death. <u>No error</u>
         C   D   E

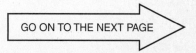

GO ON TO THE NEXT PAGE

3   3   3   3   3   3   3   3   3   3   3

24. When <u>one cuts away</u> the dead and dying limbs
             A
of a tree, you not <u>only</u> improve its appearance
               B
but also increase its <u>chances of</u> <u>bearing</u> fruit.
                   C   D
<u>No error</u>
  E

25. Except for the night watchman <u>and I,</u>
                        A
<u>everyone</u> <u>had gone</u> home for the day;
  B   C
<u>the two of us</u> were the only persons left in
      D
the building. <u>No error</u>
               E

26. <u>Unfortunately,</u> some doubt <u>exists whether</u>
      A   B
women's salaries <u>will ever achieve</u> parity with
              C
<u>men.</u> <u>No error</u>
  D   E

27. <u>To those</u> <u>who</u> upheld the belief that Earth
   A   B
did not move, Galileo's theory that Earth

<u>circles</u> the sun was <u>disturbing</u> unorthodox.
  C   D
<u>No error</u>
  E

28. <u>According to</u> Macchiavelli, a ruler
    A
maintains his position <u>by virtue of</u> his
                   B
<u>ability toward governing</u> and his
            C
<u>knowledge of</u> his rivals' weaknesses.
        D
<u>No error</u>
  E

29. For <u>most</u> of American history, women lacked
    A
the right to vote: <u>not until</u> the early twentieth
              B
century <u>was</u> the franchise <u>granted to</u> women.
       C   D
<u>No error</u>
  E

GO ON TO THE NEXT PAGE

3 3 3 3 3 3 3 3 3 3 3 3

The passage below is the unedited draft of a student's essay. Parts of the essay need to be rewritten to make the meaning clearer and more precise. Read the essay carefully.

The essay is followed by six questions about changes that might improve all or part of the organization, development, sentence structure, use of language, appropriateness to the audience, or use of standard written English. In each case, choose the answer that most clearly and effectively expresses the student's intended meaning. Indicate your choice by blackening the corresponding space on the answer sheet.

---

[1] It is difficult to deny that the world of music has changed greatly in the past thirty years. [2] The style, sound, technology, and lyrics of music have been altered greatly. [3] In the last three decades, several new categories of music have come into being.

[4] One reason why music has changed so greatly is that artists use music as a tool to publicize certain social messages. [5] Although many artists of the 1970s used this method as well, their issues were not as severe that banning their album was possible. [6] For example, one rap-singer, Ice-T, used his album to promote "cop-killing." [7] The idea was so offensive that many believed the album should be banned. [8] The controversy caused by Ice-T made the Arista record company refuse to continue production of the album.

[9] Another way in which music has changed is lyrics. [10] When you listen to certain heavy metal or rap groups, one may notice foul and obscene language used. [11] Some of the references to sex are shocking. [12] In past eras, such language in recorded music was unheard of.

[13] Technological changes in music have occurred. [14] With the advent of highly advanced musical devices and many digital effects, the sounds of music have been completely altered. [15] Rock and roll was invented in early 1950s. [16] When you listen to heavy metal, you hear more distorted guitar sounds than in music of the 60s and 70s. [17] In the era of electronic instruments, the

variety of possible sounds is incredible. [18] Present day sounds could never have been achieved in previous years because the technology was not at hand. [19] New music utilizes electronically produced sounds never heard before. [20] Computers generate everything from the human voice under water to the sound of whales. [21] There are no limits to what the music of the future will sound like.

30. Which of the following is the best revision of the underlined segment of sentence 5 below?

    Although many artists of the 1970s used this method as well, their issues were not as severe that banning their album was possible.

    (A) the issues were less severe than those which caused banning their album to be possible.
    (B) their issues were not as severe that their albums were in danger of being banned.
    (C) they never raised issues that could have caused their albums to be banned.
    (D) the issues they raised were not serious enough that banning their album was a possibility.
    (E) they raised less serious issues and banning their albums was not likely.

31. In view of the sentences that precede and follow sentence 10, which is the most effective revision of sentence 10?

    (A) Listening to certain heavy metal or rap groups, lyrics containing obscenities are often heard.
    (B) Obscene language is common in the songs of heavy metal and rap groups.
    (C) Certain heavy metal and rap groups use foul and obscene language.
    (D) Obscenities are often heard when one listens to the lyrics of certain heavy metal or rap groups.
    (E) Listening to obscene language and listening to the lyrics of certain heavy metal and rap groups.

GO ON TO THE NEXT PAGE

3 3 3 3 3 3 3 3 3 3 3

32. In the context of the entire essay, which revision of sentence 13 provides the most effective transition between paragraphs 3 and 4?

(A) Technological changes in music also have occurred.

(B) Also, technology has changed musical sounds.

(C) Noticeable changes in music's sounds have come about through technological changes.

(D) Changes in musical technology has changed musical sound, too.

(E) But the most noticeable change in music has been its sound.

33. In a revision of the entire essay, which of the following sentences most needs further development?

(A) Sentence 3
(B) Sentence 7
(C) Sentence 8
(D) Sentence 19
(E) Sentence 20

34. Which of the following sentences should be deleted to improve the unity and coherence of paragraph 4?

(A) Sentence 14
(B) Sentence 15
(C) Sentence 16
(D) Sentence 17
(E) Sentence 18

35. With regard to the organization of the entire essay, which is the best revision of sentence 2 in the introductory paragraph?

(A) In the past thirty years, not only the style, sound, and technology has changed, but the lyrics have, too.

(B) Having undergone a change in the style, sound, and technology, musical lyrics have altered also.

(C) Changes in musical sound have occurred, while the technology and lyrics have tremendously altered the style of music.

(D) Musicians have transformed today's music in style and sound, creating new lyrics and using new technology.

(E) Along with changes in sound and technology, the lyrics of music have changed, too.

STOP

IF YOU FINISH BEFORE TIME IS CALLED, YOU MAY CHECK YOUR WORK ON THIS SECTION ONLY. DO NOT WORK ON ANY OTHER SECTION IN THE TEST.

Section 4

TIME—25 MINUTES
24 QUESTIONS

For each of the following questions, select the best answer from the choices
provided and fill in the appropriate circle on the answer sheet.

Each of the following sentences contains one or
two blanks; each blank indicates that a word or
set of words has been left out. Below the sentence
are five words or phrases, lettered A through E.
Select the word or set of words that best completes the sentence.

Example:

Fame is ----; today's rising star is all too soon
tomorrow's washed-up has-been.

(A) rewarding   (B) gradual
(C) essential   (D) spontaneous
(E) transitory

Ⓐ Ⓑ Ⓒ Ⓓ ●

---

1. Despite the current expansion of fencing
association membership in America, the
governing body of world fencing fears that
fencing could be in danger of _____ if it does
not become more _____ to spectators.

(A) monotony…intelligible
(B) overcrowding…resistant
(C) extinction…accessible
(D) corruption…cordial
(E) remoteness…handy

2. Precision of wording is necessary in good
writing; by choosing words that exactly convey
the desired meaning, one can avoid _____.

(A) redundancy
(B) complexity
(C) duplicity
(D) ambiguity
(E) lucidity

3. Despite the _____ size of her undergraduate
class, the professor made a point of getting to
know as many as possible of the more than 700
students personally.

(A) negligible
(B) modest
(C) infinitesimal
(D) daunting
(E) moderate

4. Biographer Janet Malcolm maintains that biography is a spurious art, for the orderly narrative
it creates is _____; the "facts" aren't facts at all,
but literary _____.

(A) illusory…inventions
(B) genuine…commonplaces
(C) informative…allusions
(D) brilliant…triumphs
(E) sincere…criticisms

5. Something in Christopher responded to the
older man's air of authority: he looked _____; ,
accustomed to _____

(A) magisterial...command
(B) monumental...intimidate
(C) diffident...domineer
(D) masterful...obey
(E) decisive...fret

GO ON TO THE NEXT PAGE

Read each of the passages below, and then answer the questions that follow the passage. The correct response may be stated outright or merely suggested in the passage.

Questions 6–9 are based on the following passages.

Both passages relate to the career of the abolitionist Frederick Douglass. Passage 1 comes from the introduction to a collection of his short prose. Passage 2 is excerpted from Douglass's letter to his former master, written while Douglass was in England.

Passage 1

To elude slave catchers, the fugitive slave Frederick Baily changed his name, becoming Frederick Douglass, abolitionist spokesman
Line and author. When he published his autobiogra-
(5) phy, however, Douglass exposed himself to recapture: federal laws gave Douglass's ex-master the right to seize his property. Douglass traveled to Britain, where slavery was illegal; there he worked to gain support
(10) for America's anti-slavery movement. After two years, British friends unexpectedly bought his freedom, allowing him to return home to continue the fight. Some abolitionists criticized Douglass, however, saying that by let-
(15) ting his freedom be bought he acknowledged his master's right to own him.

Passage 2

I have often thought I should like to explain to you the grounds upon which I have
Line justified myself in running away from you . . .
(20) We are distinct persons, and are each equally provided with faculties necessary to our individual existence. In leaving you, I took nothing but what belonged to me, and in no way lessened your means for obtaining an *honest*
(25) living . . . I therefore see no wrong in any part of the transaction. It is true, I went off secretly; but that was more your fault than mine. Had I let you into the secret, you would have defeated the enterprise entirely; but for

(30) this, I should have been really glad to have made you acquainted with my intentions to leave.

6. In Passage 1, the word "property" (line 7) most nearly means

(A) parcel of land
(B) right of ownership
(C) characteristic trait
(D) personal possession
(E) particular virtue

7. As described in Passage 1 (lines 10–16), the attitude of the abolitionists to the purchase of Douglass's freedom can best be characterized as

(A) enthusiastic
(B) indifferent
(C) negative
(D) envious
(E) sympathetic

8. Compared to Passage 2, Passage 1 can be described as

(A) figurative rather than literal
(B) expository rather than argumentative
(C) rhetorical rather than unembellished
(D) descriptive rather than factual
(E) subjective rather than objective

9. The "enterprise" to which Douglass refers in Passage 2 (line 29) is

(A) a financial transaction
(B) the letter to his former master
(C) his escape from slavery
(D) his return from England
(E) the means of earning an honest living

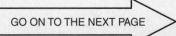
GO ON TO THE NEXT PAGE

Questions 10–15 are based on the following passage.

In this excerpt from The Way to Rainy Mountain, *the writer N. Scott Momaday tells of his grandmother, a member of the Kiowa tribe, who was born at a key time in Kiowa history.*

I like to think of my grandmother as a child. When she was born, the Kiowas were living the last great moment of their history.
Line For more than a hundred years they had con-
(5) trolled the open range from the Smoky Hill River to the Red, from the headwaters of the Canadian to the fork of the Arkansas and Cimarron. In alliance with the Comanches, they had ruled the whole of the southern
(10) Plains. War was their sacred business, and they were among the finest horsemen the world has ever known. But warfare for the Kiowas was preeminently a matter of disposition rather than of survival, and they never
(15) understood the grim, unrelenting advance of the U.S. Cavalry. When at last, divided and ill-provisioned, they were driven onto the Staked Plains in the cold rains of autumn, they fell into panic. In Palo Duro Canyon they aban-
(20) doned their crucial stores to pillage and had nothing then but their lives. In order to save themselves, they surrendered to the soldiers at Fort Sill and were imprisoned in the old stone corral that now stands as a military museum.
(25) My grandmother was spared the humiliation of those high gray walls by eight or ten years, but she must have known from birth the afflic-tion of defeat, the dark brooding of old warriors.
(30) Her name was Aho, and she belonged to the last culture to evolve in North America. Her forebears came down from the high coun-try in western Montana nearly three centuries ago. They were a mountain people, a mysteri-
(35) ous tribe of hunters whose language has never been positively classified in any major group. In the late seventeenth century they began a long migration to the south and east. It was a journey toward the dawn, and it led to a

(40) golden age. Along the way the Kiowas were befriended by the Crows, who gave them the culture and religion of the Plains. They acquired horses, and their ancient nomadic spirit was suddenly free of the ground. They
(45) acquired Tai-Me, the sacred Sun Dance doll, from that moment the object and symbol of their worship, and so shared in the divinity of the sun. Not least, they acquired the sense of destiny, therefore courage and pride. When
(50) they entered upon the southern Plains they had been transformed. No longer were they slaves to the simple necessity of survival; they were a lordly and dangerous society of fighters and thieves, hunters and priests of the sun.
(55) According to their origin myth, they entered the world through a hollow log. From one point of view, their migration was the fruit of an old prophecy, for indeed they emerged from a sunless world.

10. The author of this passage indicates in lines 12–16 that the Kiowas waged war predomi-nantly because they

(A) feared the Comanches
(B) wanted more land
(C) were warlike in nature
(D) had been humiliated by the cavalry
(E) believed they would perish otherwise

GO ON TO THE NEXT PAGE

11. Compared to the Kiowa warriors, the cavalry-men were

   (A) more idealistic about warfare
   (B) exceptionally fine horsemen
   (C) vulnerable to divisiveness
   (D) unswerving in determination
   (E) less given to brooding

12. The author's grandmother directly experienced

   (A) imprisonment at Fort Sill
   (B) the bleak attitude of the older Kiowa men
   (C) the defeat at Palo Duro Canyon
   (D) the loss of the tribe's provisions
   (E) surrender to the white soldiers

13. The author views the Kiowas of the late seventeenth and eighteenth centuries with a sense of

   (A) urgency
   (B) ambivalence
   (C) remorse
   (D) admiration
   (E) irony

14. By "their ancient nomadic spirit was suddenly free of the ground" (lines 43 and 44), the author most nearly means

   (A) the wanderers were now free to worship the sun
   (B) the acquisition of horses liberated them to rove more freely
   (C) they did not have to pay the Crows for the gift of horses
   (D) the oldest of the migratory Kiowas lacked ties to the soil
   (E) they no longer believed in the earth spirits of their ancestors

15. An "origin myth" (line 55) as used by the author is

   (A) a theory of reproduction told to Native American children
   (B) a religion the Kiowas learned from the Crows
   (C) a type of tale known only to Kiowas
   (D) an explanation of how the Kiowas came into being
   (E) a natural tale about trees and the sun

Questions 16–24 are based on the following passage.

This passage is from a book written by a contemporary American surgeon about the art of surgery.

One holds the knife as one holds the bow of a cello or a tulip—by the stem. Not palmed nor gripped nor grasped, but lightly, with the
Line tips of the fingers. The knife is not for press-
(5) ing. It is for drawing across the field of skin. Like a slender fish, it waits, at the ready, then, go! It darts, followed by a fine wake of red. The flesh parts, falling away to yellow globules of fat. Even now, after so many times, I
(10) still marvel at its power—cold, gleaming, silent. More, I am still struck with dread that it is I in whose hand the blade travels, that my hand is its vehicle, that yet again this terrible steel-bellied thing and I have conspired for a
(15) most unnatural purpose, the laying open of the body of a human being.

A stillness settles in my heart and is carried to my hand. It is the quietude of resolve layered over fear. And it is this resolve that
(20) lowers us, my knife and me, deeper and deeper into the person beneath. It is an entry into the body that is nothing like a caress; still, it is among the gentlest of acts. Then stroke and stroke again, and we are joined by other
(25) instruments, hemostats and forceps, until the wound blooms with strange flowers whose looped handles fall to the sides in steely array. There is a sound, the tight click of clamps fixing teeth into severed blood vessels, the snuf-
(30) fle and gargle of the suction machine clearing the field of blood for the next stroke, the litany of monosyllables with which one prays his way down and in: *clamp, sponge, suture, tie, cut.* And there is color. The green of the cloth,
(35) the white of the sponges, the red and yellow of the body. Beneath the fat lies the fascia, the

GO ON TO THE NEXT PAGE

④ ④ ④ ④ ④ ④ ④ ④ ④

tough fibrous sheet encasing the muscles. It
must be sliced and the red beef of the muscles
separated. Now there are retractors to hold
(40) apart the wound. Hands move together, part,
weave. We are fully engaged, like children
absorbed in a game or the craftsmen of some
place like Damascus.
    Deeper still. The peritoneum, pink and
(45) gleaming and membranous, bulges into the
wound. It is grasped with forceps, and opened.
For the first time we can see into the cavity of
the abdomen. Such a primitive place. One
expects to find drawings of buffalo on the
(50) walls. The sense of trespassing is keener now,
heightened by the world's light illuminating
the organs, their secret colors revealed—
maroon and salmon and yellow. The vista is
sweetly vulnerable at this moment, a kind of
(55) welcoming. An arc of the liver shines high and
on the right, like a dark sun. It laps over the
pink sweep of the stomach, from whose lower
border the gauzy omentum is draped, and
through which veil one sees, sinuous, slow as
(60) just-fed snakes, the indolent coils of the intes-
tine.
    You turn aside to wash your gloves. It is a
ritual cleansing. One enters this temple doubly
washed. Here is man as microcosm, represent-
(65) ing in all his parts the Earth, perhaps the universe.
    I must confess that the priestliness of my
profession has ever been impressed on me. In
the beginning there are vows, taken with all
(70) solemnity. Then there is the endless harsh
novitiate of training, much fatigue, much sacrifice. At last one emerges as a celebrant,
standing close to the truth lying curtained in
the ark of the body. Not surplice and cassock
(75) but mask and gown are your regalia. You hold
no chalice, but a knife. There is no wine, no
wafer. There are only the facts of blood and
flesh.

16. The passage is best described as
    (A) a definition of a concept
    (B) an example of a particular method
    (C) a discussion of an agenda
    (D) a description of a process
    (E) a lesson on a technique

17. The "wake of red" to which the author refers
    (line 7) is
    (A) a sign of embarrassment
    (B) an infectious rash
    (C) a line of blood
    (D) the blade of the knife
    (E) a trail of antiseptic

18. In line 8, "parts" most nearly means
    (A) leaves
    (B) splits
    (C) rushes
    (D) shares
    (E) quivers

19. The "strange flowers" with which the wound
    blooms (line 26) are
    (A) clots of blood
    (B) severed blood vessels
    (C) scattered sponges
    (D) gifts of love
    (E) surgical tools

20. In writing of the "strange flowers" with which
    the wound blooms (lines 23–27), the author
    is being
    (A) technical
    (B) derogatory
    (C) ambivalent
    (D) metaphorical
    (E) didactic

GO ON TO THE NEXT PAGE

21. The word "engaged" in line 41 most nearly means

  (A) compromised
  (B) engrossed
  (C) delighted
  (D) determined
  (E) betrothed

22. In lines 48–50, the comment "One expects to find drawings of buffalo on the walls" metaphorically compares the abdominal cavity to

  (A) an art gallery
  (B) a zoological display
  (C) a natural history museum
  (D) a prehistoric cave
  (E) a Western film

23. In creating an impression of abdominal surgery for the reader, the author makes use of

  (A) comparison with imaginary landscapes
  (B) contrast to other types of surgery
  (C) description of meteorological processes
  (D) evocation of the patient's emotions
  (E) reference to religious observances

24. One aspect of the passage that may make it difficult to appreciate is the author's apparent assumption throughout that readers will

  (A) have qualms about reading descriptions of major surgery
  (B) be already familiar with handling surgical tools
  (C) be able to visualize the body organs that are named
  (D) relate accounts of specific surgical acts to their own experience of undergoing surgery
  (E) remember their own years of medical training

STOP
IF YOU FINISH BEFORE TIME IS CALLED, YOU MAY CHECK YOUR WORK ON THIS SECTION ONLY. DO NOT WORK ON ANY OTHER SECTION IN THE TEST.

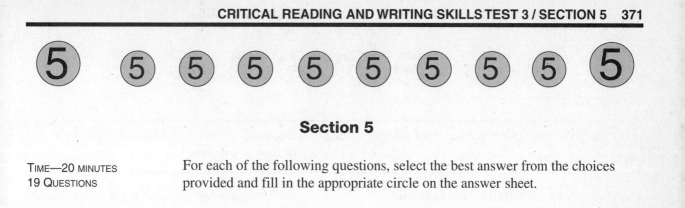

Section 5

TIME—20 MINUTES
19 QUESTIONS

For each of the following questions, select the best answer from the choices provided and fill in the appropriate circle on the answer sheet.

Each of the following sentences contains one or two blanks; each blank indicates that a word or set of words has been left out. Below the sentence are five words or phrases, lettered A through E. Select the word or set of words that best completes the sentence.

Example:

Fame is ----; today's rising star is all too soon tomorrow's washed-up has-been.

(A) rewarding   (B) gradual
(C) essential   (D) spontaneous
(E) transitory

Ⓐ Ⓑ Ⓒ Ⓓ ●

---

1. A subway modernization program intended to ____ a host of problems ranging from dangerous tracks to overcrowded stairwells has failed to meet its schedule for repairs.

   (A) augment
   (B) initiate
   (C) deplore
   (D) disclose
   (E) eliminate

2. To astronomers, the moon has long been an ____, its origin escaping simple solution.

   (A) interval
   (B) ultimatum
   (C) enigma
   (D) affront
   (E) opportunity

3. The amusements of modern urban people tend more and more to be ____ and to consist of the ____ of the skilled activities of others.

   (A) strenuous…contemplation
   (B) healthful…enjoyment
   (C) solitary…sharing
   (D) passive…observation
   (E) intellectual…repetition

4. As matter condenses out of the thin disk of hot gas and dust revolving around a new sun, it ____ into larger particles, just as snowflakes stick together as they fall.

   (A) crashes
   (B) protrudes
   (C) coalesces
   (D) evaporates
   (E) dissolves

5. The term *mole rat* is a ____, for these small, furless rodents are neither moles nor rats.

   (A) pseudonym
   (B) digression
   (C) misnomer
   (D) nonentity
   (E) preference

6. Einstein's humility was so ____ that it might have seemed a pose affected by a great man had it not been so obviously ____.

   (A) spurious…genuine
   (B) convincing…assumed
   (C) profound…sincere
   (D) heartfelt…hypocritical
   (E) modest…contrived

GO ON TO THE NEXT PAGE

The questions that follow the next two passages relate to the content of both, and to their relationship. The correct response may be stated outright in the passage or merely suggested.

Questions 7–19 are based on the following passages.

These passages are portraits of two fathers. The first appeared in a contemporary novel, the second in a memoir written in the 1990s by a person looking back on experiences in the San Francisco Bay area.

Passage 1

In 1948 my father was serving his second term as sheriff of Mercer County, Montana. We lived in Bentrock, the county seat and the
Line only town of any size in the region. In 1948
(5) its population was less than two thousand people. . . .

Many of the men in Mercer County had spent the preceding years in combat. (But not my father; he was 4-F. When he was sixteen a
(10) horse kicked him, breaking his leg so severely that he walked with a permanent limp, and eventually a cane, his right leg V-ed in, his right knee perpetually pointing to the left.) When these men came back from war they
(15) wanted nothing more than to work their farms and ranches and to live quietly with their families. The county even had fewer hunters after the war than before.

All of which made my father's job a rela-
(20) tively easy one. Oh, he arrested the usual weekly drunks, mediated an occasional dispute about fence lines or stray cattle, calmed a few domestic disturbances, and warned the town's teenagers about getting rowdy in
(25) Wood's Cafe, but by and large being sheriff of Mercer County did not require great strength or courage. The ability to drive the county's rural roads, often drifted over in the winter or washed out in the summer, was a much more
(30) necessary skill than being good with your fists or a gun. One of my father's regular duties was chaperoning Saturday night dances in the county, but the fact that he often took along my mother (and sometimes me) shows how
(35) quiet those affairs—and his job—usually were.

And that disappointed me at the time. As long as my father was going to be sheriff, a position with so much potential for excite-
(40) ment, danger, and bravery, why couldn't some of that promise be fulfilled? No matter how many wheat fields or cow pastures surrounded us, we were still Montanans, yet my father didn't even look like a western sheriff. He
(45) wore a shirt and tie, as many of the men in town did, but at least they wore boots and Stetsons; my father wore brogans and a fedora. He had a gun but he never carried it, on duty or off. I knew because I checked, time
(50) and time again. When he left the house I ran to his dresser and the top drawer on the right side. And there it was, there it always was. Just as well. As far as I was concerned it was the wrong kind of gun for a sheriff. He should
(55) have had a nickel-plated Western Colt .45, something with some history and heft. Instead, my father had a small .32 automatic, Italian-made and no bigger than your palm. My father didn't buy such a sorry gun; he con-
(60) fiscated it from a drunken transient in one of his first arrests. My father kept the gun but in fair exchange bought the man a bus ticket to Billings, where he had family.

GO ON TO THE NEXT PAGE ⟶

Passage 2

Line   He was good-looking, in a Southern,
(65) romantic poet sort of way. He needed those
good looks, one of the aunts said; why else
would my otherwise sensible mother have
married a man like him, an actor-writer
hyphenate who lived on dreams and spent his
(70) free evenings carrying a spear at the Opera
House. But that was in later times, when he
had moved out of the rundown communal
house in the Berkeley Hills, leaving my
mother and the ever-changing cast of nominal
(75) uncles and aunts to patch the ancient water
heater and pump out the basement when the
overpressured valve finally blew. He needed
separateness to write, he said, solitude, something we'd never given him, and he was tired,
(80) tired of being dragged from his study to tend
to the latest household eruption that bubbled
up "like gas from a Calistoga mud bath," he
said, with relentless regularity.

He looked tired by then, as tired of us as
(85) we were of him, of forgotten birthdays and
surprises that failed to surprise. When he did
bring us a present, I even wondered why, for it
was always somehow off: last season's hot toy
no one played with any more, or a complicated
(90) model no boy could assemble without a
father's help. Which we never got. He was an
actor, after all, not tech crew, an artist, not
someone who could fix a toy.

If he was an actor, we were props at best.
(95) Reluctant ones—had there been a Plantagenet
Pleasure Faire, he would have strutted his
hour as Wicked Dick III, while Geoffrey and I,
thrust into burlap sacks, were hauled off, two
little princes in shabby tights, to be disposed
(100) of elsewhere. That was his glory, kinging it.
Living History,[1] he called it, and in the early
days he followed the fairs up and down the
state, living the Renaissance first in Agoura,
then in Marin, finally winding up the acting
(105) season with Victoria's England in San
Francisco or even Oakland for one or two
slow years.

Not that anyone ever hired him to act the
king. No, he was a minor figure even on that
(110) rude stage, a charming but lesser nobleman in
Elizabeth's court, an attentive councilor in
Victoria's entourage. But he shared the perks
of royalty, such as they were, stood center
stage in black velvet pantaloons while the
(115) September sun burned overhead, or posed
handsomely (in a Prince Albert coat, no less)
as the royal party made its way through the
Christmas crowds at Dickens Fair. Why he
stuck to it, I never understood. Certainly not
(120) for the pay.

Between fairs he wrote, or thought of
writing, shut up in his study, into which we
children were not allowed, or did research for
his one-man-shows (in which he played a
(125) series of writers, one per show, so that one
year we saw his Edgar Allan Poe, another
year, his Ambrose Bierce). He was a writer, or
at least a writer once removed, writing down
other men's words and speaking them as if
(130) they were his own. At times it seemed he
thought they were his own, he paraphrased
them so freely, vamping upon the themes of
The Devil's Dictionary.[2] And he probably
thought we were his own as well, as little
(135) acquainted with us as he was. And so we were,
if only by example and heredity.

---

[1] Since the 1960s, California's Living History Centre has pro-
duced fairs and festivals in northern and southern California.
The Renaissance Pleasure Faire is set in the time of Queen
Elizabeth I; the Dickens Christmas Fair and Pickwick Comic
Annual, in the time of Queen Victoria.
[2] A book of diabolical epigrams by Ambrose Bierce.

GO ON TO THE NEXT PAGE

7. In Passage 1 the narrator uses the parenthetical material (lines 8–13) to

   (A) suggest that his father became sheriff to compensate for his disability
   (B) highlight the difference between his father and other men in Mercer County
   (C) justify his father's peaceful nature
   (D) belittle his father
   (E) indicate that the voters felt sorry for his father when they elected him sheriff

8. Mentioning that Mercer County "had fewer hunters after the war than before" (lines 17 and 18) is the author's way of saying that

   (A) the men had had their fill of shooting and death
   (B) the men worked long hours and had no time for hunting
   (C) the narrator's father prevented the men from hunting
   (D) the men thought hunting was too dangerous
   (E) many of the hunters were killed in the war

9. By describing his father's work clothes (lines 44–48), the narrator is suggesting that his father

   (A) wanted to dress like other men
   (B) didn't take the sheriff's job seriously
   (C) was pretty dull
   (D) was a nonconformist
   (E) was concerned about his image

10. By wishing that his father had a gun with "some history and some heft" (lines 54–56), the narrator means

   (A) an antique gun
   (B) a more expensive gun
   (C) a gun used in the war
   (D) a gun that could be worn in a holster
   (E) a more impressive gun

11. In Passage 1 which of the following best describes the narrator's feelings about his father?

   (A) Regret
   (B) Hostility
   (C) Resentment
   (D) Affection
   (E) Indifference

12. The narrator of Passage 2 compares himself and his brother to "props" (line 94 because they

   (A) reinforced their father's image as a parent
   (B) were assets to theatrical productions
   (C) were physical objects handled onstage
   (D) supported their father's dramatic efforts
   (E) possessed essential attributes their father lacked

13. In line 110, "rude" most nearly means

   (A) roughly made
   (B) deliberately impolite
   (C) highly vigorous
   (D) inconsiderate
   (E) tempestuous

14. The narrator mentions his father's sharing the perks of royalty (lines 112–118) in order to emphasize that his father

   (A) had gone far in his chosen field
   (B) wanted to share these privileges with his children
   (C) had a particularly regal demeanor
   (D) demanded only the best for himself
   (E) received very little for his efforts

GO ON TO THE NEXT PAGE

15. In Passage 2, which of the following is NOT
an accurate description of the narrator's father?

(A) He was not dependable to his children.
(B) He enjoyed being the center of attention.
(C) He had an appealing appearance.
(D) He was well liked by those who shared his
home.
(E) He was uncomfortable with his
responsibilities.

16. The narrator's purpose in writing this portrait
of his father was

(A) to show readers the effects of a bohemian
lifestyle on one man
(B) to help himself understand his complex
feelings toward his father
(C) to illustrate the importance of open communication among members of a family
(D) to tell about the difficulties of his boyhood
(E) to praise his father, a man he both loved
and feared

17. In which respect is the portrait of the father in
Passage 1 similar to the portrait in Passage 2?

(A) In both passages we see the father through
the eyes of a young boy.
(B) Both passages portray the father as deficient in some important way.
(C) In both passages we get to know intimate
details of the father's life.
(D) Both passages tell us as much about the
narrator as about the father.
(E) Both passages imply that the narrators
would like to emulate their fathers.

18. As presented in the two passages, the relationship between each narrator and his father is

(A) loving
(B) competitive
(C) cautious
(D) distant
(E) tense

19. The authors of both passages come across as

(A) loyal sons
(B) intolerant of their fathers
(C) respectful of their fathers
(D) rebellious sons
(E) puzzled by their fathers

STOP

**IF YOU FINISH BEFORE TIME IS CALLED, YOU MAY CHECK YOUR WORK ON THIS
SECTION ONLY. DO NOT WORK ON ANY OTHER SECTION IN THE TEST.**

⑥ ⑥ ⑥ ⑥ ⑥ ⑥ ⑥ ⑥ ⑥ ⑥

Section 6

TIME—10 MINUTES
14 QUESTIONS

For each of the following questions, select the best answer from the choices provided and fill in the appropriate circle on the answer sheet.

Some or all parts of the following sentences are underlined. The first answer choice, (A), simply repeats the underlined part of the sentence. The other four choices present four alternative ways to phrase the underlined part. Select the answer that produces the most effective sentence, one that is clear and exact, and blacken the appropriate space on your answer sheet. In selecting your choice, be sure that it is standard written English, and that it expresses the meaning of the original sentence.

Example:
The first biography of author Eudora Welty came out in 1998 and she was 89 years old at the time.

(A) and she was 89 years old at the time
(B) at the time she was 89
(C) upon becoming an 89 year old
(D) when she was 89
(E) at the age of 89 years old

Ⓐ Ⓑ Ⓒ ● Ⓔ

---

1. Not everyone are afraid of earthquakes, but this unwarranted confidence does not mean that earthquakes are not dangerous.

   (A) Not everyone are afraid of earthquakes, but
   (B) Because not everyone are afraid of earthquakes,
   (C) While not everyone are afraid of earthquakes, but
   (D) Not everyone is afraid of earthquakes,
   (E) While not everyone are afraid of earthquakes,

2. Volunteering on political campaigns can help students become a more attractive candidate for jobs in government.

   (A) become a more attractive candidate for jobs
   (B) become a more attractive candidate for a job
   (C) become more attractive candidates for jobs
   (D) becoming as candidates more attractive for the jobs
   (E) to become as candidates more attractive for the job

3. The technological marvels of modern medicine is of little comfort to most of the 45 million Americans who are not covered by health insurance.

   (A) medicine is of little comfort to most of the 45 million Americans who are not covered by health insurance
   (B) medicine are of little comfort to most of the 45 million Americans they are not covered by health insurance
   (C) medicine are for little comfort for most of the 45 million Americans whom health insurance does not cover
   (D) medicine is of little comfort to most of the 45 million Americans that health insurance fails to cover
   (E) medicine are of little comfort to most of the 45 million Americans who lack health insurance

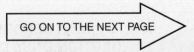
GO ON TO THE NEXT PAGE

4. The artist Georgia O'Keeffe <u>provoked strong reactions, and they often contradicted one another</u>.

   (A) provoked strong reactions, and they often contradicted one another
   (B) provoked strong, often contradictory reactions
   (C) provoked strong reactions, frequently they contradicted one another
   (D) provoked strong reactions, often they contradicted each other
   (E) provoking strong, often contradictory reactions

5. Many job-seekers attempt to exaggerate their qualifications <u>but typically failing</u> to impress their interviewers.

   (A) but typically failing
   (B) but it is typical that they fail
   (C) but fail, typically,
   (D) however they fail typically
   (E) but with their typical failing

6. Walter had initially derided the new, energy-efficient automobiles on <u>sale, then eventually he was convinced of the value</u> of fuel economy.

   (A) sale, then eventually he was convinced of the value
   (B) sale, then eventually the value convinced him of
   (C) sale, but eventually he was convinced of the value
   (D) sale, but eventually convincing himself of the value
   (E) sale; however, eventually being convinced of the value

7. <u>Arriving at the scene of the accident, the victims of the crash were treated by the paramedics</u>.

   (A) Arriving at the scene of the accident, the victims of the crash were treated by the paramedics.
   (B) After they had arrived at the scene of the accident, the victims of the crash were treated by the paramedics.
   (C) As soon as they had arrived at the scene of the accident, the paramedics were treating the crash victims.
   (D) Arriving at the scene of the accident, the paramedics will treat the victims of the crash.
   (E) Arriving at the scene of the accident, the paramedics treated the victims of the crash.

8. The author of the ethics column, a follower of Ayn Rand <u>argued that one should always place your self-interest first</u>.

   (A) argued that one should always place your self-interest first
   (B) argues that one should always place your self-interest first
   (C) argued that one should always place one's self-interest first
   (D) argued that one's self-interest should come before your concern for others
   (E) argued that one always should place our self-interest first

9. When I told you that you needed to use elbow grease to clean that filthy floor, <u>I assumed you would recognize that I was employing</u> a figure of speech.

   (A) I assumed you would recognize that I was employing
   (B) I assumed you recognizing that I was using
   (C) I assumed you are recognizing that I was using
   (D) I assume your recognition of my having made use of
   (E) I assume your recognition of its being

GO ON TO THE NEXT PAGE

10. The automobile workers decided <u>to select a delegation and it would speak</u> to the management about improving working conditions in the plant.

    (A) to select a delegation and it would speak
    (B) on selecting a delegation so that it would speak
    (C) to select a delegation that would speak
    (D) to select a delegation and they would speak
    (E) on the selection of a delegation and on speaking

11. Even though she acknowledged that she was as biased in favor of her son as any other <u>parent, she maintained that her partiality did not blind her from his faults</u>.

    (A) parent, she maintained that her partiality did not blind her from his faults
    (B) parent, she maintains that her partiality does not blind her from his faults
    (C) parent, she maintained that the fact of her being partial did not blind her to his faults
    (D) parent, she maintained that her being partial did not blind her from his faults
    (E) parent, she maintained that her partiality did not blind her to his faults

12. John Corry's account of Lincoln's speech at Cooper Union provides historical context, narrative <u>drama, and it cogently analyzes one of the seminal texts</u> of our nation's history.

    (A) drama, and it cogently analyzes one of the seminal texts
    (B) drama, and it presents a cogent analysis of one of the seminal texts
    (C) drama, but it cogently analyzes one of the seminal texts
    (D) drama, thus it has cogently analyzed one of the seminal texts
    (E) drama, and a cogent analysis of one of the seminal texts

13. The national marine sanctuary known as the Flower Gardens, located in the <u>Gulf of Mexico, home to some of the most spectacular banks of coral and sponges to be found</u> in this part of the world.

    (A) Gulf of Mexico, home to some of the most spectacular banks of coral and sponges to be found
    (B) Gulf of Mexico, home to some of the most spectacular banks of coral and sponges that were found
    (C) Gulf of Mexico, is home to some of the most spectacular banks of coral and sponges to be found
    (D) Gulf of Mexico, home to some of the most spectacular banks of coral and sponges we found
    (E) Gulf of Mexico, home to some of the more spectacular banks of coral and sponges found

14. Pupils of this venerable professor have termed him at once infuriating because of his disorganization <u>but his erudition is nevertheless an inspiration</u>.

    (A) but his erudition is nevertheless an inspiration
    (B) although he is inspiringly erudite
    (C) and inspiring because of his erudition
    (D) while being so erudite as to inspire them
    (E) while being so erudite that he inspires them

STOP

IF YOU FINISH BEFORE TIME IS CALLED, YOU MAY CHECK YOUR WORK ON THIS SECTION ONLY. DO NOT WORK ON ANY OTHER SECTION IN THE TEST.

ANSWER KEY

Section 2

1.	**B**	5.	**B**	9.	**A**	13.	**E**	17.	**E**
2.	**B**	6.	**B**	10.	**D**	14.	**D**	18.	**B**
3.	**C**	7.	**B**	11.	**D**	15.	**A**	19.	**B**
4.	**E**	8.	**A**	12.	**C**	16.	**C**	20.	**C**

21.	**D**
22.	**E**
23.	**C**
24.	**E**

Section 3

1.	**B**	7.	**D**	13.	**C**	19.	**A**	25.	**A**	31.	**B**
2.	**E**	8.	**D**	14.	**A**	20.	**B**	26.	**D**	32.	**E**
3.	**C**	9.	**D**	15.	**B**	21.	**E**	27.	**D**	33.	**A**
4.	**A**	10.	**B**	16.	**B**	22.	**A**	28.	**C**	34.	**B**
5.	**C**	11.	**C**	17.	**B**	23.	**E**	29.	**E**	35.	**D**
6.	**C**	12.	**D**	18.	**D**	24.	**A**	30.	**C**		

Section 4

1.	**C**	5.	**A**	9.	**C**	13.	**D**	17.	**C**	21.	**B**
2.	**D**	6.	**D**	10.	**C**	14.	**B**	18.	**B**	22.	**D**
3.	**D**	7.	**C**	11.	**D**	15.	**D**	19.	**E**	23.	**E**
4.	**A**	8.	**B**	12.	**B**	16.	**D**	20.	**D**	24.	**C**

Section 5

1.	**E**	5.	**C**	9.	**C**	13.	**A**	17.	**B**
2.	**C**	6.	**C**	10.	**E**	14.	**E**	18.	**D**
3.	**D**	7.	**C**	11.	**A**	15.	**D**	19.	**E**
4.	**C**	8.	**A**	12.	**C**	16.	**B**		

Section 6

1.	**D**	5.	**C**	9.	**A**	13.	**C**
2.	**C**	6.	**C**	10.	**C**	14.	**C**
3.	**E**	7.	**E**	11.	**E**		
4.	**B**	8.	**C**	12.	**E**		

ANALYSIS OF TEST RESULTS

I. Check your answers against the answer key.

II. Fill in the following chart.

Sentence Completion Number Correct _____	Section 1 (Questions 1–8) _____		Section 4 (Questions 1–5) _____	Section 5 (Questions 1–6) _____		Total _____
Reading Comprehension Number Correct _____	Section 2 (Questions 9–24) _____		Section 4 (Questions 6–24) _____	Section 5 (Questions 7–19) _____		Total _____
Sentence Improvement Number Correct _____		Section 3 (Questions 1–11) _____			Section 6 (Questions 1–14) _____	Total _____
Error Identification Number Correct _____		Section 3 (Questions 12–29) _____				Total _____
Paragraph Improvement Number Correct _____		Section 3 (Questions 30–35) _____				Total _____

III. Interpret your results.

Sentence Completion	Number Correct _____
Reading Comprehension	Number Correct _____
Sentence Improvement	Number Correct _____
Error Identification	Number Correct _____
Paragraph Improvement	Number Correct _____
	Subtotal _____

Guessing Penalty: Subtract 1/4 point for each incorrect answer. _____
(Do not take off points for questions you left blank.)

TOTAL SCORE _____

	Sentence Completion Score	Reading Comprehension Score	Total
Excellent	18–19 Correct	43–48 Correct	60–67
Very Good	14–17 Correct	33–42 Correct	46–59
Good	11–13 Correct	25–32 Correct	35–45
Fair	9–10 Correct	20–24 Correct	28–34
Poor	6–8 Correct	12–19 Correct	17–27
Very Poor	0–5 Correct	0–11 Correct	0–16

	Sentence Improvement Score	Error Identification Score	Paragraph Improvement Score	Total
Excellent	21–25 Correct	13–18 Correct	6 Correct	38–49
Very Good	15–20 Correct	10–12 Correct	5 Correct	28–37
Good	8–14 Correct	7–9 Correct	4 Correct	17–27
Fair	5–7 Correct	5–6 Correct	2–3 Correct	11–16
Poor	3–4 Correct	3–4 Correct	1 Correct	5–10
Very Poor	0–2 Correct	0–2 Correct	0 Correct	0–4

SCORE YOUR OWN SAT ESSAY

Use this table as you rate your performance on the essay-writing section of this model test. Circle the phrase that most accurately describes your work. Enter the numbers in the scoring chart below. Add the numbers together and divide by 6 to determine your total score. The higher your total score, the better you are likely to do on the essay section of the SAT.

Note that on the actual SAT two readers will rate your essay; your essay score will be the sum of their two ratings and could range from 12 (highest) to 2 (lowest). Also, they will grade your essay holistically, rating it on the basis of their overall impression of its effectiveness. They will *not* analyze it piece by piece, giving separate grades for grammar, vocabulary level, and so on. Therefore, you cannot expect the score you give yourself on this model test to predict your eventual score on the SAT with any great degree of accuracy. Use this scoring guide instead to help you assess your writing strengths and weaknesses, so that you can decide which areas to focus on as you prepare for the SAT.

Like most people, you may find it difficult to rate your own writing objectively. Ask a teacher or fellow student to score your essay as well. With his or her help you should gain added insights into writing your 25-minute essay.

	6	5	4	3	2	1
POSITION ON THE TOPIC	Clear, convincing, & insightful	Fundamentally clear & coherent	Fairly clear & coherent	Insufficiently clear	Largely unclear	Extremely unclear
ORGANIZATION OF EVIDENCE	Well organized, with strong, relevant examples	Generally well organized, with apt examples	Adequately organized, with some examples	Sketchily developed, with weak examples	Lacking focus and evidence	Unfocused and disorganized
SENTENCE STRUCTURE	Varied, appealing sentences	Reasonably varied sentences	Some variety in sentences	Little variety in sentences	Errors in sentence structure	Severe errors in sentence structure
LEVEL OF VOCABULARY	Mature & apt word choice	Competent word choice	Adequate word choice	Inappropriate or weak vocabulary	Highly limited vocabulary	Rudimentary
GRAMMAR AND USAGE	Almost entirely free of errors	Relatively free of errors	Some technical errors	Minor errors and some major ones	Numerous major errors	Extensive severe errors
OVERALL EFFECT	Outstanding	Effective	Adequately competent	Inadequate, but shows some potential	Seriously flawed	Fundamentally deficient

Self-Scoring Chart

For each of the following categories, rate the essay from 1 (lowest) to 6 (highest)

Position on the Topic _____

Organization of Evidence _____

Sentence Structure _____

Level of Vocabulary _____

Grammar and Usage _____

Overall Effect _____

TOTAL _____

(To get a score, divide the total by 6) _____

Scoring Chart (Second Reader)

For each of the following categories, rate the essay from 1 (lowest) to 6 (highest)

Position on the Topic _____

Organization of Evidence _____

Sentence Structure _____

Level of Vocabulary _____

Grammar and Usage _____

Overall Effect _____

TOTAL _____

(To get a score, divide the total by 6) _____

ANSWER EXPLANATIONS

SECTION 2

1. **B**   The contrast here is between *revivals* (new productions of old plays) and original productions.

2. **B**   "But" signals a contrast. In the Ice Ages, musk oxen ranged or roamed over much of the Northern Hemisphere. In recent times, however, they have been *confined* or limited *to* the far northernmost regions.

3. **C**   The comparison suggests society is an *organism* made up of many parts serving different role or *functions*.

4. **E**   By definition, someone *credulous* or gullible readily *believes* things without having much reason to do so.

5. **B**   "Instead" signals a contrast. The missing word must be an antonym or near-antonym for "physically changes." Something *static* or unchanging by definition does not physically change.

6. **B**   To be sometimes harsh and sometimes gentle is to act in *contradictory* ways. Such inconsistencies in behavior might well make someone seem an *inexplicable* enigma, a mystery that could not be explained.

7. **B**   To debunk the subject of a biography is to expose the false claims about that person's virtues, to poke holes in the legend, so to speak. The subject of this biography, however, deserves the praise she has been awarded. She is even better than tales paint her, *surpassing* her legend.

8. **A**   To come up with or invent a name for something new is to *coin* a term.

9. **A**   To say that today's chocolate lovers would not find the Aztec's "food of the gods" heavenly is a *humorous understatement*. More likely, their reaction would be like that of the Spanish explorers who described the unsweetened chocolate beverage as food for pigs!

10. **D**   In describing the Aztec beverage as "fitter for hogs than men," the explorers were being scornful or *derisive*.

11. **D**   Use the process of elimination to answer this question. The author uses a metaphor: Salk's release of the vaccine was "the opening shot in a war." Therefore, you can eliminate (A). The author cites a statistic: polio claimed 600 new victims in 2001. Therefore, you can eliminate (B). The author quotes Salk, a historic figure whose legacy lives on. Therefore, you can eliminate (C). The author makes several assertions. Therefore, you can eliminate (E). Only (D) is left. It is the correct answer. The author never *describes a process*.

12. **C**   In helping wipe out a disease that had crippled children for centuries, Salk did an *amazing*, stunning amount for humanity.

13. **E**   Throughout the passage, the author praises Moore's "sweet confection," demonstrating its strengths and showing reasons for its popularity over the years. Thus, the passage chiefly serves to *explain the enduring appeal of this classic example of light verse.*

14. **D**   Moore did not invent any new myths. However, he *transformed the old myths* of Kris Kringle the sled driver and Saint Nicholas the bishop into our archetypal Santa Claus.

15. **A**   Moore uses sources from a variety of traditions—Norwegian, Dutch, possibly even American. To compose something out of elements drawn from such a variety of sources is by definition to be *eclectic*.

16. **C**   To delineate Santa Claus is to depict or portray him. The *illustrator* Thomas Nast closely based his illustrations of Santa Claus on Moore's own words.

17. **E**   One contrasts Moore's St. Nick with Irving's in order to see just how very good and imaginative a job Moore did compared to Irving. Moore goes beyond Irving in furnishing Santa with steeds,

naming these steeds, and differentiating them from one another. In doing so, he shows considerable *creativity*.

18. **B**   We never think of questioning what the poem says because, like the poem's protagonist, we are too awestruck by what we see to ask any questions. We view what occurs *with astonishment and awe*.

19. **B**   The author disregards or *dismisses* the sneers of the professional deconstructionists (literary critics, members of a literary school with little respect for light verse). He believes the lasting popularity of the piece should outweigh the deconstructionists' petty criticisms.

20. **C**   The phrase "that goes for 'The Raven'" means "that also *holds true for* 'The Raven.'" The author is asserting that he has not ignored the claims of popular favorites like "Casey at the Bat" and "The Raven" in saying Moore's poem is probably our most popular American poem.

21. **D**   "Mere" popularity here means *simple* popularity, considered apart from any other quality a work of art might possess.

22. **E**   A moribund reader is someone figuratively dead or *insensitive to the verse* he or she reads. (*Moribund* literally means approaching death; dormant.)

23. **C**   The author presents this pair of rhyming words as one of Moore's "Muse-inspired" better pairings. Clearly, he regards Moore's use of these words with both *delight* in the rhyme and *admiration* for the rhymester.

24. **E**   The author does not bother to summarize the story of "A Visit From Saint Nicholas" for the reader. He refers blithely to its anapests and alliteration, mentions its protagonist (whom someone unfamiliar with the poem, not knowing any better, might have confused with Saint Nick), and generally assumes that anyone reading his article will *already be familiar in great detail with Moore's poem*.

SECTION 3

1. **B**   Wordiness. Choice B makes the writer's point simply and concisely.

2. **E**   The suggested revision tightens this ineffective compound sentence by eliminating the connective *and*.

3. **C**   Wordiness. Choice C deftly cuts the unnecessary words.

4. **A**   Sentence is correct.

5. **C**   Misplaced modifier. Whom did the police coerce? Not the confession, but the defendant!

6. **C**   The suggested revision tightens this loose, sloppy compound sentence by eliminating the connective *and*.

7. **D**   Dangling modifier. Ask yourself who was reading Pope's epigrams. Choice D rewrites the sentence so that the participial phrase *Reading the epigrams of Alexander Pope* correctly modifies *I*. (Although choice C also rearranges the sentence so that the opening phrase modifies *I*, it introduces an error in verb tense.)

8. **D**   Error in subordination. The use of the subordinate conjunction *Although* emphasizes the contrast between Tolkien's literary and scholarly specialties.

9. **D**   The writer is focusing on Waters. The use of the active voice here reinforces this emphasis.

10. **B**   Sentence fragment. The elimination of the comma and of *by which,* together with the interchanging of *brought* and *water* creates a correct sentence.

11. **C**   Informal redundancy. The structure "*Because . . . is* the reason" is inherently redundant. Choice C eliminates the redundancy, strengthening the sentence.

12. **D**   Lack of parallelism. Change *and not in* to *and not through*.

13. **C**   Error in pronoun-antecedent agreement. The antecedent, *technology*, is singular; the pronoun should be singular as well. Change *they* to *it*.

14. **A**   Error in usage. The phrase *scarcely no* is a double negative. Replace it with *scarcely any*.

15. **B**   Adjective-adverb confusion. Change *exceeding* to *exceedingly*.

16. **B**   Error in subject-verb agreement. The subject of the sentence is *limerick* (singular); the verb should be singular as well. Change *are* to *is*.

17. **B**   Sentence fragment. If you eliminate the conjunction *and*, you will have a correct sentence, with the noun *drivers* as the subject of the main clause.

18. **D**   Lack of parallelism. Change *how to pitch* to *pitching*.

19. **A**   Error in pronoun choice. Students are people, not things. Change *which* to *who*.

20. **B**   Error in subject-verb agreement. Be on the lookout for sentences in which the subject follows the verb. Here, the subject is *bandits* (plural); the verb should be plural as well. Change *lurks* to *lurk*.

21. **E**   Sentence is correct.

22. **A**   Dangling modifier. Change *Upon dressing, you* to *Once you have dressed it, you*.

23. **E**   Sentence is correct.

24. **A**   Error in pronoun choice. Change *one cuts away* to *you cut away*.

25. **A**   Error in pronoun case. *Except for* requires the objective case. Change *and I* to *and me*.

26. **D**   Error in logical comparison. Compare women's salaries with men's salaries, not with men. Change *men* to *men's*.

27. **D**   Adjective-adverb confusion. Change *disturbing* to *disturbingly*.

28. **C**   Error in idiomatic usage. Change *ability toward governing* to *ability to govern*.

29. **E**   Sentence is correct.

30. **C**   Choice A contains an awkwardly expressed clause that begins *which caused*. Choice B contains a faulty comparison: *not as severe that*. Choice C accurately revises the sentence. It is the best answer. Choice D contains an awkwardly expressed clause that begins *that banning*. Choice E contains faulty diction. The conjunction *and* is not an effective connecting word in the context.

31. **B**   Choice A contains a dangling participle and a weak passive construction. Choice B accurately continues the thought begun in sentence 9. It is the best answer. Choice C contains redundant language: *foul* and *obscene*. Choice D contains a weak passive construction (*Obscenities are often heard*) and is wordy. Choice E lacks a main verb; therefore, it is a sentence fragment.

32. **E**   Choices A and B are adequate, but dull, transitional statements. Choice C is a wordier version of (A) and (B). Choice D contains an error in subject-verb agreement; the subject *changes* is plural, but the verb *has* is singular. Choice E serves as a good transitional statement that highlights the most important change in music discussed in the essay. It is the best answer.

33. **A**   Only Choice A requires development, since no mention is made in the essay of "new categories" of music. All the other choices are factual statements that require no further elaboration.

34. **B**   All choices except (B) contribute to the discussion of changes in musical sounds brought about by technology. Choice B, however, wanders from the topic.

35. **D**   Choice A unnecessarily repeats the phrase *in the past thirty years* and contains an error in subject-verb agreement. Choice B is awkwardly expressed and confusing. Choice C fails to list the changes in music in the proper order. Also, it groups *technology and lyrics* together, as if they worked in concert to alter contemporary music's style. Choice D succinctly and accurately states the main idea of the essay. It is the best answer. Choice E, by subordinating the initial clause, gives the lyrics of music undeserved importance.

SECTION 4

1. **C**   "Despite" signals a contrast. Right now, fencing in America is in a stage of growth; the fencing association's membership is expanding. However, the association fears that fencing will not grow but die out (face *extinction*) if spectators cannot understand what's going on. Thus, fencing needs to become more *accessible* (comprehensible).

2. **D**   Precise wording reduces the chances of *ambiguity* (confusion about meaning).

3. **D**   It would be a *daunting* (discouraging) task to get to know over 700 people in the course of one semester. Such a large group is in itself *daunting*.

4. **A**   "Spurious" means false or fake. Malcolm argues that biographers make up or *invent* the facts they narrate, so the orderly narrative you read and take as historically true is actually *illusory* (deceptive; unreal).

5. **A**   By definition, *magisterial* means authoritative or *commanding*.

6. **D**   The "property" that Douglass's ex-master sought to reclaim was a *personal possession* that had been lost to him, namely, his former slave Frederick Douglass.

7. **C**   The abolitionists criticized Douglass for letting his British friends purchase his freedom. They were clearly *negative* about the action, considering it politically incorrect.

8. **B**   Passage 1 is clearly *expository*: it presents information about a historical figure. Passage 2, in contrast, is *argumentative*: in it, Douglass justifies his actions, giving his grounds for running away.

9. **C**   The enterprise that Douglass kept secret from his former master was his plan to *escape from slavery*.

10. **C**   The author states that warfare for the Kiowas "was preeminently a matter of disposition rather than of survival." In other words, they *were warlike in nature*.

11. **D**   The author comments that the Kiowas "never understood the grim, unrelenting advance of the U.S. Cavalry." They lacked the *unswerving determination* that kept the cavalrymen pursuing their foes long after a band of Kiowas would have changed its course.

12. **B**   Born too late to experience the actual fighting and famine, the author's grandmother did experience *the bleak,* cheerless *attitude* of the defeated warriors, "the dark brooding" *of the older Kiowa men*.

13. **D**   Describing the Kiowas as "a lordly and dangerous society of fighters and thieves, hunters and priests of the sun" (lines 53 and 54), members of a courageous and proud tribe, the author clearly regards them with *admiration*.

14. **B**   Before they acquired horses, the Kiowas were tied to the ground, forced to move slowly in the course of their journey toward the dawn. Once they had horses, however, they were *liberated to rove more freely*; their wandering spirit was no longer tied down.

15. **D**   The Kiowas' origin myth describes how "they entered the world through a hollow log." Thus, it is *an explanation of how they came to be* on Earth.

16. **D**   Step by step, the author traces the course of a surgical procedure, from the initial grasping of the scalpel through the opening incision to the eventual sensory exploration of the internal organs. In doing so, he is *describing a process*.

17. **C**   As the surgeon draws the knife across the skin, it leaves a thin *line of blood* in its wake (path or track passed over by a moving object).

18. **B**   To part the flesh is to *split* or separate the skin.

19. **E**   The "strange flowers" with their looped handles are the hemostats, forceps, and other *surgical tools* attached to the opening.

20. **D**   To write of one object by using a term that normally indicates a different object, suggesting a likeness between them, is to make an implicit comparison, that is, to be *metaphorical*.

21. **B**   The simile "like children absorbed in a game" indicates that in this context "engaged" means *engrossed* or deeply involved.

22. **D**   Primitive drawings of buffalo and other wild beasts still exist in *caves* in which *prehistoric* humans dwelled.

23. **E**   Writing of "ritual cleansing," entering the "temple" of the human body, the truth hidden in the "ark" or holy place, the author is referring to priestly or *religious observances* (rites).

34. **C**   The author freely uses technical names for various *body organs*—"fascia," "peritoneum," "omentum"—tossing in occasional descriptive adjectives or phrases as if he assumes the reader is already *able to visualize* these organs in some detail. Readers without much background in anatomy might well feel the need for additional information about these organs (size, function, specific location) in order to appreciate the passage fully.

SECTION 5

1. **E**   A modernization program logically would attempt to *eliminate* or get rid of problems.

2. **C**   Something that cannot be solved with ease remains a mystery or *enigma*.

3. **D**   If you simply watch or *observe* the skilled activities of others, you are *passive*, that is, inactive.

4. **C**   The key phrase here is "stick together." Small particles of matter join together to form larger ones. In other words, they coalesce.

5. **C**   A *misnomer* (incorrect designation) by definition misnames something. The writer here is arguing that mole rats have been given the wrong name.

6. **C**   Einstein's humility was not a pose that he put on for an audience. His *profound*, deep humility was clearly *sincere* (genuine; unfeigned).

7. **C**   Throughout the passage, the narrator, a small boy, wishes that his father had been a tougher, more heroic sheriff. *To justify his father's peaceful nature* to himself as well as to his reader, he explains why his father had not gone to war like other men.

8. **A**   We are told that, when the men returned from war, they "wanted nothing more than to work their farms and ranches and to live quietly with their families." In essence, the war veterans *had had their fill of shooting and death*.

9. **C**   The narrator disapproves of his father's clothes. At least the other men "wore boots and Stetsons." All told, the boy thinks that his father is *pretty dull*, especially for a sheriff in Montana.

10. **E**   The boy wishes that his father carried a "nickel-plated Western Colt .45," perhaps one that had been carried by a gunslinging sheriff in the old West. In short, his gun should to have been a *more impressive* firearm.

11. **A**   The passage is tinged with the boy's *regret* that his father was not a tougher, more glamorous sheriff. In fact, he says that aspects of his father's job "disappointed" him.

12. **C**   Theatrical properties or props are usually movable items (not costumes or furniture) that actors use onstage during a performance. Note how the author describes the boys' likely fate, to be hauled offstage as if they were inanimate *physical objects* (lines 94–100).

13. **A**   The stage is rude in the same sense that "the rude bridge that arched the flood" is rude: it is a *roughly made*, somewhat primitive structure.

14. **E**   The narrator uses the phrase "such as they were" to dismiss the supposed perks or privileges of stage royalty. Considering that his father's reward was to stand under a hot sun wearing a heavy costume, it is clear that his father *received very little for his efforts*.

15. **D**   Given that he forgot their birthdays and never helped them fix their toys, the narrator's father clearly was "not dependable to his children." He "enjoyed being the center of attention": he gloried in acting like a king and starring in one-man shows. He "had an appealing appearance," evinced by the good looks that attracted his wife. He "was uncomfortable with his responsibilities," tired of dealing with household problems. All he lacked was the liking of *those who shared his home*, who grew to be as tired of him as he asserted he was of them.

16. **B**   The narrator has told the story of his father to better *understand his complex feelings toward his father*, who abandoned his family responsibilities in pursuit of ambitions the narrator neither shares nor fully understands.

17. **B**   The authors of the two passages portray their fathers as *deficient in some important way*. The father in Passage 1 is not tough and courageous enough to suit his son, and the father in Passage 2 is flawed in many ways—from his inability to succeed in his career to his destructive self-centeredness.

18. **D**   Neither son seems to have a close relationship with his father. In essence, they are *distant*.

19. **E**   The author of Passage 1 seems to be asking how a man can be both a sheriff in Montana and a wimp at the same time. It's *puzzling* to the boy. The author of Passage 2 analyzes his father closely,

but not with a sense of confidence in his findings. In many ways the father remains *puzzling*. As the passage says, the author never understood why the father endured his low-paid, uncelebrated career as an actor working for fairs.

SECTION 6

1. **D**   Error in subject-verb agreement. When used as a subject, *everyone* takes a singular verb. Change *Not everyone are* to *Not everyone is*.

2. **C**   Shift in number. The noun, *students*, is plural; its complement should be plural as well. Change *candidate* to *candidates*.

3. **E**   Error in subject-verb agreement. The subject, *marvels*, is plural; the verb should be plural as well. Change *is* to *are*.

4. **B**   Wordiness. Choice B makes the writer's point simply and concisely.

5. **C**   Sentence fragment. Replacing the present participle, *failing*, with the verb, *fail*, corrects the fragment.

6. **C**   Run-on sentence. Do not link two independent clauses with a comma.

7. **E**   Dangling participle. Ask yourself who arrived at the scene of the accident. Was it the victims? No, they were already present. Only choice E rewrites the sentence so that the participial phrase *Arriving at the scene of the accident* correctly modifies *paramedics*. (While choices C and D have *paramedics* as the subject of the main clause, they introduce new errors involving the sequence of tenses.)

8. **C**   Error in pronoun choice. Avoid shifting from one pronoun to another within a single sentence. Change *your self-interest* to *one's self-interest*.

9. **A**   Sentence is correct.

10. **C**   Wordiness. The removal of the connective *and* tightens the sentence, making it more effective.

11. **E**   Error in idiomatic usage. The verb *blind* takes the preposition *to*. Change *from* to *to*.

12. **E**   Lack of parallelism. Choice E has parallel structure.

13. **C**   Sentence fragment. Choice C supplies the missing verb, *is*.

14. **C**   Lack of parallelism. Choice C makes the parallel clear by neatly linking its similar elements with the connective *and* to produce a balanced sentence.

NOTES

THERE'S ONLY ONE PLACE TO TURN FOR TOP SCORES...

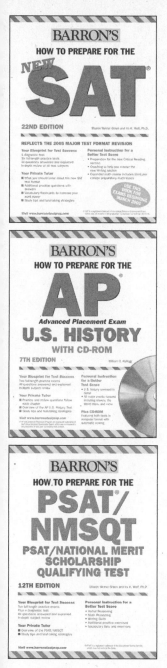
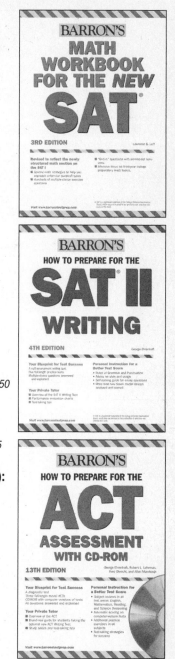

NOTES